NARRATIVE OF A FIVE YEARS EXPEDITION
AGAINST THE REVOLTED NEGROES OF SURINAM

JOHN GABRIEL STEDMAN

Narrative
of a Five Years Expedition
against the
Revolted Negroes of Surinam

Transcribed for the First Time from the Original 1790 Manuscript

*Edited, and with an Introduction and Notes, by
Richard Price & Sally Price*

All rights reserved, including without limitation the right to reproduce this book or any portion thereof in any form or by any means, whether electronic or mechanical, now known or hereinafter invented, without the express written permission of the publisher.

This book has been brought to publication with the generous assistance of the Menil Foundation and the National Endowment fro the Humanities.

Originally published by The Johns Hopkins University Press.

Copyright © 1988, 2010 by Richard Price & Sally Price

978-1-5040-2929-2

Distributed in 2016 by Open Road Distribution
180 Maiden Lane
New York, NY 10038
www.openroadmedia.com

*This edition is dedicated
to Stedman's maroon adversaries
who staked their lives on the attainment of
freedom, justice, and peace.
And to their present-day descendants
who refuse to forget.*

Contents

Preface and Acknowledgments
IX

Introduction
XIII

Stedman's 1790 "Narrative"
1

Editors' Notes to Stedman's "Narrative"
631

Appendix A: Flora and Fauna Identifications
673

Appendix B: Sources for Literary Citations
687

References Cited
699

Preface and Acknowledgments

Unlike all previous publications of John Gabriel Stedman's *Narrative*, the present edition is based on Stedman's personal copy of the 1790 manuscript rather than on the heavily edited first published edition of 1796. We present the text of the manuscript intact (except for minor typographical adjustments, described below); our own commentary appears separately, in the Introduction, Notes, and Appendixes.

The preparation of Stedman's 1790 manuscript for publication began in 1978, when we first confirmed its authenticity and significance at the James Ford Bell Library, University of Minnesota. Richard Price conducted the first years of research alone; Sally Price joined him as coeditor in 1982. A large number of people have contributed to the preparation of this edition. With apologies in advance for any inadvertent omissions, we wish to express our gratitude to all of them for sharing so generously their time, energy, and knowledge. While acknowledging our debt to them, we also take full and unambiguous responsibility for any errors, whether of fact or interpretation, that may still remain.

At the University of Minnesota, Professor Stuart B. Schwartz first alerted us to the manuscript's presence, expressed continued interest in our progress over the years, and eventually offered useful comments on a draft of the Introduction. Dr. John Parker, curator of the James Ford Bell Library, facilitated our editorial task with both courtesy and expertise at every stage, making available a microfilm copy of the "Narrative" for our use in Baltimore, arranging to purchase Stedman's manuscript diaries when we discovered that they were on the market, answering our queries about the transcription of problematical passages, and commenting on the Introduction. Carol Urness, also of the James Ford Bell Library, helped us with many details and offered encouragement when it was most needed during our stay in Minneapolis. William A. Wood, assistant director of the University of Minnesota Press, warmly supported our efforts during the years when our shared expectation was to publish with that house, and then, when circumstances changed, graciously encouraged the transfer of the project to the Johns Hopkins University Press.

Professor G. E. Bentley, Jr., of the University of Toronto generously and patiently counseled us at nearly every stage of this project. His unmatched knowledge of William Blake and the late eighteenth-century art of the book helped suggest many new avenues for us to explore. He has undoubtedly saved us from making many of the sorts of errors that are almost inevitable when one crosses as many disciplinary boundaries as we do in this edition.

In Baltimore (and later in Minneapolis), Scott V. Parris took on the tedious job of producing a provisional transcription of the approximately 865-page handwritten manuscript in 1979–80; he also contributed significantly to the early analysis of differences between the 1790 manuscript and the 1796 first edition, helped us to decide on the shape of our publication, and made a number of important comments on the Introduction. Rebecca B. Bateman cheerfully devoted long hours of library research to clarifying particular allusions in the "Narrative" and took responsibility for the often-difficult transcription of diary entries. Mark Rasmussen and Robert Newman provided references for many of Stedman's literary citations. And undergraduates in several classes at Johns Hopkins contributed their insights to our understanding of Stedman's life and times.

Colleagues at Johns Hopkins were consistently generous with their time and knowledge, no matter how seemingly arcane our queries. Jerome Christensen, Lowell Edmunds, Jack P. Greene, Josué V. Harari, Lieselotte E. Kurth, Georg Luck, Jerome J. McGann, Stephen Orgel, and Peter Sacks helped us track down many of the more elusive of Stedman's literary citations and foreign language quotations. William C. Sturtevant offered specialized advice throughout our years of work and made useful comments on the Introduction. Ronald Paulson also offered expert advice on the Introduction, sharing his special insights about the literary influences on Stedman's style and imagery.

Colleagues from other institutions also helped in various ways at every stage. We would like to thank James T. Collins, David Dabydeen,

PREFACE AND ACKNOWLEDGMENTS

Robert N. Essick, David V. Erdman, P. H. Hulton, Paul J. Korshin, Thomas V. Lange, Peter Linebaugh, J. F. M. Macleod, H. T. Mason, Susan McKinnon, Sandra Ann Niessen, Elizabeth Traube, and Gerald P. Tyson. We are particularly grateful to Stanley L. Engerman, who commented on a draft of the Introduction. We would also like to acknowledge the kindness of Claude Lévi-Strauss, who continues to represent for us the epitome of Old World erudition (see note to page 199).

In the Netherlands, Professor R. A. J. van Lier encouraged our work and very kindly made available to us his full correspondence with the botanical and zoological experts who contributed to the plant and animal identifications for his 1971 edition of the 1796 *Narrative*. Dr. Silvia W. de Groot made useful comments on a draft of the Introduction, and Dr. Wim Hoogbergen provided some important clarifications regarding the Boni Wars. Dr. M. E. van Opstall of the Algemeen Rijksarchief answered all our queries with celerity and good humor and provided photographic prints of archival materials. Mr. S. Emmering shared with us his considerable bibliographic knowledge. Professor H. Hoetink, at several stages, personally facilitated our research endeavor. And in Suriname, Drs. Gloria Leurs, director of the Surinaams Museum (as well as Jimmy Douglas, her predecessor) offered us hospitality, cooperation, and the resources of the museum's fine library.

In Germany, the hospitality of Hilda Emge–von Barton Stedman helped make our interviews with her aunt, Hilda von Barton Stedman, both enjoyable and productive. In England, John Maggs provided information on the book trade that was crucial in our attempt to piece together the history of the manuscript, and both B. A. Sharpley and Kate Ward of Louth, Lincolnshire, also contributed importantly to that endeavor. The late spinster "cousins," Hilda von Barton Stedman and "Daisy" Pym, who last helped us when they were ninety-four and ninety-eight years old, respectively, hold a very special place in our memory; they represent a precious link with the past, and their contributions enriched our lives as well as this book. In Paris, Leah Price's intimate knowledge of the novels that Stedman read and enjoyed, from *Tom Jones* to *Peregrine Pickle,* led to the identification of a number of otherwise elusive literary allusions; we are also grateful to her for sensitive comments on earlier drafts of the Introduction.

Kareem Zuhair produced the photographic prints used for this edition. Photographing the frustratingly uneven surfaces of a two hundred-year-old book required delicate compromises for almost every plate; when choices had to be made between the clarity of an illustration and its imprint (caption, plate number, etc.), we consistently favored the former. Niko Price served as our adviser for computer problems and produced the genealogy in figure 11. The final preparation of the manuscript benefited from the blue pencil of Carol Ehrlich, whose care and knowledge in copyediting an earlier one of our books inspired us to place a special request for her collaboration on this project.

The Interlibrary Loan department of the Milton S. Eisenhower Library at the Johns Hopkins University patiently put up with our myriad requests for obscure items; this edition owes much to their assistance, as well as to that of Pierre Berry and other members of the library's staff. The staffs at the New York Public Library, the John Carter Brown Library, the British Library, and the Bodleian Library also facilitated our tasks at various times, as did those of the Algemeen Rijksarchief and the Gemeentelijke Archiefdienst Utrecht.

During 1981–82, R. P.'s work on this project was supported in part by the Johns Hopkins University and in part by a Senior Fulbright Fellowship in the Netherlands at the Rijksuniversiteit Utrecht and the Rijksuniversiteit te Leiden, where Profs. Bonno Thoden van Velzen and Adam Kuper were, respectively, our gracious academic hosts. We are especially grateful to the Editions Program of the National Endowment for the Humanities, which helped support the research for this project.

The cover inset, as well as the *Narrative*'s frontispiece and finis page, are reproduced from the editors' copy of the large paper hand-colored 1796 first edition. All other illustrations from the *Narrative* are reproduced from the plain 1796 first edition—the majority from the editors' copy but some from the copy in the James Ford Bell Library, University of Minnesota.

Finally, we wish to thank John Szwed who, however indirectly (1985: 227, line 26), helped us realize that Baltimore is indeed the place "whose oriole is not an oriole," and who helped attune us to the niceties of annotations of the following sort:

Lines 747–748: a story in the magazine about a Mrs. Z.
   Anybody having access to a good library could, no doubt, easily trace that story to its source and find the name of the lady; but such humdrum potterings are beneath true scholarship.

INTRODUCTION

In 1759, when Voltaire needed a setting for his satirical discussion of New World slavery, he turned to Suriname.

> As they drew near the town they came upon a Negro lying on the ground wearing only half his clothes, that is to say, a pair of blue cotton drawers; this poor man had no left leg and no right hand. "Good heavens!" said Candide to him in Dutch, "what are you doing there, my friend, in that horrible state?"
> "I am waiting for my master, the famous merchant Monsieur Vanderdendur."
> "Was it Monsieur Vanderdendur," said Candide, "who treated you in this way?"
> "Yes, sir," said the Negro, "it is the custom. We are given a pair of cotton drawers twice a year as clothing. When we work in the sugar mills and the grindstone catches a finger, they cut off the hand; when we try to run away, they cut off a leg. Both these things happened to me. This is the price paid for the sugar you eat in Europe." (*Candide,* chap. 19)

By this time, Suriname had developed into a flourishing plantation colony and had earned a solid reputation, even among such rivals as Jamaica and Saint Domingue, for its heights of planter opulence and depths of slave misery. Stedman's "Narrative" makes clear on almost every page that Voltaire's choice of mid-eighteenth-century Suriname was chillingly on target.

The colony was founded in 1651 by the English but was ceded six-

INTRODUCTION

teen years later to the Dutch, who built it into "the envy of all the others in the Americas" (Nassy 1788, 1:56). By the mid-eighteenth century, it was said to be producing more revenue and consuming more imported manufactured goods, per capita, than any other Caribbean colony (ibid., 2:40). The local plantocracy was, to borrow Gordon K. Lewis's phrase about the Caribbean more generally, "crassly materialist and spiritually empty . . . the most crudely philistine of all dominant classes in the history of Western slavery" (1983, 109). As Stedman describes, planters were routinely served at table by nearly nude house slaves, who also fanned them during their naps (and sometimes all night long), put on and took off all of their clothes each morning and evening, bathed their children in imported wine, and performed other similar tasks; wealthy planters in the capital often had forty or fifty such hand-picked domestic slaves. The estates that generated this wealth were large by comparative standards: an average sugar estate had a slave force of 228, more than seventeen times as large as contemporary plantations in Virginia or Maryland (R. Price 1976, 16). Likewise, Suriname's slave population, which came from a variety of West and Central African societies, contained an unusually high ratio of Africans to Creoles, and of recently arrived Africans to seasoned slaves. The colony's ratio of Africans to Europeans was also extreme—more than 25:1, and as high as 65:1 in the plantation districts. (For comparison, Jamaica's ratio in 1780, "the highest in the British West Indies," was 10:1 [Craton 1975, 254].)

Marronage plagued the colony from its earliest years, as slaves escaped into the rain forest that grew up almost to the doorsteps of the plantations. By the mid-eighteenth century, "the colony had become the theater of a perpetual war" (Nassy 1788, 1:87), and organized bands of maroons kept planters living in constant fear for their lives and in constant risk of losing their investments. The 1760s witnessed a tremendous increase in the extension of credit by Amsterdam bankers, as Suriname planters mortgaged their estates and engaged in ever-increasing conspicuous consumption. By 1773, when Stedman arrived in what he called "this Blood Spilling Colony" to help quell the most recent maroon depredations, heavy speculation, planter absenteeism, and rapid changes in plantation ownership were posing a serious threat to the colony's viability. In short, this was a maximally polarized society—some three thousand European whites, who must have sensed that their world was coming unglued, living in grotesque luxury off the forced labor of some fifty thousand brutally exploited African slaves.

Stedman's *Narrative* has been much admired (and has gone through

INTRODUCTION

more than twenty editions in six languages). It has also been much misunderstood. Although some commentators have accepted the work uncritically, as a soldier's unproblematical eyewitness account of unvarnished truths, and others have regarded it as some sort of abolitionist tract, we feel that its real significance stems from its being neither. Comparison of Stedman's text with his unpublished Suriname diaries and with other contemporary Suriname sources permits us to analyze the complex ways in which he constructed his work, while living in very changed personal and political circumstances, a decade after the events that it describes. The text consists of a half-dozen interwoven strands—the romance with Joanna and his efforts to gain her freedom; the military campaigns against the rebel slaves; his relations with other soldiers, particularly his commanding officer, Fourgeoud; the description and investigation of exotic flora and fauna; the description of Amerindian and African slave life; and, most important, the description and analysis of relations between planters and slaves—all structured by a chronological framework taken from his Suriname diaries. Stedman himself provides considerable assistance to the critical reader: a keen observer who, in his more than four years in the colony, moved comfortably through an unusual variety of contexts in this rigidly stratified society, he took pains, throughout his "Narrative," to distinguish his sources and to separate first- and second-hand accounts. Much of what he reports indeed derives from first-hand observation, but even his reports of hearsay represent key primary data, in that they disclose rich details about everyday plantation discourse.

Ironically, the power of Stedman's indictment of plantation slavery stems in part from his middle-of-the-road political position. Precisely because he was no abolitionist, Stedman's accounts of the behaviors and attitudes of Suriname's masters and slaves take on special authority. It is true that Stedman was caught in a paradox not easily seen at the time: "to the extent that cruelty was inherent in slavery, humanitarian amelioration [of the sort advocated in the text by Stedman] helped perpetuate cruelty" (Jordan 1968, 368). Yet Stedman's descriptive prose and illustrations, of both planter decadence and slave dignity, transcend his stated political views. It is as if he saw and understood and wrote and drew something more than he was prepared to admit to himself or to others. His original "Narrative," here published for the first time, stands as one of the richest, most vivid accounts ever written of a flourishing slave society. Whatever his own mixed intentions in writing and publishing it (and we discuss these in detail, below), others began using versions of his work for the antislavery cause as soon as they appeared, and—in part because his own critical apparatus is relatively accessible

INTRODUCTION

to us today—we can find in these pages a unique vision of an often-terrible past world that allows us better to understand our own.

"Studying to be Singular"

At the age of forty-two, having retired from military service in the Scots Brigade to a country house in Devonshire, John Gabriel Stedman wrote a rollicking account of the first twenty-eight years of his life (until his departure for Suriname), "principally . . . to amuse miself," but also for "my friends during my life[time]," and then afterwards, perhaps, "for all sorts of peaple to read" (*1786, 20 bis*).[1] Adopting the tone (if not quite matching the style) of *Tom Jones* or *Roderick Random*, Stedman envisioned his younger self as fearlessly iconoclastic and rebellious, jumping from one merry prank or drunken brawl to the next, and from one (often, married) woman's bed to another, all across the face of the Netherlands. The first child of a commissioned officer in the Scots Brigade and his Dutch wife, he described his boyhood (spent largely with his parents in Holland but partly with a paternal uncle in Scotland) as chock-full of misadventures and abrasive encounters of every description. The "premier mobile of all hurly-burly's, and street battles, which were my greatest delight" (*1786, 6*), he was "cald by some a good nut for the Devil to Crack, and By others a good fire stick to light his furnace" (*1786, 4*). Although his talent for drawing was "universally admired" (*1786, 5 bis*), he rejected his parents' attempts to arrange for him to study with painters in Holland "from merely a motive of pride—scorning to be instructed by block heads" (*1786, 5*).

Stedman depicted a childhood filled with the same kinds of experiences, attitudes, and personal relationships that were to characterize his years in Suriname. He dwelt, for example, on his early feelings of being tormented by authority figures, first in his interactions with the servant who accompanied him on a trip from Holland to Scotland (whom he consistently referred to as "my tyrant") and subsequently in his relationship with the cold, stern uncle who served as his guardian and tutor for two years; later, in Suriname, such feelings came to dominate his stormy relationship with his commanding officer, Colonel Fourgeoud. According to the autobiography, his volatile reaction to the personal injustices committed by these unsympathetic figures was also well developed long before the outbursts and impulsive acts of destructive rage that pepper his Suriname "Narrative." When, for example, his French instructor refused to honor a bet about how long it would take the ten-year-old Stedman to memorize a difficult passage, he claimed to have

INTRODUCTION

shattered instantly "in ten thousand pieces [the teacher's] beloved statue of Erasmus . . . although I knew I must be whipt for it the next moment" (*1786, 7*). And he reported that in Scotland he protested his uncle's harshness through a full range of rebellious acts—from milking cows into his hat to startling old women by firing pistols behind their backs (*1786, 3 bis*).

Stedman was proud of being unusually sensitive, even in an age of pervasive and modish sentimentality. He described the intensity of his empathy for all creatures from early childhood, which paralleled his troubled reactions to much of what he later witnessed in Suriname. For example, he wrote that when eight years old he cried "til I actually fell in convulsions" over seeing a fish broiled alive, and suffered "unspeacable mortification" at the slow torture of a cock by a group of boys (*1786, 6 bis*). These feelings were softened by neither age nor experience; in a 1787 letter of advice to his son, he urged him to "rejoice in good nature not only to man—but to the meanest insect—that is the whole Creation without exception[.] Scorn to hurt them but for thy food, or thy defence" (*14 January 1787*);[2] and a diary entry written just two years before his death noted, "a poor cow hamstrung by the infernal butchers. May God damn them" (*1795*).

Throughout his life, Stedman regularly interceded in order to alleviate the suffering of both people and animals. He described how, as a child, he went to great lengths to avoid drowning a mouse that had been discovered in the house; for this disobedience he was later whipped (*1786, 6 bis*). He recounted how, in the rain forest, after shooting but not killing a monkey, he was forced to put the animal out of its misery with his bare hands:

> my heart felt Seek on his account; here his dying little Eyes still Continued to follow me with seeming reproach till their light gradually forsook them and the wretched Creature expired. never Poor Devil felt more than I on this occasion, nor could I taste of him or his Companion when they were dress'd, who afforded to some others a delicious repast and which ended the Catastrophe. (p. 141)

In describing one of his rare battlefield encounters with rebel warriors, Stedman admitted that "my Sensibility Got so much the Better of my Duty, And my Pity for these poor miserable, illtreated People Was such, that I Was rather induced to fire with Eyes Shut . . . than to take a Proper Aim, of Which I had Frequent Opportunities" (p. 405). And when a lone, elderly rebel appeared in his camp, Stedman gave orders that he should not be harmed and left him some biscuits, beef, and rum (p. 562). In planters' homes he quickly interceded to prevent punishment to slaves (e.g., by paying for five plates broken by a slave girl to "save her from horrid whipping" [*24 February 1773*]). And back in England, a diary entry mentioned "a mouse dead in the snap and cold, by care once more revived" (*16 May 1792*).

In his own writings, Stedman's concern for animals was explicitly related to the characteristic Enlightenment belief in the "wonderfull chain of Gradation, from Man to the most diminitive of the above Species [here referring to monkeys] . . . who if wisely viewed and desected, bear such general resemblance with /nay little difference from/ myself" (p. 144). From this perspective, Stedman saw Africans as the close kinsmen of both nonhuman primates and himself: "does not the face, Shape, and Manner of the african Negroe /whom in every respect I look on as my brother/ I say does this not often put us in Mind of the Wild Man of the Woods or *Orangoutang?*" (p. 144).[3]

The passions that are so prominent in Stedman's account of his tragic romance with the mulatto slave Joanna appear also in his memories of childhood; for example, he describes himself at age eleven weeping bitterly over parting from a school companion named Alida Paris (*1786, 2 bis*). But he depicted most of his relationships with women as of an entirely different kind. Indeed, his self-image as a Lothario, and the sometimes unexpected advances this led to, developed long before the famous incidents in which Suriname slaves and planters' wives alike repeatedly forced themselves upon him. As he pictured himself in his youth,

> I was certainly much beloved amongst the girls, but particularly of a certain sort, not by the best of them . . . on account of my person which was without vanity allowd to be a lure for most of women species—I had a Je ne say qwoy about me, of the fasquinating kind, which attracted the girls as the eys of the Rattlesnake attrakts Squirls, and unaccountably persuades them to submission. (*1786, 18, 29*)

Stedman larded his autobiographical sketch with amorous adventures. He told in some detail how, at age seventeen, he was tricked into entering the bedroom of an elderly, foul-breathed woman, "half dres'd en negleegee," who gripped his hand and pulled him, struggling, into an unwanted embrace (*1786, 10 bis*). After various similar encounters during the subsequent months, his diary records that "one Gauseman's servant maid commits a rape on me," to which he appended the marginal note, "I acknowlege miself at this time one of the compleetest fleks and was verry careless of what was to become of me" (*1786, 15*). Nonetheless, he persisted in his adventures, having by then (he says) read "Joseph Andrews, tom Jones, and Roderick Random which heroes I resolved to take for my models" (*1786, 15*)—by which he seems to have meant models of the real-life (rather than merely literary) variety. "R. Random," he added, "I liked best and in imitation of he [I] emedately fell in Love at the Dancing assembly with a Miss diana Bennet whom I shall call narcissa [after the heroine of that book]" (ibid.). And accordingly, he followed that infatuation not only by falling "desperately in love" very soon after, but also by taking advantage of the frequent sexual opportunities that were coming his way. The wife of his landlord, for example, on the excuse that Stedman was ill, "pays me frequent visits in my bedroom[.] I treat her like Joseph did potiphars wife and prefer her maid Maria Bymans"—which preference ultimately ends this rather complex domestic farce when the landlady, "mad with jealousy . . . in consequence [causes] Maria Bymans and poor I [to be] turn'd out of the howse at the same time" (*1786, 16;* see also the scene in *Joseph Andrews* in which Joey begins to be called Joseph as Lady Booby unsuccessfully attempts to seduce him [Fielding 1742: bk. 1, chap. 5], as well as Genesis 39).

Stedman seems to have thoroughly enjoyed being (and depicting himself as) a merry prankster. During his childhood, after having had an argument with his brother, he first threatened to hang himself and then let his brother discover him hanging, apparently lifeless, by a rope from the rafters, "my Eys turnd up—my head on one shoulder—and my tung down over my chin . . . which [the truth having eventually been discovered] occatoind a curious scene of mirth and consternation" (*1786, 14 bis*). Or again, believing that his mother was favoring his brother, he decided to interrupt her while she was "with a group of fine Ladies . . . sipping theyr limonade in the moonshine," by "quietly strip[ping] miself in the howse and running through the middle of them stark naked. . . . The allarum was to me exceedingly entertaining" (ibid.). During his later youth, his practical jokes and related exploits became more closely involved with drinking, brawling, and sex, as he sometimes visited three bawdy houses in a single night, shared various women with his friends, watched his "best mate . . . cohabit with [a girl they had just picked up] on a publick country road," and so on (*1786, 19 bis*). And right alongside his affectedly penitent asides to the effect that "I am ashamed almost of my scandalous life" (*1786, 20 bis*), or that "nothing could be more wild than I was at this present time" (*1786, 19 bis*), he always liked to remind his readers that, nevertheless, "none could have a better heart, however strange tis truth" (ibid.).

Stedman viewed himself, with a certain pride, as a perpetual misfit because of his principled refusal to pay homage to the conventions of his day. In 1785, during the period when he was writing the autobiographical account of his youth, he noted in his diary that

> in all places I have been beloved by the inhabitants when known but at first cald mad in Scotland, mased [confused] in England, fou [crazy] by the namurois [Belgians], gek or dol [crazy or mad] by the Duch, and law [Sranan for insane] by the negros in Surinam, owing intirely to my studying to be singular in as much as can be so. (*29 November 1785*)

Stedman's "studying to be singular" followed him to the grave.

> Before he died he expressed a wish to be interred, as our kings and queens were formerly, at midnight and by torchlight and, of all the odd things, he wanted to lie at Bickleigh, side by side with Bampfylde Moore Carew [known as the King of the Gypsies]. (Snell 1904, 138)[4]

In defense of his writings, Stedman consistently championed the cause of artless candor, asserting, for example, that "some stuff to be sure may lie hard in sour stomachs," but that "I neither wryte for profit nor applause—purely following the dictates of nature, & equally hating a made up man and made up storry" (*1786, 5 bis*). This same dedication to reporting things exactly as he saw them, regardless of the consequences, is also reiterated frequently in his Suriname "Narrative" and used there to justify many of the very passages that were eventually excised by the publisher in the version that finally went to press.[5]

Stedman's diaries make clear that eighteenth-century Europe was a world in many ways extremely distant from the Europe of our own day. Certainly the way in which death had to be accepted as part of everyday experience jumps out from his pages with startling regularity. The diaries and autobiography record, for example, that

> when, but a boy at scool, my most loving scool companion ... was snached away by the smallpox. ... When a cadet, my best friend ... was run through the heart by an artillery man, in a duel ... when ensign, my best companion ... in a fitt of Frensy, poisoned himself [*1786, 8*]; my nephew, a Lieut in the 64th Ret. was kild by his horse [*February 1792*]; we saw a most dreadfull execution of 7 malefactors 2 of whom were hang'd, and 5 were broak upon the rack, without ever having done murder but once or twice in self defence [*1786, 18 bis*]; I saw a rascal for comitting murder, executed on the rack [*1786, 26 bis*]; in France a 14 headed guillottine [was] invented. ... [and] above 4200 prisoners ... [were] all waiting to be put to death. (*31 December 1793*)

The sense of strangeness and distance that the modern reader may feel reading Stedman on eighteenth-century Suriname, then, is not

INTRODUCTION

solely a function of that colony's exotic history. Though his Suriname descriptions may seem, for example, to include a startling number of untimely deaths (the death of sailors from drowning, of slaves from punitive tortures, of soldiers from lack of proper food in the rain forest, and of colonists from tropical diseases), they should be read in the broader context of the contemporary European world, which Stedman and his intended readers used as their point of reference. As Darnton has recently reminded us, perhaps with just a touch of hyperbole, plebeian eighteenth-century Europe now seems "an almost inaccessible world . . . a world so saturated with violence and death that we can barely imagine it" (1984, 34–36).

"A Five Years Expedition"

In 1771, friendless, in debt, and saddened by the recent death of his father, Stedman resigned himself to "the desperate ressourse of going as a common sailor to North America or the Mediterranean, or even up the Baltick incognito for a voyage not longer than 9 months" (*1786, 29 bis*) in order to accumulate enough cash to pay off his debts. For the previous eleven years, since the age of sixteen, he had been serving—first with the rank of ensign, then as lieutenant—in the Scots Brigade, in the pay of the Dutch Stadthouder, defending various Low Country outposts. In response to a call for volunteers to serve in the West Indies, he left Holland on 24 December 1772 on the frigate *Zeelust*, with the rank of captain (by brevet), and arrived in Suriname on 2 February 1773. His stay in the colony, which lasted just over four years (rather than the hyperbolic five proclaimed in the title of the "Narrative"), resulted in one of the most detailed "outsider's" descriptions ever written of life in an eighteenth-century slave plantation society. Stedman's ongoing and intimate dealings with members of all social classes, from the governor and the wealthiest planters to the most oppressed slaves, gave him special opportunities to observe and describe the full panorama of Suriname life.

Stedman was part of a corps of eight hundred European volunteers—professional soldiers trained for the battlefields of Europe—who were sent to Suriname by the Dutch States-General to assist the beleaguered local troops then fighting against marauding bands of escaped slaves in the eastern region of the colony. In 1760 and 1762, the two largest groups of maroons (the Djuka and the Saramaka, settled along the upper Marowijne and Suriname rivers, respectively) had won their independence by treaty, after a century-long guerrilla war against

XXI

the colonists. But the succeeding decade witnessed unexpected and lively hostilities involving newer maroon groups that lived just beyond the borders of the flourishing Cottica and Commewijne River plantations, trapped between the slave society of the coast and the free Djukas and Saramakas (who, as part of their treaties, were pledged to turn over to the colonists any new maroons they encountered). Between 1768 and 1772, the frequency of raids on plantations by these small new groups, and of military expeditions sent after them, increased tremendously.

By 1772, the entire Cottica-Commewijne plantation economy was grinding to a halt as great numbers of slaves began "deserting" to these nearby maroons, who by then were not only destroying plantations almost at will (carrying off slave women, tools, weapons, and ammunition) but even successfully capturing outlying colonial military posts. Citing the "awful and sad circumstances of the colony" caused by the "audacity of the runaways" (and having decided as a matter of principle not to negotiate peace treaties with them), Governor Nepveu and his council requested, and received, professional troops from Europe, among whom was Stedman.

We now know that the maroons against whom Stedman and his comrades fought consisted of a number of very small bands—at the height of their strength no more than a total of several hundred men, women, and children.[6] Organized primarily according to the plantations on which they had served as slaves, these maroon groups periodically banded together, split apart, and rejoined, depending on the immediate military situation and on the shifting alignments of their leaders—the charismatic Boni and his "father," Aluku; their major allies, Coromantijn Codjo and Suku; and other lesser-known chiefs such as Kwami, Aricot, and Puja van La Paix. Between 1769 and 1776/77 (when the surviving members of these groups crossed over the Marowijne River to settle in French Guiana), they lived in some twenty different villages or camps, never staying long enough for more than a single harvest of crops, sometimes forced to move even more quickly when discovered by a colonial commando sent out to burn their houses and fields.[7]

The most dramatic single battle of what has come to be known as "The First Boni War" (1765–77) actually unfolded several months before Stedman's arrival in Suriname. In April 1772, troops of the Suriname government had discovered Boni's palisaded village, Boucou, which was surrounded by a deep swamp fordable only by secret paths hidden just below the water level. For five months, as Boni somehow managed to continue sending out raiding parties that destroyed plan-

Figure 1. Boucou, during the final siege, with the attackers' camp in the foreground (1772). A, officers' barracks; B, storehouse; C, soldiers' barracks; D, Negroes' huts; E, kitchen; F, watch-house; G, path or trace to the gardens. Drawn by J. F. Frederici, commander of the Rangers. As Boni's people finally fled the village, they taunted their attackers, "shout[ing] out to us that their old village [Boucou] was [now] called 'Mi Sal Lossij' [I may be taken] but their new one was 'Jou no sal vindij' [You will not find it]" (de Beet 1984, 100; and see pp. 84–86, below). Algemeen Rijksarchief.

INTRODUCTION

tations and terrorized the colonists, government troops attempted unsuccessfully to conquer his besieged stronghold. In July, the government made the "desperate" but sage decision to create an elite corps of fighting men, the "Neeger Vrijcorps" (whom Stedman referred to as "Rangers")—116 slave volunteers, purchased specially from their planter-masters for the purpose, who were promised their freedom, a house and garden plot, and military pay in return for fighting the maroons.[8] Although in their first attempt to storm Boucou two Rangers drowned trying to cross the swamp and twelve others were captured (and then maimed or executed), these troops displayed "unexpected" courage and perseverence, and within a month the government had purchased and manumitted another 190 slaves to join the corps of Rangers.

In September 1772, a heavily armed force, including the enlarged corps of Rangers, finally took Boucou, killing at least five men and capturing twenty-five women, four men, and nineteen children who were unable to escape with the rest of the population. Chief Boni had successfully resisted the siege for five long months, demonstrating impressive strategic acumen while relying on his gods to control the rains so that his adversaries could not cross the swamp. But the fall of Boucou—in which near-starvation seems to have played the decisive role—was a serious military and moral blow to Boni's people; within weeks, some one hundred to one hundred twenty additional maroons from the community were captured wandering in the forest (some even turning themselves in to the colonists) and another fifty to sixty were shot by patrols.[9]

Stedman's arrival in Suriname in February 1773 coincided with a rare moment of optimism on the part of the colonists. Boucou had just fallen; Boni was on the run; the plantations, for the moment, seemed secure. Almost immediately, however, Colonel Fourgeoud (commander of the newly arrived troops) and Governor Nepveu began to argue about the further conduct of the war, and this conflict lasted until Fourgeoud's departure nearly five years later.[10] For example, Nepveu stood firmly behind an ambitious plan to construct a "protective cordon" ninety-four kilometers long, a kind of Great Wall of China, consisting of scores of manned posts along a road ten meters wide that would mark off the boundaries of the civilized plantation zone from the forest and its marauding maroons, while Fourgeoud disdained such "passive" defenses;[11] Nepveu wished to depend heavily on the recently formed corps of Rangers, while Fourgeoud was suspicious of its relative independence and mistrusted the Africans' "unorthodox" fighting tactics; Nepveu greatly feared renewed hostilities with the already "pa-

XXIV

INTRODUCTION

Deez Krijgsman is FOURGEOUD, wiens heldevuist en moed
In 't Surinaamsch gewest de veiligheid herstelde,
De bosschen vaagde van al 't plonderziek gebroed,
Dat, Jaaren achter een, den nijvren planter kwelde.
Hij Stierf, na zoveel dienst tot aller braven smart,
Maar zijn gedachtenis leeft eeuwig in hun hart.
                                       F. LENTFRINCK

Figure 2. Colonel Louis Henry Fourgeoud. Engraving by Th. Koning, ca. 1778, apparently after a painting made by Stedman in 1775 (see n. 36 (d), below). The memorial poem by F. Lentfrinck reads (roughly): "This Warrior is FOURGEOUD, whose hero's fist and courage / Restored the security of Suriname, / Sweeping the forests clean of the plundering swarms, / Who, Year after year, tormented the industrious planter. / He Died, to the regret of all good men, having served so well, / But his memory lives forever in their hearts."

cified" Saramaka and Djuka, while Fourgeoud believed he could count on their active support in fighting Boni and the other new "rebels." Amidst these ongoing disagreements about overall strategy—complicated by the existence of the corps of Rangers and the troops of the Society of Suriname, initially under a command structure distinct from Fourgeoud's forces—military activity of one kind or another nevertheless continued throughout the period of Stedman's stay in the colony.

Again and again, Boni or one of his allies would stage lightning-quick assaults on plantations, and one or another of the colony's forces would pursue them through the forests, destroying any fields and villages they were able to discover. Captured maroons were often forced to serve as guides for these expeditions, but it seems clear—both from Stedman's "Narrative" and from other contemporary documents—that most of the military expeditions against these maroons were fruitless. Stedman's own experience was typical in this respect: on seven campaigns in the forest, averaging three months each, he engaged in only one battle, the taking of Gado Sabi in 1774. (His moving descriptions of this encounter, graphically portrayed in the frontispiece [where the burning village appears in the distance], make clear that even this great "victory" served mainly to chase the courageous but miserable rebels farther into the forest [see pp. 389–411].) The war, then, was characterized by the colonial troops' criss-crossing, more or less blindly, vast expanses of treacherous forests and swamps, with the maroons—through an efficient system of spies and lookouts—almost always remaining at least a step ahead, and often setting fatal ambushes for their pursuers. In the end, however, Fourgeoud's general strategy of cruising the forests proved successful in driving out the maroon guerrillas, though at the cost of enormous loss of life among his troops; some eight hundred thirty additional men were sent from Holland in 1775 to supplement the original contingent of eight hundred, yet only a couple of hundred lived to return to Europe.[12] For Fourgeoud's men and the government troops did finally manage to make the eastern forests of Suriname so uncomfortable that Boni and his people (by this time only some two hundred to three hundred strong) chose to settle in French Guiana, crossing the Marowijne River by canoe in two groups, in 1776 and 1777, just before Fourgeoud's own departure for Holland.[13]

"My Little Wrytings"

In addition to the manuscript of the "Narrative," completed in 1790, Stedman left diverse notebooks and papers that have helped us piece

INTRODUCTION

together the history of the work from its beginnings in the form of a log kept in Suriname in the 1770s through the various stages of writing, editing, and negotiating with the publisher that led to the first edition of 1796.

Stedman's log of daily events during his years in Suriname recorded details of his personal life (from dinners with planters to nights spent wenching), military activities, and anecdotes about the natural and social worlds around him. Throughout his stay in the colony, Stedman divided his time between two settings that could not have stood in sharper contrast. The homes of planters, where he was a frequent guest, were notable even in the context of New World plantation societies for both the opulence and the decadence of their daily life. The military campaigns in the rain forest were extended ordeals of frustration, danger, malnutrition, sickness, and death. Stedman's way of coping with these contrastive settings seems to have involved both his consciously chosen role as scientific observer (which encouraged him to distance himself from much of what he witnessed) and his incurable romanticism (which encouraged intimate personal involvements and a responsiveness to the natural beauty of the colony, even during the most trying moments of his stay). His easy movement between different social settings owed much to his linguistic facility; he spoke English, Dutch, French, and, most important, Sranan (the English-based creole that was the everyday language of slaves and many whites—see p. 515).

Faithfully, he kept on-the-spot notes—sometimes jotted down on cartridges or even on "a Bleached bone" when writing paper was not available (p. 578)—and then strung them together in a small green notebook that once lay briefly at the bottom of the Commewijne River before being recovered and dried out for later consultation (p. 369), as well as on ten folded sheets of foolscap, written on both sides.[14] From the outset, Stedman had the intention of some day expanding these notes into a book. On the final page of his "small green almanack," covering 29 October 1772 to 29 April 1774, he wrote, "This Small Journall is written with the greatest attention, founded on facts allone by Captt. John G. S——n, who Shall explain it more at large one day, if Providence Spares him in life."

In addition to his practice of keeping up a diary no matter what the circumstances, Stedman systematically studied and drew whatever caught his curious eye. He described, for example, how on a military campaign in the forest,

> while we were Unsuccessful in taking the Rebels I Availed myself of Taking a Draft of Every Animal, reptile, or Shrub, that I thought Could

XXVII

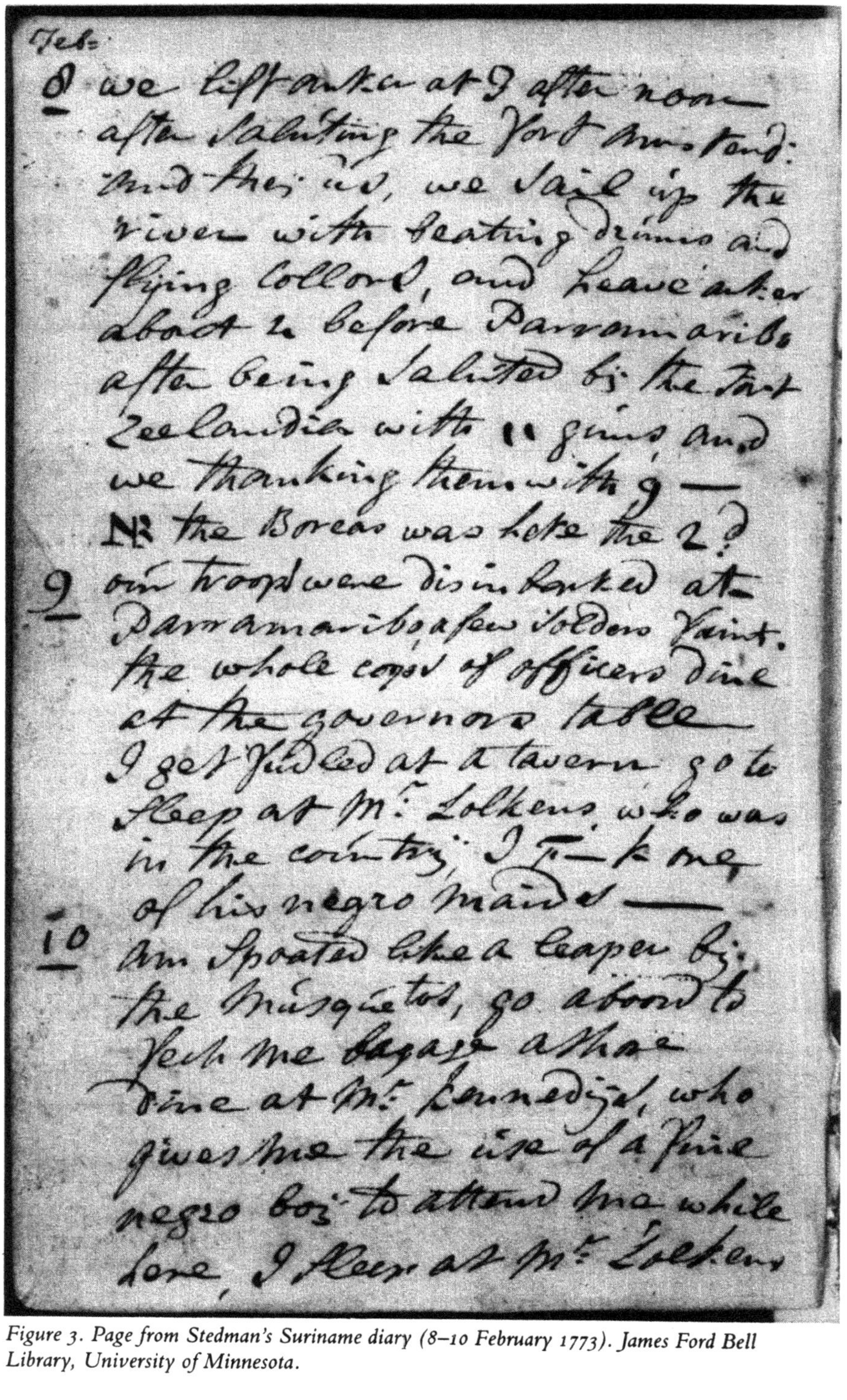

Feb:

8 — we left anker at 9 afternoon after saluting the fort Amsterdam and Thesius, we sail up the river with beating drums and flying collors, and heave anker about 2 before Parramaribo after being saluted by the fort Zeelandia with 11 guns and we thanking them with 9 —
N: the Boreas was here the 2?

9 — our troops were disimbarked at Parramaribo a few soldiers faint. the whole corps of officers dine at the governors table I get fudled at a tavern go to sleep at Mr Lolkens who was in the country, I F—k one of his negro maides —

10 — am spoted like a leaper by the Musquietos, go abord to fech me bagage ashoar dine at Mr Kennedys, who gives me the use of a fine negro boy to attend me while here, I sleep at Mr Lolkens

Figure 3. Page from Stedman's Suriname diary (8–10 February 1773). James Ford Bell Library, University of Minnesota.

INTRODUCTION

Illustrate my Little Collection of Natural Curiosity, which I now began to form some Idea of Exhibiting one Day to the Publick if I was Spared to return to Europe. (p. 347)

Similarly, Stedman avidly collected both natural and ethnological "curiosities," some of which he presented to the Leverian Museum, others to the Prince of Orange upon his return to Europe (*1796, May 1796*, p. 620), and some of which have been recently rediscovered at the Rijksmuseum voor Volkenkunde in Leiden. These latter include the oldest extant Afro-American banjo in the world, collected by Stedman from a slave in Suriname (see R. and S. Price 1979; Whitehead 1986).

After his return to Europe, Stedman composed the retrospective autobiographical sketch covering his life prior to the Suriname expedition and continued to keep a diary, recording personal matters, noting financial dealings, listing his correspondence, and summarizing the major political events that occurred in Europe each month. Some of these diaries were kept in a bound *dagwyser* [datebook], others in a thin, marbled-paper notebook, still others on fifty-one loose folded sheets of foolscap and two other loose sheets; the entries vary significantly in their length and inclusiveness, and there are some years (e.g., 1779–83) for which no materials have been found at all.[15]

As we set out to reconstruct the stormy publication history of Stedman's book, we first worked with these materials in the form in which they had been published by the English antiquarian Stanbury Thompson (1962, 1966), who had bought them from a London junk dealer about 1940.[16] However, it quickly became apparent that Thompson's work confused as much as it elucidated. Examination of the original notebooks and papers that Thompson had used (which are now in the James Ford Bell Library at the University of Minnesota) revealed that, not only had he inserted his own commentary into that of Stedman without in any way distinguishing the two, but he had changed dates and spellings, misread and incorrectly transcribed a large number of words, translated Dutch words (and mistranslated Sranan words) into English, reordered words and even whole passages, rephrased column lists as prose, included passages that had been carefully crossed out by Stedman, and deleted other passages without apparent reason—all this without indicating in his publication where the alterations had been made.

Thompson also took it upon himself (perhaps mimicking eighteenth-century practice, perhaps from his own personal post-Victorian sensibilities) to insulate his readers from shock. He published Stedman's Suriname diary entry for 12 March 1773, for example, as "Dine at Ken-

INTRODUCTION

nedy's," but discreetly omitted to print Stedman's next sentence, "3 girls pas the night in me room." He reworded Stedman's entry for 8 January 1774 at many points and deleted the observation that the piranhas that infest the creeks and rivers of Suriname were known locally as "p——k biters."[17] Thompson obscured an allusion to the inebriated state of the publisher of the "Narrative" at the time he wrote Stedman "an insolent epistle" in September 1795 by transcribing the (clearly written) word "wine" as "w——," and he modified in similar fashion Stedman's frequent references to "turds." More significant, Thompson took Stedman's characteristic and unambiguous diary references to having "f——d" one or another woman (or having been "f——d" by same) and printed them as "fooled," altering the interpretation of several key incidents.[18] It should be clear, then, why, in preparing our new edition of Stedman, we have relied exclusively on those manuscript diary pages now at the University of Minnesota, rather than on Thompson's flawed book.

According to his diary, Stedman began working on the "Narrative" on 15 June 1778—just a year after returning to the Netherlands from Suriname, and only a few days after receiving from Sir George Strickland (the man to whom he dedicated the 1790 "Narrative") an offer "to get my West Indies voyage published, which I promised to write" (*10 June 1778*).[19] In September 1784, having married a young Dutch woman, he moved to England, and in May 1785 they settled at Tiverton in Devonshire, where he continued the writing and began enlisting the support of subscribers for the publication.

His diary entries for these years were dominated by mundane domestic matters, such as financial worries, children's and animals' health, gardening activities, the weather, trips with his wife, problems with servants, attendance at church and social events, horseback riding, moving his family from one rented house in Tiverton to another, thefts in the neighborhood, taxes, births and birthdays, minor marital disputes, and his own ill health.[20] Family responsibilities were a constant burden; as he commented on 20 November 1789, soon after the birth of his third child, "between wives and children—nurses and maids—dogs and cats—mice and rats rats and mice—fleas and lice, I am plagued out of my senses." The diaries we have for these years are incomplete and erratic and contain almost no mention of the progress of his projected book. He seems to have worked at it steadily throughout the period, however, and—in spite of his numerous travails—made clear in 1787 that "My only ambition remaining is to se my little wrytings made publick" (*18 January 1787*).

The daily log that Stedman kept during his "five years" expedition

Figure 4. "John Gabriel Stedman. Capt. Scotch Brig. Stuarts Regt." Oil portrait by C. Delin, 1783 (when Stedman was thirty-nine years old). Stedman Archive, Haus Besselich, Urbar, Germany. Courtesy of Hilda von Barton Stedman.

INTRODUCTION

in Suriname reflected the perspective of a bright and independent young officer—unattached, adventurous, and barraged with new physical, emotional, and social experiences. By the time that he had married and settled down in England, however, he had become committed to a family-oriented existence that could not have contrasted more dramatically in its bourgeois domesticity to the heady experiences he had had in Suriname. From this perspective, both geographically and culturally distanced from Suriname, he exhibited a strong tendency to romanticize the personal relationships of that period of his life. The "Narrative," then, should be read in part as Stedman's retrospective and somewhat idealized vision of his youth in Suriname, written from the perspective of a significantly changed personal situation. Surprisingly, perhaps, the events of the 1790 text closely follow the diaries that Stedman kept in Suriname. Although the diary entries tend to be brief and cryptic, compared to the more elaborated descriptions in the "Narrative," discrepancies or contradictions are rare.[21] However, one major transformation did take place: the depiction of his relationship with his "Suriname wife," Joanna.[22] This in turn had significant repercussions for his treatment of interracial sexual relationships in the "Narrative" more generally.

Stedman's daily log from his early months in Suriname leaves no doubt about the frequency of his sexual encounters with slave women (continuing his pattern of frequent transactions with Dutch prostitutes in the years before). On 9 February 1773, the very first night after his arrival in Paramaribo, Stedman laconically recorded in his diary, "sleep at Mr. Lolkens . . . I f——k one of his negro maids." During the following months, his notes about dinner companions were frequently complemented by mention of his sleeping partners.

> a negro woman offers me the use of her daugter, while here, for a sertain soom[.] we dont agre[e] about the price. (*22 February 1773*)
>
> soop in me room with two mallato girls. (*25 February 1773*)
>
> B——e comes to me and stays the whole night. (*26 March 1773*)
>
> J——a, her mother, and Q—— mother come to close a bargain [of formalized concubinage] we me, we put it of for reasons I gave them. (*11 April 1773*)
>
> Dine and soop at Lolkens— B——e and J——a both breakfast with me, I call meself Mistire. (*12 April 1773*)
>
> B——e sleeps with me. (*13 April 1773*)
>
> J——a comes to stay with me. (*23 April 1773*)

xxxii

INTRODUCTION

The rather different account that Stedman gave of this same period in his 1790 "Narrative" minimized the frequency of everyday, quasi-commercial sex between white men and slave women and strongly romanticized his own relationship with Joanna. While not actually denying in the 1790 manuscript that Mr. Lolken's "negro maid" (whom he depicts there as being extremely insistent) stayed with him that first night, he discreetly chose to "draw a Sable Curtain" over the climactic scene (p. 43); his disagreement about the price of the girl who was offered to him by her mother was transformed, in the 1790 version, to a curt refusal based on his shock and moral disapproval of a mother offering her daughter "to be what she pleased to call my Wife"; and neither his activities with "B——e" nor those with the other, unnamed mulatto girls were ever mentioned in the 1790 text. Also removed, between the diaries and the 1790 depiction, were important aspects of Joanna's role as a sexual partner. There is no mention of her sleeping with Stedman (either alone or with "B——e") until well after they became good friends; the very telling scene in which her mother offers her to Stedman for a price is deleted wholesale; and in general, the early stages of their relationship are rephrased by Stedman to elevate Joanna from the role of a slave girl providing routine sexual services, as part of a commercial transaction, to the status of a pure and noble beauty, a true Sable Venus, whom Stedman first began to worship from afar.

Emblematic of this shift is the fact that Stedman's early diary references to Joanna usually identify her (along with other slave women who slept with him) by her first initial only, while in the 1790 manuscript she joined the ranks of more respectable characters in the "Narrative," being referred to by her full name. In the course of the 1790 text, Stedman developed the romantic image fully; a passage from chapter 13 conveys the characteristic tone of his retrospective portrait of Joanna and includes an example of his frequent practice of "adapting" well-known verse (in this case from *Paradise Lost*).

> Not Adam and Eve in Paradise could Enjoy a greater Share of felicity, than we now did—free like the roes in the forest and disintangled from every care and fashion, we breathed the purest Ether in our walks, and refresh'd our limbs in the Cooling limpid Streams, health and Vigour were now again my portion, while my Mulatto flourished in youth and beauty, the envy and admiration of all the River Comewina—
>
> Here in close recess,
> With flowry Garlands and sweet Smelling herbs,
> Espoused Eve did deck her nuptial bed,
> And heavenly Quires the hymenaean Sing;

Figure 5. "*The Voyage of the Sable Venus, from Angola to the West Indies.*" Colored engraving by W. Grainger, after a painting by T. Stothard. Also published in Edwards 1794, 2:27, to illustrate Edwards's dreadful seven-page "The Sable Venus, An Ode (Written in Jamaica)." The iconography is characteristic of the years when Stedman was writing the "Narrative." Courtesy of Judith Johnston, New York.

INTRODUCTION

> What Day the genial Angel to *her friend*
> Brought her in naked Beauty more adorn'd,
> More lovely than Pandora, whom the Gods
> Endow'd with all their Gifts. (p. 260)

These alterations and embellishments were clearly important to Stedman in projecting an image of his own conduct in the colony that now seemed appropriate, from the perspective of his life as a middle-aged gentleman established with his wife and children in the English countryside, and in preserving the memory of a woman whom he had indeed come to love. Motivated by very personal considerations, these alterations had the effect of distorting Stedman's descriptions of an important aspect of contemporary Suriname life. While his diaries depicted a society in which depersonalized sex between European men and slave women was pervasive and routine, his 1790 manuscript transformed Suriname into the exotic setting for a deeply romantic and appropriately tragic love affair.

In terms of social and cultural description, the major distortion these changes produced was the treatment of a local institution that had come to be referred to as "Suriname marriage" (see van Lier 1949, chap. 3). The features that distinguished this arrangement from traditional European marriage were its commercial dimension (with the European man paying an agreed-upon sum to a member of the slave woman's family), its temporal limitation (to the period of the man's residence in the colony), the nature of its initiation (through a secular rather than a religious ceremony), and its ready availability to already married men. Stedman alluded to this kind of arrangement in speaking of Joanna's own mother, a slave named Cery, who had "attended [Joanna's white father] with the Duties of a Lawful Wife" (p. 88). And in the 1790 "Narrative," he also outlined the terms of the institution more generally, though never in any way associating it with his own relationship with Joanna:

> I must describe this Custom which I am convinced will be highly censured by the Sedate European Matrons—and which is nevertheless as common as it is almost necessary to the batchelors who live in this Climate; these Gentlemen all without Exception have a female Slave /mostly a creole/ in their keeping who preserves their linnens clean and decent, dresses their Victuals with Skill, carefully attends them /they being most excellent nurses/ during the frequent illnesses to which Europeans are exposed in this Country, prevents them from keeping late Hours knits

for them, sows for them &c•—while these Girls who are sometimes Indians sometime Mulattos and often negroes, naturally pride themselves in living with an European whom they serve with as much tenderness, and to whom they are Generally as faithfull as if he were their lawfull Husband to the great Shame of so many fair Ladies, who break through ties more sacred, and indeed bound with more Solemnity, nor can the above young women be married in any other way, being by their state of Servitude entirely debard from every Christian priviledge and Ceremony, which makes it perfectly lawfull on *their* Side, while they hesitate not to pronounce those as Harlots, who do not follow them /if they can/ in this laudable Example in which they are encouraged as I have said by their nearest Relations and Friends.

• —of this Habit even the Clergymen are not Exempt witness the Rev. Mr. Snyderhaus, Mr. Talant, &c. (pp. 47–48)

"Suriname marriage" was both well defined and widespread in the colony, and from the perspective of those who knew Stedman and Joanna, it clearly served to delineate the terms of their relationship. It was at once the framework for the most meaningful personal relationship in Stedman's life and the embarrassing reminder of Joanna's servile status. A decade after he left Joanna, and several years after her death, Stedman seems to have dealt with this awkwardness simply by denying that his situation fit the mold of other "marriages" between Europeans and slaves in the colony. In the 1790 "Narrative," he repeatedly stressed that he had intended to make Joanna his legal Christian wife in Europe; and at the same time, he chose not to mention the special "Suriname wedding" that he celebrated according to local custom on 8 May 1773. In denying that his relationship with Joanna was the product of its colonial time and place, Stedman drew on then-current European sentimental ideals to elevate it, in retrospect, to an example of pure and faithful love (which effectively captivated European audiences—see below). "Suriname marriage," meanwhile, became a vague, hastily discussed abstraction in the 1790 "Narrative," even though it was being reported by a man whose personal life had centered on it for more than four years.

"To Make Them Publick"

In the spring of 1787, Stedman's diary began to mention the reactions of the friends to whom he showed parts of what he was then calling his "Journal" (later to become the 1790 "Narrative") and his efforts to se-

INTRODUCTION

cure their financial backing for its publication.[23] On 8 February 1791—almost thirteen years after he had begun its composition—he sent a copy of the full manuscript as well as a list of seventy-six subscribers (for ninety-two copies) to his publisher, Joseph Johnson, in London.[24] At the same time, he posted "proposals" to potential subscribers in London, Edinburgh, York, Liverpool, Bath, Bristol, Exeter, Portsmouth, and Plymouth. During the next several weeks, his correspondence (presumably regarding subscriptions for publication) continued to expand dramatically; on 28 February 1791 he noted that he had by then sent out proposals "to Cambridge and Oxford Coledges [and] to about 30 towns at home and abroad. Besides to a number of Private English gentlemen."

Stedman's financial arrangements with Johnson are not fully clear. Stedman was able to guarantee a sum to Johnson by having raised, as of early 1791, ninety-two subscriptions at a guinea each. By date of publication in 1796, the list of subscribers had grown to two hundred (for 208 copies), in large part due to Stedman's incessant letter writing and personal solicitations, drawing on his Dutch, Scottish, and Suriname connections (including some of the participants in the events of the "Narrative"), on his acquaintances in Devonshire and London, and on career military officers elsewhere.[25] Johnson had apparently agreed, upon accepting the manuscript in 1790, to pay Stedman "£500 & chance for 1000" should the book prove successful (*2 February 1792*), and in 1793 Stedman requested and received an advance of £212.10.0 (*25 December 1793*).[26] This was not, then, a form of the common late eighteenth-century agreement for "publishing by subscription" in which the author went to the publisher as employer to employee (Hepburn 1968, 10–11), but it was not an uncommon arrangement (G. E. Bentley, Jr., personal communication, 1984). Stedman seems to have sold Johnson the complete rights, and it seems clear that, during the six years the book was in press, Stedman's role vis-à-vis Johnson was not dissimilar to that of a modern author whose manuscript has been accepted by a publisher: ultimately dependent about all decisions regarding production details (typeface, illustrations, print run, pricing), as well as about matters of editorial modification.

Johnson was a prominent figure in radical British political and intellectual circles during the late eighteenth century. A shy, taciturn bachelor, he nevertheless entertained a particularly active social group in his home over his bookshop, regularly bringing together men and women interested in art, literature, and politics for dinner and discussion on Sundays and occasional Tuesdays (Tyson 1979, xv, xvii). His regular guests included authors whom he published, such as Thomas Paine,

INTRODUCTION

Joseph Priestley, William Godwin, Erasmus Darwin, Richard Price, Mary Wollstonecraft, and Henry Fuseli. Between 1790 and 1796, Stedman often participated in these evenings when he was in London.

Johnson's interests ranged widely, and he published works of theology, medicine, moral philosophy, science, poetry, children's literature, feminism, and politics, as well as *The Analytical Review*. Of particular importance—both in his general publishing career and in his treatment of Stedman's "Narrative"—were his political views, which have been characterized as "moderate radicalism" (Tyson 1979, 139), but which often grazed the edge of official acceptability. "Both lucky and shrewd, he managed for a time [during the mid-1790s] to pick politically sensitive books that espoused radical sentiments while staying within the law against seditious writings" (135). But though he managed to walk this thin line for several years, Johnson was finally arrested in 1798, ostensibly for selling a pamphlet by Gilbert Wakefield (a reply to the Bishop of Llandaff's patriotic, anti-French *An Address to the People of Great Britain*), which concluded, "Great revolutions are accomplishing: a general fermentation is working for the purpose of general refinement through the universe" (158).[27] It seems clear that Johnson's handling of Stedman's "Narrative," which he published just two years before his arrest for sedition, was affected by his general concern during this period about staying within the law.

"80 Engravings Design'd from Nature on the Spot"

Johnson began to work on Stedman's manuscript as soon as he received it in early 1791, focusing his attention first on the formidable logistics of getting Stedman's approximately 106 "drawings" (mainly watercolors) engraved for eventual inclusion in the book. At the time Stedman submitted his manuscript and artwork, he envisioned eighty-three engraved plates (many consisting of two separate images on a single page) including a frontispiece, and in fact Johnson eventually published all but two.[28] Johnson, like other contemporary publishers, "had to employ the best engravers he could afford, and he had to match the genius of the engraver to that of the painter whose work he was to recreate" (Bentley 1980, 64).[29] He also had to match engravers to appropriate subject matter and, in Stedman's case, to decide which original works merited the extra expense of "name" engravers.

Johnson seems to have sorted Stedman's artwork according to such criteria and to have farmed it out quickly to his engravers. Thirty-five of the published plates are unsigned and remain unattributed. Of these, all but three seem to have been executed in 1791, soon after Johnson commissioned them; they include most of the fish, bird, and plant depictions and are, for the most part, uninspired journeyman work.[30] Two similar natural history plates are dated 1791 and signed by A[nker] Smith. Fourteen plates, mainly depicting animals and the majority also dated 1791, were executed and signed by [Inigo] Barlow, a frequent engraver of natural history subjects. The seven plates that include Stedman's most important maps and plans were engraved by a cartographic specialist, T. Conder, all but one in 1791. And a single plate depicting a "Female Quadroon Slave" was engraved by Perry in 1794, rather late in the book's production; though executed in stipple, it seems otherwise to have been directly modeled on the engraving of Joanna that had been produced by the better-known Holloway the previous year.

Johnson engaged four "name" engravers to execute the remaining twenty-two plates. In 1796, when his own *Analytical Review* announced the imminent publication of Stedman's book, there was special mention of the eighty [sic] plates "executed by Bartolozzi, Blake, Holloway, Benedetti, &c. &c.," and an early review of the work praised these engravings as being "in a style of uncommon elegance" (*Critical Review*, January 1797, 60). Francesco Bartolozzi, a Royal Academician and undoubtedly the most expensive of the engravers who worked on Stedman's plates, signed three—two full-page, rather stylized figures executed in characteristic stipple, and the more compositionally ambitious Stedman self-portrait that serves as the frontispiece (chronologically the final plate to be produced for the book). Michele Benedetti was engaged early in the project to engrave the two Amerindian depictions, which he accomplished in 1792 in a style similar to that of Bartolozzi. And T. Holloway was given the task of engraving a single important plate, Stedman's beloved Joanna, which he executed in 1793 in a style reminiscent of Blake's work for the book.[31]

William Blake's sixteen plates "have long been recognized as among the best executed and most generally interesting of all his journeyman work . . .[and] particularly in the large paper copies with the engravings colored by hand, are some of [his] most interesting and important book illustrations" (Keynes 1971, 98; 1969, 10). Undoubtedly, they include the most arresting visual images in the *Narrative*. With the notable exception of an overwhelmingly ordinary depiction of local fruits and vegetables (pl. 52), each of Blake's engravings successfully blends his own inner vision with Stedman's, producing works that express, for example, in the case of slave tortures (pls. 11, 35, 71) extraordinary power and pathos, in the case of his wonderfully humanoid monkeys and the skinning of the giant anaconda (pls. 18, 42, 19) sprightly humor, and in the case of his emblematic representation of the three interdependent continents (pl. 80) demure but unmistakable sensuality.

Blake effectively matched his engraving techniques to Stedman's subjects. His moving depictions of slaves were viewed by one scholar as "figures shaped by heavy linear nets placed against [contrastive] landscapes etched in a notably free and open style . . . their representations bound to the pictorial equivalent of the social system which imprisons them" (Essick 1973, 503–6; see also Essick 1980, 52–53). In contrast, his *finis* page engraving of "Europe supported by Africa & America" manages an almost airy representation of what another scholar glossed as "three comely nude women tenderly embracing each other, the Negro and the European clasping hands in sisterly equality" (Erdman 1952, 244). Thirteen of Blake's plates are signed by him and dated December 1792 and 1793; three others are almost certainly his and are dated December 1793 and 1794 (pls. 25, 55, 71—Keynes 1921; Erdman 1952, 244; Bentley 1977, 622). In addition, his signature on the very ordinary plate 52, combined with Stedman's expressed satisfaction with Blake's work for the book as early as 1 December 1791, suggests that some of the other unsigned and routine journeywork in the book may also be his.

As Bentley has written, "Engraving is always a work of translation in which the graphic conventions are different from those of the artist with a brush or pencil" (1980, 63), but Blake often "overstep[ped even] the usual barriers between designer and engraver," imprinting his own vision on his journeyman graphic works (Essick 1980, 51). Consequently, there has been lively scholarly interest in the relationship between Stedman's original "drawings"—long presumed to be lost—and Blake's engravings modeled after them. Essick (drawing on Smith 1960) has made an ingenious argument by analogy about "the subtle alterations that Blake probably brought to the Stedman designs" by introducing the better-documented transformations that Blake effected in 1792 (the same year he worked on many of the Stedman plates) upon a preliminary wash drawing by Governor King of "A Family of New South Wales." As Essick notes, "The family is a scruffy little group in the drawing, and the faces seem more like simplified caricatures than careful representations. Not only has Blake altered the disposition of the figures, but he has transformed poor and naked aborigines into noble savages" (Essick 1980, 53).[32]

In a similar fashion, Erdman suggests that Blake must have taken liberties with Stedman's intentions. Referring to the *finis* page, he notes that while Stedman, in the 1796 text, "expresses an 'ardent wish' that all peoples 'may henceforth and to all eternity be the props of each

INTRODUCTION

Figure 6. "*A Family of New South Wales.*" Left: *Wash drawing by Governor King.* Right: *Blake's engraving, made after King, for Hunter,* An Historical Journal of the Transactions at Port Jackson and Norfolk Island, *1793 (plate dated 1792). From Essick 1980, figs. 40, 41.*

other' since 'we only differ in colour, but are certainly all created by the same Hand' . . .[in Blake's plate] Europe is *supported* by her darker sisters, and they wear slave bracelets while she has a string of pearls—a symbolism rather closer to the historical fact" (1952, 244). But this interpretation, clever as it is, seems wide of the mark: the beautiful contemporary hand-colored versions of this plate (in which Blake and/or Stedman may even have played a supervisory role—see below) suggest that Blake's and Stedman's intentions were both more egalitarian and more similar. For what Erdman calls "slave bracelets" are represented in color as shining gold ornaments, and his "pearls" become, in color, simple blue beads.

During the mid-1790s, the relationship between Stedman and Blake was quite close; they repeatedly dined together, Stedman entrusted his business affairs to Blake when not in London, Stedman sent gifts (geese, a sugar cruse) to the Blakes, and they had a very active correspondence (all, apparently, now lost). Yet Stedman did not know Blake personally before 1792 at the earliest, and the fruit of their relationship, in terms of practical influence on their respective published works, was strictly one-way; while Stedman had completed his work on the "Narrative" well before he met Blake, Stedman's manuscript and drawings, as well as his various meetings with Blake, seem to have exerted a significant influence on Blake's own thought. For example, "The persons and problems of Stedman's *Narrative* reappear, creatively modified, in the text and illustrations of Blake's [1793] *Visions* [*of the Daughters of Albion*]: the rape and torture of the virgin slave, her pride in the purity and equality of her soul, and the frustrated desire of her lover and husband" (Erdman 1952, 245). And there are numerous detailed textual and visual parallels between Theotormon's love in this poem for the gentle Oothoon, whom he is unable to set free, and Stedman's love for the enslaved Joanna (ibid.; see also Paulson 1983, 89–95).

Stedman's influence extended to other Blake works as well. Though Blake "shrank from signing his engraving of this bloody document, 'The Execution of Breaking on the Rack' [Stedman's pl. 71] . . . the image of the courageous rebel on the cruciform rack bit into his heart, and in the Preludium of *America* [1793] he drew Orc in the same posture to represent the spirit of human freedom defiant of tyranny" (Erdman 1969, 231). Likewise, the plate for Blake's "A Poison Tree" in *Songs of Experience* (1794) seems to echo the Stedman/Blake "Rack" (Davis 1977, 56). Stedman's graphic description and depiction of the South American vampire bat (pp. 206, 428, pl. 57)—which he also calls the "Spectre of Guiana"—seem also to have impressed Blake, whose own haunting Spectre in *Jerusalem* takes on many of its specific characteristics (Erdman 1969, 234; Bogan 1976; but see also Appendix A, s.v. *Vampier,* below). The snake that three figures sit astride in Blake's *America* (1793, 11) seems to be an imaginative ninety-degree transposition of the anaconda he engraved that same year for Stedman's plate 19—with similar neck harness and straddling figure and the same overall contours. And even Blake's famous "Tyger! Tyger! burning bright / In the forests of the night" and its accompanying illustration from the 1794 *Songs of Experience* may well be related to Stedman's "Tiger-Cat . . . its Eyes Emitting flashes of Lightning" (p. 359) or his "*Red* Tiger . . . Eyes Prominent, and Sparkling Like Stars" in the nighttime forest (p. 359), as well as to Stedman's drawings for plate 48 (see also Paulson 1983, 97–110).

Stedman's diaries and his few surviving works bear witness that he worked in several graphic media—pen and ink, watercolors, and oils—and he often used "drawings" as a generic term. We believe, however, that most or all of his originals for the "Narrative" were watercolors, which he sometimes referred to as "paintings" (see, for example, p. 10). In the absence of evidence to the contrary, Stedman's artistic skills have generally been presumed to have been negligible. For example, Ray writes of Stedman's "modest ability as a draftsman," based on the two works known to him (nos. 6 and 7 in n. 35, below) (Ray 1976, 9), and Keynes thinks that "it seems probable that they [Blake's prints] were not very exact copies" (1971, 100). Such judgments may, however, be overly hasty. Stedman himself took special pride throughout his life in his artistic aptitudes and accomplishments. Writing of his early artistic promise, he commented that

> my talents for drawing were so universally admired that my parents were advised not to neglect them—but to Encourage me since I would make a figure by proper cultivation not inferiour even to Rubens or van Dyk.•
>
> • This was the real and general opinion. (*1786, 5 bis*)

His later writings report frequent praise for his drawings and paintings from critics in many walks of life—from poets and playwrights to some of the finest painters of the age, including the miniaturist Richard Cosway, the Royal Academicians John Francis Rigaud and Ozias Humphry, and, apparently, Sir Joshua Reynolds himself, "who Signalized it [Stedman's collection of drawings, especially those later engraved as pls. 4, 8, 53, and 61] With a verry high Compliment as Verry Expressive, And upon the whole an Excellent Performance" (p. 392; see also *10 December 1786, 4 April 1787,* and *22 October 1789*).[33] Without question, Stedman considered himself a far better artist than writer, and his contemporaries seem to have shared his opinion.

We have been able to uncover 15 drawings and paintings by Stedman. Unfortunately, they do not permit a full assessment of his artistic skills nor, therefore, of the role he ultimately played in shaping the major engravings for his book. None of them served as models for the full-page figures that constitute the book's most powerful images; only one was used at all, and that for a half-page engraving.[34] Nevertheless, they do attest that his own work was ethnographically careful and accurate—considerably more so than many of the engravings modeled after it.[35] In addition to the 15 works that we have found and to the 104 (or perhaps 105) others that he submitted to Johnson in 1791, Stedman produced a large number of others whose locations (in spite of our several years' intensive search on three continents) remain unknown to us.[36]

A comparison of Stedman's watercolor entitled "Manner of Sleeping &c. in the Forest," made in 1776, with the 1791 half-page engraving that Barlow modeled on it for the 1796 *Narrative,* reveals a number of significant changes. In reorienting the scene from vertical to horizontal, Barlow transformed Stedman's excellent depiction of the multilayered

Figure 7. "Manner of Sleeping &c. in the Forest." Top: *Stedman's original 1776 watercolor. 14.6 × 10.5 cms.* Bottom: *1791 engraving by Barlow, after the watercolor, for the 1796 first edition of the* Narrative *(pl. 73 [top]).*

Figure 8. Stedman's house at Plantation L'Esperance (The Hope). Top: *Stedman's pen-and-ink sketch, 1776, to which he affixed the following key:* "1. The room where I dined, painted, and wrote letters &c. 2. Joanna's room, where we slept &c. 3. Was the gallery. 4. Was the kitchen for Quaco. 5. Was the hen-house. 6. The yard for ducks, and 2 sheep, a hog &c. 7. Palisades all round. 8. The entry and bridge" (Thompson 1962, 194). Bottom: *Engraving by Barlow, 1791 (probably after a Stedman watercolor based on this sketch), for the 1796 first edition of the* Narrative *(pl. 73 [bottom]). See note 35 (2), below.*

tropical forest into a bare savannah, adding the edge of a river or creek in the foreground; he omitted the slave who is offering Stedman a calabash container as well as the slave who is diligently blowing on the fire; he altered the characteristically African squatting-relaxing posture of another slave into a typically European head-in-hands sitting position; he eliminated the tobacco pipes that Stedman and one of his slaves were enjoying at the end of a long day of campaigning; he turned the pieces of clothing drying over the fire as well as the two pet parrots, which Stedman had carefully delineated, into vaguely defined forms; he altered Stedman's accurately drawn carrying chests into coffinlike boxes, moved the saber, and deleted the powder pouch and wallet hanging from the roof; he moved the fire off to one side, apparently not understanding that it served to keep Stedman warm and hold mosquitoes at bay during the chilly tropical nights; and he smoothed out the rough palm leaf roof of the shelter to resemble English thatch.

The overall chronology of plate production is not fully clear. Johnson seems to have had the plates dated in large batches, annually, to establish copyright; forty-eight are dated 1 December 1791, five 1 December 1792, twenty-one [Monday] 2 December 1793, six 1 December 1794, and one 1 December 1795. The watermark for all leaves with engravings, in those plain and hand-colored 1796 copies that we have examined, includes a date of 1794, suggesting that the actual printing of all of the plates for the book was done at about the same time (as was standard publishing practice), probably in late 1795 (see below).[37]

Stedman first recorded his reactions to seeing what Johnson's engravers had produced when he noted that, shortly before 1 December 1791, he had received "above 40 Engravings from London some well some verry ill." These included several by Blake that particularly pleased Stedman: "I wrote to the Engraver blake to thank him twice for his excellent work but never received any answer" (*1 December 1791*). Stedman soon began sending "corrections" to the engravers, via Johnson, and he participated actively in the platemaking by sending such corrections even after the text had begun to be printed: on 5 June 1795, six months after he had received his final plate (the frontispiece) from Bartolozzi, he noted in his diary, "take home My Spoilt M. Script & repair all plates." We can surmise that Stedman was quite exacting in his attention to the way his "drawings" were engraved; on his 1790 manuscript "Directions for the Plates," he kept a running log in penciled symbols of plates still "to correct," and these included at various times at least eight of Blake's sixteen, all three of Bartolozzi's, Holloway's "Joanna," and many others.[38] This log also offers the only indication that it was Stedman himself who supplied the drawing of five

Figure 9. Two examples of Stedman's maritime watercolors (see n. 35 [9–15], below), and the vignette from the title page of the 1796 Narrative. *Left: "A Ship at Anker." Right: "A Dutch Frigate." Watercolors, Stedman Archive, Haus Besselich, Urbar, West Germany. Courtesy of Hilda von Barton Stedman. Bottom: Vignette.*

ships sailing into the distance—even though they are not included in the 1790 manuscript—that appears as a vignette on the title page of each of the 1796 volumes.

Johnson printed an unknown (but apparently very small) number of 1796 first editions on large paper with "the plates admirably coloured by hand" (Keynes 1971, 103).[39] During the 1790s, the first great age of English illustrated book publishing, hand coloring was already common practice for illustrated works. "Printshops sold their merchandise either colored or plain, depending upon the tastes and pocketbook of the purchaser" (Essick 1980, 121). Often, the colorists were political refugees from the Continent, and it was common for these workers (usually women) to work at long benches, assembly line fashion, each applying a single color. Publishers constantly experimented with ways to cut the costs of coloring; just around the corner from Blake's house during the 1780s, one publisher set up a school to train boys to color, to avoid the expense of adult miniaturists (Bentley 1980, 65).

We do not know the details of how the Stedman plates were colored.[40] However, a comparison of his original watercolor for plate 73 [*top*] with contemporary hand-colored examples suggests that either Stedman or a master colorist with access to Stedman's original watercolors made the specimens that the other colorists used as models.[41] For there is a remarkably close correspondence between the colors of the original and the engravings, which would have been unlikely without direct copying; in both, for example, Stedman's lapels are precisely the same shade of pink, his jacket the same blue, and his trousers the same gray. We know nothing, either, of the financial arrangements between Johnson and his engravers, but one not-uncommon contemporary arrangement was for the engravers to be paid in kind with copies of the book.[42] In this case, it is even possible that Blake—who was close to both Johnson and Stedman during the period—had a hand in coloring copies for his own benefit. But we have no hard evidence either way.

"THE BOOK GOOD FOR NOTHING"

Although the production of engravings for the *Narrative* spanned the entire period 1791–95, editorial work on the text seems to have started only in 1794, when Johnson quietly engaged William Thomson to serve as *"literary dry-nurse"* to the "Narrative." At Johnson's behest, Thomson rewrote Stedman's manuscript sentence by sentence, producing a new text "with a celerity unequalled, perhaps, on the part of any other man"

INTRODUCTION

(Anon. 1818, 2:110). Though Stedman came to regard Johnson as "the demon of Hell" (*May 1796*) because of the many changes wrought on his manuscript, Stedman apparently remained unaware—right up to his death soon after publication—that it was actually Thomson, a professional editor and ghost writer, who was directly responsible for causing his book to be "mard intirely" (*24 June 1795*).

William Thomson (1746–1817) was described in an obituary written by a lifelong acquaintance as

> one of the most extraordinary men of letters of the present age.... with an exception to poetry, [his name] is connected with almost every species of composition, and it would be impossible to write the history of the literature of the reign of George III. without assigning him a place, if not very elevated, at least somewhat conspicuous among the authors of that period. (Anon. 1818, 2:74)

After completing theological studies in Scotland, Thomson was given his own parish, in a presbytery renowned for its "religious gloom and fanatical austerity" (ibid., 86–87). In this setting of "puritanical orthodoxy," he "acquired the character of a *bon vivant* and pleasant companion, rather than that of a godly minister" (87), and his employment there was, by mutual agreement, short-lived. Thomson then moved to London (ca. 1780), where he sought to become a man of letters and was eventually enlisted to "revise, correct, and finish" a manuscript on King Philip III of Spain, following the death of its original author (93). As a result of the favorable response to this work (and his being awarded "the unsolicited degree of LL.D. from the University of Glasgow"), his reputation grew, and, among other literary activities, he was "not unfrequently employed either to revise or review the works of living authors" (94). During the next several decades, he wrote professionally in an astonishing variety of formats—from pamphlets and newspaper articles to novels and plays, as well as works of biblical commentary, military tactics, political and scientific history, and world travel, under both his own name and pseudonyms. By the time he made the acquaintance of Joseph Johnson during the early 1790s and had begun to frequent his literary evenings (once falling asleep and snoring aloud during a *tête-à-tête* with Mary Wollstonecraft), Thomson was devoting himself largely to writing travel accounts on, for example, the Western Hebrides and on Norway, Denmark, and Russia—working from notes provided by the "authors" to produce the final texts (102–6). Johnson's selection of Thomson to edit Stedman's "Narrative" was, then, hardly surprising.

On 25 May 1795, Stedman got his first glimpse of the manuscript he

INTRODUCTION

had given Johnson in 1791, noting laconically in his diary, "12 chapters printed & mard." Thenceforth until his death two years later, Stedman's life became a tormented struggle to repair what he saw as the damages inflicted upon his work. His relations with Blake and with Luke Hansard (Johnson's printer for the *Narrative*) remained friendly throughout the period; he entrusted his business affairs to Blake when he was away from London and parts of his manuscript to Hansard, as a way of keeping it out of Johnson's hands. But Stedman's irritation with Johnson knew few limits, and he was often consumed by anger and frustration at the publisher's stubborn and "uncivil" refusal to respect his wishes. By June 1795, he was referring in his diary to "My Spoilt M. Script" (*5 June 1795*); "on Midsummer day" he complained of receiving "the 1s. vol. of my book quite mard[,] oaths and sermons inserted &c" (*24 June 1795*); and shortly after, he remarked, "My book mard intirely[.] am put to the most extreme trouble and expence. . . . ba[w]dy oaths lies & preachings in my unhappy book" (ibid.).[43] He also mentioned "a hot quarl with Johnson" (ibid.). In August the problems continued: "Johnson uncivil all allong"; in December, after Johnson had sent him a "blur'd index," he concluded that "the book good for nothing"; and on 17 January 1796, he wrote what was probably his final letter to his brother's wife in Holland: "My book was printed full of lies and nonsense, without my knowledge. I burnt two thousand vols., and made them print it over again, by which they lost 200 guineas. You have no idea of the villainy and folly I have to deal with."[44] In this same month, Stedman sent his printer new front and back matter for the book:

I sent besides to London Hansard—
a compleet index above 650 names
a compleet list of 200 subscribers
a compleet direction for 80 plates
a compleet errata with 60 faults
a compleet table of 30 chaps. contents
a compleet form for a title page
a compleet preface—and

a compleet Dedicn. to Prince of Wales of which he was made acquainted by General S= Leger who was wrote to by Major Wemyfs of II Regimt[.] I charged Hansard not to trust the above papers with Johnson who I would now not save from the gallows with only one of them so cruelly was I treated—and I declare him a scoundrel [i.e., challenge him to a duel?] without he gives me satisfaction. (*1796*)

In May, Stedman was still complaining: Johnson "again torments me by altering the Dedication to the P. of Wales &.—he being a d———nd

L

INTRODUCTION

eternal Jacobin scoundrel" (*May 1796*). But by the middle of the month, Stedman's travails were over: "the whole or most of my publication of which I send away the last cancels so late as the middle of May 1796—having been in hand no less than 7 or 8 long years" (*May 1796*).

A close reading of Stedman's diary makes clear that Thomson must have produced an entirely new manuscript (now lost) from Stedman's 1790 text, and that it was from this new manuscript that Johnson, in 1795, had Luke Hansard print what he then thought would be the first edition.[45] We now believe that the often-faint pencil "cancellation" marks across many passages on Stedman's personal copy of the manuscript (now at Minnesota) were made by him during the summer of 1795, as he read in anger through the printed pages for the first time, noting to himself what Johnson (actually Thomson) had deleted or altered.[46] Comparison of Stedman's marks with the 1796 first edition suggests both the extensiveness of the changes that Johnson/Thomson had expected to be able to make in Stedman's text, and Stedman's success in getting a certain number of the alterations reinstated.

From the summer of 1795 until early 1796, Stedman spent much of his time in London, negotiating with Johnson about the differences between the text he had completed in 1790 and the altered version. Stedman's diary and related evidence make clear that what emerged as the 1796 first edition was an unhappy compromise. Stedman, like many battered authors, eagerly waiting to have his work published and to receive royalties (and buffeted by rapidly declining health), felt it necessary to concede on many of the points of difference in order to reinstate those passages he cared about most (and which Johnson was willing to publish). Stedman's insistence on not simply accepting the version that Johnson had printed allegedly cost the publisher two hundred guineas, presumably in printer's fees and paper costs. In the end, Stedman seems to have come to terms with Johnson, settling for a book that was rather different from the one he had written. Just before the complete 1796 first edition was to appear (in its final, "negotiated" form), he wrote, "I have overcome them all, and at last, in one month's time, the book comes out, and so soon we can make up accounts" (Thompson 1966, 75).

A Comparison of the Texts of 1790 and 1796

Although Stedman was quite unprepared for the massive revisions that were made of his 1790 manuscript, he had always expected some professional editing to take place. In his 1790 "Advertisement to the

INTRODUCTION

Reader" he implied that his manuscript might benefit from being "properly prepared for the Eye of the Publick by the able Pen of a candid and ingeneous Compiler" and that, before publication, it would need to be "Maturely and fully digested" (p. 25). The actual editing that Thomson did at Johnson's behest ranged from this expected kind of minor rephrasing—often designed to "improve" Stedman's direct, sometimes coarse soldier's language—to substantial alterations of Stedman's views on race, slavery, and social justice, obliterating or warping significant aspects of his Suriname experience and the social commentary he had intended to share with his readers. In this section, we attempt to describe and analyze these editorial modifications, providing sufficient examples to establish the relationship between the Minnesota manuscript, which Stedman finished in 1790 and which is published here for the first time, and the well-known and much-published version first brought out by Johnson in 1796.

Purely stylistic changes—in spelling, punctuation, and phrasing—were effected throughout. We offer two characteristic examples, to illustrate the extent of this type of general editing. The first forms part of Stedman's description of the encounter between government troops and the rebels of Boucou; the second is part of the account of his own arrest in the forest for insubordination.

| 1790 (pp. 84–85). To through a *facine* bridge over the Marsh was then projected but this Plan after several weeks had been spent in the attempt and a great many Men shot dead in the execution was also frustrated and drop'd—during which time the two little armies kept popping and blackguarding each other at a shocking rate. Having desisted from carrying over the above bridge, and no hopes of getting through the Marsh into the Fortress, besides the ammunition and victuals growing considerably less. . . . | 1796 (1:82–83). It was then projected to throw a fascine bridge over the marsh, by the troops; but this plan, after several weeks had been spent in the attempt, and a number of men shot dead while employed upon it, was of necessity laid aside. Thus every hope of passing through the marsh into the fortress being frustrated, and the food and ammunition being considerably lessened. . . . |
| 1790 (pp. 433–36). we Proceeded on till we Entered the Camp; at Which Moment I was met by the Adjutant, And put Under an Arrest by the Commanders Orders | 1796 (2:148–49, 154). The reader may judge of my mortification, when I inform him, that, instead of receiving the approbation of my commander, as I certainly de- |

LII

to be tried by a Court Martial Under Pretence of having quitted the Rear Guard Without his orders. . . . No Sooner Was I Sat Down at this Place /where was Also kept a Post of the Society Troops/ than I was Accoasted by Several deputies sent me from Col: Seybourgh With an Offer of being set at Liberty Providing I Would Acknowledge before two Commisarys, that I had been Justly arrested Which I Refused.	served, I was immediately on my arrival in camp put under an arrest, to be tried by a court-martial for disobedience of orders. . . . We were scarcely arrived at this post, than I was accosted by several deputies from Colonel Seyburg, who earnestly intreated that I would only acknowledge myself to have been in fault, assuring me that I should then be set at liberty, and all would be forgotten. As I was conscious, however, of my own innocence, I could not in common justice criminate myself.

There were many other types of largely stylistic alterations. In a number of cases, the order of paragraphs was shifted, footnotes were incorporated into the text, textual material was placed in footnotes, the selection of poems was altered, verse was rephrased as prose, foreign-language quotations were translated (in both directions; e.g., Fourgeoud's "I am Undone" became "*Nous sommes perdus!*" [p. 413; 1796, 2:120] and "*vincere out mory*" became "victory or death" [p. 116; 1796, 1:128]), and there was, throughout, an extensive weeding out of Stedman's Latin quotations and biblical allusions.

Some of the rephrasing designed to "correct" Stedman's occasional coarseness caused alterations mainly in tone or color, lending a certain flatness to Stedman's lively and picturesque descriptions. For example, his reference to a "Smouse" was changed to read "Jew" (p. 116; 1796, 1:127), his "Quacks" were transformed into "surgeons" (p. 176; 1796, 1:249), "a Couple of hungry whores" became "a brace of the frail sisterhood" (p. 616; 1796, 2:393), and a portion of his description of a dalliance with a slave woman was changed from "[she gave me] such a hearty kiss—as had made my Nose nearly as flat as her own" to the briefer and more delicate "[she] imprinted on my lips a most ardent kiss" (p. 43; 1796, 1:20). Likewise, scatological references were systematically purged. For example, the 1796 publication omitted the passage that described Colonel Fourgeoud's joy, after a discouraging day of vainly pursuing his rebel slave foes through the forest, at finding a pile of "reeking S—— [declaring] he was now perfectly sure of following the Enemy," upon which a grenadier embarrassedly stepped forward to admit "*this was me and please your Honour*" (p. 214; 1796, 1:264); and Stedman's report that "some suppose" that the unusual sound produced by the bird called the *trumpeter* "is made by the nose . . . and others that it comes forth through the Anus" was edited to omit the latter phrase (p. 213; 1796, 1:262).[47]

For related reasons, no doubt, a number of sexual allusions were deleted by the editor. For example, Stedman described how the sadistic mistress of a plantation "from a Motive of *Groundless* Jealousy . . . put an end to the Life of a young and beautiful Quadroon Girl, by the infernal means of plunging a red hot Poker in her Body, by those parts which decency forbids to mention," but the 1796 version removed the final phrase (p. 115; 1796, 1:126). Likewise, when Stedman related how "the pious Mother of the Charity-House [in Paramaribo] Nephariously Kept Flogging the Poor Slaves dayly because they were She said Unbelievers," the editor deleted his accompanying observation: "the Men she Always Strip'd *Perfectly* Naked, that not a *Single* Part of theyr Body might Escape her Attention—to what is Religion Come at Last?" (p. 472; 1796, 2:198). Similarly, his claim that howler monkeys are so lascivious that they "sometimes Attack the female of the Human Species" was censored (p. 502; 1796, 2:236);[48] his statement that not only are Negroes' "Necks . . . Thicker than Ours . . . [but] their Genitels Conspicuously Larger" was also excised (pp. 512–13; 1796, 2:252); the fact that a "Cowskin" with which "during Breakfast 7 Negroes were Again tied up and Flogg'd" was in fact "the Dried Penous of a Bull" was omitted (p. 555; 1796, 2:307); and even his personal, deeply felt statement about the "pleasure [of] rambling naked when the occasion will permit it" apparently overstepped bounds of conventional propriety and was deleted (p. 138; 1796, 1:160).

Stedman's editor also made a consistent effort to mute evidence of his "wilder" side (which Stedman himself had already toned down considerably between his diaries and his 1790 "Narrative"), and much of the wenching, hard drinking, brawling, and dramatic temper tantrums reported in the 1790 manuscript was altered or simply deleted. A representative example, describing an incident during the outward voyage to Suriname, may illustrate the more general process:

> **1790** (p. 34): Having received a severe fall on the Quarter deck by its being wet and Slippery and finding myself otherwise exceedingly low spirited I had recourse to daily bathing in sea water, and also made use of a Cheering Glass of Claret with two *anchors* of which /being about 20 Gallons/ each Officer was provided, besides his own Stock /but part whereof had been industriously filshed from me and which I detecktd from the back of a hencoop/. by these Means I found such a considerable benefit that in a few days after, I was perfectly recover'd of my Complaint but so exasperated that I took revenge on a locker with above 300

INTRODUCTION

Consealed Eggs, which I stove in and bedaubd the whole Cabin with Yolks.

1796 (1:14): Becoming extremely low-spirited towards the close of our voyage, I now had recourse to daily sea-bathing, and to a chearing glass of claret, two ankers of which had been provided for each officer, independantly of his own stock. These means proved efficacious, and I found myself in a few days perfectly recovered from my complaint.

Sometimes, this type of editing, though apparently minor, caused the loss of significant descriptive information. Stedman reported graphically, for example, how on board the ship bound for Suriname, "dinners were sometimes served up in the very Tubs employed by the Surgeons to void the filth of the Seek" (p. 33), but in published form the tubs were more politely characterized simply as being "of not the most cleanly appearance" (1796, 1:12). Likewise, Stedman's reference to the "overgrown Widows, Stale Beauties, and overaged Maids" of Suriname (p. 49) who mistreated their young female slaves out of jealousy was discreetly deleted. And even the telling observation that "All the mulatta-, negroe- and Indian Slaves in the Colony go bare footed—and naked above the waist" was excised (p. 41; 1796, 1:18). Moreover, in the course of such minor editing, a number of careless errors were introduced—misspellings of foreign words (bananabeck/banarabeck [p. 109; 1796, 1:117]), alterations of dates (with those in the 1790 version corresponding to Stedman's diary entries [pp. 39, 175; 1796, 1:16, 207]), and so on. And Stedman's editor was not above exaggerating facts for effect—for example, increasing the size of the weight attached to a female slave as punishment from "3 Score pounds or upwards" to "at least a hundred pounds" (p. 39; 1796, 1:15).

Stedman himself was responsible for making two changes between the versions of 1790 and 1796—the dedication and the final pages of the work. Stedman dedicated the 1790 manuscript to Sir George Strickland, who "from . . . first seeing my Original drawings seem'd to patronize them" and who had been the first to encourage him seriously to write up and publish his Suriname experiences (*10 June 1778*). By 1796, for reasons that are nowhere spelled out, Stedman had sought and received permission to dedicate the work instead to the Prince of Wales (*1796*). Johnson, apparently objecting to the new dedication on political grounds, attempted to alter it (*May 1796*), but we have no indication of the precise nature of the argument nor which of the two antagonists won out in the end.

The final pages were also changed, at least partly by Stedman. In the 1790 "Narrative," after describing the untimely death of his dear and

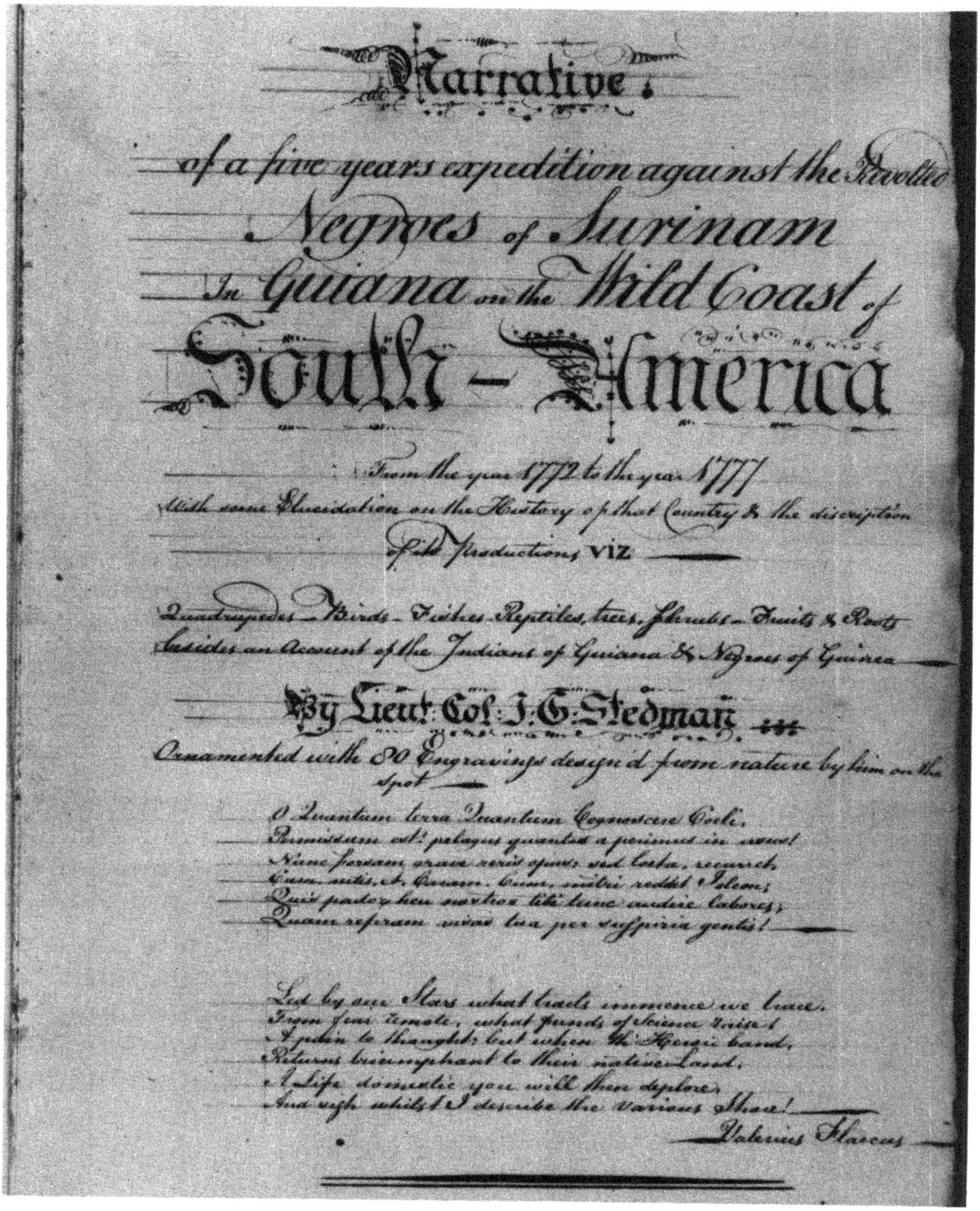

Narrative

of a five years expedition against the Revolted Negroes of Surinam In Guiana on the Wild Coast of South-America

From the year 1772 to the year 1777

With some Elucidation on the History of that Country & the discription of its Productions VIZ

Quadrupedes — Birds — Fishes, Reptiles, trees, shrubs — Fruits & Roots besides an Account of the Indians of Guiana & Negroes of Guinea

By Lieut. Col. J. G. Stedman

Ornamented with 80 Engravings designed from nature by him on the spot

O Quantum terra Quantum Cognoscere Cœli.
Permissum est pelagus quantus a periments in usus!
Nunc fortuna graves rerum opus, sed terra, recursh,
Cum artis, et Rerum, tum artis reddit Idem;
Quis paulo hen mortis tibi tunc audire labores;
Quam referam visus tua per suspiria gentis!

Led by our Stars what tracts immence we trace.
From sene to sene, what funds of science rise!
I peten to thoughts but where th' Heroic band,
Returns triumphant to their native Land,
A Life domestic you will then deplore
And sigh whilst I describe the various Shore!
 — Valerius Flaccus

Figure 10. Title page of Stedman's 1790 "Narrative." James Ford Bell Library, University of Minnesota.

INTRODUCTION

virtuous Joanna, Stedman added a long memorial poem, mentioned his marriage that same year to "a young Lady ... of a very Respectable Family in Holland" and the birth of their first "English" children, and then proudly commented that Johnny Stedman (his son by Joanna) was "at this moment on board of the *Southampton* Frigate ... ready to Strike a blow at the Spaniards should they dare to Quarrel with the Kingdom of Great Britain" (p. 626). In contrast, the 1796 version omits all but the barest mention of Joanna's death (a change probably effected by the editor) and then adds a poem to the recently drowned Johnny, Stedman's "An Elegy on my Sailor" (2:402–3, previously published in a 1795 issue of the *Weekly Entertainer* [Thompson 1962, 375]).

A third such alteration remains mysterious, and Stedman himself makes no direct reference to it in his diaries. The 1790 title page clearly lists the author as "Lieut: Col: J: G: Stedman." (The same designation appears both on the title page of the manuscript autobiography he completed in 1786 and in his formal instructions about his return address that same year [Thompson 1962, 287].) We know that Stedman was promoted by the Prince of Orange from captain to major, and from major to lieutenant colonel in the Scots Brigade in 1777 and 1783, respectively (1796, 2:395; p. 622).[49] Indeed, the prepublication announcement of the book in Joseph Johnson's own *Analytical Review* (February 1796, 223) listed the author of the *Narrative,* which "in a Short Time will be published," as "LIEUT. COL. STEDMAN." Yet the title page of the 1796 book styled him, rather, "Captn. J. G. Stedman."

In the 1790 preface, Stedman defiantly defended his right to criticize others freely "till I shall have found out the Reason why Vice ought not to be Expos'd to the World as well as Virtue made Conspicuous" (p. 10). Yet, being aware of the risks of libel, and afraid that some of his criticisms "might tend to expose him both to great Confusion, and even Danger," he expressed his intent for the published version, rather than "omitting publick or private transactions ... to insert both the one and the other ... [but] with initial Letters" (p. 25).[50] In accord with these instructions (and, undoubtedly, with an eye on Fox's recently passed libel law), the names of many individuals mentioned pejoratively in the 1790 "Narrative" were abbreviated in the 1796 publication. For example, Mrs. Stolker, who reportedly drowned a baby for crying and then gave the mother 300–400 lashes for trying to retrieve its body from the river, was referred to in 1796 as "Mrs. S——lk——r" (p. 267; 1796, 1:329). Similar abbreviations are used in the 1796 first edition for the names of two clergymen who kept slave concubines (p.

47; 1796, 1:26), for the captain "who in 1781 threw 132 living Slaves into the Sea to perish" (p. 81; 1796, 1:78), for the plantation owner whose clandestine flight from Suriname caused Joanna and her fellow slaves to be put up for sale to pay his debts (p. 175; 1796, 1:208), and many others. And some personal criticisms were deleted altogether, for example, the acquittal of an officer (identified only by an initial even in the 1790 manuscript) whose cruelty resulted in his lieutenant "leaping out at the Cabbin Window and ending his Existence" (p. 81; 1796, 1:78).

Stedman, no more hesitant to find fault with the scientific observers who preceded him than with cruel slave owners or military officers he knew in Suriname, frequently criticized the misleading reports of "too many Authors . . . among whom are Men of genius and Learning," and suggested that "some indeed may have erred from Ignorance or wrong information, but numbers from a motive of Pride, and presumption, have been with impunity permitted to vend of their shamefull impositions on the too Credulous Public" (p. 164; cf. 1796, 1:198). Many of the controversies he addressed in this realm—with Merian, Buffon, Fermin, Bancroft, and others—were printed in the 1796 book, but others were suppressed. For example, in his assessment of a report by "*Alexander Garden* M[.] D. F. R. S." on the electric eel, the following passage was excised: "nor have I ever heard of any ones being kil'd by them according to this Gentlemans Account," as was the general statement that followed: "and in this manner I shall make it my business to Confute all the Errors that come within the Circle of my Compass, by whatever Author they may be Stated without exception, as a Duty to Myself in Particular, and to the World in General" (p. 115; 1796, 1:126).[51]

Stedman's sharpest personal criticisms in the 1790 manuscript were reserved for his commanding officer, Colonel Fourgeoud, and it is here that the 1796 publication was most extensively edited. Frequent allusions to the sausages, hams, claret, and other delicacies on which "the old Gentleman" dined while his soldiers were forced to subsist on the most meager (and often worm-infested) staples are consistently toned down or deleted (pp. 209, 229–30, 274; 1796, 1:258, 282, 339). Also carefully edited were reports that Fourgeoud systematically neglected the well-being of his troops (p. 164; 1796, 1:197), invented tasks "for the mere purpose of thus persecuting me to Death" (p. 225; 1796, 1:277), and "having found every means to kill me ineffectual," tormented Stedman by confiscating his cartridges and slandering his friends (p. 226; 1796, 1:278). The rough edges of Stedman's similarly adversarial, though briefer, relationship with another commanding

INTRODUCTION

officer, Lieutenant Colonel Seybourgh, were also systematically smoothed over in the 1796 publication. For example, the descriptions of Seybourgh's sadism toward his troops and much of the detail and emotion surrounding Stedman's false arrest by Seybourgh ("my infamous Foe") in the forest were simply deleted, as was the general remark that "Col: Fourgeoud, Lieut: Col: Seybourgh & Myself by this Time so Effectually hated each Other that no Triumvirate was ever more Compleat" (pp. 339, 433; 1796, 2:24, 149).

Stedman's reactions to Fourgeoud's sadism and favoritism, which ranged from fantasies about murdering him (p. 210; 1796, 1:259) to images of relinquishing himself to Hell for the "Satisfaction of seeing him [Fourgeoud] burn" (p. 281; 1796, 1:349), were generally deleted from the 1796 publication, as were his thoughts about reporting the colonel's "neglect of duty" directly to the Prince of Orange or other authorities (p. 285; 1796, 1:355). Similarly deleted was Stedman's disclosure that Fourgeoud had actually received his commission on the basis, not of merit, but of financial gain to the men who nominated him: "those who Recommended this man to Such a distinguished Rank, & Office . . . proceeded from self interest Alone to be Reinburs'd the money that he Was in theyr debt" (p. 617; 1796, 2:394). And sarcastic as well as simply disrespectful allusions to Fourgeoud (e.g., as "the Hero" [p. 284; 1796, 1:354] or "this Sod" [p. 188; 1796, 1:227]) are converted to more polite forms of reference, as are Stedman's many pejorative comparisons of Fourgeoud to, for example, tyrants, bedlamites, or reptiles (pp. 225, 227; 1796, 1:277–78). Not all of Stedman's criticisms of Fourgeoud were deleted in the 1796 publication, and there are even a few cases in which they were slightly embellished (p. 571; 1796, 2:332). But in general, the muting of the adversarial relationship between these two strong-willed soldiers probably represents the single most frequent alteration of Stedman's manuscript for publication.

Stedman's descriptions of sexual relations between European men and African women were subtly but systematically changed between 1790 and 1796. The frequency and importance of such relations were diminished, at the same time that the social distance between the partners was emphasized. Emblematic of these changes is the 1790 passage that elaborates on Stedman's diary entry for his first night in the New World ("sleep at Mr. Lolkens . . . I f——k one of his negro maids" [9 February 1773]):

> having knocked once or twice at the door—it was opened by a Masculine young *Negro-woman*, as black as a Coal . . . I was fatigued and longed for some rest—thus made a signal that I wanted to sleep—but here I was truly brought into great Distress—for she again misunderstanding me

INTRODUCTION

> had the unaccountable assurance to give me such a hearty kiss—as had made my Nose nearly as flat as her own—I knew not what to do or how to keep my Temper and disentangling myself with some resentment flung into my sleeping apartment but here *wousky*[52] pursued me again—and in Spite of what I could say pulld of[f] my Shoes and my Stockings in a Moment. Heavens, I lost all patience. This Young Woman to be sure was as black as the Devil, to be short as the rest of this adventure can afford but little instruction or entertainment to the reader. I shall beg leave to draw a Sable Curtain over it. (pp. 42–43)

In contrast, the 1796 publication related the incident until the removal of Stedman's shoes and stockings, but carefully avoided any direct or indirect reference to the sexual encounter itself, and it added a comment—not present in the 1790 "Narrative"—about the characteristic servility of "female negro slaves . . .[in all] the West India settlements" (1796, 1:21).[53]

Stedman"s relationship with Joanna, one of the leitmotifs of the book, was changed in a similar direction by means of a large number of subtle, individual alterations. Descriptions of the deep emotional bonds between Stedman and his mulatto lover were in general either deleted or elevated to a purely literary plane; and the text was repeatedly rewritten to stress the inequality of their respective positions in society.[54] A single example may convey some idea of these changes. In the 1790 "Narrative," Stedman described his chagrin at learning that Joanna was about to be transferred to a new plantation

> at the mercy of some rascally Overseer—Good God; I flew to the Spot in Search of poor Joanna and found her bathing with her Companions in the Garden.
>
> But lo! with graceful Motion there she Swims
> Gently removing each Ambitious Wave
> The crowded waves transported Clasp her Limbs
> When, When, oh when shall I such freedoms have
> In vain ye envious Streams So fast he flow
> To hide her from a lovers ardant Gaze
> From every touch you more transparent grow
> And all revealed the beautious Wanton plays
>
> But perceiving me She darted from my presence like a Shot, when I returned to Mrs. Demelly and declared without the least hesitation no less than that it was my intention /if such could be/ to Purchase to Educate & to make even my lawfull Wife *in Europe,* the individual Mulatto Maid *Joanna* which I relate to the World without blushing or being

ashamed of while Mrs. Demelly gazed upon me with Wild Astonishment.

- —This is here regularly done twice a Day by all the Indians Mulatto's Negroes &c—and which Constitutes so much to theyr health and to their Cleanliness—while by the Europeans /some few excepted/ this Salutary Custom is never put in *practice*. (p. 98)

But Stedman's editor substituted for this passage, simply:

Good God!—I flew to the spot in search of poor Joanna: I found her bathed in tears.—She gave me such a look—ah! such a look!—From that moment I determined to be her protector against every insult. (1796, 1:99)

Stedman's own version, characteristically, dwells on Joanna's beauty and clearly states his intention to raise her to his own status by education and by making her his lawful wife. The edited version, saying nothing of her beauty,[55] emphasizes Joanna's pitiable condition (bathed in tears rather than bathing with her companions) and makes Stedman her protector and patron, rather than her lover-aspiring-to-be-her-husband. These changes seem to have been just what the reading public wanted: the *British Critic* noted with approval, "The tale in particular of Joanna, and of the author's attachment to her, is highly honourable to both parties" (November 1796, 539).

Stedman's views on slavery, the slave trade, social justice, and organized religion were also substantially and systematically altered for the 1796 publication. At the time that he was writing the "Narrative" during the 1780s, his positions were well within the mainstream of contemporary educated British opinion—ambivalence and equivocation about slavery and the trade as institutions, combined with genuine compassion for oppressed humanity (see, for example, Anstey 1975, 91–153; Davis 1966, 391–421; 1975, 420–21, passim; Lewis 1983, 94–238).[56] While Stedman was far from being (like Johnson, Blake, and others of that circle) a republican or abolitionist sympathizer, within the contemporary spectrum of public opinion he was equally far from being a political conservative. With his feet firmly planted in the middle of the political road, Stedman saw himself as arguing equally against men such as Clarkson who exhibited the "enthusiasm of ill placed Humanity [Humanitarianism]" and those who would "persevere in the most unjust and diabolical barbarity . . . for the sake of drinking rum, and eating Sugar" (p. 168).[57]

INTRODUCTION

In his 1790 "Narrative," Stedman rehearsed the whole panoply of already well-worn arguments in favor of the continuation of slavery and the trade, including (among others) the Lockean claim that captives in just wars may legitimately be enslaved (p. 170; see Sypher 1942, 76–83); the commonplace apologetic that, with just laws, Africans "may live happier in the West Indies, than they ever did in the Forests of Africa," and far happier than the oppressed hordes of laborers, prostitutes, soldiers, and others, in Europe (p. 171; see also Goveia 1956, 78–79); the argument that sailors, "the props, and bulwarks of every Mercantile-Nation," are far better off working on slave ships than having to be "hang'd to keep them from Starving" in times of peace (p. 171); the political-economic warnings about the advantages France would gain, and the attendant doubling of the price of sugar and rum, should the trade be abruptly ended (p. 172); and even the semantic reminder that "slavery" was a mere word that had come to have misleading connotations and that it might better be replaced by "Menial Servant," since many slaves were in fact better off than "Prentices in England" (p. 173; see also Davis 1966, 395). Motivated, he claimed, by a dual concern for "the *African*" (whom he explicitly said he "loved") and for "this *glorious Island*," Stedman urged Parliament to focus on amelioration—the passage and rigid enforcement of laws that would protect the rights of enslaved Africans as human beings—and thus "make the Slaves in our West India Settlements perfectly happy, with even an Accumulation to the Wealth of their Masters" (p. 173). The key for Stedman was to enforce the rule of just law, and he styled a "Cancer" those current West Indian "laws which are deaf to the cry of the Afflicted Dependants, While the Master is invested With that unbounded de[s]potism Which ever ends in a Tirannical Usurpation" (p. 534; see also p. 542).

Stedman's editor made a consistent attempt to slant his "moderate" opinions, as expressed in the 1790 "Narrative," in the direction of a rigid proslavery ideology for the 1796 first edition, at the same time deleting many of his observations that suggested the common humanity of Africans and Europeans. And he often altered Stedman's middle-of-the-road humanitarianism and strong penchant for cultural relativism to read almost like Edward Long's (1774) acidulous proslavery apologetics. In the 1790 "Narrative," Stedman frequently depicted the African as Natural Man, exactly like you or me but for the mixed blessings of European "civilization": "the *Africans* in a State of nature, Are not that Wretched People Which they are by too Many ignorant European Wretches Represented" (p. 369); "the africans are not so intirely destitute of morality and even Religion as a number of ignorant Euro-

LXII

INTRODUCTION

peans imagine" (pp. 72–73); "their own Religion being much more Comodious [than ours], and not so much divested of Common Sence as numberless Stupid Europeans imagine" (p. 171); and yet more forcefully, "the African Negroes though by Some Stupid Europeans treated as Brutes Are made of no Inferior Clay but in every one Particular are our Equals" (p. 514). By 1796, all of these passages (and others like them) had been expunged and, in their place, the "national character of [the African] people" was now described as being "perfectly savage" (1796, 1:203).

Likewise, Stedman's occasionally ambivalent but generally laudatory assessments of the character of the Saramaka and Djuka Free Negroes, whom he depicted as carefree, state-of-nature forest dwellers in 1790 (p. 172) were transformed in 1796 to make them brute savages. While the "Narrative" admitted that they "have indeed behaved indifferently well ever since the forgoing treaty" (pp. 73–74), even though the Society of Suriname had repeatedly reneged on "Sending the Yearly *Presents*" according to the treaties (p. 510), the 1796 edition deleted both these observations and asserted flatly that there are no "marks of civilization, order, or government among them, but, on the contrary, many examples of ungovernable passion, debauchery, and indolence" (1796, 1:203).

Realizing that "the anti-slavery writer accents every trait that identifies the Negro with the white man" (Sypher 1942, 5), Stedman's editor tried to weed out his frequent and, in themselves, seemingly minor comments to this effect. To cite but three examples: Stedman at one point credited the rebel Negroes with what he called "humanity" for sparing the lives of his own men, but by 1796 the editor had completely altered his intentions by simply changing the word to "hurry" (p. 154; 1796, 1:183); Stedman's footnote explaining that "the word *negroish* is verry ill applied when meant to discribe greediness or Self interest" was deleted by the editor (p. 524; 1796, 2:265); and while Stedman had directly compared "Black Women [with] theyr Sparkling Eyes.—Ivory Teeth, and remarkable Cleanliness All over" to "the to[o] many Languid Looks, Sallow Complexions, deform'd Bodies, And Broken Constitutions, of our European Contriwomen," this passage (like others on the physical beauty of Africans) was deleted wholesale (p. 369; 1796, 2:62).

Similarly, many of Stedman's blunt general remarks about the pervasiveness of misconduct and debauchery among European planters were muted or deleted, as were his several statements of this sort: "those planters who dare so inhumanely to persecute theyr Slaves without a Cause deserve in my opinion no better treatment [than to have

INTRODUCTION

their slaves revolt]" (p. 75; 1796, 1:69). More generally, Stedman's editor tried to sharpen the thrust of what he apparently viewed as the book's incipient antiabolitionist message by adding new, topical, and unequivocal statements against immediate abolition to the 1796 preface:

> it must be observed that LIBERTY, nay even too much lenity, when *suddenly* granted to illiterate and unprincipled men, must be to *all* parties dangerous, if not pernicious. Witness the *Owca* and *Sarameca* Negroes in Surinam—the *Maroons* of Jamaica [who had rebelled in 1795], the *Carribs* of St. Vincent [who had also just rebelled], &c. (1:v)

And, just to be sure, he added a still more explicit and longer passage arguing, in contrast to the thrust of Stedman's 1790 "Narrative," that slavery in Suriname is far worse than that in the British West Indian colonies, where "our [British] planters have by their own laws most humanely restrained . . .[the] unlimited infliction of punishment . . . exercised so commonly in Surinam" (1796, 2:289–90).

Stedman's Voltairean skepticism about organized religion apparently offended his editor as well. As with slavery and the trade, Stedman took pains to make clear that he was not opposed to the institution itself (p. 525), but rather to its widespread corruption—in this case by "hypocrites," among whom he seems to have numbered most British clergymen as well as the Moravian missionaries sent out to convert the Indians and Africans in Suriname. Here is a characteristic passage, excised by Stedman's editor, who had, after all, once been a minister:

> As for the moravian missionary's that are Settled Amongst them to Promote theyr faith &c. I have no Objections, Providing their morals go hand in hand with theyr Precepts, but without Which they ought /like a Pack of Canting Hypocritical Rascals deserve/ to be Strip'd naked, then tar'd & Feathered by the negroes, & flog'd out of the Colony. (p. 595; cf. 1796, 2:363)

Some of Stedman's views on other social issues seem to have been altered in response to rapidly shifting political currents (and with an eye on the recent sedition law). For example, his lengthy and inflammatory criticisms of conduct in the British navy, with direct comparisons of sailors to slaves (and the identical conclusion that just treatment would lead to both greater efficiency and happiness), were very largely deleted (see, for example, pp. 77–78; 1796, 1:73). And, similarly, his political passages relating to British-American relations were consistently altered (e.g., p. 182; 1796, 1:218).

We now believe that the alteration of Stedman's "Narrative" to make it less radical (and more proslavery) was matter-of-factly effected by his editor, William Thomson, largely on his own initiative.[58] We know that

INTRODUCTION

at the same time Thomson was rewriting the "Narrative" line by line, he was also "actively engaged in writing tracts in defence of the slave-trade," commissioned by proslavery groups "holding forth *golden temptations* to needy men of letters" (Anon. 1818, 2:108). And the period immediately after 1792 witnessed a broad public reaction against the antislavery movement—in part an anti-Jacobin backlash following the French Revolution, in part horror at the 1791 slave rebellion in Saint Domingue and bitterness at the subsequent death of more than forty thousand British soldiers sent to quell the nascent Haitian Revolution. Thomson's political alterations of the "Narrative," then, not only may have squared with his own views; they also seem to have been in step with changing public opinion and to have protected the book against the new sedition law, and they might even have been expected to help sell a few additional copies of the work.

We suspect that Johnson, who must have focused more on the overall impact he thought the book would have, paid little attention to what he assumed to be largely technical editing on Thomson's part, and that he gave Thomson's text to the printer without first having compared it carefully to Stedman's original. Only after Stedman saw the printed pages in 1795—when it was too late to restore most of the altered text (much of which, after all, had been changed quite subtly)—would Johnson have realized, from Stedman's complaints, the extent of the changes. And Johnson probably argued to Stedman, in fact with some justice, that the overall message of the book had not really been changed at all. Although Thomson had systematically edited out such explicit passages as "thus in 20 Years two millions of People are murdered to Provide us with Coffee & Sugar" (p. 533; cf. 1796, 2:279), Johnson understood that the *Narrative* (with its numerous chilling eyewitness accounts of barbaric tortures of slaves and its graphic accompanying illustrations) would, even in its edited form, stand as one of the strongest indictments ever to appear against plantation slavery. And public reaction bore him out; upon publication, the *Analytical Review* claimed:

> It will be impossible to peruse the numerous relations of shocking cruelties and barbarities contained in these volumes without a degree of painful sympathy, which will often rise into horrour. Many of the facts are indeed so dreadful, that nothing could justify the writer in narrating them, but the hope of inciting in the breasts of his readers a degree of indignation, which will stimulate vigorous and effectual exertions for the speedy termination of the execrable traffic in human flesh, which, to the disgrace of civilized society, is still suffered to exist and is, even in christian countries, sanctioned by law. (September 1796, 225–26)

INTRODUCTION

And the influential *Critical Review* (January 1797, 53) observed, similarly, that "we have never opened any work which is so admirably calculated to excite the most heart-felt abhorrence and detestation of that grossest insult on human nature,—domestic slavery."

A History of the Minnesota Manuscript

Despite several years of research (in England, Germany, the Netherlands, France, and Suriname), we cannot definitively trace the path of Stedman's manuscript "Narrative" from the house in Tiverton where he died in 1797 to its present home in the James Ford Bell Library at the University of Minnesota. But while available evidence does not constitute conclusive proof, it does allow us to reconstruct a trajectory that we consider highly likely. Two collateral branches of Stedman's family provide the key data (fig. 11).[59]

During the early 1790s, while the "Narrative" and its accompanying illustrations were in press, Stedman kept the original manuscript with him at Tiverton (apparently traveling with it while correcting proofs in

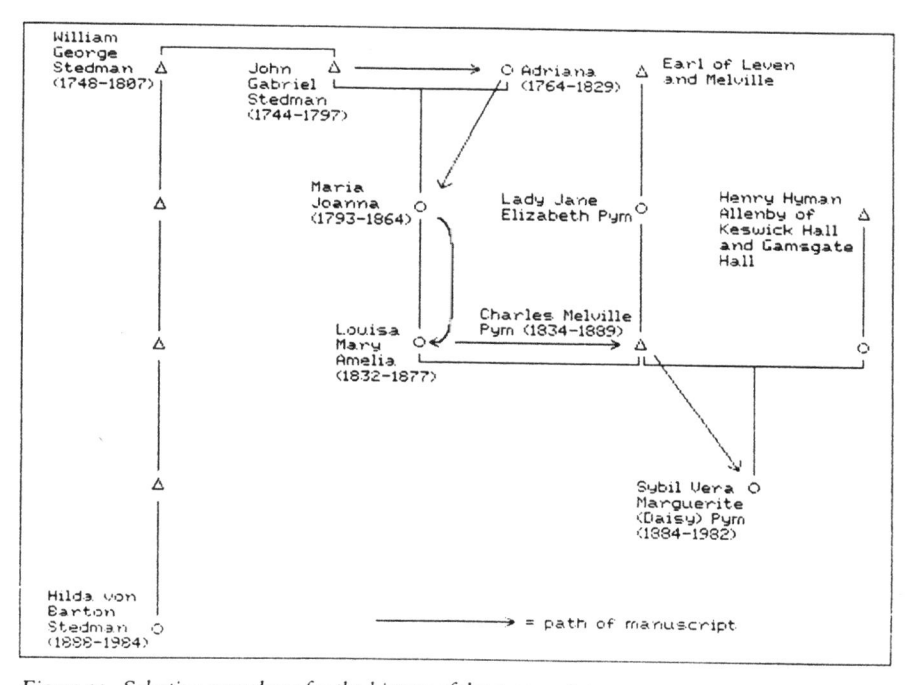

Figure 11. Selective genealogy for the history of the manuscript

LXVI

1795 in London). After Stedman's death in 1797, his widow, Adriana, changed residence several times but finally settled down in Maastricht, where she lived with a servant, close to the house of their youngest daughter, Maria Joanna, and her husband. In 1829, Adriana died there; Maria Joanna handled her mother's affairs, and we presume that she took possession of her father's manuscripts and papers at that time. Years later, one of Maria Joanna's daughters, Louisa Mary Amelia, married Charles Melville Pym and moved to his estate at Woodpark (Ballyclough, County Cork, Ireland), bringing Maria Joanna to live with them. When Maria Joanna died there in 1864, Louisa Mary Amelia in turn took over her affairs, including the papers originally belonging to her own grandfather, John Gabriel. Soon thereafter, Louisa Mary Amelia and Charles moved to Yorkshire, where he assumed the post of rector of Cherry Burton, and where she became mentally ill, eventually dying, childless, of "Acute Mania" in the "Lunatic Hospital St. Giles."[60] After his wife's death, Charles remarried and in 1884 had a daughter, Sybil Vera Marguerite ("Daisy") Pym, who we now have reason to believe was the last legitimate private owner of the "Narrative."

Daisy Pym was orphaned at about age five and lived her entire active life at Louth, Lincolnshire. Along with two younger brothers, she was raised by servants; she later lived with a single servant, never marrying. Sometime around 1950, she received a visit from a distant German "cousin," Hilda von Barton Stedman, great-great-granddaughter of John Gabriel's brother, and an avid family historian. This postwar meeting between Daisy and Hilda provides the central link in our chain of evidence.

Hilda, whom Richard Price first met in 1980 (and who died five weeks after her ninety-sixth birthday in 1984), lived in a medieval abbey, Haus Besselich, on a beautiful hillside facing Koblenz am Rhein. This magnificent home, part of which she had turned into a family archive, had been bought in 1834 by her grandfather, himself the grandson of John Gabriel's brother (Schlegel 1980, 76);[61] until World War I, there was frequent visiting back and forth across the Channel by Stedman family members.[62] In 1980, while R. P. was conducting research among the papers and books at Haus Besselich, Hilda related a story that she was to reiterate on other occasions: not long after the end of World War II, she had visited a distant cousin in England who possessed a large stack of John Gabriel Stedman's papers and manuscripts. This woman, however, vigorously disliked the Stedman side of her family, calling John Gabriel "a terrible man," vehemently denying any interest in the papers, and not even allowing Hilda to see them except from across the room. Not only had John Gabriel married a "black" woman, she explained, but her own parents' families were much more distinguished—"The Earl of Such and Such and Lady So and So" (as Hilda mimicked her). Hilda also mentioned that this cousin was much older than she and would be perhaps 110 years old if still alive. A many-months'-long attempt to retrieve the name and address of this distant Stedman relation from the then-92-year-old Hilda's lively but erratic memory finally bore fruit through the good offices of her niece, who found written in an old address book in one of Hilda's desks, "Miss S. V. M. Pym," with an indication that she was a Stedman descendant, and an address in Louth.[63]

In May 1982, R. P. was finally able to locate and visit Miss Pym, then in her ninety-eighth year (just six months before her death), at Mablethorpe Hall Old People's Home, near Louth. Although Daisy proved considerably more charming than informative during the tea-time visit, owing to memory confusion, information provided by her solicitors and her two closest friends in Louth has allowed us to reconstruct something of her attitudes about John Gabriel Stedman and his manuscript.

The genealogical information in figure 11 helps explain the negative attitude toward John Gabriel Stedman that Hilda repeatedly attributed to Daisy in her conversations with us.[64] For not only did Miss Pym's own ancestry indeed include earls and ladies; her connection to the Stedman family was solely through her father's first marriage, to John Gabriel's granddaughter, who had died, presumably with considerable disgrace to the family, a certified lunatic. Nevertheless, we believe that upon the early death of her parents (about 1890), Daisy became the grudging keeper of John Gabriel's papers, including his manuscript of the "Narrative."

In the mid-1960s, Daisy—then an octogenarian—moved into the Mablethorpe Home, leaving her own house, with its contents intact, in the care of two close friends who lived nearby. Soon thereafter, two younger relatives independently visited the house, removing "a chest of drawers and some other things," according to Daisy's friends.[65] Sometime in late 1965 or early 1966, "two Brighton knockers, very disagreeable chaps," appeared at the door of a well-known London bookseller, peddling a bound manuscript, cheap.[66] Within a few weeks of its purchase, and despite the fact that the very knowledgeable bookseller's assistant suspected that the manuscript was the original copy of Stedman's *Narrative,* "the guv'nor" (his boss) insisted on selling it at a low price to a Danish bookseller then making his London rounds. (These transactions occurred in sufficiently quick succession so that the London bookseller failed to notice the existence of a small original

INTRODUCTION

watercolor by Stedman [see fig. 7], which lay between two leaves in the middle of the volume.) In March 1966, not long after the manuscript had been removed to Copenhagen, Dr. John Parker, curator of the James Ford Bell Library, was shown the manuscript by Rosenkilde & Bagger, Booksellers, and arranged for its purchase. Some twelve years later, Professor Stuart Schwartz of the Department of History, University of Minnesota, apprised us of the existence of a Stedman manuscript that he had seen in the James Ford Bell Library and that he thought might be of interest. R. P. arranged to examine it in the fall of 1978; at that time, he confirmed the identity of the manuscript and began the research that led to the present edition.

THE PRESENT CRITICAL EDITION

The 1790 manuscript of Stedman's "Narrative" consists of front matter, thirty chapters, and back matter. The front matter includes five blank unnumbered pages, on the fourth of which Stedman had pasted his personal bookplate containing his coat of arms; a verso page labeled "I" with the penciled word "Frontispiece"; a (recto) title page written in embellished letters and labeled "II" (see fig. 10); a blank page labeled "III"; a dedication page (IIII), a blank page (V); a preface (VI–XI); a table of contents (XII–XVI); a list of the (yet-to-be-engraved) plates with directions for placing them in the text (XVII–XVIIII); and an "Advertisement to the Reader" (XX). The verso of XX is marked "N° I" and is intended for the first numbered plate. The next recto is paginated "1" and begins the text, which continues through page 825 on consecutively numbered pages that contain the thirty chapters, each one following directly upon the last rather than beginning on a new page; those pages intended for plates are left free of text.[67] After a blank unnumbered page, the back matter consists of an index (I–VII), a blank page (VIII), a list of the "Gentlemen Officers" in Fourgeoud's regiment (VIIII), translations of many of the Latin passages given in the text (X–XIIII), a poem recounting Stedman's outward voyage to Suriname (XV–XVIIII), a list of subscribers for the "Narrative" (XX–XXI), a financial account of subscription income and related expenses (XXII–XXIII), and five blank pages.

The manuscript, bound in quarter calf and old marble boards, measures thirty-four × twenty-one centimeters. Some of the watermarks say "T. Chorlock"; others, "I Taylor"; others display a crest or escutcheon. Footnotes, indicated by large inked dots (• or ••) in the text, are placed at the bottom of the pages, except when they do not fit there

LXIX

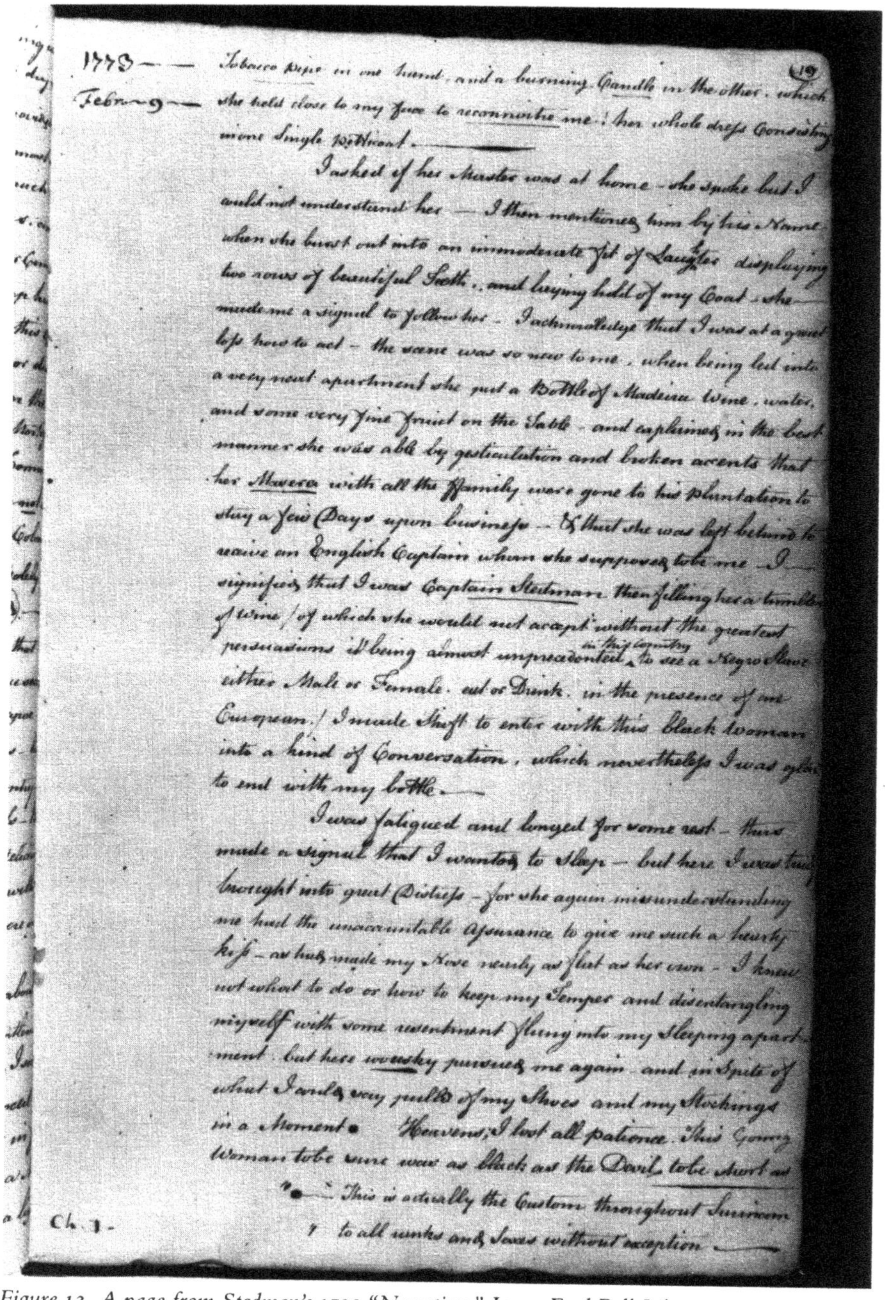

1778 — Tobacco pipe in one hand, and a burning Candle in the other, which
February 9 — she held close to my face to reconnoitre me; her whole dress Consisting
in one Single Petticoat. —

I asked if her Master was at home — she spoke but I
could not understand her — I then mentioned him by his Name,
when she burst out into an immoderate fit of Laughter, displaying
two rows of beautiful Teeth; and laying hold of my Coat. She
made me a signal to follow her. I acknowledge that I was at a great
loss how to act — the scene was so new to me. when being led into
a very neat apartment she put a Bottle of Madeira Wine, water,
and some very fine fruit on the Table — and explained in the best
manner she was able by gesticulation and broken accents that
her Master* with all the family were gone to his Plantation to
stay a few Days upon business — & that she was left behind to
receive an English Captain whom she supposed to be me — I
signified that I was Captain Stedman. then filling her a tumbler
of wine (of which she would not accept without the greatest
persuasions, it being almost unprecedented in this country to see a Negro Slave
either Male or Female. eat or Drink in the presence of an
European) I made Shift to enter with this Black Woman
into a kind of Conversation, which nevertheless I was glad
to end with my bottle. —

I was fatigued and longed for some rest — thus
made a signal that I wanted to Sleep — but here I was truly
brought into great Distress — for she again misunderstanding
me had the unaccountable Assurance to give me such a hearty
kiss — as but made my Nose nearly as flat as her own. — I knew
not what to do or how to keep my Temper and disentangling
myself with some resentment flung into my Sleeping apartment. but here instantly pursued me again. and in Spite of
what I said very quickly of my Shoes and my Stockings
in a Moment. ● Heavens, I lost all patience This Young
Woman to be sure was as Black as the Devil, to be short as

●— This is actually the Custom throughout Surinam
† to all ranks and Sexes without exception —

Ch. 1.

*Figure 12. A page from Stedman's 1790 "Narrative." James Ford Bell Library,
University of Minnesota.*

INTRODUCTION

and are written vertically in the margin. The script itself represents the labor of "two perfect youths" whom Stedman employed as amanuenses; the change in handwriting occurs on page 385, at the beginning of chapter 16. Throughout, occasional corrections and additions have been made in pen in Stedman's own handwriting; some marks and annotations were also made in pencil.

The pages produced by the two copyists are distinguishable in several respects. The second copyist had more florid handwriting, was somewhat more prone to errors (e.g., repeated words and dropped letters), indented paragraphs more rarely, and utilized upper case letters to begin words much more frequently. In addition, he differed from the first copyist in his spelling, usually writing "sick" (rather than the first copyist's "seek"), "watter" (rather than "water"), "swimming" (rather than "swiming"), "musket" (rather than "musquet"), "severals" (rather than "several"), "padrols" (rather than "patroles"), and so on.

Our complete critical edition includes all of the original front matter and the full text of the thirty chapters; the back matter has been omitted except for the list of "Gentlemen Officers," the list of subscribers, and the translations of Latin passages (which have been incorporated into Appendix B, our notes on literary citations).[68] In the "Directions for the Plates That are Intended for the History of Suriname," we have added plate numbers (taken from the imprints of the engravings in the 1796 first edition). The original manuscript is available to scholars for consultation at the James Ford Bell Library of the University of Minnesota.

The preparation of the handwritten eighteenth-century text for a computerized twentieth-century printer has entailed a number of decisions about spelling, punctuation, spacing, and inclusiveness. Because the idiosyncrasies of the original text do not generally obscure meaning for modern readers, and because the 1790 manuscript has been subjected to more than its fair share of editorial meddling in previous editions, both we and the authorities on eighteenth-century manuscript editing whom we consulted felt that it would be most useful to produce a relatively unaltered transcription rather than a modernized text. We have therefore reproduced the original punctuation (e.g., dashes instead of periods) and spelling (which often, for example, writes "verry" for "very," "ashoare" for "ashore," "Fourgeond" for "Fourgeoud," "waste" for "waist," and so forth). We have, however, added clarifications, always in square brackets, when needed for intelligibility, for example transcribing "of" as "of[f]" (as in "he even ordered an indian Chief to have his head struck of[f] on account of some domestick Misdemeanor" [p. 62]), or following the Dutch word "of" by its English

INTRODUCTION

translation ("or") when Stedman, who was bilingual, used it inadvertently (as in "the Aborigenes of [or] Indians of Guiana" [p. 301]). We have included as normal text those words or letters that were added in pen in the manuscript with a caret, in Stedman's hand. In general, we have ignored pencil substitutions of single words or punctuation (often being unable to determine their origin), as well as the lighter pencil cancellation marks discussed on page LI, above; we have, however, accepted occasional penciled spelling corrections when they lend intelligibility. We have retained the use of slashes (/) to open and close parenthetical remarks and have tried to follow faithfully the capitalization of words used in the original manuscript—though the distinctions between, for example, upper and lower case *p*'s and *a*'s were not always clear. We have deleted quotation marks on those longer quotations that we print indented, as well as in a few places in chapter 20, where the passages they enclose are not in fact quotations; we have not followed the eighteenth-century practice of opening each line of indented citations and footnotes with quotation marks. In general, we have used one-en dashes for the copyists' shorter in-sentence dashes and one em for their longer "stop" dashes (which they used as alternatives to periods); the actual physical length of both kinds of dashes in the manuscript is variable. We have omitted the one- or sometimes several-word overlap between pages that was employed by the copyist who penned the second half of the manuscript, as well as repeated words or phrases that are obvious copying errors. Words that are underlined in the 1790 manuscript have been printed in italics in this edition. Finally, we have deleted the dates that were penned in the margin of the manuscript, marking the placement of each with a printer's mark (❧) and indicating the dates covered on each page by means of running heads.

Editions, Translations, Abridgments, and Reprints of Stedman's Narrative

The following listing includes all editions, translations, abridgments, and reprints of Stedman's *Narrative* known to us, plus a representative indication of the current location of copies available for consultation. (For pre-twentieth-century editions, we list one location each, when known, for the Netherlands, Great Britain, the United States, and Suriname. Given the rapid, ongoing computerization of bibliographic data bases, more extensive listings seem unnecessary here.) Items marked with an asterisk have not been seen by us; we do not list several "editions" that are mentioned in other bibliographies because we believe

INTRODUCTION

them to be "ghosts" (e.g., based on the bibliographer's having seen simply a prospectus for an item, or a citation in another bibliography, rather than the item itself).

1. 1796   Narrative, of a five years' expedition, against the Revolted Negroes of Surinam, in Guiana, on the Wild Coast of South America; from the year 1772, to 1777: elucidating the History of that Country, and describing its Productions, Viz. Quadrupedes, Birds, Fishes, Reptiles, Trees, Shrubs, Fruits, & Roots; with an account of the Indians of Guiana, & Negroes of Guinea. By Captn. J. G. Stedman. illustrated with 80 elegant Engravings, from drawings made by the Author. London. Printed for J. Johnson, St. Paul's Church Yard, & J Edwards, Pall Mall. 1796.
2 vols., Demy 4to. Vol. 1: frontispiece, engraved title page, and pp. xviii, 14, *11–14*, 15–30, *29–30*, 31–276, *275–76*, 277–407, verso blank, (7), plus 38 plates (one of which is folded) and 2 folded maps, numbered 1–40; vol. 2: engraved title page and pp. iv, 404, (7), 40 plates (one of which is folded), numbered 41–80. (See also n. 39.) This is the first published edition, from which all other editions, translations, and bowdlerizations have been made. The page numeration repeated with asterisks in both plain and colored 1796 issues appears to be a printing error, without significance for the editorial history of the Narrative.
Koninklijk Bibliotheek, British Library, James Ford Bell Library (University of Minnesota), *Surinaams Museum*

2. 1796   Idem no. 1.
Large paper issue (Royal 4to), with all plates colored by hand. (See also n. 39.)
British Library, James Ford Bell Library

3. 1797   Stedman's Nachrichten von Surinam und von seiner Expedition gegen die rebellischen Neger in dieser Kolonie in den Jahren 1772 bis 1777. Ein Auszug aus dem Englischen Original. Mit einer Karte und Kupfern. Mit allergnädigsten Freiheiten. Hamburg, 1797. bei Benjamin Gotttlob Hoffmann.
8vo, pp. (4), iii–xiv, 522, "druckfehler" (1). 7 plates

and folded map. Pp. viii and ix are misnumbered iiiv and xi, respectively. This is an abridged edition, with no chapter breaks, translated by Christian Wilhelm Jacobs and Friedrich Christian Kries. "Voreninnerung" (iii–xiv) signed by "C. W. Jacobs" and "F. Kries." Published as vol. 8 of a series, *Neuere Geschichte der See- und Land-Reisen*. The work has an additional series title page, which, other than adding the name of the series, is identical to the other title page except that the publisher's name is correctly spelled Gottlob. The seven plates and one map were redrawn for this edition by Meijer, L. Hoppe, and Frentzel, mimicking the style of the originals—fine stipple on the plates originally engraved by Bartolozzi, heavy linear nets on those originally by Blake, etc. Plates are drawn after Stedman's 1796 pls. 6, 7, 19, 32, 40, 61, 69, and 76.

Universiteitsbibliotheek Amsterdam, New York Public Library, Surinaams Museum

*4. 1797 Stedmans Nachrichten von Suriname, dem letzten Aufruhr der dortigen Negersclaven und ihrer Bezwingung in den Jahren 1772. bis 1777. Auszugsweise übersetzt von M. C. Sprengel. Halle, in der Rengerschen Buchhandlung. 1797.

2 vols. in one, 8vo, pp. 279, (1); 222. An abridged translation. (See also no. 5.)

British Library, John Carter Brown Library

*5. 1797 Idem no. 4.

Vols. 8 and 9 of Sprengel's *Auswahl der besten ausländischen geographischen und statistischen Nachrichten zur Aufklärung der Völker und Länderkunde.*

British Library, John Carter Brown Library

6. 1798 Voyage à Surinam et dans l'Intérieur de la Guiane, contenant La Relation de cinq Années de Courses et d'Observations faites dans cette Contrée intéressante et peu connue; Avec des Détails sur les Indiens de la Guiane et les Nègres; Par le Capitaine J. G. Stedman; traduit de l'Anglais par P. F. Henry: Suivi du Tableau de la Colonie Française de Cayenne. Avec une Collection de 44 Planches in-40., gravées en taille-douce, contenant des Vues, Marines, Cartes Géographiques, Plans, Portraits, Costumes, Ani-

INTRODUCTION

maux, Plantes, etc. dessinés sur les lieux par J. G. Stedman. A Paris, Chez F. Buisson, Imprimeur-Libraire, rue Hautefeuille, no. 20. An VII de la République.

3 vols., 12mo, pp. (4), viii, 410; (4), 440; (4), 506, errata (1). Atlas in 4to. Publisher's autograph preceding title page is dated 1 Brumaire, An 7 [23 October 1798]. This is an abridged translation that omits, for example, the poetry that appeared in the original. It includes, following the abridged Narrative: "Supplement au Voyage à Surinam, et dans l'intérieur de la Guiane. [par] Le. C. Lescallier, ancien Ordonnateur de la Guiane"—a commentary on Stedman's natural history materials, written specially for this edition (vol. 3, pp. 229-42); "Notions sur la Culture des Terres basses"—four letters relating to tropical agriculture (pp. 243-348); and "Tableau de la Colonie de Cayenne," by P. F. Henry, the translator (pp. 349-464). The accompanying Atlas includes 44 numbered plates, four of which are folded, engraved after the originals by Tardieu l'aîné. Of all the plates redrawn after the 1796 originals, these are in our opinion the most successful. Some are regrouped, e.g., combining Stedman's pls. 2 [*top*] and 3 [*top*] into a single plate, eliminating his pls. 2 [*bottom*] and 3 [*bottom*]; some images are reversed; clouds are generally added to the blank skies of many of the images; and the stippling in, for example, the frontispiece has been changed to line engraving. Nevertheless, Tardieu's plates come closest to the originals in capturing Stedman's spirit and intent. The plates are drawn after Stedman's 1796 frontispiece plus all or part of pls. 1-4, 6-8, 10, 11, 14, 16-20, 23, 28, 30-32, 35, 39-43, 47, 49-51, 53-56, 60, 61, 65, 68-70, 73, 76, 78, 79.

Bibliothèque Nationale, Universiteitsbibliotheek Leiden, British Library, James Ford Bell Library

*7. 1799   Reize in de binnenlanden van Suriname, door Kapitein John Gabriël Stedman. Met plaaten. Naar het Hoogduitsch door J. D. Pasteur. Leiden: A. & J. Honkoop.

2 vols. in one, 8vo, 6 plates and 1 map. Apparently, this is a translation of no. 3.

Koninklijk Bibliotheek, Surinaams Museum

INTRODUCTION

*8. [1799?] I. G. Stedmann's Reisen in Surinam, für die Jugend, bearbeitet von M. Chr. Schulz. Neue Auflage mit V illuminirten Kupfertafeln. Berlin, in der Schüppelschen Buchhandlung. [n.d.]

8vo, engraved title page, and pp. iii–iv, 180. 4 plates. An abridged German juvenile edition. (We have also seen this edition listed as 1805.)

John Carter Brown Library

9. 1799–1800 Reize naar Surinamen, en door de binnenste gedeelten van Guiana; door den Capitain John Gabriël Stedman. Met plaaten en kaarten. Naar het Engelsch. Te Amsterdam, by Johannes Allart.

4 vols., 8vo, 41 plates. Vols. 1 and 2 dated 1799; 3 and 4, 1800. An abridgement that follows closely no. 6 and, in fact, seems to have been translated largely from that edition rather than from no. 1. Following the Narrative are "aanghangzels" (vol. 4, pp. [67]–308) consisting of translations of the (non-Stedman) materials about French Guiana originally published in no. 6. The plates are unsigned except the frontispiece, engraved by Reinr. Vinkeles, but all seem to have been drawn after those by Tardieu l'aîné for no. 6 rather than after the plates in no. 1. The plate selection also follows the French edition except that two plans—Stedman's pls. 54 and 78—are omitted in this edition. The plates are generally poor, relative to those in no. 1 or no. 6, with systematic degradation of the character of nonwhites, e.g., the face of "Graman Quacy" (Stedman's pl. 76) is redrawn to look dull-witted or almost moronic.

Koninklijk Bibliotheek, James Ford Bell Library, Surinaams Museum

10. 1800 Capitain Johan Stedmans Dagbok öfwer Sina Fälttåg i Surinam, jämte Beskrifning om detta Nybygges Inwånare och öfriga Märkwärdigheter. Sammandrag. Stockholm: Tryckt i Kongl. Ordens Boktryckeriet hos Assessoren Johan Pfeiffer.

12mo, pp. (6), 306, (14), with one plate facing p. 74. An abridged Swedish translation by Samuel Odmann. The single plate is engraved by C. C. Furutrad after Stedman's pl. 19.

Universiteitsbibliotheek Leiden, James Ford Bell Library

INTRODUCTION

*11. 1800 Kleines Magazin von Reisen zur angenehmen und belehrenden Unterhaltung der Jugend. Nach den neuesten deutschen und ausländischen Originalwerken, bearbeitet von Schulz. Erstes Bändchen mit 5 Kupfertafeln. Berlin 1800, bey Oehmighe dem Jüngern.

Colored frontispiece, engraved title page, and three color plates engraved by L. Hoppe. 8vo, xii, 180 pp. An abridged German juvenile edition. The redrawn plates combine images from various of the plates in no. 1. Our correspondents suggest that this edition may be nearly identical to no. 8.

12. 1806 Second edition, corrected, of no. 1.

2 vols., 4to. Vol. 1: frontispiece, engraved title page and pp. xviii, 423, verso blank, (4), plus 38 plates (one of which is folded), and 2 folded maps; vol. 2: engraved title page and pp. iv, 419, (5), 40 plates (one of which is folded). Title page identical to no. 1 except that above the vignette is added "Second Edition corrected," and "Th. Payne" replaces "J. Edwards" (who had retired from business several years earlier) as Johnson's copublisher on the final line. The colophon reads, "Luke Hansard, printer, near Lincoln's-Inn Fields." Text corrections are simply typographical, though the whole text has been reset. This edition, like no. 14, sometimes appears hand colored, but this was always done much later.

British Library, James Ford Bell Library, Surinaams Museum [colored]

13. 1809[?] Curious Adventures of Captain Stedman, During an Expedition to Surinam, in 1773; Including the Struggles of the Negroes, and the Barbarities of the Planters, Dreadful Executions, the Manner of Selling Slaves, Mutiny of Sailors, Soldiers, &c. and Various Other Interesting Articles. London: Printed for Thomas Tegg, III, Cheapside . . . [Verso of title:] T. Plummer Printer, Seething-Lane. [n.d.]

8vo, pp. (2), 7–26. Folded frontispiece (reproduced in our fig. 13e). This bowdlerization of the *Narrative,* written in the third person ("says our author . . ."), focuses on scenes of torture, descriptions of planters' lives, and geographical descriptions of Suriname. (This pamphlet also includes, on pp. 26–28,

Flagellation of a Female Samboe Slave.

A

Esclave Samboe, déchirée de coups de Fouet.

B

Eene SAMBOE Slavin, wier lichaam door zweepslagen is van één gereten.

C

SCHIAVA SAMBOE, LACERATA DALLA FUSTIGAZIONE.

D

INTRODUCTION

Figure 13. (a–d, left; e, above) *Comparison of engraving styles.* (a) *Engraving by William Blake, 1793, for Stedman's pl. 35;* (b) *Engraving by Tardieu l'aîné for 1798 French edition;* (c) *Engraving by Reinr. Vinkeles for 1799–1800 Dutch edition;* (d) *Engraving by Acqua for 1818 Italian edition;* (e) *Anonymous engraving entitled "The Barbarous Cruelty inflicted on a Negro—at Surinam," 1809, for* Curious Adventures of Captain Stedman *(no. 13). It was, presumably, depictions of the kind in (e) to which Lord Bentinck referred when he described how, during the general elections of 1831, "to rouse the feelings and passions of the people . . . there were placed before half the hustings in the kingdom full-length pictures of white planters flogging negro women" (Hansard 1848, 37).*

"The Loss of His Majesty's Ship, Romney," an extract from a topical letter unrelated to Stedman's adventures.)

New York Public Library

14. 1813 Reissue of the sheets used in no. 12.

Only the date on the title page is altered; Johnson, who died in 1809, is still listed as publisher.

Koninklijk Bibliotheek, British Library, New York Public Library

15. 1818 Viaggio al Surinam e nell' Interno della Guiana ossia Relazione di Cinque Anni di Corse e di Osservazioni fatte in questo interessante e poco conosciuto Paese dal Capitano Stedman. Versione dal francese del Cav. Borghi. Corredata del Ritratto dell'Autore; di una Carta geografica, di rami colorati, ed accresciuta

di note e di un supplemento del Traduttore sulle altre parti della Guiana, nè visitante, nè descritte dal sig. Stedman. Milano, dalla Tipografia di Giambattista Sonzogno.

4 vols., 12mo, pp. xix, (1)–275, (1), 6 plates, folded map; 275, (1), 4 plates; 278, (1), 4 plates; 259, (1), 3 plates. Published in the series *Racolta de' viaggi più interessanti esequiti nelle varie parti del mondo, tanto per terra quanto per mare, dopo quelli del celebre Cook, e non pubblicati fin ora in lingua italiana*. The plates are drawn after Stedman's pls. 4, 7, 8, 11, 19, 32, 35, 39, 49, 53, 55, 61, 68, 69, 76, and his musical note transcription in no. 1, vol. 1, p. 245. The frontispiece is an engraved portrait of Stedman by L. Rados, after Stedman's 1796 frontispiece. Fourteen of the other sixteen plates were redrawn by Acqua, who took considerable liberties with the originals, and these were colored, often garishly, by Lazzaretti and V. Banieri. The redrawn body proportions and clothing, as well as the colors chosen, often suggest to us southern Italian peasants as much as scenes from Suriname.

James Ford Bell Library

16. 1824　Joanna, or the Female Slave. A West Indian tale. Founded on Stedman's Narrative of an Expedition Against the Revolted Negroes of Surinam. London: Printed for Lupton Relfe, 13, Cornhill; Constable and Co., Edinburgh; and R. Milliken, Dublin.

12mo, pp. i–xi, 1–176. An abridged, stylistically altered version of no. 1, without plates. Published as part of the ongoing debate about General Emancipation, which the anonymous compiler, in his preface, argues is "neither practicable nor desirable," instead advocating "the abolition of cruelty."

British Library, Library of Congress

17. 1834　"Joanna." In The Oasis, Mrs. [Lydia] Child, ed., Boston, Benjamin C. Bacon, pp. 65–105.

Consists almost wholly of extracts from no. 1, with occasional brief summaries of deleted portions. Contains a workmanlike depiction of Joanna, engraved by G. G. Smith after Stedman's pl. 8, plus an untitled and unsigned engraving identical to the

INTRODUCTION

penultimate one in no. 18. The editor's note makes clear the thin line U.S. abolitionists then walked, noting of Stedman that "He is the hero of his own story; and I leave him to tell it in his own words. Should any fastidious readers be alarmed, I beg leave to assure them that the Abolitionists have no wish to induce any one to marry a mulatto, even should their lives be saved by such an one ten times."

Library of Congress

18. 1838   Narrative of Joanna; an Emancipated Slave, of Surinam. (From Stedman's Narrative of a Five Year's Expedition against the Revolted Negroes of Surinam.) Boston: Published by Isaac Knapp, 25, Cornhill.

16mo, pp. (3–4), 5–57, plus unrelated antislavery verse, 59–64, and a listing of antislavery works for sale by the publisher (8). Reprinted from no. 17 but with some new plates. Frontispiece ("Joanna") as in no. 17, engraved by G. G. Smith, plus four very crude engravings, with only the third even vaguely based on the 1796 originals: "Joanna at the slave market" and "Joanna visiting Capt. Stedman, at 'The Hope'" (both between pp. 18–19), "Capt. Stedman's residence, 'The Hope'" (between pp. 40–41), and "Capt. Stedman's taking final leave of Joanna" (between pp. 54–55).

University of North Carolina Library

19. 1960   Voyage à Surinam par le capitaine Jean-Gabriel Stedman. Edition établi et présentée par Michel Rouzé selon la traduction originale de P.-F. Henri [*sic*]. Paris: Le Club Français du Livre.

8vo, frontispiece, title page, and pls. 41 and 8 badly reproduced from the 1796 colored edition, [editor's] preface [i–v], pp. 1–343, 19 plates (reproduced from 1798 French edition). A one-volume abridgment, following fairly closely the Henry translation of 1798.

20. 1963   Expedition to Surinam being the narrative of a five years expedition against the revolted negroes of Surinam in Guiana on the wild coast of South America from the year 1772 to 1777 elucidating that country and describing its productions with an account of Indians of Guiana and negroes of Guinea by Captain

INTRODUCTION

John Stedman newly edited and abridged by Christopher Bryant and illustrated with engravings selected from the earliest edition themselves made after drawings by the author. London: Folio Society.

8vo, frontispiece, [i–v], Introduction [vi–viii], 1–239, 12 plates. A "modernized" abridgment. The plates have titles reset; imprints and engravers' signatures are omitted.

21. 1971 Narrative of a five years' expedition against the revolted Negroes of Surinam in Guiana on the Wild Coast of South America from the years 1772 to 1777. Elucidating the history of that country & describing its productions, viz. quadrupedes, birds, reptiles, trees, shrubs, fruits, & roots; with an account of the Indians of Guiana and Negroes of Guinea by Captain J. G. Stedman, illustrated with 80 elegant engravings from drawings made by the author[.] Printed for the Imprint Society[,] Barre, Massachusetts.

2 vols., 4to. New edition of no. 1, with introduction and notes by R. A. J. van Lier. The reproductions of the plates omit the imprints.

22. 1972 Idem no. 21, using the same sheets, but bound in one volume. Amherst: University of Massachusetts Press.

23. 1974 Reize naar Surinamen en door de binnenste gedeelten van Guiana[.] I–IV [.] Opnieuw uitgegeven naar de oorspronkelijke editie Amsterdam 1799–1800[.] Met inleiding en aantekeningen door Prof. Dr. R. A. J. van Lier[,] Hoogleraar aan de Landbouwhogeschool te Wageningen. Amsterdam: S. Emmering.

4 vols. in two. Facsimile reprint of no. 9, plus a Dutch version of the introduction and notes written by van Lier for nos. 21 and 22.

24. 1988 Narrative of a Five Years Expedition against the Revolted Negroes of Surinam. Edited, and with an Introduction and Notes, by Richard Price and Sally Price. Baltimore: Johns Hopkins University Press.

25. n.d. Stedman's *Surinam:* Life in an Eighteenth-Century Slave Society. Edited by Richard Price and Sally

INTRODUCTION

Price. (Abridged paperback edition of no. 24, in preparation.)

Stedman's *Narrative* also inspired more purely literary and dramatic works as well as various graphic imitations. In 1804, Franz Kratter published a play based on the *Narrative*, *Die Sklavin in Surinam*, at Frankfurt; five years later a Dutch translation, *Stedman, toneelspel in vijf bedrijven*, appeared in Amsterdam. In 1840, the popular novelist Eugène Sue published a two-volume romance based loosely on the *Narrative*, *Les Aventures de Hercule Hardi* (published in English translation in 1844). Two Dutch novels have also drawn on Stedman: Herman J. de Ridder's *Een levensteeken op een dodenveld* (1857) and Johan Edwin Hokstam's *Boni* (1983). Most recently, David Dabydeen has written a set of powerfully evocative poems, in Guyanese Creole and English, which are loosely related to Stedman's work—*Slave Song* (1984). And a number of artists, in addition to those who redrew the original plates for the Dutch, French, German, Italian, and other editions, produced works based on the original engravings: for example, the Dutch military painter Jan Hoynck van Papendrecht made colored drawings after Stedman's book (now at the Koninklijk Nederlands Leger en Wapenmuseum, Leiden), as did the American illustrator Tom Jones (Jones, Elting, and Gero 1981). The decorative borders on nineteenth-century Suriname maps often included scenes drawn after Stedman (see, for example, Universiteitsbibliotheek Amsterdam, map 26-32-42). And Stedman's engravings continue to turn up as illustrations in unexpected settings. Recently, while touring an open-air exhibit of Amerindian petroglyphs in Guadeloupe, we saw large blow-ups of three Stedman plates (actually, the Tardieu l'aîné redrawings of the originals for the 1798 French edition) being used, with no indication that they depicted scenes from Suriname, as illustrations of the lifeways of the pre-Columbian inhabitants of that island.

Notes to the Introduction

1. In our Introduction, all references in italics are to Stedman's manuscript diaries, now at the University of Minnesota. Most such references list day, month, year (e.g., *2 February 1792*), but for those cases in which Stedman did not specify day and month we simply list the year (e.g., *1795*). During 1785-86, Stedman wrote a series of retrospective diary entries—in effect, an autobiography covering the period 1744-72—which we refer to here as *1786;* our page references to this manuscript correspond to the complex handwritten numeration system employed by Stedman (see also n. 15, below). In transcrib-

INTRODUCTION

ing Stedman's diaries, as well as the "Narrative" itself, we retain the slashes (/) that he generally used in lieu of parentheses. (For fuller discussion of transcription conventions, see pp. LXXI–LXXII.)

2. Stedman's letter was considered sufficiently admirable to be published during his lifetime in the *Weekly Entertainer* and several other such periodicals and, in 1819, in R. Turner's *The Fashionable Letter Writer* (Thompson 1966, 62–63); the full text was also published by Thompson (ibid.).

3. During the course of the eighteenth century, the idea of the Great Chain of Being was invoked both to emphasize the differences between Europeans and Africans (Jefferson's famous argument that Negroes stood exactly halfway between whites and the highest apes [see Jordan 1968, 490] or Long's lengthy proof of "the natural inferiority of Negroes" that was capped by the rhetorical question of whether they were not "a different species of the same GENUS" [1774, 2:352–77]) and to stress their common humanity (as Stedman often did—sometimes invoking Linnaeus's nonhierarchical principles of natural classification [e.g., p. 514]). For an excellent discussion of these issues, see Jordan 1968.

4. Stedman refers to "*Bampfield-Moore-Carew*" in the "Narrative" (p. 229) and seems to have regarded him "as a kindred spirit . . . [for whom he] felt particular esteem and admiration" (Snell 1904, 138). Carew (born in either 1693 or 1703) was the son of a Devonshire rector who ran off and joined the gypsies at an early age, was accused of swindling and fled to Newfoundland, and returned to England where he eloped with the daughter of an apothecary and was chosen King of the Gypsies. Convicted of vagrancy, he was transported as a prisoner to Maryland, escaped to the Indians, successfully posed as a Quaker in Pennsylvania, returned to England, won prizes in the lottery, and died in either 1758 or 1770 (Stephen and Lee 1967–68; Thompson 1966, 80; van Lier 1971, xii). Stedman was, in fact, buried near the Gypsy King at Bickleigh, according to his own "odd" wishes (Snell 1904, 138).

5. Stedman's position regarding the expression of unvarnished truths was characteristic of contemporary authors of illustrated travel accounts.

> A further consequence of the scientific (that is, factually motivated) travel description is its favoring of a plain, rhetorically unornamented, and seemingly artless style. . . . The struggle to find an innocent mode of literary and visual expression that would convincingly do justice to the novelty of the material circumstances encountered is discussed in the preface to every notable relation of a voyage of discovery published between the middle of the eighteenth century and the middle of the nineteenth. (Stafford 1984, 28)

6. Excellent analyses of the internal structure of these groups, with rich, previously unpublished supporting documents, may be found in de Beet 1984 and Hoogbergen 1985. The reader interested in military aspects of Stedman's "Narrative," which we have chosen not to cover in detail, is urged to consult those works. Considerable further military data relating to these wars may be found in the voluminous correspondence of Stedman's commander, Colonel

INTRODUCTION

Fourgeoud, now in the Algemeen Rijksarchief (Coll. Fagel); although we have read through many of these materials, their level of detail places them beyond the scope of this essay.

7. Stedman's "translations" of the names of maroon villages, which he "thought so verry *Sentimental*" and which have been taken at face value by many readers of the "Narrative" (e.g., Bubberman et al. 1973, 62; Counter and Evans 1981, 272), are in fact the fanciful products of a romantic sensibility. "Kebree me," which Stedman renders as "Hide me O ye Surrounding Verdure," means simply "Hide me"; "Boucoo," which Stedman translates as "It shall moulder before it Shall be taken," means, rather, "fog" or "mold" (and most likely referred to the swampy location of the village); and so on (p. 400). More accurate accounts of the names and locations of the villages to which Stedman refers in the "Narrative," including excellent maps, may be found in de Beet 1984 and Hoogbergen 1985.

8. Blacks had long provided the numerical core of antimaroon military expeditions in Suriname, but during the early and mid-eighteenth century they had always been nonmanumitted plantation slaves, used in unarmed support roles (R. Price 1983b). In 1770, for the first time, a corps of free "coloureds" and blacks (not specifically manumitted for this purpose) was formed (the so-called Corps Vrije Mulatten en Neegers), but they met with little military success. In contrast, the Neeger Vrijcorps, or corps of Rangers, formed in 1772, was unusually effective and became especially feared by Boni and his allies, as various testimonies of captured maroons attest (de Beet 1984). (Since the mid-nineteenth century, scholars have used variant, sometimes overlapping names for the troops formed, respectively, in 1770 and 1772: among modern authorities, de Groot insists that only the former should be called "Vrijcorps" and that the latter should be called "Korps Zwarte Jagers" [1970; 1975; personal communication, 1984]; but Hoogbergen, citing Wolbers [1861, 319–24] as well as his own research, reports finding little documentary evidence for the latter term in the Dutch archives and prefers the nomenclature we adopt here [1984; 1985; personal communication, 1984].) Stedman himself had no doubts about the superiority of the Rangers over his European troops, "*one* of these free negroes . . . [being] Preferable to half a Dozen White men in the *Woods* of Guiana" (p. 396). For comparative materials on the use of black troops by Caribbean colonial governments during slavery, see Buckley 1979.)

9. Stedman describes the siege and fall of Boucou from second-hand sources (pp. 84–86). The documents in de Beet 1984 provide far richer eyewitness descriptions, by both soldiers and members of Boni's group. See also de Groot 1975 and Hoogbergen 1985.

10. Fourgeoud, a personal friend of the Prince of Orange, was a rather eccentric, obsessive Swiss-born professional officer who had earlier served the Dutch in putting down the great Berbice slave rebellion of 1763 (Hartsinck 1770).

11. A much smaller cordon path had already been constructed in 1770 in the eastern coastal region. Nepveu's more ambitious cordon was, in fact, built

between 1774 and 1778, and it soon had more than one thousand men stationed permanently at its various posts (Bubberman et al. 1973, 64; Essed 1984, 52–53; see also pp. 543 and 585). This cordon, maintained at least in part until 1842, did not, however, achieve its purpose.

12. These figures are taken from van Lier (1971, xiv). Stedman claimed that a total of twelve hundred troops were sent to Suriname, with less than one hundred returning (p. 607; but see also p. 511). Essed cites yet different figures (1984, 121). But Hoogbergen, though giving slightly different dates from ours for the arrival of the troops from Holland, nonetheless gives a total very similar to ours—sixteen hundred fifty men (1985, 186, 224, 228–29).

13. It was not until 1789 that Boni's people once again commenced hostilities in Suriname territory, initiating what has come to be called the Second Boni War (1789–93); see Hoogbergen 1984, 1985.

14. Years later, Stedman wrote of the "small green almanack that I Carried in my pocket during the Expedition through Danger—Disease, Famine, water, Smoak & Fire—& which long & Constant Hardships having so much defaced the Above little Green Book that its most Recent Contents became to all but to myself unintelligeable" (p. 8). This notebook (9 × 15 cms) and other Suriname fieldnotes are now at the James Ford Bell Library, University of Minnesota. Though some passages are difficult to read, they are on the whole legible. The ten loose sheets of writing paper, like those that Stedman used for his post-Suriname diaries, are technically "flat foolscap," measuring approximately 13 × 16 inches.

15. The autobiographical sketch, though written in 1785 and 1786, often adopted a presentist perspective, taking on the style of diary entries written contemporaneously with the events reported. The diaries also include at least some comments written well after the dates under which they were entered, though this is apparent only from a careful reading. Thus, in the entry dated 21 April 1778, Stedman reported giving his mother "Security for 50f per annum. . . . I payd til 6 May 1779." In the entry for 24 February 1785, he noted receiving "news that W. Macbeath was drownd which was afterwards proved to be falce"; this comment was followed by one dated 27 June stating, "the raport of W. Macbeaths being drownd contradictid." And for 1 December 1791, he recorded that "I wrote to the Engraver blake to thank him twice for his excellent work but never received any answer."

16. Thompson relates how,

about the year 1940 . . . I acquired the journal from a junk dealer in Pimlico, London. The man submitted the sheets (the journal comprised of about one hundred loose pages, letters, etc.) to me as a job lot, all mixed, all jumbled together, creased, and partly torn, for a few shillings. . . .

"'Ere guv'nor! a pile o' old letters cheap. A dollar the lot. Tek 'em out a mi' road," were his words.

A quick glance at a few sheets assured me of the fact that I had in my possession an original old 18th century manuscript journal. (1966, 131–32)

INTRODUCTION

In the late 1960s, before Thompson's death, John Maggs visited him and arranged to purchase Stedman's diaries and letters; in 1981, we were able in turn to arrange for them to be acquired from Maggs Brothers by the James Ford Bell Library. We do not know the path by which these materials traveled from Stedman's house in Tiverton, upon his death in 1797, to the Pimlico junk dealer in 1940. But we suspect that they may have been passed down, along with the manuscript of the "Narrative" itself, to Miss Pym, who may have simply disposed of them as worthless clutter in the late 1930s (see pp. LXVI–LXIX).

17. This image had also apparently troubled the editor of Stedman's "Narrative" who, during the 1790s, excised the final six words of the author's comment about the piranhas snapping off "the fingers and breasts of women and private Parts of Men" (p. 131; 1796, 1:149).

18. Sometimes, instead of "fooled," Thompson printed "***" (e.g., 1962, 115); and once he replaced Stedman's clearly written "fuk" with a dash and an explanatory footnote that read "Become intimate" (1962, 185).

19. We were unable to locate the entry for this day in Stedman's handwritten diaries; the reference is taken from Thompson (1962, 216).

20. Stedman's finances throughout the period were strained. Before leaving for England, he had managed to sell his military Company for one thousand pounds to a Dutchman, but he expended relatively large sums getting settled in his new home (Thompson 1962, 234–37). Stedman's only steady income throughout his years in England seems to have come from the army. By an act of Parliament in 1783, he and his fellow Scots Brigade officers who had resigned their Dutch commissions and returned to England because of British-Dutch hostilities were put on the half-pay list of the British army, according to their rank abroad (p. 622). Eventually, in 1793, Stedman's half-pay as major was changed to full pay, when he was offered that rank in the British service (*14 October 1793*); soon after he retired on full pay (*5 June 1795*).

21. There are occasional exceptions, as when Stedman succumbed to the temptation to "correct" or embellish an observation after the fact in order to create a desired effect. For example, an anaconda that he reported at the time he saw it to be 18 feet long grew, in retrospect, to be "22 feet and some inches," and still "but a young one, come to about its half-Growth" (*26 August 1773*, p. 147). And, where the diary merely notes "the air Poisoned by mosketos," the "Narrative" states, "So very thick were the Musquitoes now that by Clapping my two hands against each other I have kill'd in one Stroke to the number of 38 upon my honour" (*19 July 1773*, p. 127).

22. Stedman's European marriage took place on 2 February 1782 (Thompson 1962, 234). Joanna died, possibly from the effects of poison, on 5 November 1782; Stedman did not learn of her death until August 1783. In spite of his sentimentality about Joanna throughout the "Narrative" (and despite his fudging of this chronology there—pp. 624–25), he seems to have decided well before her death to keep her simply as a precious memory and not to seek to bring her to Europe. Similarly, soon after his return to Holland from Suri-

name, Stedman divested himself of his personal slave, "my true & Faithful Black boy *Qwaccoo,*" by making a present of him to the Countess of Rosendaal (p. 620).

23. See entries for 22 April, 7, 15, and 27 May, and 13 August 1787; see also 22 October 1789.

24. Johnson, who in 1790 had agreed to publish the "Narrative" (*2 February 1792*), finally published it in 1796, with the bookseller James Edwards, who is written down on Stedman's 1790 "List of Subscribers" for "12 Coppies" (p. 628). Only Johnson's name appears as publisher on the imprints of the plates for the 1796 *Narrative,* and other evidence suggests as well that Edwards was a largely silent partner in the transaction.

25. See note to page 628 for the names of the subscribers added between 1791 and 1796.

26. When the book was finally published in two quarto volumes in 1796, its price was quoted variously as £2.12.6, £2.14.0, and £3.3.0 (*British Critic,* November 1796, 536; *Critical Review,* January 1797, 52; *Analytical Review,* September 1796, 225).

27. During and after his six months in the King's Bench Prison, Johnson continued his publishing activities but at a reduced pace. Many of his personal relationships with writers also deteriorated, some on the grounds that he was becoming neglectful in his handling of manuscripts and book orders. William Wordsworth complained that he failed to make his books available to potential buyers; Samuel Coleridge attempted to withdraw the copyright for one book from him and publish it elsewhere; and his old friend Joseph Priestley, who repeatedly expressed frustration at Johnson's sloppiness in handling orders, settling accounts, and answering letters during this period, finally broke off all relations with him a few months before the publisher's death in 1809 (Tyson 1979).

28. The two exceptions are labeled in Stedman's 1790 "Directions for the Plates" as "Snake" or "Slake," intended for manuscript page 234 and apparently related to the description there of a wounded maroon named Snakee (see pp. 206–7), and "the Chastisement call'd Spanso Bocko," a punitive torture described in detail on manuscript page 720 (p. 556), where the reader is referred to a plate that Johnson may have deleted because of its particularly grisly character, anticipating such commentary as appeared in the *British Critic* (November 1796, 539): "The representations of the negroes suffering under various kinds of torture, might well have been omitted, . . . for we will not call them embellishments to the work."

29. The plates would have cost Johnson at least £5 each and probably a good deal more, making a total of £400 at the very least (G. E. Bentley, Jr., personal communication, 1984).

30. There are indications that many of these were produced by anonymous engravers employed in Bartolozzi's workshop, and a certain number may have been executed by an engraver named Simpkins (*May 1796*).

31. Sitwell, in fact, incorrectly attributes "Joanna" to Blake (1940, facing

INTRODUCTION

140); similarly, Keynes incorrectly attributes "Joanna," but to Bartolozzi, at the same time misdating it as 1794 (1971, 100).

32. Smith, who was the first to make this comparison, concluded that "there is no finer expression of the idea of the noble savage in visual art than Blake's engraving." Smith also suggested that the male Loango slave in Blake's engraving for Stedman's plate 68 was "a graceful and dignified . . . embodiment of youthful masculine beauty [that] may be compared with the striding male figure in *A Family of New South Wales*" (Smith 1960, 128–29).

33. Stedman's amanuensis wrote "Sir *John* Reynolds," and, as the whole long passage in which the name appears was deleted from the 1796 *Narrative*, there is no further evidence regarding its accuracy. A check of relevant biographical dictionaries, however, reveals no Sir John Reynolds alive at the time, and—given the clear mention of Cosway, Rigaud, and Humphry, as well as Stedman's earlier report that his paintings had been "with pleasure Contemplated . . . [by] the immortal Reynolds" (p. 10)—it seems almost certain that he intended to refer to Sir Joshua.

34. That Stedman's watercolors for the book's engravings have (with one exception) apparently not survived may not be surprising, since drawings given to engravers were ordinarily discarded after they were published (G. E. Bentley, Jr., personal communication, 1984). Nevertheless, Stedman's pencil annotations on his "Directions for the Plates" made during the early 1790s were apparently intended to indicate which "drawings [were] not [yet] returned," which led us to search widely but ultimately without success, in public repositories and private collections of prints and drawings, for any surviving watercolors. We suspect that if any of these materials still survive they would have been kept with the manuscript itself until the mid-1960s, in Louth, Lincolnshire; however, they were not among the materials offered by the knockers to the London bookseller in 1967 (see pp. LXVI–LXIX).

35. We are aware of fifteen surviving artworks by Stedman:

1. Original watercolor for Stedman's plate 73 [*top*], "Manner of Sleeping &c. in the Forest," drawn in 1776 and engraved by Barlow in 1791. 14.6 × 10.5 cms. Discovered tucked between the pages of the 1790 manuscript. James Ford Bell Library, University of Minnesota. (See fig. 7.)

2. [Printed reproduction of] pen-and-ink sketch of Stedman's house at Plantation L'Esperance (The Hope), as it was in 1774. Drawn from memory 23 December 1776 directly into Stedman's diary. Engraved (quite probably from a watercolor, like no. 1, made by Stedman after this sketch) by Barlow, as plate 73 [*bottom*], where it is entitled "Rural Retreat—The Cottage" and is indeed made to resemble an English cottage more than the palm-roofed house of Stedman's sketch. The pages containing the sketch were removed from the diary between their publication by Thompson (1962, 194) and the acquisition of the diary by the University of Minnesota, and their current location is unknown. (See fig. 8.)

INTRODUCTION

3. [Printed reproduction of] pen-and-ink sketch, "Plan of my hutt," drawn 23 December 1776 into Stedman's diary. Same history as number 2 (see Thompson 1962, 193; see also p. 564).

4. [Printed reproduction of] pen-and-ink sketch of "Indian hutt in which I lived at Java Creek, in December 1775," drawn 24 December 1776 into Stedman's diary. Same history as numbers 2 and 3 (see Thompson 1962, 196).

5. [Printed reproduction of] pen-and-ink sketch of "a small house . . . which I built in imitation of the rebel Captain Bonny's," drawn 24 December 1776 into Stedman's diary. Same history as numbers 2–4 (see Thompson 1962, 196).

6. Original watercolor drawing of a horse and groom, probably depicting a scene from 1777: "bought a Verry handsome English horse & put my Black boy *Qwaccoo* in a Brillant Livery" (p. 618). 10½ × 7⅝ in. (*Pace* Keynes [1971, 100], who misread a Stedman diary entry of 5 August 1778; this drawing was not given to Ferrier at that time, nor does it represent "Huyzing's groom.") Mounted opposite the frontispiece in the copy of Stedman's 1796 book inscribed by him to Lieutenant Colonel Ferrier, Pierpont Morgan Library, Collection of Gordon N. Ray. (For a reproduction, see Ray 1976, 9.)

7. "Lewis, Duke of Brunswick, &c. &c. &c. Late Field Marshal in the Service of Holland." Drawn and engraved by Stedman, published 24 December 1784 by F. Jones, London, and sold as a separate plate at one shilling. Stedman had served under his command for more than twenty years and had met him in 1772 (*2 November 1772*). A flowery letter from Stedman to the duke, written in French and dated 24 February 1785, announced the publication of the portrait and expressed his personal admiration; the text is transcribed in Thompson 1962, 252–53. Atlas van Stolk, Kat. no. 4523, Rotterdam. (For a reproduction, see Thompson 1962, facing p. 265.)

8. Pen-and-ink sketch of the Stedman coat of arms, drawn ca. 1785 directly into Stedman's diary (*1786, 1*). Stedman noted there that "the Supporters—viz—a Sirin or Mermaid alluding to the sea: and a Spread Eagle to Austria—are of my own choice and invention and which my Family have full right to bear." (For a reproduction, see Thompson 1962, facing p. 25.)

9–15. Small watercolors of ships at sea, undated and unsigned. They are titled, in Stedman's hand, "A French Frigate"; "A Dutch Frigate"; "Whale Taking"; "A Chase"; "A Ship at Anker"; "A Fresh Gale"; "Before the Wind." Hilda von Barton Stedman, who received the drawings from her father, told us in 1980 that he had told her that Stedman himself had given them to his grandfather (Stedman's brother's son), who left them to him. Stedman Archive, Haus Besselich, Urbar, West Germany, Collection Hilda von Barton Stedman. (See fig. 9.)

XC

INTRODUCTION

36. According to Stedman's diaries, he made some of these in multiple versions. We list here those about which we have information:

a. Various unspecified works depicting Suriname scenes given by Stedman to Fourgeoud before 1776 and sent to Holland to be engraved at the request of the Heren van Amsterdam (part owners of the colony of Suriname) (*29 January 1776*).

b. A miniature model of "my Cottage /in Which I lived at the Hope/ on an Oblong Board About 18 inches in Length which being entirely made of the manicole tree & Branches like the Original, it Was a masterpiece." Made ca. December 1776 [see n. 35 (2)]. "Sent in a Present to my Friend Mr. Degraaff at Paramaribo, Who Since Placed it in a Cabinet of Natural Curiosity's at Amsterdam" (p. 565).

c. "a Painting of his [Fourgeoud's] own Figure Marching at the head of his Troops in a Deep Swamp and which picture he sent to the Prince of Orange, and the Duke of Brunswick as a Proof of What he and his Troops Underwent in Surinam" (p. 339). Presented by Stedman to Fourgeoud 20 April 1775. A similar or identical drawing is described by Stedman on page 402 and was engraved by Blake in 1794 as plate 55.

d. A "painting" of Fourgeoud's "Figure at Large, in his bush Equipage, which Was to be Engraved at the Expence of the Town of Amsterdam . . . [executed] on a Large Sheet of paper With China ink" on 29 May 1775 (p. 352). Reported by Stedman as being in transit to Amsterdam on 29 January 1776. An engraving apparently based on this painting was executed by Th. Koning and published, apparently as a kind of obituary-memorial, about 1778, accompanied by a heroic poem about Fourgeoud written by F. Lentfrinck. (See fig. 2.)

e. "Plan, And Birds-Eye-View of All the Encampment of Magdenbergh," given by Stedman to Fourgeoud in June 1775, who then sent it to the Prince of Orange and the Duke of Brunswick "As a Proof of his Military Manoeuvres &c" (p. 359). A similar drawing served as the model for the book's plate 51 [*top*].

f. "Paramaribo," given to Joanna's defender, Mrs. Godefrooy, 5 January 1776. This is apparently a "neat copy" of the drawing or painting that served as the model for the book's plate 30.

g. "Alkmaar," a depiction of Mrs. Godefrooy's own cacao plantation, given her by Stedman on 8 March 1776. A similar "view" served as the model for the book's plate 10 [*top*].

h. Portrait of Mr. Cornell, about whom we have no other information than that he gave Stedman "some Paints" (*3 February 1776*).

i. Portrait of Mrs. Godefrooy, given her by Stedman on 11 March 1776.

j. Portrait of Mr. Goetzee, a planter, given him by Stedman on 13 September 1776.

k. View of "A la Bonheur," a coffee plantation owned by Mr. De Graav, presented to him by Stedman on 13 September 1776.

INTRODUCTION

l. Portrait of Mrs. Goetzee, whom Stedman considered particularly sadistic in her treatment of slaves, given her by him 26 September 1776. (Both she and her husband were apparently poisoned by their slaves several years later [p. 555].)

m. Four watercolors representing all his plantations, given by Stedman to Mr. Goetzee on 9 November 1776 (p. 558).

n. "18 Figures in Wax," which Stedman personally presented to the Prince of Orange on 24 September 1777 at Loo, Gelderland, "made by myself for his Musaem . . . they Represented the free *Indians of Guiana* & negroes *slaves of Surinam* in Different Occupations on an Island Supported by a Crystal Miror, & Ornamented with Solid Gold" (p. 620). See note to page 620.

o. "A collection of wax-work viz negro, indi: &c. . . . which bears the admiration of all that se it" (*9 January 1778, 21 February 1778*). Stedman began what was apparently his second wax creation on 9 January 1778 and finished it on 21 February. On 4 March it was transported to Lieutenant Colonel Ravens, a man with whom he dined several times during 1778.

p. "A view of Tiverton," given to Martin Dunsford, author of *Tiverton Memoirs* (*13 November 1793*).

q. "A view of Arlington House [Devon]," given to Mrs. Chichester 13 November 1793 (for her biographical data, see Thompson 1962, 333).

r. Oil portrait, possibly of William Blake, presented by Stedman to Blake in June 1795.

37. The paper size and details of the watermark differ for the colored issue, however, indicating a separate printing about the same time.

38. The Blake plates marked "to correct" were plates 7, 25, 35, 49, 55, 68, 76, and 80. More generally, the correspondence between the dates printed on the plates and Stedman's often-obscure running-log pencil marks is unclear. For example, Stedman's diary clearly records the frontispiece as being the final plate to be executed, but it is dated 1794, while another Bartolozzi plate (pl. 4), which Stedman also marked "to correct," is dated 1795.

39. The hand-colored issue is Royal Quarto (with the four copies for which we have measurements having page sizes of 30.3 × 23.4, 29.7 × 23.5, 29.5 × 23, and 29 × 23 cms); the ordinary issue is Demy Quarto (with the two copies for which we have measurements having page sizes of 26.6 × 21.5 and 26.3 × 21 cms). Keynes states that the colored issue has a faulty "imprint in the first volume in two lines: *London/Printed by J. Johnson &c.*" (instead of on one line, "London. Printed for J. Johnson. St. Paul's Church Yard, & J. Edwards, Pall Mall. 1796," which appears in the ordinary issue as well as in the second colored volume [1971, 103]), and the colored copy in the James Ford Bell Library matches his description. However, the imprint in the first volume of our own colored copy is "correct," that is, identical to those in the ordinary issue and the second colored volume. Perhaps the error in the imprint cited by Keynes was caught and corrected partway through the printing pro-

cess. The irregularities in pagination are identical in the ordinary and large paper editions (see p. LXXIII), but there is at least one printing discrepancy between the two: the pagination for page 301 both in our large paper copy and in that in the James Ford Bell Library reads "10ɛ." In any case, the papers for these nearly simultaneous issues—including the plates—are different, though both sets bear a 1794 watermark.

40. We believe (as, apparently, did Keynes [1971, 103]) that all the original 1796 hand-colored copies are on large paper, which distinguishes them from copies colored later—often a century after publication. Likewise, all large paper copies we have seen (or corresponded about) are hand colored.

41. This was a general practice for large illustrated books at the time (Tooley 1954, v).

42. It has been suggested that Blake may have been among the subscribers to Stedman's book (Bentley 1977, 623, 695), as "Blake (Mr. Wm) London" appears in the 1796 subscription list. But it seems more likely to us that this was instead "the William Blake of Aldersgate-street . . . who contributed a guinea to the London Abolition Society in 1788" (Erdman 1969, 230). None of the other engravers' names appears in the subscription list to Stedman's book, and though Blake was the only engraver with whom Stedman had a close personal relationship (which could explain a subscription), it seems to us more likely that this same circumstance would have caused Blake to obtain gratis any copy he might have owned.

43. The diary entry for 24 June includes events covering a number of days.

44. Unfortunately, this letter was among those few items that disappeared between Thompson's publication of Stedman's diaries and letters (1962 and 1966) and their acquisition by the University of Minnesota. Our only source for it is Thompson (1966, 75), whose carelessness in transcription always leaves room for doubt.

45. It would seem that Johnson expected this printing to be the final one and not just "proofs," since Stedman allegedly found two thousand copies to burn. It seems clear that the plates were not among the materials that Stedman claims to have destroyed.

46. This conclusion is based on a complex series of inferences, including statistical analysis of marked and unmarked passages. Because both Thomson's manuscript and the printed pages produced from it are lost, however, we can compare the markings on the 1790 manuscript only against the 1796 first edition, not against the printed text that Stedman had before him as he made them.

47. Stedman's book, even in its edited (1796) form, still falls squarely within the stylistic temper of his age and exhibits the characteristic rhetoric of its genre. In her study of the contemporary illustrated travel book, Stafford points to an "emphatically masculine" style and notes that "a hardy virility thus became a peculiar prerogative of the traveler's scientifically educated eye" (1984, 49). After citing various supporting examples she singles out one author who "captures this attitude best, stating [in 1821] that he composed in a 'natural

INTRODUCTION

and manly language as it would become an English naval officer to write'" (ibid., 50).

48. Tales of lascivious monkeys, apes, and orangutans ran rampant through eighteenth-century travel literature. It is an indication of Stedman's lack of racialism, relative to his contemporaries, that he depicts the potential mate of his howler monkeys as the (generalized) female of the *human* species, rather than specifying—as was common practice—the female African or Hottentot (see, for example, Jordan 1968, 229–30, 490–93).

49. His corresponding promotions in the British Service culminated in his appointment to lieutenant colonel in May 1796 [*14 May 1796*].

50. Stedman's fears were not merely abstract; among the subscribers to his book, for example, were two people bearing the same surname as Mrs. Nagel, whom Stedman had originally described as "a hott bich" (*5 March 1776*) but who appears more anonymously and decorously in 1790 (483) and 1796 (2:211) simply as "Mrs N."

51. One reviewer dryly criticized Stedman's excessive penchant for finding fault with previous naturalists, especially Merian, by noting that Stedman

> intimates that some of the figures in that lady's History of Surinam Insects are not sufficiently accurate. Could that justly celebrated lady be revived, to take a view of Captain Stedman's publication, there is great reason to apprehend that she, in her turn, would censure some of the representations there given, and, perhaps, be not a little surprised at some of the author's observations on her own performance. (*British Critic,* November 1796, 540)

52. See note to page 43, below.

53. Stedman's descriptions of this encounter clearly touched on themes that fascinated the European audience. A passage from a contemporary satirical account, describing a visit to a Barbados plantation, displays similar concerns:

> Towards the evening the gentleman [the narrator's planter host] asked me if I would look at his hen negroes. I accepted the proposal, and we walked along a rank of about thirty females of that species. He then asked me how I liked them. I said that perhaps it was owing to prejudice that I did not think them very amiable. After supper he conducted me to my apartment, where I was surprised to find a very pretty mulatto girl. My friend told me, that as I did not seem to like any of his hen negroes, he had sent to a planter of his acquaintance to borrow a beauty of a somewhat lighter hue. I thanked him, told him there was no occasion for such an attention, and expressed my sorrow at his incurring such an obligation on my account.
>
> "Oh!", answered he, "that is nothing; I shall lend him one of my people to work at his sugar-mill tomorrow, which you know is much the same thing." Though this extraordinary attention of the West-Indian shocked the morality of my ideas, yet, as I have always made it a rule to conform to the customs of the countries I visit, I invited the young mulatto girl to get into bed.
>
> "Ki, Ki!" cried the tawny beauty, starting back with the greatest

marks of astonishment. Upon my renewing my solicitations, she told me that it was a liberty she could never think of taking; that the mat at the bed-side was destined for her bed; and, "if massa," said she, "want ee chambepot, he will put he hand out of bed; if he want me, he will puttee out he foot."—There was something droll in this arrangement, but however, it was convenient, and I thought it a thousand pities that Providence should visit so hospitable a country with such frequent hurricanes. (Corncob 1787, 70–71)

54. Changes in the Joanna story between the 1790 and 1796 versions are somewhat less consistent than other substantive editorial alterations. The motivation for one addition—the mention of Stedman's "wedding" to Joanna (1796, 1:106)—remains unclear to us, as it seems inconsistent with most of the other changes. We would speculate, however, that the editor's attempts to depersonalize the relationship throughout the text may have caused Stedman, when he first saw the edited version in 1795, to insert this passage as a step toward righting the balance. And the fact that he referred to a "decent wedding," rather than to "Suriname marriage," may have been his way of circumventing the problems that had caused him to leave out any mention of the ceremony in 1790 (see p. XXXVI).

55. The deletion of references to the beauty of African or mulatto slaves, as well as to their personal cleanliness relative to local Europeans, was frequent throughout the work (as was the complementary deletion of Stedman's various comments about the unattractiveness of European women in Suriname).

56. These views seem to have been shared by the extremely popular poet James Thomson, author of *The Seasons* (1730), whom Stedman quotes frequently in the "Narrative," and who, "had he written when the evils of the trade were more widely known, . . . might have been the greatest poet of antislavery" (Sypher 1942, 160). Thomson shared with Stedman an abhorrence "of cruelty to animals . . .; his preference of country to town; his rhapsodies on domestic love . . .; his contrast between the misery of the poor and the heartless luxury of the rich" (Beers 1899, 112). And, like Stedman, Thomson knew the West Indies firsthand; he was at once "the earliest poet of pseudo-Africa" and "one of the most insistent voices in praise of British freedom and British commercial expansion—neither entirely unrelated to the slave-trade" (Sypher 1942, 160, 163).

57. Stedman himself, of course, had not only been "married," Suriname-style, to a slave (Joanna), he had owned the young slave "Qwacco" (whom he had purchased for 500 florins) until 1777, when he bestowed "my true & Faithful Black boy" upon the Countess of Rosendaal to become her butler (pp. 340, 620). And on 20 February 1792, Stedman's diary unequivocally records, "I refuse Mr. Samson & parson Land to put my name on the petition for the abolution of slaves" [i.e., for the abolition of the slave trade].

58. With the evidence at hand, it is not possible to be absolutely certain that all these changes were made by Thomson. Johnson's influence can, we feel, be fairly ruled out in this regard, since his views on slavery, the slave trade, natural

rights, and similar issues were considerably more radical than Stedman's, and since he had consistently been willing to publish books espousing these positions (Tyson 1979). We cannot, however, be sure that Stedman himself did not contribute some of the changes discussed in this section. His views on slavery could, logically, have hardened along with British opinion more generally. Yet Stedman's developing friendship with Blake during the period and his many diary entries serve no notice that his views had in any way changed. He clearly remained throughout a staunch Royalist (pitted, in this respect, against that "eternal Jacobin," Johnson) but, apparently, every bit as addicted to sentimental antislavery poetry, to romantic reminiscences about his Suriname experiences, and to the fight against social injustice and cruelty as ever. Given Stedman's documented reaction to the text that Johnson printed in 1795 and the lack of any evidence that his own views had changed substantially between 1790 and this time, the scenario that we trace seems to be the most likely explanation of these particular editorial transformations in the "Narrative."

59. Our genealogical evidence comes from family papers and interviews kindly provided by Hilda Emge–von Barton Stedman and her aunt Hilda von Barton Stedman, as well as from Thompson (1966).

60. An official copy of her death certificate, dated 23 August 1877 at Bootham, York, and now in the James Ford Bell Library, states that she had been "Wife of a Clergyman of the Church of England." Presumably, the placement of this record with the diaries was a result of the research that Stanbury Thompson, who owned the diaries from 1940 until sometime in the 1960s, conducted in the course of writing his two books (1962, 1966).

61. Shortly after Hilda's death, the archives in Haus Besselich, to which she had devoted so much care, were permanently transferred to the nearby Abtei Rommersdorf, under the jurisdiction of the Landeshauptarchiv Koblenz (Hilda Emge–von Barton Stedman, personal communication, 1984).

62. Joan Plummer Scott (nee Stedman) of Lanton Tower, Jedburgh, Roxburghshire, reports that during her grandfather's lifetime, around the turn of the century, the Scottish and German branches met quite frequently and that before World War I her father stayed at Haus Besselich as a little boy (personal communication, 1982).

63. We later learned that in 1967 Hilda had written similar, though (in retrospect) unintentionally garbled, information to G. E. Bentley, Jr., who had inquired about the possible existence of Blake materials in her archives: "We have a quantity [of] family papers for this period in our archives. It exist[s] still [with] one lady: 'Miss S. V. M. Pym—Orme Gardens (17 East Gate), Louth, Lincolnshire, England'[.] This lady is the last from the branch of John Gabriel Stedman. . . . I have heard that she has a lot of old papers" (G. E. Bentley, Jr., personal communcation, 1982). Hilda must already have been suffering from occasional memory confusion, since she had in fact visited Daisy and seen the papers some years earlier.

64. Joan Plummer Scott (nee Stedman) reported similarly—and without prompting from us—that "I remember Hilda . . . saying some rather sad

INTRODUCTION

things about Miss Pym, whoever that was" (personal communication, 1982).

65. We have been able to contact the person who is said, by the custodians of the house, to have removed the chest of drawers, but he denies any knowledge of Stedmaniana; the other relative in question, who lives in the south of England not far from Brighton, has not replied to our repeated inquiries. Unfortunately, the solicitor who handled Miss Pym's affairs until the 1960s, and who—it is said—would have known exactly what she did and did not own in the way of Stedmaniana, is (like so many of Miss Pym's contemporaries) now deceased.

66. In British parlance, "knockers" are sharp-eyed men who, getting a foot in the door by one fast-talking means or another, offer to buy a painting, book, or other unsuspected valuable for a pittance from an innocent, usually elderly, person in need of cash, and then unload it quickly in another town, no questions asked. "Brighton knockers" are said to be "the worst of the lot."

67. The pages left blank for plates are generally odd-numbered (recto) pages. However, in the "Directions for the Plates," two even-numbered pages (154 and 544) are listed (though pp. 151 and 541 are the ones left blank for these plates in the manuscript); page one is listed as containing a plate, even though the page facing it is left blank for that plate in the manuscript; and plates are listed for pages 211 and 234 (with only vague designations, and apparently as additions to the original listing), even though those pages are not left blank in the manuscript and no plates were included in their respective positions in the 1796 publication.

68. The index was devoted largely to a listing of natural history species, which is here superseded by our own notes on flora and fauna (Appendix A); and Stedman's poem (which, though bound with the manuscript, was almost certainly not intended to be published with it) has recently been published separately (R. and S. Price 1985).

NARRATIVE OF A FIVE YEARS EXPEDITION
AGAINST THE REVOLTED NEGROES OF SURINAM

"From different Parents, different Climes we came,
At different Periods"; Fate still rules the same,
Unhappy Youth while bleeding on the ground;
'Twas Yours to fall — but Mine to feel the wound.

Narrative
of a five years expedition against the Revolted Negroes of Surinam In Guiana on the Wild Coast of South–America

From the year 1772 to the year 1777

With some Elucidation on the History of that Country & the discription of its Productions **viz**
Quadrupedes–Birds–Fishes–Reptiles, trees, Shrubs–Fruits & Roots besides an Account of the Indians of Guiana & Negroes of Guinea

---

by Lieut: Col: J: G: Stedman

Ornamented with 80 Engravings
design'd from nature by him on the Spot

O Quantum terra Quantum Cognoscere Coeli,
Permissum est! pelagus quantos aperimus in usus!
Nunc Forsam grave reris opus: sed loeta, recurret,
Cum rutis, et, Caram. Cum, mitri reddet Iolcon;
Quis pador heu nostros tibi tunc audire labores;
Quam referam visas tua per suspiria gentis!

Led by our Stars what tracts immence we trace,
From fear remote, what funds of Science raise!
A pain to thought; but when th'Heroic band,
Returns triumphant to their native Land,
A Life domestic you will then deplore,
And sigh whilst I describe the various Shore!
         Valerius Flaccus

DEDICATION

To Sir George Strickland of Boynton Barː
 Sir—
   The Compliment of a dedication particularly to men of Rank and Quality being of late become little better than a paultry piece of pompous Flattery & Formality, & too often Accompanied by interesting views, I will so far deviate from the unmanly mode as freely to Assure you that neyther your Superior taste for natural Curiosity however Conspicuous or whatever Service you may have it in your Power or Inclination to render me were my inducements—But Simply a pleasing recollection of that warmth with which you from yr first seeing my Original drawings seem'd to patronize them—Accompanied with that open Friendship which on our first meeting Abroad you not only Profest but since have Firmly prov'd to entertain for me—These Alone Sir are my motives for presuming to dedicate to you the Premises of my untutor'd pen & pencil—while the only favour I ask of you in Return is to Believe that however Common a Dedicatory Epistle I have the honour to be with the most uncommon Regard as well as with the Deepest Respect—
             Sir
                 Your most Obedː
                 and most Humble Servː
                     John: Glː Stedman

Preface to the Manuscript

A Soldier or Sailor ought to be a man of Courage & by Heav'ns I will not appear before the Tribunal of Critics with that Squeeking Tone & Trembling Accent us'd by so many of my poor Contemporaries, however ample the Field for exercising theyr Spleen & ill temper against me—But boldly will I first plead my Cause & after that like the dying Indian Submit to my doom without a Shrink or a Complaint—

To begin then—I am going to be told that my Narrative besides its not being interesting to Great Britain has neither stile, orthography, order, or Connection—Patcht up with superfluous Quotations—Descriptions of Animals without so much as proper names—Trifles—Cruelties—Bombast &c. to all which Accusations I partly plead Guilty—I say partly, but with very great Sincerity—Next that some of my Paintings are rather unfinish'd—That my plants fully prove I am nothing of a Botanist—And that the History of Joana deserves no place at all in this Narrative—Guilty—Still besides all which I may be perhaps mistaken in a few of the Dates &c. &c.—& now for my defence—D——n order, D——n matter of fact, D——n ev'rything I am above you all—This is too bad—But I will Honestly & Candidly endeavour to Counterbalance the scales of my destiny by Stating a few unavoidable & incontravertable facts–& then even try to kick up the beams by putting in such other Engredients as will I hope Suspend the most bitter Critick in the Air—

PREFACE

In the first place—His present majesty's Reign being replete with new Discoveries, and the Colony of Surinam not appearing as yet to have been very much explored by any British Subject have induced me to make publick my itinerant remarks to the inhabitants of this Kingdom—

Next—most of the following sheets being Compiled from a small green almanack that I Carried in my pocket during the Expedition through Danger–Disease, Famine, water, Smoak & Fire—& which long & Constant Hardships having so much defaced the Above little Green Book that its most Recent Contents became to all but to myself unintelligeable—I say these Circumstances assuredly ought fully to account for the want of Stile Elegance &c—& which by interlarding them with a few Quotations from better Writers I only meant to make more palatable to some of my Readers—the Linæn names may easily be added by the Connoisseurs—the Trifles leapt over–while the Cruelties ought to serve in deterring others from puttin them in practice—and the bombast must stop the holes—

As for my Drawings they were Generally taken from Nature yet most of the Animals having been dead when they were brought to me ought in some measure to plead for that want of Action which may Chance to be found in a Few—And in regard to my being no Botanist, I answer—that the delicate investigation of Plants with Spectacles is not the work of one reader in one Hundred—

In short all these are Defects & Blunders which plain Faith in the Annex'd narrative must help to wipe away where the Dangers & Distresses I have surmounted will appear incredible to all, but such as have Experienc'd a Similar fate & these Can be but few—I have Conversed with men who sail'd round the World with Admir! Anson & Spoke with others who were present when Cap! Cook was Shot dead at Owhyhee—These men saw much & Encounter'd great Hardships but whose Narrow Escapes & Wretchedness Comes no more in Competition with the fatalities that I have Experienc'd than a trip o'er the Channel ought to be compar'd to the Adventures of Alex! Selkirk on the Island of Juan Fernandos—

During these was I Supported by a Gentlemans Daughter Reduced to the Situation of a humble Slave to whose memory after saving my life so often I am assuredly indepted ev'ry gratitude in my Pow'r—

Then let this be my apology for inserting a name so dear to me & Which was never pronounc'd but with the greatest regard nay even Respect by all who had the good fortune to know her—while as to an Oversight in the dates it Can matter but little if she makes her first appearance on a Friday or if I first landed in Guiana upon a Monday—

PREFACE

If now what I have said has not Sufficient weight then let me add that besides having been debarr'd from a Classical Education & being next to a stranger in this Country, I have even had very little time for Lecture & still less for Compiling this Laborious work, Which was never once Corrected or indeed wholy intended for the Press—That in this Arduous task after spending a life of hury yet in obscurity I never was assisted but Constantly interupted by domestick Occurrences—& that my Encouragement was so very little, as to have been Frequently told by the Grave ones that not an Englishman would understand in the End what I had put to paper, yet still I persevered with an undaunted Resolution, or if you think proper presumption til I had accomplish'd my Views—

This Reader—This open Confession alone ought to be a recommendation to the Book annex'd to people who are not slaves [to] Fashion & prepossed by Froth & Flumery–nay so little do I indeed pretend to be a writer alamode that I feel myself very much at a loss how to give this Preface a More proper Conclusion than it had a Beginning and which I am well Convinc'd many fine Fellows will Call out, it is not the Thing—but let it be consider'd that I write from the Feelings of an officer & nor more nor less than–simple truth unmask'd—an officer well acquainted that either overdone delicacies or very Rustick food can please but the palates of a Few—while wholsome homely fair is usually best Relished by the Generality of mankind—& such is the mess he offers to all Ranks Capacities ages & Sexes without Distinction—which may also be Call'd an Ample field or Garden wherein Carefully sorting the Weeds many very beautiful Flowers may be Cull'd in wand'ring along—nay even a mine in which by those who know how to Separate the dross from the mettal many Valuable drops of Gold & even some inestimable Gems may be Discover'd—what have I said?—I to hope for merit after my learn'd Kinsman's performance was Tax'd to be either without originality or information*—yet, O Heavens how should I laugh aloud to be told that my unstudied theme posses'd both the one & the other—Be that as it may my vanity will not permit me to pass by in Silence that I have Corrected many other authors & that as many of my Friends have read even this Journal if I must Credit them with uncommon pleasure & Instruction—but all the world to be sure are not ones friends—Linæus himself has also been Guilty of imperfections—& in the Celebrated Miss Merians Surinam Drawings I pledge my Honour to point out many Faults—

And now a word or two relative to the Expedition against the Re-

---

* —Do. Stedman author of Lælius & Hortensia

volted negroes—perhaps the most uncommon expedition that was ever undertaken by wonderful man—In this for the Liberty I have assumed to take with the Character of the Commander in Chief, & a few others I Scorn to make the smallest Consession till I shall have found out the Reason why Vice ought not to be Expos'd to the World as well as Virtue made Conspicuous—This prerogative I know might be disputed me by some Nations, but is rather applauded in a Land of Liberty where the principals of Humanity are Naturally engrafted on the Subject as the British Oak is the natural produce of the Soil—Happy Island—may Guardian Angels protect thee long & long—& if in thy Sight I have any merit at all conceal it not—but if from such the Sheets thou art going to peruse are totally divested—Strike home—yet let not the blow be fatal since time & Gentle usage who knows may mend me—

But S'wounds I feel I am Stooping to Low—the native petulancy of my temper almost witholds my pen—I who present mankind with no less than 30 Laboreous Chapt.^{rs} in which natural History is promoted—the Olive Indian admir'd—the sable negro slave Supported—& the black European expos'd to the naked eye, while the whole is Variegated with the most beautiful Landscapes, & the Account of my military wanderings through an unbounded forrest—I who excibit alone a small Musaeum of above one Hundred Original paintings & who dare to Censure most other works of the kind in which eyther the writer or the painter have never seen the spot which they describe—while here both the first & the last are the works of my own hands—while even the ingenious Cowley has with satisfaction perus'd the one, & the immortal Reynolds with pleasure Contemplated the other—no—To see my work damn'd without Redemption—I Spurn the thought—And at all Hazards for the Laudableness of my motive do I think myself entitled to thanks from the publick, as well as to Reproaches for the Defects in the Execution—

But Hark—I hear the Ladies say—Good Lord what a strange man is this we have got to deal with?—Then know my pretty girls that I have live'd amongst the wild people—yet where nevertheless I have been taught to know that affected modesty is neither more or Less than the Quintessance of unaffected impertinence—

Shall I Proceed?—but I am forgetting that I now live in a Civiliz'd Country where an elegant compliment even unmeant is Frequently more acceptable than the naked truth painted in the purest Colours of Black & white—let such individuals however remember that

PREFACE

Non, qui Sidonio Contendere Callidus ostro
Nescit Aquinatem potantia vellera fucum,
Certius Accipiet damnum propiusque medullis,
Quam qui non poterit vero distinguere falsum.

And now Farewell to the Inditious few who have a heart to put up with thy neighbours imperfections & know how to peruse With Candour & Desernment who like the noble honey bee extract food & Sweetness from those very flowrs where the Vulgar drone & the Wasp meet with nought but insipidity & perhaps Suck poison—

Farewell do I say principly to thee O hardy youths who art the props of this Glorious Island by thy machless Valour–whose manliness as well as Generosity with equal justice & Conspicuity redound all over the Globe—

And ye O british fair—impress'd with a Sense of the deepest respect do I approach thy Shrine—thou who art the pride of Nations by thy dazling & unrivel'd beauty, as must as by thy enlightn'ed understanding & Tender Sensibility which so much distinguish thy finer feelings from others of thy Sex—accept of my most Ardent wishes for thy Lasting Welfare—while that Confidence which I place in the goodness of your hearts Cannot but prompt me to think that one day when we shall be better Acquainted, you will not only shake off that prepossession which a Hundred to one my unaccountable Stile has induc'd you for the present to take up against me—but at intervals throw down the Book—& with a Sigh exclaim in the Language of Eugenious—Alas poor Stedman—

Table of Contents

Chapter 1st   p. 27

Insurrection amongst the Negroes in Dutch Guiana–
An Expedition sets out from the Texel–Short account of the Voyage–
the Fleet arrives in the River Surinam–Reception of the Troops–
Sketch of the Inhabitants &c.

Chapter 2nd   p. 51

General Discription of Guiana–Of the Colony of Surinam
in particular–account of its earliest Discovery–is possest by
the English–By the Dutch–Murder of the Governor Lord Somelsdyk–
The Settlement taken by the French & ransom'd

Chapter 3rd   p. 66

History of the first Negroes revolting–Causes thereof–
Distracted state of the Colony–Forced Peace concluded with
the Rebels–Mutiny of Sailors and Soldiers–remarks on rebellion
in general–A word of advice to young Officers &c.

CONTENTS

Chapter 4th p. 79

Short interval of peace and plenty–the Colony plunged in
new Distress by a fresh insurrection and nearly ruined–
Review of the Troops for its defence–An action with the Rebels–
Gallant behaviour of a Black Corps till the arrival
of Col. Fourgeonds Marines

Chapter 5th p. 87

The scence [scene] changes–Some account of
a beautiful Female Slave[–]The manner of travelling in Surinam–
The Colonel explores the situation of the Rivers–
Barbarity of a planter–wretched treatment of the Sailors &c–
Sensibility

Chapter 6th p. 102

Account of a dreadful Execution–Fluctuating state of
political Affairs–Short glimps of Peace–An Officer shot Dead–
his whole party cut to pieces and a general alarm renewed
throughout the Colony–Hospitality &c

Chapter 7th p. 119

Armed Barges are sent up to defend the Rivers–Discription of
the Fortress new Amsterdam–A Cruise in the upper parts
of Rio Cottica and Pattamaca–Great Mortality amongst the Troops [–]
view of the Military post at Devils Harwar

Chapter 8th p. 151

Three Estates burnt and the Inhabitants Murder'd by the Rebels[–]
real Picture of Misery and Distress–
Speciman of a March through the Woods of Surinam–
Col. Fourgeond and the remaining Troops leave Paramaribo

CONTENTS

CHAPTER 9th P. 162

Some diseases peculiar to the Climate—Groop of newly imported
Negroes going to be sold—Reflections on the Slave Trade—
Their Voyage from Africa—Manner of selling them in the Colony—
discription of a Cotton plantation

CHAPTER 10th P. 181

Col. Fourgeond marches to the Wana Creek—Harrasses the Enemy—
Account of the Manicole Tree with its various uses—
March to the Mouth of Coermoetibo River—Some Rebels taken—
Shoaking treatment of a wounded Captive Negroe

CHAPTER 11th P. 209

The Troops March back to the Wana Creek—the Rebels pass near
the Camp pursued without success—great distress for
want of water—Mineral Mountains—Sample of Wickedness
in a Superior—the Troops arrived at La Roshelle in Patamacca

CHAPTER 12th P. 232

Discription of the town of Paramaribo and Fort Zalandia—
Col. Fourgeond marches to the river Marawina—a Captain wounded—
Some privates Shot—Strange Execution in the Capital—
account of Fort Somelsdyk—of the Hope in Rio Comewina

CHAPTER 13th P. 253

A Sugar plantation discribed—Domestic Happiness in a Cottage—
Further account of Fourgeonds opperations—Dreadful cruelties
inflicted by some Overseers—
Sketch of resentment by a rebel negro Captain

CONTENTS

Chapter 14th   p. 273

Col. Fourgeond to Paramaribo–Sample of ignorance in a Surgeon[–]
Example of virtue in a Slave–Ferocity in a Commander–
the Troops reenter the Woods–Account of Loango Dancing–
proof of the Force of Natural affection

Chapter 15th   p. 301

Description of the Aborigines or Indians of Guiana–their Food–Arms–
Ornaments–Employments–Diversions–Passions–Religion–
Marriages–Funerals &c.–of the Charibee Indians in Particular–
their trade with the Europeans

Chapter 16th   p. 321

Reenforcement of fresh Troops arrives from Holland–
Encampment on Mount Magdenburgh in Tempatee Creek–
Remarkable instance of Lunacy in a Negroe–
Moutains–Beautiful views– the Sick are sent to Europe

Chapter 17th   p. 340

New samples of unprecedented Barbarity–
Occurances on mount Magdenbergh–prices of Provisions at
Paramaribo–Description of a new animal–
Great Mortality amongst the Troops in Tempatee and Comewina River

Chapter 18th.   p. 356

A Tiger taken in the Camp–
Fatal recounter of a party with the Rebels who kill several of the
Troops and force them back–
Definition of a Planter of Surinam–Contagious distemper–
Suicide–Scene of primitive Nature

CONTENTS

Chapter 19th   p. 371

The Troops march to Barbacoeba in Rio Cottica–Frensy Fevers–
Gratitude in a English Sailor–
Discription of the Government of Surinam–Some account of a
noted American during the late War–
Scene of unprecedented Generosity

Chapter 20th   p. 389

A Rebel Negroe described–Bush fighting–Sentimental Expressions
of the African Blacks–The Town of Gado Saby
taken by Col. Fourgeond–Superstition–
Wonderful Shifts–and great Generalship in the Enemy

Chapter 21st   p. 412

Spirited Conduct of the Rangers and Rebels–A Skirmish–
fine scene of Brotherly affection–the Troops return to
Berbacoeba–plan of the Field of Action &c.–A Slave kill'd by the
Ooroocookoo Snake

Chapter 22nd   p. 425

Allarm in the Pirica River–A detatchment marches to its relief–
Ambuscade–wonderfull effect of the Biting of a Bat–Scene in a
Quabmire [Quagmire]–Sketch of the inquisition–and return of the
Troops to Coermoetibo Creek

Chapter 23rd   p. 444

Second march to Gado-saby–Account of a living Skelaton–
Enchanting landscapes–Devastation–the Commander in Chief falls
sick and leaves the Camp–some Rebels taken–
discourse on the existance of Mermaids–heavy rains–desease–
Famine–misery–&c

CONTENTS

Chapter 24th p. 463

Two Volunteer Companys erected of Free Mulattoes & free Negroes–
discription of the Arowowca Indian Nation–
Col. Fourgeond Regiment receives order to sail for Europe–
Countremanded–reenter the Woods–trade of the Colony–
Discription of a Cacau Estate–Sample of sable Heroism

Chapter 25th p. 488

Singular Method of detecting a Thift–The strange Escape
of a Frog–Rencounter between the Rangers and Rebels–
Amazonian feat in a negroe Female slave–wonderful sagacity in
wild Bees–the Regiment receives a second order to return to Europe

Chapter 26th p. 506

The Troops on Board–still ordered to disembark–great dejection–
Mutiny–Insolent Conduct of an Ouca Negro Captain–
near two hundred sick sent to Holland–General discription of the
Affrican Negroes–Of unhappy and Happy Slaves

Chapter 27th p. 543

The rape of the Sabines–Shoking Execution and Affrican
Fortitude[–]Description of an Indigo Plantation–the spanso Bocco
a punishment–Troops again reenter the woods–
the Expedition draws to a conclusion

Chapter 28th p. 559

The Rebels fly for protection to Cayenne–third March
to Gado-saby–a second reinforcement of Troops arrived from
Holland–Shipwreck of the Transport Paramaribo–
March to Rio Marawina–dismal picture of distress & of Mortality–
yᵉ Colony restored

CONTENTS

CHAPTER 29th P. 581

Some account of a remarkable negroe–the troops prepare for
Europe–Description of a Coffee plantation–plan of reform for
the Encrease of population, and universal Happiness–
one more sample of Hellish Barbarity, and Example of Humanity–
the Regiment embarks

CHAPTER 30th P. 606

The Ships weigh anchor and put to Sea–review of the troops–
account of the voyage–the arrival in the Texel–
discription of the pampus near Amsterdam–final debarkarcation in
the town of Bois le Duck–the Death of Col. Fourgeond–
end of the Expedition[–]Short History of the late Scotch Brigade,
Conclusion

Directions ffor the Plates

That are Intended for the History of Surinam

❦

[frontispiece "From different Parents, different Climes we came"		2]
1. Map of Guiana		28
2. The Flying Fish and the Dolphin of the Moderns		35
3. View of the Constable Rocks off Cayenne, and the Saw Fish		37
4. A Negroe Female with a Weight chain'd to her Ancle		40
5. The Fruit call'd Avoira, and the Shaddock Apple		45
6. The Map of Surinam		52
7. A Coromantyn Free Negroe or Ranger Armed		83
8. Female Mulatto Slave of Surinam [Joanna]		89
9. Sprig of the Tree Tamarind		91
10. View of the Estate Alkmaar, & the representation of a &c		93
11. A Negroe Hanged Alive by the Ribs to a Gallows		105
12. The Toucan and the Fly Catcher		110
13. A Private Marine of Col: Fourgeouds Corps		121
14. View and Plan of the Fortress call'd Amsterdam		123

DIRECTIONS FFOR THE PLATES

15.	The Laguana Lizard of Guiana, and the Aligator of &c	129
16.	The Ai and the Unan or the Sheep and the Dog Sloth	133
17.	View of the Post Devils Harwar, & the Arm'd Barges &c	137
18.	The Mecoo and the Kishee Kishee Monkies	143
19.	Skinning of the Aboma Snake shot by Captn Stedman	149
20.	Order of March through the Woods of Surinam	156
21.	The Blue and Yellow and the Amazon Macaw	165
22.	Group of Negroes as Imported to be Sold for Slaves	167
23.	Sprig of the Cotton Tree	179
24.	The Armadilla and Porcupine of Guiana	186
25.	Sculs [written in pencil]	190
26.	The Manicole and the Cocoa Nut Tree Snake [canceled]	195
27.	The Agamy and Powesse or Wild Turkey	212
28.	The Military Post Vreedenbergh, & view of three &c	219
29.	Azure Butterfuly of S.e Amarica	228
30.	View of the Town of Paramaribo with the Roads and Shipping from the &c	235
31.	Plan of the Town of Paramaribo	238
32.	Female Quadroon Slave of Surinam	243
33.	The Rajew of [or] Stag of Guiana & the Werrobocerra or Small	251
34.	The Sugar Cane in its 4 Different Stages	256
35.	The Flaggellation of a Samboe Female Slave	265
36.	The Spurwing'd Water hen & the red Carlew of Surinam	275
37.	The Pingo Waree or Wild Boar of Guiana & the Pecary or Mexican Hog	287
38.	The Plantain Tree & the Banana	298
39.	Indian Family of the Carribee Nation	307

DIRECTIONS FFOR THE PLATES

40.	Arms, Ornaments, and Furniture of the Indians	319
41.	View of Lesperance or the Hope, and view of Clarenbeck &c	325
42.	The Quato and Saccawinkee Monkies	331
43.	Sprig of the Arnotta and Roucou Tree	335
44.	Blue and crimson Butterfly of S: America, & the Palm Tree Worms	337
45.	The Anamoe and Green Parrots of Guiana	345
46.	The Wood Rat of Surinam, & the Grisson	351
47.	The Fresh Waterfish call'd Dago Fisee, and the Numara	354
48.	The Jaguar or Tygar of Terra Firma, & the Tygar Cat of Surinam	361
49.	A Surinam Planter in his morning dress	365
50.	The Mountain Cabbage and Maureecee Tree	374
51.	View of Magdenbergh, and view of Calais & the Creek Cassewinica	378
52.	Limes, Capsicum Mamee Apple &c	380
53.	A Rebel Negroe Arm'd and on his guard	391
54.	Gradation of Shades between Europe and Africa	399
55.	March through a Swamp or Marsh in Guiana	403
56.	Plan of the Principal Field of Action between the Rivers Cottica &c	417
57.	Murine Oppossum of Terra Firma & the Vampire of Guiana	430
58.	The Agouti or Indian Coney & the Paca or spotted Cavey	437
59.	The Hippopotamus & the Manatee of &c	455
60.	View of the Camp at the Javah Creek & view of the Encampment &c	461
61.	Indian Female of the Arowaka Nation	467
62.	Green Butterfly of S: America, & the Rattle Snake & Dipsas of Guiana	473
63.	Sprig of the Cocoa or Chocolate Tree	481

DIRECTIONS FFOR THE PLATES

64.	The Musk Melon, Water Melon & Pine Apple	485
65.	The Humming Bird, with its Nest and Grass Sparrow	491
66.	Manner of catching Fish by the spring Hook, & by the Baskit	497
67.	The Yellow Wood Pecker and Woodo Louso Foulo	501
68.	Family of Negroe Slaves from Loango	535
69.	Musical Instruments of the African Negroes	539
70.	View of the Settlement call'd the Jew Savannah, and the Blue Bergh &c	545
71.	The Execution of breaking on the Rack	548
72.	Sprig of the Indigo plant	553
	The Chastisement call'd Spanso Bocko [canceled]	
73.	Manner of Sleeping &c in the Forest & rural Retreat–the Cottage	566
74.	The Tamandua and Coati Mondi	570
75.	The Spoon Bill, & the Jabiru of Guiana	580
76.	The Celebrated Gramman Quacy	583
77.	Sprig of the Coffee Tree	587
78.	Regular plan of a Coffee Plantation	589
79.	The Shark and Remora	610
[finis page]	Europe supported by Africa and America	619

Advertisement to the Reader

It is Humbly requested by those who do this Manuscript the Honor of reading it, to keep it perfectly clean particularly from greasy spotts, as it has cost the Author a prodigeous deal of labour Patience and expense to have it Compleated even in its present state however inaccurate—but which defects are to be greatly ascribed to its being wrote in haste and coppy'd by two perfect Youths, without it was ever either revised or corrected—It is also to be observ'd that /the whole not being intended for the Press/ Secresy and Discretion are expected, and that not a single Line whatever of the Sheets annex'd is to be coppied—The more so as many Gentleman's Names are mentioned in it and private transaction related which however interesting to the Author himself and to his particular Friends might tend to expose him both to great Confusion, and even Danger—were they literaly under their present Dress to appear before the publick—and which assuredly can only be the Wish of his Enemies, amongst which number he should be sorry to rank those few whom he intends to trust with the perusal of the Pages annext[—]But should this Narrative where every Thing is now put down at Random ever be deem'd worthy of the Press, and be properly prepared for the Eye of the Publick by the able Pen of a candid and ingeneous Compiler, in that case the Author so far from omitting publick or private transactions is fully determined to insert both the one and the other, that is with initial Letters, and proper restrictions, and after having been Maturely and fully digested.

Chapter 1st

*Insurrection amongst the Negroes in Dutch Guiana—
An Expedition sets out from the Texel—Short account of the Voyage—
The Fleet arrives in the River Surinam—Reception of the Troops—
Sketch of the Inhabitants &ᶜ*

The exploring of Foreign Countries having of late so much taken up the attention of the publick & with so much success, particularly since the first discoveries of the immortal Captⁿ *Cook,* besides which thinking that the Colony of *Surinam* in Dutch Guiana was not as yet perfectly known to this Kingdom, not to mention the pressure of my Friends–were the Principal Motives that induc'd me to throw in my mite & not my abilities as an Author, neyther as a painter, never having been teach'd the art of Drawing–thus but little brillancy can be expected from eyther my pen or my pencil–

> No Art without a Genius will prevail,
> And parts without the help of Art will Fail
> But both ingredients jointly must unite
> To make the happy Character Compleat.

Then let Truth, Simple Truth alone be my Apology–more so since in the Army & Navy ought ever to be met with the Fewest Compliments but the greatest sincerity—this Stamps the Gentleman—& thus without Further Circumlocution I come to the point by boldly setting out on the Subject—

A most dangerous Revolt having broke out in the Colony of Surinam amongst the negro-slaves who were Arm'd & assembled in the woods threat'ning immediate destruction to that settlement, determin'd the states of the united Provinces to send out a fresh Corps of

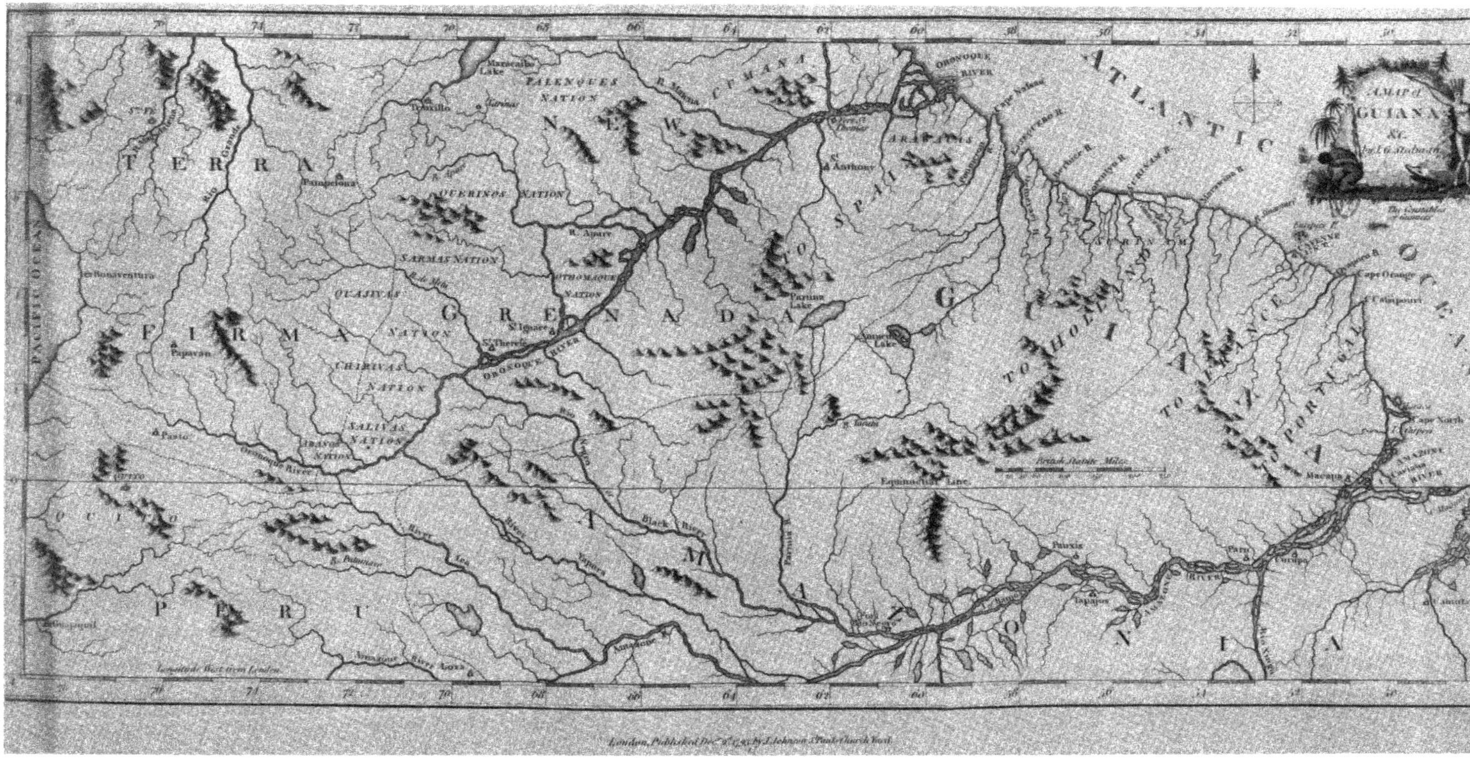
A MAP of
GUIANA
&c.
ATLANTIC OCEAN
PACIFIC OCEAN
TERRA FIRMA
NEW GRENADA
CUMANA
PERU
QUITO
ORONOQUE RIVER
PALENQUES NATION
QUERINOS NATION
SARMAS NATION
CHIRIVAS NATION
SALIVAS NATION
TO HOLLAND
TO FRANCE
TO PORTUGAL
Cape Orange
Cape North
Equinoctial Line
Black River
Maracaibo Lake
Papayan
Pauxis
Macapa

1772—OCTOBER 28, NOVEMBER 1, 12, 22, DECEMBER 3, 7, 8, 13

500 Volunteers in 1772 to act Conjuntly with the troops already there, in Quelling the Insurrection & preventing a general massacre—at this time I was Lieutenant in the Honble Genl Stuarts Regiment of the Scots Bregade in the Service of Holland when impress'd by the Prospect of Preferment usually annext to so Hazardous a Service & in the hopes of Gratifying my Curiosity in exploring a Country so Little known–I offered myself to be one of the party–& had the honour to be Accepted by his Serene Highness the prince of Orange who immediately advanc'd me to the rank of Captn by *Brevet* in the new Corps intended for the expedition under Col: Fourgeoud a Swis Gentleman from Geneva near the Alpin mountains, who was invested with the supreme Authority & Appointed to be our Commander in Chief •—

Having taken the Oaths of Fidelity on the 12.th of Novr provided myself with a Case of Pistols & otherwise prepard for the Voyage I took my last Farewell from my old Reg.^t & other Friends & repair'd to the Island of Texel where many of the Troops were already assembled to be put on board–& where in rowing ashore I had nearly perish'd by the Boats sinking in the surff in company with one *Campbell* & one *Macdonald* two young officers—The Island of Weeringen was however the general Spot of Rendezvous and here our Commander in Chief arriv'd on Decr 7th when he was Saluted by 3 Cheers from the whole Corps in General—Three Transport Ships lay in the Texel Roads to receive us on board & on the 8th of Decr the troops being form'd into Companys & Created to a Reg.^t of marines, were embark'd & only waited for the first fair wind to set sail to South America—At our Embarcation we were Saluted with 7 Guns from each Ship in particular, which Compliment was again return'd by 3 Cheers from the Soldiers my station being with Colonel Fourgeoud—

We lay wind bound in the Roads for Several days during which time a Mr Hesseling one of our officers most unluckily was Seiz'd with the *Small*-Pox which might have infected the whole Ships Company, and to prevent which he was hoisted over board, and ordered a Shore on a place call'd the *Helder*, w[h]ere I accompanied him in an open boat, and where his Malady encreasing he was left behind when the fleet sailed for Surinam—

At my returning on board the Surgeon declared that he saw the Symtoms of the same disorder on myself and I was next ordered a Shoare on the Island of *Texel*. there I past my Quarantine between hope

---

• —Each officer was permitted to *Reenter* his old Reg.^t if he Survived to Return again to Europe, where his place was kept open during the whole time of the expedition for the purpose of putting it in his offer.

29

and fear the best I could However the Surgeon proved to be mistaken, and after much uneasiness of mind, I got once more on board in perfect Health and Spirits Just before the Signal Gun was fired for the fleet to weigh Anchor—which circumstance cannot but induce me to advise those destined to a Naval or Military Life to avail themselves of the Art of innoculation in order to avoid a painful Anxiety to themselves and a most dangerous Infection to their fellow Creatures—

Dec. 24th–at Eight OClock in the morning with a fresh breese from E.N.E and the most beautiful Weather, our small fleet put to Sea in Company with above a hundred other Vessels, bound for different parts of the Globe, and under Convoy of the *westellingwerf* and *Boreus* Men of War—how applicable the following lines?

> This day a Day in Days of Yore
> Our fathers never saw before
> This Day a Day tis ten to one
> Their Sons shall *never see* again—

The three Transports were new frigate built Ships each carrying Flag Jack and Pendant by order of his Serene Highness, and from 10 to 16 Guns while the Officers kept wach on the Quarter Deck and did Duty as is usual in the Navy•

Having safely got without the Soundings—we Saluted the Men of War once more with 9 Guns from each vessel, which Compliment was the last time returned with an equal Number And we kept Course down Channel while at Sea our fleet though small made a very Splendid Appearance—

—Sic transit Gloria Mundi—

The 4 first Days we passed *Northforeland* the *Isle of Wight* and *Portland* point where the *westerlingwerf* Convoy being spring aleak left us and ran into Plymouth for Repair—

The wind now freshened as we came near the Bay of Biscay where the Mate of the Vessel made me take particular Notice of a kind of *Sea Swallow,* which is commonly known by the name of the *Storm Bird,* as it is supposed to give Seamen Notice of an approaching Tempest—This Bird is of a very deep blew Colour and approaching to black with some variegated tinges throughout—The Size may be near that of a large Martin or Swallow with the feet of a Duck the toes being joined by a

---

• —I must here not omit to Mention that our Hammocks with which, and proper bedding Our Officers as well as private Men were provided were all Slung *athort* Ships, Contrary to the general method used at Sea /Viz/ *fore and* aft which we found to be by experience both very convenient & roomy—

Membrane and the Wings of a most extraordinary Length with which it flies Swifter and longer than any bird existing, Skimming with an incredible velocity round the Horison—Its bill is long, and Sharp pointed, and it lives entirely upon fish. The cause of this Birds giving Notice of an approaching Storm is not from its instinct of Philanthaophry towards Man as some have foolishly been pleased to assert, but its flying before the Tempest proceeds only from the more natural instinct of its hastening to avoid it. If the wind blows very high it is never upon the wing but thus overtaken floats on the Surface of the waves—

The next day being January 2nd 1773 we had as was expected a very hard gale of Wind at N.N.E. with double reefed topsails and haches lay'd fore and aft which made the poor Soldiers very seek—Off *Cape Finister* we lost sight of the *Boreas* Man of war, and of the *vigilence* transport who had both parted Company with us during the Gale. Thus remaining but 2 Vessells out of five and being now without any Convoy we prepared the Ships for defence against the rude *African pirates* should any of them chance to fall in with us—

January 4th A Stout Ship cast up to windward in the offing which Bearing strait down upon us we took to be an Algerine Cruiser but which proved to be the *Boreas Man a war* who joined us in a little time thereafter. From this date the Men were daily exercised by Shooting with Marbles at a Mark /from the Quarterdeck/ which was suspended to the yards arm the best Marksmen being encouraged by a dram of Brandy—

The 14th in the Morning Watch we past the Tropicks where the usual Ceremony of *Ducking* was ransom'd for tipping the Sailors with some Silver in an old Shoe that was nailed to the Mast for the purpose. About this time the Convoy most unluckily lost one of her best Seamen, the Boatswains Mate, who by his too great intrepidity pitched from the fore yards arm in the waves—his presence of mind in calling to the Captain, *be not alarmed for me Sir,* in the certain Hopes of meeting with relief attracted peculiar Compassion since no Assistance of any kind was offered to him in Consequence of which after Swimming a Considerable time within view, the Misfortunate Young Man went to the Bottom—

We now were got into the Trade Winds, which blow perpetually East and differ with the monsoons in these last being only periodical—

There we saw several *Dolphins* which make a beautiful appearance in the water, and seem to take pleasure in following the Ships—The Dolphin of the ancients which is of the Grampus kind, and who has been so much the predilection of the Poets on account of its Philanthrophy

&c is found by the Moderns to possess the very reverse Qualifications, being exceedingly destructive, and voracious, while those Bounds and Gambols which it makes near the Ships in place of giving pleasure, are looked on by the Mariners as a prediction of approaching bad weather—What in my Opinion alone makes the modern Dolphin or Dorado /which is supposed to be of the same species/ so much attract our Attention is the unrivaled and dazling brilliancy of its Colours in the Sea—its back being all along like enamelled with Spots between azure blue and a reflecting light Sea green, which Shine conspicuously on a dark Ground, and make the fish appear as bespangled with the richest jewels, while the belley is of a lightish and the fins and Tail of a beautiful Golden die—Its length is from 5 to 6 feet, and of a slender tapering make from the head towards the Tail, which projects with two large horns—and something in the form of a *Cresent,* the Head juts out with a lengthened kind of Snout—The Jaws of which are armed with Small Teeth—its eyes are large and Scales exceedingly small, while one remarkable fin runs over its back from the one extremity to the other—

The Weather here became from day to day more warm which made it very Comfortable while I generally spent my time Mast High above my Shipmates by reading a Book for amusement in the round tops, or hawling a Rope for exercise and whose Company in the Cabbin could not be very desirous owing to Sea Sickness, and other complaints being most of them fresh water Sailors, one or two who had belonged to the navy excepted, and a few of those gallant Officers who helped to Quell the negro insurrection in the Colony of *Berbice* in 1763 of which Colonel Fourgeoud was one—so little were they used to being on board that a Lieutenant *Du Moulin* was thrown over the Ships gunnel by a roll of the vessel and must inevitably been drown'd, had I not grasped him in the fall as I chanced to stand without board upon the main chain Wails—Here one of our Officers made an Experiment on the pressure of water by sinking a well corked Bottle several fathoms deep, fixed to a Line with a Lead, when either the Cork is forced into the bottle or the bottle itself broke to pieces.

I here made also a most Salutary Remark which however trifling and insignificant it may appear to many must be of the greatest Consequence to Sailors,-viz-that in the Cloaths, Bedding, or Linnens of the Seamen no *vermin* can exist in hot Climates, while yet at the same time they Continue on the Head, at least such we experienced it in our vessel to the great Consolation of the Ships Company besides which it was attested to be usual by one or two oldpeople of the crew—

Here the Sea Swarms with an Animal that seems to Sail on the Surface of the Water with a side wind, and is vulgarly called by the Seamen a *Portuguee manowar*, whether this is the *Nautilus,* or the *Argonauta* of *Linnoeus* I am not naturalist sufficient justly to determine thus shall content myself with saying that this Annimal appears above water like a Ladies fan expanded with a beautiful red border the lower extremity of which is fixed in a thin Shell by the way of a boat, which it sinks, rises to the Surface, and guides to and fro at discretion by means of 6 *Tentacula* or limbs that are used by the Animal like oars—I shall only add that when those animals are touched by the Hand they occasion a very painful tingling which continues for some time—

The 18th it blew very fresh, and heavy Seas washed over the vessel—in helping this day to reef the Main top sail for amusement I had the Misfortune to loose my bunch with all my Keys which dropped into the Sea from the yard arm as I threw my foot over the braces; and which trifling accident I should not relate had it not proved to me an insurmountable inconvenience during the rest of the voyage since I could come at nothing of my own private property—And the more so while the whole Ships Company *Officers included* lived on salt provisions alone, a *pig* and a couple of *lean Sheep* excepted whose legs had been broke by the rolling and pitching of the vessel & which dinners were sometimes served up in the very Tubs employed by the Surgeons to void the filth of the Seek, while we *must* impute this abominable negligence to *Monsieur Laurant* Colonel Fourgeoud's French *Valet de Chambre,* and which delicacies I have often Supplied by a Salt-Herring slic'd up with Onions that I purchased from one of the foremast-Men and Converted In Salamagundy. This manner of living on Salt Beef, Pork, Peas, &c like the Common Sailors /whilst *splash* whent the Carion and *plump* went the Cabbages, and the water was no better than it ought to be/ was introduced by the Care of our *prudent* Commander in Chief who like a wise father of his People wished to make us accustomed to what we were to meet with when we should be encamped in the woods of Surinam   Besides from a generous Intention of regaling the South American Inhabitants on European refreshments, such as live *Sheep, Hogs, fowls, Ducks, Baconhams–harts-Tongues preserv'd-Greens, pickles, Spices* &c all of which were on board in profusion and provided by the Town of Amsterdam

But good Intentions do not always meet with their Reward, since the *worms,* without any ones permission laid hold of the whole *dead* stock for themselves /what had Life only escaping their Rage/ who were for a punishment together with their plunder plunged overboard into the ocean

Another Inconveniency arose from this plan which was that Gentlemen not being altogether composed like foremast-Men severals began to give Symptoms of the Scurvy and even of another *loathsome* indisposition that shall be nameless   However by *patience* flour of *Brimstone* and *Butter I* for one had the good fortune to weather those *trifling* Evils but the weakness of discontent still remained, Myself and one or two more dared to complain, we even dared to Sigh, and wish for better usuage, my Sighs in particular reached the ears of the Commander in Chief, and I had *ever* after cause to repent of my presumption, our precious Souls were however not neglected, since prayers were every day read from the Quarter deck by a Corporal who acted as Chaplain, but who unluckily was since detected in Committing a Crime that will not bear to be mentioned

The 20th about this time we saw numbers of *flying fish* this animal the *Exocoetus volitans* of Linnaeus is about the Size of a Herring—its back is flat and of an olive brown Colour the Sides and Belly of a resplendent Silvery white the mouth Small the eyes large the tail bifurcated and the Scales hard, Smooth and Silvery the pectoral fins serve this fish at times for wings, yet no longer than whilst they are wet, when it drops back into the Sea. they are of a golden Colour at the upper Surfaces and beautifully variegated near the Edges with blue Spots, their length is as long as the Body, its flight which is occasioned by the Pursuits of the Dolphins, and other large fishes is always streight forward and generally of short duration till it redips its fins in the Sea. the throwing themselves so frequently on board vessels, and sticking in the Shrouds is not to avoid the danger of Sea Birds as some writers have been pleased to assert, but in my opinion simply because they are obstructed in their flight by an Object which probably they can neither see nor turn away from—I here only shall add that the flying fish is of different Species, is both the prey of the Scaly, and of the feather'd Creation—and that it often meets his doom in that Element to where it made application for its Safety—

22nd Having received a severe fall on the Quarter deck by its being wet and Slippery and finding myself otherwise exceedingly low spirited I had recourse to daily bathing in sea water, and also made use of a Cheering Glass of Claret with two *anchors* of which /being about 20 Gallons/ each Officer was provided, besides his own Stock /but part whereof had been industriously filshed from me and which I detsckted from the back of a hencoop/. by these Means I found such a considerable benefit that in a few days after, I was perfectly recover'd of my Complaint but so exasperated that I took revenge on a locker with above 300 Consealed Eggs, which I stove in and bedaubd the whole Cabin with Yolks—

The Harangus Volans, or Flying Fish.

The Dorado, or Dolphin of the Moderns.

London, Published Dec.r 1.st 1791 by J. Johnson, St Paul's Church Yard.

1773—JANUARY 30, 31

- 30th Hazy weather the Ships bring to & heave the lead at 13 fathom foul water—
- 31st we pass'd several large black Rocks to windward called the *Constables*—and cast anchor near the *Euripice or Devils* Islands off the Coast of South America—the Euripice Islands are situated about 24 Miles from the French Settlement of Cayenne bearing due N.N.W. North Latitude 5 Degrees and 20 Minutes—they are a ridge of small uninhabited Rocks and very dangerous for Shipping. Here the Current runs Continually from S.E. to N.W. at the Rate of 60 English Miles in 24 Hours—thus whatever Vessel Chances to Sail past the mouth of the River Surinam must make a considerable round without which she can certainly not regain it—

To Day we saw the *Narval* or Sea Unicorn and one or two large *Sea Turtles* floating past the Ships Side. the *first* is a large fish with a long and straight extuberance on its nose like a tapering twisted Rope—This fish appeared to be about 6 or 8 feet in Length though some are 40 or 50, and that of its horn about 4 which is thought to be when polished not inferior in either whiteness or hardness to Ivory, and which weapon is dreadfully offensive to many fishes, especially the *whale* to whose nature the Narval seems to have some affinity, being also of the viparous kind, and oftener found in Cold than in Warm Climates The female it is said wants that anterior extuberance, which is so remarkable in the Male. This Animal by some authors has been Confounded with the *Sword Fish*–to which however it bears not the Smallest Resemblance, another call'd the *Saw fish* has also a projecting bone of 3 or 4 Feet long, but, this is flat and on both sides, armed with strong Sharp pointed Spikes, and which give it the form of a Saw—This *Saw* which is Covered over with a rough, slimy, darkish Colour'd Skin that covers the whole Annimal begins to spread itself near the Eyes—and thus continues spreading in breadth till far behind them it forms the head in a flatish triangular figure—and terminates in two Species of fins—above the Eyes are two large holes, which I apprehend to be the Organs of hearing, and not as Some Supose for Spouting Water—almost directly under them is a large orifice, something in the form of a half moon apparantly without teeth which is the mouth, and between this and the underpart of the spicked *Saw* are the Nostrils. the Body of the Sword fish is not much larger than the head, with two strong dorsal fins the one near its middle the other near the Tail—which is partly bifurcated, raised perpendicular, the longest part upwards without rays—and all covered over with dark skin, the belly is of a lighter Colour, near the anus are two ventral fins next each other and from which project the genitals as is usual in male Sharks in two large excressences

View of the Constable Rocks, off Cayenne, from N.E.

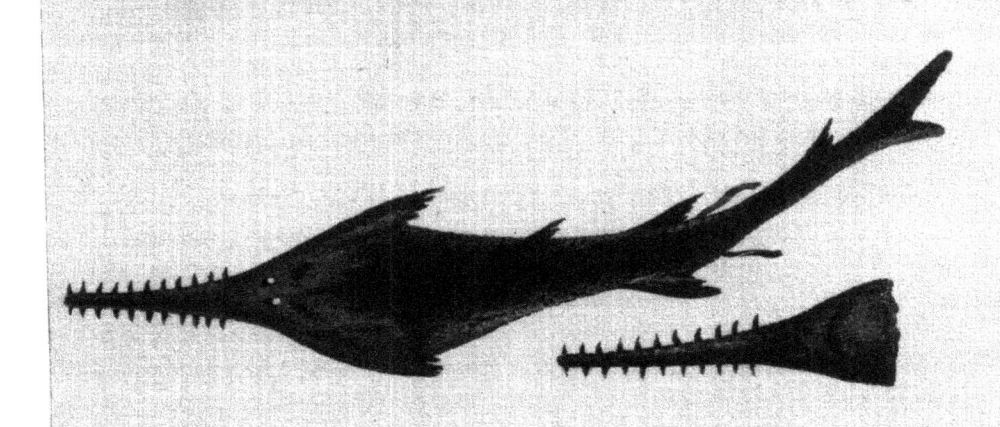

The Saw-Fish, & part of the Head reversed.

London, Published Dec.r 1.st 1791, by J. Johnson, St Paul's Church Yard.

like thongs, the whole forming a very hideous Appearance—this fish fights with the largest whales—till the Sea is allaround died with blood—seldom quitting its adversary till it has vanquish'd or kill'd it—I have seen this monster out of the water and its whole length measured about 15 feet—

The *Turtles* are divided into two Species, which the people of Surinam generaly distinguish by the names of *Calapee* or Green Turtle, and *Carett*, the Calapee weighs sometimes above 400 pounds weight, and has a flattish Shell—the Carett weighs not so heavy neither is its food recon'd so delicious, while its shell /which is most valuable/ is more convex. both these animals lay their Eggs /which are round, about the Size of billiard balls, and good eating/ on the Sands to a very considerable number where they are hatched by the Sun. the manner of taking them is by turning them on their backs with hand Spikes when they are discovered on the Shoare which prevents them from escaping back in the water til they can with convenience be transported, in Surinam they are bought and kill'd by the Butchers, who sell their flesh like Beef Mutton &c to the Inhabitants. the turtles are mostly in Season in the Months of February, March, April and May—

Feb. 1st We weighed Anchor and having kept course till the Evening, we came to an Anchor again, off the river *Marawina* which has been fatal to many Ships by mistaking it for the River Surinam to which its entry bears a very great Resemblance, this River being so very Shallow even at High water that Ships of any burthen immediately get a Ground—

2nd The fleet entered the beautiful River *Surinam* with a fine breeze, and at 3 oClock P.M. dropt anchor before the new Fortress called *Amsterdam* where the *Vigilance* transport had arrived 2 Days before us, and which place I shall afterwards describe—The fortress immediately saluted the Ships from the Batteries and got the Compliment return'd when a long Boat with one of our Captains was dispatched to *Paramaribo* to give the *Governor* notice of the Troops being arrived in the Colony—

Here the Air was perfumed with the most odoriferous Smell in Nature by the many Lemons, Oranges, Shaddocks &c with which this Country abounds—

During this the Company's walk'd on Shoare, and in the Fortress, to refresh themselves, where I accompanied them and waited on the Commandant Colonel De *Ponchera* of the Society or Colony Troops—

Now all were got Safe on *Terra-Firma* prayers and Hymns were laid aside as useless bables while Swearing and Cursing became their Substitute, If this is generally the Custom I know not. but that it ought not to be such I dare maintain since either to be a Hypocrite, or altogether abandoned is equally despisable—

When stepping on Land the first object I met was a most miserable Young Woman in Chains simply covered with a Rag round her Loins, which was like her Skin cut and carved by the lash of the Whip in a most Shocking Manner. Her Crime was in not having fulfilled her Task to which she was by appearance unable. Her punishment to receive 200 Lashes and for months to drag a Chain of several Yards in length the one end of which was Lock'd to her ancle and to the other End of which was a weight of 3 Score pounds or upwards. She was a beautiful Negroe Maid and while I was Meditating on the shocking Load of her Irons I myself nearly escaped being rivitted by Fascination—I now took a draft of the wretched Creature upon paper which I here present to the Sympathizing Reader and which inspired me with a very unfavourable Opinion of the Humanity of the Planters residing in this Colony towards theyr negro Slaves—

Here I found the Grass very long and very Coarse, which covered us all over with most disagreeable Insects–by the Colonists called *Pattat* and *scrapat* lice—the first is so small that they are scarsely visible—the 2nd are something larger and have the form of a *tick* or dogs louse, they both stick fast to the Skin, and occasion the most disagreeable itching—in the rainy Season they are reconed the most numerous, and to walk bare footed is supposed the best way to avoid them, they adhering generally to the Cloaths with greater ease, and of course in greater Numbers, from which they immediately find their way to the quick. from this inconveniency we only got rid at our Return on board, by washing the parts infested, with the Juice of *Lemons* or *Limes* which gave us great consolation—

3rd Several Officers of the Society or Colony troops, with a number of other gentlemen Came to visit us on board, and to Welcome us into the Colony, who Complimented us with a great Quantity of Fruits, Vegetables & other refreshments. they were Row'd in most elegant Barges or *tent Boats* by 6 or 8 Negro's, mostly Accompanied with Flags & small bands of Musick, which vessels I shall afterwards more amply describe—

But what astonish'd me most of any thing was to see the *barge men* all as naked as when they were born, a small strip of Check or other Linnen Cloth excepted, which pass'd through between their thighs to Cover what decency forbids us to expose, & was simply Drawn /before & behind/ over a thin Cotton string that is tied around theyr Loins. these men look'd very well—being healthy Strong & young, theyr skin

A Female Negro Slave, with a Weight chained to her Ancle.

London, Published Dec.r 1.st 1793, by J. Johnson, S.t Paul's Church Yard.

Shining & almost as black as Ebony, the Colonists Generally using their handsomest Slaves to row their boats Serve at Table &c—but wide different from these were 1 or 2 Canoos fill'd with half Starv'd ematiated wreches that Came along side our Ships, begging bits of saltbeef or dried Fish from the Soldiers & who would even fight for the value of a bone.

    4.th To Day Col: Fourgeoud took a Trip in Cognotio to the Town of Param? and return'd in the Evening—

    5.th a Mr *Rynsdorp* came on board who introduc'd to Col: Fourgeoud our Commander in Chief 2 *Black Soldiers* being manumitted Slaves, & who had been Lately form'd into a Corps to the number of 300—these 2 men Mr R. shew'd us as Samples of that valiant body, which had sometime before so gallantly distinguish'd itself for the welfare of the Colony & which I shall in proper place make mention of—

This Day I wrote to my Friends in Europe the account of our safe Arrival, being still at Anchor before the fortress *amsterdam* where the Heat between Decks and even above board was almost insupportable—

    6th I receiv'd a most polite invitation from a Mr Lolkens a planter, /to whom I had been Recommended/ to Accept of his house and Table at Param? which is the Capital of the Colony—

    8.th We at last once more weighed anchor, taking leave of the fortress with 9 Guns each which it returned, and sailing up the river Surinam with beating Drums, flying Colours and a Guard of Marines on the Quarter Deck we finally dropt anchor before the Town of *paramaribo* at 4 o Clock P. M. within Pistol Shot of the Shore, having been saluted by the Citadel *Zelandiea,* with Eleven Guns on our arrival, which Compliment was returned by the Man of War and by the Transport Ships. But here description fails—

> The neatness of the Town–the grandeur of the Shipping—
> The verdure of the woods–and beech adorned with naked Jetty beauties•
> Surinams Silver Streams–Guianas gilded Crest—
> The air perfumed with more than fragrance–and Phoebus ever smiling

    This Night we all once more slept on board–and the next morning at 6. OClock the Troops were disembarked under a general rejoicing which was demonstrated by all the Ships in the Roads being in full dress and an incessant firing of Guns being kept up till the whole Corps

---

• —All the mulatta- negroe- and Indian Slaves in the Colony go bare footed–and naked above the waist Somtimes with the addition of a Shawl or handkerchief thrown negligently over one Shoulder—

was landed—having been on board exactly 63 Days viz. wind bound 16–at Sea 40 and in the river Surinam 7–during all which time but one single Marine died of the fleet which was very remarkable and another Poor Man was discovered to be lunatick.

At this time all the Inhabitants of Paramaribo ran out and flocked together to see the newly arrived Troops—and well they might, for a finer Corps was never seen in any Country of flourishing Young Men the eldest scarce past 30 all neat and clean, drest in new uniforms & Caps ornamented with twigs of Orange *blossom*

Having thus paraded on a large Green Plain between the Citadel and the Town before the Governors house, and during which time several Soldiers fainted by the heat it being still in the dry season the Companies marched into Quarters which were provided for their Reception, whilst the Officers were entertained with a most elegant Repast by the Governor. this entertainment had much the greater Relish after living so long upon salt provisions, and the Governors Civelity was the more astonishing–since our Commander had begun to Compliment him–by drawing up his Regiment with their backs to his palace, what reasons this Gentleman had for acting in this manner I know not, nor did I think any body else, but true it is that so early began the animosity between the two Commanders /to the great Mortification of all the officers in the Corps/ who were by their Commissions independant of each other, except *in employing* us or *not* employing us, which depended alone on the Governor of the Colony and Counsel, But *where* or in *what manner* was vested solely in the Power of our Commander in Chief Colonel Fourgeoud—

The festival was no less truly Magnificent—I shall only say that the choicest Delicacies of Europe and America mixed together were served up in Silver Plate, by a Score of the handsomest Indian Negroe and Mulatto Maids in the world, drest in the finest India Chintses—but all naked above their Middle, according to the Custom of the Country, and adorned in the richest manner with Golden Chains–Medals–Beads–Bracelets–and sweet smelling flowers–and that while the most delicious wines Sparkled in gilded Chrystals and were poured out with profusion–the fruits presented on richest Japan at the Desert were one Composition of Charm and Ambrosia—

Having enjoyed this superb entertainment till about 7 O.Clock I went in search of the house of M*r* *Lolkens* the gentleman who had so kindly come to invite me while I was on Board, I soon found out the place of his residence, where my reception chanced to be so *ludicrous* that I beg leave to relate the Particulars in full. having knocked once or twice at the door—it was opened by a Masculine young *Negro-woman,* as black as a Coal, holding a lighted *Tobacco pipe* in one hand, and a burning *Candle* in the other, which she held close to my face to *reconnoitre* me! her whole dress Consisting in one Single petticoat—

I asked if her Master was at home—she spoke but I could not understand her—I then mentioned him by his Name when she burst out into an immoderate fit of Laughter displaying two rows of beautiful Teeth, and laying hold of my Coat she made me a signal to follow her—I acknowledged that I was at a great loss how to act—the scene was so new to me, when being led into a very neat apartment she put a Bottle of Madeira Wine, water, and some very fine fruit on the Table— and explained in the best manner she was able by gesticulation and broken accents that her *Masera* with all the Family were gone to his plantation to stay a few Days upon business—& that she was left behind to receive an English Captain whom she supposed to be me—I signified that I was *Captain Stedman* then filling her a tumbler of wine /of which she would not accept without the greatest persuasions it being almost unprecedented in this Country to see a Negro Slave either Male or Female eat or Drink in the presence of an European./ I made Shift to enter with this black woman into a kind of Conversation, which nevertheless I was glad to end with my bottle—

I was fatigued and longed for some rest—thus made a signal that I wanted to sleep—but here I was truly brought into great Distress—for she again misunderstanding me had the unaccountable assurance to give me such a hearty kiss—as had made my Nose nearly as flat as her own—I knew not what to do or how to keep my Temper and disentangling myself with some resentment flung into my sleeping apartment but here *wousky* pursued me again—and in Spite of what I could say pulld of my Shoes and my Stockings in a Moment.* Heavens, I lost all patience. This Young Woman to be sure was as black as the Devil, to be short as the rest of this adventure can afford but little instruction or entertainment to the reader. I shall beg leave to draw a Sable Curtain over it—only observing that from this Small Sample the general Character of the negro Girls may be decided which may serve to put young Europeans on their Guard who may chance to visit the West India Settlements—and who do not always escape with impunity—

10th Having now breakfasted on a dish of Chocolate, and no appearance of the planters soon returning—I took my leave of his House and his Black Maid Servant, and having visited the Soldiers in their Quarters I was by the Quartermaster conducted to a very neat House of my

---

* —This is actually the Custom throughout Surinam to all ranks and Sexes without exception—

own, which if it was unfurnished it was not uninhabited Since leaving my Captains Commission which was of parchment in the window, it was eat by the *rats* in the first night and which annimals and *Mice* are exceedingly plentiful in this Country—

This day all the live stock consisting in Hogs Sheep, Ducks, and Fowls, and intended for our Supply at Sea, /but having weathered the Voyage as other Passengers/ were escorted to the head Quarters under the immediate eye of our Commander, and their Protector, whilst above 60 Cags of fine preserved Vegetables, and as many westphalia Hams, /that were found still remaining but *rotten*/ were thrown into the river Surinam to feed the Sharks.

Both Officers and Men still continuing to exist on bread and Cheese for all allowance and which we must impute to the hurry and Confusion annex'd to our debarcation &c. I was politely regaled by my next door neighbour a Mʳ *Halfhide,* the only *Londoner* then resident in the Colony—

However those little Difficulties were soon surmounted by the remarkable Hospitality peculiar to the Inhabitants of this Settlement, which deserve my highest Encomiums—since I no sooner got my Baggage carried on Shore, and began to put my little House in some order, than the Ladies sent me Tables–chairs–mirrors–plate, china–Glasses–and all other Furniture that I wanted whilst the Gentlemen /who gave me a general invitation/ overloaded me with presents such as Madeira Wine–Porter–Cyder–Rum–Sugar and Lemons–besides some delicious fruits particularly the *Shaddock* which is of a most agreeable Taste between Sweet and acid it grows on a Tree which is supposed to be transported from the Coast of Guinea by one Captain Shaddock and whose Name it still retains in the English West India Islands, but in Surinam is called *pompolmoeso.*

> ————Exotic of Cerean dye
> Sweet acid of Spring of an injur'd Sky,
> O *Shaddock* like thy Country Captive led
> And doom'd to grace the board her Children spread

It seems to be of the Orange kind but as large as the Head of a Boy of 8 or 10 Years old, its skin is exceedingly thick of a bitterish taste and of a pale Yellow or Citron Colour–of this fruit there are two Species–of the flesh of the one is white, that of the other a beautiful pale red–and may be eat without any restraint—It is even reckoned wholesome by the Inhabitants who are for the most part remarkably fond of it—

I shall here also take the opportunity to describe the *awara* or avoira

The Fruit called Avoira.

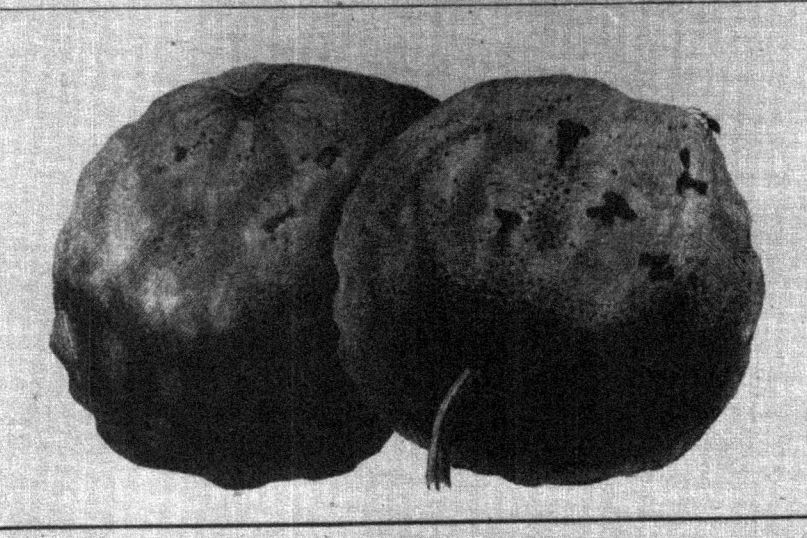

The Shaddock Apple.

London, Published Dec.r 1.st 1791, by J. Johnson, St Paul's Church Yard.

not for the Goodness of its taste but for the richness of its Colour which is of a deep Orange approaching red. this fruit which is of an oval Shape and near the Size of an Orleans-plum grows on a species of palmtree and is much esteemed by the negroes who make rings of the Stone with cyphers, initial letters &c for the Europeans, it being exceedingly hard, and as black as Jet or Ebony. the flesh is very thin on this Stone and exactly the Colour of Gold but I must return to my Journal

11th This morning my Face–Breast–and Hands were all over Spotted like a leopard, occasioned by thousands of Muskitos which flying in Clouds had kept me Company in my new Quarters during the night– and to the Stings of which vermin I had actually been insensible by the fatigues of a sea Voyage of which I had not yet got the better, by a Scorching Climate &c—

The *Muskitos* are a Species of large Gnats. they are inconceivable numerous in the rainy season, and on the banks of rivers or Creeks where they in a cruel manner attack new comers from Europe, whom by instinct they sting in preference to the Colonists—they suck the blood till they can scarcely fly, leaving large knobs or blotches behind which Cause an itching that cannot be expressed–indeed their horid buzzing Musick is sufficient to make one Sweat, which deservedly gives them the name of *Devils Trumpeters*—in the evening the candles are no sooner lighted than they are stuck full of them, they fly into the drink and into the victuals, nay even ones mouth and Eyes are not perfectly free—the cure of their Stings is to bathe the parts with Lime or Lemon Juice and water which may be also called no bad preservative—the Inhabitants burn Tobacco in their Apartments just before they are going to shut the Windows, which ought to be at *sunset* viz, at 6. OClock, when the Tobacco Smoake sets them a flying and the negro Girls help to drive them out by the wind of their Petticoats which they throw off without the least reserve every evening thus in *Quirpo* to battle with the Gnats or Muskitos—some people have Slaves to fan them the whole night during their Sleep–especially the Ladies–except such as have green gauze doors to their beds the generality of the Inhabitants usually Sleeping in Hammocks which are covered with a large Sheet suspended on a tight line straight over them something in form of an awning of a Ship which convenience I having wanted, was the cause of my distressed Situation—

Here are also a larger Species of those insects, which are called *Mawkers* in the Colony–their Sting is very painfull–but being less numerous than the Muskitos they are not such a grievous Plague to the Inhabitants

15. I was entertained at the House of *Colonel Texier* the Commander of the Society Troops

About this Time Colonel Fourgeoud was acquainted by the Governor and Counsel that the Rebel Negroes seeming now so quietly disposed without offering any more Injury to the planters &c The Colony had no further use for our Troops which could be very well defended by those of the Society and by the new Corps of *black rangers,* and in Consequence of which we were at Liberty to return to Europe when we thought proper, without deviating from our Duty. Some received this news with pleasure, and others with reluctance–whilst the Transports which had still been kept in Commission were ordered to be put in ballast for our departure, However by a petition signed by Most of the Inhabitants in opposition to the Governor and Counsel we were again desired to remain, which after some Canvasting being by all parties agreed on the wooding and watering of the Ships was ordered to be Stopt—

19th To Day I was invited to dine with a Mr Kenedy who was remarkably civil to me. he not only told me that his Carriage, riding Horses and Table were entirely at my Service, but gave me the use of a fine *Negro Boy* to carry my umbrella while I shoul[d] remain in the Colony.

22. But what was my astonishment at Seeing an elderly negro woman this Morning enter my Room who did no less than present me her Daughter to be what she pleased to call my Wife; being recovered from my Surprize I had so little Gallantry as to refuse the old Lady's offer which I however did in a civil manner. while a trifling Present ended the Ceremony to their Satisfaction and they both curtseing decently departed.

Having still nothing to do I must describe this Custom which I am convinced will be highly censured by the Sedate European Matrons– and which is nevertheless as common as it is almost necessary to the batchelors who live in this Climate; these Gentlemen all without Exception have a female Slave /mostly a creole/ in their keeping who preserves their linnens clean and decent, dresses their Victuals with Skill, carefully attends them /they being most excellent nurses/ during the frequent illnesses to which Europeans are exposed in this Country, prevents them from keeping late Hours knits for them, sows for them &c*—while these Girls who are sometimes Indians sometime Mulattos

---

* —of this Habit even the Clergymen are not Exempt witness the Rev. Mr Snyderhaus, Mr Talant, &c

and often negroes, naturally pride themselves in living with an European whom they serve with as much tenderness, and to whom they are Generally as faithfull as if he were their lawfull Husband to the great Shame of so many fair Ladies, who break through ties more sacred, and indeed bound with more Solemnity, nor can the above young women be married in any other way, being by their state of Servitude entirely debard from every Christian priviledge and Ceremony, which makes it perfectly lawfull on *their* Side, while they hesitate not to pronounce those as Harlots, who do not follow them /if they can/ in this laudable Example in which they are encouraged as I have said by their nearest Relations and Friends.

Many of these Sable Colour'd Beauties will however follow their own *Panchant* without restraint whatever, even refusing with contempt the greatest acknowledgements offered by the Champions on whom they bestowed their favours, and which they profer without any kind of Ceremony to the first other favourite who may chance to strike their fancy—These are the disinterested Daughters of pure Nature, while others must be rewarded for their Charm, but will go so low as a dram or a broken tobacco pipe.

Having apologised to the modest Reader for this ingenious Sample of the Surinam way of Living I shall go forward—

At more than 20 Families my board was now Dayly spread to partake of their Hospitality when I thought it convenient so that notwithstanding our Gentlemen having formed a Regimental Mess, I had very Seldom the Honour to profit by their Company. In short all seemed to vie with each other who was to shew the newly arrived troops the greatest marks of politeness, and entertainments went round like the Guns go round the Tower on a Day of Publick rejoycing, a M.̲ Rynsdorpt having invited no less than the whole Corps without exception on a very superb Dinner–accompanied with Musick &c nor did it stop here–Balls–Card assemblies and Cavalcades were daily recreations–till even upon the river, for Captain Van de Velde inviting us the same evening on board the Boreas Man of war gave the Company a very genteel Supper in the Cabbin after which we danced on the Quarter Deck under an Awning or large Sail Spread over it in the form of a tent till 6 oClock in the morning–and after this again we took an airing with the Ladies in their Carriages—

Thus in place of fighting the Enemy we seemed to come over for nothing else but idle dissipation which was carried on to such a Length that it absolutely knock'd up several of our Officers—

At this I took proper warning and at once leaving the others to enjoy theyr Splendor I retired from all public Company as the only means of preserving my health in a Climate where an European is so much debilitated by perpetual perspiration /even when he does nothing but sit still/ that the Smallest Exercise and particularly excesses must be to him of the most pernicious Consequence•—

Luxury and dissipation in this Country are carried to the extreme and in my opinion must send Thousands to the Grave, the Men are generally a set of poor wither'd mortals—as dry and sapless as a squeesed lemon—owing to their intemperate way of living such as late hours—hard drinking—and particularly their too frequent intercourse with the negro and mulatto female sex, to whom they generally give the preference before the creole Ladies and many of whom really deserve that preference by their remarkable Cleanliness and youthfull vigour when compared to the fair Women of this Colony—who are a poor languid generation with complexions not much better than that of a drum Skin, a very few perfect beauties set aside—whose delicate features—elegant shape—and graceful air—are certainly unexceptionable—

But all Things may be carried to excess and from this excess it is that I have known many wives outlive 4 Husbands but never a Man wear out 2 wives—Is it then to be wondered that the poor illtreated Ladies should be Jealous of their Spouses and so bitterly take revenge on the causes of their disgrace—the negro and Mulatto Girls whom they persecute with the greatess bitterness and most barbarous tyranny Or is it to be wondered that the unmarried with so little reserve should snap at any new comer from Europe; It certainly is not, and I myself have already being persecuted by overgrown Widows, Stale Beauties, and overaged Maids till I have lost my Temper on the occasion notwithstanding they were possessd of opulent Fortunes•• Nay it was even publickly reported that two of them had fought *a Duel* on account of one of our Officers.

During all this fine piece of Business and having nothing better to do in my retirement, I resolved for my amusement to write a short *History of the Colony of Surinam* and to take such *Drawings* upon Paper as I thought worth my attention. In which plan /besides consulting the best, and most modern authors/ I was since much befriended by the Governor Mr *Nepveu* who not only himself gave me a deal of Infor-

---

• —So very unhealthy is guiana allowed to be that in a fit of low Spirits while at Sea & from a Supposition I shoul[d] no more return to Europe, I had the delicasy of dropping overboard the miniature portrait and lock of hair given me as a keepsake by a very beautiful young Lady to prevent its ever been found in my possession and propogate ungrounded Suspicions—

•• —it is a true observation that the tropical Maids & Musquitos generally attack the new come Europeans by instinct—in preference to the west india Setlers—

mation and showed me several Manuscripts, but also sent me regularly every Morning such Shrubs Annimals &c. as I desired to Copy, it having been ever my Study notwithstanding a Coolness between our Commander and this Gentleman to keep friends with both parties if possible and independent of that Duty which I owed Colonel Fourgeoud as my Commander in Chief to treat the Governor of the Colony w.th that respect which I thought was due to his dignity his rank and his conduct. In which I was supported by several Officers of the Corps, nor was the Cause of Annimosity ever rightly known that subsisted between those two veteran Field Officers.

Oh that I might live to merit Popes Epitaph on the ingenious Sir Godfrey Kneller—But o how vain these hopes!

> Living great Nature fear'd he might outvie
> Her Works—and dying fear'd herself may die

Let me however now try to fulfil what I have undertaken–and commence with the earliest remembrance of Surinam after giving first some general account of Guiana—

Chapter 2nd

General Discription of Guiana—Of the Colony of Surinam in particular—Account of its earliest Discovery—is possest by the English—by the Dutch—Murder of the Governor Lord Somelsdyk— The Settlement taken by the French & ransom'd

Guiana by some call'd the wild Coast is situated in the N.E. Division of South America or *Terrafirma* and between 8 Degrees 20 Minutes North and 3 Degrees South Lattitude* being about 680 Geographical Miles in Breadth and between 50 and 70 Degrees 20 Minutes west Longitude from the Meridian of *London* which makes it about 1220 Miles in Length—

It is bounded by the River *Viapary* or *Oronoque* on the N.W. and on the S.E by the river *Maronon* or *Amazon*—On the N.E it is washed by the atlantick ocean and has Rio Negro or black River on the S.W which form it in a kind of Island, and Seperate it from *new granado, Peru* and the *Brazils*.—

Notwithstanding *Guiana's* being situated under the Torrid Zone, The heat is here a great deal more Supportable than on the Coast of *Guinea*** Guiana being daily tempered by cooling Sea breezes whereas on the Coast of Africa the wind blows continually from the Land, and it is so scorchingly hot by its traversing so many sandy deserts. These Easterly winds which generally blow between the Tropicks and incline either N.

* —And not between 7 d.N. and 5 d.S. according to Doctor Bancroft

** —I never made the experiment by a barometer but the heat is still so very intense that it is sayd to rise above 120 degrees, and that Sailors have been known to broil thin Slic'd Beef by the Sun on the fluke of the anchor and boys to let up a *Kite* which has been parch'd before it came to the Ground—

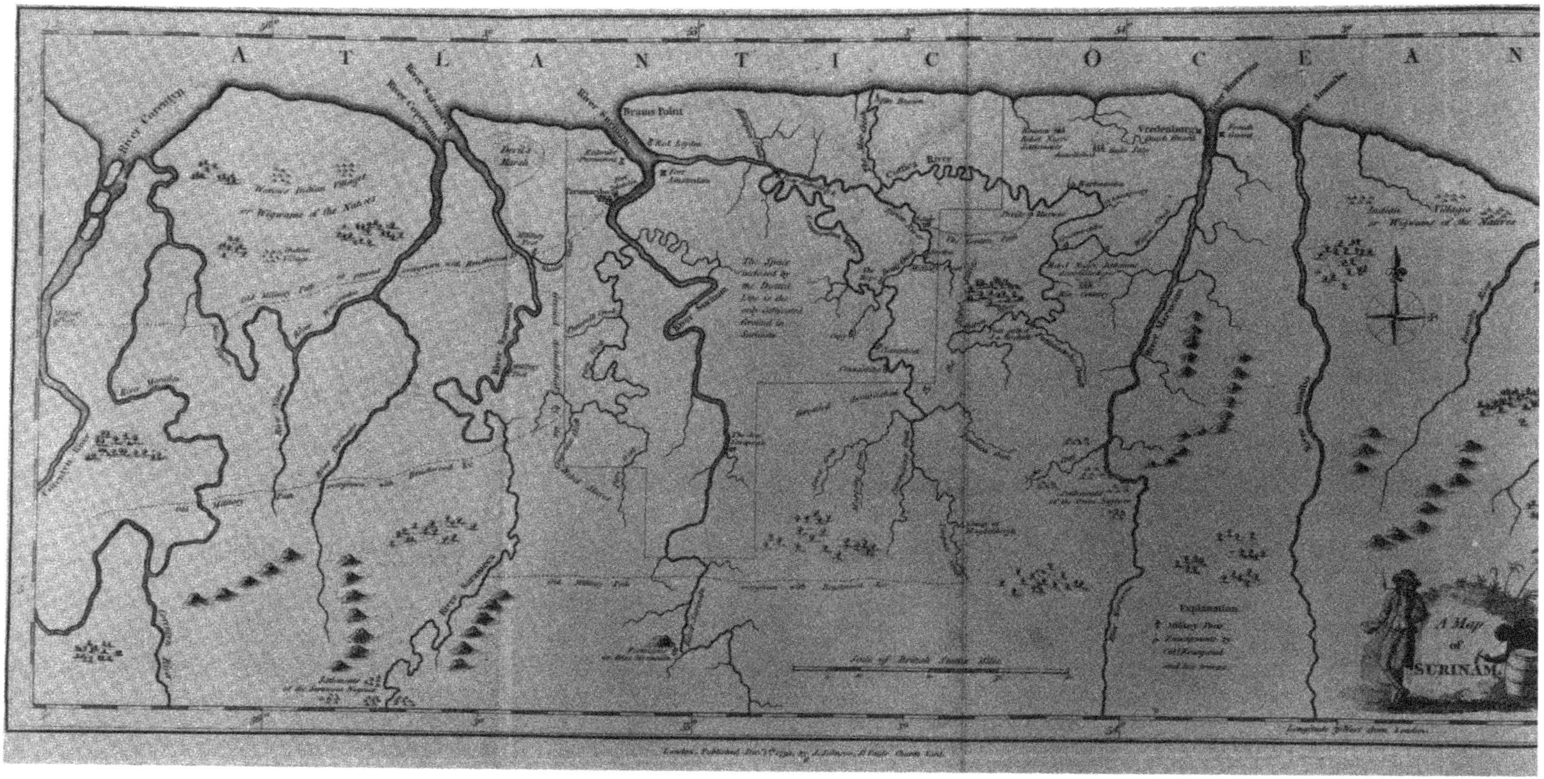
A T L A N T I C   O C E A N
River Coretyn
River Saramaca
River Coppename
River Surinam
Braams Point
Vredenburg
Cottica River
A Map of SURINAM
Explanation

1773—FEBRUARY 28

or S. as the Sun is N. or S. of the Equator, are called the *Trade Winds* by which the Air is mostly refreshed on the Coast of Guiana at the making of the Tides, yet only from 8 or 10 in the morning till about 6 OClock in the Evening, the *Land Zephyr* being very seldom or almost never heard to wisper during the nights, which are nevertheless quite fresh and Chilly—and even sometimes very cold especially towards the morning—occasioned by thick fogs and vapours which exhale from the Earth and which dampness makes them exceedingly unwholesome—

The length of Day and Night in Guiana is nearly the same the Sun rising the whole year round at about 6 oClock and setting at the same hour in the Evening—which never varies much above 40 Minutes•—

The rainy Season may be called the winter of this Country—and the dry Season its Summer, which divide the year as cold and warm weather divide it in Europe with this difference that here they have of each kind two /Viz/ two *rainy* and two *dry* Seasons, which are distinguished by the Appellation of the *greater,* and the *Smaller*—the two latter not being called thus because the rains and the Sunbeams are less violent But because they are supposed to last only half as long as the former. Thus the year is allowed to be divided in this Country but in my Opinion the two rainy Seasons must be equal in Length that is generally Speaking—since these downfals of water only happen when the Sun is vertical which near the line it is twice a Year and certainly of equal duration; the great and small *dry* Season are easily accounted for, the first for instance beginning in Surinam when the Sun is about to cross the Equator on its way to the Tropick of *Capricorn,* often in the Month of October, when a continual drought and scorching heat must take place till its return in March and this is properly called the great dry Season—then having past over the Inhabitants on its way to the Tropick of *Cancer* during which Time it rains prodigiously and without intermission till near June it leaves a short space of parching heat till about July and this may be called the Small dry Season—after which the waters again incessantly keep pouring down till October••

• —Not 13 Minutes according to Mr. Hartsink—

•• —How Mr. *Guthrie* should only begin his dry Season at the North tropick, when the Sun is vertical at the tropick of Capricorn, or how he should make it last till the Sun is again vertical at Cancer: viz. from the beginning of Janr. to the latter end of May I acknowledge Surpasses my Comprehension. Doctor Bancroft must also in this particular be mistaken when he makes the 2 *dry* Seasons of an equal length, but here Dr. Fermyn gives the most Judicial account by saying it is generally dry whether between the Tropics on one Side of the Equator, while the great Luminary is gone to the other Side by which he alludes to *two* Seasons in the year which indeed is oftener the consequence than 4—

53

The Clouds thus following the Sun Shew the wisdom of Providence* in a most conspicuous light—Since without these Floods of water pouring down when the Sun is perpendicular over the Inhabitants, neither animal or vegetable could exist by the penetrating force of its rays, the dry Season being still the most unhealthy particularly to the strongest Constitutions by the desolutions of those fluids or humours which are in the most vigorous always the most repleat, and to use D.̲r Fermyns words the burning heat is sometimes so excessive as to produce a perspiration so abundant and continued that water so soon as drunk will exhale at the pores as from a wet Sponge when pressed

I only shall observe that these Seasons vary very much one year with another—as winter and Summer sometimes come sooner or later in Europe nay that even the weather varies sometimes continually in one Day for which I must leave others to account, And that their Seperation from each other is always attended with very loud claps of Thunder and vivid Flashes of lightening which continue for several Weeks together often killing the Inhabitants and their Cattle while the Hurricanes are at certain periods truly tremenduous.

The face of this Country is in some Places Mountainous dry and barren—but in general the Soil is exceedingly fruitful and Luxurious in its kind being the whole Year overspread with a Continual Verdure while the Trees both bear blossom and ripe fruit at the same time and present an everlasting Spring. this general vegetation in *Surinam* particularly, must not only be attributed to the rains and warmth of the Climate, but also to its low and Marshy Situation where it is cultivated by the Europeans, and which situation /tho' not so healthy/ answers best for the Purposes of the Planter, the fields overflowing by the Swelling Rivers and producing Crops of Sugar Canes without replanting sometimes *ten* to *one* that are produced in the West India Islands by which they may not improperly be Compared to the Banks of the River Nile in Egypt

The Uncultivated parts of Guiana** are covered over with immense forests—Rocks and Mountains*** /some of the latter impregnated with *Minerals* of different kinds/ intermixed with very deep Marshes or

---

• —A word not once mentioned in Lord Ansons voyage round the World—

•• —Surinam is less cultivated than formerly owing to the frequent insurrections of the negro Slaves who have ruined most of the distant plantations, as demonstrated in the annex'd Map of this Colony—

••• —Here D.̲r Bancroft again commits an error in asserting that for the distance of near 50 Miles from the Sea not so much as a Hill is to be met with

Swomps and large healths [heaths] or Savanas. The stream along the Coast runs Continually Northwestwards as I have mentioned, and the Shore is almost inaccessible by Rocks—banks, Quicksands—bogs—prodigious bushes—and impenetrable Brushwood by which it is lined and closely interwoven—

Guiana abounds with very beautiful rivers witness the Oronoque and Amazon, by which as I have mentioned it is bordered, and which rivers may with Justice pass for two of the largest in America if not in the whole World—

This part of Terra Firma is only occupied by the *Portuguese Spaniards* and *Hollanders,* a small Settlement called *Cayenne* excepted, which is situated between the River Marawina and cape Orange, and which belongs to the French—

The Portuguese Dominions in Guiana Stretch along the River Amazon—and those of Spain line the Banks of the River Oronoque—

The *Dutch Settlements* which are Spread along the Sea side, viz, The Western or Atlantic Ocean from Cape Nassau to the River Marawina, are *Essequebo—Demerary—Berbice* and *Surinam**—as they are distinguish'd on the Map before this work. Of all these the last is the best and largest and the description of which as I have promised I intend to make the principal Subject of my Narrative—In the year 1657 the Dutch also established a small Colony in the river *poumeron,* which was in 1666 demolished by the English and in the Year 1677 they again began to erect another Settlement in the River *Wiupokko* or *Oyapoco*[.] But this was like the former that same Year demolished by the French—

The limits of Surinam are a wreath of the rivers *Kanze* or Canje on the west—about 40 Miles from the river Corrantyne & /according to its owners/ the river *Sinamaree* on the East, but the French dispute this point by keeping a Military post at the *Marawina* positively insisting on that River to be their property beyond which indeed the Dutch possess not one foot of *Cultivated* Ground—By the first its length should be 240 Miles—but if the River Marawina is to be reckoned /as I think it ought to be/ the *ne plus ultra* of Surinam, in that Case it only measures 180 Miles at 60 in a Degree of proper land along the Coast of the Atlantick Ocean—

The principal Rivers that belong to this Settlement are the River *Surinam* from which the Colony takes its Name—the *Corantine*—the *Copename*—and the *Serameca*—also the Marawina[—]but of all these Rivers the first alone is navigable—all the other three and even the River *Marawina,*

• —They also have two Islands Curacao & Saint Eustatius

being indeed very broad and long but at the same time so Shallow and so crowded with Rocks and small Islands, that they are of little Consequence to Europeans nor are their banks inhabited, except by some of the Indians, or natives of the Country—

The River Surinam whose Mouth is situated at about 6 Degrees North Latitude is broad at the Entry near 4 English Miles and deep from 16 to 18 feet at low water Mark the tide rising and falling above 12 feet–this breadth and depth is continued from its Mouth upwards for a Distance of 8 or 10 Miles when it divides itself in two branches, keeping its own windings to the South S.E for a length of upwards 120 Miles all navigable for small craft, after which it turns duly to the South with Islands and Small cataracts, its source never being discovered by Europeans—

It is here to be observed that all large vessels after entring this River ought to be kept rather near the East Shore of it, the opposite Side being very full of Shoals till before the Town of Paramaribo which is about 18 Miles from its Mouth—

The other branch into which this large River is divided is named *Comawina* and keeps due East for about 16 Miles with a depth of about 3 or 4 Fathom water at high water mark, thus not navigable for any Ships of burthen that go deep but its breadth may be computed to about 2 Miles; here the River Comawina is again divided in two branches with its own Name to the S.E for a length of above 50 Miles–and that of Cottica to the E.S.E for more than 40 Miles, when this last takes a Meandring turn to the S.S.W. for a Distance of about 24 or 30 Miles—

In all these Rivers which dont run straight but Serpentine ways are discharged a number of very large Creeks or Rivulets–the whole having their banks inhabited by Europeans and Cultivated with most beautiful Coffee, Sugar, Cacao, Cotton, & Indigo plantations and which form the most delightful Prospects that can be imagined to the People that Travel and which is in this Country always done by water the Soil being generally unadapted to make Roads and in some places the woods &c. absolutely impenetrable, a small path of Communication between Paramaribo and the River Saramaca being the only practicable Road that I know in the whole Settlement—

The Rivers of which the Banks are uncultivated, such as the Corrantine–Copename–Serameca–& Marawina Merit but little description Thus I only shall say that they are generally from 2 to 4 Miles broad–exceedingly Shallow and crowded with Quick Sands–small Islands and Rocks which form a Number of beautiful cascades or waterfals &c—

In the River Marawina is often found a curious Stone or Pebble which is known by the name of the Marawina Diamond, and which being polished bears a very great resemblance to that most valuable Gem, in Consequence of which it is often set in Rings, Eardrops, Bracelets &c—

In all the above Rivers without Exception the Water rises and falls above 60 Miles from the Entry occasioned by the stoppage of the freshes by the Tides, yet fresh water may generally be met with about 24 or 30 Miles from the Mouth of any of these Rivers—

For watering Ships that of the River Surinam is reckoned the most excellent which the Sailors fetch so far as the Jew Savanah being above 40 Miles from the Town of Paramaribo—

The worst thing for Ships in these Rivers is that their bottoms are often attacked by a kind of water worms which danger is best prevented by frequently Careening them in order that they may be properly cleaned scraped calked and payd for which use the *Coaltar* invented by the Earl of *Dundonald* and for which a patent of 12 Years was granted is here recommended as preferable to any other—

It is here high or Low water nearly every 6 Hours & half, the Spring tides rising regularly twice a Month when the Rivers swell to a considerable Degree which as I have already mentioned is often of Infinite benefit to the planters—

I must now say something of the defense of the above Rivers which however I propose to describe more at large on another Occasion—

On the East Side of the Mouth of the River Surinam is a small Promontory Call'd *Braams Point* which I think originally had been named *Prams* or *Parhams* point, after Francis Lord *Willoughby of Parham,* to whom this Settlement was given by King *Charles* the second in 1662, and which Spot is supposed to be the first on which the said Lord Willoughby should have landed which was in 1652–ten years before the royal Charter–be that as it may this *point* is not fortified, but about 8 Miles upwards are two Redoubts one on each Side of the River–that on the East Shore is called *Leyden*–the other *Purmerent*–and a little higher up is the new fortress call'd *Amsterdam* built on the point of Land which seperates the two Rivers, *Surinam* and *Comewina* from each other, and *whose* fire crossing itself with that of the two *Redoubts* protects the entry of both Rivers—

On the seperation between the River *Comewina* and *Cottica* about 16 Miles from Fort Amsterdam is a Fortress called *Somelsdyk* which commands the two opposite Shores /viz, that of Rio Comewina–and Rio Cottica—

Near the Town of Paramaribo–and about 6 or 7 Miles from the fortress Amsterdam, is the Citadel which bears the name of *Fort-Zelandia,*

1773—FEBRUARY 28

protecting the Town and all the Shipping in the roads—

Besides all this there are Military Posts on the Rivers *Corrantyn–Sarameca–*and *Marawina*, next a strong Guard at the Mouth of the *Mott Creek* about 30 Miles below the river Surinam, where a fire Beacon or light House is erected on the Coast to warn the Ships bound for that River that they are past the Mouth of the dangerous River Marawina which Guard also fires a few Guns to let the Colony know that Ships are within view, and steering for the Coast—

Up the higher parts of the rivers Surinam–Comewina[–]and Cottica–are also continually kept *advanced Guards* to protect the Inhabitants from inland invasions by the Indians or run away Negroes—In all these Consists the principal defence of this Settlement besides a small arm'd *Bark* or *garda Costa* which cruises to and fro between the rivers Marawina and Berbice to give intelligence in case of any threatening emergency to the Colony—

I had almost forgot to mention that a Path fortified with Military posts had been projected and was actually begun from the upper part of the river Comewina till the River Saramaca–but the Plan did not take–and the above Line which was called the *Orange Path* is at present over grown to a Wilderness—

Having thus fully described the Surface of the Country in *General* with its boundaries Rivers &c–I shall now proceed by giving an Account of the earliest Discovery and most remarkable Revolutions of this once so flourishing Colony *Surinam* in particular, which escaped being visited by the gallant Admiral *Rodney* the last war—

That part of Terra Firma which is called *Guiana* or the Wild Coast and in which lies the Colony of Surinam Is said to have been first found out by *Christopher Columbus* a Genoveese in the Year[—]

1498. From where he was sent home in Chains, the others mention that it was not discovered till the Year—

1504 By one *Vasconunes* a Spaniard, It is a part of that Country to which was given the name of *Terra Firma* Because after finding out *Cuba* to be an Island–This Spot was the first main-Land or Continent the Europeans set their foot upon—

1595 It was visited by Sir Walter *Rawleigh* under Queen Elizabeth who sailed up the River *Oronoque* above 600 Miles in search of the supposed *Eldorado* for finding the Gold Mines—

1617 He once more attempted the same Undertaking being the Year before his Execution at Westminster by King James 6th[—]

1634 One Captain *Marshall* with about 60 English-Men were discovered in Surinam imployed in planting Tobacco according to the relation of David *piterse devries* a Dutchman who Spoke with them upon the Spot—

1640 Surinam was inhabited by the *French* who were obliged to leave it soon thereafter on account of the frequent invasions which they justly suffered from the Caribian Indians for having in imitation of their Neighbours the Spaniards treated them with the most barbarous Cruelties—

1650 This Colony being vacant Francis Lord Willoughby of Parham by K. Charles the second's Permission sent their one vessel equipped by himself to take possession of it in the Name of his royal Master—a little after which he sent 3 Ships more—one of them carrying 20 Guns—all these were well received by the Indians or Inhabitants of the Country with whom they entered into Friendly treaties and a sort of negociation—

1652 Lord Willoughby went over himself and having made several good and wholesome Laws and regulations for the Government and defence of the Colony returned back to England from where he continued to supply that Settlement at his own Expence with Men and Ammunition—

1662 On the second day of June the Colony of Surinam was granted by Charter of Charles 2nd King of Great Britain to Francis Lord Willoughby of Parham and at the said Lords desire to be divided with *Lawrence Hide* Esqr second Son of Edward Earl of Clarendon who was then high Treasurer of England for them and their descendants forever, the Original Record of this Charter, to be found in the Chappel of the Rolls—

1664 The English captured new Netherland since that called New York from the Dutch—

1665 They were now in a prospering way in Surinam mostly by planting Tobacco—and cutting of valuable Timber, with which this Country abounds, they had also raised above 40 fine Sugar plantations and built a strong Fortress of hewn Stones for their defence, notwithstanding some suppose that *this* was done by the Portuguese at what Period is uncertain, while the French strenuously dispute that point and insist it was the work of Monsieur *Ponsert de Bretigny* when they had possession of this Country be that as it may it lies about 16 or 18 Miles from the Mouth of the River Surinam, and this industrious Settlement found themselves perfectly happy in a small Town they had built under its Walls—But their felicity lasted not long for during the war's between Charles the 2nd and the united provinces, the Dutch having been Drove from the Brazils by the Portuguese in 1661 took the Colony of Surinam

1773—FEBRUARY 28

from the English in 1667 under the Command of one Captn Abraham *Cruisen*–who was sent out for that purpose by the province of Zeeland, with 3 Ships of War and 300 Marines–the English Commander William Biam lost the Settlement of Surinam by Surprize when above 600 of the best Men in the Colony were at work on the Sugar Plantations–witness the loss of the Dutch who in Storming the Citadel had but one Man kild on the occasion and who having planted the Prince of Oranges Flag on the Ramparts, gave now to this Fortress the Name of *Zeelandia,* and that of *new-Middleburgh* to the Town of Paramaribo–after making the Inhabitants amongst other Contributions pay one hundred thousand Pounds weight of Sugar, and sending a number of them to the Island of Tobago. All this happened in February and in July following the Peace was concluded at Breda. But most unluckily for the new Possessors of Surinam it was concluded unknown to the English Commodore Sir *John Harmans* who in October that very same Year having first taken Cayenne from the French entered the river with a strong Fleet of 7 Ships of war 2 Bombketches &c and retook the Colony from the Dutch killing on this occasion above 50 of their Men and destroying 9 Pieces of Cannon in Fort Zeelandia–the greatest part of which he shot to rubbish—

The new Inhabitants were now in their turn put under Contribution, and the Dutch Garrison transported Prisoners to the Island of Barbadoes—

At the discovery in Surinam that the Peace had been concluded in Europe between *England France* and *Holland* before Commodore *Harmans* retook the Colony from the Dutch a deal of Tumult and disorder took place among the Inhabitants about who was their lawfull Sovereign till at last by an Order of King Charles this Settlement was restored to the Dutch in 1669 when twelve hundred of the old Inhabitants English and Negroes together left it who all went to settle on the Island of Jamaica And at the end of the succeeding war it was Confirmed by the Treaty of *Westminster* that Surinam should be their lawfull property forever in exchange for the province of new York which accordingly took place in the Year
1674 and after which Period the Colony of Surinam was never more in the possession of Great Britain•—
1678 One Mr Heynsius was now Governor of the Colony and one Captn Lightenbergh Commanded the Troops

---

• —Of *new York* not one word is mentioned by either Mr *Hartsink* or Mr *Fermin* the only Dutch others [authors] of Note that have wrote on the Subject

1773—FEBRUARY 28

The Dutch for the first few Years enjoyed but little Satisfaction in their new Possession being daily harassed by the invasions of the *Caribian* Indians who could not bear them—So well as they had done the English—and murdered several of them—besides the province of Zeeland to whom this Colony properly belonged being perpetually at variance with the other united Provinces about the Sovereignty of this Settlement, and not being by themselves able to support the great expence that was requisite for its preservation and defence—at last resolved to sell the whole to the Dutch west india Company which they did in the Year

1682 for the Sum of 23,636 Pounds Sterling including all the warlike stores Ammunition &c amongst which were 50 Pieces of Cannon with a Charter from their High and Mightinesses the States general to be free of Duty for 10 Years. But few Months after this the West India Company notwithstanding the above Charter of Indemnification finding the other necessary expence of the Settlement *also* to[o] great for them again transferred two thirds of the Colony of Surinam The one to the Town of *Amsterdam* the other to the House of *Somelsdyk* /at the same price for which they had bought it in

1683/ And which three together form'd a Society to whom by a resolution of the States general /yet under Continual Sanction of their High and Mightiness/ was sometime afterwards intrusted the Sole, and entire direction of Affairs in this Country—

Such was the Situation of Affairs in Surinam and in such a Manner finally all Matters were Settled, when *Cornelis van Aarssens Lord of Somelsdyk*—as being one of the Proprietors himself went over in Person with 300 Men besides the Felons as we send them to Botany Bay, and at his Arrival in

1684 Took the Commande as Governor General of the Colony. He now Created a Court of *Policy* to help in the Administration of Justice—but with the Members of which, and also with the Inhabitants he lived in Continual Differences, so that they sent several Complaints against him to Europe—notwithstanding he had made a favorable peace with the *Caribian–Warowa–*and *Arowakka* Indians and besides with a few run away Negroes, that were settled at *Rio* Copename since the English had possession of the Colony—

However this unfortunate Gentlemans Reign lasted but a short space of Time, viz, till the Year

1688 when on the same Day both the Governor and the Commandant under him, were murdered by their own Soldiers which was alledged to be owing to their having not only forc'd the Men to work like Negroes in digging Canals &c—but also forced them to subsist on very bad and short Allowance which at last had drove them to this desperation—•

I am sorry to say this treatment is too often the Consequence in some Settlements, as I shall prove and indeed the only Cause the Prisoners offered to give in their defence for Committing this horrid act of Cruelty—

I hope it will not here be thought out of place if I describe a few of the Particulars that attended this most daring undertaking—

The Governor was walking under a grove of Orange Trees near his House with Mr *Verboom* the Commander of the Troops when unexpectedly 10 or 12 arm'd Soldiers /seemingly drunk/ accosted them and immediately asked for less work, and more subsistence; his excellency the Governor drawing his Sword to drive them back was instantaneously shot through the body, and died upon the Spot—while Mr Verboom who received but one wound expired the 9th day there after—This done the rioters march'd in Triumph to the Fortress Zeelandia, accompanied by several accomplices which they took without resistance and made themselves masters of the Gunpowder and victualling Magazines. after this the Garrison having join'd them they all form'd a Ring, chose out amongst them a Commander in Chief and several other officers, to whom they all Swore to be true as also to each other to the last drops of their blood. what is very remarkable, is that their new Chief that very Afternoon ordered the body of the Massacred Governor Somelsdyk to be enter'd in Fort Zeelandia with decensy and military Honors while the great Guns were fired from the walls and 3 rounds with Small arms by the Rebels—

The Magistrates, and other inhabitants of Surinam now saw themselves in a sad dilemma, and obliged even to enter in a Capitulation with the rioters in the Fort, for fear of further Consequences, the principal articles of which were that they should evacuate Fort Zeelandia, for which they were to receive a few hundred Pounds, then to be embarked on board the Transport Ship *Salamander*—and permitted to quit the Colony without Molestation to set sail for what part of the world, they should think proper[.] accordingly they all to the amount of above One hundred were shipped—but no sooner did they prepare to weigh Anchor for their departure then independant of the Capitulation

• —Somelsdyk had the Character of a Tyrant; he was under the mask of Religion—Brutal—Despotick—hasty and Cruel—he even ordered an indian Chief to have his head struck of[f] on account of some domestick Misdemeanor to which he could not claim especially in those days the smallest Shadow of Authority—the indian having acted according to what he thought right by his own laws and in his own native Country—

1773—FEBRUARY 28

/which had been no further intended than a Stratagem to Subdue them/ the Ship *Salamander* was boarded by several Small Vessells, arm'd and man'd for the purpose, the rebels forced to surrender themselves at discretion—and a few days after tried for Murder & Rebellion, when eleven of the Capital Ringleaders were executed—three of whom were broke alive upon the rack, and 8 hang'd on the Gallows in irons—the rest all got their pardon—but being no longer to be depended on from time to time were discharged from the Colonys Service when others could be got to replace them which was the end of this Melancholy Catastrophy—

1689 The year following his Widow offered to transfer her Portion in this Settlement to King William 3rd but to no purpose, while one Mr Scherpenhuyzen was sent over to Surinam from Holland with a fresh supply of Men and Ammunition to take the Command in place of the late Lord Somelsdyk as Governor of the Collony. Mr Scherpenhuyzen at his arrival found every Thing in the greatest Confusion to which he immediately put the speadiest Means of redress—he established a Court of *Justice* which differed with that formed by his Predecessor Governor Somelsdyk /and was called the Court of *Policy*/ in this particular, that the former has got the management of all the warlike and Criminal Affairs—& the latter that of all civil process—and money matters, both of which Courts remain to this Day and of which the Governor of the Colony is always president—

This Gentleman was also very diligent in establishing many good Laws and institutions—and had just begin to put the Colony in a proper State of defence against its home and foreign Enimies, of which at this Time it stood greatly in need, when war was declared between France and the united Provinces—and the same year of his arrival the Settlement of Surinam, attacked by Admiral *Ducasse* with a strong Fleet—which however Governor Scherpenhuysen most manfully beat of after they had already begun to Cannonade the Fort Zelandia—

1692 One *Jeronimus Clifford* an Englishman was condemned to be hanged, which was exchang'd to Seven Years Imprisonment in the Fortress Somelsdyk on pretence of having insulted the Magistrates, who had arested him for Debt However on application to the Court of Great Britain he was set at Liberty in 1695 by desire of the King when he made a Demand of 20,000 Guineas on the Colony for Damages and false Imprisonment—which being refused, his Heirs have Continued to claim since 1700 to so late as 1762 but hitherto without any Satisfaction—

During the succeeding wars that happened in 1712 the French Commodore Jasques Cassard met the same treatment from Governor de

Gooyer which Ducasse had met from Scherpenhuysen but four Months after he returned with better Success, and put the Colony under Contribution for a Sum of about 56,618 Pounds Sterling—

It was on the 10th of October that he entered the River of Surinam with 6 or 8 Ships of War accompanied by a number of small Vessels on which fleet were embarked 3000 Men—The largest Ships were

Le Neptune of 74 on which he himself Commanded
Le Temeraire of 60
Le Rubis of 56
La Vestale of 48
La Parfaite of 48
and La Meduse of 36 Guns

The 11th Cassard sent a Longboat with a white Flag and an Officer, to treat with the Inhabitants, Concerning their being willing to pay Contribution or not, which if they refused to do—he threatened to Bombard the Town of Paramaribo,* now cald new Middleburg about their Ears. However the boat was obliged to return on board without any Satisfactory Answer—

The River Surinam just before Fort Zelandia being above a Mile in Breadth—la Meduse and several flat bottomed vessels with French, being favoured by a very dark Night, now found means to sail up past Paramaribo without having been observed by the Dutch—with an intention to plunder the Sugar and Coffee Plantations that lay situated above that Town but on the 15th, the Defendants prepared two large flat bottomed barges fill'd with Conbustible Matter—such as Tar-barrels &c. and anchored them on the other Side of the River—directly opposite to the Town—to which fire being put set them both in a blaze, and discovered the smallest Boats of the Enemy as they tried to get up the river through the night, who did this time not escape without Damage by the Guns of the Fort and those of the trading vessels that lay in the Roads, who sunk some of them and drowned a great number of their Crews—this Stratagem however did not hinder Cassards people who had passed, to pillage and set on fire the P[l]antations while he himself having at last anchored before the Town of Paramaribo, threw above

• —In the Year 1667 Capt.n Abraham Cruisen gave that Town the name of new *Middleburg*—but it was before and after called nothing but Paramaribo which is said to be the true *Indian* Name and should signify—the *Spot of Flowers*—This is the general Account—but in my opinion not only *Parhams point*—but the *Para* Creek and the Town of *Paramaribo*, nay even the great Water Called the *Golden Parima* or Parhama Lake took their Names from Francis Lord Willoughby of *Parham*, whom as I have mentioned received this Settlement from Charles the Second King of Great Britain, and was one of the first Possessors of this beautiful Country—Surinam is also call'd a Province by the Dutch, but mostly known by the name of Colony, Settlement, &c

30 Shells into it, and kept close Cannonading both that and Fort Zelandia till on the 20th of October when he sent a Second Message with his Adjutant to the Dutch and asked them finally if they would Capitulate and pay Contribution or not—and which if they now dared to refuse he threatened Fire Death & Destruction to the whole Settlement—

The Dutch seeing their ruin inevitable if they persisted asked for a 3 Days Cessation of Hostilities to deliberate, which being granted they at last complied with Commodore Cassards demands and accordingly on the 27th a treaty of 23 articles being settled between them, they pay'd the demanded Contribution of 56,618 Pounds Sterling to the French but mostly in Sugar Negroe-Slaves &c.—having but little Gold or Silver in the Colony—this done the Commodore Jasques Cassard weigh'd on the 6th of December 1712 and with his whole fleet left the Settlement of Surinam—

Chapter 3rd

*History of the first Negroes Revolting—Causes thereof—
Distracted state of the Colony—Forc'd Peace concluded with
the Rebels—Mutiny of Sailors and Soldiers—remarks on Rebellion
in general—A Word of Advice to young Officers &c*

No sooner was this unfortunate Colony delivered from its outward Enemies, than it was attacked by inward ones of a more fierce and desperate nature—

The Caribean and other Indians had indeed in former times often disturbed this Settlement but with these a peace being Established as I have mentioned after the arrival of Governor Somelsdyk in this Colony, they have inviolably kept it ever since–living in the greatest Harmony and Frienship with the Europeans—

The revolted Negroe Slaves are the foes I now intend to Speak of–and who may with truth be called the Terror of this Settlement if not the total loss of it—

From the earliest remembrance some run away Negroes have sculked in the woods of Surinam, but these were of very small Consideration till of later times /viz/ about the Year 1726 or 28 when by their hostile Numbers increasing and mostly being armed besides bows and Arrows with Lances and *Firelocks* which they had pillaged from the Estates, they committed Continual Outrages and depradations upon the coffee and sugar Plantations–both from a Spirit of revenge for the barbarous and inhuman treatment which formerly they had received of their masters & from a view of carrying away plunder such as Gunpowder [–]Balls–Hatchets &c–in order to provide for their Subsistence and defense—

These Negroes were mostly Settled in the upper parts of the River

Copename and Serameca—and from which last they take the name of the *Serameca Rebels* which distinguishes them from other Gangs that have revolted since—

Several Commands of Military and Plantation people were now sent out against them—but were of very small effect, in their bringing them to Reason by Promises, or in getting them rooted out by blows—

1730 A most shocking Execution on Eleven poor Captives was then experimented—to terrify if possible their Companions—and thus to make them return to their Duty[.] One Man was hanged alive with an Iron hook struck through his Ribs upon a Gibbet—and two others being chain'd to Stakes were burnt to death by Slow fire—Six women were broke alive upon the rack—and two Girls were decapitated—through which Tortures—they went without uttering a Sigh—

1733 Three Indians were also decapitated, for having kill'd 3 french deserters which shows how far the Civil Law now extends in this Country.

1742 A Charter for 12 Years, and *Ground* to the Circumference of about 40 Miles was granted by the Surinam Society to one *Willm Hack* to dig for minerals, but the profits not being able to reimburse the expence the Scheme was drop'd and the mineral project abandoned—

But I must return to the negroes, on whom it appears the inhuman *Carnage* that I have mentioned above, had very little Effect, indeed quite the reverse Since it enraged the Serameca Rebels to such a Degree that they became dreadful to the Colonists which lasted for several years successively and who no longer being able to support the expences and fatigues of Sallying out against them in the Woods—besides the great losses and terrors which they so frequently sustained by their invasions—at last resolved to treat for Peace with their sable Enemies—

Governor Mauricious, who was at this Period at the Head of the Colony accordingly sent out a strong detachment to the Rebel Settlement at the Serameca River—for the purpose of effecting if possible the so much wished for peace, which detachment after some Skirmishing with the strugling Rebel parties at last arrived at their head Quarters where they demanded and obtained a parly—and when a treaty of Peace consisting of 10 or 12 Articles was actually concluded between them in 1749 as had been done before in 1739 with the rebels on the Island of Jamaica—

The Chief of the Sarameca Rebels was a creole Negroe call'd Captain *Adoe*, who now received from the Governor as a present, a fine large Cane with a Massive silver Pummel, on which were Engraved the Arms of Surinam—as a mark of their further independence and a preliminary of the other presents that were to be sent out the Year following as Stipulated by treaty particularly arms and Ammunition when the Peace was to be *finally* concluded—

To the Governor, *Adoe* then returned a handsome Bow with a Compleat case of Arrows, which had been Manufactured by his own hands, as a token that during *that* time on his side all Enmity was ceased and at an end—

This affair gave great Satisfaction to some, indeed to most of the Inhabitants of Surinam who now thought themselves and their effects perfectly secure—while others look'd on this treaty as a most hazardous resource—nay as a sure step to the Colonys inevitable ruin—

Be that as it may I cannot help thinking with the latter that independent of Governor Mauricious good intentions nothing can be more dangerous than making a forced friendship with People who by the most abject Slavery and bad usage were provoked to break their Chains and shake of[f] the Yoke to seek revenge and Liberty, and who by this trust being put in them have it in their power to become from Day to Day more formidable—

Nor can I help thinking on the contrary that the insurrection having already rose to such a pitch, the Colonists ought to have continued Fighting against it while they had a nerve to strain, or a hand left to draw a Trigger, not from a motive of Cruelty, but for the political good of so fine a Settlement while if taken at the worst it is still better to loose one's Life with one's Fortune Sword in hand, than to live in the Perpetual dread of losing both by one general Massacre—

That best of all was never to have drove these poor Creatures to such extremities by constant ill treatment Speaks of itself—while at the same time it is certainly true that to Govern the Coast-of-Guinea Negroes well, nay even for their own benefit—the strictest discipline is absolutely necessary, but I ask why in the Name of Humanity should they undergo the most cruel Racks and tortures entirely depending upon the despotic Caprice of their Proprietors and overseers which it is well known to be too generally the Case throughout all the West Indies, and why should theyr bitter Complaints be never heard by the Magistrate that has it in his Power to redress them?—because *his worship* himself is a planter, and scorns to be against his own Interest—such is most truly the Case, and such is no less truly lamentable, not only for the sake of the Master and the Man—but also and chiefly for that of one of the finest Colony's in the west indies being by such unfair proceedings put in the utmost danger and difficulty[.] However it is to be supposed that Exceptions do here take place, as they do in all other circumstances, God forbid they should not—and I myself have seen and even at different times been eye Witness where the Plantation slaves were treated with the utmost Humanity where the hand of the Master was seldom lifted but to caress them, and where the eye of the Slave sparkled with Gratitude and affection—

Let us now step forwards and see what were the fruits of making Peace with the Saramaca Rebels—

In 1750 which was the Year thereafter, the promised presents were dispatched to Captain *Adoe* when the detachment that carried them were Attacked on their March and every Soul of them murdered on the Spot by a desperate Negroe called *Zamzam,* who not having been consulted at the peacemaking had put himself since at the head of a strong party—and now carried off the whole stock /consisting of Arms and Ammunition Checker'd Linnens Canvas Cloth–Hatchets–Saws–and other Carpenters Tools besides Salt Beef–Pork–Spirits &c/ as his own private property and besides which *Adoe* suspected, the delay was intended to cut their throats, by a new supply of troops /which he was told was/ coming from Europe—

By this accident the peace was immediately broke–Crueltys and ravages increased more than ever, and Death and Destruction once more raged throughout the Colony—

In 1751 this Settlement was in the utmost distress and Confusion when by request of the Inhabitants *Baron Spoke* was sent to Surinam with 600 fresh troops taken from the different Regiments in the Dutch Service who continued to pay them* and orders at his arrival to change the members of the Court—send Governor Mauricious to Europe to account for his Proceedings /who never more returned having in 1753 asked and obtained his Dismission after being Honourably acquitted from the Charge laid by his Enemies against him/ and ad interum to officiate himself as Governor of the Colony—

Baron Sporke found every thing indeed in the greatest disorder the disunion having even broke out between the inhabitants and their Rulers, and to which it was highly necessary /as Scherpenhuysen did before/ to apply the most beneficial and speediest means of Redress which this Gentleman did, and died the Year after, when a general distraction again took place—

In 1757 Things were come from bad to worse /when one Mr *Cromelyn* was Governor of this Colony/ by a new Revolt being broke out in the Tempate Creek amongst the negroes owing to nothing but their being so cruelly treated by their Masters, which fresh insurrection was of such serious Consequence /they having joined themselves to 16 hundred other run away Negroes already settled in 8 different Villages be-

• —the other expences were paid ¼ by the Society and ¾ by the Inhabitants—

tween *Tempaty,* and the River Marawina, alongst the banks of the *Jocka Creek*/ that after repeated Battles and Skirmishes /they being all well armed as I have mentioned/ without much success for the Colonists or any hopes of Quelling it—they saw themselves once more reduced to sue for Peace—with their own Slaves as they had done in 1749 with the Rebels of Serameca—but which was as I have said since, broke in 1750 by the irrascible conduct of the Rebel Negro, Zamzam—

During this last revolt a Captain *Mayer* of the Society troops being tried for *Cowardice* by a Court Marshall and found guilty was condemned to be shot through the head, he was accordingly led to the place of Execution where after every thing was ready, he was pardoned by the Governor, who not only shewed him ever Civility but preferred him to the rank of Major—

To let the whole World now see that Blackmen are not such Brutes as the generallity of White ones imagine—I must beg leave to mention a few of the principal Ceremonies that attended the ratification of this Peace—

1760 The first thing was another parly proposed by the Colonists which was to be sure agreed to by the Rebels when the last not only desired, but absolutely insisted that the Dutch should send them yearly amongst a great variety of other articles, a handsome Quantity of fire Arms and Ammunition as Specified in a long list made up of broken English by a Negroe whose Name was *boston* and was one of their Captains—

Next Governor Cromelyn sent two Commissioners /as some since have been sent over the ocean/ M:r Sober and M:r Abercrumby who marched through the woods escorted by a few Military &c–to carry some presents to the Rebels Preliminary to the ratification of the peace for which they now went finally to treat—

At the Arrival of the above Gentlemen in the Rebel Camp at the *Jocka Creek* they were introduced to a very handsome Negroe called *Araby* who was the chief of them all, and born amongst the last 1600 that I have mentiond in the Forests, he received them very politely and taking them by the Hand, desired they would sit down by his Side upon the Green–at the same time assuring them they needed not be under any apprehensions of evil since coming in so good a Cause, not one intended, or even dared to hurt them—

But when the above mentioned Captain Boston perceived that they had brought a parcel of Trinkets, such as Knives[–]Scizars–Combs–and Small Looking Glasses–and forgot the principal Article in Question /viz/ Gunpowder Fire Arms and Ammunition he resolutely stept up to the Commissioners and asked in a Thundering Voice if the European imagined that the Negroes could live on Combs and Looking Glasses, adding that one of each was fully sufficient to let them all see their faces with Satisfaction while a single Gallon of *Mansany* viz. Gunpowder—should have been accepted as a proof of their trust—but since that had been Omitted, they should with his will, never more return to their Countrymen till every article of his List should be fulfilled—

A Negroe Captain called *Quacoo* now interfered Saying that these Gentlemen were only the Messengers of their Governor and court and as they could not be answerable for their Masters Proceedings they should certainly go back to where they came from without Hurt or Molestation, or even he Captain Boston should dare to oppose them—

The Chief of the Rebels then ordered Silence—and desired Mr Abercrumby to make up a list himself of such Articles as he Araby should name him—which that Gentleman having done, the Rebels not only gave him and his Companions leave peaceably to return with it to town—but their Governor and Court a whole Year to deliberate on what they were to chuse Peace or War—unanimosity [unanimously] swearing that during that interval all animosity should cease on their Side—after which having entertained them in the best Manner their Situation in the Woods afforded they wished them a happy Journey to Paramaribo—

One of the Rebel Officers upon this occasion represented to Mr Sober and to Mr Abercrumby, what pity it was that the Europeans who pretend to be a civilized nation—should be so much the Occasion of their own ruin by their inhuman Cruelties towards their Slaves

> we desire you /continued this Negro/ to tell your Governor and your Court that in case they Want to raise no new Gangs of Rebels, they ought to take care that the planters kept a more wachful eye over their own properties and not so often trust them in the hands of a parcel of Drunken Managers and overseers who by wrongfully whipping the Negroes—debauching their wives and Children—neglecting the Sick &c are the ruin of the Colony and wilfully drive to the Woods such Quantity's of Stout handsome People who by their Sweat got your Subsistence without whose hands your Colony must drop to nothing—and to whom at last in this pitiful manner you are Glad to come and ply for friendship—

Mr Abercrumby now begged of them to be accompanied with one or two of their principal Officers to Parimaribo where he promised they should be vastly well treated &c but the Chief Araby answered him with a Smile that such was time sufficient a year thereafter when the peace should be *thoroughly* concluded that then even his Youngest

Son should be at their service to receive his education amongst them, while for his subsistance and even for that of his descendants he should take the sole cure upon himself without ever giving the Christians the smallest trouble—

After this the Commissioners left the Rebels and all arived safe and sound at Paramaribo—

The Year of deliberation being ended the Governor & Court sent out two fresh Commissioners to the Negro Camp to bring the so much wish'd for peace to a thorough Conclusion which after a deal of Canvasing and Ceremonies on both Sides, and the Presents being promised to the Negroes according to their wishes /as *some* Nations pay Tribute to the Emperor of Morocco/, at last was finally agreed on, while as a proof of their Affection to the Europeans, the Negroes indiscriminately insisted that each of the Commissioners should during their remaining stay in the Rebel Camp take for his constant Companion one of their handsomest Young Women—treating them with Game fish fruit and the best of all that the forest aforded, intertaining them without intermission with Musick Dancing and Cheering, besides firing one volley after another, when they returned also contented to Town—

This done the above presents were sent to the Negroes near the River Marawina by the indentical M.r *Mayer* who had formerly not dared to fight against them escorted by 600 Men Soldiers and Slaves and which Gentleman had nearly baffled the whole business by Contrary to his Orders and from a Pucilaminous principle delivering all the presents to the Rebels without Receiving the hostages in Return, However fortunately *Araby* kept his Word, and sent down 4 of his best officers as pledges to Paramaribo. By this the peace was perfectly accomplished when a treaty of 12 or 14 articles was signed by two white Commissioners and 16 of Araby's black Captains in 1761, which Ceremony took place on the Plantation *Ouca* in the River Surinam where all the parties met, this being the Spot of Rendezvous appointed for the purpose, after four different Embasys had been sent from the Europeans to the Negroes—

But signing this treaty alone was still not look'd on as sufficient by the Rebel Chief Araby, and his People, who all immediately Swore an Oath, and insisted on the Commissioners to do the same after the manner in practice by themselves, not trusting intirely they say'd on that made use of by the Christians, which they had seen too often broke, whereas for a Negro to break his Oath is absolutely without Example• which plainly argues that the africans are not so intirely destitute

• —Of this at least I never saw or heard of an instance during all the Time that I lived in the Colony—

of morality and even Religion as a number of ignorant Europeans imagine and which I hope still more clearly to demonstrate on other occasions—

The Solemnity made use of on this Day Consisted in both parties letting themselves with a Lance or penknife a few drops of blood from the Arm into a Callebas or Cup with clean spring water in which were also mixed a few particles of dry earth, and of which all present were obliged to drink a draught upon the Spott, Europeans and Africans without Exception, which they call drinking each others blood—having first Scattered a few Drops upon the Ground, when theyr *Gaddoman* or priest with upcast Eyes and Stretched Arms, took Heaven and Eearth to Witness and with a most audible Voice and awfull manner, invoked Gods Curse and Malediction on all such as should first break through this sacred treaty made between them from that Moment henceforth to all eternity to which the multitude Answered *da So* which Signifies in their Language Amen—

> Then loudly thus before th'attentive Bands,
> He calls the Gods, and Spreads his lifted hands;
> O first and greatest power whom all obey,
> Who high on Ida's holy mountain Sway;
> Eternal Jove! and you bright Orb that roll
> From East to West! and view from Pole to Pole!
> Thou Mother Earth! and all ye living Floods!
> Infernal Furies, and Tartarean Gods,
> Who rule the Dead, and horrid woes prepare
> For perjured Kings, and all who falsly Swear!
> Hear and be Witness—
>   From the same urn they drink the mingled Wine
> And add Libations to the Pow'rs divine.
> While thus their Prayers united mount the Sky;
> Hear mighty Jove! and hear ye Gods on high!
> And may their blood who first the League Confound
> Shed like this Wine, disdain the thirsty Ground;

The Solemnity being ended Araby and each Captain was presented /to distinguish them from other Negroes as the Serameca Capt.ⁿ *Adoe* had been before in 1749/ with a fine large Cane and Silver pummel on which were also engraved the Arms of the Colony—

The above mentioned Negroes are called *Aucas* after the name of the Plantation w[h]ere the Peace Articles were Signed by which Name they are distinguished from those of *Serameca* which I have already described—

The *Auca* Negroes have indeed behaved indifferently well ever since the forgoing treaty—fortunately for the Colony of Surinam from which they must yearly receive /as I have said amongst a number of other Articles/ a handsome Quantity of ball and Gun powder—

This Year viz, 1761, the Charter was also renewed to the West India Company by their *High and Mightinesses* for the Term of 30 Years longer, as it had been before in 1670–1700 and 1730 for a loan of about 5 Million Sterling at the rate of 6 Pr Cent, payable by the said West India Company—

This same Year 1761 the peace was also a Second time concluded with the *Serameca* Rebels who were at present Commanded by a Negro call'd *Wille* instead of their former Chief *Adoe* who was dead—but this Second peace was unfortunately a *second* time broke by a Rebel Captn called *Muzinga* who had received none of the Presents, and which Presents had been again on their way to the Chief *Wille* as they had been formerly on their way to the Chief *Adoe*—cut off and Captured by the individual and Enterprising Devil *Zam Zam*—

However with this indifference that none of the detachement that were sent with them were now murdered as on the preceeding time, or even one single person hurted.

The above Captn Muzinga now fought desperately against the Colonists—he gave battle face to face and beat back above 150 of theyr best Troops that were sent out against him killing numbers, and taking away all their baggage and Ammunition—

However very soon after this, when the real Cause of *Muzinga's* discontent was known. Means were found out and adopted to pacify this gallant Warrior by making him receive and share the presents sent out by the Colonists on an equal footing with his brother Heroes, when Peace was a *third* & last time concluded in 1762 between the *Serameca* Rebels and the Colony—and which has Providentially been kept sacred and inviolable the same as with the Negroes of Ouca to this day—

The Hostages and chief Officers of both the above menti[one]d Negro Cohorts, on theyr arrival at Paramaribo were entertained at the Governors own Table, having previously paraded in State through the Town, accompanied by his Excellency, and in his own private Carriage—

By theyr Capitulation with the Dutch the above *Ouca* and *Serameca* Rebels must yearly receive as I have mentioned, a handsome Quantity of Arms and Ammunition from the Colony. for which those have received in return the Negroes promises of being their faithful alies, to deliver up all desertors for which to receive proper premiums, never to appear arm'd at Paramaribo above 5 or 6 at a time & also to keep theyr Settlement at a proper distance from the Town, or Plantations. the Serameca Negroes at the River Serameca—and those of the Ouca Negroes near the River Marawina—where one or two White Men call'd *Postholders* were to reside amongst them in Quality as a Species of Envoys—

Both these tribes were now supposed, in all 3000. and but few Years after by those that were sent to visit theyr Settlements /including Wives and Children/ computed to be no less than 15 or 20000 people, they are already become overbearing and even insolent brandishing theyr silver headed Canes under the Noses of the Inhabitants by way of derision and independence, forcing from them liquors, and verry often Money—And which if they refuse putting them in Mind how /when they were theyr Slaves/ they murdered theyr Parents, and theyr Husbands, from what I have just mentioned, and theyr Numbers encreasing from Day to Day I must conclude that should ever the peace be once more broke, the above new allies will become the most dreadful foes that ever the Colony of Surinam will have to deal with. Besides the Example and encouragement these treaties give other Slaves to revolt even without provocation against theyr Masters—and Obstinately to fight for the same priviledges, while at the same time those planters who dare so inhumanely to persecute theyr Slaves without a Cause deserve in my opinion no better treatment, yet this most assuredly too often is the consequence•—

Having thus far dwelt on the Subject of negro Slaves revolting against theyr Masters I shall now say something Concerning Sailors and Soldiers rebelling against theyr Commanders—after mentioning that in 1763 the Town of Parrimaribo would have been burnt down to the Ground without knowing to what to ascribe the Cause, had it not been prevented by the Courage and intrepidity of the Sailors, who at the hazard of theyr lives alone prevented the general Conflagration—

The same Year a Mutiny broke out on board the outward bound East-india-Man *Neimburgh* Commanded by Captain *Ketell,* the crew, /consisting chiefly of French and German Desertors who had been Kidnapped in Holland/, rose in Arms against their Superiors, and having murdered most of the Officers and warrant Officers, while others were put in Chains, Carried the Vessel to the Brazils, where the Capital ringleaders going a Shoare, and living in riot and dissipation soon discovered what they were to the Portuguese Governor, in Consequence of which they were all taken into Custody, but theyr accomplices on

• —It was about this very time that the rebellion in the Colony Berbice between the Planters and the Slaves was at the highest—

board suspecting what had happened, imediately slipped their Cable, and set Sail for the Island of Cayenne, where their piracy was put to an end—for the french seizing both Ship and Crew delivered the one and other to the Colony of *Surinam* where in 1764 seven of the most Guilty were executed on board the same Vessel which they had Captured, then at anchor in the roads before the Town of Paramaribo—viz—one was decapitated, and 6 hanged to the Yards Arm, whose heads were also chopp'd of[f] and planted on Iron Spikes upon the beech in a cage that was made for the Purpose. the others who had been taken by the Portuguese were sent from the Brazils to Amsterdam after which they were also executed in Texel Roads on board the *Westellingwerf* Man a War, which Ship was one of the Convoys sent out with us from Holland; then their bodies were gibbeted in Iron Harness and placed for Example alongst the Coast—

This same Year also 3 of the Society or Colony Soldiers who had been Guilty of Mutiny and desertion were yet executed in *Surinam* but as their case is perhaps the most peculiar in its kind, that ever existed I must also beg leave to give some Account of its proceeding—

During the time of the Insurrection amongst the Negro Slaves in the Colony of Berbice which happened in the Year 1761, /and where they had not been treated so cruelly as in other Colonys/ Not only a regiment of Marines /Commanded by Colonel de Salve and which now belongs to General Douglas/ was sent over from Holland to that Settlement, but also the neighbouring Colonies sent troops to their Assistance in order to Subdue if possible the revolt in the Berbice, and in this they soon succeeded since the Woods in that part being of small extent, they are easily penetrated, which both prevented the Rebels from forming Settlements, and often discovered them to their pursuers in Consequence of which after numbers had been shot dead and others taken Prisoners, the rest were forced to surrender themselves at discretion, and implore for Mercy, which was politically granted to numbers, /some scores excepted/ or they must have been Starved to Death for want of Subsistance—

During these troubles it happened that an Officer and about 70 Men sent from the Colony Surinam to help those in the Colony Berbice, had been posted on the Banks of the River *Corrantine*—This detachment together with a party of Indians, who are natural enemies to the Negroes but friends to the Europeans had one Day beat the Rebels in a skirmish—having killed several of them and retaken about 20 or 30£ Sterling in Value which effects the Negroes had Pillaged from the neighbouring Estates—but the officer who commanded this detachment having unwarrantably distributed this booty amongst the Indians alone without giving Share to his Soldiers, discouraged them to such a Degree that they revolted, and deserting theyr Commander took their March for the river Oronoque through the Woods, in hopes of soon falling in with the Spanish Settlements and being relieved; But how Miserably were these Deluded Men mistaken, and disappointed in their desperate undertaking by meeting the Rebels or bush Negroes on the Second or Third day of there March—These notwithstanding the Soldiers solemn protestations that they were come without any evil intentions towards them and their intreaties to let them pass by unmolested nevertheless suspecting that this Party had been sent out to Spie and betray them, artfully proposed that they sho[ul]d lay down their Arms at Mercy, which they the deserters stoopidly having complied with, the Rebels immediately /having dressed them in one Rank and pick'd out 10 or 12 to assist them in attending the Sick and Wounded, Repairing their Arms, and trying to make Gunpowder in which however they since Miscaried/ Condemned all the others to death which was instantaneously put in Execution and above 50 of those Misfortunate Men were one by one shot dead upon the Spot—

It can well be supposed that those who were sav'd alive by the Negroes must have Spun out but a very Melancholy existence amongst them, and the most of whom died within but very few Months after by ill treatment hardships and want, and when the Rebels surrendered themselves to the Europeans at discretion, the few remaining miserable wretches that were still found in Life were directly loaded with Irons, and sent back from the Colony Berbice to Surinam where 3 of them as I have said above were Executed in the Town of Paramaribo one being hanged, and 2 broke alive upon the Rack, which ended all their Sufferings; one of these wretches was a frenchman call'd *Renauld* who seemed to have inbib'd the Spirit of the negroes by living amongst them even unto Death, comforting his accomplice who was a German and tied down upon his back by his side, Just ready to receive the dreadful blows, and bidding him keep a good heart, that the voyage of Life would soon be over, while his own bones were breaking by the Executioner with an Iron bar. The ringleading Negroes were roasted alive by half dozens in a shocking manner being chain'd to Stakes in the Middle of Surrounding flames without uttering a Groan or a Sigh—

Permit me here to make a short observation on the usuage of the navy and Army in the west Indies as I have done before on that of the Negro Slaves—

The Sailor and the Soldier who are on Duty in the Colony if taken proper care of are certainly two of the most useful members in helping to Support it what strong Spirited and willing drudges are they when properly protected and Encouraged by theyr Commanders—How careless are they of theyr own Lives—and how ready and fearless of Danger to protect theyr Officers if they are well supported and are but fairly dealt with—but I am Sorry to say that such is wide distant from being always the Consequence and that to[o] often at least with some nations the Sailor the Soldier and the Slave but differ in the name—

How many times have I seen a Stripling Officer Pride himself in making Sink below a ropes-end or a bamboe the poor old withered and veteron Sailor or Soldier—who might, by Age at least, have been his father and by Skill & Experience his Commander—

And how often have I heard the Groans of the helpless and agonising young Man—allowed to die for mere neglect and want where both the proper attendants and necessary comforts in plenty might be had, and with but Little trouble while his naked trembling and half Starved Companions exausted with navy and military hardships and fatigue had Scarsely strength sufficient left to carry him to the Grave—

A proper Subordination and discipline is certainly the foundation of all good order in which either too much Severity or too much lenity /of which However I think but very few Examples can be produced in the west indies/ is dangerous, and striking at its root points directly to over through [overthrow] it—

But why should things be so frequently carried to Extremes, and why should not a certain Medium be kept in View which tends so much to Secure the happiness of both the Ruler and the Subject and Strengthen the Bands of Society in General—

Yet such God knows is but too seldom thought of, those Gallants and brave Gentlemen excepted who by their Humanity /and which goes hand in hand with valour/ are an Ornament to the Human Species, while pity it is that by the Carelessness of so many others /especially Young Officers/ about the welfare of their Soldiers and Sailors, to whom the whole Care and trust of these useful creatures is given, and who ought to Pride in making theyr Lives at least Supportable, such Numbers of Stout able and blooming young Men are now dayly swept to the Grave—whole crews and Companys of whom if properly look'd after might have lived for Years to the Good and the Glory of theyr Country—

But let us wave these Melancholy Scenes of Blood and human woe and pursue what has happened in the Colony of Surinam during its short flourishing State—

Chapter 4th

*Short Interval of Peace and plenty—the Colony plunged in
new Distress by a fresh Insurrection and nearly ruin'd—
Review of the Troops for its defence—An Action with the Rebels—
Gallant behaviour of a Black Corps till the arrival
of Col Fourgeoud's Marines*

1764 Gold and Silver Specie being Scarse cards were Stamped which passed for Cash to the amount of £40000 Value with a discount of 10 P.r Cent—

1765 A great Hubbub was made here on account of a free Negro Woman call'd Eliz. *Sampson* going to be married to an European, she was worth above a hundred thousand pound Sterling inherited from her Master whose Slave she had formerly been and having addressed herself to their High and Mightinesses her Request was Granted, and accordingly being Christened she entered in the Lawful Bond of Matrimony with one M.r Zubli—

1766 This Settlement was visited by an earthquake which however happened to do very little Damage—

1769 The whole Coast was in fire from Cayenne to Demarary[–]this happened in the dry Season when all the woods are parched by the heat—and the underwood choaked with dryed leaves the flames which were supposed to be kindled by the negligence of the Indians or Rebels were so violent, that they threatened distruction to several Estates—and during the night appeared like the representation of Hell from the Sea, while the Eastern Wind made the Smoak so thick throughout the day, that one could not see another at the distance of 6 Yards while the Smell was almost insupportable—

1773—FEBRUARY 28

This same Year a Quantity of rock Christal was discovered in the inland parts of Dutch Guiana•—

1770 The house of Somelsdyk sold its Share or portion of the Colony of the Town of amsterdam for the Sum of 63636£ Sterling, So that now that City holds in it two thirds and the other third still belongs to the West india Company, which as I have said form together *the Society* of Surinam—

The Colony seem'd now in a prosperous and flourishing way since the making of the Peace with the Serameca and Ouca Negroes, and every thing was peace and in good order[.] The Inhabitants /as I mentioned/ thought themselves and their Effects now perfectly Secure—So that nothing but Mirth and discipation was thought of which was even push'd to Lavishness and profusion—

Surinam look'd like a large and beautiful Garden Stocked with every thing that nature and Art could produce to make the life of Man both Comfortable to himself and useful to Society all the Luxuries and Necessaries for Subsistance were Crowding upon the Inhabitants while the five Sences seem'd intoxicated with bliss and to use an old Expression Surinam was a Land that overflowed with Milk and Honey—

But this delusive felicity, this Life of Wantonness and thoughtless decipation alas lasted not Long—The Planter wanted to get rich too soon without the wretchedness of the Slave came into Consideration till finally drunkenness, Luxury Riot and all manner of Vice and Debochery became predominant—while even Cruelties by several Masters towards theyr Slaves /notwithstanding the destruction that so lately threatened them/ rather Encreased than deminished—and at the same time /as I have mentioned before/ the bad example of the making peace with the Serameca and Ouca Negroes Stimulating the other Slaves to revolt in the same way in hopes of meeting with the same Success where [were] the Complicated Causes that the Colony was again plunged in its former Abiss of Difficulties; the most beautiful Estates /in this Settlement call'd Plantations/ were again seen some blazing in flames, and others laid in Ashes, while the reeking and mangled bodies of theyr Inhabitants were Scattered alongst the Banks of the river *Cottica,* and theyr effects pillaged by theyr own Negroes, who all fled to the woods Men Women and Children without exception. These new revolters were distinguished by the name of the *Cottica Rebels* where theyr hostilities begun, and theyr numbers augmenting from Day to Day they soon became as formidable to the Settlement as the *Serameca* and *Ouca* Negroes had been before them, and were just going to give the finishing

• —And governor cromelyn Succeeded by Governor Nepvew—

1773—FEBRUARY 28

blow to the Colony of Surinam in 1772.—Now all was Horror and Consternation—And nothing but a general Massacre was expected by the greatest Majority of the Inhabitants who fled from theyr Estates and Crowded to the Town of Paramaribo for Protection[.] In this dilemma of affairs the Inhabitants were now obliged to come to the distracted resolution of *limiting the Game upon itself,* that is to say of forming a regiment of *Manumitted-Slaves* to fight against their Countrymen thus set Negro to battle against Negro* which providentially had the desired effect. these *brave*** Men acting wonders above expectation in Conjunction with the Colony or Society troops whose strength alone was no longer thought sufficient to defend this Settlement at present, besides wch the Society of Surinam made application to his Serene Highness the Prince of Orange for Assistance and in Consequence of which a Corps of *Marines* /all Volunteers/ was immediately embodied, draugh[t]ed from the different regiments in Holland of this /as I mentioned/ the Command was Given to Colonel *Fourgeoud* and it was in this Corps that I had the honour to be appointed a Captain—

I shall now give some Account of in what the Surinam Army *white* and *black* consisted, and then proceed to a detail of theyr gallant behaviour before our fleet arrived to their assistance—

The Regular Troops that belong to the Society of Surinam are intended to be 1200 Men when compleat divided into two Batillions paid partly by the Society and partly by the Inhabitants—But they never can produce that number in the Field owing to many Complicated reasons as theyr dying on the Passage—theyr seasoning to the Climate—theyr dangerous and fatiguing Duty—theyr being shot, lost, in the Woods, &c—besides this number of reinforcement of 300 more was now sent them from the Town of Amsterdam—but of these unlucky wretches scarse fifty were landed fit for Service having shared a fate on theyr passage by the inhumanity of theyr Leader M.^{r} H—— little better than that which the poor african Negroes experienced since by the barbarous Captain *Coolingward* who in 1781 threw 132 living Slaves into the Sea to perish, M.^{r} H—— having starved and tortured by unecessary hardships almost all the whole of his reinforcement to Death And forced his Lieutenant /not Longer able to bear, or be witness to the inflixion of his Tyranny/ to seek redress in the waves, by leaping out at the Cabbin Window and ending his Existence–M.^{r} H—— was honourably acquitted—

* —I have made some mention of them in the 1.st Chapter page [41]

** —thus cald by the Europeans alone—

81

1773—FEBRUARY 28

The Military in Surinam are composed of several very good and Experienced Officers and well innured to the Service, but for theyr private Men I can indeed say little to boast of, being a Composition of Scum-Composed of all nations–ages shapes–and sizes & by chance wafted together from all the different Corners of the Globe, yet notwithstanding which they fight like little Devils, and have on many different Occasions been of infinite Service to this Settlement—

Here is also a small Corps of Artillery being part of the 1200 which I must acknowledge to be very fine in all respects—

As for what they please to call theyr Militia they are a few Gentlemen excepted who command them such a set of dastardly Scarcrows, that they will absolutely not bear to be mentioned as fighting Men—

But now for the new raised Corps of Manumitted Slaves, who though in number but 300 have proved to be of as much Service to the Colony, as all the others put together greatly owing to the Strength of theyr Constitutions, theyr wonderful activity, perseverance &c—

These Men were all Volunteers, mostly Stout Strapping able young fellows, picked from the different Plantations–who received for them theyr full Value in Money—none were accepted but such as were reputed to be of a very good Character and indeed they have since in my own presence given astonishing proofs of theyr fidelity to the Europeans and theyr valour against the revolters—their Chief Leaders are 3 or 4 White Men call'd *Conducters,* to whom they pay the Strictest Obediance–and one or two of whom generally attend them when they set out on any Enterprize or March of Consequence, every ten privates have one Captain who Commands them in the forest by the different Sounds of his horn–as the boatswain Commands the Sailors or as the Cavalry of Europe are Commanded by the Trumpets in the field, by which they advance, retreat, attack or Spread &c. they are Arm'd only with a firelock and Sabre, but of both which weapons they understand the management in the most Masterly Manner—they generally go naked by preferance in the woods excepting trowsers* and a scarlet Cap on which is theyr number, and which /besides theyr *parole* or watchword which is *Orange*/ distinguishes them from the *rebels* in any Action to prevent disagreeable mistakes—

Having thus discribed the forces of Surinam I shall now proceed in Order with my Narrative—

I have already said that the newly revolted /call'd the Cottica/ Rebels–were just going to give the finishing blow to the Colony in 1772 And I shall now relate how this Catastrophe was prevented—

* —They have of late Years been decorated with Green Uniforms &c—

A Coromantyn Free Negro, or Ranger, armed.

London, Published Dec.r 2d 1795, by J. Johnson, St. Paul's Church Yard.

1773—FEBRUARY 28

These Negroes being Commanded by a desperate fellow named *Baron*, had erected a strong Settlement between the rivers Cottica and the Sea Coast not far distant from the river Marawina, from where they sallied forth to commit theyr depredations on the Plantations—I call it strong because like an island it was naturally surrounded by a broad infoardable Marsh or Swamp which prevented all Communication except by private paths under water known only to the rebels alone and before which *Baron* had placed loaded Swivels which he had plundered from the neighbouring estates, besides its being fenced and inclosed on every Side by several thousand strong Palisades made it no Contemptible fortification—to this Spot Baron gave the name of *Boncou*, or Mouldered intimating that it should perish in Dust before ever it should be taken or even discovered by the Europeans—This nest however after many marches, and Countre-Marches was at last disclosed* by the vigilence and perseverance of the Society troops, and the black Soldiers or *Rangers* /which I shall Call them for the future theyr Service being Chiefly like that of the rangers in *virginia* who are sent out against the Cherokee Indians,/ And now it being determined that these Sable foes should be beseiged and rooted out, a strong detachement of white and black troops were sent against them under the Command of one Captain *Myland* to head the first; and Lieut. *Fredeiricy* a Spirited young Officer with the *Conductors* to lead the Later and which detachment on their Arrival at the above Marsh were obliged to Encamp upon its borders not being able to pass through it on account of its unfoardable deepness—

On the discovery of the troops, the bold Negro Baron imediately planted a white flag within their View, which he meant as a token of defiance and independance, when an incessant firing began on both sides which was of very little Effect. To through [throw] a *facine* bridge over the Marsh was then projected but this Plan after several weeks had

---

* —Another Settlement of the Rebels was well known to exist in a Corner of the Colony known by the name of the *Lee shore* and Situated between the Rivers Surinam and Serameca but here the Situation by Ma[r]shes, Quagmires, mud, and water is such that it fortifies them, from any attempts of Europeans whatever, nay they are even Indiscoverable by negroes, except by their own, So thick and impenetrable is the forest on that Spot, and overchoaked with thorns–briers, and underwood of every Species. from under these Covers nevertheless these Sable Gentry Sally forth in small parties during the night to rob the Gardens and fields surrounding Parramaribo and carry of[f] the young Women they chance to meet with—In this diabolical wilderness once was lost for 2 or 3 days and nights as he went out a shooting a Young Officer called *Freiderecy* of whom I am in a little time to take further notice, and who would probably never more have been heard of had not Governor *Cromelyns* precaution by ordering one Gun to be fired after another, given him an opportunity to find his way back and thus restore him once more to his friends—

been spent in the attempt and a great many Men shot dead in the execution was also frustrated and drop'd–during which time the two little armies kept popping and black-guarding each other at a shocking rate. Having desisted from carrying over the above bridge, and no hopes of getting through the Marsh into the Fortress, besides the ammunition and victuals growing considerably less and the loss of a great many men, things were come to such a Crisis that the Seige must have been broke up and the Troops marched back to Paramaribo had not the rangers by their indefatigable efforts–and /however strange to think/ inplacable bitterness against the rebels found out and discovered to the Europeans–the underwater Paths of Communication to *Boucou*, severals being shot and drowned in the execution of this material piece of Service—

Captain Myland with the Regulars now foarded the Swamp on *one* side and making designedly a *faint attack* on the fortress drew Baron with all his rebels to its defence as was expected, while Lieut. Fredericy /having with the rangers cross'd the Marsh on the *other* side/ had the opportunity of leaping with his black party /who were eager like so many blood hounds/ over the Pallisades Sword in hand without opposition—

A most terrible Carnage now ensued while several Prisoners being made on both Sides, and the Fortress of Boucou was taken[–]But Baron* with the greatest number of the Rebels escaped in the Woods, having first found means to cut the throats of 10 or 12 of the *rangers* who had lost their way in the Marsh and whom he seized sticking in the Mud–Cutting of[f] the Ears–nose–and lips of one of them–whom he in this Condition returned Living to his friends–where however the miserable Man soon expired—nor could Lieut. Frediricy himself have so well escaped during the Action that took place within the Fort, and where in the first onset nothing but Negroes were Engaged, had he not been favoured by Darkness, by Smoke, and a black crape being covered over his face–which prevented him to be distinguished by the rebels

* —This Baron who /as I mentioned/ was the head of all the Cottica rebels, had formerly been the Negro Slave of one Mr *Dhalbergh* a Swede who had made him a favourite on account of his Genius; who had teached him to read and write and bred him a Mason–he had also been with his Master in Holland, and was promised his Manumition on his return to the Colony—But Mr Dhalberg breaking his Word in regard to his Liberty and selling him to a Jew, Baron obstinately refused to work in Consequence of which he was publickly flog'd below the Gallows–and which usuage the Negro resented so much that he from that Moment Swearing revenge against all Europeans without exception flew to the woods, where putting himself at the head of all the Rebels his Name became dreadfull to the Colony and in particular to his former Master Dalberg declaring Solemnly he should never die in peace, till he should have washed his hands in the Tirants blood—

from out amongst his Dusky Companions•—

Such was the War we were come to wage in Surinam and in which I frankly declare I should never have engaged had I known any other way to push my fortune—

That the rangers and rebels must be the most inveterate Enemies can very well be accounted for–Since notwithstanding the first are useful and true to the Europeans, they are certainly look'd upon by the Second as Traytors–and betrayers of theyr Countrymen–being both the one and other party originally *Africans* from the Coast of Guinea–or Creoles born in the Colony of Surinam—

The taking of Boucou was now greatly Spoke of and deem'd a very severe Crush for the rebels, in which both the regulars, and rangers, indeed behaved with unprecedented intrepidity and Courage, while independant of Captain *Mylands* gallant Conduct—Lieut. *Fredericy* was particularly taken Notice of, who was presented by the Surinam Society with a beautiful Sabre–firelock–and brace of Pistoles Mounted in Silver, and Ornamented with the marks of his Merit, besides the rank of Captain—

Indeed the whole detachment without exception white and black Met with the greatest Marks of Content and Approbation—

In this State were the public Affairs of this Settlement in One thousand seven hundred and Seventy three when our fleet drop'd Anchor before the Town of Paramaribo—

• —A few of the *Negroes* indeed wear trowsers Shirts and Jackets in the Woods, the *regulars*, are but seldom seen to wear more, both the officers and Private Men dressing alike, and as light, and as plain, as possible—

Chapter 5th

The scene changes—some account of
a Beautiful Female Slave—The Manner of travelling in Surinam—
The Colonel explores the situation of the Rivers—
Barbarity of a Planter—wretched treatment of the Sailors &c—
Sensibility

As I have already in the beginning of this Work given some account of our incorporation, our voyage, our Landing and our reception in this Colony in Feb. 1773 which may be deem'd a Species of Introductory Chapter—and having discribed the Colony of Surinam in its boundaries and revolutions from its earliest discovery, in the 2, 3 and 4 Chapters–I shall now continue my Narrative by linking *our* little Corps to the General Chain of events, and write from what I have experienced by local and occular demonstration—

Having before said that from our Arrival till for several Weeks after, we seem'd to be landed in Guiana for nothing but idle dissipation till viz. Feb-27–I shall now proceed from March 1ˢᵗ the same Year, and just about the beginning of the rainy-Season, when our Life of Mirth and Joviality still continued, and diversify the mind of the reader after the preceeding Scenes of Horror by giving of a Description of the beautifull Mulatto Maid Joanna*—

This fine young Woman–I first saw at the house of a Mʳ *Demelly* Secretary to the Court of Policy where I daily breakfasted, and of whose Lady, *Johanna* aged then but 15 Years was a verry remarkable favourite—

Rather more than middle Size–She was perfectly streight with the most elegant Shapes that can be view'd in nature moving her well-

• —A Mulatto's between white and black—

form'd Limbs as when a Goddess walk'd—Her face was full of Native Modesty and the most distinguished Sweetness–Her Eyes as black as Ebony were large and full of expression, bespeaking the Goodness of her heart. With Cheeks through which glow'd /in spite of her olive Complexion/ a beautiful tinge of vermillion when gazed upon–her nose was perfectly well formed rather small, her lips a little prominent which when she spoke discovered two regular rows of pearls as white as Mountain Snow—her hair was a dark brown–next to black, forming a beauteous Globe of small ringlets, ornamented with flowers and Gold Spangles—round her neck her Arms and her ancles she wore Gold Chains rings and Medals–while a Shaul of finest indian Muslin the end of which was negligently thrown over her polished Shoulder gracefully covered part of her lovely bosom–a petticoat of richest Chints alone made out the rest bare headed and bare footed she shone with double lustre carrying in her delicate hand a bever hat the crown trim'd rown[d] with Silver—The figure and dress of this fine Creature could not but attract my particular notice, as she did indeed of all who beheld her, which induced me to ask of Mrs Demelly in the name of wonder who she was that appeared so much distinguished above all the rest of her Species in the Colony, and which request this Lady obligingly granted—

> She is Sir said she the Daughter of a respectable *Gentleman* named Kruythoff [•] who has besides this Girl 4 Children by a black Woman call'd *cery* the property of a M^r D:B—— on his Estate call'd *Faukenburgh* in the upper part of the river Commewina—Some few Years since Mr Kruythoff made the offer of above one thousand Pound Sterling to M^r D:B—— to obtain Manumitions for his Ofspring which being inhumanly refused it had such an effect upon his Spirits that he became frantick, and died in that Melancholy State soon thereafter, leaving in Slavery and at the discretion of a Tirant 2 boys and 3 beautiful Girls, of which the one now before us is the eldest [••]–the Gold Medals &c which may seem to Surprize you are the Gifts which her faithful Mother /who is a most deserving Woman towards her Children and of some Consequence amongst her own Cast/ received from her father before he expired, and whom she ever attended with the Duties of a Lawful Wife—M^r D:B——

• —This Gentleman was well known by Mr Greenwood, who now lives in Leicester fields—

x —and 30,000 pound Sterling for his dutch relations—[penciled note added in margin in Stedman's handwriting]

•• —In Surinam all such Children go with the Mother that is if she is in Slavery her Ofspring are her Masters property, should theyr father be a prince without he obtains them by purchase—

Joanna

London. Published Dec.r 2.d 1793, by J. Johnson, S.t Paul's Church Yard.

however got his just reward for having since drove all his best Carpenter Negroes to the Woods by his injustice and Severity he was ruined to all intents and purposes, obliged to fly the Colony, and leave his Estate &c— to the disposal of his Creditors, while one of the above unhappy deserters a Samboe*–had been the Protector of Cery with their Children–by his industry. his name is *Jolycoeur* and now the first of Barons Captains whom you may have a Chance of meeting in the Rebel Camps, breathing revenge against all Christians—

Mrs D. B—— is still in Surinam being arrested for her Husbands debts till Faukenbergh shall be Sold by execution to pay them, which Lady now lodges at my house where the Unfortunate *Johanna* attends her, in whom she prides and treats with much tenderness and distinction—

Having thanked Mrs Demelly for her Relation of Johanna in whose Eye was started the precious pearl of Simpathy I took my leave and went to my Lodging in a State of Sadness and Stupefaction—

However insignificant and like the Stile romance this Account may seem to some, it is nevertheless a Genuine fact, which I flatter myself may not be disinteresting to many others—
When reflecting on the State of Slavery altogether, and my Ears being Stund with the Clang of the Whip and the dismal Yels of the wretched Negroes on whom it was inflicted *Sling-Slang* from morning till Night and when considering that this might one day be the fate of the Unfortunate Mulatto Maid I have above described–should she chance to fall in the hands of a Tirrannical Master or Mistress I could not help cursing the barbarity of Mr D.B.—— for having withheld her from a fond parent who by bestowing on her the education of a Lady, would have produced in this forsaken plant /now exposed to every rude blast without protection/ an ornament to Civilized Society—

I became Melancholy at all this and as it were to Counterbalance the general Calamity of the miserable Slaves that Surrounded me, I began to take more delight in the pratling of my poor Negroe boy *Quacoo*, than in all the Fashionable Conversation of the polite Inhabitants of this Colony—My Spirits were deprest, and in the Space of 24 hours I was very ill indeed, when a cordial a few preserved *tamarinds* and basket with some fine Oranges were sent me by an unknown Person. this and letting about 12 Ounces of blood recovered me so far that on the 5th I was able for Change of Air to accompany a Mr *Macneyl* who gave me a most pressing invitation to his beautiful Coffee Plantation Sporksgift in the *Matapica* Creek—

But before we set out I will here take the opportunity to say some-

* —A Samboe is between a Mulatto and a Negroe—

Sprig of the Tamarind Tree.

thing of the *Tamarinds*, this Fruit is produced on a Tree about the Size of a large Apple Tree—the trunk being very streight and covered with a brownish colour'd bark, the twigs are slender arched and knotty, producing leaves and a pod which I can best describe by the annext representation where **A** is the leaf natural Size **B** the extremity of the branch **C** the fruit green and unripe **D** the pulp brown in perfection and **E** the purple kirnels or Stones that are inclosed within it The upper parts of the leaves are a darker Green than underneath–upon the whole forming a very agreeable Shade on which account the tamarind trees are frequently planted in Groves as poplars are in Europe, the Male and Female Species bearing a remarkable distinction in their Colour that of the first having the deepest Hue—I shall not presume to say any thing of the Medicinal Qualities of this or any other tree in Guiana which are as Amply, as I believe Justly, described by Do. *Bancroft* in his Letters to Do. *Pitcairn,* Fellow of the Royal College of Physicians in London–&c except in mentioning such efficasy as I have found them to possess by experience—and which consists in the pulp alone which when preserved is a most delicious refreshment in hot climates, it is also a laxitive–and when disolved with water makes a very cooling and agreeable beverage, correcting the humours and much recommended in all diseases, particularly in hot Fevers—

Let us now proceed to the Estate Sporksgift for which Plantation we set out from Paramaribo in a tent Boat, or barge, rowed by 6 or 8 of the best Negroes belonging to Mr Macneil, every body as I have said travelling by water in this Country—These barges I cannot better describe than by comparing them with those that accompany what is usually Stiled the *Lord Mayors Show* on the River Thames, only being less in Magnitude, though some are very little less in Magnificense–if gilding Flags Musick and every conveniency can be call'd such they are often row'd by 10 and sometimes by 12 Oars and being lightly built, with a most astonishing Swiftness, while the rowers never stop from the moment they set of[f] till the company is landed at the place of destination continuing to tugg night and day sometimes for 24 hours together and Singing a Chorus all the time to keep up theyr Spirits when /theyr naked bodies dreeping with Sweat like post horses/ they headlong one and all plunge into the river to refresh—

> The Wanton Courser thus, with reins unbound
> Breaks from his Stall, and beats the trembling Ground
> Pamper'd and Prowd, he seeks the wonted tides
> And laves in height of blood, his shining Sides—

We now passed a number of fine Plantations but I could not help taking

View of the Estate Alkmaar, on the River Commewine.

Representation of a Tent Boat, or Plantation Barge.

particular Notice of the Cacao Estate cald *Alkmaar* situated on the right side in rowing up the River Commewina, which is no less Conspicuous for its beauty than for the goodness of its proprietor, the invaluable Mrs Elizth *Danforth,* now Widow Godefrooy as shall be seen on many different occasions—

At our Arrival on the Estate *Sporksgift* I had the pleasure to see a Manoeuver which gave me the greatest Satisfaction as also to an American one Captain *Bogard* who was our Companion on this Jaunt—

The Scene consisted in Mr Macneyls on the Moment after we were Landed turning the Overseer out of his Service–and ordering him to depart from the Plantation in an inferior boat call'd a *Ponkee*• to Paramaribo, or to where he thought proper–which was instantaneously put in Execution–he having by bad usuage and cruelty caused the death of 3 or 4 Negroes–after which all the Slaves got a Holly Day and a present of some Rum which was spent in festivity by dancing and Clapping hands in a Green before the dwelling house Windows—

The Overseers sentence was the more ignomious and galling as at the time of his receiving it a negro foot boy who was buckling his Shoes was call'd back and he desir'd to buckle them himself, which verifies the old Proverb, that set a beggar a horseback he rides to the Devil—

I should here give an Account of the Management of a Coffee Plantation–but neither my health or my time permitting me such for the present I must reserve it for another Occasion–and only say that the Spirited Conduct of this Planter–the Joy of his Negroes–the Salubriety of the Country air–and the Hospitable Manner in which we were entertained at his Estate where on the 8th of March we drank the Prince of Oranges health had such an effect on my Constitution and my spirits that on the 9th I returned if not recovered greatly benefitted to Paramaribo—

But I should be Guilty of Partiality did I not relate one Instance which throws a Shade over the Humanity of my friend Macneyl••– Having observed a handsome young Negroe go very lame while the others were Capering and dancing and enquiring for the Cause of it– this Gentleman told me himself, that being accustomed to run away from his work he had been obliged to hamstring him–which was that he had cut through with a knife the large tendon above one of his

• —A *ponkee* is a flat bottomed Boat of 4 or 6 Oars Something like a Square-toed-Shoe. Sometimes it has a tent and Sometimes not—

•• —Thus relentlessly I am going to hear Friends and Foes.—

heels—however severe this despotick Sample of bad usuage may appear it is nothing Comparable to what I will make appear in the Sequel—

On our Return in the Town of Paramaribo the news was nothing but a few dreadful Executions, the *Boreaus* Manawar Captain Van de velde being Sail'd for Holland, and Colonel Fourgeoud having on the 8th being the Prince of Oranges Aniversary entertained a large Company with a ball *en Militaire* in the Officers *Guard-room*—the Musick consisting in 2 fidlers, who had nevertheless the Conscience to make him pay 120 Duch florins for rosin and Catgut[.] About this time I was also attacked by a distemper call'd the *prickly-heat*—by the Colonists rootvont[.] it consists in all the Skin taking a Colour like Scarlet occasioned by small pimples, and itching inconceivably—under ones Garters or any place of Close Confinement the fricksion is almost insupportable—with this Plague all new comers from Europe are soon infected—the Cure is to bathe the parts with the Juice of Limes and Water, as for the bites of Gnats or Musquetos notwithstanding all this the Prickly heat is allowed to be healthy by the Inhabitants, which may be true Since from that Period my health and Spirits were perfectly reestablished• and now again I was as happy as Paramaribo could make me—

Now Colonel Fourgeoud Set out with a barge to inspect the Situation of the River Comewina in case the actual Service of our Troops should be wanted. being at his departure Saluted by the Guns in Fort Zelandia, and by those of the Ships in the roads—which Compliment I acknowledge did astonish me after the Coolness that took Place and now was rooted between him and the Governor of the Colony—

I took myself another trip with a M.r Charles Ryndorp who row'd me in his Barge to 5 beautiful Coffee estates and to one *Sugar* Plantation in the *Matapica*, *Paramarica* and *Werapa* Creeks, the discription of which last call'd *Schoonort* I must also refer till another Occasion, but Where I saw one Scene of barbarity which I cannot help to relate—

The Victim was a fine old Negro Slave who having been /as he thought/ undeservedly sentensed to receive some hundred lashes by the lacerating whips of 2 Negroe drivers—he during the Execution pull'd out a Knife which /after having made a fruitless thrust at his persecutor the Overseer/ he plunged up to the heft of his own bowels, repeating the blow till he dropt down at the tirants feet, for this crime he was /being first recovered/ Condemned to be Chain'd to the furnace, that

• —See a Curious Paper Something Similar to this Subject in the London Review and European Magazine for July 1785.—Page 30—

1773—MARCH 30, APRIL 6, 13, 14, 20, 27

distils the kildevil* there to keep in a perpetual fire night and day, by the heat of which he was all over blistered till he should expire by Infirmity or old Age indeed of which last he but had little chance. he shew'd me his Wounds with a Smile of Contempt which I returned with a Sigh and a small Donation nor shall I ever forget the Miserable Man—who like *cerberus* the dog of hell was loaded with Irons and Chained to everlasting torment. as for every thing else that I met on this little tour, I must acknowledge to be elegance and Splendor, and my reception Hospitable above my Expectation—but these elision fields could not dissipate the Gloom that the infernal furnace had left upon my Spirits a damp of such a dusky nature that no faint Sun shine can evaporate—

Of the Coffee Estates that of Mr Limes call'd Limeshope was the most magnificent and may be deem'd with Justice one of the richest in the Colony; we now once more on the 6th of April returned safe to Paramaribo—

Here The *Westerling-Werf* Manowar, Captn Crass was arive'd from Plymouth in 37 Days and in which port he had put to Stop a leak, having parted Company with us /as I said/ off Portland in the end of December 1772—

Today Dining at the house of my Friend Mr Lolkens to whom I had been /as I first mentioned/ recommended by Letters—I was an eye witness of the unpardonable Contempt with which Negro Slaves are treated in this Colony, by his Son a boy not more than 10 Years old, when sitting at table, giving a Slap in the face to a gray headed black woman for by accident having touched his powdered hair, as she was serving in a dish of *Kerry;* I could not help blaming his father for Patronizing the Action who told me with a Smile the Child should not longer offend me as he was the next day to Sail to Holland for Education to which I answered that I thought it was high time—at the same Moment a Sailor passing by broke the head of a Negroe man with a bludgeon for not having Saluted him with his hat—Such here is the State of Slavery—

Now Colonel Fourgeoud departed with a barge to Rio *Surinam* to explore the Situation and banks of that River—To Day Died Captain Barends one of the Masters of the Transports which were still kept in Commission in Case they should be wanted for our return to Europe[.] I can here not pass by one or two of the Singular efforts of Frensy

---

* —Kildevil is a Species of rum which is distilled from the Scum and dregs of Sugar chaldrons, it is much drunk in this Colony and the only Spirits allowed the Negroes when they get any—Many Europeans also from a point of Oeconomy make use of it to whom it proves no better than a Slow and pernicious Poison—

Fevers so common in this Country, viz, a young fellow on board the Westellingwerf this day with an old rusty Knife absolutely *Castrated* himself yet he shortly after recovered, while another going at an unseasonable hour to List for a Soldier the officer being disturbed in his Sleep desired him to go to *the Devil* the Young Man answered "very well Sir," run to the river and drowned himself imediately—

Five or Six Sailors now were buried every day whose Lamentable fate I cannot pass by unnoticed, they actually being used worse than the negroes in this Scorching Climate, where besides rowing large flat bottomed barges up and down the rivers day and night for Coffee Sugar &c–and being exposed to the burning Sun, and heavy rains, and besides Stowing the above Commodities in a hold as hot as an Oven—they are obliged to row every upstart planter to his Estate at a Call, which saves his Cash and his negroes and for which they receive in return *nothing*–many times not so much as a mouthfull of meat and drink paliating hunger and thirst by begging from the Slaves a few banana's or Plantains eating oranges and drinking water, which in a little time relieves them from every Complaint by Shipping them of[f] to Eternity—at Paramaribo they are no better treated, where like horses they must /having unloaded the Vessels/ drag the Commodities to the distant Storehouses, being bathed in Sweat and bullied with bad Language, Sometimes with blows, while a few Negroes are ordered to attend, but not to work by the direction of theyr Masters which many would willingly do to relieve the drooping Sailors to whom this must be exceedingly disheartining and on whom his task falls with double and trible hardships–the Planters also employ those Men to paint their howses clean their Sash Windows, and do numberless other Menial Services for which a Seaman was never intended–all this is done to save their Cash and theyr Negroes as I have said while by this usage thousands are Swept to the Grave who by their profession alone might have lived for many years thereafter, nor dare the West India Captains to refuse theyr men without incuring the displeasure of the Planters and seeing theyr Ships rot in the Harbour without a Freight–nay I have heard a poor Sailor wish to God he had been born a Negroe and beg to be imploy'd amongst them in Cultivating a Sugar or Coffee Plantation–all this is truly Shamefull and Calls loudly for imediate redress—

I now enquired of M*rs* Demelly what was become of the amiable Joanna, who told me that her Lady M*rs* D.B.—— had escaped to Holland on Board the Boreas Manowar under the protection of Capt*n* *van de velde* who like a true *Perseus* had broke her Chains, and rescued this *Andromeda* from the Jaws of the Monster Persecution, and that her

1773—APRIL 27

young Mulatto was now at the house of an Aunt a free woman from where she expected by the Creditors every moment to be sent to the Estate Friendless, and at the mercy of some rascally Overseer—Good God; I flew to the Spot in Search of poor Joanna and found her bathing with her Companions in the Garden•—

> But lo! with graceful Motion there she Swims
> Gently removing each Ambitious Wave
> The crowded waves transported Clasp her Limbs
> When, When, oh when shall I such freedoms have
> In vain ye envious Streams So fast he flow
> To hide her from a lovers ardant Gaze
> From every touch you more transparent grow
> And all revealed the beautious Wanton plays

But perceiving me She darted from my presence like a Shot, when I returned to Mrs Demelly and declared without the least hesitation no less than that it was my intention /if such could be/ to Purchase to Educate & to make even my lawfull Wife *in Europe,* the individual Mulatto Maid *Joanna* which I relate to the World without blushing or being ashamed of while Mrs Demelly gazed upon me with Wild Astonishment—

In this passage my Youth must plead my Cause—nor should it at all have been inserted were it not for reasons to be met with in the Sequel. while to those alone who have read the history of *Incle* and *Yarico* as related by the Spectator with pleasure and *approved* of that Gentlemans Conduct—I here make an Apology—

I next went to the house of my Friend Mr Lolkens who happened to be the administrator of *Faukenbergh* Estate, and asking his assistance I intimated to him my Strange Determination—having recovered from his Surprize and Stared at me an interview at once was proposed and the beauteous Slave produced trembling in our presence—Reader if you have perused the fate of *Lavina* with applause /though the Scene admits of no Comparison/ reject not the destiny of *Joanna* with Contempt. It was she who had sent me the Cordial and Oranges in March— when I was nearly expiring and which she now modestly acknowledged before us both was in gratitude for having pitied her Situation— But as to live with me anyhow she absolutely refused it not, she said, from a want of friendship, or insensibility of the Honour I did her— But from a Sence that she must be parted from me soon, should I

• —This is here regularly done twice a Day by all the Indians Mulatto's Negroes &c—and which Constitutes so much to theyr health and to their Cleanliness—while by the Europeans /some few excepted/ this Salutary Custom is never put in *practice*—

return to Europe without her, and a Convixion of her inferior State in *that* part of the world should she ever accompany me there; in which Sentiments firmly persisting she was permitted decently to withdraw and return to the house of her Aunt—I recommending her from my Soul to M:^r Lolkens, and begging she might be continued at least at Parramaribo, which privilege this Gentleman humanely was pleased to Grant her, while I once more yet only to Some apologize for this wonderfull digression—Here it ends–

And Now came the news, that in the end of this month the *rangers* having discovered a rebel Village, had attacked it, and carried of[f] three Prisoners, Leaving 4 others shot dead upon the Spot whose right hands chop'd of[f] and *barbacued* or dried in Smoak they had sent to the Governor at Paramaribo—•

On receiving this news Colonel Fourgeoud imediately left the River Surinam–and on the 1st of May returned to Town in expectation of his Regiment being employed on actual service but there it also ended, and we still were allowed to linger away our time, each after his own private fancy, while the rangers were reviewed on the 4th in the Fort Zelandia at which Ceremony I was present, and must confess that this Corps of black Soldiers—had a truly tremenduous appearance; warriors whose determined and open aspect could not but give me the greatest Pleasure to behold them—they received the thanks of the Governor for theyr manly behaviour and faithful Conduct—besides which they were entertained with a rural feast at the Publick expense at Paramaribo: and were having invited theyr wives and Children the Day was spent in Mirth and Conviviality, without the least disturbance nay even with decorum and propriety to the great Satisfaction of the Inhabitants—

The *Westelling* Werf Capt:^n Crass now Sail'd for Holland but first for the Colony of Demerary.–thus both our Convoys having left us–things began to look as if we should Still be employed on Actual Service, and for which on our returning to Europe we began to have great reason to wish–not only our Officers but our private Men begining to be debilitated by the relaxation of the Climate and Some by a discontinued Debauchery. So common to all ranks in this Settlement; the later dying by half douzins every day, as hard Labour and bad treatment had kill'd the poor Sailors, which clearly demonstrates that all Excesses are mortal to Europeans in Guiana But Men will lessen what they-do-not imitate Since I myself notwithstanding my former Resolution of living retired now relapsed in the vortax of discipation–Not only becoming Member

• —For every Rebel Prisoner a reward is paid of 25 florins–& for every right hand fifty being nearly 5 Pound—

of a Club, and Partaking of all the polite Amusements, but plunging in every extravagance without Exception, however I got the reward that I deserv'd, and all at once became so ill by a fever—that I was not expected more to recover: in this Situation did I lay in my hammock till the 17th with only a Soldier and my black boy to attend me, and without another friend, Seekness being so common in this Country, and every one having so much ado to mind themselves, that neglect takes place betwixt the nearest acquaintances—but this is not the Case with the Inhabitants who perhaps are the most Hospitable People on the Globe to Europeans, these Philanthropysts not only cramming the Sick with 20 different cordials at a time, but crowding theyr apartments with as many different Condolers who from Morning till night Continue prescribing, insiting, bewailing, and lamenting friend and Stranger without exception—and this lasts till the patient often becomes delirious and expires—who is thus by friendship crushed to Death, like the more nimble Inhabitants of the forests are hugged, till they die by the embraces of their overfond parents, and this must inevitably have been my Case between the two extremes of neglect and prodigality, had not this morning entered my apartment to my unspeakable Joy and Surprize, the valuable Mulatto Slave *Joanna* accompanied by one of her best friends—She said she was acquainted with my forlorn Situation—That if I still entertained of her the same good Opinion, her only request was that she might be allowed to wait upon me, till I should be recovered, which I readily granted, and by her unremitting Care and attention had the good fortune so far to regain my health and Spirits, as to be able in a couple of Days after to take an airing in Mr Kennedy's Carriage—

I now renewed my wild Proposals of purchase of Education, and of transporting her to Europe with the greatest Cincerity but these were now all once more rejected with this humble declaration—

> I am born a low, contemptible Slave, to be your Wife under the forms of Christianity must degrade you to all your Relations and your Friends, besides the expence of my Purchase and Education, but I have a Soul I hope not inferior to the best European, and blush not to acknowledge that I have a regard for you who so much distinguishes me above the rest—nay that now independant of every other thought I shall pride myself /by in the way of my *Ancestors*/ to be yours all and all, till fate shall part us, or my Conduct Shall give you Cause to Spurn me from your Presence.

which was Spoke with downcast looks, and tears dropping upon her heaving bosom—& while she held her Companion by the hand. From this Instant the Beauteous Maid was mine, nor had I ever after cause to repent it as shall be seen more particularly in the Sequel—Now pale envy do thy utmost, while I shall continue to Glory in this Action, as much as this virtuous Slave did pride in making me her choice—

Having only added that I this day made her a present of different Articles to the value above 20 Guineas I shall drop the asure Theme—

But the day following what was my verry great Surprize at seeing my Gold all returned upon my Table—this enchanting Creauture having carried every Article back to the Merchants—

> your generous intentions allone Sir /Said she/ are sufficient But allow me to tell you that any Superfluous expence on my Account–I will look on as deminishing that good Opinion which I hope you have, and will ever entertain of my disinterestedness, and upon which I shall ever put the greatest value—

Such was the genuine Speech of a Slave who had simple nature for her only education–and the purity of whose refined Sentiments stand in need of no Comment, which I was now determined to improve by every care—I shall now only add that Gratitude to her Superior virtues, and particular attention for me, and my Duty to the World in General, by producing such a Slave upon the Stage, could have alone induced me to dwell on a Subject, which I am convinced must attract me so much censure, while if but with a few my Motive will plead for my Presumption, I shall lay easy under the Burthen—

this evening I visited at M.̲ʳ Demellys who with his Lady congratulated Me on my recovery from Sickness, while at the same time however Strange, with a Smile they wished me Joy with /what by way of good humour they were pleased to call/ my Conquest which *M.̲ʳˢ Demelly assured me was not a little Spoke of in Paramaribo, as Censured by some, applauded by others, but she believ'd in her heart envied by all—Now Reader prepare for Scenes of a more dusky nature—

* —a more well educated woman was not in the Colony—

CHAPTER 6th

*Account of a dreadful Execution—Fluctuating state of
political Affairs—Short glimps of Peace—An Officer shot dead–
his whole party cut to pieces and a general alarm renewed
throughout the Colony—Hospitality &c*

* Now Died our Lieutenant Collonel *Lantman* while a number of our Officers lay Seek—amongst whom at last /in place of Joy and discipation/ pale Mortality began to take Place, & which from Day to Day encreased amongst the private Men at a most Lamentable rate—
* Next day Were inter'd with Military Honours the remains of the deceased Lieut. Colonel, in the centre of the Fortress *Zelandia*–where all criminals are imprisoned–and all field Officers Buried–and where I was not a little Shock'd to see the Captive rebel-Negroes–and others–clanking their Chains, and roasting *Plantains* and *yams* upon theyr graves–which I could not help putting me in mind of so many helish fiends in the Shape of African-Slaves, tormenting the Souls of their European persecutors, in which number by the *Navy* or *army* ought with Justice not to be included who come not to inspire Revolts but to Quell them—From out these gloomy Mansions of dispair, this very day seven Captive-Negroes were selected who being led to the place of Execution by a few Soldiers which is in the Savana, and where the Sailors and Soldiors are inter'd, 6 were hanged and one broke alive upon the rack, besides which one White Man before the court house was scurged by the publick executioner–who is in this Country always a black–But what makes me take particular Notice here was the Shameful injustice of showing a Partiality to the European who ought to [have] known better by letting him escape with a slight Corporal Punishment, while the poor african who is destitute of precept Laws,

for the same crime, viz, Stealing money out of the Town Hall—lost his Life under the most excrusiating Torments through which he manfully went without heaving a Sigh or Complaining, and while one of his Companions with the rope about his neck and just going to be turn'd of[f] gave a hearty laugh of Contempt at the Magistrates who attended the Execution—I ought not to omit that the Negro who flog'd the White Man inflicted the Punishment with the greatest Marks of Commisseration all which *almost* had induced me to deside between the Europeans and Africans in this Colony—that the first were the greatest barbarians of the two—a name which tarnishes Christianity and is bestowed on them in too many Corners of the Globe, with what real degree of Justice I will not take on me to determine

Having testified how much I was hurted at the cruelty of the above execution—and Surprized at the intrepidity with which the Negroes bore theyr Punishment—a decent looking Man stept up to me—

Tho /said he/ Sir—you are but a new commer from Europe—and know very little about the african Slaves without which you would testify both less feeling and Surprize—Not long ago /continued he/ I saw a black man hang'd alive by the ribs, between which with a knife was first made an insision, and then clinch'd an Iron hook with a Chain—in this manner he kept living three days hanging with his head and feet downwards and catching with his tongue the drops of water /it being in the rainy season/ that were flowing down his bloated breast while the vultures were picking in the putred wound, notwithstanding all this he never complained and even upbraided a negro for crying while he was flog'd below the Gallows*—By calling out to him—"*you man? da boy fasi*"—"*are you a Man you behave like a boy*"—Shortly after which he was knocked in the head by the More Comiserating Sentry who stood over him—with the but[t] end of his Musquet**—another Negro /said he/ I have seen *Quartered* alive who after 4 Strong horses were fastened to his Legs and Arms, and after having had Iron Sprigs drove home underneath every one of his nails, on hands and feet—without a motion he first ask'd a dram and then bid them pull away without a Groan—but what gave us the greatest entertainment /continued he/ were the fellows Jokes, by desiring the Executioner to drink before him—in case there should chance to be poison in the Glass, and bidding him take care of his horses least any of them should happen to Strike backwards—as for old Men being broke upon the rack and young women roasted alive chain'd to Stakes there can be nothing more common in this Colony—

* —all Negroes cry out for Mercy while they are flog'd, in hopes of having thereby the lesser Punishment—but never no never where no Mitigation is expected—

** —of such an Execution Mr Greenwood of Leicesterfield was one eye Witness—

I was putrifyed at the inhuman detail, and breaking away with a curse from the Damnable Spot of laceration Made the Best of my way home to my own Lodgings—

🙘 A Promotion now took place and was preferr'd to be Lieut Colonel Major *Westerlo,* whose place was filled in by Captn *Bequer.* what makes me mention this promotion more particularly is because it shows Colonel Fourgeouds unlimitted Power of filling up every vacancy however under the Sanction of his Serene Highness the Prince of Orange—

🙘 Having now received a supply of Provisions from Holland and absolutely doing no Service in the Colony it is resolved on all Sides that we shall go home, our Regiment notwithstanding its being paid partly by the united Provinces still being exceedingly chargeable to the Society and the Inhabitants, who conjunctly paid all other Expences, thus in the hopes of Sailing in the middle of June, the transports were ordered a Second time to Wood–Water–and otherwise prepare–I must say nothing of what I felt on this occasion however not long.

🙘 Since the next day getting Intelligence that a Plantation was demolished and the Overseer Murdered by the rebels we were a second time desired to stay by request of the Governor and the Inhabitants–& in Consequence the 3 Transports which had since Feb. 9th till now been kept

🙘 waiting at a great expence•–were finally put out of Commission and the victuals stowed at the head Quarters in temporary Storehouses erected for the purpose—

Now all the minds of the People began to be Quieted, knowing the ultimating of what the Troops were come here for–viz: to go on actual Service, and protect the Inhabitants & which was certainly much better for both, than to linger away an Idle Life at Paramaribo—

🙘 Our Officers and men seem'd now in excellent Spirits and this being his Britannicks Majesties Birthday Mr Kennedy, Macneyl, and myself forgot not to drink the Kings Health, and success to the Colony of Surinam—

🙘 When again on the 7th to our inutterable Surprise we were actually for the 3rd time officially acquainted that things seeming quiet–and tranquility reestablished the Colony of Surinam had no further use for our Services—these sudden changes did not fail to cause a great deal of discontent amongst the Military and amongst the Inhabitants—Cabals were form'd that threatened to break out in a Civil Contest–Some charging the Governor as jealous of the unlimitted power that was vested in Colonel Fourgeoud, who by many people was blamed as abusing of that power–by not treating the Governor with that Civility

• —at the expence of 80 florins P^r day each being above 2000 Guineas—

A Negro hung alive by the Ribs to a Gallows.

which he might have done without deviating from his own Consequence, thus while one Party swore we were the bulwarks of the Settlement by keeping the rebels at bay—the opposition hesitated not to call us the locusts of Egypt who were come to live on the fat of the Colony. be that as it may, but it made our life very uncomfortable while a great number of us could not help thinking that between the two we were very ill used—and I myself in particular had cause to feel very unhappy—

This same day while at dinner on board a Dutch Vessal in the roads, the Company were alarmed at the most tremenduous Clap of Thunder that ever I heard in my Life killing several Negroes and Cattle•—

In short on the Eleventh the Ships were again taken in Commission and ordered with all possible expedition to prepare for our Departure—while every one was making himself ready for the voyage—

Our Quitting the Colony of Surinam being at last fully determined upon, I received a Polite Invitation from a Mr Campbel who was lodged with a Mr Kerry at my friend Kennedys to accompany him on a visit to the Island of Tobago, where I might recruit my debilitated health and dejected Spirits, the first being not perfectly recover'd—and the 2nd in a drooping Condition and henceforth from there to return by the leeward Islands to Europe

This was to me a most glad and agreeable offer all things considered, and which I should with all the pleasure imaginable accepted of had not my making application for this favour to Col: Fourgeoud been prevented by the news received on the 15th which was no less than that an *Officer* of the Society troops was shot dead by the rebels and his whole Party consisting of about 30 Men cut to Pieces and which threw the whole Colony once more into Confusion and Consternation; the above Gentleman whose name was *Lepper* and only Lieut was much the Cause of this Misfortune By his too great Courage and Intrepidity—without either temper or Conduct•• of which I cannot omit relating the particulars—

It being now in the heart of the short dry Season this officer being informed that between the Rivers Patamaca and upper Coermootibo, a village of negroes had been discovered, by the rangers some time before, he now insisted with *this* Small party which was only a detachment from the Patamaca post to sally through the woods and attack

---

• —This very day the City of Guatimala in old Mexico was swallowed up by an Earthquake, when 8000 Families instantly Perished—

•• —this Gentleman formerly belonged to the life Guards in Holland from where he had fled after Stabbing his Antagonist through the heart with his Sword in a Duel—

them—But the rebels being apprized of his intention by theyr Spies /which they never want/ imediately marched out against him when they laid themselves in an ambush near the borders of a deep Marsh through which Lieut: Lepper with his party were to pass on theyr way to the Rebel Settlement—no sooner were these unfortunate Men got in the Swamp till near theyr armpits than their black Enemies rushed out from under Cover and shot them dead at pleasure in the water without they could return the fire more than once, their Situation preventing them from Loading. they indeed might have strove to get upon the beech had not a general Confusion taken place by the sudden death of their over Gallant Commander who /being imprudently distinguished by a Gold laced hat from amongst the rest,/ was shot through the head, in the first onset—the few that scrambled out of the Marsh upon the banks were imediately butchered in the most barbarous manner—while 5 or 6 were taken prisoner, and carried alive to the Settlement of the Rebels, whose Melancholy fate I shall in proper place describe, as I had it from those that were eye witness to it—and which ends this dismal Catastrophe—

Now all Paramaribo was in an Uproar—some parties so vehement that they were ready to tear the Governor and Counsel to pieces for having dismissed Colonel Fourgeoud with his Regiment, while others ingeniously declared that if we were intended for no more use than we had hitherto proved to be of, our company could without Ceremony be dispenced with—all this could not be but Exceedingly Galling for our Officers, who wished nothing more than to be employed on actu[a]l Service for the good of the Colony of Surinam, thus while our Chief did on the one Side not escape from Censure, on the other side the most bitter Lampoons were spread through the Town against the Governor and his Counsel, *libels* of such a black and inflamatory nature that no less than a thousand Gold Ducats were offered as a reward to the discoverer of theyr author, with a promise of secreting his name if he required it—but the whole was to no purpose and neither author or informer made their appearance while the general Clamour still continuing the Governor and Counsel were forced /as they had desired us a 3rd time to Sail for Europe,/ now a 3rd time to petition us to remain in Surinam, and protect the distracted Situation of the Colony—to this Petition we once more condescended and the Ships were actually a 3rd time put out of Commission—We however Still continued doing of nothing to the unspeakable Surprize of every one—the only Duty hitherto having consisted in a Subalterns *guard* at the head Quarters to protect the Chief, his Colours, his Storehouses, Pigs and Poultry, which Parade regularly mounted every day at half past 4 O'Clock and to where our Gentlemen Squired the Ladies—and another guard on board the transports, till the provisions were stowed a Shoare in the Magazines a few field days excepted, when the Soldiers were drill'd for pomp alone in a burning Sun till they fainted—I cannot continue any further without giving some Sample of these two extraordinary Men who were greatly by theyr inveterary and opposition to each other the Cause of our undesided, and fluctuating manner of proceeding, and the outlines of which two Characters may assist in unrevelling the riddle—For what in the name of wonder were we so plagued in Surinam?—

As the ingrediants of flattery or fear make but a small part of that Gentlemans Composition who gives *them*—and who pretends perfectly to have known both; the reader may depend on having them painted in their Original Colours, however strong the Shades—but—

—Vera dicuntur Obscursis—

Governor Nepveu was said to be a man of Sense more than Learning and was indepted alone to his artful & cunning manner for having rose to this present dignity from Sweeping the Hall of the Court house—by which he also from nothing found means to accumulate a most Capital fortune and to command respect from all ranks who had any dealings with him—they never daring to attack him but at a distance—his Comportment was affable but ironical, without ever losing the Command of his Temper all which made him have the appearance of a Man of fashion, and Carry every thing before him as he wished, he was generally known by the appellation of Reynard, and was most certainly a fox of too much artifice to be run down by all the Hounds in the Colony—

Colonel Fourgeoud was quite the reverse he was impetuous Passionate Self sufficient and revengeful, he deserved not the Name of Cruel to individuals but was a Tirant to the Generality and the Death of hunddrids by his sordid avarice and oppression, with all this he was partial ingrateful and confused—but the most indefatigable Man for hardships and fatigue that ever yet was known—which like a true *buccaneer* he bore the most Heroic Courage, patience and perseverance he was also affable to the private Soldiers, but of his Officers he was the bane—he had read but had no Education to digest it—in short few Men could talk better but in *many occasions* none act worse—

Such were the Characters given of our two Commanders, which I shall not Contradict and whose opposition to each other could not miss to Gall the happiness of the Troops, and as I have said promote the fluctuating State of political affairs in this dejected Colony where by appearance we were Still come to do nothing—

1773—JUNE 20

    Thus having still none of Colonel Fourgeouds warlike achievements to discribe, I shall give an Account of one of his *Pets,* which he was very fond of This was a bird call'd the *Towcan* and in Surinam bananabeck or cojacai from either its bill having some resemblance to that fruit, or from its loving to feed on it, perhaps from both and which kept hopping tame amongst his Poultry—

The *Towcan* is no larger than a tame Pidgeon and yet its beak is no less than 6 inches if not more this bird is shap'd like a Jackdaw, carrying its tail alwais Perpendicular except when it flies—its Colour is black except a little white under the throat and breast which is bordered by red in the form of a Crescent reversed—and a few feathers above and under its Tail Some white & some crimson the head is large with a blueish ring round the Eyes of which the iris is Yellow, and its ashcoloured toes are much like those of a Parrot, but its remarkable beak deserves the most particular attention which is Serrated and of a Sise so improportioned to its body, this beak however /which is arched/ is as thin as parchment and consequently very light it is yellow on the top and on the Sides a beautiful Scarlet inclosing a tongue which is very much like a feather—The Towcan feeds on fruit especially pepper and as I have said is very domestick—

I shall here also take the Opportunity to describe another tame bird which I saw with Pleasure at the house of Mr Lolkens, and which I take to be what we call the *Flycatcher.* they call it in this Country Sun fowlo because when it extends its wings, which it often does, on the interior part of each wing appears the most beautiful form of a Sun—this bird is about the Size of a woodcock and of a Golden Speckled Colour—its legs are verry long, and also its slender Bill which is perfectly streight and very pointed—with this it darts at the flies while they creep, with such wonderful dexterity and Swiftness that it never once misses its object, which seems to make its principal food, and which make it both useful and entertaining; this bird might with some degree of Propriety be stiled the *perpetuim Mobilae* its body making a Continual horisontal Motion and its tail keeping time like the Pendulem of a Clock—Having discribed these two Contrasts in their appearance I must add that neither they nor any other bird in Guiana notwithstanding their beautiful plumage ever sing with any degree of Melody perhaps 3 or 4 excepted whose Notes are Sweet but not variegated, and of which I shall speak in proper Season—which shows that Nature has destributed her favours equally to all her Sons and Daughters

I must however not forget to mention one like the mock-bird, and the *Caribean-Wren* of which last only I am now to take particular Notice, this bird which is call'd by the Sable Colonists *Gado-fowlo* the bird

The Toucan & the Fly-catcher.

London, Published Dec.r 1.st 1794. by J.Johnson, S.t Paul's Church Yard.

of God—/probably from its familiarity, inoffensiveness, and its delightful Musick/ is rather larger than the English Wren to which its Plumage much resembles—it frequently perches upon the Window Shutters, with the docility of the robin, where from its Enchanting Warblage it has been Honoured by many with the name of the South-America Nightingale—

But I must proceed with my Narrative, the 21 died *Mr Renard* one of our best Surgeons, who was buried the same Afternoon and which is very requisite in this hot Country where putrefaction so very soon takes place, and more especially when the patient dies of a *putred-fever* which are in this Colony extremely frequent. this loathsome disease first appears by bilious vomiting, lowness of Spirits, and a Yellow Cast of the Countenance and Eyes—and without plenty of lime or lemon juice is internally used, which is allowed to be one of the best remedies, the distemper becomes fatal and certain Death in few Days is the Consequence—

The *Belly-hatty* or dry Gripes which is also a common Complaint in this Country, and not only causes excrusiating Pains, but is exceedingly dangerous, had now also attack'd a great number of our People—as to the Causes of this disorder—I can give no certain account of but the Cure is generally by taking inwardly—the *Castor-Oil* by the mouth, and having it injected by the rectum with a few other prescriptions—it consisting in an obstinate Costiveness that Can by no other means be overcome—indeed it was lamentable to see the State to which were already reduced a Corps of the finest flourishing Young fellows, the best of whose blooming fresh Complexion was now changed to the Sallow Colour of old Parchment—Officers and Soldiers were indeed riding post haste on the highway to eternity—and all hitherto to no purpose, tho some People chus'd to indict that the whole was no more than a Political Scheme to have another Regiment added to the War Establishment in holland, as Colonel *Desalves-Marines* had been before but to which others chose to give but very little Credit—be that as it may we all stood a Chance of in a few Months longer to be not Shot—but literally carressd to Death—if walking in the Moonshine til Midnight with a groop of Lady's in a constant evaporation may be call'd so, to which was generally added Wine and Water—a few old fashion Songs—and the most insipid Conversation. In short on the 27 we again lost by Death the Gentlemanlike Lieut Colonel *Baron de Gersdorph* who was very much regretted by every one, while the *Grim King* of Terrors Conscientiously beginning at the head of the Corps with the field Officers could not but give some Consolation to the Inferior gentry who were preferr'd in

1773—JUNE 27

their places by Colonel Fourgeoud which Commander in Chief Continued himself as firm as a rock—

Major Becquer was now made Lieut Col. and a Cap.! Roekoph advanced to rank as Major—

The European Animals that live in this Climate are no less debilitated and deminutive than the fair human Species—*Beef* for instance is both• Smaller and not near so delicate as it is in Europe owing to its perpetual perspiration and the Coarseness of the Grass on which it feeds, which is not so good as that of the Salt Marshes in Somerset—indeed this must be true since on the banks of the Oronoque they ran wild, and are sold by the Spaniards for two Dollars per head, while a single piece of ready roasted beef is often sent from Europe to Guiana as a most valueable and delicate present & on which the planter puts a greater value, than the Alderman on venison or Turtle—

The manner of this long preserving the meat when roasted is by putting it in a blocktin box or Canister then filling up the empty Space with Gravy or dripping till it is perfectly covered over, after which the box must be made fast and Soudered round about so that neither Air or Water can penetrate by which means I was told that it may be with safety carried round the Globe—

The *Sheep* of this Country are so small that when skinned they seem not larger than what is call'd Young Lamb in White-Chaple Market. they have no horns or wool but streight hair, and are to an European but verry indifferent eating the more so since all Beef Mutton &c—must be consumed on the day that it was kil'd, which makes it tuff, while keeping it longer makes it liable to putrefaction. both the above Species are unatural to Guiana and the breed has been imported from the old Continent—So also was the breed of the *hog* but with an uncommon Degree of better Success and do *these* Animals in my Opinion thrive better in Guiana than in Europe; the hogs are here large fat, good and plentiful, they feeding on any thing that comes in their way, and on the Estates are often fattened with green pine-Apples of which they are exceedingly fond—and which grow so spontaneously in this Climate—as for the *Poultry* nothing Can thrive better—the Common *fowls* are here as good, and as Common as in England but less, and their Eggs more sharp-pointed. a smaller species of the *Dunghill* kind with rumpled inverted feathers seem natural to Guiana, being reared inland by the Indians or natives—The *Turkeys* are very fine and so are the *Geese* but the *ducks* are excellent being of the large *Muscovy* Species with Crimson

• —This I am surprized to be contradicted by Do. Bancroft who says it improves in Size in South America while one Bullock may often be produced in Smithfield Market who will weigh down two of the largest in Guiana—

1773—JUNE 27, 29

Pearls betwixt the beak and the head, these are here Juicy fat and in Great plenty—I must here make a remark that the *hog* and *Duck* which lives upon any thing and which waddles in Mire and in Dirt are the two Animals for the Kitchen which thrive the best of any in this Country—

At last the hour arrives—and all the officers and men are ordered to be ready at a Minutes warning to set out on actual Service—Now all was in a stir—and each now preparing to do wonders—while our little Corps was already Melted from 530 able Men to about 3 fourths of their number, by Death and Sickness, the Hospital being crowded by invalids of every kind

I think it will here not be amiss before we set out on our Exploits to give a regular list of our *Primo Plano, Pay* and *table Money* Eleven florins make about 1£ and which consisted in—

—General List of Rank—Pay-and Table Money in the Corps—

N°.	RANKS.	PAY.	TABLE.	IN ALL
1	Colonel and Chief	/4400	/1200	/5600
2	Lieut Colonels	2000	1000	3000
1	Major	1800	1000	2800
3	Captains	800	400	1200
4	D° by Brevet	650	400	1050
7	Lieutenants	500	200	700
7	Second D°	450	200	650
7	Ensigns	400	200	600
1	Adjutant	600	300	900
1	D° Assistant	400	200	600
1	Quarter Master	500	200	700
2	D° Assistants	400	200	600
1	Volunteer	—	—	—
3	Surgeons	500	200	700
3	under D°	240	100	340
3	Mates	143	100	243
1	Apothecary	500	200	700
1	Stuard	300	100	400
3	Cooks	300	100	400
22	Serjeants			
36	Corporals			
406	Private Men			
1	Drum Major			
8	Drums			
2	Negroes			
3	Domestiques			

All those mentioned within the brackets, were paid by the week—and got their allowance in Effects, destributed to them regularly every Monday

Total: 530 able Men when we saild out of the Texel—

1773—JUNE 29

The *Volunteer* was a young M.^r **H** entrusted to the Care of Col. Fourgeoud who showed him never the smallest attention—The 2 Negroes were one *Akera* and *Gowsary* two desperados who had been both rebel Captains in the Colony *Berbice* and who by taking *Atta* theyr Chief and Delivering him to the Governor of that Settlement had escaped from the Gallows, and were now both private Soldiers in our Regiment—by these two Men the most inhuman Murders had formerly been Committed on the Europeans in the Year 1762 when the revolt was in the above Colony—

Before we left Paramaribo I had the opportunity of seeing two very extraordinary Animals of the Aquatic tribe, the one was in Mr *Roux*['s] Cabinet of Curiosities, and is call'd in the Colony *Jackee*, in Latin *Rona Piscatrix*, this fish is about 8 or 10 inches long without Scales exceeding fat and delicate which I can testify by Experience since that time, and is found in all Narrow Creeks and Marshy places—But what is extremely remarkable, is that this Creature however incredible it may appear absolutely changes to a perfect frog, but not from a frog to a fish, as Merian, Zeba and some random Historians[*] have been pleased to assert, and of which truth I was this day fully Satisfyed by seeing the above Animal desected and Suspended in a Bottle with Spirits, when the two hinder legs of a very small frog made theyr appearance, growing inside from that part of the back to which usually the intestines are fixed, to my very great astonishment—my discriptive parts clearly demonstrate that I am no naturalist, abiding Simply by what I have seen—I nevertheless humbly presume to suppose in *this Case* that the *Jackee* is neither more or less than a Tadpole arived to the compleat Maturity of a fish before it takes its transformation—

The other I saw at the house of my friend Kenedy. this was what D.^o Bankroft cals the *Torporific* and others the *Electrical Eel*—and which Do: Fermyn supposes to possess the same Qualities with the Torpedo. this wonderful Animal is of a Lead Blue Colour—Shaped something like an Eel with one large fin that runs below it. from head to tail, not unlike the keel of a Ship and only lives in fresh water its length is call'd by some 3 feet, and by others not less than 4 or 5 times as large[**]—when this Animal is touched by the hand, or any rod of Metal or hard wood it communicates a shock the impulse of which produces the same effect as electricity—This shock Do: Bankroft /in my Opinion wisely/ supposes not to proceed from any Muscular Motion but equally emitted from every part of the body—And Do: Fermyn has assured me that the

---

[*] —Mr Hartsink and I am sorry to say in this Mr Westley—

[**] —Mr Greenwood of Leicester fields has told me himself to have kil'd one of Eleven feet Long—

Shock of this Electrical Eel has been Communicated to him through the bodies of 8 or 10 People who stood hand in hand for the purpose of trying the Experiment—

For my own part all that I can say about this Animal is that I saw it in a Tub full of water where it appeared to be about 2 feet long–that I threw of[f] my Coat, and having turn'd up my shirt Sleeves, tried above 20 different times to Grasp it with my *hand* but all without Effect, receiving just as many Electrical Shocks as I touched it, which I felt till in the top of my Shoulder, to the great Entertainment of Mr Kenedy to whom I lost a small wager on the Occasion. The Electrical Eel Swims forwards or backwards at pleasure, and may be eat with the greatest Safety–it is even by many People call'd delicious—That this Animal must be touched with both hands before it gives the Shock I must take the liberty to Contradict, having experienced the Contrary Effect and that they should be found in Surinam above 20 feet long never yet came within the reach of my knowledge as both is asserted by *Alexander Garden* **M D.F.R.S.** in his Letter to John Ellis Esq. **F.R.S** dated Charles Town South Carolina August 14th 1774–nor have I ever heard of any ones being kil'd by them according to this Gentlemans Account—and in this manner I shall make it my business to Confute all the Errors that come within the Circle of my Compass, by whatever Author they may be Stated without exception, as a Duty to Myself in Particular, and to the World in General—

This day I was also informed of some Cruelties which I must Still relate before my Departure, as motives to deter others from the abominable Practices. Some at which Humanity must Shrink and Seeken—what Reader will believe that a *Jewes*[s] from a Motive of *Groundless* Jealousy /for such her Husband made it to appear/–I say who can believe that this unprecedented Monster put an end to the Life of a young and beautiful Quadroon Girl, by the infernal means of plunging a red hot Poker in her Body, by those parts which decency forbids to mention, while for a Crime of such a verry hellish nature, the Murderer was only banished to the Jew Savanah, a Village I shall afterwards describe besides paying a trifling fine to the Fiscal who is a Magistrate—

Another Young Negro Woman having her ancles chained so close together, that she could hardly move her feet, was knocked down with a Cane by a Jew, till the blood streamed out of her head, her arms and her naked Sides—

Still a third Israellite had dared to Strike one of my Soldiers for having made water against his Gardenfence, on this Rascal I took revenge for the whole fraternity by wresting the offending weapon out of his hand which I instantly broke to thousand pieces on his Guilty naked pate—

I nevertheless was just enough to flog another of my Men out of the Regiment for picking a Smouses Pocket, So Jealous are the Dutch Soldiers of what they please to call a point of Honour, that were a thief to be known in the ranks, the whole Regiment would lay down their Arms—this etiquet is not amiss and would be of no bad Consequence to be introduced in some other Armeys, where a thief is as good as another if he is born to be 6 feet high—

Enough—of Cruelties, but which I am obliged to relate, and which I hope will make it the more excusable when I introduce Sometimes Scenes of a more lively Nature however inconsistent with either natural History or the account of a Military Expedition—I wish to diversify the Sable Scenes of Horror, by the more cheering Sunshine of Content, And to variegate this Work in such a manner /if possible/ as to make it please both the Stern Grim Philosopher, and the Youthful, the beautiful and innocent Maid; This shall ever be my desire and my Study—

This day also Colonel Fourgeoud Issued the following Orders, viz, that in Case on any Military Duty it ever happened that 2 Officers or under Officers of equal rank should meet the one of *his* Corps the other of the Society that in that Case the first should take the Command, independent of the others Seniority, without the latter bore a higher Commission—And now for *vincere out mory,* with the wooden walls of the Colony the props of Surinam viz. half a Dozen of Crazy old Sugar Barges, such as are used by the Colliers on the Thames only being roofed over with boards which made them have the more the appearance of so many *Coffins*[—]How well they deserved this Name I am afraid I shall too soon make appear by the number of Men they have buried—

With one of these Vehecles of destruction departed this very day for the Jews Savanah up the river Surinam Major Medler 2 Subalt.ⁱ 1 Serjeant 2 Corporals and 28 Men, Thus after having been kept fidling, dancing, and dying for 5 Months at Paramaribo the Manoeuvres were fairly begun—

To day departed for the River Comewina one Capt.ⁿ 2 Subalt.ˢ—1 Serjeant 2 Corporals and 18 Men—I cannot help making mention of a very singular Circumstance that happened to the Captain Just Mentioned, whose Name is *Tulling Van Olden Barnevelt* the first day we landed in this Colony—Having entered the Lodgings on which he was billetted—his Landlady declared that she should ever pride herself in showing all the Civility in her Power to either Marines or Navy Officers, as she owed her Life to one of them who had some Years before picked her up in an open boat with several others, after they had 16 Days being tosted about without either Compass, Sail or Provisions /a little Sea bisquit and water excepted/ in the Atlantick ocean. To make the Story short Cap.tⁿ Tulling Van olden Barnevelt was the individual Officer who had saved her from the Jaws of Death, he having at that time belonged to the Navy as Lieut of a Dutch Man of War—

To Day departed also another Barge with 2 Subalt.ˢ one Serjeant one Corporal and 14 Men Commanded by Lieut Count Randwyck to the river Pirica—In the evening having entertained some Select Friends at my house–remembering the Motto—

Ede bibe lude nam post Mortam nulla est voluptas

And /my lost bunch of Keys being renewed at 5 S.ʰ Sterl: each*/ I having lock'd up all my effects, I took my last farewell from the lovely Joanna to whose Care I left my all and herself to the protection of her Mother and Aunt with my directions for putting her to School till my return after which–I at last marched on board, with 4 Subalt.ˢ 2 Serjeants 3 Corporals and 32 Men, under my Command, to be divided in 2 barges, and bound for the upper part of the River Cottica–Now my Mulatto—

—Cast a mournfull Look
Hung on my hand and then dejected Spoke
Her Bosom laboured with a boding Sigh
And the big tear stood trembling in her Eye

The above Barges were all arm'd with Swivels–blunderbusses &c–and provided with allowance for one Month theyr orders were /that which went to the Jew Savanah excepted/ to cruise up and down the rivers while each barge had a Pilot and was rowed by Negro Slaves, 10 of which were on board for the purpose and which made my Compliment including my black Boy Quaco exactly 36—

With this Ships Company was I stowed on my Hencoop–while on my Lieut.ˢ Barge were but 29 People thus had they rather more room— I must take Notice that from our first Landing in Surinam till now our Private Men were paid in Silver Coin, which the Captains had proposed to exchange for card Money at the rate of 10 P.ʳ Cent gain for *them*, by which the poor fellows would have benefitted between 2 and 300 Pound Sterling P.ʳ Year to buy Refreshment—But Colonel Fourgeoud insisted they should Continue to receive their little Cash in Coin which in small Sums was no more value than paper and I thought un-

* —All Iron work is exceedingly dear in this Colony and takes rust imediately from the perspiration occasioned by the great heat of the Climate—

1773 — JULY 2

accountably hard, Since this was hurting the whole without profit to one single Individual—

One thing more I must remark and I have done which is that all the Officers who were now going out upon Duty Continued to pay at the Mess—which cost each Captain at the rate of £40 and for which in his barge he was to receive after the rate of 10£ thus lost 30£—and this consisted in Salt Beef* pork and Peas, on an equal footing with the private Soldiers a few bottles of wine excepted—which was peculiarly hard for me and my officers, as we were going to be Stationed where absolutely no refreshment of any kind was to be met with, being surrounded with the most horrid and inpenetrable woods, beyond the hearing of a Cannon-Shot from any port or plantation whatsoever— This was not the Case with the other barges which were Stationed in the middle of Pease and plenty being within view of the most beautiful Estates—we were pitied by all ranks without exception, who foreseeing our approaching Calamities Crowded my barge with the best of what they had to give us, and which they insisted upon my accepting of—while Gratitude claims my Specifying their Generosity on the annex'd small List—Just as I found it—

24 bottles of best claret	6 Bottles of Muscadelle wine
12 D? of Madeira	2 Gallons of Lemon Juice
12 D? of English Porter	2 Gallons of Grinded Coffee
12 D? of D? Cyder	2 large Westphalia hams
12 D? of Jamaica Rum	2 Salted Bullocks Tongues
2 large Loaves of white Sugar	1 Bottle with Durham Mustard
1 Gallon of D? Candy	12 Spermacety Candles—

Having humbly beg'd my Readers Pardon for this Minute insertion to which I was alone induced by wishing to give a Sample of the Hospitality of this people, and endeavouring to show that if many of the Inhabitants of the Colony of Surinam are the dregs of the Creation by their Cruelties, brutalities &c others by their hospitality and tender feelings are an Ornament to the human Species. I say having apologized for this and perhaps some other too great Liberties—I shall end this Chapter, and prepare for the ensuing Voyage—

* —Vulgarly calld Irish Horse—though verry Justly—

Chapter 7th

Arm'd Barges are set up to defend the Rivers—Discription of the Fortress new Amsterdam—A Cruise in the upper parts of Rio Cottica and Pattamaca—Great Mortality amongst the Troops— view of the Military Post at Devils Harwar

At 4 O'Clock in the morning the fleet cast of[f] from theyr Moorings, and with the Ebtide row'd down as far as the fortress New Amsterdam where being wind bound we dropt Anchor of[f] the Battery—

I hope it will here not be out of Character to describe the dress of our Marines, which was blue turn'd up with Scarlet–Short Jackets– leather Caps, armd with a Musquet Saber and Pistol–a large wallet or knapsack across one Shoulder and theyr Hammocks Slung over the other–while in the woods they wore trowsers and check Shirts with short linnen frocks as more adapted to the Climate, indeed they Still look'd as if each Soldier could devour a Tyger by himself but how in a little time these strong and flourishing young Men were Metamorphos'd to a parcel of Smoak dried Scarcrows—My Pen is not sufficient to discribe—

I now having reviewed my forces, viz, Myself 4 Subalterns 2 Serjeants 3 Corporals 32 privates*–2 Pilots 20 Negroes and my black boy Quacco being altogether 65–next numbered them–placed the Arms Consisting in blunderbusses Swivels &c Stow'd the Luggage, and slung the Hammocks with Propriety: I then perused my Orders which consisted in Cruising up and down *Rio* Cottica between the Society Posts la *Rochell* at Patamaka and *Slands welvaeren* above the last Plantation, to prevent the Rebels from Crossing the River, to ceize or kill them if possible,

---

* —we never made use of drums [drummers] except at Paramaribo while in the Woods &c we made them serve as private Marines—

1773—JULY 3

and protect the Estates from their invasions in all which /if necessary/ I was to be assisted by the troops of the Society on the above Posts with whom I was also to deliberate on the proper Signals to be given in case of any alarm—

Having now also the time and opportunity I think it will not be Improper to use them both in giving the reader some Account of the Fortress call'd New *Amsterdam*—This piece of Fortification was begun in the Year 1734 and finished in 1747—It is built in the form of a regular Pentagon with 5 bastions, being about 3 English Miles in Circumference–Surrounded by a broad foss that is supplied from the River and defended by a Covertway well Palisaded[.] Its foundations are a kind of Rocky Ground, and its principal Strength by water a large bank of Mud off the Point Supported by a strong Battery of Cannon which prevents even flat bottomed Vessels from making any Approach in that Quarter and by crossing the fire of the Guns with the opposite Redoubts *Leyden* and *Purmerent,* protects the entry of both the River Surinam and Comewina—It has besides Powder Magazines and victualling offices well provided–all the other necessary buildings for the Supply of a strong Garrison and even a Corn Wind Mill, and Cistern that will hold above a thousand Hogsheads of fresh Water, and indeed it had need since according to my Opinion it will take the whole Army of Surinam to hold out a proper Seige for any length of time, adjoining the fortress is also a large Spot of Ground, well Stock'd with Plantains, yams &c to feed the Society Slaves that are keep'd here at the Colonys Expence to work at the Fortifications, under the inspection of a proper Overseer—On this Fort is generally keep'd a small Garison commanded by an Officer of the Artillery which makes all vessels whatever bring to, show their Colours and Salute them with 7 Guns each, which Compliment is answered with 3 Guns from the Battery and the hoisting of a flag on the Ramparts—I only shall add that this fortress is on the N.E. side surrounded with bogs and impenetrable bushes–and that the Spot was formerly called the Tigers Hole from *that,* and its very low and Marshy Situation.—

Having described fort New Amsterdam I must not leave it without taking Notice of a very remarkable fish which is always seen in great Quantities on its banks and has absolutely 4 Eyes Swimming constantly with 2 above and 2 under water these fishes are about the Size of a Smelt and Swim in Shoals with incredible Velocity; they seem principally to delight in brackish water, are no bad eating it is say'd, and are call'd *Coot-Eye* by the Inhabitants of the Colony—for some Account of this fish see Gordons Geographical Gramar where he speaks of the Dutch Settlements in Guiana—

A private Marine of Col. Fourgeoud's Corps.

London, Published Dec.r 2.d 1793, by J. Johnson, St. Paul's Church Yard.

1773—JULY 3-7

This Evening my Sentinel being insulted by a rowboat who dam'd him and his whole Crew for a parcel of useless Hectoring and Swaggering bullies, I imediately man'd the Canoo—and gave chase—but by the help of hoisting a small Sail and a dark night the rogue who kept course towards brams point had the good fortune to escape my resentment—

In the morning up Anchor and having doubled the Cape row'd with the flood till we arive before *Elizabeths Hope* a beautiful Coffee Plantation where the Proprietor Mr *Klynhams* inviting us ashoare show'd us every Civility in his Power besides loading my barge with refreshing fruits vegetables &c—He pitied our Situation he said from his heart and foretold the Miseries we were going to struggle with the Rainy Season being just at hand or indeed already commenced by frequent Showers accompanied by loud Claps of thunder "As for the Enemy" said he,

> you may depend on not seeing one single Soul of them they knowing better than to make their Appearance in Publick while they may have a chance of seeing you from under Cover, thus Sir take care to be upon your Guard—But the Climate, the Climate will murder you all. However (continued he) this shows the Zeal of your Commander who will rather see you kill'd at any rate than allow you any longer to eat the Bread of Idleness at Paramaribo

which he accompanied with a Squeeze by the Hand when we took our leave and the beautiful Mrs *Dutry* his Daughter shed tears at our departure, this Evening we anchored before the *Matapica* Creek—

I here created my 2 barges to Men of war and Christen them the *Charon* and the *Cerberus*•—by which Names I shall distinguish them during the rest of the voyage. we now kept rowing up the River Cottica, having past since we entered Rio Comewina the most enchantingly beautiful Estates of Coffee and Sugar which line the banks of both these rivers at the distance of one or two Miles from each other—

My Crew having walked and Cook'd their dinners ashoare on the Plantation *Lavanture* we anchored in the Evening before *Rio Pirica*—

We row'd still further up Rio Cottica and went a shoare on the Estate *Alia*—at all the above Plantations we were most hospitably received, which now begun to diminish as the River here begins to grow Manowar [narrower]—this Evening anchored before the Estate *Lunenburgh*—

we continued to keep Course, and having walk'd a shoare on the

---

• —The sudden Death and wilful Murder would not have been out of Character—or less applicable but with these Epithets I had at that time not yet the honour of being acquainted—

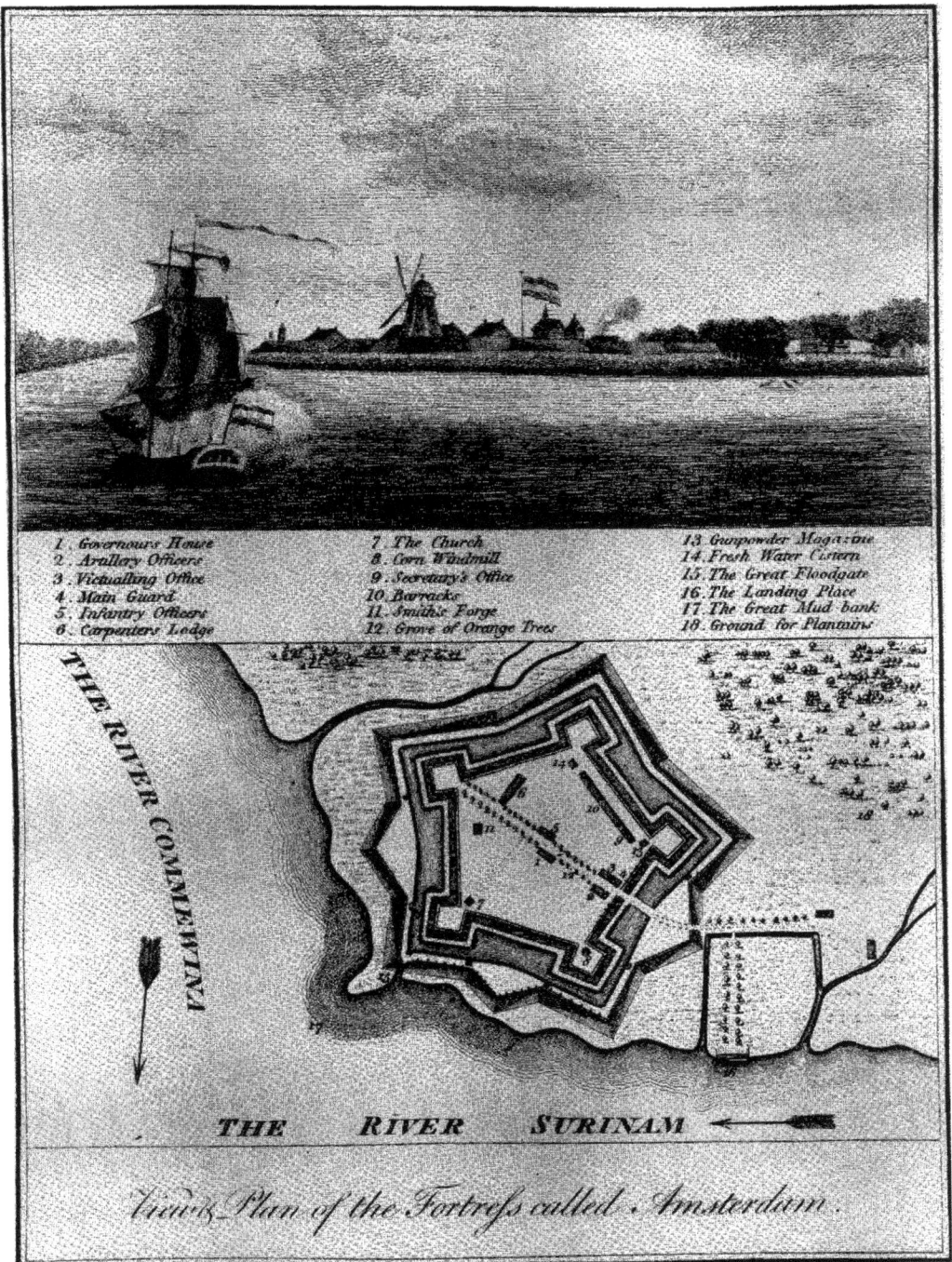

1. Governours House	7. The Church	13. Gunpowder Magazine
2. Arillary Officers	8. Corn Windmill	14. Fresh Water Cistern
3. Victualling Office	9. Secretary's Office	15. The Great Floodgate
4. Main Guard	10. Barracks	16. The Landing Place
5. Infantry Officers	11. Smith's Forge	17. The Great Mud bank
6. Carpenters Lodge	12. Grove of Orange Trees	18. Ground for Plantains

THE RIVER COMMEWINA

THE RIVER SURINAM

View & Plan of the Fortress called Amsterdam.

T. Conder Sculp.

London, Published Dec.r 1.st 1791, by J. Johnson, S.t Pauls Church Yard.

Estate *bockkesteyn* / being the last Plantation up the River Cottica on the right, except one or two small Estates in Patamaca / at night we cast anchor at the mouth of *Coopmans* Creek. today the Charon was on fire but soon extinguish'd•

We again kept rowing upwards and at Eleven OClock A.M cast anchor off the Port Slanswelvaren which was guarded by the Troops of the Society—Here I Slept ashoare with all my Officers to wait on Captain *Orzinga* the Commander and deliver 3 of my seek Men in his Hospital where I saw such a sight of Misery and wretchedness as baffles all Imagination. this place having formerly been calld *Devils Harwar* on account of its so very great unhealthiness a name by which alone I shall again distinguish it as much more Suitable than that of *Slanswelvaren* which signifies the welfare of the Nation—

Here I saw a few of the wounded wretches who had escaped from the Engagement in which Lieut. *Lepper* with so many Men had been kill'd one of whom told me the particulars of his own Miraculous Surviving—which were so very wonderful and at the same time so Authentic that I think them highly worth relating to show what in this Climate a Soldier is exposed too—

> I was shot Sir /said he/ with a Musquett bullett in my breast and to resist or escape being impossible I, as the only means left me to save my Life through [threw] Myself down amongst the deadly wounded and the dead without moving hand or foot; here in the Evening the Rebel Chief Surveying his Conquest ordered one of his Captains to begin instantly with cutting of[f] the Heads of the Slain in order to carry them home to theyr village as Trophys of their Victory which Captain having already chopp'd of[f] that of Lieut *Lepper* and one or two more said to his friend *Son de go Sleeby caba Mekewe liby den tara dago tay tamara*, the Sun is just going we must leave the other dogs till to morrow, Saying which /continued the Man/ as I lay upon my bleeding breast with my face resting upon my left Arm he dropd his Hatchet into my Shoulder by way of Gesticulation and made the fatal wound you see and of which I shall perhaps no more recover—I however lay quite Still till they went away carrying along with them the Mangled Heads of my Comrades and 5 or 6 prisoners alive with their hands tied on their backs who never more since have been heard off[.] when all was quiet and it was very dark I found means on my hands and feet to creep out amongst the Carnage & get under Cover in the forest where I met another of our Soldiers who was less wounded than Myself and with whom after 10 days wandering in torment and despair without bandages not knowing which way to go, and only one Single Loaf of black bread for all Subsistence between us

• —however contrary to reason—

we at last arrived at the Military Post of Patamaca emaciated, and our wounds creeping in live worms and Corruption—

I gave the miserable Creature half a Crown, and having agreed with Capt.ⁿ Orzinga upon the Signals we left this Pest house of the human Species and Steping on board my Man of War row'd up till before a place call'd *barbacoeba* where we once more came to an Anchor—

    We still rowed further up the River till we came before the *Coermoetibo* creek and where we finally moored the fleet as being the Spot of my head-Station by Colonel Fourgeouds Command. here we saw nothing but water, wood, and clouds which had an extremely solitary appearance—

    I detach'd the Cerberus to her Station viz. upper Patamaca & for which place she row'd imediately with a long list of Parols according to my orders but which were never of any Service—we now tried to cook the Victuals on board, our furnace being a large tub fill'd with Earth and we succeeded however at the expense of almost having Scald'd one of my Men to death, and the hazard of setting the Barge once more on fire.—we having no Surgeon along with us this Office was left to my Care together with a small Chest of Medicines and I perform'd so well that in a few Days the Marine was recovered—

    To prevent the same Accident again I sought an opening in the Creek above named, which having found not very far from the Mouth, I ordered my Negroes to build a Shade and my men to dress theyr victuals below it placing Sentinels around them to prevent a Surprise and in the Evening we return'd to our Station—This we continued to do every day till the 14.th when we row'd down to barbacoeber—

    There we did build another Shade for the same purpose and then /the rain already beating through my decks/ rowd down to Devils Harwar for repair where I put one of my Negroes Seek in the Hospital—

    I got my deck caulk'd, and payd, and did send the account of our Arrival to Colonel Fourgeoud—

    We returnd to Coermoetibo Creek having lost an Anchor amongst the roots of *Mangrove* that on both Sides line the Banks of all the rivers in the Colony—the *Man Groves* are two Species the red, and the white, but the former is that which I now Speak of—It arrises from a number of roots that emerge above Ground for Several feet high before they join together and form the trunk which is both large and tall—the bark is gray out-side but inside red and used for tanning Leather[.] its Wood is reddish hard and Good for building &c but the most remarkable is that from its extended branches and even its trunk descend thousands of ligneous Shoots like the ropes of a Ship which droping to the Earth take root, and again reascend forming for a great Circumference an inpenetrable thicket, while like so many props they do keep the tree Steady in all Weathers—the White Mangrove grows Mostly in the more distant places from the Water—This Evening my Sentinel when it was very dark call'd out he Saw a Negroe with a lighted tobacco pipe cross the coermoetibo Creek in a Canoo, which made us all leap out of our hammocks when one of my Slaves declared it was no more than a *fire flie* on the wing–which actually was the Case—these Insects are above an inch long with a round pack under the belly of a transparent Greenish Colour which in the dark gives a light like a Candle, its eyes are also very luminous[.] upon the whole by the light of a Couple of these flies one may very well see to read small print, there is another Species that are Smaller and only are observed when they fly elevated, at which time they appear like intermitting Sparks of fire, emitted from the fordge of a blacksmith—

Today I having nothing else to do Shot a bird which is here call'd a *tigri-fowlo* or Tiger-bird but which I take to be one of the heron Species–it is about the same Size but of a reddish Colour covered over with regular black Spots from which it has derived its name its bill which is long and Streight as also its legs and toes are of a pale Green Colour and seems to tell that it lives upon fish the neck is also long from which hangs down a kind of hoary feathers, on the head which is Small it has a roundish black Spot and its eyes are a beautiful Yellow—

By a Water Patrole from the Cerberus I receiv'd intelligence this Evening that the Men begun to be Seekly

I now also getting Information that on the Spot where we had dressed our Victuals in the Coermoetibo Creek, and which is on the Rebel Side of the River, a strong detachment had lately been Murdered by the Enemy ordered the Shade to be burnt to the Ground and the meat to be dress'd on board the barge—Here all the Elements now seem'd to oppose us–the *Water* pouring down like a deluge by the heavy rains forced itself fore and aft in the vessel where it set every thing a float–the *Air* poisoned by Miriads of Musquitoes that from Sun Set to Sun Rising regularly keep'd us Company, and prevented us from getting any Sleep–besides besmearing us all over with blood and blotches–the *Smoak* of the fire and the tobacco /which we burnt on their Account/ ready to choak us–and not a footstep of *Land* to cook our Salt Provisions in Safety–to all this misery we added that discord broke out between the Marines and the Negroes, on whom promises or threats having no weight–I was obliged to have recourse to other Means–viz,–I tied up the ring leaders of both parties and after ordering the first to be well flog'd, and the latter to be horsewhipt for an hour–

I pardoned them all without one Lash—this had equally the effect of the Punishment, and Peace was perfectly reestablished but to prevent approaching disease was totally out of my reach—I had indeed been told

> If you Phisitians want these are the *best*
> good air A chearful Mind Spare diet Moderate Rest—

I had also read Doctor *Armstrongs* beautiful poem upon health where he recommends *Air, exercise, diet,* and *recreation,* but here all was to no purpose—

We now row'd down till before the *Casepoere* Creek in hopes of Meeting some Relief, but were equally as bad So very thick were the Musquitoes now that by Clapping my two hands against each other I have kill'd in one Stroke to the number of 38 upon my honour—

We again rowd down to Barbacoeber during which we saw one or two beautiful Snakes Swim across the River and where by Stepping a Shoare under the Shade I have mentioned we met with a little relief I now had recourse to the advice of an old Negroe—"Cramaca /said I/ what do you do to keep your health"—

> Swim every day twice or thrice Sir /said he/ in the Water, this *Masera* not only serves for Exercise where I can not walk but keeps my Skin clean and cool while the poares being open, I enjoy a free Perspiration, without this by unperceivable filth the poares are shut—the Joyces [juices] Stagnate and Corruption must inevitably follow.

having recompenced the old Gentleman with a Dram I instantly Strip'd and plung'd headlong into the River I had however no sooner taken this leap than he call'd to me for Gods Sake to return on board which having done with much astonishment he put me in Mind of the *Aligators,* besides a fish which is here call.ᵈ *Pery*—

> both these Sir /said he/ are exceedingly dangerous, but by following my directions you will run no hazard—you may Swim as naked as you was born but only take Care that you Constantly keep in Motion for the Moment you are Quiet you run the risk not only of their Snapping of[f] a Limb but of being drag'd yourself to the bottom—•

I acknowledge his Account rather made the [me?] backward[.] still seeing the Example with Success, I had the resolution to follow it and

• —This is confirm'd by Do: Bancroft who says the Indians in Swiming take Care to Continue in Motion by which means the fish are frightened and keep at a distance but Mʳ Wesley has been egregiously mistaken when he asserts that this King of the Reptiles cannot bite under Water, as I shall in future prove the Contrary by Occular Demonstration—

reap'd the benefit so long as I was in the Colony—this Negroe also advised me to walk barefooted and thinly dressd,

> now is the season Masera /say'd he/ to use your feet to become hard by walking on the Smooth boards of the Vessel the time may come when you will be obliged to do so for want of Shoes in the middle of thorns and briers as I have seen some others–custom said he massera is second nature our feet were all made alike do so as I advise you and in the end you will thank old Cramaca—as for being thinly dress'd /continued the Negroe,/ a shirt and trowsers is fully sufficient which not only saves Trouble and expense but the Body wants *Air* as well as it does Water, thus bathe in both when you have the Opportunity—

I from that moment followed his wise Counsel to which besides being Cleanly and Cool I in great part ascribe the Preservation of my life—

I now often thought on Paramaribo where I enjoyed all the delicasies of life, while here I was forced to Shift much worse than any Savage yet should I not have repined [= complained] had any one profitted by our Sufferings, but I am forgetting the Articles of War, viz, bluntly obey and ask no Questions

Having mentioned the *Aligator* in Surinam call'd the *Kaiman* I shall here give some account of that very destructive Anthropophaga–it is an Amphibious Annimal and found in most Rivers in Guiana–its Size is from 4 to 18 or 20 feet in length the tail as long as the Body both of which are on the upper part indented like a Saw its Shape being Something like a Lizard–the Colour on the back is a Yellowish brown approaching black variegated on the Sides, with Greenish Shades the belly being a dirty white the head is large with a Snout and Eyes something resembling those of a Sow, the last immoveable it is sayd and guarded each by a large Protuberance or hard knob, the Mouth and throat extremely wide are beset with double rows of teeth that can Snaip almost through a bone, it has 4 feet arm'd with Claws 5 before & 4 behind and hard Sharp pointed Nails–this whole Annimal is covered over with large Scales and a Skin so thick that it is invulnerable even by a Musquet Ball except in the head or the belley where it is most liable to be wounded, its flesh is eat by the Natives but is of a Musky taste and Savour owing it is said to a kind of bags or bladders inside of each Limb, the Aligator lays its Eggs the Size of those of a Gooze in the Sand on Shoare to a great number where they are hatch'd by the Sun, the Males eating the Greatest Quantity of them, on Land this Animal is not Dangerous for Want of Activity but in the rivers where he is often seen lurching for his Prey with his Musle alone above Water,

The Leguana or Iguana Lizard of Guiana.

The Alligator or Cayman of Surinam.

1773—JULY 21, 22

Something like the Stump of an old Tree, he is truly tremenduous for all that comes in his Way—yet for Man he is afraid as I have said during the time he keeps his hands and feet in Motion but no longer, some Negroes even have the Courage to attack, and vanquish the Aligator in his own element, notwithstanding his violent Strength and unequall'd ferocity he being particularly fond of human flesh—

In Surinam is also found the *Crocodile* which differs in this with the Aligator that his body is more Slender & is absolutely not so ferocious—it is I think erroneously say'd that of both the above Animals the upper Jaw alone is Moveable*

In this Country are Lizards to the Size of 5 or 6 feet but that Species which is here call'd the *Leguana* and by the Indians the wayamaca is seldom above 3 feet long from the head to the extremity of the Tail—it is covered over with Small Scales, reflecting very brilliant Colours in the Sun—the back and legs being of a dark blue, the Sides and belly of a Yellowish kind of Green as also the bag or loose Skin which hangs under its throat. it is Spotted in many Parts with brown and black and its eyes are a beautiful pale red while the Claws are of a deep Chesnut Colour—

This Lizard like the Aligator has its back and tail indented which both are formed into a Sharp edge it lays its Eggs upon the Sand—is often seen amongst the Shrubs and plants where the Indians shoot it with bow and Arrow who esteem its flesh as a great delicacy, nay they are even sold dear at Paramaribo and bought as a Dainty by many of the White Inhabitants who are exceedingly fond of it—this Creature's bite is extremely painful but seldom attended with bad Consequences—

Having today sent my Serjeant and 1 Man sick to the hospital at Devils Harwar we now row'd again to the head-Station before Coermoetibo Creek—

Here to Day one of my Negroes catch'd some fish amongst which was the torporific Eel already described, which he dress'd and eat with his Companions—the others were the *Pery* & *Que Quee* the Pery was that mention'd by the old Slave as very dangerous—this fish is sometimes near 2 feet long of a flatish make Scaly and of a blewish Colour, the Mouth large and thick set with Sharp teeth, which are so strong and the Pery so voracious that it frequently Snaps of[f] the feet of

---

* —at Maestricht in 1781 I saw the head of a Crocodile putrified which had been then dug out of Mount-Saint Piere the body of which by Calculation must have Measured above 60 feet long. Query when or how did this trophical Animal come there, yet there with Astonishment I beheld it—

Ducks when Swiming—nay even the fingers and breasts of women and private Parts of Men—by not having kept moveing while in the Water—the *Que-Quee* may be call'd a fish in Armour being covered over from head to tail with brown Coloured moveable rings Slyding the one over the other and joined like those of a lobster or an Iron harness which serve for its defense in place of Scales, this last is from 6 to 10 Inches with a large head, and of a roundish Shape—both the Pery and the Que-Quee are very good eating—but I must for some time lay aside the descriptive parts and return to my Journal—

    This being the day appointed Between Capt.ⁿ Orzinga and me to try the Signals, at 12 OClock precisely the whole Blunderbusses and Swivels were fired at Devils Harwar on board the Charon, and on board the Cerberus still Stationed at Patamaca, which afterwards proved to be ineffectual and to no purpose, no one having been able to hear the report of the Guns fired by the other—during this however I met with a Small accident viz, by firing myself one of the blunderbusses which having placed like a Musquet against my Shoulder I received such a violent Stroke by its repulsion as through [threw] me backw.^{ds} over a large hogshead with Irish beef, and had nearly dislocated my right Arm—this it seems was owing to my Ignorance of the Manoeuvre, as being since told that all such Weapons ought to be fired under the hand /especially when they are heavy charged/ and when by swinging round the body at once with the Arm the force of the Repulsion is broke without effect—My inserting this is only to show in what manner heavy loaded Muscatoons ought always to be fired, especially since without any Aim the execution of their wide Mouth is equally fatal—

    Getting now an account by a Canoe that came down from Patamaca that the Cerberus was in danger of being attacked by the Enemy who had been Spied hoverring round about her, and the river where she was moor'd being very narrow I imediately /having row'd the Charon up till before the Pinneburgh creek/ mann'd the Yoll as being the most expeditious, and went myself with 6 Men to her Assistance, when the whole proved to be a false alarm and in the Evening return'd back to our Station—in rowing down I was surpriz'd to be haild by a human Voice, which beg'd me for Gods sake to step ashoare, this I did with 2 of my Men when I was accosted by a poor old Negro Woman imploring me for some assistance, it seem'd she was the property of a Jew, to whom belong'd the Spot of Ground where I found her, & where the Poor Creature lived quite alone in a hut not larger than a Dogs Nest, Surrounded by a Wildnerness except a few *Plantain* trees, *Yams* and *Cas-*

1773—JULY 26, 27

sava• for her Support[.] She was of no more use to work on the Great Estate and was banished here only to Support her Masters right to the Possession Since this Spot had been ruined by the Rebels—having left her with a Piece of Salt Beef Some Barley and a bottle of Rum I took my leave when she offered me in Return one of her *Cats,* but to no purpose the row Negroes firmly insisting that she was a witch—which shows that Superstition reigns not only in Europe—

In this Creek the banks of which on both sides are Covered with Mangroves, thorns and briars, we found floating on the Surface of the Water a kind of large white *nuts* which seem'd to have drop'd themselves by ripeness from the Shell, they were sweet crisp and exceedingly Good eating, but I neglected to enquire from what tree they were produced—a kind of Water Shrub call'd the *Mocco-Mocco,* is here new to be met with in great Quantities. it grows about 6 or 8 feet high thick at bottom, jointed and prickly all the way to the top where it is very Small & divided in 3 or 4 large Smooth Oval leafs, which possess almost the Quality of blistering by the violence of theyr drawing and attraction—coming near the Charon in the Evening I found my Sentinel fast asleep—which enraged me so much that having quietly entered on board the barge I fired my pistole closs to his Ear Just over his head, Swearing I should the next time blow it through his brains, the whole Crew flew to theyr Arms and the poor fellow had nearly leap'd in the Water while Mitigation was certainly here his due, since by the Musquitoes none could dose only now and then by intervals excepted—

We now returned to Coermoetibo Creek where this Day my Negroes having been ashore to cut Wood for the furnace brought on board a poor Animal alive with all its 4 feet chop'd off with the bill hook and which lay still in the bottom of the Canoo, having freed it from its torment by a blow in the head, I was acquainted that this was the *Sloth* call'd *loyaree* or *Hiaey* by the natives on account of its plaintive voice, it is about the Size of a Small Water-Spaniel with a round head Something like that of a Monkey, but its mouth is remarkably large its hinder legs were much Shorter than those before to help it in climbing•• being each armd with 3 tremenduous Sharp Claws, which are all its defence and which had induced my Slaves to Commit the above Amputation, its eyes are languid and its Motion is so slow, that it takes 2 days to get to the top of a Moderate Tree from which it never descends while a leaf

• —which I shall discribe on another Occasion—

•• —Not longer according to Mr Hartsink—

The Ai, & the Unau; or the Sheep & Dog Sloth.

London, Published Dec.r 2nd 1795, by J. Johnson, St. Paul's Church Yard.

or a bud is remaining, beginning its devestation first at the top, to prevent its being Starved in coming to the bottom when it goes in Quest of another, making incredible little way when on the Ground— Of these Animals there are two Species in Guiana distinguished by the names of *Sicapo* and *Dago* loyaree viz. the Sheep and the dog Sloth which some Authors call the *Ai* and the *Unan* the first has a long kind of clowdel[?] hair of a Greenish Gray like faded Grass and only 28 Ribs the others hair is lank and of a reddish Colour its head is not so round, it has 46 Ribs and only 2 Claws on each foot, this and both being of a roundish figure makes them look more like an excressence in the trunk than like an Animal feeding on the Tree which often prevents them from being discovered by theyr Enemies–the Sloth has a soft squeeking Voice like a young Cat; is different in its generative parts, from all other Quadrupedes and is eat with avidity by the indians and negroes

Now came down from Patamaca in an open Canoo and burning Sun Lieut. Stromer the Commander of the Cerberus in a violent fever, drinking Cold Water from the River for all relief, also a Jew Soldier* of the Society Port La Rochelle with the account that the Rebels had actually past the Creek above the last Estate two days before as had been reported viz, from E. to W. at the same time delivering me a Negro Woman and sucking Child who had formerly been Stole by the Rebels, and now had found means to make her Escape. from below I received also the news that Major Medlar had sent to Town from the Jew Savanah 2 barbaccu'd hands of the Enemy kill'd by the rangers–that an Officer and 10 Men were landed at Devils Harwar with Provisions under my Command, and that one of my Seek Men there had died– yet an Order from Fourgeoud to seek out if possible a dry Spot to build a Magazine—I now having detached my Lieut. Mr *Hammer* to take the Command of the Cerberus at Patamaca instantly weighed, and row'd down till before the Casipoery Creek where we past such a Night as no Pen can discribe being crowded with all Sorts of People, the Seek Groand, the Jew prayd, the Soldiers Swore, the Negroes beg'd, the Women Sung the Child Skweek'd the fire Smoaked, the Rains poured down and the whole Stunk to such a Degree that I vow to God I began to think myself little better off than in the black Hole of Calcutta. Heaven and Earth all seemed now to Conspire against us, however at 6 oClock next Morning the Joyful Sun broke through the Clouds, and I drop'd down with the Charon til before Devils Harwar—

Here now I delivered my Seek Officer and 5 Seek Men besides my

• —Several Jews were Soldiers in the Society Troops—

other Passengers, on whom I had done all that was in my Power but that was very little & having also stow'd the newly arriv'd Provisions in a proper place. I onced more returned to my Cursed Station where I came to an Anchor on August the first—

&. Now between the Showers we saw great Quantities of Monkeys of which I shot one and having had no fresh Meat for a Long time I got it dress'd and eat it with a good appetite, we were at this time really in a Shocking Condition, not only wanting refreshment but all the Mens Shoes and Hammocks were rotting from day to day being /besides mostly wet/ composed of the very worst Ingredients sent from Holland—

&. Got the Account that Lieut. Stromer was dead at Devils Harwar—

&. We drop'd down till before that Place to bury him decently but such was utterly impossible, since having contrived to make a Coffin of old boards, the Corps[e] drop'd through it before it reach'd to the Grave and afforded absolutely a shocking Spectacle, we nevertheless found means to go through the rest of the Interment with some decorum, having covered it over with a Hammock by way of a Pall, and fired 3 Volleys by all the Troops that had strength to Carry Arms, this over I regaled the Officers on a Glass of Wine, and once more took farewell of Devils Harwar on the 6th, having first wrote Colonel Fourgeoud that the Rebels were past above La Rochelle and that I had found a Spot for a Magazine at Barbacoeba, Also the Death of my Lieut Mr *Stromer,* and recomended my Serjeant /who had been an officer Hussars/ for advancement

I think /to give the reader some Idea of this Spot/ I will here take the opportunity to discribe it—This was in former times a Plantation but is now entirely occupied by the Military who keep here a Post to defend the upper parts of the River Cottica—the Soil is elevated and dry, which makes it the more remarkable that it should be so very unwholesome yet such it certainly is, and here hundreds of Soldiers had been buried—it lies on the Right Side of the River—in going upwards and had some time ago a Path of Communication with the River Pirica /on which were a few Military Guards/ but which is now little or not frequented and overgrown in a perfect Wilderness. The buildings in Devils Harwar are all made of the *Pina* or *Manicole* Tree, which Tree and the manner of using it for Houses &c I shall afterwards I hope compleatly describe, but now must content myself /on account of want of time/ with only saying that on this post the buildings consisted in a Dwelling for the Commanding Officer with 4 very good rooms, another Ditto for the Subalterns, a Good lodge for the private Soldiers, an hospital for the

Seek /which is large and roomy, and so it had need being never without Inhabitants/ a Powder and Victualling Magazine, proper Kitchens, a Bakehouse &c besides a Well with fresh Water. the Society Troops also keep a Stock of Sheep, pigs, and Poultry at this place to use only for the Hospital alone, here was at this time yet a Cow which had been allotted for the Rangers after *Boucou* was taken, but the feast had not been kept at this place. She had now a Calf and afforded Milk for the Officers to theyr Tea &c, but for we poor Devils in the barges were nothing at all of the kind. Some of the Officers here also had little Gardens with Sallads &c. what makes Devils Harwar so unhealthy in my opinion are the Miriads of Musquitos that hinder the People from taking rest, and the Quantity of *Chigoes* or Sand fleas, which here abound, a dangerous insect, of which I must also reserve the discription till another occasion—

I Arrived now again at Coermoetibo Creek, where I resolved to make a landing on the West Shore at every hazard, for my *own* Soldiers to cook their beef, and barley /it being just as well to be shot by the Enemy at once, as to be kill'd on board the Charon by Inches,/ however this was a difficult task, all that Shore being so very Marshy, and overgrown with every kind of underwood that we could hardly put our new project in Execution–till at last my Negroes having made a temporary kind of bridge /to Step from the Yol upon a Small Speck of dry Ground/ and having form'd a slight Shade of Manicole Leafs to keep of[f] the Rayn, we found means to keep in a fire, and be a hundred times better than we were on board the Charon—

But here our Danger was certainly also much greater since an old Rebel Settlement was not very far from this place call'd *Pinneburgh* /from a neighbouring Creek though others say it got this name on account of the Sharp Pins stuck in the Ground like *Crowfeet* or *cheval-de-frise* with which the Rebels had formerly fortified and defended it,/ and notwithstanding this Village had been demolished it was well known that the Rebels still often visited the Spot, to pick up some of the ryst, Yams and Casadas, which the Ground Continued /in its barren State/ to produce for /now and then/ a temporary Subsistence, and was I almost morally convinced that the Rebels who had lately past above La Rochelle in Pattamaca were at this Moment incamp'd at the above Spot *Pinneburgh,* ready to Commit some Depredations, on the Estates In the Rivers Cottica or Pirica, if not to attack our selves for which reason I always keep'd double Sentinels round the landing place, and orders that no Man should be allowed to speak or make any manner of noise while on that Spot, in order to hear even the Smallest rusling of a Leaf and prevent danger by vigilance and Alacrity—

View of the Post Devil's Harwar, on Rio Cottica.

The Armed Barges, commanded by Capt.ⁿ Stedman.

London, Published Decr 1.st 1791, by J. Johnson, St Paul's Church Yard.

1773—AUGUST 8

To Day my other Officer *Macdonald* fell seek but refused to be sent to Devils Harwar on account of leaving me thus quite by myself—I have say'd that we had no Surgeon but a parcel of Medicines, these which consisted in emitics–Laxatives–and Powders /of which I knew not the proper use/ I at their desire dayly distributed to the Men, who loading their Hammocks [stomachs] with heavy salt Provisions and no exercise, had actually sometimes need of art to assist nature, while these briny Meals of Pork and beef, Col: Fourgeoud insisted on, to be much wholesomer food in a tropical Climate than fresh provisions– which he say'd by the heat corrupted in the Stomack whereas the others underwent a proper digestion and this may be perfectly true for those whose Stomacks were strong enough to support the Argument but of such were but few on board either the Cerberus or the Charon–I had also some Plaisters on board the barge, but these were indeed very soon expended by the running ulcers which covered over all the Crew, and this was easily accounted for, since in this Climate /where the Air is impregnated with Miriads of invisible annimalcules/ the Smallest Scratch imediately becomes a running Sore, and scraching must be daily occupation, where one is covered over with Musquitoes &c I have say'd the best Antidote and cure was lemon or lime acid, but this we had not; the next is never to expose an open wound or even the smallest Scratch to the Air but the Instant they are received to cover them up with a grey Paper wetted with Spirits, or any kind of Moisture, So that it may Stick to the Skin—for my own part no Man could still continue to be more healthy, wearing nothing but my long trowsers and check Shirt loose at the Collar and turnd up in the Sleeves, nay even when the Sun was not too hot, I stript altogether to the Buff, and every day twice Continued to plump into the river—by this I was always cool and clean–besides there is a kind of pleasure in rambling naked when the occasion will permit it, which I always envied the Indians and Negroes, and of which only those few can have any Idea, who have tried the experiment, and delight in following these rules, which kind nature by an unerring precept has prescribed them–I also dayly used a cheering Glass of Wine having first hung it a few fathoms under Water which made it much more cool and agreeable—But during all these hardships, I must not forget that our troubles were recompensed by a few *Marcusas* that we found in this place, which had been left there standing since the Estate many years by-gone had been destroyed. they were indeed but one single old Tree; But the Marcusas rather grows on a Shrub, to speak properly and consists in a delicious fruit of an oval form, and of an Orange or Golden die the blossom like the passion-flour; most are larger, and some less than a hens Egg, and are in the same manner broke open, when they inclose an ash Colour Succulent Jelley full of Small Seeds, which one drinks out of the Shell being Sweet mixed with acid, of a delicious flavour, and so cool that it put me in mind of Ice Mamelade. another thing were the beautiful Butterflies particularly those of an azure blew, which are exceedingly large and between the Showers Skimd and hover'd amongst the Green boughs, to which their Ultramarine line, brightened by the Sun, bore the most enchanting Contrast, but as I could not catch one of them I must delay any further description—

This Eevening we heard the Sound of a Drum which We could Suppose to be no other than that of the Rebels, nevertheless we determined to Continue dressing our Victuals ashoare, keeping on our Guard /according to the advice of M:r Kleyhans/ who had exactly foretold what now befel us—

This Day M:r Macdonald was much Worse, however by seeing me receive a Letter from Col: Fourgeoud he seem'd to revive, /as we did all/ expecting now to be reliev'd from our horrid Situation. But what was our Mortification at Reading that we were Still to Continue on the cursed Station /by his order who like a true General was Relentless of our Misery and Complaints/ which Letter was accompanied by a present of fish hooks and tackle, to make up for the deficiency of other refreshments, and indeed Salt Provisions which began dayly to grow both worse and less—

Timeo Danaeos et Dona ferentes.
—virgil—

And so it was, while the whole Crew bore distraction in their Countenances declaring they were Sacrificed to no manner of purpose and while the Negroes sigh'd, pronouncing the Words *Ah Poty backera.* however by a few Tamarinds, Oranges, Lemons and Madeira Wine which were by this Occasion sent me by my best *friend* at Paramaribo, I found means to give not only to my Officers, but also to my drooping Soldiers some relief—but this cheering Sunshine could not last Long and the Day following we were as much distress'd as ever—when I had once more recourse to the nimble fraternity of the forest, and brought down 2 Monkeys with my Gun from the top of the Mangroves, where they were Skipping not by Douzens but by Hundreds—

Sent 2 Men seek to the Hospital. this Evening again heard the Drums—

By a Hurricane about Noon the Charon broke loose from her Anchors and was drove a Shoare, getting her upper Works terribly damaged by the Stumps of Trees &c that hung over The River while the

Water from the Clouds broke in upon us like a torrent—

- Came down seek from the Cerberus the other Officer S. Lieut. *Baron Ower* whom at his Request I ventured to send down to Paramaribo—I now received another Letter from Collonel Fourgeoud with a little Money for the Men to buy refreshments where nothing was to be met with, but not a Word of our going to be relieved—
- S: Lieut Cattenburgh fell Seek next at Devils Harwar where he had the Care of the last come Pork and Peas—
- Ordered En: Macdonald /Who was rather better/ to take the Command in his Place, and send him imediately to Paramaribo also get Report that the Cerberus having only 4 private Men left was retired to the Post at La Rochelle—
- I sent 2 of my Men to her Assistance and ordered her back to her former Station—
- I at last fell Seek myself and upon the whole was now truly in a Pitiful Condition, deprived of both my Officers and my Serjeant, my Men upon the three Stations /viz. the 2 barges, and Devils Harwar together/ melted down to only 15 from the 42 without a Surgeon or Refreshment surrounded with a black forrest, and exposed to the Mercy of a relentless Enemy should he be Inform'd of our defenceless Situation—the remaining few declaring they were doom'd to destruction, and who could hardly be prevented from rising in rebellion, and going down the River Cottica with the Charon against my orders. but how little reason is there in a Common Soldier, had they only Considered that our Commander in Chief had other Fish to fry at Paramaribo, Where he made wise Plans for his ensuing Campaigns, and wrote Letters to Holland with an account of his already begun Exploits, which to be sure had a much better grace, and more martial appearance from the number of Dead, /no Matter in what manner they were kil'd/ that where [were] mentioned in their bloody Contents, Indeed I myself was not altogether free from making some unfavourable reflections, such as that the Enemy having cross'd the Pattamaca Creek, A few troops from all Quarters ought to have march'd against them, that is from *La Rochelle, Devils Harwar* and the *River Pirica,* when betwixt the three, the Enemy might have been /if not intirely rooted/ at least call'd to a very severe account for their Presumption—besides by Appearance saving the Lives and Property of those Victims, which after such incursions are generally devolted to theyr rage. But all such reflections and many more we must impute to the effects of a frenzy fever, which seem'd already to have affected my Pericranium—
- I was rather a little better this Day and between the fits of the fever Shot a Couple of large black Monkeys, to make some broth, by way

of Refreshment, which /however uncommon and Strange it may appear to the reader/ I had /nevertheless/ found to be extremely good, while this may be owing in part to my being in Want of other fresh provisions—

But as the killing of the one was attended with such Circumstances, as for ever after had almost deter'd me from going a Monkey hunting I must beg leave to relate them as they happened—Seeing me on the Side of the River in the Canoo the Creature made a Stop from Skipping after his Companions, and /being perch'd on a branch that hung over the Water/ examined me with attention and the greatest Marks of Curiosity, no doubt taking me for a Giant of his own Species, while he shewed his teeth perhaps by way of laughing—chattered prodigiously—and kept dancing and shaking of the bough on which he rested with incredible strength and velocity—at this time I lay'd my Piece to my Shoulder and brought him down from the Tree plump in the Stream but may I never again be more Witness to such a Scene, the Miserable Annimal was not dead but mortally Wounded, thus taking his Tail in both my Hands to end his torment, I swong him round and knock'd his head against the Sides of the Canoo with such a force, that I was covered all over with blood and brains; but the Poor thing still continued alive, and looking at me in the most Pitiful manner that can be conceived, I knew no other Means to end this Murder than by holding him under Water till he was drown'd, while my heart felt Seek on his account; here his dying little Eyes still Continued to follow me with seeming reproach till their light gradually forsook them and the wretched Creature expired. never Poor Devil felt more than I on this occasion, nor could I taste of him or his Companion when they were dress'd, who afforded to some others a delicious repast and which ended the Catastrophe—

That Monkies are no bad food may easily be accounted for, especially when young, since they feed on nothing but fruit, nuts, Eggs, young birds &c they being both frivivorous and Carnivorous; and indeed in my opinion *all* young Quadrupedes are eatable, but when one Compares those kill'd in the Woods to those filthy disgusting creatures, that disgrace the Streets, no wonder that they should turn the Stomach of the most famished. as for the wild ones I have eat them boild, roasted, and stew'd, and found their flesh white juicy and Good; the only thing which disgusted me—being their little hands, and their heads, which when dress'd by being depriv'd of the Skin look like the hands and the Skull of a young infant—I have already observed that they are in Guiana of many different Species, and according to Do. Bancroft from a large *Orangoutang* to the very small *Sanguinkee*, however of the former I never have heard Speaking while I was in this Country, as for the latter I shall discribe him in his turn when he shall give me the opportunity, and only now give an account of those whom I have met with on this Cruise

That which I shot the 2^d Inst. is what is call'd in Surinam *Meecoo,* it is near the Size of a Fox and of a reddish gray Colour with a black Head and very long tail—those I kil'd the 10th were indeed exceedingly beautiful, and much more delicate when dress'd than the former, they are call'd the *keesee-keesee* by the Inhabitants, are about the Size of a rabbit and most astonishingly nimble—their Colour is reddish all over the body and the tail, which is long, and the extremity of which is black, but orange are its four feet—the head is very round the face milk white with a round black pach in the middle, in which are the mouth and the nostrils, and which give it a Mask-like appearance, its eyes are black and remarkably lively—these Monkies we saw dayly pass along the Sides of the river, Skipping from Tree to Tree, but mostly about Midday, and in very numerous bodies, regularly following each other like a little army with their young ones on their backs not unlike little knapsacks, their manner of travelling is by the formost walking to the extremity of a bough, from which it bounds. On the extremity of that belonging to the next Tree, at a most astonishing distance, and with such wonderful activity and precision that it never once misses its aim, while all the others, one by one, /and even the females with theyr little ones on their backs which Sticks fast to the mother like burs/ perform the same leap with the greatest seeming fasility and Safety; they are also remarkable in climing up alongst the nebees, or natural ropes, with which many parts of the forest are interwoven—and make it look like the rigging of a fleet at anchor. The Monkeys I am told have Sometimes two young but of their sucking them like the human Species I have been a Witness. this kind towards Sun set clamber up to the tops of the Palm trees /some of which are above One hundred feet in height/ where they sleep Safe in the large diverging branches—the *keesee-keesee* is such a beautifull and delicate form'd Creature, that it is by many people keep'd as a pet to a Silver Chain, besides its Mimice[?] Drolleries, its good nature, and chirping voice which pronounces *Peeteeco-Peeteeco* without intermission—they are easily tamed and the way to take them is by a strong Glue, made by the Indians, and which is something like our European bird Lime—The other Species of which I gave the horrid account were call'd by my Negroes *Monkee-Monkee* the only thing further that I can say of them is that they are in Size between the two former described, and all over black—one thing I ought not to omit which is very remarkable viz that one morning I saw from my barge a

The Mecvo & Kishee-Kishee Monkeys.

Monkey of this kind, down to the Waters edge, rincing his Mouth and appearing to clean his Teeth with one of his fingers—he was first discovered by one of the Slaves who pointed him out to me to my astonishment. the last thing I shall now say further upon this Subject /without the Smallest Pretensions to a Connoiseur in natural Philosophy, as may to[o] easily be perceived throughout the discriptive parts of this no less labourious work/ is that the wonderfull chain of Gradation, from Man to the most diminitive of the above Species, is too conspicuous not to inspire me with humility, and think more of these wandering little objects, who if wisely viewed and desected, bear such general resemblance with /nay little difference from/ myself, not only in theyr external and internal form, but in many of theyr actions and pursuits, which are by us cal'd instinct; and by following which they never Err; while Man the proud Lord of the Creation with all his reason, is so many times conducted in a bogue [bog], from where he can no more be extricated. does not the face, Shape, and Manner of the african Negroe /whom in every respect I look on as my brother/ I say does this not often put us in Mind of the Wild Man of the Woods or *Orangoutang*? While on the other hand what is *this* still'd more than a large Monkey? I acknowledge the theme almost to[o] delicate to bear investigation—here I shall end it for the present, after Still adding that the above Animals are Sociable, that they are very tenatious of life, as I have showed, and that the usual distinction between what are call'd *Monkeys* and *Apes,* consist in this, that the first have all tails, of which the latter are divested, and which /never having met with in Guiana/ I believe more to be the Inhabitant of Asia and Africa, than of that part of the new World distinguished by the name of South America. the Monkeys are often Mischievous near the Plantations where they Commit depredations on the Sugar Canes &c yet of which I but one time have been a Witness & which I shall Circumstantially mention as it occurs in the Course of my Travels—

Speaking of Animals, I must also mention the *Otters* here call'd *Tavous* who in the Coermoetibo Creek frequently attracted our Attention by their disagreeable Noise; being amphibeous they live mostly upon fish, are about 3 feet in length, gray colour'd, and all over bespeckled with white, their legs are short and arm'd with 5 webfooted Claws, the head is round, the nose beset with whiskers like a Cat, the Eyes are Small and placed above the Ears; the Tail is very short—this Animal moves awkwardly upon land but in the rivers proceeds with great velocity—In Guiana are also Sea otters that are much larger but which I never saw—

I have mentioned that I Yesterday was better but this day was exceedingly ill indeed, not being able to sit up in my Hammock under which the black boy *Quacoo* now lay crying for his Master—

The poor Lad himself fell Seek, while I sent 3 more men with a hot fever to Devils Harwar—now also came the melancholy account that the officer M.ʳ *Ower* was also dead–having expired on his Passage downwards at the Estate Alia, where he was buried; in short my Ensign M.ʳ *Cattenburgh* who went since to Paramaribo died next, and nothing else was now expected more for me who was at this moment in a burning fever, forsaken by all my Officers and Men, without a friend, or assistance of any kind, except what the poor remaining negroe Slaves could afford to give me in boyling a little Water to make some tea—one Consolation I feel while I am writing this, which is that my hardships have a chance to attract some Pity, and who would not undergo a little Pain to see the Pretty Girls sigh for their Sufferings? while he that was the unecessary Cause shall be detested. but all things have an end, and at last so had this, since this very afternoon I received an order from the *great* Colonel Fourgeoud, to come down with both the barges till before the Devils Harwar /, but, *neplus ultra,*/ where I was again to take post a Shore and relieve Captain Orzinga of the Society Service who with his Men was to go to La Rochelle in Patamaca to Strengthen the troops already there. Ill as I was this had such a great effect upon my Spirits, that I imediately ordered the Cerberus down to the Mouth of the Coermoetibo Creek, where she join'd me that same Evening—

at last far[e]well infernal place and having weigh'd Anchor we row'd down as far as Barbacueber during which time a Circumstance happened, which is perhaps more worth relating than all the other Exployts put together of this diabolical cruise—and which I shall relate with that Simplicity to which I propose adhearing throughout the course of this whole narrative, despising as much that show of the Marvellous which is so common in too many Authors, as on the other hand by a becoming Spirit, I dispise that barbarity which disgraces to[o] many Commanders—

Resting in my Hammock between the Paroxisms of my fever about half way between Coermoetibo and barbacueber while the Charon was floating down, The Sentinel call'd to me that he had seen and challenged Something black and moving in the brushwood on the beach which gave no Answer and which from its thickness he concluded must be a Man—I imediately drop'd Anchor and having mann'd the Canoo, ill as I was, I step'd into it, when we row'd up to the Place mentioned by the Sentinel; here we all stept ashore to reconnoitre, I suspecting this to be no other than a rebel Spy, or Stragling Party detached by the enemy–when one of my Slaves named David declared it was no Negroe, but a large amphibeous Snake which could not be far from the beach, and I might have an Opportunity to Shoot it if I pleased but to this I had not the Smallest inclination from its uncommon Size, from my Weakness, and the difficulty of getting through the thicket, which seem'd impenetrable to the waters edge and I ordered to return on board; the Negro then ask'd me liberty to step forwards and shoot it himself, ashuring me it could not be at any distance, and warranting me against all Danger; this Spirited me so much that I determined to take his first advice, and kill it myself, providing he was to point it out to me, and bail the hazard by Standing at my Side, from which I Swore that if he dared to move I should level the piece at himself, and blow out his brains without Judge or Jury, and to which he agreed; thus having loaded my Gun with a bal Cartridge we proceeded, *David* this was his name cutting away a path with the bill hook—and a marine following with 3 more loaded firelocks to keep in reddiness; we had not gone above 20 Yards through mud and Water /the Negroe looking every way with an uncommon degree of archness and attention/ when starting behind me he call'd out, *me see Snakee,* viz, that he saw the Snake coild under the fallen leafs & rubbish of the trees. "D———n you rascal /said I/ then stand before me till I also see him or you are dead this instant," and this he did, when with very much difficulty I perceived the head of this monster distant from me not above 16 feet moving its forked tongue, while its Eyes seem'd to emit fire by their brightness—I now resting my piece upon a branch to take a proper Aim fired, but missing the head the ball went through the body, when the animal struck around and, with such astonishing force, as cut away all the underwood around him with the facility of a Scythe mowing grass, and by flouncing his tail made the Glare and dirt fly over our heads at a considerable distance, during which Manoeuvre we all ran to the river and crowded into the Canoo—the negro now intreated me to renew the Charge ashuring me he would be quiet in a few Minutes, and at any rate persisting in the Snakes neither being able or inclined to pursue us /which he undertook to prove by walking before me till I should be ready to fire;/ I again did undertake to make the Trial, the more while he said that his first starting backwards, had only proceeded to make room for myself. I now found him a little removed from his former Station but very Quiet, with his head as before out amongst the fallen Leafs, rotten bark, and old Moss; I fired at it imediately, but with no better Success than the other time, the Snake sending up such a cloud of Dust and dirt as I never saw but in a whirlwind, and made us once more all betake to our heels for the Canoo, where now being heartily tired of the exploit I gave orders to paddle* for the barge; but the Slave Still intreating me to let him kill the Animal I was actually induced to make one third and last attempt in Company with himself; thus having once more discovered the Snake we discharged both our pieces at once, /not unlike the Story told of Robinson Crusoe with Friday,/ However with this good Effect that he was now by one of us Shot through the head, when David the Slave /leaping with Joy before the monster as his namesake the King had done before the Ark/ fetched the penter or boat-rope in order to drag him to the Canoo—but this again was a difficult Jobb since the creature notwithstanding its being mortally wounded still Continued to make such twists and wreathes as made it dangerous for any one to come very near him, however the negro having made a running noose, through it over his head with much dexterity, after a few fruitless attempts to make an Approach—and now all taking hold of the rope we haul'd him to the beach and tied him to the Stern of the Canoo to take him in tow, being still alive, where he keep'd Swimming like an Eel & I having no Relish for taking such a Ship Mate on Board—whose length /notwithstanding to my astonishment all the Negroes declared it to be but a young one, come to about its half-Growth/ I measured to be 22 feet and some inches, and its thickness like that of my black Boy Quacoo, who might then be about 12 Years old, and around whose waste I since measured the Creatures Skin—

Being arrived along side of the Charon the next thing was what now to do with this huge Animal when it was determined to bring him ashore at Barbacoeba to have him Skin'd, and take out the Oil &c. this we Did, when the negroe David having climb'd up a Tree with the end of the rope, let it down over a strong forked branch, and the other Negroes hoisted the Snake up in Suspence, this done David with a sharp knife between his teeth now left the Tree, and clung fast upon the Monster which was still twisting, and began his Operations by ripping it up and stripping down the Skin as he descended, which though the Animal could now do him no hurt; I acknowledge had a terrible appearance, viz, to See a Man Stark naked, black and bloody, clung with Arms and legs around the Slimy and yet living Monster—however his labour was not in vain since he not only dextrously finished the operation, but provided me with /besides the Skin/, above 4 Gallons of fine Clerified fat or rather Oil, loosing perhaps as much more, which I delivered to the Surgeons at Devils Harwar for the use of the wounded

* —in all Canoes are used Padles in stead of Oars—

Men in the Hospital and for which I received their hearty thanks, it being deem'd particularly for Bruises, a verry excellent Remedy—at Signifying my Surprize to see the Snake still living after he was deprived of his Intestines and Skin *Cramaca* the old Negro assured me, he would not die till after Sun Set; the Negro's now cut him in Slices in order to dress him and eat part of him, they all declaring he was exceedingly good and Healthy, which to their great Mortification, I refused giving my assent to—and we row'd down wth the Skin to Devils Harwar—

Having thus described the manner in which he was kil'd I shall now give some Account of the Animal itself, which is mentioned by many different Authors, and of which several Skins are preserved in the British and Mr Parkinsons Museums. It is call'd by Mr Westley *Lyboija* and *Boa* in the British Anciclopedia, to where I refer the reader for a perfect Account and an excellent Engraving of this wonderful Creature, which is in the Colony of Surinam call'd *aboma*—its length when full grown is sometimes 40 feet and more than 4 feet in Circumference its Colour is a Greenish black on the back, A fine brownish Yellow on the Sides, and a dirty white under the belly—the back and Sides being Spotted with irregular black rings, of a pure white in the middle, its head is broad and flat, Small in proportion to the Body with a large Mouth beset with a double row of teeth, a forked tongue, and two bright prominent Eyes; it is all covered over with large Scales some about the Size of a Shilling and under the body near the Tail arm'd with two strong *claws* like Cock Spurs, to help its seizing its Prey—it is an amphibious animal, that is to say, it delights in low and Marshy Places where it lays coild up like a rope and concealed under all kinds of Moss rotten Timber and dried leafs to ceize its prey by Surprize, which from its great bulk it has no activity to pursue—this consists when Hungary in any thing that comes within its reach, no Matter what, a Sloth, a Wild Boar, a Stag, or even a Tiger, around which having twisted itself by the help of its claws, So that it can not escape, it next breaks by its irresistable force every bone in the Annimals body, which it then covers over with a kind of Slime or Saliva from its mouth to make it Slide, and at last gradually sucks it in till it disappears.—after this the aboma cannot shift his Station on account of the great knob or knot, which the Swallowed Prey occasions in that part of the body where it rests, till it is digested, which would hinder him from Sliding alongst the Ground, and during which time the *aboma* wants no other Subsistence. I have been told of negroes being devoured by this Animal, to which I willingly give Credit should they chance to come within his reach during the time of his affamation and which proprietys of seizing their prey long fasting &c I believe to

The skinning of the Aboma Snake, shot by Cap.ⁿ Stedman.

1773—AUGUST 26

be common in many /if not in most/ other Snakes nor do I apprehend that its flesh is in any ways pernicious to the Stomach which look'd beautifully white, had the appearance of fish, and I should never have refused the negroes from eating it had I not observed a kind of dissatisfaction amongst the remaining Marines for going to give the Negroes the use of the Kettle to boil it. the bite of this Snake is said not to be venemous, nor do I believe it bites at all from any other impulse than hunger—

I shall only add that having nail'd its Skin on the bottom of a Canoo, and dried it in the Sun /Sprinkling it over with wood ashes to prevent it from Corruption/ I sent it to a friend at Paramaribo from where it was since sent to Holland as a Curiosity—

However Strange this account may seem to many readers, let them peruse that given by a Gentleman in the Island of Ceilon, /who saw a Tiger kill'd there by a Snake he calls the *Anacanda* but in a quite different manner/, and theyr wonder will cease in an instant, which gentlemans relation is so very marvellous, that /independent of what I have experienced, I acknowledge/ it Staggered my faith as no doubt my account may do that of many others—and that the *aboma* has the power of fascination or attracting Animals within its reach /as mentioned by Do: Bancroft/ I am obliged to contradict, this being a Quality, I not without difficulty attribute even to the rattle Snake independent of all that has been said upon the Subject—and of which I shall speak in proper time and place convenient

In short this Job being ended, we also made an end of the Cruise by in the night dropping down for the last time till before the Society Post Devils Harwar in order next day to take possession—

Chapter 8th

Three Estates burnt and the Inhabitants murder'd by the Rebels—
real picture of Misery and Distress—
Speciman of a march through the Woods of Surinam—
Col. Fourgeoud and the remaining Troops leave Paramaribo

Stepping a Shoare I now relieved Captain Orzinga with his Men, and took the Command of this Place, having been on board the Charon exactly fifty Six Days or Eight Weeks, in the most wretched Condition that can be discribed—hoping now to get the better of my Complaint, by the help of a few refreshments as Milk &c and the Society Troops /above One hundred in number/ being to set of[f] next day with my empty barges to La Rochelle in Patamaca, I now review'd my Marines, when I found that I had left out of 5 Officers but 2 both Sick the other 3 being dead besides one Serjeant 2 Corporals and only 15 privates being the remainder of 54 healthy people on the 2nd day of last July— This Army was not more than sufficient to defend, the Hospital Crowded with Sick, the Ammunition and Victualling Magazine, &c on a Spot where lately had been kept 300 Soldiers, particularly while the Enemy were lurcking not far off in Consequence of which the Society Captain reinforced me with 20 of his Men and all was well; next in the Evening he entertained me and my 2 Subalterns on a Supper of *fresh-meat* both roasted and boild to our great comfort and Surprize, but which since to my unspeakable Mortification, proved to be the individual poor Cow with her Calf on whom we had built all our hopes for a little relief, which one of his Sentinels had shot by a wilful mistake during the former night, and by which Captn Orzinga for the Sake of one Mouthfull, deprived us all from that lasting Comfort on which we had placed our hopes, and which we stood /being emasiated/ so very much in need of, while this Action /however trifling it may appear/, independant of his former Politeness, I could not help thinking exceedingly ungenerous—

🙰 In the morning at last the Society troops row'd up to Patamaca when examining the 20 Soldiers they had left me they proved to be the refuge of the whole Party, with agues, wounds, ruptures, and rotten limbs most of whom next day were obliged to enter the Hospital—

🙰 Having bastonated my late pilot for Stealing from the Soldiers, I sent a report to Colonel Fourgeoud that I had taken post, and acquainting him of my weak Situation ask'd for a proper Reinforcement—this Evening again 2 of my Men having died—all things now being regulated and Settled I thanked Heaven in the expectation of getting at last some rest, still being weak and with these cheering hopes retired at 10 OClock at night to my hammock, but this tranquility was of short duration, Since having scarsely shut my Eyes I was awaked by my Serjeant, and the following Letter put in my hands sent by an express from the Captain of the Militia or bargers in Cottica—

Sir—
This is to acquaint you that the Rebels have burnt 3 Estates by your side, *Suyingheyd* [= de Zuinigheid], *Peru,* and *L'Esperance,* the ruins of which are Still Smoking and that they have cut the throats of all the White Inhabitants that fell in their hands as on their retreat they must pass close by where you are posted, be on your guard. I am in haste
Yours &c
was Sign'd Stoeleman

I imediately Started up, conscious of my defenceless Situation, and the express who brought the Letter having Spread the news the moment of his landing, I had no need to turn out the Soldiers, the few that were well not only but the whole Hospital breaking out, several of whom in Spite of my opposition crawling on hands and feet to their Arms, drop'd dead upon the Spot, nor may I ever behold such a Scene of Misery and distress here lame, blind, Seek, and wounded, in the hopes of preserving a wretched existance rushed upon certain Death, and could only be compared to the Distressed Army and Navy at Carthagena Commanded by the British Admiral *Vernon*—whom Thomson describes viewing his dying forces, in the beautiful following lines

—You Gallant Vernon Saw
The miserable Scene; you Pitying Saw.
To Infant weakness sunk the Warriors Arm,
Saw the deep racking pang; the ghastly form,

The lip pale quivering, and the beamless Eye,
No more with ardour bright.—

    I was myself in a very weakly condition indeed, however we continued to lay all night upon our Arms, during which time I press'd the express to add one to the number being determined to Sell our lives as dear as possible, but no Enemy appearing in the morning we buried the dead in theyr hammocks, not a board to make a Coffin to be met with on the whole post—I now lost all Patience, and had the audasity to write to my Commander /besides what had happened/ that my last Men stood upon the brink of the Grave by hardships and for want of being properly supported /the verry waiters of the hospital being deserted the moment of my Arrival here, who had gone to Paramaribo/ indeed our whole number was now melted down to but 12 Men to protect 12 buildings while we had no more than 2 verry Small chests of Ammunition to defend them and no retreat for the Seek, all the Barges being gone to Patamaca, and the last Canoo with my letter to Colonel Fourgeoud, I having set adrift that belonging to the express who was bookkeeper of a neighbouring Plantation, to prevent him or any other from making theyr Escape. in this Situation I was now obliged to make Slaves to Soldiers whom I arm'd with a hatchet not daring to trust them with a firelock—and in short acknowledge I found myself in great difficulty, While this whole night we again watched under Arms, and in the Morning found dead 2 more of my poor Soldiers on the Ground—

    I now began really to think we were all devoted to distruction, while the Men regardless of all order /Selff-preservation excepted/ throughout aloud [allowed] the most bitter Invectives against their Persecutor the Gallant Fourgeoud, which I could not prevent; nor can I help remarking the generalship of the rebel negroes who had keept laying on the lurch Just til the removal of the Society Troops from Devils Harwar, and who ceised the very first day of their departure, convinced of its being guarded only by my Seek, and emasiated Soldiers in order to Commit there Depredations on the Cottica Estates, well knowing that my Force was not sufficient to pursue them, nay hardly to Stand in my own defence. however all this was much according to my expectation while on the Contrary had my Strength timely been Sufficient they could never have escaped at least from being cut off in their retreat; especially if the Troops in Rio Pirica, had acted Conjunctly with those in Cottica by Padroleing the cordon or Path between the 2 rivers, and across which the Rebels twice were unavoidably obliged to pass—

But what use was it for me to make reflections, which now could no more avail, besides the hazard of being Censured by the martial Train for daring to find fault with my Commander many of *which-Gentlemen* by the general Rule of Military etiquet must never, nay can never Err—

≥ We now waited once more till morning and then bury'd another of my poor Men, while I yet cannot conceive how any one could Survive such toil, in such a debilitated State, and in a tropical Climate, yet such Some did though few, while I at last being persuaded that the Rebels must have past the Cordon, without having thought proper to pay us a visit on their retreat, determined to let those few wach no longer but to let them die their own natural Deaths—at last in the evening when all was too late came down by water from the Post La Rochelle to our Assistance 1 Officer and 10 Men–I having had but 9 left to do the duty—But to what purpose now?

≥ Another Man died—I at this Time once more reviewed my forces which amounted exactly to 7 Marines, the few Scarecrows of the Society excepted–however the Chance of our getting our throats cut was at this time over, thanks alone to the Pusilanimity, perhaps even to the humanity of the rebel-Negroes, against whom by heavens we could have made little more resistance than a field of Grasshoppers against a flock of Carion Crows—

≥ I now received a Letter from Colonel Fourgeoud Condoling me on the loss of so many good Officers, acquainting me that I was to be reinforced, and that at my recommendation My Serjeant M.r Cabanns was appointed an Ensign which gave me pleasure, and happened apropo, Since to Day poor Ensign Macdonald was sent down very seek to Paramaribo. I answered to all this that "I was obliged to him, as I could no longer be accountable for whatever Consequence happened, where I was left to defend a whole River with none but seek People, without even sufficient Ammunition, and who were hourly expiring for want of proper Medicines or even so much as a Surgeon to attend them," here being none but one or two Surgeons Mates belonging to the troops of the Society, who could do little better than draw blood, and cut of[f] a beard or a Corn upon Occasion but nothing else of any Consequence and this letter imediately departed—

≥ I buryd another of my Marines—

≥ One died again, and I had not one remaining who was not ill or his feet Swel'd with the insects call'd Chigoes, all these poor Men being mostly Germans, who had been accustomed to a healthy Climate in their own Country[.] In short I began now to be reconsiled to putting my last Man under Ground, and to leap into the Grave after him myself—when finally arrived from Paramaribo a barge with the proper reinforcement, Ammunition, Provisions, Medicines—a Surgeon &c &c and an Order from my Chief for me to trace out the tract of the rebels imediately on the Quandom Communication Path call'd the Cordon, between Cottica and Pirica, and to write him the result of my Discovery, also that he intended to keep his Magazines at Devils Harwar and was not to make use of the Spot I had found out for that use at Barbacueber—

I now prepared to march next Day myself in quest of the grand Discovery which would have been much grander indeed had it been more timely and then placed the Ammunition and Provisions in the Magazine—

As the manner of marching in this Country is so very different from that in Europe I shall here before we set out accurately discribe its proceeding—

In the first place in Surinam no such thing is practicable as three or even two ranks, thus no marching by Divisions, Platoons, or yet by files,—but the whole party being dres'd in one rank face to the right, and every Man follows his leader, the Negro Slaves being interspersed between the Men to be guarded themselves, as well as what they carry and which Manner of Marching is Cal'd Indian-file—for instance for a detachment of 60 Men and Consisting in 1 Captain, 2 Subalterns, 2 Serjeants, 4 Corporals, 1 Surgeon, and 50 Privates, ought to be employed at least 20 Negro Slaves, which are pay'd to their Masters at the rate of 2 Shillings Sterling Per Day by the Colony, and to which this is a much greater expense than would be horses or waggons, which can in this Country not be employ'd for Military Service—

The manner of interspersing them amongst the troops is as follows; the first or foremost are generally 2 Pioneers viz 2 Negros with bill hooks to cut away, so as to make a practicable Path, with 1 Corporal and 2 Men to recconnoitre the front; and in case of necessity to give the Alarm, and then 1 Subaltern, 6 Privates, and a Corporal, which forms the *van* or advance-Guard; then follows at some distance the *Corps* or Main-body in 2 divisions, being in the first 1 Captain, 1 Corporal[,] 12 privates, 1 Surgeon, and 2 Negroes to carry the Powder; in the 2^d are 1 Sarjeant and 12 privates; and then again folllows at some distance the *rear-Guard* or Corps deserve Consisting in one Subaltern, 1 Serjeant, 1 Corporal, 18 privates, and 16 Negroes, to carry the Medicines, beef, bread, Spades[,] axes, kettles, kildivil or rum, the Officers boxes, the Seek &c. the 3 last of all being one Corporal, and 2 Men at some distance, to give the alarm in case of an Attack by the Enemy as the others had orders to do in the front; which ends the train[.]

References to the above March.

Van (A)
1. Two Negroes with Bill hooks to open a Path.
2. One Corporal & two Privates, to cover the Van.
3. One Subaltern, Six Privates, & one Corporal.

Main Body (B)
1. The Captain or commanding Officer.
2. The Surgeon.
3. Two Privates, to cover the Powder.
4. A Negro with a Box of Ball Cartridges.
5. Two Privates.
6. A Negro with a Box of Ball Cartridges.
7. Eight Privates.
8. One Corporal.
9. Twelve Privates.
10. One Sergeant.

Rear Guard or Corps de Reserve (C)
1. A Subaltern Officer.
2. Two Privates.
3. Three Negroes, with Medicines, Kettles, Axes, Spades &c.
4. Two Privates.
5. Three Negroes with Salt Beef, Salt Pork &c.
6. Two Privates.
7. Three Negroes, with Black Bread, or Rusk Biscuit.
8. One Private.
9. Two Negroes, with Kill-devil, or New Rum.
10. One Private.
11. One Negro, with the Captains Provisions.
12. One Private.
13. One Negro, with Provisions for the two Subaltern Officers.
14. One Private.
15. Three Negroes to carry the Sick & Wounded.
16. Six Privates.
17. One Sergeant.
18. One Corporal & two Privates, to cover the Rear.

Marks to be cut on the Trees on a March.

	A +	B ‡	C ‡
Fourgeoud's	1st Column, Sub A.	2d Ditto, Sub B.	3d Ditto, Sub C.
	D #	E #	F #
Society's	1st Column, Sub D.	2d Ditto, Sub E.	3d Ditto, Sub F.

Order of March thro' the Woods of Surinam.

London Published Decr. 1st 1791 by J. Johnson, St Pauls Church Yard.

1773—SEPTEMBER 7, 8

&. Every thing being ready as much as possible according to the above Rules for my Small Party, Consisting in myself, Subaltern Officer /of the Society M*r* *Hertsbergh*/ 1 Surgeons Mate, 1 Guide, 2 Serjeants, 2 Corporals, 40 Privates, and only 8 Negro-Slaves to cut open the Passage and carry the luggage, we faced to the right at 6 OClock in the Morning, and Sallied forth in the Woods, keeping Course directly for the Pirica River—

Having marched till about 11 OClock on the Cordon, I discovered as I had expected the track of the Rebels in their retreat, by the marks of their footsteps in the Mud broken bottles Plantain Shells, barbacued fish, and fresh ashes where they had made a fire, bearing by appearance towards Pinneburgh already mentioned—

I had now found the nest to be sure, but the birds were flown, and to whom to attribute this Mistake I must leave to the derision of the Judicious—In short we continued our March till 8 OClock when we arrived at the Society Post *Soribo* in Pirica, in a most shocking Condition, having waddled through Water and Mire above our hipps, Climb'd over heaps of fallen trees, creep'd underneath them on our bellies—Scratched and tore by the thorns or macas that are here of many kinds, Stung all over by the Patat or Scrapat lice, ants, and *wassy-wassy* or wild bees, fatigued to death by marching in a burning Sun, and the last 2 hours in hells darkness, holding each other by the hand, and having left 10 Men behind, some with agues, some stung blind, and some with their feet full of Chigoes—being at *Scribo* in the most Hospitable manner received by the Commanding Officer, I went to my hammock with a fever. the *wassy-wassy* or Surinam honey bee, is not larger than an English blew-bottle-fly and black, they are never keept in hives but Swarm wild in the forest; where they build in hollow trees, or between the forked branches, their nests being some as large as an inflated Cows bladder, to which they bear no bad resemblance both in Colour and Smoothness, except in being less regularly Oval; from these abodes /when they or the branch are inadvertantly touched/ buz forth thousands of warriors, which little flying Army is Extremely redoubtable, pitching always by instinct on the Eyes, the lips, and in the hair, from where they cannot soon be extricated, their Stings generally occasioning a fever, and swelling the Parts so verry much that they occasion blindness for several hours; their honey is a dark brown liquid, and so is their wax but gummy being both of little Consequence—

&. I was now a little better but neither myself or my Men able to march back, while the other Captain, sent a Small Party of his Soldiers to pick up the poor Marines I had lost the day before, and of whom they brought with them 7 being carried in Hammocks tied to poles, each by 2 Negroes, the other *three* having scrambled back to Devils Harwar

During this I wrote a 3ᵈ Letter to Colonel Fourgeoud couched in such terms as few people would do to their Commander in full Senses but the truth viz, that I had found what he wanted, that also with proper Support I might have cut of[f] the Enemies retreat, in place of finding their footsteps, but that now all was to[o] late and the party knock'd up to no purpose—which I was since told insenced him so much that he was like to spit fire on the occasion and roard like a ramping lion—

Being now sufficiently refreshed to renew my March we left *Scribo* at 4 OClock in the morning, and at 4 OClock P.M arrived /after undescribable Sufferings, like so many miserable wretches/ at Devils Harwar, tore to rags, covered over with Mud and blood, and our thighs and legs cut and Scratched from top to bottom by the Prickles, and flogging of the branches, most of the Men being without Shoes and Stockings, by necessity; while I, and who had done this March in the same Condition from choice, absolutely had Suffered the least of the whole party, by having inured myself gradually to walk barefooted on the barges. at Devils Harwar I found arrived to take the Command now Lieut. Col. *Westerloo,* and a Quarter Master, his troops being only expected the next Day; this made me exceedingly happy, hoping at last to meet with some relief; and having ceded him my written orders, the Magazine Hospital &c &c. I Strip'd, and plung'd into the river to wash my Self and take a Swim, and by which /being very much overheated/ I found myself greatly refreshed, while upon the whole I seem'd quite to revive, particularly on receiving a Quantity of fine fruit, Jamaica rum, Wine Sugar &c from Joanna, who had been informed that I was dead some time before; but how did my blood chil when the Quartermaster told me as a Secret, that my Serjeant one fowler had /having first got drunk with my wine/ offered violence to this virtuous woman, and that he was to be at Devils Harwar next day when I should see the marks of her just resentment on his face—Heaven and Earth, I Swore imediate destruction to the villain, and having ordered a Negro to Cut 12 bamboe Canes, I retired like one enraged Swearing to assassin him, inch by inch—

Now arrived two Subalterns, with a 2ᵈ barge full of Men, Ammunition, Medicines, and Provisions, which no sooner were marched into Quarters, and Stowed, than I sent for the hopeless *fowler* whose face being in 2 places wounded, I locked up in a Room, and without asking one Question broke Six of the bamboes over his head, till he escaped all bloody out at the Window, and my resentment Gradually abated—

He certainly had suffered much, but nothing equal to what were my Sensations, at being Still further informed that Colonel Fourgeoud had deprived her of all my Effects, which he had Sealed and locked up in an empty Store room, in case of my decease which by appearance he Expected while my house was given to another, and by which means I could not get so much as a clean Shirt to exchange with my So disgracefull Tartars [tatters]—Nevertheless by the hopes of going down myself I was supported—The other news of more Importance was that the Hero in person with most of the troops had at last left Paramaribo which he had Divided on Devils Harwar, in Rio Cottica; at the Estate Bellair in Rio Pirica; and at the Estate Clarenbeck, and Crawassibo, in Rio Comewina; at which last he had established his head Quarters, and from where conjunctly with the troops of the Society, and the Rangers, he intended to Sally forth in Quest of the Rebels; while he had ordered the infernal barges all to be relieved at last and theyr remaining troops to reinforce the Posts above mentioned•—which the Soldiers observed /to give the Devil his Due/ was a very wise and well plan'd regulation—

I was now extremely poorly, and low—However prepared to go this Evening to Paramaribo, in consequence of which I waited on Colonel Westerloo to ask his Commands—but who now /without Ceremony/ told me /not only/ that I was devoted to Destruction by Colonel Fourgeoud, for having dared to find fault with his wise Manoeuvers and which was certainly too true, but that he had orders as a proof of it not to let me be removed to Paramaribo, till I should be bed-fast dying and unable to move—the effect that this Answer made on my Spirits I shall not attempt to discribe, Suffice it to say that I lost all reserve at once and having cursed the cause of my Distress publickly, and allow'd, against whom I throughout [threw out] the most bitter imprecations, as the Wilful Cause of my Death, I strold in the Adjoining Woods, unarm'd, and in the Condition of a frantick, deliberating whether to end my own existence or not; the last prevail'd, and returning home I now drank such a Quantity of Jamaica rum, to alleviate my Distress, that it had nearly prevented me from forming resolutions of any kind for ever after—

Now came the news from *Patamaca,* that the Rebels on their repassing the River above La Rochelle, had again destroyed a Small Estate, and murdered its proprietor a M! *Nyboor*—It was either this time, or it happened since, that an Overseer escaped by the help of a Negro Boy, who desiring him to leap into a Canoo, and lay in it down flat upon his

• —none of the barges lost any number of Men those I commanded alone excepted—

belly, leap'd himself into the Water, where by Swiming with one hand and Guiding the Canoo with the other he ferried his Master Safe over the Creek Patamaca, through a Shower of Musquet bullets, the Rebels firing upon them all the time but without execution; however for this Material Piece of Service he was recompenced the Week after, with 300 Lashes by the same Master, for having forgot to open one of the Sluces or flood Gates—on this Act of Gratitude, I shall make no Comment, but proceed—I have given an account of my miserable State Yesterday and which to day if possible, was encreased—I was now truly mad with grief and determined to exchange my wretched Situation one way or another—My resolution gave me Strength, and I once more stept up to Lieut. Colonel *Westerloo,* insisting that I *would* be transported, or that I should attribute to him, as well as to his low Protector *Fourgeoud,* the Cause of my approaching Death, which the Surgeon now declared, without my request was granted, must inevitably follow verry Soon; a Consultation was then held in which by some it was agreed that I was verry Ill indeed, but by others that I was *only* out of my Senses, while one dared to declare, he thought that both, the first and last, was no more than a farce, repeating the 13 verse, of the 21st Chapter in the 1st Book of Samuel—"And he changed his behaviour before them, and feign'd himself mad in their hands, and scrabbled on the doors of the Gate, &c"

This piece of ashurance absolutely made me laugh However in place of like David being hushed, I now Swore by Death and Damnation, that I should Certainly take revenge on the *modern King of Gath* at all hazards, if I was here keep'd a State Prisoner much longer; when at last it was agreed on that I was certainly *insane,* and a boat ordered to row me emediately down to Paramaribo, but no White Servant to attend me, who being a Soldier could not be Spared on the Post, where he added *one* to the number of *one-hundred,* and which was no bad Generalship in this new Commander, who had besides from the first day of his Arrival, begun to *Palisade* himself all around, and ordered his Sentrys to call twice, *that all was well* during the night, which had the double Advantage of making him sure of it himself, and of persuading the Enemy that theyr number was the double, Should they chance to be heard; and which help'd at least in keeping them at bay, well knowing of what consequence the loss of a good Officer is to the State, should the Cruel Negroes ever think to return. In short I took my leave of the above Gentlemen /, who had most of them by their good behaviour, of late being promoted from *private* Serjeants/, while my poor and only Ship Mate M^r *Do Hammer* was Still doom'd to remain on Devils Harwar; and resting upon a Negroes Shoulder, I at 12 OClock at noon walk'd to the Waters Side, where Stepping in the boat, I left this human *butchery* & where I had burried so many brave fellows, & row'd with 6 Negroes and my black boy to the Town of *Paramaribo*—here I arrived on the 14ᵗʰ, at 2, OClock in the morning, but I having no residence of my own, was most Hospitably received at the house of a Mʳ *De Lamarre* a Merchant, whose Wife was Joanna's Sister, and for which last he imediately dispatched a Servant to the house of her Aunt.—And another for a Physician, I being extremely ill indeed, which was the end of this brilliant, this Fruitful expedition; after an Absense of 2 Months, and 12 days, during which time I am convinced that the Simpathising reader has often felt for us and to whom I renew my most unfeigned appology for dwelling so long upon my own Subject; yet which I could not very well avoid, and keep up the Connection, while far from Glorying in any one of my private Actions, I only State them to expose the weakness of human nature, and as a Guide for others, in like Circumstances /in some Measure/ to rule their Conduct with more Propriety—

CHAPTER 9th

Some deseases peculiar to the Climate—Groop of newly imported Negroes going to be sold—Reflections on the Slave Trade—The Voyage from Africa—Manner of selling them in the Colony—discription of a Cotton Plantation

I now found myself in an elegant and well furnished Apartment, encouraged by the hopes given to me by the Physician, carrest by my friends, and supported by the Care and attention, of the inestimable Joanna—

One Captain *Brant* having at this time the Command in Colonel Fourgeouds absence he sent me this Morning my Trunks and baggage, which had been seal'd up, and which when looking into them, I found that I had Enemies at home as well as abroad, Since most of my Shirts, books &c, were now eat to moulders by the *Blatta* or *Cockroach* cald *Cakrelaca* in Surinam, nay even my Shoes also were destroyed, of which I had brought over 12 pair new from Europe, they being extremely dear and bad in this Country—

This insect which is of the beetle kind, is one Inch and sometimes about 2 inches long–oval, flat, and of a dark reddish brown Colour; by getting in betwixt the crevisses of lockers, chists, or boxes, it not only there deposits its eggs, but Commits its ravages on linnen, Cloth, Silk, or any thing that comes in its way; besides getting in the victuals, or drink of any kind makes it extremely loathsome, where it leaves the most nautious Smell, Stinking worse than a bug–as most West India Vessels /especially those loaded with Sugar/ bring them home in great quantities, I shall say little more about them, only that they are seldom seen to fly, but creep very fast, and that the best /and I think only/ way to keep the boxes free of them, is by placing them on 4 empty wine bottles keept free from dust, which by their Slipriness prevents their asscending, and getting in through the Key holes, or even the smallest openings in the bottoms—but which precaution had been neglected by my good friend Colonel Fourgeoud—however I found linnen sufficient for present use, and by the industry of Joanna soon was provided in a new stock—none can conceive the Comfort I felt, after being properly dress'd, and shifted, my Mental faculties were recruiting apace, while my fine Constitution greatly Contributed to the recovery of my health—poor *Macdonald* being still ill at Mr Kennedys who had humanely given him an Asylum at his return from Devils-Harwar—

Having now time I enquired about the fatal-Fowlers conduct, when to my surprise I was informed, that he had indeed got drunk as was reported to me, by which he had fallen amongst the bottles, and cut his face, but that he never had attempted the smallest *rudeness,* so far the reverse that his enibriation had proceeded from his Sorrow, at seeing both *me* and *Joana* so ill treated, and my things transported against his inclination—I now was exceedingly hurt at my past Conduct, and upbraided by the *Cause* of it, as I deserved, to whom I promissed to be fowlers friend for ever after, and kept my Word—

&. My fever began now much to abate, but I was infected with another disorder peculiar to this Climate & which I am afraid, I Shall be able, but indifferently to discribe–it is called in Surinam the *Ring-Worm,* and consists in large scarlet irregular Spots particularly on the under parts of the body, and which increase in Magnitude from Day to Day, unless prevented by timely application–these Spots are surrounded with a kind of hard, Scrufulous border, that makes them look in my opinion something like *land-Maps* and which are as troublesome by their itching, as the itch, pric[k]ly-heat, or the Sting of the Musquitoes, and so very infectious, that if one chances to sit on a chair, emediately after another who has the disorder, he is almost certain to catch it–it is I believe endemial, very ill to get rid off, and the best cure, to rub it with a Composition of refined-*Salt-Petre, Benjoin*–flower of *brimstone,* and *white-Mercury* mixt with fresh-butter, or hogs-lard–inconceivable are the many troubles to which one is exposed in this Climate—

&. I now again relapsed, and was twice drawn blood in one day. this Morning I was visited by poor Mr *Henaman,* the young volunteer I have once before mentioned, who looked like a Ghost, and was left seek at Paramaribo to shift for himself by Colonel Fourgeoud, notwithstanding this fine Gentleman owed great part of his good fortune to his Family—

&. I now again being a little better, was exalted from living like a Savage, to the Temporary Command of the few Troops left at Paramaribo /Captain *Brandt* being ordered to Join Fourgeoud in Rio Comewina/ when the Colours, regiments Cash &c were transmitted to my own lodging, and a Sentinel placed before my Door; and from which Moment I began to show my Power, by discharging the Sower gripe-gut-wine, which had been bought for the Seek Officers as well as Men, and which I supplied, from the Money now in my Possession, with good wholesome claret; while I was sorry not to have it in my power to exchange the Salt-Beef, Pork, and Peas, that were left for the Hospital also in fresh provisions; but this was particularly forbid by the Commander, while the butter, cheese, and tobacco was taken away, and for which they got one Quart of Oil amongst 10, and their bread reduced to 2 Pound for a whole Week, and while the Officers were left to Shift for themselves, or put up with the same allowance, notwithstanding they keept on paying their Quota to a Regimental Mess, which now *no more* existed—

I now for the first Time did take the Air on horseback, in Company with young M.? Heneman, though we could not ride above 3 English Miles distance out of Town, on a Species of gravel, that leads to the Wanica-Path, and which I have already mentioned, to Communicate with the River Serameca, as the only Practicable road in the Colony. during this little Jaunt which /on account of the dry Season being Commenced/ we did at 6 oClock in the morning, we saw a great many of these large fine-looking birds called *Macaws* and in Surinam called *Ravens* from their Proportion to the Parots, which may be look'd on as a kind of Tropical Crows; the *Macaws* are divided in different Species, of which I shall only discribe 2, preferring to say nothing, in preference to what I cannot support, as I am sorry too many Authors have done already, and among whom are Men of genius and Learning; some indeed may have erred from Ignorance or wrong information, but numbers from a motive of Pride, and presumption, have been with impunity permitted to vend of their shamefull impositions on the too Credulous Public—

The *Blew-and-Yellow-Macaw* is as large as a barn door fowl, with short legs and a crooked bill, like that of a parrot—the former dark colour'd, with black claws, too and too; the latter also black, the upper Mandible alone Moveable; its tail is like a Wedge, and Consists in a few very long and Streight feathers, the back of this bird from the head /the top of which is a Sea green/ to the extremity of its tail, is the most beautiful azure blew die that can be imagined, while underneath, its whole body is of a Pale orange Colour; round its eyes it is perfectly white, interspersed with black Rings, Composed of very small feath-

The Blue & Yellow & the Amazon Macaw.

London, Published Dec.r 1.st 1791, by J. Johnson, St Paul's Church Yard.

ers—the other is call'd in Surinam the *Amazone-Macaw* this is rather less than the former, its tail, legs, and bill, are formed in the same manner, but the latter is of a dirty white; the head neck and breast of this bird is of a bright Scarlet; round the Eyes alone excepted, where it is white with black rings; its wings may be said to be divided by bars in 4 Colours, being Scarlot at the top, next Green, then Yellow, and blew down to the extremity of the tail, theyr variety and brightness, being Divinely beautiful in the Sun—All the Macaws fly in Couples, have a Shrill disagreeable Shreek, bite Severely theyr bill being very hard and Sharp, and which is of great use to them in Climing; they are easily tamed, and may be teached to Speak like other Parrots—the Indians frequently bring them to Paramaribo, who sometimes part with them for a bottle of rum, or for a few fish hooks.

This Evening arrived seek from the head Quarters /at the Estate *Crawassibo* in Comewina/ Colonel *Texier* the Commanding Officer of the Society Troops—which Gentleman had intended to have marched Conjunctly with Colonel Fourgeoud, through the Woods in Quest of the Rebels—But whose Constitution /already weak/ not being able to support the Commander-in-Chiefs regimen of living on *Salt* provisions, had begun to flag from the beginning, till he was sent home to Paramaribo in this drooping Condition—

The fever had now left me and the Ringworm began to abate—but the Misery and hardships which I had so lately undergone still broke out my Constitution—by 2 enormous *boils* on my left thigh, which entirely prevented me from Walking—however my Physition ordering me dayly to take the Air when I had the opportunity I waited to day on his Excellency the Governor of the Colony by the help of my friend Kennedys Chaise, and from where returning homewards, I Stopt the Carriage at the Waters Side, to behold a groop of human beings, who had deservedly attracted my particular attention, and which groop I shall Circumstantially endeavour to discribe—They were a drove of newly imported *Negroe's* Men, and Women, with a few Children, who had just landed from on board a Guinea-Man that lay at Anchor in the roads to be sold for Slaves to the best bidder in the Colony, and were such a set of living atomatons, such a resurrection of Skin and bones, as justly put me in mind of the last trumpet; seeming that moment to be rose from the grave, or deserted from the Surgeons Hall at the old Bailey—and of which no better discription can be given than by comparing them to walking Skeletons covered over with a piece of tand leather—

2— And the Lord caused me to pass by them round about and

Group of Negros, as imported to be sold for Slaves.

London, Published Dec.r 1.st 1793, by J. Johnson, S.t Paul's Church Yard.

> behold there were many in the open valey and lo they were very dry—
>
> 3— And he said unto me Son of Man can these bones live? And I answered O Lord God thou knowest
>
> Ezekiel 37.—2-3—

before these wretches /who might be in all about 60 in number/—walked a Sailor, and another followed behind, with a bamboe rattan; the one serving as a Shepherd to lead them along, and the other as his Dog to bite them occasionally should any one lay behind, or wander away from the blisted flock; while at the same time equity claims of me to acknowledge, that in place of all those horrid and dejected Countenances that are with so much industry discribed in Pamphlets and Newspapers, I perceived not one Single down-cast look amongst them all, and that the *bite* of the bamboe was inflicted with the utmost moderation by the Sailor who nine times out of ten exchanged it to a *bark* or a *Grin*—Having view'd this sad Cluster of my fellow Creatures with amasement, I drove home to my lodgings with no less Humiliation—where I noted down what I could learn from the best Authority, both *white* and *black,* what is really the fate of these people, from the last moment of theyr liberty in Africa, to theyr present period of their Slavery in America, and which I shall endeavour to relate, together with a few of my own unbiassed Sentiments upon the Slave trade, /which is now so much in Agitation/ with that becoming Candour and impartiality, which not only every Gentleman but every Man, should pride himself in being possessed of—

I have since read Mr Clarkson's Essays, and read them with pleasure—I have read all the debates, and newspaper Controversies—and still heard more Arguments on the Subject, but find myself obliged to say /with that same bluntness which is perhaps too conspicuous throughout this whole Work/, that *most* of the learned Gentlemen in many Cases, have err'd on *both* sides; some by mis Information and prejudice, and others by Stuborness and passion; and which errors I will point out with manliness should I be damn'd by them altogether— It is idle from a principle of Humanity alone to persist in supporting such Arguments as are Confutable by Common sence, especially when founded principally on information, /providing Peoples Ears will be open to Conviction, by those who ought to know better by experience, and if not, *then* it is only spending their lungs to no purpose, and firing their powder at the Sparrows/ while it is equally absurd, for the sake of drinking rum, and eating Sugar, to persevere in the most unjust and diabolical barbarity; the enthusiasm of ill placed Humanity, being in my opinion equally as pernicious to Sosiety on one side, as the practice of ill grounded cruelty is winkedly destructive on the other.—In short, In the Evening *those Negroes* who were not sold, were return'd to their Companions on board the Guinea-man, to be paraded the same manner next day—

Here we will leave and take a retrospect view of those People in theyr own Country—All the World knows the extent of Africa, and that the greatest part, nay almost the whole, is what the Europeans call unsivilized. nevertheless not only the African negroes, but all the rest of the human Species, nay even the Animal Creation, live under a Species of Government, to where they flock, either prompted by fear for protection, or influenced from a Motive of avarice, to augment their Wealth; these Governments in Africa are small, and each ruled by a private king or Prince, /who like in all other Governments, counterballances the lower Class of his Subjects in the Scale of Misery, while the middle Station alone enjoy real Happiness/, theyr little Kingdoms encreasing so fast by Population, that like other great ones they clash together, and Millions are destroyed on both Sides, and well it is, /however little our narrow Conception to see it/, that the alwise Creator has ordered *war* this generally, and from all times; since like throughout all the other links of the Creation—as one fish lives upon another, Man would eat Man, and prey upon his brother without it. I acknowledge the many Arguments in favour of waste *lands* and industry, but I may as well use the Argument of waste *Water,* or waste *Air* and which human remarks, come not in the Smallest Competition in the always Scale of Omnipotence; Man can and ought but see at a certain distance and no farther—and it would be just as absurd to ask the Question why as it is in Popes lines to ask—

Why has not Man a Microscopic Eye?
The reasons Plain because Man's not a fly.

No more is he a God, thus let him keep within his limitted bounds, judge the Small Circle allotted to be within his Compass and Conception, but leave a *universe* to be governed by the great fountain of nature alone, submitting to its events with resignation. Nay I will even venture to say that *War* is just as necessary to prevent a general Stagnation on the Globe, as are our passions, nay the Circulation of the very blood that is in our veins to keep us healthy—does not the whole Creation from the invisible insect go to War, and make way for each other? nay do not the very Elements clash together, and enter in tremenduous convulsions—as the one proceeds from natural Causes to thin and purify the Air, So does the other to thin and preserve the human Species, who ever have, and ever will be thind, if not by *war,* by hurricanes, Pest, Scarcety &c, and whom it is just as necessary to diminish as it is to weed vegetables, or plants in a Garden—in order to give room to some, by destroying others, and prevent /as I say'd before/ one general Stagnation, which Arguments I shall end by observing with the Author above Quoted, that in my humble Opinion, *whatever is, is right* whatever Dreadfull the apparant Consequences.

If it is then allowed that war is as necessary evil proceeding from natural Causes, and that its horrors and devestations are at times, as necessary amongst the Sable Africans, as amongst the fair Europeans /who even derive from it Honor, and Glory/ the Question rests, on which of the 2 Continents are felt the greatest Calamities, and the most People destroyed by its Effects?—the Answer is evident, if we compare the Magnitude of uncivilized Africa, to the dimensions of hostile Europe, /bursting from every Corner with Smoak and fire & which carries even its dier and pestilential Effects to every other Quarter of the Globe/ and I candidly ask, if in 50 such *battles* as are described by the ingenious M:r *Clarkson* /kindled for the Capturing of Slaves, and of which but few Examples can be produced/ are Committed half the ravage, and destruction, that sometimes rages in *one* of our *british* Sea Engagements, both in regard to friend and foe?—Certainly not.—then what are the result of the Africa Wars?—the Result is, that great numbers of prisoners are taken on both Sides, which are eyther doom'd to be kil'd afterwards, or to be sold for Slaves in the Coast & the *last,* however dispisable, being to most Men still Preferable to Death.—

This clears their Country I Say and These 100000 /Spoke of to be/ transported yearly, are shurely but a very small proportion, to the Millions, that in all Europe annually expire under the name of Liberty, loaded with the pangs of want & disease, and crushed under the galling chains of oppression. nay while the very oppressors themselves, bend under the weight of that Gold, extorter'd from the brow, and distill'd by the Sweat of their drooping Subjects.—from all which I must conclude that *this trade,* or buying of negroe Slaves, is not so bad a thing as some try to support. while the effects that follow it, are alone the Complicated Evils, under which lay groaning, the too helpless African negroes & whose lives if properly looked after might /at the same time without being less usefull/ be made incomparably more happy, than those of eyther our Sailors, or Soldiers.—These are obliged to go, and be drownd or shot abroad, to get a pernicious Subsistance for their little starving families at home & to which they are to[o] often drag'd, lock'd short in Irons, contrary to their Capacity, or inclinations not to speak of above 50,000 helpless young Women, who independent of their genius, and beauty, must for the Sake of a loathsome temporary Subsistance, parade the Streets of our Metropolis in all Weathers, exposed to all thats Horrid, till they die unpitied upon a dunghill, in the middle of their own Countrymen, Starved, destested, kik'd, and wallowing in Corruption—How Dreadfull this account, Yet all this bustle /viz. what happens in Africa, the same as what happens in Europe/ seems so perfectly necessary to me, that it stands not in need of the smallest investigation, as it is a perfect truth, that from a private evil, is derived a general good—while Still more I am surprized, that *that* Humanity which induces people to plead across the Atlantic Ocean, till in the internal parts of Africa, and America, should not inspire them to begin at home with their own Countrymen, and Countrywomen first, where the needy who stole to support the cries of nature, and the relentless assassin are equally punished, and thousands of whom /as I have just observed/ independant of the many So Laudable Almshouses and Charitable Institutions, /erected as lasting Monuments of Honor throughout the Island of Great Britain/ stand much more in need of their assistance and Protection, than the Negro Slaves of Guinea, the greatest number of whom, under a well regulated Government, may live happier in the West Indies, than they ever did in the Forests of Africa—And as to theyr becoming Christians, they may /a few of them Excepted/ have a Chance of becoming a parcel of canting Hypocritical Rascals, like too many of theyr protecttors, and use it as a Cloak to impose upon the ignorant, but will never *chuse* to know more of that Sacred Institution, than they already do of Snow, their own Religion being much more Comodious, and not so much divested of Common Sence as numberless Stupid Europeans imagine—Besides I cannot help thinking it ungenerous thus wishing to deprive the West India *Planters* of their Property, by a Sudden abolition of the Slave Trade, who after their many hazards, and their loss of health, Wealth, and time, have no other Method of procuring a Subsistance for their families & which when cheapest is always to[o] dear bought—as for the *Sailors* imployed in it great numbers of them perish I acknowledge, but who if not died in this Way, would possibly have been obliged, to pick your Pockets for a Subsistance, and in Company with too many of theyr unfortunate Ship Mates, have been hang'd to keep them from Starving—it being very well known that these poor Men /who are the props, and bulwarks of every Mercantile-Nation/ have no Provisions made for them in times of Peace, and that the brave Tar, who has escaped a watery Grave during the War /to protect your Life and Property/ is often only saved to exchange it for an Airy one when it is over—thus better go to the Coast of Guinea to buy Negroes—

And As for the *Political*-good of the Nation that is to be derived by this humane abolitian, it is too conspicuous to pass it over in Silence—

Great Britain it is observed has already lost her 13 American Colonies /as some say/ by wishing to make a free People to Slaves, and now about to lose all her West India Settlements by in reverse, wishing to make Slaves to free People—for all which loss her Sons now have /at the hazard of peeping through a halter/ nobly emigrated to Bottany Bay, which being a new thing to be sure is preferable to old Baubles and Guigaws, and will no doubt in time not only make up for the loss of all America, but prove a most blessed acquisition for the nation—besides forcing us to go to foreign Markets to buy at double Price, has the good Effect of showing our Generosity to our french, and Spanish Neighbours—of keeping our Men from getting drunk at home with Jamaica Rum—And our Women from Spoiling their teeth by eating Sugar.—these are the Complicated Advantages which are likely to result should an Abolition of the Guinea Slave Trade take place, while should an Emancipation in the Islands have happened, one Negro would have cut anothers throat for hunger•—

But if we really wish to keep our remaining antiatlantick possessions that lay between the Tropicks, I in that Case do maintain, that they can never be cultivated but by Negroes alone Neither the fair European, or the American Indian, being adequate to the task—then the Grand Question that remains to be solved is—are these Negroes to be Slaves or a free People—to which I answer without hesitation—*dependent, &* under proper restrictions /a few very industrious individuels only excepted[/]—not so much even for the Sake of the European as for that of the African himself, with whose passions, debauchery and indolence, I am perfectly acquainted, and who like a Spirited Horse, when unbridled often Gallops to destruction himself, while he tramples under his feet all that he meets with—they would indeed in time provide for their *imediate* Subsistance but would no more think /at least for Ages to come/ of amassing Wealth by industry than their Countrymen the *Orangoutang;* of which the 20000 *Ouca* and *Serameca* free Negroes that are settled in Surinam, and which I have before mentioned, are a Glasing Instance; who neither want land, time, hands, or the proper tools for Cultivation, but will ten times sooner be employed in dancing, drinking, and catching fish, or killing a boar or a tiger, than in planting either Coffee—Sugar—Cacao—Cotton or Indigo—and by which their *Wealth* in a short time might be encreased, not only beyond a Possibility of want, but even to affluence for themselves and for their descending Posterity to many generations—the too much aspiring after *which,* has indeed made as many miserable in the State of Civilization, as it has made

• —That is in a few weeks—

happy if not more;—and am I of Abe *Renalds* Opinion, that the *natural-Man* /amongst which Class I rank the present generation of negroes/ in a free State, and even in a State of dependance, is the happiest of the two, providing while he is curb'd he is also indulg'd with some liberty, no Mortal being perfectly free,—and while he enjoys without restraint the Compleat Necessaries of Life, I think the name of *Slaves* /with which he is branded, and which sounds so odious in the Ears of those not acquainted with the many indulgences which he certainly reaps under a good Master/ might be exchanged to that of a Menial Servant—Query, what are the Prentices in England?—

I love the African Negroes, which I have showed on numberless occasions, and whatever wrong Constructions may be placed on what I have said on this Subject–I wish from the bottom of my heart that my *Words* may be the Anticipation of what shall be pronounced by that Illustrious body the British Parliament upon the Subject; but should it not be so I take Liberty to prophesy, that thousands and thousands shall repent it, and more be ruined by the rash proceeding, while it is not less for the benefit of the *African* than for that of this *glorious Island* that I have Spoke them, being neither interested the one way or the other, and for which I pledge my Honour; while as a further Proof I Shall throughout the Course of this narrative, still take the further liberty of pointing out such measures as, may make the Slaves in our West India Settlements perfectly happy, with even an Accumulation to the Wealth of their Masters—

It is said the West Indies can supply itself with Slaves in point of population.—I deny it not when in some course of time, such proper regulations shall have taken place–then, and not till then, All may be happy and Contented together without loss to the *Publick,* or to the *individual,* who first went to settle in these tropical burning Climates, under the Sanction of the British Legislature and to whom he with Justice still looks up for Protection—That such an Amendment *alone* for the present may take place and not a Simultaneous emancipation of the Negroe Slaves I pray and plead for and also that it may be crown'd with every success, after which time only and not before, I shall pride, and Glory, in the intire Abolition of a trade, which is at present certainly carried on with unbounded barbarity and usurpation.—This much for Africa in General, and now once more for her Sons in particular—

From what I have said above it clearly appears that numbers of the negroes offered for Sale have been taken in battles, and made Prisoners of–while many others as M.r Clarkson wisely observes, have been Scandalously Kidnapped, and some others transported for Offences &c Of

1773—OCTOBER 6

all which I shall produce a few Examples in the future—

These groops of People then are Marched from every inland part to the factories, erected by different nations upon the Coast, where they are Sold, or more properly Speaking bartered like the other Productions of their Country, viz. as Gold..elephants-teeth &c to the Europeans for bars of Iron, fire Arms. Carpenters tools. checkred linnens, hats, knives, Glasses. tobacco, Spirits &c—next they are embarked for Exportation, during which time they without Contradiction feell all the Pangs that Mental, or Corporal, Misery can inflict—being tore from their Country and th.r dearest Connexions, stow'd hundreds together in a dark stinking hold, the Sexes being Seperated, while the Men are kept in chains to prevent an insurrection—In this manner are they floated over turbulent Seas, not certain what is to be their destiny, and generally fed during the Passage with Horse Beans, and Oil, for all Subsistance.—but all Captains are not *Cooling Woods,* and these Pangs are often alleviated with better food by the more humain, so far that none or few of the Cargo die during the Passage, and the whole crew arive healthy in the West Indies—I even remember one instance where the Capt.n, Meat, S.r Mate Surgeon & Boson and most of the Sailors having expired at Sea, So that the remaining few could not work the Ship without the Negroes assistance, yet these last having been well treated help'd at least to run the Vessal upon Shoare, by which they not only saved many lives—but tamely and even chearfully allowed themselves to be fetched, and sold as I have above mentioned to who would please to buy them•—

Having wafted them over the Atlantick Ocean I will now breefly proceed with the manner in which they are disposed of—No sooner is a Guinea-Man arrived than all the Slaves are led upon deck, where they are refreshed with pure Air, Plantains, bananas, Oranges &c, and being properly clean'd washed, and their hair shaved in different figures of Stars. half moons &c, /which they generally do the one to the other (having no Razors) by the help of a broken bottle and without Soap/ I say after this, one part of them is sent a Shoare for Sale, decorated with Pieces of Cotton to serve as fig leafs, arm bands beads &c being all the Captains Property, while the others Spend the day dancing hallooing, and clapping hands on board the Vessel—I having thus sufficiently described theyr figures after landing we now shall suppose to see them walking along the Waters Side and through the Streets, where every planter picks out that number which he stands in need of, to supply

• —this vessal had her Captain murdered the voyage before last and now belong'd to Capt.n Grim—

those wanting by Death Desertion &c. and for which he makes a Bargain with the Captain good Negroes costing from 50 to 100 Pound each—Amongst these should a Woman chance to be pregnant her Price is Augmented accordingly—while I have known the Captain of a Dutch Guinea-Man who acknowledged himself to be the father, possess the unheard of Brutality of doubling the Value by selling his own Ofspring to the best Bidder, but for which he was highly Censured by his Companions, one rotten Sheep not disgracing the whole flock—The next thing is before the bargain is struck to let the new acquisitions one after another mount upon a hogshead or a table, where they are visited by a Surgeon making all the different figures and gestures with Arms and legs of a merry Andrew upon the Stage, to prove their Soundness or unsoundness, after which they are adopted by the buyer, or cast as he thinks proper—If he keeps them the Money is paid down—and the new bought Negroes imediately branded on the breast or the thick of the Shoulder by a Stamp made of Silver with the inicial letters of the Masters Name as we mark furniture or any thing else to authenticate the property—But these hot Letters which are about the Size of a Sixpence occasion not that pain that may be imagined, and which blisters being directly rub'd with a little fresh butter is perfectly well in the Space of 2 or 3 Days—No sooner is this Ceremony over and a new name given to the newly bought Slave than he or she is delivered to an old one of the same Sex and sent to the Estate, where each by his Guardian is properly kep'd clean, instructed and well fed, without working for the Space of 6 Weeks, during which Period from living Skeletons they become Plump and fat with a beautiful clean Skin till disfigured by the lash of the cruel Whip which too generally follows from the hands of the too relentless Overseers—Here I must leave them for some time and Continue my Narrative after observing that the Negroes are composed of different Nations or Casts such as the

abo	Congo	Loango	pombo
bonia	gango	N'Zoko	wanway-&c
blitay	konare	Nago	
Coromantin	kiemba	Papa	

with most of which I have found means to get acquainted and of which I shall speak more Amply in proper place and Season—

The Surgeon now having lanced my thigh, I this day Scrambled out, and once more saw the selling of Slaves to the best bidder, Heavens shall I relate it[?] amongst whom was now my inestimable Joana, the Sugar Estate Faukenburgh with its whole Stock being to day sold by Execution to defray by Dividend the Creditors of its late Possessor M.

D. Borde, I now felt all the Horrors of the Damn'd bewailing my unlucky fortune that did not enable me to become her Proprietor my self and figuring in my Mind her ensuing dreadfull Situation—Me thought I saw her, mangled, ravished, ridiculed, and bowing under the weight of her Chains calling aloud for my assistance–I was miserable–Indeed I was truly wretched labouring under such Emotions as had now nearly deprived me of all my faculties, til restored by the assurances of my Friend Mr Lolkens, who providentially was appointed to Continue Administrator of the Estate during the absence of its new Possessors Messrs Passelege & Son at Amsterdam and who had bought it and its dependants for only 4000 Pound—I say till restored by the Assurances of my Friend /who brought Joana again to my presence/ that in every Service which he could render either to myself or her /and which he had now more in his Power than ever, the Estate at present belonging to only two Masters/ no Efforts on his Side should be wanting–which promise I desired him to keep in remembrance and in which he since nobly persevered as shall appear—

I now being informed that Colonel Fourgeoud had left Crawassibo Estate and entered the Woods just above the Plantation Clarenbeek on his way to the Wana Creek to try if he could not fall in with the Rebels, requested by a letter that I might join him there so soon as I should be recovered, and having Ship'd off this Day for the last mentioned Estate Clarenbeek /where an Hospital was also erected/ a Chist with Medicines and all the Quacks that had been left at Paramaribo, I imploy'd Mr Greber the Surgeon of the Society on my own Authority and at the Regiments expense to attend the Seek Officers and Soldiers who were left in Town destitute of Cash and now without assistance–while I also ordered to be purchased two *more* Anchors of best Claret for theyr Support thus properly availing myself of my Command which at best could but last a few Days longer—

This Evening departed my Friend De la Mare with his 25 free Mulattos to the River Surinam he being a Captn of the Militia and they being infinitely preferable to the European Scarcrows—

I was now so far recovered as to be able to ride out every Morning when the following ludicrous adventure happened on the Road that leads to Wanica—here a Mr Van de-vel-de bragging how fast his horse could Gallop, proposed to me to run a race and to which I agreed providing he was to take the Start at 20 paces distance. Off he went, when a little after my English Horse passing his galloway like a Shott it Sprung rider and all through a hedge of thick limes and left Mr Van de velde not in the dirt like Doctor Slop by Obadiah but like Absalom hanging among the branches—

1773—OCTOBER 17, 18

The Horses in Surinam are little better or larger than Jack Asses /except those that are brought from North America, or Holland, which last are generally employed for Carriages/ yet they are useful in the Sugar Mills where Mules are also very much made use of which are carried over from Barbary and sometimes sold so high as 50 Guineas— none of these are natural to Guiana but as many other Animals have been imported and become the Inhabitants of the Climate while to save unecessary repetitions I will here give the following accurate list of such Quadrupedes as are not peculiar to the new Continent

the Elephant	Sheep	Wild Goat
the Rinoceros	Goat	Small Guinea Stag
Hipopotamus	Hog	Rabit
Cameleopard	Dog	ferret
Camell	badger	rat
Dromedary	Sable	Mouse
Lion	Stot or ermine	fat Squirrel
Tiger	hiaena	Gardin Squirrel
Panther	Jackall	Marmot
Horse	Genett	Ichnewman
Ass	Civett	Jerboa
Zebra	Cat	Maki and
Ox	Antelope	several kinds of
buffalo	Chamois Goat	Monkeys—

Should the number on this list seem rather great, I in that case refer to the Celebrated Count De Buffon from where it was extracted—

This Evening arrived seek from Devils Harwar Ensign Matthew one of the Officers by whom I had been relieved—

And this day he was already followed by his Commander and my friend Colonel Westerlo supported by 2 Soldiers, who had ridiculed me for Complaining after being on board the cursed barges so many Weeks, while these Gentlemen had been out but a few days and always on Shoare, this last having attempted to accompany the old Colonel Fourgeoud to wana /whom he had joined at La Rochelle in Patamaca/ but had been knocked up after making his first Entry in the woods—I was at dinner with a Mr Day when I saw him pass by a miserable Spectacle, and independant of what had past at Devils Harwar I having a regard for this Gentleman started up immediately got him a Coach in which I accompanied him to his Lodgings and where having placed a Centinel before his Chamber door to keep out the rabbel, I sent for one Doctor van Dam besides a Doctor Kissam an American to attend him—forbidding all other Communication, that of an old

Negro Woman his Man Servant and Black Boy /bien-venu/ excepted by which I apparently preserved his Life—

    Came down seek Lieut. Count de Randwyk—

    Ditto. Ensign Coene also and at last my poor old Shipmate Lieut Hamer who had till now been kept at Devils-Harwar being near 4 Months till overcome by Disease he had got leave to be transported to Paramaribo—which shows what a Cursed place was Devils Harwar to the Troops—

    This Morning was sent me by the Governor a Cotton twig which I coppied and now having the time I will give the discription of that usefull Comodity which has only been Cultivated in Surinam since about the Year 1735 but not with advantage till about the Year 1750 or 52. it consists in different kinds, but I shall confine myself to that which is the most Common and the most useful in this Colony—This Species of Cotton grows upon a Tree which is about 6 or 8 feet high[,] bears before it is a Year old and produces two Crops annually of each about 20 Ounces in weight—the leaves are something like those of the Vines, of a bright green and the feebres [fibers] of a Cinnamon Colour—The Cotton balls which are some as large as a Small hens Egg and divided in three Parts grow on a very long Stalk and in a triangular Pod which is first produced by a yellow flower and when ripe opens of itself when it discloses the globular Contents as white as fleaks of Snow and in the middle of these are contained small black seeds, form'd not unlike those that are usually found into grapes—

The Cotton tree will prosper in any kind of tropical Soil and comes to very good account if the Crops are not Spoilt by a too long rainy Season it being Cultivated with so very little trouble and expense, having nothing to do but to plant the Seeds at a little distance from each other, when each Seed as I have said produces the Year of its being put in the Ground. The Seperation of the Seeds from the Pulp is the Work of One Man only by the help of a Machine made for the Purpose after which the Cotton has undergone all its necessary process, and is put in bales of between 3 and 4 hundred Pound Weight each for Transportation, which bales ought to be well moisted at the time of Stowing it, to prevent the Cotton from Sticking to the Canvas—in the Year before my Arrival in Surinam were exported from this Colony to Amsterdam and Rotterdam alone near 3000 bales of Cotton which produced about 40,000 pound Sterling•—Best Estates make 25000 lb

This ingredient is Spun in the West Indies by a rock and Spindle, /such as was offered to Hercules, by Omphale Queen of Lydia,/ and

---

• —the avaridge price has been from 8 to 22d p^r lb weight—

Sprig of the Cotton Tree.

London, Published Dec.r 1st 1791 by J. Johnson, St Paul's Church Yard.

extremely fine, when by the Sable Queens it is knet in Stockings &c one pair of which are Sometimes sold for the price of a portegee Jo, or 2 Guineas

The Indians or natives of Guiana make very good hammocks of Cotton also which they barter with the Inhabitants at Paramaribo for other Commodities. in the annexed plate **A** is the twig itself **B** the Pod **C** the Cotton ball and **D** the Seed—but on a Smaller Scale than nature–I should here also describe the coffee cacao Sugar and Indigo Cultivations, but must reserve them till they offer me the Opportunity[,] having made it my Plan to Speak of things only as they occur which is more pleasant to myself, and better adapted to diversify the mind of the reader—

Being now perfectly recovered, I resolv'd to Join Colonel Fourgeoud at the Wana Creek—without waiting his orders—and accompany him on his excursions through the forest, in consequence of which having first cropt my hair as being more convenient and cleanly in the Woods, and provided myself with the necessary bush equipage, such as Jackets Trowsers &c. I waited on the Governor to ask his Commands and who entertained me in a most polite manner and told me that what I was now going to suffer would Surpass what I had already undergone. I nevertheless persisted in wishing to go as I Sayd without waiting an Order from the Chief and accordingly applied to the Magistrates for a boat and the necessary Negroes to transport me which being promised for the following day I gave over the Colours and Regiments Cash, with the Command of the remaining Seek troops to a Second Lieut Meyer the only healthy Officer then at Paramaribo—Indeed the Collors, the cash, and the Seek Soldiers were of equal use to us in Surinam, the first never having been displayed except at our landing–the 2^d invisible to all except to Col. Fourgeoud–and the 3^d dying the one after the Other—

Chapter 10th

Col: Fourgeoud Marches to the Wana Creek—Harrasses the Enemy—Account of the Manicole Tree with its various uses—March to the Mouth of Coermoetibo River—Some Rebels taken—Shoaking treatment of a wounded Captive Negroe

Being now ready to set out upon my Second Campaign I repair to the Water Side at 6 O Clock in the Evening where in place of a tent boat, I found a greasy Yoll with a few Drunken Dutch Sailors to row me to an Estate in the River Comewina from where they were going to fetch their Captain back to Paramaribo and from which place I might if I pleased beg the rest of my Passage upwards, or shift for myself in the best manner that I was able—I had already one foot in the boat when reflecting that I was going voluntarily on a hazardous expedition without being ordered, and from a motive of wishing to serve a parcel of ungrateful Gentry I repented and stept back upon the Shoare where /Swearing I should not move to theyr defense till such time as I should be decently transported, should the whole Colony be on fire,/ I was seconded by all the English and Americans in the town, and a general hub bub took place, the Dutch exclaimed against the expense of a tent boat which would cost them 30 Shillings, when they could have the other for nothing, while the others declared them a parcel of Shabby Rascals, who deserved not the smallest protection from Colonel Fourgeouds Troops—A Mob now gathered and a riot ensued, before M:r Hardegens Tavern at the Waterside while hats wigs. bottles and Glasses flew out at his Window[.] the Magistrates were next sent for to no purpose and the fighting continued in the Street till 10 OClock at night, when I with my friends fairly keep'd the field, having knocked down several Sailors, planters, Jews, and Overseers and lost one of my

Pistoles which I threw after the rabble in my Passion, nor would it have ended here had not M! Kennedy who was Member of the Court of Polisy and two or three more Gentlemen whom he brought with him found means to appease the whole dispute by declaring I had been badly used, and should have a proper boat the next day, after which we all sat down and drank away the night till the Sun rose the next morning—

Having now sleep'd and refreshed myself a few hours, I was waited on by 4 American Captains–viz, Cap! Timmens of the Harmony, Capt. Lewis of the Peggy, Capt. Bogard of the Olive Branch and Capt. Minet of the America, who insisted on my refusing any vessal whatever from the Colony this time and on their sending me up in one of their own boats man'd by their own Sailors only, to which each Contributed alike–and do I declare that independant of the threatening rupture between Great Britain and her Colonies/, and which seemed then upon the eve of breaking out in an open flame,/ nothing could surpass the warm heart and friendship which these Gentlemen proved to possess not only for me, but for every individual that bore a british Name or had any Connection with that glorious Island for which they all Swore to have still the greatest regard that could be, but not for its administration, which they said was a rotten one, and of which I have heard them wish to chop of[f] the head with one blow of the hatchet, rather than they should be the Cause of setting a Son to fight against his own father, or one brother against another, and upon the whole making go to War 2 nations that are so nearly allied by the sacred ties of Consanguinity, by friendship, and every thing else, but declaring that if it must be so, they would stand out till they had Spilt the last drops of theyr blood before they should yield to what they pleased to call a Scandalous oppression, and usurpation of theyr rights, theyr liberties, and theyr property—In short I accepted of their very polite proposal, when having received a letter from M! Kennedy to deliver to one of the Militia Captains a M! N. Reeder in the River Comewina, with orders to send me further up in a proper tent boat, and having arranged Matters so at home that neither Colonel Fourgeoud, or the Cockroaches could hurt me, I shaked hands with my Mulatto, and at 6 in the evening repaired once more to the Water Side escorted by my English and American Friends, and where having drunk half a dozen bowls of Punch we seperated, and I departed for my Station, they having hoisted the Colours on board of all theyr vessals in the roads and at the boats going of[f] saluting me with 3 Cheers to my great Satisfaction, and the Mortification of the gaping Scum by which we were surrounded, and which Compliment being returned by the boats Crew, and 3 Voleys from my fusee we soon row'd out of Sight of Paramaribo—

Being come to the fortress N. Amsterdam we were obliged to Stop for the return of the tide to row up the River Comewina, during which time I was genteelly entertained with a Supper by the Society Officers Quartered there but at 12 O Clock set off again, and having row'd all night I breakfasted with Capt. Macneyl in Matapica Creek, /he having been one of General Sporks Captains in 1751 who had also given him this Estate from which it takes its Name/ after which we once more set out and arrived at the Plantation Charlotten-burgh, where I deliverd M.ʳ Kennedys Letter to M.ʳ Reeder and who promised next morning to assist me.

So very insensed was I at the usage I had met with at Paramaribo, and so well pleased with the English Sailors that I ordered the Tars a dinner of 12 roasted ducks and gave them 36 bottles of Claret, Being my whole Stock, besides a Guinea and my Compliments to theyr Captains, when with the Ebb tide they took theyr leave and row'd down to their vessals as well pleased, and as drunk as Wine or Strong Spirits could make them—

I now pursued my Voyage upwards as far as the Estate Mondesir—

I came to Lapaix having view'd the ruins of the three Estates Zuynigheyd, Peru, and L'Esperance, which had been burnt when I commanded at Devils Harwar—Here one of the Overseers gave me an account of the whole Catastrophe and particularly of his own Miraculous Escape–which I shall relate in his own Words—

> the Rebels Sir /say'd he/ had allready surrounded the Dwellinghouse in which I was, before I knew of theyr being on the Plantation–and were employ'd in Setting fire to the 4 Corners of it, so that running out of doors was rushing on Certain Death; in this dilemma I fled to the garret where I lay myself flat upon of the beams, in the hopes of their dispersing soon, and my Stil escaping before the building was burnt down, but in this I was disappointed, as they remained, and at the same time the flames encreased so fast that the heat became insupportable where I was & I had no other alternative left but to be burnt to death, or to leap from a high garret window in the middle of my exasperated enemies, this last however I resolved upon and had not only the good fortune to alight unhurted upon my feet, but to escape without a wound–through amongst them all, /while cutting and Slashing at me with Sabers and bill hooks/ and pursuing me to the River Side in which I plunged myself headlong, but not being able to Swim immediately sunk to the bottom, nevertheless /said he/ I still kept my full presence of mind–and while they concluded me to be drownd found means by the help of the Moco-Moco

and Mangrove roots, to bring myself both under Cover of the impending verdure, and just so far above water with my lips as to continue in a State of respiration, till all was over; they having kill'd every other body and I was taken up by a boat from my verry distressed Situation—

These were his very words when in Spite of the Aversion I have to overseers in general I could not help congratulating the poor fellow on his having escaped from the wrath of the 4 Elements—

- I arrived at Devils Harwar—Oh Cursed Spott—
- I now at last row'd up the Coermoetibo Creek where having tied the boat to a Tree which over Spread it by its thick branches we quietly lay down to Sleep during the night myself and Quacoo in the tent upon the benches, and the Negroes under the Seats, whom I ordered alternately to keep Watch, and awake me if they heard the least rus[t]ling in the Woods, forbidding them all absolutely not to Speak or make any Noise to prevent the Rebels, who were hovering at both Sides of the Creek from hearing us, and cutting all our throats without distinction, at least myself who was the only white Person amongst them all, I was confident could not escape their fury; I say after these precautions we all lay down and I never slept more soundly in my life from 9 OClock
- till about 3 in the Morning but when Quacoo and myself were both suddenly thrown down from our benches by the boat all at once keeling upon one Side, while all the Negroes leap'd overboard in the Water—I instantly now cock'd my Pistole, and jumping out of the tent call'd aloud what was the matter, well determined to blow out my own brains sooner than be taken alive by such a relentless Sad Enemy; for the Space of a few Seconds I got no Answer, when at last the boat again suddenly redressing itself /by the motion of which I was thrown now of[f] my feet, / one of the swimming Negros call'd out, *kay Mimasera da wan See Cow,* and to my great happiness it proved to be no other, than the *Manatee* or Sea Cow which is called in Cayenne the Lamentyn, but of which Animal for the present I can say nothing more than that by the account of the Negroes it had Sleep'd under the boat which by its awaking had been lifted up, and thrown upon one Side, and again redress'd itself when the Manatee made its escape from underneath it— I not so much as having seen the Creature nor indeed hardly they, owing to the darkness of the night which lasted some hours after, but during which Time we had no more Inclination to go to rest at last the Suns bright beams began to dart through the Trees and guild the nodding foliage, whom I having addressed something in Doctor Armstrongs Language—

Hail Holy light first born of heaven and only less than God—

We cast off from our Moorings, and continued rowing up Coermoetibo Creek /which was now very narrow/ till near noon, when we saw a Smoak, and at last came to the mouth of the Wana Creek, which also waters out in the Marawina, and which was the Spot of rendevous but where the troops were not yet come, and opposite to which were encamp'd a few of the rangers to guard the provisions that were waiting the arival of Colonel Fourgeoud and his Party from Crawassibo, and last from Patamaca—

One of the Rangers having to day kill'd a *tattu* or *Armadilla*, call'd in Surinam *Capasee*, I shall here discribe it

This Animal is with propriety sometimes Stiled a hog in Armour, its head and ears being much like those of a roasting Pig and its whole body covered over with hard Shells like Shields, sliding in moveable rings like those of the Qui-Qui fish already mentioned the one over the other, except on the Shoulders and the rump which are covered something like the turtle, with one Mass of Solid immoveable bone call'd by some a Quiras and a helmet—Of this Creature there are many Species in Guiana, the largest being from the Snout to the tip of the tail above 3 feet in length of a reddish Yellow Colour and Marked all over with hexangular figures—its eyes are Small the tail long and thick at the root, and tapering gradually like a Carrot towards the Point, is covered over like the Body with moveable rings—this Animal has four Short legs, with 4 toes, armd with 2 large claws on the fore feet, and 5 on those behind—The Armadillo walks generally in the night time being seldom seen through the day, and sleeps in burrows under Ground which it makes with great dispatch and facility, and in which it Sticks so fast that the strongest Man cannot pull it out having its tail in both hands; when attack'd or afraid it forms itself into a round ball like the hedge hog making its Quiras and helmit meet together, in which are inclosed its head, feet, &c but what Guard is invulnerable to destructive Man? none. this Creature feeds on roots, fruits, insects, birds &c and when dress'd appear'd to me no bad dish, though in general it is reckoned no great delicasy, only the Indians in particular being extremely fond of it—

I shall here also take the opportunity to say Something of the *Guiana-Porcupine* called here guinea-Maccaw and by some Adjora—this Animal which is from its Mussle to the root of the tail sometimes 3 feet in length is all over covered with hard Pricles, the feet, the face, and part of its tail excepted, which Prickles are about 3 Inches long, yellow at the root a dark chesnut colour in the middle and white at the points and which are extremely Sharp, highly polished, and moveable, serving for the creatures defense, and which when irritated it dresses in

The Armadillo, & Porcupine of Guiana.

London, Published Dec.r 2.nd 1793 by J. Johnson, S.t Paul's Church Yard.

1773—NOVEMBER 2

array, and makes a formidable appearance before its adversary; at other times these prickles lay flat on its back something like the bristles of a Sow; the head of the Porcupine is of a roundish make and join'd to the body by a remarkably thick short neck. its eyes are large bright, and placed near the ears, which are very Small and round, it never bites and on each side of its nose has long whiskers verry like the Otter or the Cat—its feet are shaped very much like those of a Monkey, which assist it in climbing of trees to seek its food, and in which its long tapering tail is also very Serviceable, which like a fifth limb, it twists about the branches—and is near the extremety covered over with hair like the face, the underpart near the tip only excepted, which is perfectly callous and black as are also the inside of all its feet—

The Hedge hog of this Country is I think little different from that of the old Continent, being about 8 or 10 Inches in length, covered over with Pale Yellow Prickles, but hair on the face, and under the belly, which is rather more Soft and longer than in the hedgehog of Europe— It has dark brown Spots like eye brows over its Eyes, and no Ears but auditory holes, and 5 toes with bended Claws on each foot, its tail is very Short, and its defence consists in forming itself to a round ball or Clew, in the manner of the Armadillo—its food consists in fruit roots, vegetables insects &c and makes no bad dish for the Indians or natives of the Country—

Colonel Fourgeoud not being yet arrived, I amused myself with Swimming, and padling up the mouth of the deep Wana Creek with a Canoo, during which time a *M.* *Rulach* one of our Officers who was with me made me observe /in the top of a Mangrove tree/ a battle between a Snake, and a frog, /and for the greater authenticity that frogs are to be found in trees, I refer the Reader to the London Review for March 1785 Page 199, where in the Abbe *Spallanzanis* desertation upon frogs, the *tree-frog* is particularly mentioned/ but finding this Animal amongst the branches did not nearly so much excite my Surprize as the engagement itself, which I shall distinctly relate, and in which the poor frog lost the battle—indeed when I perceived him his head and Shoulders were already in the Jaws of the Snake, which last seemed to me about the Size of a large kitchen poker—and had its tail twisted around a tough limb of the Mangrove, while the frog who appeared to be the Size of a Mans fist, had to my great astonishment lay'd hold of a twig with the Claws of its hinder legs, as with Small hands—In this position where they pulling both for Life, and forming one Streight Line between the 2 branches, and thus I beheld them seemingly Stationary and without a Struggle—Still hoping the poor frog might extricate himself by his excertion; but the reverse soon was the Consequence, when the

Jaws of the Snake gradually relaxing, and by their elasticity forcing [forming?] an incredible orifice—the body and fore legs of the frog little and little disappeared till finally nothing more was seen than the hinder feet and claws, which he at last let go from the twig, and was Swallowed alive by suction down the throat of his formidable adversary, from where he gliding down some inches further, at last rested, forming a knob or knot, at least 6 times as thick as the Snake, and whose Jaws and throat emmediately contracted, and reassumed theyr former natural Shape—the Snake being out of our reach we could not kill him with Conveniency to take any further Examination, thus left him, he continuing in the same attitude without moving, and twisted around the branch—

One party of the Troops now being arrived, and incamp'd on the **S.W.** Side of the Coermoetibo Creek about one Mile above the Mouth of the Wana—I went with a Couple of Rangers to pay them a visit, when Major *Roehkopf* the Commanding Officer informed me that Colonel Fourgeoud had marched last from Patamaca in two Collomns of which he was the one, while the other was hourly expected—and that the rest of the regiment was divided in the rivers *Cottica, Pirica* and *Comewina,* excepting those that were Seek in the Hospital at Paramaribo—I was now in excellent health and good Spirits and in the hopes of being reconsiled to Fourgeoud by this Voluntarily Proof of my Seal [zeal] for the Service, I returned to the rangers Camp to wait his arrival—I was indeed well acquainted with his irreconsilable Temper, and at the same time conscious of my own wild, and Ungovernable Disposition, when I thought myself ill treated but soon forgot trifling injuries, and was now determined by my active and affable behaviour to make this Sod my friend if such was possible—

In Short the wished for hour arrived, and being apprized of Colonel Fourgeouds approaching, I went half a Mile from the Camp to his rencounter, acquainting him that I was come *Pour Participer de la gloire* and to serve under his immediate Command which he having answered with a bow, I returned it and we marched together in the rangers Camp—The news of this March consisted in their having taken from the Enemy 3 Villages, particularly one called the rice Country on account of the great Quantity of rice which they here found, Some ripe, Some in full blossom, but which /leaving the huts or wigwams intire*/ they had all destroyed after driving the Rebels to flight, who were commanded by one *bony* a relentless Mullatto, who was born in the forest, and had nothing to do with *barons* Party that had lately been drove from

• —this was not necessary as they are built with so very little Trouble—

Boucow—that they had found 7 Sculls stuck upon Stakes, under which lay mouldering the bodies above ground, and part of the garment and which discovered them to be the remains of the unfortunate *Lieut Lepper* and 6 of his Men; in Consequence of which they were all buried immediately also that they had taken Prisoner a *Woman* who declared that the *White Men* taken alive at the engagement as I have related with Lepper, had one by one been Stript by the Negroes so soon as they arrived in the rebel Village or rice Country, where they had by bonys orders been flog'd to death, for the recreation of theyr Wives and their Children; this was an Act of Cruelty in *bony* which was quite reverse in the Character of *Baron* and who independent of all his threats and Menaces, it was well known had sent back different Soldiers to Paramaribo, whom he might have kil'd, even helping to Conceal them from his enraged accomplices, and assisting them with provisions, well knowing they were not the Cause of the disturbance, while not a *ranger* could escape his fury /as I have mentioned before/ that had the misfortune to fall in his hands—The other news was, that the whole Party nearly being Starved for want had conjuncly called out for Bread—Bread—Bread, theyr being Still plenty in the boxes, but which had been keept back 3 Days, in exchange for the rice above mentioned, when the Officers to show their Zeal had rushed with kock'd Pistoles and drawn Swords in amongst the Men, and /indiscriminately laying hold of the first in their way/ had unluckily Seized a Poor Man named *Schmidt* and whom /notwithstanding all the others Swore he was innocent/ they had for an Example to the rest, bastonaded between 2 Corporals, till the blood gushed out of his Mouth like a fountain, which ended the revolt—While one of his Conductors named *Mangol* Scorning to be under Colonel Fourgeouds Command had left him, without asking his Consent, after which he left the Service altogether—These were the Particulars of the March in both Collomns, From Crawassibo in Comewina till the Wana Creek—

While I was now about Noon resting in my Hammock very Contentedly, I was accosted by my friend Lieut. *Campbell,* who acquainted me with tears in his Eyes that the Evening before, Colonel Fourgeoud had to the Officers of the Surinam Society given, not only of myself and of him, but of all the Officers and private Men belonging to that brave and gallant Corps, the Scots brigade in the Dutch Service, the most diabolical Character that could be invented—I imediately Started up, and having got Campbells Information Confirmed, went to Fourgeoud and asked him in Publick, what was the cause of this Slander behind my back—he said it was owing to my petticoat trowsers only, which I wore for coolness and conveniency something like the High-

The Sculls of Lieu.t Leppar & Six of his Men.

London, Published Dec.r 2.d 1795, by J. Johnson, S.t Paul's Church Yard.

landers of Scotland, and he was pleased to call indecent, as for the rest of what was said on my Account he charged with it M.' *Stoelman* the Captain of the Cottica Militia, as being the first propogator, but who at this time was absent, to all which I answered *the thiefer like the better Soldier,* and having swore revenge against this assassin of my reputation besides promising to lengthen my trowsers in the dutch way, we seperated, but an hour after which I received orders immediately to cross the coermoetibo Creek and be henceforth under the Command of Major Rughcoph who was with his party or Collomn at this time incamped on the S. Side of the Mouth of Wana Creek; force is indeed the ruling Principle in Military Affairs, says a certain Author, and upon the whole had the ingenious Advice given to a Commander in Chief, in one of the British Magazines, been read by Colonel Fourgeoud, I should have imagined he had copied it Sentence after Sentence, since by g———d nothing could better correspond—Being arrived in Major Rughcopfs Camp where having got a Couple of Negroes to Serve me, the first thing was to build a hut, or more properly speaking a Shade over my Hammock, to keep me free from the rain and the Sun shine and which was done within the Space of one hour—as the process of building these huts is of very material Consequence throughout this expedition, where we never used any tents, and during which time several thousands of the above huts were erected, I will describe the manner in which it is carried on—the more as being extremely curious, and useful on many other occasions—Curious because neither Hammers or Nails, or indeed any kind of Carpenters tools are required, a strong cutlass or billhook only excepted, and usefull as they are instantly raised, and form not only lasting, but the most delightful and convenient Habitations, with even 2 Stories above each other if required—for all this nothing is wanted but 2 things, the first the *Manicole* by the french called *Latanie* and here Prasella or the pina[?] tree, and the second the *nebees* call'd by the French *Liannes* the Spaniard *Bajorcos* and in Surinam *tay-tay*—

The *Manicole* Tree which is of the Palm tree Species is mostly found in Marshy places, and is always a proof of a rich and Luxurious Soil, it is about the thickness of a Mans thigh very streight and grows the height of from 30 to 50 feet from the ground, the trunk which is jointed at the distance of 2 or 3 feet is of a light brown Colour hard externally for the thickness of about half an Inch, but pethy [pithy] like the English Elder and good for nothing within, except near the top where the wood becomes Green, and incloses, a delicious kind of white food—call'd Cabbage, and which being peculiar to all the palm trees—I shall on another Occasion amply discribe—On the top of all this the Manicole tree Spreads in beautiful green boughs with leafs hanging Streight downwards like Silk Ribbons, which forms it into a kind of an umbrella; The manner of using it for building Huts or Cottages, is by cutting the trunk in Pieces of as many feet long as you wish to have the partition high, for instance 7 feet, which pieces are next Split in Small boards, the breadth of a Mans hand, and devested of their pethy Substance, when they are fit for immediate use; having Cut and prepared as many of these laths as you will want to surround your Dwelling you have nothing to do but to lash them in a perpendicular position, and close to each other to 2 cross bars of the same tree fix'd to the corner posts, all which is cut and shaped with the bill hook alone, and tied together by the nebees, or tay-tay which I think have here derived theyr name from *to tie*–, since the English had possession of the Colony.

The *nebees* are a kind of ligneous ropes of all Sizes, both as to length and thickness that grow in the Woods and which climb up alongst the trees in all directions, and are so plentiful and wonderfully dispersed that like the ligneous Cordage of the Mangroves /as I have said before/ they make the forest appear like a large fleet at anchor, killing many of the Trees by mere Compression, and entwining themselves with each other to the thickness of a Cable of a Ship, without any kind of foliage, which makes them sometimes have a wonderful appearance, particularly when asscending lofty trunks, in a Spiral manner to the top, from which they next hang down to the Earth, take root and reassend. sometimes the thin nebees are so closely interwoven, that they have the appearance of fishing nets, and game can not get through them; these nebees are exceedingly tough, and may be used for mooring large vessels to the Shore—Having only added that some of them are poisnous, especially those that are flat, grooved, or angular, I shall proceed to the roofing of the Cottage—This is done by the green boughs or branches of the same Manicole tree that made the Walls, and in the following manner–each bough which I can compare to nothing so well as to the Shape of a feather and which is as large as a Man, must be split from the top to the bottom in 2 equal halves as you would Split a Pen, when a number of these half boughs are tied together by theyr own verdure, and form a bunch, next you take these bunches and tie them with nebees one above another upon the roof of your Cottage as thick as you please, and in such a manner that the verdure which looks like the mane of a horse hangs downwards—this covering which at first is green, but soon takes the Colour of the English Reed-thatching, is very beautiful, lasting, and close, and finishes your house as I have said without the help of a hammer or a nail, the doors, and windows, tables, Seats &c are made in the same manner also—enclosures for Gardens the Same or other places for keeping of Cattle—and by this conveniency it is that the rebel Negroes never want good houses, which if burnt to ashes to day, are again perfectly rebuilt to morrow, however never in the places where they have been discovered by Europeans; while the Indians in place of the Manicoles generally cover their wigwams with *tas* or with *trooly,* of which I shall Speak on another occasion—I ought not to forget that the Seed of these trees consists in a Spatha near the top of 30 or 40 knotty feebres, forming in a Species of broom for which they are used throughout the Colony—thus while the Manicole affords you a House, it assists you also in the means to keep it clean, besides the Cabbage which indeed as I have said is found in all the other Palm trees &c—but the hut that I now lay under was not built in the Convenient manner above described, which was not requisite for the Short time that we generally were in one place; it consisting only in a roof or Cover without any Walls; the manner of erecting these little Shades /which every private Soldier does for himself[/] is simply by planting 4 forked Poles in the Ground at such a distance that your Hammock can conveniently hang between them, next to rest 2 short poles Strong enough to support your weight in the above forks, the one at the head and the other at the feet, and to which are lashed the clews [end knots] of your hammock, on the *outer* extremities of these are lay'd t[w]o Long Sticks, and on them again 2 short ones, and thus alternatively 2 long, and 2 Short, which all diminish in proportion as you finish, till your Sky light looks like the rafter of a Ship, on the top of which you scatter the Manicole branches as they are *viz* without either splitting or tying them, and as thick as the Season my require, when your temporary fabrick is completely finished, which keeps you dry as well as your boxes, and under the rafters of which by the help of the nebees you hang your fuzee, Sword, pouch, pistoles &c—

As I have been discribing the Manicole tree I will here also give some Account of the *Cocoa-Nut* Tree, as I think it resembles that the most of all the Palm Species; This Tree which is so much esteemed, as affording to Man food, Cloathing, shelter &c possesses not in my opinion all those Qualifications, but is well worth particularly to be taken Notice of—it grows like the former in a tall jointed trunk sometimes, 10, or 20 feet higher and also much thicker, but never so perpendicularly-Streight, while its bark is of a gray Colour, hard without but pethy within /as I said like the Elder in Great Britain/ its branches are larger and of a deeper green than those of the Manicole tree, but are equally divided, with penated leaves on both Sides, which in the other I compared to green Ribbands & while neither they hang so Streight downwards nor are the branches so regularly arched, which makes them have more the appearance of large feathers, and which spring up at the top as they fade in proportion at the bottom; the Cocoa Nut tree also produces a Cabbage in its Summit, but is to[o] valuable on account of its fruits to be cut down for the Sake of such a Paultry gratification—These nuts it produces at the Age of 6 or 8 Year old after which it is never seen without them–they grow usually 6 or 8 at one stalk which diverges from the heart of the tree, are the Size of a Mans head, but more cilindrical, dark green, and as it were divided in three–being divested of a thick fibrous husk or bark something in the manner of our Walnuts, the Cocoa Nut appears dark brown, rough, and triangular, at one end pointed, and at the other blunt, where it has 3 round holes, fill'd with a pethy Substance—This nut is exceedingly hard and requires to be broke with a hammer, or saw'd through the middle to come at the nourishment; When young this consists in a white liquid which I can compare to nothing better than to Milk and Water mix'd with Sugar, and which is an exceeding Cool and agreeable beveridge, but at a riper period this is form'd into a Crisp Kirnel, which adheres close to the inner Side of the Shell for about half an Inch thick, while it remains perfectly hollow within—this Kirnel which has a fine flavour and tastes like the liquid is good eating, and the Shell of the Cocoa Nut itself, which is capable of taking a high polish, is often convested into Cups, punch Spoons Small vases &c which when trim'd with Silver or Gold, and Sometimes curiously engraved make a very beautiful appearance upon the Side board—

> From yonder Monarch of the lofty grove,
> Pluck me the Cocoa harbinger of Love;
> Besect its Shell, the Milky Liquid pour
> The Nut fair form'd shall grace my native bower,
> Or Carv'd by inds, and deck'd with burnish'd Gold
> A pleasant potion to my love shall hold

In the Plate adjoining **A** is the Manicole tree, **B** the trunk Split into Laths, **C** the nebees to tie them together, **D** the leaf split from the top downwards, and **E** the same tied into Bunches; **F** is the Cocoa Nut Tree, **G** the figure of one of its branches, **H** the Cocoa Nut in the green husk & **J** the same devested of that outer Substance—
And now once more for my Narrative—

This Morning being return'd from a Padrole with 20 Marines and 20 Rangers, and sitting round a Species of Table to take some Dinner with the other Officers I was rudely insulted by a Captain *Meyland* of the Society troops, who as I say'd with Lieut. Fredericy had taken boucou, and who was Colonel Fourgeouds Contryman and Friend—The afront

The Manicole & the Cocoa Nut Tree

consisted in Meylands handing round to each a drop of claret, he having indeed but one bottle left, and in an impertinent manner excepting me alone whom he desired to give over the glass after it was already in my hand—I justly suspecting these were the fruits of my Commander in Chief recommendation, as had been reported to me by Campbell, endeavoured to appease the furious Swish, by a proper apology, telling him, I had inadvertantly erd not imagining I was to be distinguished from the other Officers, while I also assured him it was not for the value of his wine, and which I politely gave over to my next Neighbour; but this affability had no other Effect than to make my fierce adversary worse, who by appearance mistaking it for pusilaminity, became over-bearing, and Scurilous, in which he was seconded by all the other Swish and Germains without exception—I said no more and having cut a Wing of the boil'd bird cald powessa that stood before me, /which bird had been shot by one of the rangers and given us as a relish in addition to our Salt Pork and Peas,/ I devoured it like a tyger to iritate them the more if it was possible, and left the Table with a determination *to do or die,* and take immediate Satisfaction for the bad usage. thus resolved I first went to the hut of a Seek Soldier, whose Sabre I borrow'd /my own being broke,/ on pretence of going to cut a few Sticks, after which I went in Quest of Mr Meyland, and found him Contentedly Smoking his Pipe by the Water Side while looking at one of his friends who was angling—having tiped him on the Shoulder, I hastily told him before the other that if he did not fight me that moment, I was determined to Cather his Jacket with my Sabre where he stood—he at first declared that he had only meant a Joke, and wished for Peace, but seeing me persist knocked the ashes from his pipe against the heel of his Shoe with great deliberation, and having also fetched his Sabre, walked with me alone about half a Mile out of the Camp; here I stopt him Short, and drawing my Weapon, desired him to stand in his defense which he did, but observed that as the Point of his was broke off we were unequally arm'd—and so we were his being Still near a foot longer than my own, thus calling to him that Sabres were not to thrust, but made to cut with, I offered to make an exchange but which he also refusing, I stuck my tool into the Ground, and flying at him like a fury with my hands, endeavoured to wrest his Sabre from him, till /I having hold of it by the blade/ I saw the blood trickle down all my fingers, and I was obliged to let go—I now took up my own Weapon, with which I struck at him several times but all without effect he parying every blow with the utmost facility, till at last he made a Slash at my head, with all his force, which being Conscious I would [could?] not ward off, by my Skill, I bow'd under it, and at the same instant I struck

Sidewise for his throat, but a little to[o] low, when I had the good fortune to make a gash in the thick of his right Arm, of at least 6 Inches in length, and the lips of which appeared both through his Jacket, which made his right hand hang down Streight by his Side, while I myself had not intirely escaped, his Sabre having pearsed through my hat and lining, and /though without touching my Scull/ about an Inch deep in my right Shoulder—I now insisted on his asking my pardon or firing pistoles both with the left hand, but he chose the first which ended the battle, and having put him in mind that such swish Jokes, were to an Englishman always great earnest we shaked hands, and I conducted him covered with blood to the Surgeon of his own Corps, who having sowed up the wound this brave Man went to his Hammock, who for the Space of several Weeks could do no Duty, who had been deluded /he now Acknowledged/ by Colonel Fourgeoud, and with whom I lived in the greatest intimacy ever after—but I had still some fish to fry—and that very afternoon chalenged two other Officers who had espowsed Mylands Qwarl against me at dinner, being fully determined at all hazards to establish that Character by blows, which I was like to be rob'd of by Backbiteing, and I succeeded, both acknowledging their Error, while I became all at once the darling of the Camp—

    This day both Colomns met together—and conjunctly encamped on the N. Side of the Wana Creek, still at its Mouth where it runs in the Coermoetibo, placing advanced Guard at both creeks at one Miles distance from it, and this very evening I took the opportunity of acquainting Colonel Fourgeoud that I had nearly cut off the head of his beloved Countryman in a Duel, /well knowing he must be informed of it by others/ and which trespass he was not only graciously pleased to pardon but to tell me with a Smile that I was a *brave garçon,* but in which Smiles I put no more trust than I would do in the tears of a Crocodile—

    My doubts of his Friendship were Soon verified—since my only true friend Campbell going down seek to Devils Harwar, he would not so much as allow the boat or *ponkee* to stop till I had ended a Letter directed to Joana for some clean Linnens, however a ranger /of which Corps I by this time was become a remarcable favourite/ found means to make me overtake this poor Youth in a Corialla or small-Canoo /being made out of one single piece of timber/ when shaking hands together we seperated, with tears and I never saw him more he dying few days thereafter—

    Colonel Fourgeoud now being determined to Scower the North banks of the Coermoetibo we broke up in 2 Colomns, viz. his own first and that of Major Rughcoph to which last I still belong'd following, leaving behind only a strong Guard with the Provisions, and the Seek,—before we set out I shall Specify the Essence of our orders to be observed on a March, as issued Since by the chief on the 15.th August 1774 at Crawassibo, and which /though 9 Months after this date thus rather late/ are so Judicious that they do infinite honour to his Adjutant Captn *Van Geurike*–who had the Chief hand in their Composition–in

- Art. 1—Quietness and Sobriety was strongly reccommended[—]
- Art. 2—On pain of death none to fire without receiving orders—
- Art. 3—Also Death to whoever Quits or loses his Arms[—]
- Art. 4—The same punishment for those who dare to plunder while they are Engaging the Enemy—
- Art. 5—An Officer and Serjeant to inspect the distribution of the Victuals at all times and–
- Art. 6—Each Officer to be limitted in the number of his black attendants—

The other orders were that in Case our Marines marched in 2 or 3 Divisions or Colomns, they were to mark the trees with a Sabre or billhook, to give Notice to each other where they had pass'd, in the Manner as Noticed on Plate 20 where **A B** and **C** denote Marks made by the 1st 2nd and 3rd Division or Colomn, and **D E** and **F** the Marks made by the D^o Divisions or Colomns of the troops of the Surinam Society–and which marks were to be cut only in such trees as were on the left Side of the Path in Marching—Also when the troops did march over large Sandy deserts heaths or Savanahs they were occasionally to drop small Twigs or reeds, tied together in the form of a Cross–and that in each Camp at the troops leaving the same was to be left a bottle and blank paper, but in Case any thing particular should happen, the same to be Specified thereon—next that in case of the troops being attack'd by the rebels on a March a small retrinchement was to be form'd of the baggage boxes, at the back of which, to lay down flat on the Ground the Negro Slaves, and which was to be defended by the rear Guard only, while the other troops had orders not to linger on the defensive, but vigorously with Screwed bayonets to rush in upon the enemies fire–nevertheless humanely giving Quarter to all such as should be taken alive, or Surrendered themselves to the troops at Mercy–these were the Stated rules of our future Military Conduct; but for the present I beg leave to observe, that all was the most unaccountable Hurry and Confusion—however in this pickle did we proceed,

1773—NOVEMBER 13, 14

keeping Course toward the Mouth of the Coermoetibo Creek, each Officer provided with a pocket Compass by which we were to Steer like Sailors through a dark wood, where nothing is to be seen but heaven and Earth—as at Sea nothing appears but clouds and water—thus those who were acquainted with Navigation were the best off, and run the least hazard of lozing themselves in a black unbounded forest—while those wretches who deservedly most attracted my Pity, were the miserable Negro Slaves, who all were bending under their loads, whose heads /on which they carry all burthens/ bore the ball'd Marks of theyr Servitude, who were drove forward like Oxen with a Stick and above all Condemned to Subsist on half allowance, while they did double drudgery—In Short as our bad fortune would have it though in the dry Season the rains began to pour down from the heavens like a torrent, which continued all night, and during which deluge /according to Colonel Fourgeouds Order/ we all were like true Troyans ordered to encamp without huts or other covering of any kind—Slinging our Hammocks between two trees, under which upon two small forked Sticks were placed our fire Arms, as the only method to keep the priming-powder dry in the Pan; above this piece of Architecture did I hang like Mahomet betwixt the two Load Stones, with my Sabre and pistole in my bosom, and independant of wind and Weather fell most profoundly asleep—

At 5 OClock in the Morning I heard the Sound of up, up, up, when the rain still continuing the half of the Officers and Men were Seek and I rose from my Hammock Soakd as from a Wash tub—having secured the lock of my firelock in imitation of the rangers with a piece of the bark of a Palm tree, and swallowed a dram, with a Piece of dry rusk bisquet for my breakfast, we again marched on but I ought not to forget mentioning the Negroes, who had the whole night Slept in the Water on the Ground, and were in better health than any of the Europeans; had we now been attack'd by the Enemy it is a truth we must have all been cut to Pieces, being disabled from resisting with our fire Arms, in which not only most of the Priming but even many of the Cartridges were as wet as Dung & which might have been prevented by like the buccaneers of America, having Cased and waxed down our Arms; but these were trifles not to be thought of, however one thing now happened which threatned to be no trifle, and that was that the provisions were done, and those expected to meet us in the Creek not arrived, having by some Mistake been neglected and by which accident we were now reduced officers and Men, without exception, to subsist on *one* rusk bisquet and Water for all allowance, and for 24 hours to keep us from Starvation*–while it is to be remark'd that Monsieur *Laurant* our Hero's French valet de Chamble [Chambre], one time was blown down to bramspoint and another time sunk with all the Provisions–which made some of the Soldiers declare that the Devil had mistaken *him* for his *Master;* however in the middle of this distress we were again presented by one of the rangers with a large bird call'd here *boossy-Calcoo* being a Species of wild turkey. this was a Godsend indeed and of which in the Evening it was resolved to make broth each throwing a piece of his rusk biscuit in the Kettle, and /Standing round the fire/ beginning to ladle away so soon as the broth began to boil, which had another virtue, viz, that notwithstanding its being put over at 6 OClock in the Evening, at 12 OClock at midnight the Kittle was just as full as the first Moment it had been begun Supping, though rather weaker I must acknowledge, the heavy rain having plump'd in it without intermission–during which time having no huts as the night before–I avail'd myself once more of my English *petticoat-trowsers,* which dropping from my middle I hung round my Shoulders and Continuing to turn round before the fire /like a fowl on a Spit placed perpendicularly/ I pass'd the hours rather with more comfort than my miserable Coffing Companions–all I can say of the bird above mentioned is that I thought it differed little with the Common Turkey which weigh here often above 20 pound.

The largest bird in Guiana is here call'd *Tuyew* and by others the *Emu*—it is between the Ostrich and the casuary Species I was told as I never saw one in my life and about 6 feet high from the Crown to the ground. its head is Small, its bill flat, the neck and limbs long the body round without a tail and of a Whitish Grey Colour its thighs are remarckably thick, and it has 3 toes on each foot while the Ostrich has but two; this bird it is said cannot fly at all, but runs very Swift while it flutters with its wings and is mostly found near the upper parts of the Rivers Marawina & Serameca; when Speaking about birds notwithstanding /as I have say'd/ few of them sing here with any degree of Melody, for which theyr plumage Compensate[.] I was during this March so much Charm'd with 2 in particular, that I was induced to put theyr Sweet Notes to Musick—

Those of the 1ˢᵗ rather Qwick— 𝄞 ♪♪♪♪♪♪♪ Sounded thus–

The 2ᵈ thus but Slow— 𝄞 ♪♪♪♪♪ —and that

* —*rusk-bisquit* is rye bread cut through the middle and baked or dried till it is as hard as a Stone, I have often broke it with the butt end of my fusee and glad to have it when mouldered, imp[r]egnated with worms, Spiders, Pins, broken bottles &c &c—

was all but which they sung so true, so soft, and to such proper time, that in any other place I should have been very apt to believe they were the performance of a human Artist upon his flute; as I never saw either of those birds but imperfectly and at a distance, I can say nothing more about them but that they are frequently heard in Marshy places—

Now We marched again–through Very heavy rains, which by this time had swell'd the Water so high in the woods that it reach'd above our knees, and prevented us from crossing a small Creek in our way, without the help of a temporary bridge—In Consequence of which I prevail'd on the rangers to erect One by the help of a few Slaves, & which they did in the Space of 40 Minutes, by cutting down a Streight Tree which fell directly across the Creek and to which they besides made a kind of railing–but Still with this our Commander Rughcoph was not pleased, whose temper was sowered by Misery, and whose Constitution was already broke by hardships; he call'd the Rangers *feegh Shinder-kneghte* &c–who with a Smile of Contempt left him Swearing, and cross'd the Creek some by Swiming; and others by Climing a tree, whose branches hung over it, and by which they dropt down on the opposite Shoare, in which I followed their Example, and there we stopt till the arrival of the poor trembling and debilitated Major Rughcoph, while 2 thirds of his Command were as bad as himself, but I Still Continued in perfect health–except in being much Stung by different insects, and tore by thousands of thorns or Macaws[?], particularly one Species being black prickles of several inches in length, that break in the wound, and project like the back of a Porcupine on a kind of low or dwarf palm tree cal'd the *Cocareeta,* and whose large branches diverge from the Earth like the fire of a fuse from a bomb; another cursed inconvienency to be met with throughout all the low and Marshy places in the Forest are a kind of roots cal'd *Matakee,* and more vulgarly trumpets, on account of their form resembling the windings of that Instrument, which rise above Ground like nebees 3 or 4 feet high, when they return in the Earth, take root and rise again, Continuing thus without end, and so thick that like our brambles no dog can get through between them; Over these Matakees it is extremely difficult walking; they every moment catching hold of ones feet, and frequently tripping up our heels without at every footstep one takes care to Step *clear* over them, and which for Short limb'd Men is an Absolute impossibility; with this inconveniency we were troubled throughout the whole March while we had no opportunity to fall in with any kind of good roots, or fruit for food, except a few *Maripas* which are a Species of Nuts that grow on a tall Palm tree, and are very much like the *aweyra* that I have already discribed, only larger, and of a less Orange Colour, the Stone and Kirnel being exactly the same—

We marchd again with better Wether, and arrived before noon at Jerusalem near the mouth of Coermoetibo Creek, where I had formerly during my Cruise built a Shade but which I had since burnt to prevent a Surprize from the Surrounding rebel parties—Here Colonel Fourgeoud with his drooping Soldiers was arived just a little time before us, and here now we made our appearance in such a shoaking Situation as will hardly admit of a discription, It is Sufficient to say that the whole little Army was knocked up by famine and fatigue, a very small number excepted while severals unable to walk at all had been carried upon poles by negro-Slaves in their Hammocks, and during which time we had discovered *nothing*—one thing is certainly true viz, that while the old Gentleman himself went through all the above mentioned hard ships /and to which he seemed as invulnerable as a Cannon bullet/ we had no reason to Complain of bad usage—In short I having as usual plunged in the river to wash of[f] the mire and blood occasioned by the Scratches, and taken a refreshing Swim—I look'd for my Negroes to build a comfortable hut, but in this I was disappointed they being imployed by M.r Rughcopf to build his kitchen, altho he had as yet nothing to dress in it—with this piece of Politeness for once I put up, and the rangers having made me a nice bed of Manicole Branches on the Ground /here being no trees to sling A hammock,/ and lighted a blazing fire by the Side of it. I lay quietly down next to themselves on my green Matras, where in a clear Moonshine night, And no rain, I fell a sleep as sound as a rock—But about two hours before Day break I awaked when the Moon was down, the fire was out, and I almost dead by the Cold dew, and the dampness that exaled from the Earth being so Stiff and So benumb'd that I had scarsely strength to crawl on hands and feet and awake one of my Sable Companions, however he having Kindled a new fire, I recruited so fast as at 6 OClock to be able to rise but with such excrusiating pain in one of my sides that I could not avoid groaning aloud, which to prevent Fourgeoud and the others from hearing, I hid myself in the Schirts of the Wood, but where the Pain augmenting I soon was prevented from Breathing, without the greatest Difficulty and at last fell down behind the rotten trunk of an old Cabbage Tree—here I was found by one of the Negro Slaves who was going to cut rafters, and who supposing me dead ran instantly back and allarmed the whole Camp—when I was taken up and carried in a hammock by the Care of a Captain *Medler* under proper Cover, And one of the Society Surgeons instantly sent for to attend me; by this time I was surrounded by Spectators, and the pain in my side so accute that like one in the Hydrophobia I tore my Shirt with my teeth and bit whatever chanced to be within my reach—till being rub'd by a Warm hand on my Side with a kind of Ointment the Complaint immediately vanish'd like a dream & all at once, when I was recovered and was Stedman again—Nevertheless to prevent a relapse the first use that I made of my Strength was to cut a cudgel, with which I swore to murder the *berbice ruffian geusary* who had the management of the Slaves if he did not instantaneously Set them a building for me a Comfortable hut independant of Whoever might order him the Contrary My Life being the dearest thing I had to part With and following him close at his heels with my *baton* club'd upon my Shoulder, I had the Satisfaction to be well housed in the Space of 2 hours—I must not omit that Colonel Fourgeoud during the Crisis of my Illness had given me an offer to be transported to Devils Harwar which I refused—

&. Came the news that poor Campbell had died Yesterday, and was now sent down very ill Major Rughcopf himself, who was the *Eleventh* Seek Officer during this Short Campaign; being almost Starving for want of Provisions, we here now were happily Supplied by a quantity of fish particularly the *Jackee* already discribed as changing to a frog, and the *warappa* which is of the same Sise and goodness, they being both very fat, which fish were so plentifull in the Marshes where they were left by the retreating Waters, that our Negroes catcht many with their hands, but mostly by cutting helter Skelter in the Mud with their billhooks and Sabres, after which grobling with their fingers they brought up pieces and half fishes in great abundance another fish they caught in the creek call'd *Coemma-Coemma* being from one to 3 feet long, exceedingly Sweet, but not near so delicious as the Jackee, or Warappa, which two last the Negroes generally Smoak-dry or barbacue, and which I was glad to eat without either bread or Salt, the barbacueing consists in laying the fish upon twigs of wood above the fire, where by the Smoak they dry to a consistancy that gives them no disagreeable taste, and will preserve them for several Weeks together, they requiring no other kind of dressing—

&. To Day were detached a Captain with 20 Privates and 20 Rangers to recconnoitre the demolished Village of boucow—

&. Major Rughcopf is also dead at last, and now Fourgeoud marches himself to Boucow, leaving *me* the Command of 400 Men white and black but 200 of whom were Seek in their Hammocks and out of which number I transported 30 to Die at Devils Harwar, while 60 Rangers I sent with leave down to Paramaribo, who had disgusted Fourgeoud, by Swearing his whole Operations were neither more or less than a pack a dam'd nonsense, and only fit to murder his own troops in place of the Enemy—the nature of the Negroes being such, that where they know nothing is likely to be done, they will not march, and indeed are extremely difficult to be kept in proper discipline, but on the Contrary when they expect to see the Enemy no Subordination can possibly keep them back and when they are as eager as a pack of blood hounds, fearless of danger only panting to rush upon their foe, it being really amazing to see with what degree of Skill one negro discovers the haunts of another & which can only be compared to a Dog upon the Scent—and while an *European* discovers not the smallest Sign of a Mans foot in the forest the roving eye of the *negro-ranger* catches the broken sprig, and faded leaf trod flat without ever missing it, and which indicate to him sure marks of approaching his Enemy, when as I said he can no longer be keep'd back—this to be sure is inconsistent with the modern Military tac-tic, but undoubtedly breathes that Spirit of Liberty, which in antient times alone Compleated the Valiant Soldier—and such was the native and natural Spirit still of a People who had but Yesterday been Slaves while how wide different from the Artificial Machinery of theyr European Masters, who please to call themselves the boasted Sons of Liberty—the one flying to victory like the Panting Corviser to which /with a stick to[o] often/ the other is drove like a Jack Ass; however it belongs not to me to check all Europe, which being degenerate into modern vises, it is meet should be rode with a modern Curb, yet from which I take the Liberty to exempt the *British Soldiers* and *Sailors* a braver and more generous People than Compose both its Army and Navy not existing and which also is the case in a few more Countrys where the Inhabitants fight from a national Principle witness the Highlanders of Scotland, the Grenadeers of France &c—

This Evening I avail'd myself once more of being Commandant by sending two barges for Provisions the one to La Rochelle and the other to Devils Harwar—which last brought back a box with boston bisquit sent me from Paramaribo 6 out of 10 being Stole upon the Passage

Now 2 Slaves were put in Confinement accused of having taken Pork from the Magazine, and I address'd by the troops for an examplary Punishment, the Common Soldiers dispising the Negroe Slaves as being the only People upon earth below themselves, and on whom Stupidly they look'd as the Causes of their distress; having found a large piece of pork in their Custody yet having no proof that was sufficient to call them thieves, I found myself greatly at a loss to distribute Justice with Content, both parties being so eager against each other, viz, the Europeans unmercifully accusing, and the poor Slaves vindicating their Starved Companions that the whole Camp was in an uproar—in short the first persisting in that the latter had Stole it, and they in that they had saved it to take to their families. I like a true despotick Prince ordered first a ring to be formed of the Plaintiffs, and next the Prisoners to be brought within it, also with a block and an hatchet—now the fear of my going to be too rash took the place of resentment in the Soldiers and I was implored by the very accusers to show mercy, but now stopping my Ear to all intreaty from either Side I relentlessly made a strong Negro Slave take up the hatchet and instantly Chop—the bacon into 3 equal Pieces, when giving one Share to the prosecutors, another to the Malefactors, and the 3rd to the Executioner for having sowell done his Duty, the farce was ended to general Satisfaction and no more roberies or complaints heard of in the Camp—

This Evening arrived from Devils Harwar Recovered 2 Officers of the Surinam Society Troops, one of whom calling himself Le Baron *de-Zebach* being infected with the *esprit de Corps,* Seem'd determined to espouse Captain Mylands Cause, and without Ceremony picked a Quarel with me the moment of his arrival, by saying I had call'd him a *houndsfuss*—I was amazed, and being convinced of my innocence endeavoured to explain it in a friendly manner, in which I was seconded by a Mr Rukagh one of my Officers, but the Germain in place of being appeased, grew more outrageous, and plainly told me that he insisted on Satisfaction—I never had less inclination to fight in all my Life time–thus left him without making an immediate reply with the other Officer, and walk'd to my hut in a very Gloomy mood—I had however not marched above 20 Paces when stopping Short my Spirit got up all at once, and I returned to end the Quarrel in the Moonshine, arm'd Capapee with my Sabre, and my Pistoles[.] But now the Baron was retired to his Hammock to where I dispatched Mr Rulagh with a Summonds, that if he did not instantly make his appearance to fight me, I should come in, and cut down the Clews of it with my knyfe, and then treat him as I thought a *hounds-fuss* deserved–when at last appeared a figure that shall never be effaced from my Memory—the Baron was more than middle Size, extremely thin, and his meagre visage ornamented under the nose with a pair of enormous carotty colour'd whiskers, while a white Coeue of near 3 feet adorned his back—he was in his waistcoat and walked on Stocking Soles, which were black, holed, and partly darned with white worsted. while hanging down upon his heels they discovered such a pair of Spindle Shanks as would have made a drummers teeth water, on his head was a striped worsted night Cap of all Colours, also holed, and over his breech he display'd his Valour by his Colours which hung out and the Arms of which I must not attempt to give a description of—Such was the figure that with all humiliation now beg'd my Pardon, pretending not to have understood me and which I having granted with a loud laugh and a dram of brandy faced about and Quietly reentered his Den—

Behold the Castle where the Knight resides
Of woeful figure and two Meagre Sides—

Such was the News of the night and such was the end of the Contest—

This morning early I found now that I had been attack'd by a more bloody Enemy though not so large and which was no other than a *bat* by which my hammock was all over clotted blood, and in which I lay like a Cold fowl in Gelly however as I now could not catch the usurper, I must delay giving a description of his form till I shall have the Opportunity of knocking him in the head only now observing that he had bit me deep in my great toe—

Now returned from his trip to Boucow our Colonel Fourgeoud with his Party, having surrounded 3 Stragling Rebel Negroes unarmed, as they were cutting a Cabbage tree for their Subsistance; while one of whom call'd *Pass-up* had escaped, another was taken alive, and a third with his thigh shot to Shivers by a Slug Cartridge, was first lashed hands and feet, and thus carried by 2 Negros on a Pole thrust between them in the manner of a hog or a beer barrel, bearing all the weight of his body upon his Shattered limb, which was dreeping with marrow and blood, without a plester or a bandage to cover the Wounds, and with his head hanging downwards all the time, in which manner the unhappy youth he not having the appearance of being 20 had been carried without speaking through thick and thin for about 6 Miles distance from the Camp, while he might have just as well or better been kill'd all at once or at least carried into one of the Spare Hammocks of the Soldiers—I was shocked and Surprized at this Act of barbarity in Fourgeoud whom I never saw cruel in his cool moments to an individual, indeed quite the reverse without he was opposed as sometimes he was by me, but who on this occasion was so flattered with this trophy of his victory, that every Spark of feeling and humanity was extinct—the poor young Man whose thigh was now swel'd as big as his Body being laid upon a table, I implored of one of the Surgeons call'd Pino to dress his Wounds, on which /by way of play/ he put just as many round Patches, as the Slugs had made holes, declaring he could equally never recover and singing *Dragon pour boire* during the Operation, Poor Negro! what must have been thy feelings, the fever encreased, he beg'd for some Water, which I gave him myself clean out of my hat, when he say'd *thank ye me masera,* sighd, and instantly expired to my inexpressible Satisfaction

His Companion call'd *September* had better fortune and whom Fourgeoud in hopes of making some discoveries regal'd and treated with more distinction than he did any of his Officers, while September looking as wild as a fox newly catched, was put in the Stocks during the night and *Snakee* was inter'd by the Negroe Slaves with those marks of Commisseration which his unlucky fate seem'd to claim from them, Spreading his Grave with the Green boughs of the Palm trees and offering a part of their scanty allowance by way of Libation—

&ear; Mr Stoelman the Militia Capt.ⁿ being arrived to stay one Day only in the Camp I took the Opportunity to remind Colonel Fourgeoud of what he had told me *viz.* concerning his bad tongue, which I beg'd him now to repeat in that Gentlemans hearing, as I was determined on having this point Cleared up, and to have that Satisfaction to which I thought myself intitled—when he now lay'd all the blame on Major Rughcopf who was dead–and requested of me to say nothing more about it. Heavens, I left him with Contempt, and Shaked hands with my supposed Adversary whom I told him all that had happened to his inexpressible Surprize, who took my Example and 2 hours after Quitted Fourgeoud and Jerusalem with disgust being followed by the remaining Rangers who also went to Paramaribo after theyr Companions and who as I say'd had set off six days before—

Thus were we now all Europeans the Slaves excepted and indeed a miserable Set to behold, when I was acquainted as a great Secret by one of the Surgeons Mates that the Scratch in my Shoulder /received by Capt.ⁿ Myland/ would not be cured till that Gentleman should be first perfectly recovered, and which he declared was industriously keep'd open for the purpose /though unknown to him/ by lapus infernalis blue vitriol &c—I was mad, and having damn'd the infernal Stratagem, I strip'd naked and leaping into the River washed down the wound before them all, which the next day was perfectly Sound—Such were the many vexations I had to meet with, and from which indeed others were not perfectly exempt, but who were often crushed under the burthen, while I owed my Support alone to my Constitution and my fine Spirit which never gave way–and which little annecdotes I should have past over in Silence did I not think they afforded a lively picture of human frailty, and if I am allowed to use the expression of human Wickedness—

&ear; Now was Major in Rughcopf's place a Capt.ⁿ de Borgnes and so forth, but no new Subalterns created, Fourgeoud declaring he had no more Stuff, wherewith to make them, which partly might be true amongst the Serjeants. while 2 brave Youths both Gentlemens Sons remain'd unnotic'd in the ranks, the one named *Sheffer* the other M.^r

Meyer—such ever was and ever will be the want of friends or fortune and shall I end this Chapter with that line with which Smollet begins his Roderic Random—

Et genus et virtus nisi Cum re vilior alga est—

Chapter 11th

The Troops march back to the Wana Creek—The Rebels pass near the Camp—pursued without success—great distress for want of Water—Mineral Mountains—Sample of Wickedness in a Superior— The Troops arived at La Roshelle in Pattamaca—

- We now all broke up together and leaving Jerusalem once more marched back to the Wana Creek, but did not keep exactly the track that had brought us there, while Colonel Fourgeoud independant of his former order now allow'd his remaining party to Sling their Hammocks under Cover for which he saw the great Necessity, and in which he shewed them the example, thus were we much more comfortably lodged, but not more comfortably victualled, and which the old Gentleman made up to himself by boulogn Sausages, bacon hams bullocks Tongues and a Glass of good Claret being Stores now carried by 6 Negros for his private purpose—
- We march'd again and had pleasant dry Weather the whole Day—
- ad idem–but during the night I was awaked by Monsieur Laurant, who came to tell me from his Master to make less noise—I had not spoke a word to my Knowledge, and being fatigued soon fell asleep a second time, but a second time the ceremony was repeated, when complaining bitterly of this Cruel usage, and thanking heaven that poor *Campbell* was out of the reach of his persecution, the valet declared it was nothing but a peek against the Scots, and comforted me with a pinch of Snuff tobacco—
- In short we arrived once more at the wana Creek where I found the Letter I had sent to Joanna for Linnens return'd from Devils Harwar, just as the Devil himself would have had it, however dispatching it a

second time, I went to rest with a view to recruit what I had lost the night before, but was mistaken, since I had not shut my Eyes above an hour, til I was awaked by a Sentinel sent on purpose who after shaking me 3 or 4 times by the Shoulder, told me softly at my ear I must not whistle or speak by the Colonels orders, and while Fourgeoud himself now held forth in a tremenduous voice and manner sitting up in his Hammock, and swearing a hangman was to be sent for next day who should strangle burn &c without further process whoever should dare henceforth to disobey his orders—the dark Woods echoeing and ringing with his oration, but a deadly silence reigning throughout the rest of the Camp, till I happened to break it by in Spite of my resentment bursting out in an immoderate fit of Laughter and in which I was instantly accompanied by so many others, that he began to roar like a mad bull, without being able now to distinguish one from another to my good fortune, and in which Musick he was seconded by a large toad, call'd here the *Pipa* to which Monster he actually gave shelter in his hutt, and which keept croaking during the whole night with such a Voice as could only be excell'd by that of himself, or by that of his Countryman a Swiserland bear—Morpheus now befriended me again, but to no purpose, I was condemned to die for want of Sleep, since he saw all other Methods to get rid of me had been in vain, during which time I actually began to meditate in which manner to murder him, to save myself, and as he had done too many others and in this Gloomy temper, I shall discribe the gloomy animal his dear Companion viz, the Pipa the largest of all the toads in South America if not in the World—

The Pipa is an Animal supposed by some[*] to be between and to Partake of both the Species of the Frog and the Toad; it is the most hideous of all creatures upon earth, cover'd over with a dark brown Scrophulous Skin, very uneven and marked with irregular black Spots, the hinder feet of this creature are webbed, and the toes longer than those before, thus it can both Swim and leap like a frog, in which it differs from other toads—its Size is often larger than a common duck when pluck'd and Pinion'd, and its croaking abominable, which is like all others generally during the night but what is most remarkable in this monster is the manner of its propegation, the young ones being hatcht till they become tadpoles in a kind of watery ova or Egg in which the Embrio was at first created, but in what manner to tell for me is an utter impossibility, while these Eggs are deposited in Scrufu-

[*] —By Doctor Cook—

lous Ovari or cells to a considerable number on the females back[*] where they are impregnated or faecundated by the Male. Toads are not venimus it is say'd as is generally imagined, and are even tameable, witness M.[r] *Awcott* who fed one many years[**] and Colonel Fourgeoud who keept his /for a pet, or favourite/ during the whole time of our Campeign at Wana Creek, I myself have since lodged a tame frog, and that these are eatable, viz, their thighs I also know by experience while their taste is extremely insipid[***] this much for the discription of toads and Frogs and now once more I shall go on with my Journal after first observing that the croaking of this Pipa—the Hammering of another, which sounds from sun set to sun rise, nothing but *tuck, tuck*[****] the howling of the baboons the hissing of the Tigers, Snakes &c to which added the growling of Fourgeoud and sometimes heavy rains in the bargain made the night very uncomfortable and gloomy indeed however with the rising sun my resentment forsook me, and having taken a second nap through the day, I was as well pleased, and as well after it, as the forest of Guiana could make me—

This Morning discovering a couple of fine *Powesa's* on the branches of a high tree near the Camp, I ask'd the Chief liberty to go and shoot one of them which however was bluntly refused me, on pretence that the enemy might hear the report of my Musquet who by the by knew better where we where [were] than we did ourselves, but a little after a large Snake appearing on the summit of another tree it was ordered to be shot out of it immediately—whether from fear or from Antipathy I know not, when plump down it came to the ground quite alive sliding instantly into a thicket near the Magazine—at this time I saw the intrepedity of a Soldier, who creeping in after the reptile fetched it out amongst the brambles with his hands, pretending by Superstition he was invulnerable to its bite; be that as it may but the Snake who was about 6 feet long erected its head and half its body successively to attack him, which he as frequently knock'd down with his fist, and at last with his Sabre severed him in 2 pieces, which ended the battle, and for

[*] —Do. Bancroft says they grow on the back of the Male where the females deposits the Eggs and he also calls the Pipa a venimous animal—

[**] —vide Westlys Philosophy vol. 2 Page 54.

[***] —In the Town of Maestricht they are sold in the Market being laced upon Withies or Strings—

[****] —A small Species of frogs in Surinam Whistle very much like young Ducks in England—

The Agamy, & Powese or Peacock Pheasant.

doing which he was regaled by Fourgeoud with a dram of rum—

The *Powesa,* or *Peacock-Pheasant* of Guiana, are a beautiful bird indeed, about the Size of a common turkey to which it something resembles both in appearance and taste, its feathers are a shining black except on the belly which is white its legs are Yellow, and also its bill except near the Point where it is blew, and which is arched, its Eyes are lively and bright, and on its head it is crested with a brilliant crown of black friseld feathers, that give it a noble appearance—these birds cannot fly very far, and being easily tamed may be reared for domestick uses—at Paramaribo they often sell above a Guinea apiece; another bird peculiar to guiana, cal'd by the French the *Agamee* and in Surinam *Cani Cani* I will here also take the opportunity to discribe—It is like the former near the Size of a turkey, but of a quite different make and feathers, its body which has no tail being perfectly the Shape of an Egg it is also black except on the back, where it is of a gray Colour, and on its breast where the feathers are blue and long, hanging down in a hoary manner like those of the heron the Eyes are bright, the bill which is like dowble is pointed and of a blewish green, as are also its limbs— the vulgar name of this bird is here *trumpeter* on account of the Sound it frequently makes, which bears some distant resemblance to that instrument, but from where the Sound proceeds is out of my Power to certify—Some supposing it is made by the nose, which helps to form the double bill above mentioned—and others that it comes forth through the Anus; but this I know that of all the feathered Creation together, this bird is most tameable, and the greatest Friend to Man, whom it follows, caresses and even seems to protect with the attachement of a Dog—I have seen many of them keep'd on the Estates, where like the *Powesa* they are reared for domestic uses, and feed amongst the turkeys and other Poultry—but to my Narrative—

I now received 6 Gallons of Jamaica Rum from Paramaribo and which /except two/ I gave all in a present to my Friend Fourgeoud— being now determined in Imitation of the Indians to worship the Devil from fear, *not* from adoration—

At this time 2 of our Slaves who had been out to cut Manicoles brought intelligence about 6 in the Evening, that a Gang of Rebels had past not above one Mile from the Camp headed by a Captain *Arico,* with whom they had spoke on the banks of the Coermoetibo Creek, but could not tell which way they steered their Course so much had they been frightened, in Consequence of which we got orders to pursue them by break of day and next morning, at 5 OClock all was ready, when we again broke up leaving a detachement with the Stores and repair'd to the Spot from whence came the Information where we saw a large *Palm* or *mawrisee* tree• floating in the river, and moor'd to the opposite Shore by a *nebee* which plainly indicated that *Arico* with his Men had crost the Creek, and which they do by riding astride on the floating trunk the one behind the other, and in which manner they are ferried over sometimes with Women and Children by those who are the best Swimmers—notwithstanding this plain Evidence Fourgeoud swore that it was no more than a Trick in the rebels, whom *he* said had come from where *we* supposed they were gone to, and who had only tied the tree across the river to deceive us—I and others did say what we could, but no Arguments could prevail with the Hero, and we marched directly from them, viz, *East* in place of crossing and pursuing them *West* as the rangers would certainly have done, thus we keep'd on til it was near dark, while the bread was forgot, and the whole day not a drop of Water to be met with, marching through High Sandy Heaths or Savanahs. here the Colonel pointing to a reeking S—— declared he was now perfectly sure of following the Enemy, till a Grenadier stepping forward called out *this was me and please your Honour* to the general Mirth of the Whole Corps—we now inclined a little to the right, when just before making Camp a Negro call'd out we were come to the *Wana,* and which was a Welcome Sound in my ears, thus giving him a calebas and the best part of a Quart bottle of my rum desired him to run to the Creek and make me some grog–and this he did, but the poor fellow never having made grog before in his life time powered in all the Spirits, but very little Water doubtless thinking the Stronger it was the better, which beveridge I swallowed to the bottom without taking time to taste it, and when I became instantly so much intoxicated that I could hardly keep my feet, at which actident a Serjeant of the Society making merry, I gave him a blow on his Meagre Chops with such force, that I cut the very Skin of my Knuckles upon the Jaw bone, and he went to complain to one of his Officers—we were already slinging the Hammocks when this Gentleman named *Kellar* with some others now stept up to me declaring that if I had struck the Serjeant with a Stick the Matter was nothing but as I had beat him with my fist not only the Man but the whole Corps must be disgraced by it without I made a proper atonement upon the Spot, but I most unluckily for the present being in no humour to hear his Preaching through off my Jacket declaring in my turn that in England Sticks were only made for Dogs, and fell a boxing, helter, Skelter, Men and trees, with so much fury that I actidentally tumbled back into *his* own Hammock, where

• —This tree is the largest of all the Palm Species and which I shall in course more amply give an Account of—

however they most humanely had the Civility to let me rest and where I in 5 Minutes after fell fast asleep—here I awaked about Midnight in hells torments, with my tongue and Palate parched as dry and black as my rusk bisquit; and having /not only forgot all that had happened but even/ that we were come near the Creek, I exclaimed *Good God shall we never again see Water,* which ejaculation being heard by another Society Officer named *Graff,* he instantly sent for a full Calebas of it, which he gave me accompanied with a small piece of his black bread and Cheese, and which was so good Surpassing Wine and every thing I had ever drank before, that the taste of it shall never be effaced from my Memory, nor would the rich Man *Dious* when he beg'd Water from Lazarus have drank it with a greater relish—having thanked him, and now recollecting all my blunders, I in the Morning before we marched went to M.ʳ *Kellar* to whom and the other Officers I /from my heart/ having made a proper apology and give half a Crown to the poor Serjeant, the whole was ended to Satisfaction on all Sides—

We now at last returned to our old Camp from a fruitless Cruise when Colonel Fourgeoud set the Captive Negro *September* at Liberty, who followed like a Shepherd Dog attending a flock; but our Commander in Chief was indefatigable and not only crossed and reconnoitred the West Side of the Creek himself this very day, but filling our Knapsacks, we the next morning set out again on the same track we had kept the 8.ᵗʰ he still persisting that he was to overtake the Enemy, having thus marched till towards dark we altered our Course and passed the night in an old Camp of the rebel-negroes, We having again had *no Water* the whole Day.

The next day we still proceeded, but no Enemies, or Water to be met with; the Men and Officers now began to be very faint and some of whom were already carried in their Hammocks; it was now indeed extremely hot being the very hart of the dry Season—In this dilemma we dug a hole 6 foot deep, in the bottom of which a ball Cartridge being fired a kind of Moisture began to trickle forth, but so slow, and so black, that it proved not to be of any manner of use; thus we marched on and now Encamped in an old weedy field where the Rebels sometime before had cultivated Plantains; during which Night it was truly affecting to hear the Poor Soldiers Lament for want of drink but to no purpose, and while in spite of all this Misery, Fourgeoud still persisted the third day in going forward Fourgeoud building his hopes on meeting with some Creek or rivulet to alleviate this general distress—but he was Mistaken for having again marched over burning Sands till about Noon he dropt down himself amongst a number of others a miserable Spectacle for want of an opportunity to slacken his raging thirst—and it was well that wee now ourselves were not attack'd by the Negroes, as it must have been impossible to make any resistance the Ground being strewed with distress'd Objects that appeared all to be in hot fevers; and despair now seem to Stare wild even in Fourgeouds own Countenance as he lay prostrate on the Earth with his lips and tongue parched black and while independant of what he had done me he again attracted my Pity—During all this some of the Soldiers Still devoured Salt Pork, while others kept creeping on all fours like Nebuchadnezar, and licking the Scanty drops of dew from the fallen leafs that scattered the Ground; and now I found the kindness of a Negroe when he his [is] well treated by his Master, being presented by the one attending me with a large calebas of as good Water as ever I drank in all my life to my astonishment, and this he had met with after inspeakable difficulty in the leafs of a few wild *Pine-apple-Plants* from which it is extracted in the following manner—The Plant is held in one hand and a Sabre in the other, when at one blow it is severed from the root through the thick underparts of the leafs, and is held over a Cup or calebas as you have seen the head of S.! John the Baptist held up by the hair after decapitation, and when, as the blood flows from the one, the Water flows from the other, pure, cool, and to the Quantity of sometimes a Quart from each Plant, and which has been catcht in the time of the rains by its chaneled leaves in their proper reservoirs—

Some other Negroes found the Water-Withy to help themselves but not sufficient to assist any of the dying troops

This is a kind of very thick nebee of the vine Species and which grows only in very Sandy places, which Nebee being slash'd with the Sabre in long Pieces, and suddenly held to the Mouth produces a limpid stream and affords a cool, pleasing and healthy beveridge in the Parching forest.

Being now supplied I could not help for my Soul to assist poor Fourgeoud also with Water, whose Age and Spirit with me pleaded greatly in his favour, and who being now refreshed saw himself at last obliged to turn back without any more hopes of overtaking the Enemy, while the others were carried on long Poles in their Hammocks and he still detach'd /this as his last resource/ the berbician Negro Gausarie by himself to try if he could bring him no intelligence—

We now on our retreat approaching the Well or Pit we had dug Yesterday, I Was convinced it must have clear Water by this time, thus sent *Quacoo* my boy to the front to fill one of my Gallon bottles before it should be changed to a Puddle, and thus he did, but being met on his return to me by Colonel Fourgeoud, he with the butt end of his Gun relentlesly knocked the bottle to Pieces–and doubling his Pace placed two Sentinels at the Pit, with orders to preserve the Water all for himself and his favourites—but at his moment Subordination being dead, the 2 Protectors were forced headlong in the Pitt followed by several others, who all fought to come at the Water but which being now changed in a perfect Mire Pool was good for nothing at all except /being black/ making the Divers look exactly like so many Shoeblacks—Here it ended and we slung our Hammocks in an old Rebel Camp and this done a dram of *Kildevil* was given out to each without distinction, which I never using offered my Share to my faithful Negro that had given me the Water, but here Sharp was the Word and quick the motion Since being observed by old Fourgeoud it were Snatched out of his hands, and returned in the Graybeard or earthen Jar; telling me I must either drink it myself or have None—I was exceedingly exasperated at this Mark of ingratitude, and determined in revenge to play him a Salt Water trick, which I did that very Evening by making *Quacoo* steal a whole bottle, and which I distributed amongst the poor Negro Slave and his Companions—At this Moment the good News came that fine Water was actually found to be near the Camp, when all drank hearty and Fourgeoud now ordered a warm Supper to be boild for himself, but not so much as a fire to be Lit for any body else, forbidding even the cutting of a Stick, while we were now obliged to eat our Salt beef and Pork *raw* like the Canibals—however I having tied my allowance to a string I hung it quietly over the Side of his Kettle to have it dress'd, but the black cook chancing to drop a large piece of Wood upon another by eagerness to assist me, and which alarmed Fourgeoud, I was obliged to drop my Luncheon in the Kettle and Swiftly take to my heels—The old Gentleman now swearing that somebody had cut Sticks against his orders, I quietly step'd up to his Hammock in the dark to make friends and undeceive him, and softly assured him that the whole Camp was fast asleep, but when he on pretence of not knowing me suddenly gave a loud roar and with both his hands actually catched hold of me by the Hair of the head; Still I escaped and got fairly under Cover, he calling *fire at him, fire at him,* like a true Mad Man and while all was like to rive [= split open] for laughing in their Hammocks—

Having now found out Quacoo I instantly sent him back to fetch my luncheon, he say'd *yau-Masera* and actually brought me back a piece of beef at least 10 times as large as what I had left, with which I once more had the Satisfaction to regale the Poor Slaves and which ended the damnable Day—

We now once more returned to the Wana Creek, and at last arrived in our old Camp, mostly all Knocked up, several of whom no more recovering, and having done—nothing—while the old Gentleman now regaled his friends with my rum in my presence without offering me a Drop. but which I treated with the greatest contempt–and had some left and while it was no bad entertainment to see him deal out his Loaves and fishes to some others, taking great care always to keep the largest for himself—

Here now I found a letter from the Island of *ceylon* in the East Indies where my friend & Relation Mr Arnoldus *De Ly* being Governor of *Point-de-Gale* and *Maturee* I was invited to come and find my fortune ready made, but which for the present my evil Stars prevented me to accept Of to my great grief and disconsolation—it being out of character to leave the Service at this Juncture which had it not been so, Farewell infernal place, and farewell infernal Commander—

Next day the Negro Gousarie returned from his Strole reporting he had discovered nothing who was recompensed with a few hearty Curses for his trouble—

Captain Fredericy who had marched the 20 Instant with 40 Men white and black from Jerusalem not being heard off since, It was apprehended he had met with some bad actident, and in Consequence to Day were dispatch'd 2 Captains 2 Subalterns, and 50 Men to the River Marawina for some intelligence—

The Post at the Marawina and which is cald vredenburgh consists of houses surrounded by Palisades in a kind of Square, which are all built by the Manicole trees, and with which the Woods of Guiana so much abound–on the outer Side are a Guard and 4 Sentinels, and the Fort itself is defended by several Cannon, it is situated in an opening on the banks of the river where is placed a large flag, and where the Garrison communicates with the french Post on the opposite Shore, both being situated but a little distance from the Marawina's-Mouth; to give the best idea of this Spott I here present the Reader with a view of it, as also of our Situation at the Wana Creek which however beautiful to behold on Paper was a dredfull limbo to many People; in this the 3 Camps are distinctly perceived, that of Colonel *Fourgeoud,* and of the deceased Major *Rughcopf,* on both Sides of the Wana Creek, and that late of the *rangers* which was directly opposite to its Mouth—The barges &c are to bring up provisions and to take down the Seek, however to this last was not strictly adhered, as at this very time the whole Camp was attack'd not only by the Gray, but by that dredfull distemper the bloody flux, which dayly carried numbers to the Grave, while an *emetick* or some *Physic* were the only Cures for all relief, and not a proper Surgeon to administrate them, they being all with the Hospital in Comewina and at Paramaribo—The poor Slaves were peculiarly un-

The Military Post Vreedenburgh, at the Marawina.

View of the three Encampments at the Wana Creek.

London, Published Dec.r 1.st 1791, by J. Johnson, St. Pauls Church Yard.

happy who /as I have said getting but half allowance/ lived mostly upon the produce of the Cabbage tree, Seeds, Roots, Wild-beries &c, which occasioned the first introduction of the above dangerous diseases in the Camp, and which had spread like Wild fire amongst all Denominations*—they were so Starved that they tied *nebees* or ropes about their naked bodies in the vain hopes of thus alleviating their cruel hunger—however myself and a few more escaped the infection, but I was laid up with a miserable bad cold and Swel'd foot call'd here *Consaca,* and which is not unlike Mouldy heels in Europe, it occasioning a verry great itching, particularly between the toes and issuing a Watery Kind of Substance—The Negroes are much attack'd by this Complaint which they cure by applying the Skin of a lemmon or lime, made so hot by the fire as possibly they can bear it—now was verified what I had dreaded when at Sea when I had dared to complain of our hard usage there, and of which I said I should ever after have cause to repent—also the governors prophesy when he told me at parting from Paramaribo that this Campeign should be still more disagreeable than my cruise in the barges, God in heaven knows they were both disagreeable enough–even to those that were the best treated amongst us all, but I shall go on—I have named often into what consisted our eating and drinking, viz. Salt beef Pork rusk bisquit often full of magots and water for all allowance, which dainties were dealt out regularly every 5 or 6 Days /the two former having perhaps made the tour of the World after leaving Ireland/ and were so green, so Slimy, so stinking, and sometimes so full of worms, that at other times I vow to God they would have made me cast my Stomach–but I have made no mention of what was our *furniture*—however this is done in very little time and consisted /besides our huts and Hammocks/ in a Square box or chest for each Officer to carry his linnen, fresh provisions, and *Spirits* when he had them, but of which one dram in the constitution was worth one Gallon in the Cellar, these boxes served not only as Cubboards but as chairs and tables in the camp, while on a March they were carried on the head of a negro, but we had no light after 6 O'Clock in the evening that of the Moonshine sometimes excepted when all was solemn and Melancholy beyond discription—I in particular who had expected to find the necessary conveniencys, had not so much as a trencher, or bason, fork or Spoon–for the first and Second I made a Negro's Calebas serve me the 3 I wanted not, and the fourth but seldom which I then supplied with a folded leaf in imitation of the Slaves, as for a Knife each individual carried one in his Pocket, I at last also contrived to make a

* —The bloody flux is both infectious and epidemical—

lamp by breaking a bottle in which having melted some Pork it served for Oil and a Slip of my Shirt Sleeve for a Cotton Week [wick]—one becomes exceedingly ingenious when forced by necessity and every nicety is forgot, indeed could I Now have had what formerly I left upon my Plate I should have ardently thanked God for all his Mercies; when Speaking of ingenuity I ought not to forget a number of very pretty baskets, that were made by the Negros in the Camp and which /they having teached me/ I also made to amuse myself and sent them as presents to several friends at Paramaribo. these Baskets we made were wrought with a kind of strong ligneous Cords that are found in the bark of the Cabage trees and as Do. Bancroft expresses it consists in a web-like Plexus, which is divided cross-ways in long, hard, Polish'd threads, brown and as tuff as whalebone, which threads are drawn from it and which filaments or fibers are made use of as withies are used for the purpose In England; for Punch baskets, or holding fish at umber or Quadrille nothing can be better or more beautiful but those that are large for holding fruit vegetables &c are quite different and made of a kind of bulrushes cal'd *warimbo* which are first Split and deprived of their pithy Substance, while the thin nebees make also no bad baskets—The Negroes here besides made curious Nets and even Hammocks, of the Silk grass plant, being a Species of Wild aloes that grow in the woods, the leaves are indented and prickly and contain inside *viz* longitudinally very strong and small white fibres or threads which are bruised and beat to hemp; with this are made ropes stronger than any in Europe which would answer perfectly for the rigging of Ships, and other purposes had it not been discovered that they are sooner liable to rot in the wet, this kind of hemp is so very much like white Silk, that the importation of it is forbid in many Countrys to prevent imposition by selling it for the same and more especially when mixed—By the Indians this plant is call'd Curetta, and in Surinam vulgarly Indian Soap, as it contains a Saponaceous pulpy Substance which answers for washing as common Soap for the Negroes and others— another Plant much resembling this is by the black People term'd baboon Knyfee as it sometimes cuts through the Skin to the very bone of which I myself had some trifling proofs in this Wilderness—

In the above manner the time was spent for the present while the whole Camp being without Stokings Shoes hats &c–Colonel Fourgeoud now himself walked a whole day quite barefooted, to give an Example of patience and perseverance, and keep the few remaining troops from Murmouring—in this respect I had fairly the start of them all my Skin being /the swel'd foot, or *Consaka* and a few Scratches excepted/ perfectly whole from my habit of walking *thus,* while not a sound limb was to be found amongst the rest which were running in open Sores and Corruption & for which I have already partly accounted but for which I shall Still farther Account in the following manner—While stockings and Shoes did remain they never came off from the feet of many Wearers, who after marching through Water, Mud, and Mire, in this dirty Pickle turn'd into their Hammocks, here before morning in fair Weather this dried upon theyr limbs, and in consequence occasioned an itching redness on the Skin, which scratching broke in many places, it soon became Scrufulous, and ended into open Sores and ulcers—and these from want of care and proper applications often changed in Mortifications and terrible Swellings, by which some lost their limbs and others even their Lives, without a temporary amputation did take place—Such were the causes and such the effects of what we had to struggle with, while to be sure the reader must think we suffered enough, but I shall in time prove that we still suffered more and that this was but a sample of the Piece—

In short we now got account that Captain Fredeiricy with his command supposed to be lost were safely arrived in the River Comewina, and I got a Ham and 12 Bottles of Claret sent me by one of my friends, a Captain van-*Coeverden* which I immediately gave all again in a present to Colonel Fourgeoud, only 4 bottles accepted 3 of which I drank with the other Officers, and for which in return I was once more keep'd from Sleep by one of his Sentinels, who gave me a shake regularly every hour during this whole night by the commands of his despotic Master—nothing could be more diabolically ungrateful than was this usage and having cursed myself more than once for my ill placed generosity, I threw the remaining Bottle in the river without a Cork, telling them they might now all drink wine and Water while they remain'd at the Wana Creek and be damnd, after which I went out on a Padroll with Major Des Borgnes and 40 Privates once more to try if we could still not get some account of the Negroes who had cross'd the Creek as I have say'd on the 7th Instant, being only 3 Weeks ago, and who could tell but they would be pleased to wait for us till we should overtake them—However we having drop'd down the Coermoetibo Creek with a large barge /in which we lay all night/ we stept a shore /but still on the N Side/ the next morning a few Miles below its Mouth; and immediately set out upon our March keeping course due N.E. which march Major Des Borgnes like a Hero was pleased to continue notwithstanding I put him in mind that the chist with all the Powder had been forgot; and left behind us in the barge; but what signified Cartridges where we had in reallity so little chance of seeing an Enemy now?—nothing—our next distress now was in having lost the road and being without Compass when I begging to be followed keep'd due N in hopes to come to Rio Cottica and during which we discovered the track of our Own troops /that had marched the 25.th Instant in search of Captain Fredericy and his Men/ crossing a Sandy Savanah and a little after which now following it we reentered the Wood and Slung our Hammocks

    The next morning we still continued in the same Path till at last it led in a Marsh above our middle, when we lost it, and percevering finally stood in water til under the Armpits, each carrying his Arms and Accoutrements upon his head—We were now par force obliged to return, and marching S.W. came once more to the Coermoetibo Creek where we made Camp—Here a heavy rain coming on of a sudden the same thing very nearly happened that I had met with from M.r Rughcopf at Jerusalem as my Negro having assisted in making a hut for M.r De Borgnes by my desire, was next imploy'd by his order for the Surgeons Mate and the Serjeant while I stood dreeping; having complained of this usage to no purpose, I lost all decorum, indeed grew perfectly distracted as shall be seen Just now thus—damming the cause of my Misfortune together with his Patron who had from first to last showed him the fatal example, I stept half a dozen of Pases back, and to forget my distress I all at once ran my head against a large *eta* tree till I fell in a Swoon covered over with blood—In this situation I was put in a Hammock, the Hair shaved off my head, and the Wound nearly dress'd, before I recovered by the help of volatile Salts &c, when the first object I perceived was *Des-Borgnes* in tears leaning over me, who now /not only acknowledged his fault, but/ humanely lent me every assistance, and he being certainly, independant of this neglect a Man of a Mild and good natured disposition all was made up and we shaked hands, no never more to Quarl, which ended the Year 73 in the hopes that the next might be more prosperous—

    This morning we now marched again and before noon arrived in the old Camp at Wana Creek where the report was made having done as usual—nothing—

    This day one of our Negroes presented me to my surprize with a beetle that was betwen 3 and 4 Inches in length and full 2 in breadth and is call'd here the Rhinocerous on account of its horn which is forked, black, as thick as a Quill–and bent backwards, and besides which the head has many hard knots and Protuberances this whole animal indeed is black, as also its 6 legs and its large Wings, and is upon the whole inconceiveably strong but as I have not the smallest Pretentions to be named amongst the flycatching fraternity I must leave the accurate discription of this and many other insects to the Segacious

Harway, Needham, Bradley, &c and above all to the unparalelled Sir *Joseph Banks* that Phenomenon of natural History, I having only mentioned this beetle on account of its magnitude while another Next to this in Size is the *cerfvolent* or flying-hart. flies are here in great abundance with one of which call'd *Cowflie* we were exceedingly troubled in the forest, besides many Mirriads of other indiscribable insects, the flie I am speaking of is as large as an English honey bee, Stings prodigiously deep and being fond to torment particularly horses and Cows, I can best compare it to what is cal'd the Hippo Boscus or Horse fly in Great-Britain—

At last return'd Captain Fredereicy with his party and a rebel Negro in Chains call'd *Cupido,* when Colonel Fourgeoud being finally determined to morrow to break up this infernal Campeign, he sent out a detachement of 2 Capt^{ns} 2 Sub^{tns} and 60 Privates to cruise on the way to Patamaca before him—

With Captain Frederecy came the news amongst other trifles that a Poor Devil of the Society-troops having received his Pardon on the Spot after he had already kneel'd to be shot through the head, was gone clean out of his Sences—Query would he have suffered more if the Sentence had been put in full force—

In short that I might appear as decent as Possible at La Rochelle where we intended to March to, I now wash'd my last Shirt in the Wana-Creek but was obliged to keep Swimming til it was dry by the Sun; my Letter sent for Linnen having never reached Paramaribo; and what I had brought with me being tore to rags, and tatters—

At 6 OClock in the morning now all was ready to decamp and having sent down the barges with the Seek to Devils-Harwar, we at last cross'd Coermoetibo Creek and march'd first directly South for Patamaca over Steep Mountains covered with Stones and impregnated with Minerals*–and in the Evening we incamp'd at the foot of a high hill w[h]ere we found a small rivulet of good water, and a Coppice of Manicole trees, the 2 chief ingredients required, when it is curious and indeed beautiful to behold how in the Space of an hour a green town is as it were sprung up from nothing, and a little after all the fires lighted, for now both was permitted by the Humane Commander–under which green Shades swing the troops, each in his Hammock, and on which fires, are boiling their hard fare, while in the Smoke are drying a few trowsers, Shoes and Stokings; but as I have said this last is by no

* —this again contradicts Do: Bancroft not being above 20 Miles from the Ocean where he says that no hill is to be found at near 50 Miles from the Sea—

means a general rule the greatest number preferring to let them rot upon theyr limbs—

This Night however the whole Camp was disturb'd by a diaretick-Complaint, occasioned by the Water we had here found, and which indeed was very pure, but had so much the taste of Minerals, that it was almost like that of Bath, or the German Spa, both of which I have tasted—and which evidently indicates that these Mountains might be made of use in finding Metals besides the Medicinal Quality of the Sourses, if the Dutch would go to the expence of searching in their bowels—

We now march'd the same Course again over Mountains and dales—Cosivail Mondo—and which were some so steep, that one or two of the Slaves not being able to assend them loaded, through [threw] down their burthens, and deserted not to the Enemy, but found theyr way to theyr Masters Estates, w[h]ere they were pardon'd while others tumbled down burthen and all from top to bottom—This whole Day contrary to the rule of the Seasons it happened to rain excessively, when Colonel Fourgeoud cursed the Elements, and clouds in imitation of his Patron in Tyranny and Profaneness the Spanish Duke D'Alba, who when raging in Holland, had drawn his Sword against the very Heavens—This Evening however we found our Quarters ready made, loging in the *wigwams* or huts that were left standing when the *Rice-Country* had been demolished, and Bony with his Men drove to flight, I finding in that where I lay a very curious piece of Candle that the rebels had left behind composed of bees wax, and the heart of a bull-rush.

Bonys own house where Fourgeoud loged, was a perfect Curiosity, having 4 pretty little rooms, and a Shade or piazza inclosed with neat Manicole Palisades—

The whole being excessively fatigued, Fourgeoud ordered a general rest day now, only detaching Captain Fredereicy as he knowing the Country best, with 6 Men to reconnoitre the banks of the *claas-creek* a water that issued from near this place in the upper parts of rio cottica—But there is not any peace for the Wicked, since this officer was hardly march'd when the Chiefs Eye by chance falling upon me, ordered me instantly to follow him alone, for the mere purpose of thus persecuting me to Death, and to bring him an account of what I had seen, NB on the *other Side* of the Creek—

I was enraged at this injustice, and fresh proof of his inplacable hatred, however I affected to go cheerfully till we were all again in Water til under the Arm pits, but then determined to disappoint my tormenter /by showing him I was proof to the worst that he could possibly invent to plague me, I strip'd Stark naked/ and desiring Fredericy with his Men to wait my return I with my Sabre in my teeth, plunged headlong into the Creek, and which I Swimd across by myself alone—here having ranged the opposite Shore and perceiving not a Soul to my good fortune I Swim'd back, and we all march'd into the Camp from whence we came—at Noon making my report to the Colonel Fourgeoud, he seem'd highly Surprized at what he pleased to call my temerity, he say'd it was a desperate Action which he had in reality never intended that I should perform, I was Surprized, he took me by the hand, intertained me with a bottle of my own wine devising a *vis-a-vis,* and ordered Monsieur *Laurant* to set some bacon ham before me–but who shall believe it that this repast was creeping in live Worms, while my own now his that was fresh was refused me and which exasperated me so much that I now Started up, and again left Fourgeoud, his valet, his wine, and his reptiles, with that Contempt Which they deserved alleviating my hunger with a piece of dry rusk bisquit, and a barbacued fish call'd *Warrappa*—

In Short we now all march'd again during which time Colonel Fourgeoud having found every means to kill me ineffectual, Now as his last resourse by Heavens he took my Cartridges from me, thus preventing me the very means of defence against the Publick Enemy—However his Arm bearer–Monsieur Laurant whom some pleased to call *Sancho-Pansa* and himself the chevalier *Don-Quicksote* had the humanity to give me 4 out of his Masters own private pouch, and who besides this Day showed his further Incivility in galling me by trying to slander the Character of the Honble Gen! *Stuart* and whom he knew to be my great friend and protector—this was too much and too mean—

—Pudet hoec oprobria nobis
et deci potuesse, et non potuesse reselli.–

But which however was not the Case with me for I reply'd him in publick /caring for nothing more/ that his Spite could only proceed from his having been by that Gentleman keep'd at a proper distance who knew well how to chuse his Company—Here the frensh Swish lost all temper but could do nothing worse than he had tried already, and in this fury I left him repeating from Voltaire as I went away

vas grandeur Sont des Mascarades,
Jeux d'Enfents, que tout vos projects—
Lors que la toile tombe. Empereur et Sujets,
tout Sontegaux et Camarades;

226

and while the only remaining thing to plead in his favour on these Subjects is, that being extremely fatigued he frequently drank more *Kildevil* or new-rum than his brains were able to Support, this must have been the Case; since none but a bedlemite could behave so ill as this poor Man did at times, while at other intervals, few peoples Conversation could be more agreeable; and to him shall I ever impute it alone, that some other Officers whose Company and Manners had ever been most Mild and desirable, were now by his example not only Sowered in theyr tempers, but acted in Characters in Consistant with themselves—a little after this brush I having caught one of those beautiful large Diurnal butterflies, of which I made mention during my Cruise in the River Cottica, I will not leave the woods without trying to give it a more particular discription, but limitted according to my abilities—and which small reptile is perhaps more worth the readers attention than a certain *great one* of which I so often have been obliged to Speak throughout the Course of this Work, however all that I can now say of this fine fly /I being no naturalist/ is that it measured between the extension of the Wings from tip to tip, about 7 Inches in length and that its Colour /of both superior and inferior wings/ is of such a Splendid and bright Heavenly blue, as can only be compared to the azure sky in a beautiful day, and to which not the purest ultremarine-Colour'd Sattin can approach the underside being of a lovely brown variegated with Spots, while I can not help repeating that its skim[m]ing and hovering with such a magnitude, and such a hue amongst the different Shades of green, especially in the Sun had the most enchanting appearance; of the antennae, head, thorax and abdomen I shall only say, that they were dark colour'd. This fly if I mistake not is according to the Division of Linaeus, of the Danai Species—I never saw the chrysalide or aurelia, but the caterpillar which is of a yellow grayish Colour is as thick as a large Mans finger and about 4 Inches in length the Annexd drawing I have improved from Miss Merian.—various and innumerable indeed are the charming butterflies with which the forest of Guiana abounds, by which some People who make flycatching their business get much Money, and who having Elegantly arranged them in paper boxes, with Pins stuck through them, send them off to the different Cabinets of Europe. Do: Bancroft mentions touching them with the Spirit of Turpentine as necessary to preserve them, but fixing a piece of *Camphire* in the box with the flies, has all the Effect that is required—But to proceed—this Evening we now incamp'd near the Patamaca Creek, where the poor Captive *Negroe-Woman* cried bitterly, and Scattered some Victuals and Water at the root of an old tree, by way of libation, as being

Azure blue Butterfly of South America.

London, Published Dec.r 1.st 1791, by J. Johnson, St Paul's Church Yard

the Spot w[h]ere her Husband was interr'd, and who had been Shot in some former Skirmish by the Europeans—Here Captain Fredericy and myself walking without the Skirts of the Camp in a Sandy Savanah, and discovering the fresh footsteps of a large tiger with her Young /at which time they being extremely ferotious/ we were obliged to make a sudden retreat, I measured the diameter of the dam's Claws printed in the Sand, which had the dimensions of an ordinary Pewter Plate—

Having now march'd a few hours longer the next morning we at last arrived at the Society Post La-Rochelle in Patamaca, such a Sight of thin, Starved, blackburnt, and ragged taterdemalions, and mostly without Shoes or Hats, as I think were never before beheld in any Country whatever, and which will best bear to be compared to a gang of Gipsies, while their leader was not unlike *Bampfield-Moore-Carew*, and my self at best like the forlorn Crusoe in his worst Condition, with my only cheek [checked] Shirt and the one half of my long trowsers torn away—here we now found a set of poor wretches ready to reenter the Woods that we had just left, and to undergo in the same manner the greatest misery that ever was inflicted on Sublunary Mortals—I have already Mentioned the prickly-*heat–ringworm–drygripes–putrid fevers–boils–Consaca* and *bloody flux*, to which one is exposed in this Climate—also the *Musquitoes–Patat*, and *Scrapat*-lice, *chigoes, cockroaches, ants horseflies wild-bees*, and *bats*, besides the *thorns, briars* and *aligators* and *Peree* in the Rivers and to which if added the howling of the *Tigers* the hissing of the *Serpents* and growling of Fourgeoud–the dry *Sandy-Savanahs*, unfordable *Marshes, burning-hot* Days, *Cold-& Damp* Nights, *heavy rains* and *short* allowance, people may be astonished how any one was able to Survive it–but I Solemnly declare to have Still omitted many other Calamities that we Suffered, dreading Prolixity of which perhaps I have been already to[o] often Guilty and without which I might have mentioned *Lethargies dropsies* &c &c besides the many small *Snakes Lezards Scorpions, locusts, bush-Spiders, bush-worms,* and *centipedes* nay even *flying-lice*, that one is perpetually tormented with, and in danger of being Stung by, but the discription of which cursed Company I must defer till another opportunity; so famishd was I now, that the moment of our coming here, observing a Negro-Woman Supping on *Plantain-broth* from a Calebas–I gave her half a Crown, and Snatching the bason from her hands I devoured the Contents with a greater relish than I have ever tasted any thing before or Since during my life.

When I now observed to Colonel Fourgeoud what a Pity it was not to regale his remaining Soldiers with vegetables and fresh beef or mutton, besides procuring them with hats, Stokings, Shoes &c he swore *Hannibal* had lost his Army at *Capua* by too much indulgence and damn'd the Shoemakers for not sending stronger leathers—In Short he had not only Hannibal but Horace for his Example according to the advice given in a certain Pamplet—

Ibit eo quo vis qui Zonam perdidit—

and seem'd fully convicted that no persons will behave so desperately in Action as those who are tired of their Lives.

With all this I must acknowledge, that Colonel Fourgeoud, while he had absolutely nothing left for his Officers frequently bestowed on the private Soldiers hours of his Conversation, and this was something, but as for a belly full of good Meat and Drink these were only left for himself and his favourites the Rebel-Negroes that we had taken, and who grew as fat as gueese or Turkeys in his keeping, which to be sure was a Conspicuous proof of both his Humanity and his Polity, but of neyther which he unluckily ever reaped the benefit.

Now arrived the other Party that had left Wana the day before ourselves, having taken or Seen according to Custom, *nothing,* while the Rebels knowing best who was their friend, and also the proper Season, one of them with his Wife came to La-Rochelle, and who surrendered themselves voluntarily to the Commander in Chief, while /to keep from Starvation only, having been theyr Motive/ they were as usual delivered to the Care of the Cook, to the unfortunate negro *Snaakje* alone Colonel Fourgeoud had been Cruel, but to *September-Cupido,* and the *Captive-Woman,* besides the *2 last* come Volunteers /being the only trophies of our 3-Months Campeign/ he showed every mark of lanety, and even Friendship, and *finally to me,* as he this very day acquainted me himself, that I was at liberty to go and refit at Paramaribo when I thought proper, which Proposal I gladly accepted, and that moment prepared for my departure with some other Officers, leaving behind us himself, and as I have said a gang of such scarcrows, as could have disgraced the garden or fields of any farmer in England, amongst these was a Society Captain named *Larcher;* who declared to me he never comb'd, washed Shaved, or Shifted or even put off his boots, till all was rotted from his body, and Who to be sure look'd and Smel'd, like the very Devil in person, while many other Germains ornamented their noses with long Whiskers—

At last arrived the happy hour, and taking leave of my tattered Companions, I and 5 more with a tent-boat and 6 oars row'd streight down for Paramaribo, Still in good health and in a flow of Contentment and high Spirits—

At Devils Harwar I now meet a Cargo of Tea, Coffee, Bisquit, butter, Sugar, lemmons, rum, and 20 Bottles of Clerret sent me by my

1774—JANUARY 13, 15

friends, directed to La-Rochelle, and which I again /independent and in Spite of the barbarous usage that I had so lately met with/ gave all in a present to poor Fourgeoud, 12 bottles of wine excepted, which we drank to the healths of our Wives and Mistresses in the barge, nor could I help pitying Colonel Fourgeoud, whose Age /he being about 60/ and indefatigable exertions claim'd the attention of the most indifferent, and who during this trip /if few Rebels were taken/ had certainly Scowered the forest from the River Comewina to the mouth of the Wana Creek, dispersed the Enemy, and demolished their support—

This Evening we supped at the Estate Mondesire, and from there keep'd rowing down all night and Day, roaring and singing, till the 15th at noon, when we waiting for the tide went ashore at the Fortress Amsterdam—

Here in Stepping on the landing place I can not help relating a ludicrous adventure—My good friend the Major had put on a long-ruffled clean-shirt which he had got the Lord knows w[h]ere, but he was all in rags from top to bottom besides this ornament, in this trim he walked in the fortress, while I remained alone near the boat at his desire, being almost naked and much like a Shipwrecked Sailor cast away on the coast of Damnation, however the Sentry stepping up to me, ask'd me with the greatest respect by the name of *Captain* whether the man in ruffles was not the *drum-major* of our own Regiment to which I answered in the affirmative and for which he past to my Unspeakable Mirth and Satisfaction in the fort, while I to be Sure was a Gentleman—

At last we arrived before Mr De Lamar's Door at Paramaribo, when I step'd a shoare amongst a croud of Friends, who all flock'd round to see me, and to welcome me to Town, and in the Land of the living, it having been reported that I was dead so many different times—Next was sent for my Dear, my inestimable *Joana,* but who burst in tears the moment she beheld me not only for Joy at my Still existing, but from seeing my very distress'd Situation, However these precious drops I soon kissed away, and all was happy; this ended my second Campeign and with this I put an end to the Chapter—

Chapter 12th

*Discription of the Town of Paramaribo and Fort Zalandia—
Col: Fourgeoud march to the River Marawina—A Captain wounded—
Some privates shot—strange Execution in the Capital—
account of Fort Somelsdyk—of the Hope in Rio Comewina*

Being once more arrived at Paramaribo, and having now the leizure, I think it will be high time to give some Account of that beautifull town, after only observing that being long accustomed to walk barefooted, I could not bear the confinement of Shoes and Stokings for some time which burnt and even swel'd my feet so much, that dining to day with my friend Kennedy I was actually obliged to through them off at his house, from whence he sent me home in his Whiskey—Kennedy now showed me to my Astonishment 2 letters from the unfortunate Youth *Campbell* the one directed to himself, the other to Campbells Father, which had been found in his boxes and which he had wrote before his Death acquainting them of his Dissolution, he having felt its approach by the lowness of his Health and his Spirits, yet either of which Complaints he had scorned to communicate to Fourgeoud—In these Letters he thanked them for every kindness that had been bestowed upon him, gave them a short account of what few things he had left behind, and Signed them your deceased friend Robert *Campbell*—I could not help shedding tears on hearing this Account, being perfectly convinced he had died by neglect, and a broken heart, which indeed was the Case with too many Scores of others; after this short degression I shall now give a description of the Town—

Paramaribo is Situated as I have mentioned on the right Side of the beautiful River Surinam, at about 16 or 18 Miles distance from its Mouth, and is built upon a kind of gravely rock, that is level with the rest of the Country, in the form of an oblang Square; its length is above a Mile and a half and its breadth about half as much, all the Streets which are perfectly streight, are lined with trees of Oranges, Shaddock tamarinds & Lemons which appear in everlasting bloom—while at the same time their branches Weigh down with the richest clusters of odoriforous fruit—Neither Stone or brick is here made use of for Pavement, the whole being one continued Gravel not inferior to the best Garden Walks in England, and strew'd on the Surface with Sea Shells—The Houses which are mostly two, and some three Stories high, are all built of fine timber a verry few excepted, most of the foundations are of brick, and they are roofed with thin Split boards call'd Shingles in place of Slates or tiles—

Windoes are very seldom seen here, glass being inconvenient on account of the heat, but in place of which are used Gauze frames, and sometimes nothing only The Window Shutters excepted, which are keep'd open from 6 in the morning, til 6 oClock at night—and as for a *chimney*, I never saw one in the whole Colony no fires being lighted except in the Kitchens which are always built at some distance from the Dwelling house, where the Victuals are dress'd upon the Floor and the Smoak get out by a hole made in the roof—notwithstanding all this these Timber Houses are very dear in Surinam Witness that lately built by Governor Nepvew which he declared to me had cost him above 15 thousand Pound Sterling—Here is no Spring Water to be met with, but most Houses have wells dug in the rock yet which affording but a brakish kind of beveredge are used only for the Negroes, Cattle &c. while the Europeans have reservoirs, or Cisterns, in which they catch the rain for their own Consumption & while the more Polite let it first drop through a fillering-Stone in large Jars or earthen Water-Pots, that are made by the Indians or Natives for the purpose, and barter'd at Paramaribo for other Comodities—

The Inhabitants of this Country of whatever Denomination Sleep always in Hammocks, the Negro-Slaves excepted, who mostly lay on the Ground—These Hammocks for the better Sort are all of Cotton, with rich fringes and also made and barter'd by the Indians, theyr value in Money being frequently above 20 Guineas, and neither bedding or covering is necessary, an awning excepted, to keep of[f] the Gnats or Musquitoes—Some People indeed lie in timber beds or Matrasses but in that Case they are Surrounded with green Gauze-frames instead of Curtains which let in the Air freely and at the same time keep out the Smallest insect—The Houses in general at Paramaribo are elegantly furnished, with Paintings, guilding, Chrystal Chandelliers Jars of China &c, the rooms are never paper'd or plaister'd, but beautifully

Wainscotted, and Stock'd with the neatest Joynery of Cedar, Brazil, & Mahogany—

The number of buildings in Paramaribo are Computed to be about 1400, of which the Principal are the Governors Dwellinghouse or Palace, from which through the Garden his Excellency can enter Fort Zelandia—This House and that of the Commandant which has lately been burnt to the Ground were the only brick buildings in the Colony—The Town-Hall is an elegant New Building, and Covered with Tiles, here the different Courts have their Meetings, and underneath this are the Prisons for the European Inhabitants, the Military excepted, who are Confined in the Citadel call'd Fort Zelandia,—The Protestant Church where divine Worship is done both in low Dutch & french has a small Spier, Clock, and Dial, besides which there is a Lutheran Chappel, and two elegant Jewish Synagogues, the one Germain and the other Portugueese, here is also a fine large Hospital for the Garrison that is *never empty*—The Military Storehouses, Powder-Magazines, &c are kept in the Fortress Zelandia, where the Society-Soldiers are also lodged in baracks, and some Officers in propper Pavillions—

The Town of Paramaribo has a very good road for Shipping, the river before the Town being above 1 Mile broad and containing sometimes above one hundred vessals of burthen, which are moord within a Pistol Shot from the Water-Side, and indeed there are seldom less than fourscore, which load Coffee, Sugar, Cacaw, Cotton, & Indigo for Holland, including the Guinea-Men that bring Slaves from Africa, and the brigs, Scooners, &c, that import from N. America, and the Leeward Islands, flower, Salt-herring, and Macrel, deal [= Rhine wine], boards Spirits, Sparmacety-Candles, Beef, Pork and horses, & for which they export Molasses to distil theyr rum—

This Town which is not fortified is bounded by the Roads and Shipping on the **S.E.** by a large Savanah on the **W.** by an inpenetrable-wood on the **N.E,** and is protected by Fort-Zelandia on the **E**—

This Citadel which is only Seperated from the town by a large greenplain or esplenade, where the troops assemble on different Occasions, is built in the form of a Pentagon, with one Gate fronting Paramaribo and 2 bastions commanding the river—It is very Small, but strong the whole being made of rock or hewn-Stone, round about this is a broad foss, well Supplied with water, besides some outer-Works and on the east Side fronting the River is a battery of 21 Pieces of Cannon—On one of the bastions is a clock that is struck with a Hammer by the Sentinel, who is directed by an hour Glass, and on the other is planted a large flag or Ensign, which is generally hoisted on the approach of Ships of war, publick rejoicing Days &c. having before spoke of its

View of the Town of PARAMARIBO, with the Road & Shipping, from the opposite Shore.

1774—JANUARY 16

antiquity I shall only observe that the Walls have no kind of Parapet but that they are 6 feet in thickness with embrasures—

Paramaribo is a verry lively place, the Streets being crowded with Planters, Sailors, Soldiers, Jews, Indians, and Negroes, while the river Swarms with Canoes, barges, yoals, Ships boats &c constantly going and coming from the different Estates and crossing and passing each other like the wheries on the Thames, and mostly accompanied with bands of Musick this and all the different-colour'd flags perpetually streaming in the wind, while continually some Guns are firing in the roads from the Shipping, and whole Groops of naked Girls are playing in the water like so many mermaids, can not but have a truly enchanting appearance from the beach, and in some Measure Compensates for the many Curses that one is here dayly exposed to—I might Still add the number of Carriages, Saddle Horses, and Profuseness in dress, which is truly magnificent Silk Embroidery Genua-Velvets diamonds Gold, & Silver-Lace being dayly wear, not so much as a Captain of a trading Ship appearing in less than Solid Gold buckles to his Stock, breeches &c, nor are they less refined at their tables where every thing that can be call'd deelicate is produced at any price, and served up in the newest fashion'd Silver-Plate and Japan-China—But nothing so much displays the Luxury of the inhabitants of Surinam, as the Quantity of Slaves that constantly attend them, sometimes in one family to the number of 20 and greatly upwards, an European Man or Maid Servant being almost never to be met with in the Colony—

The Current Coin as I have mentioned are Stamped Cards of which some are Value 10 florins, being about 20 Shillings, others 5 Shillings &c. besides which they have Notes from the amount of 5 to 50 Pound. Gold & also Silver being very Scarce, and which is always exchanged for the enormous interest of sometimes above 10 Per Cent, yet a Dantzig base Coin commonly call'd a *bit,* and in value something less than 6 Pence is current throughout Surinam—The Negro Slaves never receiving Paper Money which is liable to be burnt, tore by theyr Children, or eat by the rats, while a Portugueese Joannes or an English Guinea is sometimes met with, but both these are genereally used as ornaments by the Mulatto, Sambo, Quadroon, and Negro Girls—

Having this far described the Town and its fair Inhabitants who want for Nothing, as Having /besides Butchers—Meat, fowls, fish, venison, and vegetables with which last in particular the Country abounds, / all other luxuries imported, that Asia, Africa, or Europe can afford.

I say having this far gone on with this discription I shall now say something about the Prices of Provisions, which are excessively dear in general, and in particular those that come from abroad, which are here sold mostly by the Jews, and the Ship Captains, the first injoying extraordinary priviledges in this Settlement, and the latter erecting temporary Storehouses for the purpose of trade til their Ships are loaded with the produce of the Climate—

For wheat flour I have paid from one Groat to one Shilling Sterling P Lb for butter 2 Shillings, and no butchers meat under 1 Shilling and often one Shilling and Six Pence—for common fowls or Ducks from 3 to 4 Shillings a couple, and one single turkey has cost me a Guinea and a half. Egs 5 and European Potatoes 12 for 6 pence—I have bought Wine for 3 Shillings a bottle, and Jamaica-Rum for a Crown a Gallon. fish and vegetables are tolerably cheap and fruits almost for nothing, My Black Boy *Quacoo* has often come home with 40 Oranges for one Sixpence, and half a dozen Pine Apples for the same price—while limes and tamarinds one may have for Picking—

Here Houserent runs excessively high indeed, where a small room without either Chair or table comes to 3 or 4 Guineas for one Month, and a House with but 2 apartments on the same floor I have seen let for One hundred Guineas Yearly; no good Shoes to be got here under half a Guinea a Pair, and for a blew Suit of broadcloth with Silver binding I have paid above 20 Pound Sterling—

The fair or European Inhabitants in this whole Colony & who reside mostly in Town are computed /including the Garrison/ to be 5[000], and the Negroe Slaves about 75000 People, but of these last I will Speak more Particularly on another occasion, and now continue by giving some account of the *Wood* that the Houses in Paramaribo are built With & which is generally *Wana,* or *Cupy*–though many other Species are imploy'd for that purpose—The *Wana* is a light durable timber but has not a fine Grain to take a Polish, it is of a very pale red approaching Mahogany, and mostly made use of for Doors, Cubboards, tentboats or barges, &c. this tree growing to a considerable Height*—The *Cupy* tree which has some report to the wild Chestnut, may be saw'd in boards of 20 feet long, and being knotty, hard, heavy, and durable in all weathers is generally made use of to inclose the houses by way of walls, in the room of brick or Stone–this timber is of a brown Colour and will take a pretty good polish—

Having this far dwelt on the Town of Paramaribo I shall now refer the reader for a *Still better* Idea of it to the annexed Plan, and say a word or two more of its Inhabitants—Here the Guard mounts regularly every morning at 8 OClock by the Military in the fortress, besides the Burghers or Militia who keep watch all night in the middle of the

---

* —this Do. Bancroft I think Calls the Tetermer[?]—

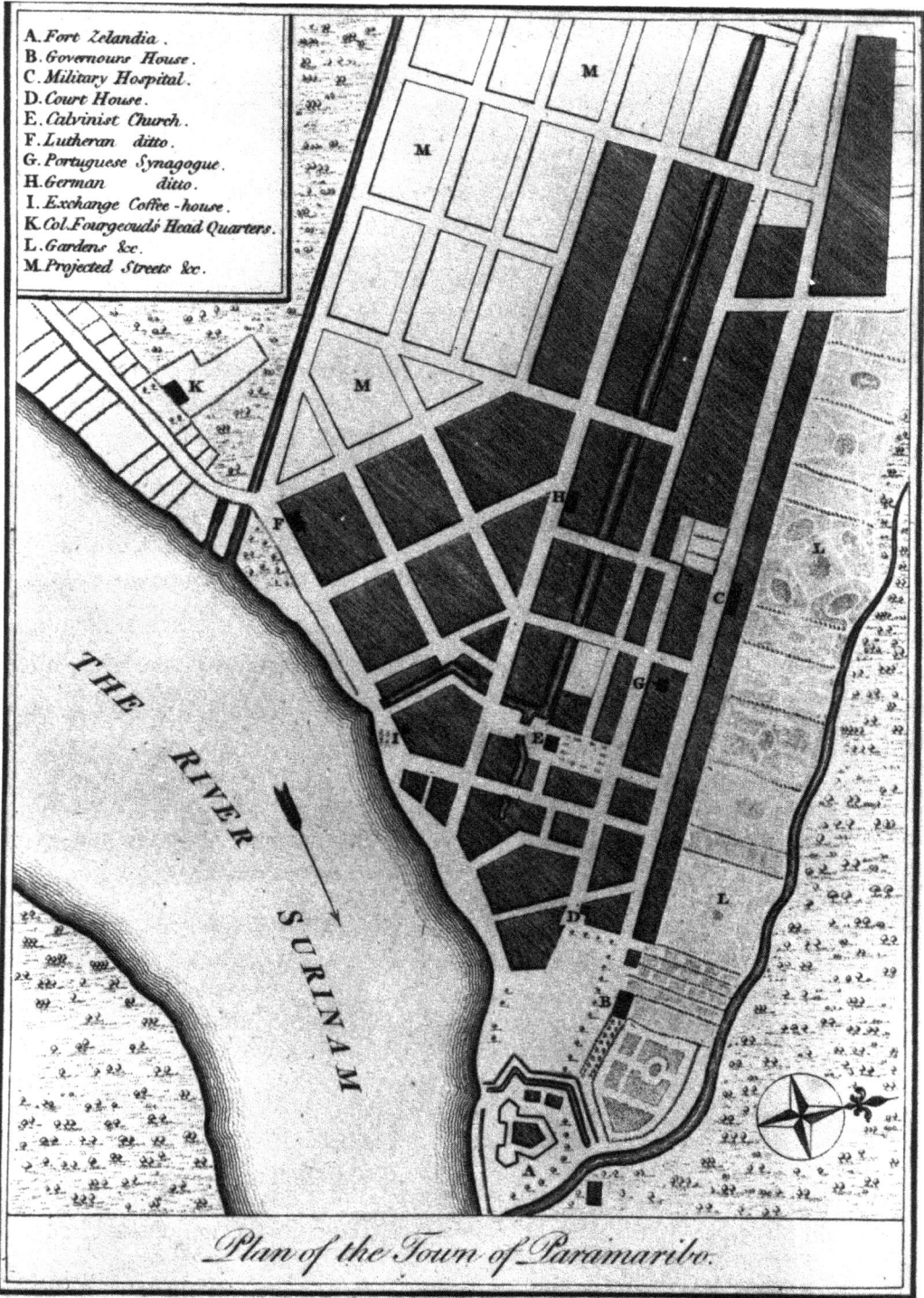

A. *Fort Zelandia.*
B. *Governours House.*
C. *Military Hospital.*
D. *Court House.*
E. *Calvinist Church.*
F. *Lutheran ditto.*
G. *Portuguese Synagogue.*
H. *German ditto.*
I. *Exchange Coffee-house.*
K. *Col. Fourgeoud's Head Quarters.*
L. *Gardens &c.*
M. *Projected Streets &c.*

THE RIVER SURINAM

Plan of the Town of Paramaribo.

London, Published Dec.r 1.st 1791, by J. Johnson, S.t Paul's Church Yard.

T. Conder Sculpsit

1774—JANUARY 16

Town—At 6 OClock **A.M** and at the same Hour **P.M** the morning and Evening Gun is fired, by the Commanding Ship in the Roads, when that Instant down come all the Flags and all the bells on board the Vessels are set a ringing & while the drums and fifes keep beating, and playing the tattoo through the Streets—From this time viz, from Sun Set, to Sun rise, the watch is set, and no negro whatever of either Sex, is alloud to appear in the Streets, or on the River without a proper Pass, signed by the Master or Mistress that he belongs to—without which he is taken up, and without further Ceremony flog'd the next morning; and at 10 OClock at night a band of black drums beat the burger or Militia retreat also through Paramaribo—

But it is after this time that the Ladies chiefly begin to make theyr appearance who delight /as I have mentioned/ above all things to have a *tete-atete* in the Moon shine where they entertain you with Sherbit* Sangree** and wine and water, besides the most innocent, and unequivocal discourse, such as the Circumstance of their last laying in, the Mental and bodily Capacities of theyr husbands, the Situation of their young female Slaves, of whom they propose you the acceptance at the Price of so much Money Per Week, payable to themselves according to theyr value in their *own* estimation—For instance having ordered half a Dozen of Girls to stand in a row the Lady tells you Sir this is a *Caleebasee* (that is a Maid) and this is not, this has only had one Husband, but this had 3 &c. thus are they not only unreserved in their conversation, but even profuse in bestowing their Encomiums on the figures, and Sizes, of such Gentlemen, as they have the honor to profit by their intertaining, and instructive Company—I ought not to omit, that to give a proof of their keeping discipline, and good order, they sometimes order the Girls to strip as naked as they were born, when you may have a better opportunity of seeing the marks of the Whip which indeed some of them are barbarously covered over with from Neck to heel; as for the Negroe Men, they go always intirely Strip'd, a small Slip of Cotton that serves as a fig leaf only excepted, in which dress they attend their Mistresses at Tea Tables, breakfast, Dinner, and Supper, without it should happen that some of them had found the means of purchasing a pair of Holland-trowsers, but in this case, should they chance to forfeit a flogging, they are by their Ladies industriously order'd, to take them off in theyr *presence,* while the other covering being soon whipt to attums, she has the better chance of beholding the effects of flagelation, besides the Preservation of the Poor Young Mans

* —a composition of water acid & Sugar

** —Water Madeira Wine Nutmeg & Sugar

breeches; thus much for the Humanity, and Modesty of the Creole*
Ladies in this Colony and which however much it may astonish some
readers is nevertheless an incontravertable fact, but every Country has
its Customs, yet from these Customs exceptions are to be made, and I
have seen Ladies in Surinam, whose Polite Conversation, and delicate
feelings would have graced the first circles in all Europe.

I had almost forgot to mention that besides the other refined amusements of feasting, dancing, Ryding, and Card Playing, they have erected a small theatre of late, where the Genteelest Inhabitants act tragedies and Comedies for their amusement and that of their friends—

No People can be neater in their dress, and cleanlier in their houses, than the Surinam.rs are in General, whose fine Linnens are not only extremely well Sow'd, and Embroidered, but so exquisitely well washed with Castile-Soap, that theyr whiteness can only be compared to Mountain Snow, and next to which the best bleached Cloth in Europe looks like Canvas—As for the Parlour floors–they are always scower'd with sower-Oranges, or lemmons, cut through the middle, which gives the house a fine fragrance, and which half a Dozen of Negro-Wenches taking one half in each hand, keep rubbing on the boards, til they are void of Juice, and during which time they keep singing a loud Chorus; Such is the Town, and such are the Inhabitants of Paramaribo, the Capital of Surinam, and indeed of all the Dutch Settlements in the West Indies–and now I must return once more to my Narrative—

Being again accustomed to *shoes* as well as ever I now visited Colonel Westerloo on board a West-india-Man, bound for Holland, viz, the Gentleman who had relieved me in Devils-Harwar, when *I* was Ill and where I had buried so many Officers, and Men, and who was now himself in such a debilitated State, having lost the Power of all his limbs, that nothing but to repatriate could possibly recover him; about this time several Officers sold their effects for ready Cash getting neyther their *pay* from Fourgeoud, or their *allowance* and for which I indeed in particular had less reason to care than most others, being dayly Entertained by my numerous friends. however for Acting in this manner it is supposed Colonel Fourgeoud had his *wise* reasons—

Walking this morning by the river Side I saw brought a shoare a fish that well merits to be mentioned on account of its Size and its Goodness being sometimes near 200 Pound in Weight**–it is here Call'd *growMuneck* or gray-frier, and is said to be of the Codfish Species, to which

* —such as are born in the Settlement of whatever Sex or Denomination—

** —here Dr Fermyn is mistaken when he calls this fish but 40lb Weight.

it bears no bad resemblance in Shape and Colour, the back being a dark olive brown and the belly white, it was cut in Slices, which were some as large as a small Drumhead, and Of which I having bought 2 for 2 florins being near 4 Shillings Stirling, I sent them in a present to Mrs Danforth where I had the opportunity to taste the best fish that ever I did eat in my life, and which in my opinion is even Superior to turbot, I shall only add that it is an Inhabitant of the Salt-Water, but is Sometimes to be met with in the rivers—These and all other kind of Salt-Water-fish are caught by the Negro fisher-Men, who are train'd up and employ'd only for that purpose by theyr Masters, and who having Sold their Cargo, are obliged to produce so much money to their Proprietor every week, and thus it is with every other trade, and ordain'd in such a manner, that if the Slaves imployed in them, chuse to be industrious they may reap considerable benefit for themselves, and even some grow *Rich*—but on the Contrary should they be idle, and indolent, so as Not to fulfil their usual task, in that Case, they are sure to be flog'd most severely—however this last is more frequently the Case on the Plantations than at Paramaribo, where I have known Slaves, to *buy* Slaves for their own use, and others buy their own liberty, or Manumission from their Masters, some others keep their Money, and if the Property of a respectable family, prefer dependance before freedom, having in the first instance nothing to care for but *one* Master, and in the second all Duties and taxes to pay, besides being in a manner dependant on all the world—I have in particular known one Negroe-black Smith, who was offered his Liberty by his Proprietor, on account of his long Servitude and exemplary behaviour—but he refused to accept of it, preferring to be the Slave of so worthy a Master—This Man had several Negro-Slaves of his own, and who work'd for himself, and no other, keep'd a decent House, with pretty furniture, and even plate, and when visited by his humane Master or Mistress entertained them with Sangree, Port or Clerret—

However these are what may be called White ravens, while in General they are treated with too much Severity, yet more particularly by the Creole-Ladies as I have said, the Gentlemen who are *such* making the lives of their Negroes at least Comfortable at Paramaribo, where if they do not always allow them to accumulate Wealth, they treat them very often even With too much indulgence—

When Speaking about Slaves I must here also mention one Class of them, call'd *Quaderoons,* that are in general very much respected on account of their affinity to Europeans, a Quaderoon being between a White, and a Mulatto, and which are verry frequent in this Colony; these young Men are frequently put to some good trade such as a

Joyner, a Silversmith, or a Jeweller, while the Girls are imploy'd as waiting Women, and teached the arts of Sowing, knitting, and Embroidery to perfection, they are generally verry handsome, and well-behaved, and being /both Sexes/ not divested of Pride they dress with a great degree of neatness, and even elegance, In short one Sees at Paramaribo not only White and black but meets

> The Samboe dark, and the Mulatto brown,
> The Mesti fair*–The well Limb'd Quaderoon.

and to give the reader still a more lively idea of these people I will discribe the figures and dress of a Quaderoon Girl as they usually appear in this Colony—they are mostly tall, Streight, and gracefully form'd, though generally rather more Slender than the Mulattos, and never go naked above the Waist as do the former; their dress consists besides often a Sattin Petticoat, covered with flowered Gause, in a close short-Jacket, made of best Holland chints or Silk, and laced before, showing about a hand breadth of a fine Muslin Shift between the Jacket and the Petticoat, as for Stokings, or Shoes, none are wore by any Slaves in the colony; but on their head, /which is mostly adorned with a beautiful bunch of black hair in short natural ringlets,/ they were [wear] a black, or white beaver-hat, sometimes with a feather, or a Gold loop & button, while their neck, arms, and anckles are ornamented with Chains, bracelets Gold-Medals, beads, &c—

All these fine Women have Europeans for their Husbands, to the no small Mortification of the Creoles & fair Sex, while should it ever be known that an European-female had kept a carnal intercourse with a Slave of whatever denomination, the first is detested, and the last loses his Life without Mercy, Such is the despotik Law of Men in Dutch Guiana, if not in the whole World over the Weaker Species—

And now to change the Subject such was the despotism of Colonel Fourgeoud, that Lieut Count-Rantwik who was to depart /being seek/ with Colonel Westerloo to Holland, was now once more ordered to remain though ill in the Colony of Surinam, and only for having said he had been ill treated by *that* Chief, which to be sure was very surprizing, from such a *humane* good-natured Gentleman; and to add to it his Justice, I shall only observe that it was now exactly one Year that all the Officers had subsisted on a *private-Soldiers* allowance of Salt Provisions, a few Weeks at Paramaribo excepted, and by which accommodation, I in particular lost presisely 30 £ but I have mentioned already that he keep'd back our Money, and why should he not keep back our allow-

---

* —between a White and Quaderoon, the others I have discribed.

Female Quadroon Slave of Surinam.

London, Published Dec.r 1st 1794, by J.Johnson, St Pauls Church Yard.

1774—FEBRUARY 1, 2, 6

ance also, it belonging not to a good Soldier to enquire after *trifles*— Nevertheless here it ended for this same Day we all got Notice that henceforth we should pay nothing, providing we could *fast*, but that if we could *not*, 10 £ Pr Annum was to be the *ne-plus ultra* of the expences for our Salt beef and Pork—

≈ But the next morning I got a still better intelligence indeed, viz, that Mr *Becquer* another of our Lieut. Colonels having scorned to partake any longer of Fourgeouds bounties had suddenly given up the Ghost, by which I became in my turn possess'd of his *vacant Company,* and this was something however dear it cost me, in heartbreak, and in Sweat yet while I thus won on one hand I lost on the other since a certain Lady /whose Husband had showed me remarkable civilities/ now made me an offer to my Astonishment which I could in Honour absolutely never accept of, besides which I had been *Sworn at Highgate;* but she still persisted, while I /refusing her favours, and Golden presents/ at last found the effects of a womans hatred and revenge, and all at once saw that Man become my Enemy who had so lately been my friend, and whose Honour I had so generously endeavoured to support from being tarnished—However I bore their frowns with resignation, and Consoled myself with the thoughts of having been proof against a trespass that too many others are proud off, and make a boast of having Committed, while in few Weeks thereafter I saw this Gentleman again /if possible/ more my friend than he had ever been before this affair did happen—

≈ In short this Evening a poor Drummer of the Society brought me a Present of some fine albicata or avigato Pears and oranges, for having supported him he said in Holland against my Servant who had knocked him down; while this mark of gratitude gave me much more pleasure, than even the loss of my late friend had given me pain. The *avigato*-Pear grows on a tree above 40 feet high. And is not unlike our Walnut trees, but the Fruit which is about the Size and Colour of a large Pear, viz. a Purple, or pale Green, is the most exquisite in my opinion of any in the Colony, or in the World; it is yellow inside, with a soft Stone like a chesnut and so good is the flesh or pulps of this fruit, so Nutricious, and Salubrious, that it is often call'd the Vegetable Marrow,• and is usually eaten with Pepper and Salt, nor can I approach it to any thing so well as to a Peach it melting in the same Manner in ones Mouth, but not so sweet, yet is incomparably more delitious—

How great thy fame O Vegetable Pear–
What fat, what Marrow can with thee compare?

• —a name given it, it is Said by Sir Hans Sloane

Long known to fame, till now unknown to Song,
Tho Britain Sigh, and Britains Monarch Long

as this fruit can never be transported—

The Oranges in Surinam are of 3 Different Species, the *Sower,* the *bitter,* and the *sweet,* all being originally imported from Spain, or Portugal—The sower Oranges are an excellent cure for Sores, and running ulcers so common in this Climate, but rather painfull, on which account their Juice is only imploy'd on those of the Negroes, whom it is supposed can bear any torment whatever—The bitter are used for preserving &c. while the sweet /which resembles the others in appearance, but have even a lucious taste/ may be used to any Quantity, without the least bad effect; and which is not the Case with that kind call'd the *China-Apples* that I will afterwards discribe; the Trees that bear all the above Species are truly beautiful, and never without fragrant blossom, or fruit throughout the Year.

Now arrived the News that Colonel Fourgeoud with the remaining troops having marched from La Rochelle in Patamacca, to Boucow, and Marawina, had been himself attack'd by the Rebels, when amongst others poor Captain *Fredereicy* marching in the Front, had been Shott through *both his thighs.* This Gallant Officer clapping both his hands on the wounds, and sitting in Water, up til his breast, to conseal the bleeding (and prevent his Situation from discouraging the rear Guard from rushing forward) til his wounds were dress'd by the Surgeon, and he carried in his Hammock by 2 Negroes—Indeed nothing can exceed the Zeal that both this young Officer, and Fourgeouds Adjutant Capt. *Van-Geurike* shoed throughout the whole expedition, who were continually with him wherever he went for 5 Years, whether their Constitutions could bear it or not, and the honour of which was the Principal Profit they derived from theyr extraordinary, and assiduous attendance, since in my Opinion Colonel Fourgeoud never yet recompensed them afterwards according to their Merit, while he abused the other Officers, and even some field-Officers worse than ever I did any of my Corporals— Thus was I not alone ill treated by this Mighty chief, though surely with more barbarity than anyone else, nor could I have suffered more had *Hider-Aly* or the Emperor of Morocco made me theyr Prisoner, the loss of my existance alone excepted—

To cut the Story short I now once more made an Offer to Join him myself in the Woods, but in place of which he sent me an order to haste to the Estate *L'Esperance,* in English the *Hope,* which I will henceforth call it, Situated in the upper part of Rio-Comewina and there to take the Command of that whole River during his absence, and which river being new to me, I was extremely happy to be sent to—

Thus having provided myself with a compleat new Camp equipage, and bought provisions, I was soon ready to depart for my new Station, but I must not leave Paramaribo, without mentioning, that during my Stay here, 9 Negro-Slaves had one leg cut off each, for having rund away from their Work at Plantation; this Punishment is part of the Surinam administration of Justice viz at the Masters desire, and was executed by M.*r* *Greber* the Surgeon of the Hospital, while the Poor Devils were deliberately smoking a pipe of tobacco, and for which he told me, he was regularly pay'd at the rate of about 6 £ Per limb—Query how many would not do the office of Jack Catch for less Money?—However independant of his great abilitys, 4 of them died after the operation, while a fifth kild himself by plucking the bandages from the Stimp, and bleeding wilfully to death during the night:—These amputated Negroes are frequent in this Colony, where they are equally useful in rowing the boats or barges of their Masters, while others are sometimes met with that want a hand, but this is for having dared to lift it against any of the Europeans, and this verifies what *Voltaire* says in his Candide.

Now for the *Hope* in the River Comewina, having first astonished all the Planters by ornamenting my black boy *Quacoos* head, with a Gold-Laced hat, Contrary to Custom for his faithful Conduct during my last Campeign in the Woods and to which Place /the hope/ I was this time sent as I ought to be, in a decent tent-boat with 6 Oars, row'd by 6 Negroes; adieu then once more My Dear Mullatto, and this Evening I came to the Estate *Sporksgift* in the Matapica-Creek—the next at Arentrust in Comewina, having past the *orleana* corruptedly call'd, the whoare-Helena-Creek, and the Fortress Somelsdyk, which as I have said at about 16 Miles above the Fortress Amsterdam, forms the separation between that and the River Cottica, commanding the 2 opposite Shores by the fire of its cannon—This fortress was built in the Year 1684 by Governor Somelsdyk whose name it Still bears, and lays in the form of a Pentagon, having 5 bastins mounted with Artillery and a foss, besides being well provided with Military-Stores, it is not large but well defended, espesially by its so low and Marshy Situation—Not far above this and on the right hand is a fine Creek call'd *Comete-Wana*—

About Mid Day I now came to the Hope, having found this whole River not less charming than I had found the River Cottica & as I have mentioned, being this lined in the same manner on both Sides with Enchantingly beautiful Estates, particularly of Coffee and of Sugar, and with the first of which it abounds principally near its Mouth—

About half way up both these rivers, are also in each a protestant Church, to where the Plantation People resort to hear divine Worship, the expense of the Parson &c being paid by the Planters—

The Estate L'Esperance or the hope, where I now took the Command is a verry fine Sugar Plantation, Situated on the left in going upwards, & at the mouth of a small rivulet call'd *bottle-Creek,* having almost opposite to it on the other Side of the river, another Creek call'd Caswinica—

The Bottle-Creek communicating both with the rivers Comewina, and Pirica, as the Wana-Creek does with Coermoetibo, and Rio-Marawina, thus may they in some degree, rather be call'd Small Channel's—

On the hope I now found the Troops were lodged in temporary houses, built of Manicole trees, and in such a low, and Marshy Situation, that by Spring-tides the whole was under water, while the Officers were all cram'd in one apartment of the same Species, and which could not miss to be extremely inconvenient, while the Planters fine house was uninhabited /by the Overseer or Manager of the Estate only excepted/—

This was rather a disagreeable Circumstance, besides its being extremely unhealthy, however I found those at the Estate-*Clarenbeek* in the same Condition, where next I visited to examine the state of the Hospital, being at best but a Cannon Shot higher up the River than myself—Indeed they were rather worse off than we by the amazing Quantity of *Rats,* that infected this place, and which were so numerous that they were visible by half-Scores at a time, destroying all the Cloaths, & Provisions, and galloping over the Peoples faces while they lay in their Hammocks during the night, and which cursed inconveniency could only be prevented by stringing Quart bottles /having first bored holes in their bottoms/ on the roaps or lashings of each Hammock, both at the head and the feet, in the manner of the Glass-beads upon a Cord, and over which /on account of their Polish/ it is impossible for the Rats to get at the Canvas, which shows that "experienca Dosit"—

Here the crowded Hospital also afforded a Melancholy Spectacle, by the Miserable Objects that it presented to my view, and upon the whole seeing nothing to invite me here I was glad to return back to the hope—My orders were here much the same as they had been in Cottica, viz. to protect the Estates from the Enemy &c. and the Paroles or Watch Words were regularly sent me by Colonel Fourgeoud—

Having here with me, one of the two Berbicia-Negroe-Captains, formerly mentioned, and named *Ackeraw,* he discovered an old decrep'd Slave call'd *Paulus* and belonging to this Estate, to be his *Brother*, whom he treated with much kindness, the Same being both surprising and Affecting—

Having nothing better to do for the present, I will discribe a few Birds, That I met with in my Walks around this Estate, in amongst these was one that is call'd in this Colony the *queese-queedee* on account of its Note, which seems to articulate that Sound, repeating it very frequently, it is about the Size of a thrush, and of a brown Colour all over, except on the breast, and the belly, where it is of a beautiful Yellow, the only thing I Can further say about this bird is that [it] is very mischievous, and an unwelcome Guest on the Plantations.–the others that /this time/ mostly attracted my attention, were wild Pigeons, of which I shot one that was very large, and by appearance, what is usually call'd the ring tail'd Pigeon of Jamaica, it was ash Coloured on the back and Sides, a lead Colour on the Tail, the belly white, and the neck reflecting a changeable Green and Purple, the iris and feet of this Pidgeon were red–besides which I saw perched on the Ground some little dwarf Pigeons, that walked in Pairs, and were not above the Size of an English Sparrow, which birds they also resembled in Colour, though rather lighter, and which I take to be the *Picui-nima* of Marcgrave, the Eyes were bright, with a yellow iris, and upon the whole these small diminutive Creatures were very pretty–they are call'd by the Dutch Steen-Duyfie, or Stone-Dove, on account of their frequently being found amongst Stones, and gravel Walks; in Guiana are also found *turtles,* but these are seldom seen near the Plantations & only frequenting the deepest resesses of the forest, where I have found their nests, built in those trees that had the Thickest foliage, I have there even stroaked them with my hand without they attempted to make any escape—they seem'd to me little different from those in Europe in regard to Colour, but rather less, and with wings of a more considerable length, than any other dove or pidgeon whatsoever•

Indeed I was charm'd with the many fine birds, and other new objects that I saw upon this Plantation, where I at last was at liberty to breathe freely, and had every reason to hope for future Contentment, and which now Promissed so Amply to make up for my past hardships, and cruel Sufferings—Here I was respected like the Prince of the River, every day invited to dine and visit on the different Neighbouring Estates, and Constantly stock'd with Game, fish, fruit, and vegetables of every kind that were sent me in Presents, thus that I scarcely knew myself from what I had been so little time before, and had very few

• —Do: Bancroft erroneously it appears calls this bird the only Dove in Guiana—

wishes remaining, when Still to augment my happiness I was most agreeably surprized by the waving of a white Handkerchief from a tent-boat, that was rowing up the river; and which soon proved to be no other than Joanna herself with her Aunt, who now prefer'd the Estate fauquenbergh /Situated about 4 Miles above the Hope, but on the opposite Side/ to the Town of Paramaribo, and to which Plantation I accompanied her that Instant—Here she introduced to me a venerable old Slave, grayheaded, and blind, who made me a present of half Dozen fowls, and was it appeared the Grand-father of my Mulatto, being now supported Comfortably since many years, by the care and industry of his numerous offspring, and telling me, he was originally from the Coast of Guinea, where he had once been more respected than were any of his Masters in Guiana—

It must seem wonderful to the World in General, to see Me so often mention this female Slave, and with so much respect, but I cannot help Speaking even with raptures, of that object who was so deserving of my attention, who alone Counterballanced all my other miseries, and who since literally saved my life, as shall be seen in the Sequel; while Independant of these Considerations, the Misfortune of her Birth and Condition, should never be a bar to prevent virtue, youth, and beauty, from gaining my esteem, but on the reverse be a Stimulative to attract it—What shall I Say further on the Subject?—nothing—and Content myself with the Consolation given by Horace to Phoceus the Roman Soldier—*Book II and Ode 4.*

>   Ne sit ancillae tibi amor pudori,
>   Xanthia Phoceu puus insolentem
>   Serva Briseis neveo colore
>   Movit Achillem.—
>   Movit Ajacem Telamone natum
>   Forma captivae dominum Tecmessae:
>   Arsit Atrides medio in triumpho
>   Virgine rapta;—
>   Barbaræ postquam cecidere turmae
>   Thessalo victore, & ademtus Hector
>   Tradidit fessis leviora tolli
>   Pergama Graiis.—
>   Nescias an te generum beati
>   Phyllidis flavae decorent parentes:
>   Regium certe genus, & Penates
>   Maeret iniquos.—

Next morning I now returned to the Hope—loaded /besides my fowls/ with ambergines, agoma, brocalay, and a few Surinam Cherries—the first are a Species of Fruit that grow in the Shape of a Cucumber, are of a kind of purple without, and white within, they are cut in Slices, and eat as other Salads, sometimes stew'd, and are very good and wholesome, the leaves of this fruit are large and Green covered over with a purple colour down,—The *Agoma* is a bitterish sort of Vegetable—the *brocaly* as in Europe, but scarcer, and the *Cherries* are ribbed, very sower, and /except when very ripe/ fit only for preserving with Sugar—

To Day I having invited some Company, we drank the Prince of Oranges health, this being his aniversary, while Colonel Fourgeoud /like a true Troijan/ still kept on Scowring the bushes, and from whom now came the news of his operations—viz—Some Shot by the Negroes, Some lost in the Woods, the Rebel Captive *Cupido* ran away with all his Chains, &c. but no Conquest of any Consequence on the Enemy while he sent me two Wounded Men to put in the Hospital at Clarenbeek, the one being terribly cut by the Rebels, who had also disarm'd him, while he had been obliged to lag behind from Necessity—Nevertheless the Chief for this Action now threatened to take away that life the Savages had Spared, and from that moment put him under an arrest, til further orders—

I now received in a present from a M.* *D'Onis* a haunch of Venison, while one of my Slaves presented me with a lesard call'd *Sapagala,* which is less in Size, and less delicious than the Leguana I have already discribed, and which is by the Indians call'd *Wayamaka,* of this last dainty however I did not partake myself, but gave it to the overseer while with the Venison I entertained All my Officers—

Of the Deer Species there are in Guiana 2 kinds, the Stag or largest call'd *Bajew* are about the Size of an English Roe-Buck, with short Curvated Horns, the Eyes are bright and full of fire, and the tail short, they are covered with a reddish-brown hair, except on the belly where it is white—these animals run and bound with amazing Strength and velocity if pursued and are frequently seen near the Estates, where they often do commit great devastations /in herds/ amongst the fields of Sugar Cane, &c. most of the Planters keeping an Indian or Negro Huntsman, they are frequently kil'd, that is by only shooting them, as hunting in this Country is literally impossible and sometimes they are taken alive in crossing the Rivers, as they often take to the Water if overheated, or with a view of escaping from their enimies—The flesh of this Stag being neither fat, tender, or Juicy, is inferior to the venison in the old Continent, notwithstanding which it is greatly esteemed by the Surinam Inhabitants—

The other Species are by the black peopl call'd the *bossee cabritta,* and

The Bajew, or Stag of Guiana.

The Wirrebocerra, or Small Deer.

by the Indians *Wirrebocerra*, these are infinitely Smaller than the former, and Still more nimble in escaping, their Skin is a Yellowish brown covered with Small White Patches or Spots, their Eyes are lively and piercing, and their Ears are narrow and Short; the Wirrebocerra never get any antlers, its limbs are small, but verry nervous and Strong, and its flesh more delicate than any of the Dear kind that ever was tasted—

Having to day visited M.ʳ & M.ʳˢ Lolkens at Fauquenbergh, we after dinner walked to a Brick manufactory call'd *appecappe*, which lays adjoining it, and is the property of Governor Nepvew, here I saw as good Bricks made by the Negroes, and as quick as I ever had seen any made in Europe, while they turn to good account for the proprietor, being not a verry common thing in Surinam, and which I only relate as a proof of the universality of the blessings of this Country, where besides the wood its for the cutting if the Inhabitants but chuse to be industrious

Being here however pester'd with Clouds of small Insects call'd *Monpeira*, I was glad to take my leave, and return to the Hope—the Monpeira are the smallest kind of Gnats, but not less troublesome than the larger Species call'd Musquetoes, flying so thick and clossely together, that they appear in the Air like [a] large Puff of black Smoak, these insects besides are so small, that they stick by half Dozens in ones Eyes, from which they can not be extricated without much Pain, and even danger—

All the above mentioned visits are here done by water, having on the hope an Elegant *tent-boat*, with half a Dozen of Negroes at my Command, which also went a Shooting for me—a fishing for me—&c—upon the whole I was here So perfectly well pleased—and So much respected, that I could have almost Capitulated never more to exchange my Situation

Chapter 13th

*A Sugar Plantation described—Domestic Happiness in a Cottage—
Further account of Fourgeouds opperations—Dreadful cruelties
inflicted by some Overseers—
Sketch of resentment by a Rebel Negroe Captain*

I have already say'd that I was happy at the Hope but how was my felicity now redoubled when this Evening Mr Lolkens, and his Lady came to visit me, and not only gave me the address of Messrs Passalege & Son in Co at Amsterdam /who as I have said were the new Proprietors of my Mulatto/, but even desired of me to take her to the Hope, where she would be better than either at Fauquenbergh or Paramaribo, which request to be sure I easily granted and instantly set about my Slaves to build her a comfortable house of Manicole trees, to be ready for her reception and convenience—While during the time of its erecting I wrote the following Letter to Messrs Passalege & Son in Co.

From the Hope in Comewina March 22nd 1774

Gentlemen—

Being informed by Mr Tierck Lolkens, the Administrator of the Estate Fauquenbergh, that you are the present Proprietors, And being under great obligations to one of your Mulatto-Slaves, named *Joanna*, who is the daughter of the late Mr Kruythoff, particularly for having attended me during Seekness—I in gratitude request of you who are her Masters, to let me purchase her Liberty without delay, which favour shall be ever thankfully acknowledged, and the ransom Money immediately pay'd by—

Gentlemen—
Your most ob.^t & most hble Servant
—John Gabriel Stedman—

Captain in Colonel Fourgeouds Corps of Marines—

1774 — MARCH 22

This Letter was seconded by another from my friend Lolkens, who much cheered my expectation with the assurance of Success—

Having dispatched these Letters to Holland and having now the opportunity also to see the whole process of a *Sugar-Plantation,* I shall here give an accurate account of it—The Same as *Schoonvort,* see M^{ch} 28.73.

The buildings usually consist in an elegant Dwellinghouse for the Planter, outhouses for the overseer, and book keeper, besides a Carpenters lodge, kitchens, Storehouses &c. and Stables if the Sugar Mills are worked by Horses or Mules, but on the Hope these were not required, where the Wheels went round by Water, being saved in Canals that surround the Estate during the Spring tides, by the means of Sluces, or floodgates, and which being let open when the Water in the Rivers is very low, the contents run out like a deluge, and set the whole Work a going

As to the Construction of a Sugar Mill [/]which is generally built at the amazing expense of from 4 to 7 or 8 thousand pound/ I can not enter into the particular discription of it, thus shall only say that the large, or *Water-Wheel,* which moves perpendicularly, corresponds with another large Wheel that is placed in a horisontal Direction, and this again with 3 perpendicular Sylanders or rollers of cast iron, that are under it supported on a Strong beam, and placed so Closs together, that when the whole is in Motion, they imbibe and crush to atoms whatever comes between them & in which manner the Sugar Cane is bruised, to Seperate the Joyce or liquor from the draff [chaff].

Those Mills that are worked by Cattle are also made on the same Construction, with this difference only that the horses or Mules answer the purpose of the horizontal-Wheel, by dragging round a large beam, like the hand of a dial—

If the Water Mills can work the fastest, and are the cheapest, they must wait for the opportunity of the Spring-tides, whereas the Cattle-Mills have always the Advantage of being ready for use when the Proprietor thinks it convenient—

Adjoining to the Mill house is a large Apartm.^{t} /both being built of brick/ in which are fixed by Masonry the Coppers or large Chaldrons to boil the liquid Sugar, and are usually five in number—On the opposite Side are the Coolers, being large Square flat bottomed wooden Vessels, in which the Sugar is put from the Chaldrons that it may Cool before it goes in the Hogsheads, and which are placed next to them on strong channeld Rafters that receives the Malasses as it dreeps from the Sugar, and conduct it in a square Cistern underneath the whole, and made for the purpose of preserving it—

Adjoining this apartment is Still a distillery, where the dross, or Scum taken from the boiling Sugar is converted in a kind of Rum, which I have before mentionned and is generally known by the name of Kildevil all throughout the Collony—

Having thus far discribed the buildings /besides which all Estates in Surinam keep a tent boat and several other small craft with a covered dock to keep them dry, and repair them/ I shall now say something of the Grounds, and the Cultivation of the Cane—

The Sugar Estates in this Colony consist often in above 5 or 600 Acres, the parts for Cultivation being divided into Squares, where the Pieces of Cane /about one foot long/ are stuck in the Ground in an obleek position but in Streight lines, and which is usually done in the rainy Season, when the Earth is well Soaked and most rich—Here the Shoots that Spring from the Joints grow for a time of 12 or 16 Months, when they become Yellow, thick like a Germain flute—from 6 to 10 feet in height, and jointed, forming a very beautiful appearance, with Pale green leafs like those of a leek, but longer and denticulated, and which hang down when the Crop begins to be ripe for cutting, during all which Period, pulling up the weeds is the principal business of the Slaves, to prevent the Canes from being impoverished by their luxurious progress—

After this the Sugar Canes are cut in pieces of 3 or 4 feet long, and /being divested of their leaves/ tied in bundells or faggots, when they are next transported to the Mill by Water /which shows the double usefulness of the Canaals/ and where within the Space of 24 hours they ought to be bruised, to prevent the Joyce from fermenting, and becoming Sower by the great heat of the climate—

I must not forget to say that some Sugar Estates have above 400 Slaves, the expense of buying whom, and erecting the buildings /the Ground excepted/ amounts frequently to 20,[000] or to 25,000 Pound Sterling—

But to give the Reader the best Idea of the Sugar Cane, which is supposed to be natural to Guiana I refer him to the anex'd Plate, where he may view it in the different Stages, though on a smaller Scale than nature, **A** Being its first appearance above the Ground, **B** the Sugar Cane come to half Maturity, **C** the same with drooping leafs in full ripeness, and **D** a piece cut of[f] at one end and broke of[f] at the other—

We shall now examine it in the Mill—here it is bruised between the working Sylenders, or the Rollers, as I say'd 3 in number, through

The Sugar Cane, in its four different Stages.

London, Published Dec.r 1.st 1791, by J. Johnson St. Pauls Church Yard.

which it passes twice, viz, once it enters and once it returns, when it is changed to dross, and its pithy-Substance into liquid, which is conducted as it is extracted through a channeld beam, from the Mill to the adjoining boiling house, and where it is received in a Species of Wooden Cistern—

So very dangerous is the work of those Negroes who enter the Canes in the Rollers, that should one of their fingers catch between them, which frequently happens by inadvertancy, the whole Arm is instantly Shattered to attoms, if not part of the Body, for which reason a hatchet is generally keep'd ready to chop of[f] the limb, before the working of the Mill can be stopped—The other danger is that should a Negro Slave dare to taste that Sugar which he produces by the Sweat of his Brow, he would run the hazard of paying the expense by some hundred lashes, if not by the breaking out of all his teeth; Such are the hardships, and Dangers to which the Sugar-Making-Negroes are exposed—

> Who toil and sweat the long laborious day;
> With Earliest dawn the ardent task begun,
> Their labour ends not with the setting Sun:
> For when the Moon displays her borrow'd beams,
> They pick the Canes, and tend the loaded teams,
> Or in alternate Watch, with ceaseless toil,
> The Rums distil, or smoaky Sugars boil.
> Ev'n while they ply this sad and sickly Trade,
> Which numbers thousands with the countless dead,
> Refus'd the very Liquors which they make,
> They quench their burning Temples in the Lake;
> Or issuing from the thick unwholesome steam,
> Drink future Sorrow in the cooling stream.—

But to proceed—From the above Wooden Cistern the Liquor is let into the first Copper Chaldron, filtering through a kind of grating to keep back the draff that may have escaped from the Mill, here having boild and being scum'd for some time, it is put in the next chaldron and so forth, til in the 5th or last, where it gets that thickness or consistancy which is required to put it in the Coolers—it is here to be observed that a few Pounds of Lime and Allum, are thrown in the Chaldrons to make it work, and granulate, while the whole is well mixed, and boild gradually Stronger and Stronger, as it proceeds towards the end, or the last chaldron—

Being next put in the wooden Coolers, the Sugar is well stired about so that the grain or body is equally dispersed, throughout the vessals, where when it becomes cold, it has the appearance of being frozen, being all over candied and of a brown glazed Consistancy, not unlike Pieces of high Polished Walnut-tree—

From these Coolers it is next put in the Hogsheads, /which are at an Average 1000 Pound weight/ where it then Settles and where /through the Crevisses, and small holes made in the bottoms/ it is purged of its remaining liquid contents, which are called Malasses, and /as I have said are received in an underground Cistern/ after which the Sugar has undergone its last operations, and is fit for transportation to Europe, where it is refined, and cast into Loaves &c. while I shall only further observe that the larger is the Grain the better is allowed to be the Sugar—NB Best Estates make 600 barrels—

I will now conclude this account, with once more repeating, that no soil in the World is so very rich, and proper for the Cultivation of the Sugar canes as is Surinam, or indeed all Guiana, which is in a manner never exhausted, and produces at an averidge 3 or 4 hogsheads of Sugar Pr Acre—

In 1771 were exported to Amsterdam, and Rotterdam alone, no less than 24 thousand hogsheads, at only about 6£ Value* each not above 1½d P.^{r} lb. which nevertheless returned a Sum of near One hundred & fifty thousand Pound Sterling, besides the great Quantity of Molasses, and Kildevil.—The first supposing 7000 Hogsheads, and which are sold to the American Islands, paying 25,000 Pound, and the second which is distill'd in Surinam for the Negroes, valued at just as much more, which makes a Sum of 200,000£ benefitted only in one Year—

The Kildevil is also drank by some Planters–but too much by the common Sailors, and Soldiers, to whom /the more so as it is always used while it is new/ it proves /as I have say'd before/ no better than a Slow, and pernicious Poison, yet it never hurts the Negroes, whose Constitutions are so much stronger than ours in a tropical Climate, but on the Contrary does them much good /particularly when at work in the rainy Season/ if they Can have the good Fortune to be indulged but with a Single dram Pr Day by their Masters, which is wide distant from being always the Consequence—

The Chaff or refuge [refuse] of the Canes next is used for fuel, or manure, and all Estates are closely surrounded by the uncultivated forest—**

---

* —It has Sometimes been Sold above 12 and 13£ pr. barrel of 1000 lb weight

** —In the Sugar Cane fields the herds of *wild Deer* often commit verry great ravages, when the pieces being Surrounded by arm'd negroes, and the Dogs set in to disperce them they are frequently Shott—

From what I have said on this subject alone the reader may form an Idea of the Riches that abound in this Country, and which nevertheless seem'd so little to Stimulate its Enemies for possessing it during the late War, while I must here make one remark—and that is, that Surinam in the possession of any other Nation than the Dutch, would instantly cease to be of its present Consequence—The Hollanders being indisputably the most patient, persevering, and industrious People that inhabit the Globe—while independent of the great Wealth that the West indies in general afford, it shall ever by my Opinion, that the Europeans could live as Comfortably without them, if not more healthy, where the want of Sugar, Coffee, Cotton, Cacaw, indigo, rum, and Brazil-Wood, can be amply supplied by honey, Milk, Wool, geneva, ale, English-Herbs, British-Oak &c—And now once more to my Narrative—

I have mentioned that my Slaves began to build a small habitation of Manicole trees for the reception of my best friend, which however was not compleated in less than the Space of 6 Days, having every Conveniency, such as a Parlour that served also for a dining room, a bed room where besides I stow'd my luggage, a Shade or Piadsa to sit under before the door, a small Kitchen detached from the dwelling, and a hen house, the whole of which was Situated in a Spot by itself, Commanding the most inchanting Prospect on all Sides, and surrounded with a Paling to keep of[f] the Cattle; My tables, Stools, Benches, and Seats being all Composed of the same identical Manicole-laths, while my Doors, and Windows, were Guarded with most ingenious Wooden-locks and keys, that were presented me by a Negro, and which were the Work of his own Manufacturing—

My House being this far finished and furnished my next Care was to Stock it with Provisions, thus I Commissioned from Paramaribo a barrel of flour, another of Salted Mackerel /which are in this Country delicious as being imported from N. America/ hams, Pickled-Sauceages, boston bisquit, &c. also Wine, Jamaica-Rum, tea, and Sugar, and a box with Spermacety-Candles, to which were added 2 Charming foreign Sheep, and a Hog sent me by Mr Kennedy from his Estate vriedyk, besides a couple Dozen of fine fowls and Ducks, given me in a present by *Lucretia* Joanna's Aunt, while fruit, vegetables, fish and Venison, flow'd to me from every Quarter as usual—

At last came down the River and arrived my Dr Joanna at the hope, in the tent boat belonging to Fauquenbergh, to whom having Communicated the Contents of my letter to Holland /which she Modestly received with downcast looks, and a blush for all reply/ I introduced her to her new Habitation, where the Plantation Slaves /as a Mark of

Respect/ immediately brought her Presents of Casada, Yams, bananas, and Plantains, and never two People were more Completely happy—

Not Adam and Eve in Paradise could Enjoy a greater Share of felocity, than we now did—free like the roes in the forest and disintangled from every care and fashion, we breathed the purest Ether in our walks, and refresh'd our limbs in the Cooling limpid Streams, health and Vigour were now again my portion, while my Mulatto flourished in youth and beauty, the envy and admiration of all the River Comewina—

—Here in close recess,
With flowry Garlands and sweet Smelling herbs,
Espoused Eve did deck her ruptial [nuptial] bed,
And heavenly Quires the hymenaean Sing;
What Day the genial Angel to *her friend*
Brought her in naked Beauty more adorn'd,
More lovely than Pandora, whom the Gods
Endow'd with all their Gifts—

Colonel Fourgeoud now soon expecting to quit the Woods, and to incamp at Magdenbergh, in the very upper parts of the river Comewina, I sent a large barge with provisions, escorted by an Officer and 20 Men, to that Spot to wayt his arrival, and receiv'd my remaining Marines which were not 20 More, excepting a small detachement at the Mouth of Caswinica Creek named Calis, and in the higher parts of which Creek at an Estate call'd Cupy, was also posted an Officer and a few Soldiers

This Morning I again was Witness to a very wonderful battle near my house between 2 Snakes, and which I must relate, the one about 3 feet long, the other no more than 14 Inches when after a long Contest of near half an hour, /during which time the many wreathes and twists were truly amazing / the largest of the 2 /having gradually Shifted his Grip/ caught the Smallest by the head and absolutely swallowed him alive—

Another observation I made upon frogs viz. that while a Negro Boy, through down some red hot Embers on the Ground, these Animals eat them with avidity without they received any visible damage from the fire, and which probably they mistook for fire-flies or something else—

Another frog I saw in the Sugar-Mill-house feasting upon a regiment of Ants, which are here exceedingly plentifull, and which with his tong /like a little dog / he lap'd up by Dozens as they Marched Past him, to my great astonishment—

1774—APRIL 4, 8, 9, 11

While Speaking about frogs I must Still mention another that regularly Sleep'd every Day on one of the beams of my Cottage, which it left as regularly every night, this was call'd by the Negroes *Yombo-Yombo* from its great power of leaping, it is very small, almost as flat as an oister Shell, Yellow with black and Scarlet Specks, and frequently found in the upper Stories of houses, to where it gets by climbing up the Walls, we thought it a pretty little Animal, and would allow no body to disturb it—

This morning while between 6 and 7 we now were interring one of my Serjeants, we heard the report of several minute Guns towards the River Pirica, in Consequence of which I detached an Officer, and 12 Men, to give assistance–who next day returned with account, that the Rebels had attacked the Estate Kortenduur–where having pillaged some Powder, &c. the Plantation Slaves alone /being arm'd by their Master/ had manfully beat them back, before he or his Men had come up to them—

Now arrived from Colonel Fourgeoud at Wana Creek a small detachement /with *September* the Captive Negro/ who related that the Rebels had Spoke with, and actually laugh'd at Fourgeoud, having overheard him deliver his orders, viz. not to fire on them, but to take them alive, while he might as well have taken so many torpedoes, and that amongst the lost in the Woods, was the unlucky Schmidt who had been lately so unmercifully beat, of which he had never recovered, and while it was prevented to give him any assistance or even try'd to restore him again, In Short independent of my Zeal for the Service, I could not help thinking myself happy out of his clutches, where nothing but misery was to be Met with, while on the Hope I enjoy'd *Orea libertas* in perfection, nor can the lines in Mr. Addisons Epistle to Lord Hallifax be better introduced than here, which were since Spoken on the 25th. July 1785 by George Dallas'd Esqr. at Calcutta—

> O Liberty, thou goddess, heavenly bright
> Profuse of bliss and pregnant with delight,
> Eternal pleasures in thy presence reign,
> And smiling plenty leads thy wanton train,
> Eas'd of her load, subjection grows more light
> And poverty looks chearful in thy Sight!
> Thou mak'st the gloomy face of nature Gay,
> Giv'st beauty to the Sun, and pleasure to the Day.

So very happy was I at present, that I thought myself not only fully Compensated for hardships past, but cheerfully ready to Submit during the remainder of my life, without a Murmur, to whatever might

1774—APRIL 11, 13, 14, 16

befal me, should it be even worse if worse was possible, However in this I confess not to have keep'd my Resolution—

- Now the whole Post was under Water, occasioned by the Spring floods having broke through the dams, that used to keep it off, which accident obliging Officers and all to walk in Water above the Knees, made it the more Comfortable for me to be pitched with my Cabbin upon a dry Spott, and to which I introduced my Dear Friend Mr *Heneman* the Volunteer, who now being entered Lieut: in my Company, was just arrived from Colonel Fourgeouds Camp at Wana Creek, with a barge full of Men and Ammunition, and the News that the remaining troops were march'd for Magdenbergh in upper Comewina, by the way of going into Quarters—The Poor Youth being emaciated with Misery and fatigue was happy to partake of the care of Joana, who was an incomparable nurse, and to whom I reccommended him from the first instant of his landing at the hope, nor was she one of those, whose looks needed to be vail'd, but who

> Undeck'd save with herself more lovely fair
> Than wood nymph, or the fairest Goddess feign'd
> Of three that in Mount Ida naked Strove,
> Stood to entertain her Guest—no veil
> Shee needed, virtue proof; no thought infirm
> Alter'd her Cheek.—

- Colonel Fourgeoud with his Troops now being come to Magdenbergh, the Officers and Troops of the Society being near 200 Men including the rangers were sent down in barges to be divided in the River Pirica, to where they March'd after landing at the hope, and during which there was on my Post such an Uproar and Confusion, that one of my Men got desperately Wounded in a Duel, a Sailor fell into the River and was drounded, and I was actually under the necessity of keeping order with my Sword, which having broke in Pieces on one of the ringleaders heads and with the hilt knocked out the best of his fore teeth, the Peace was reestablished & while such were the fruits of Colonel Fourgeouds Discipline, who while he distracted his Officers with bad usage, indulged the private Soldiers to a degree that made them pass'd all Subordination

Being at last debarassed from my unruly Guests, I sent a tent boat and 8 Oars up to Magdenbergh, to Row the Commander in Chief, with a few of his favourites to Paramaribo, and from which place he at last Permitted the wrongfully accused Count-Rantwick to sail for Holland.

- This Day most unluckily the greatest number of the Sheep belonging

1774—APRIL 16

to the Estate were poisoned by eating *Duncane* while amongst others my own, had the good fortune to escape I am sorry not to have particularly examined the duncane as it is call'd by the Negroes, of which the only thing that I can say is, that it is a kind of Shrub with a large green leaf something like that of the Docks in England, and grows Spontaneously in low and Marshy Places, Where it is instant death to whatever Animals eat its verdure, for which reason the Slaves can not be to[o] careful in rooting it out from the gras-Savana's or Meadows where Cattle are keep'd Grazing, and the more so since Sheep and Bullocks are said to be extremely fond of it, however Contrary to reason, since most Animals know by instinct to distinguish their food from their Poison—But those above mentioned being the unnatural Inhabitants of Guiana, may plead as an Exception to the general Rule, and unluckily the Sheep of the Hope having found access to a Quantity of this nuisance, by breaking through the fence of a Negros Garden where it had inadvertently been left growing, was the cause of the above unhappy Consequence—

Being entered into the discriptive Parts I will here mention a few Roots, Shrubs &c. that I here also met with in the above Negroes Garden, these were the *Yamesy*–or *Yams,* being a well known root on account of its nourishment, particularly for the Slaves through all the West Indies, this root requires a good fat Soil and will grow sometimes in Surinam to the weight of 2 or 3 score Pounds and 10,000 Pound weight upon one acre. its taste is very agreeable either roasted or boild, of easy digestion, and healthy, it is inside of a whitish Colour, and without a deep Purple approaching to black, while its Shape is very irregular, the Yams are cultivated by cutting them in Pieces like Potatoes, and by planting them a few feet distance from each other, when in the Space of 6 or 8 Months they are come to fullest Maturity and fit to be dug up, which is always known by the verdures beginning to fade and which consists in ligneous Shoots or branches that creep along the Ground like Ivy, with deep green triangular leafs, this root alone is sufficient to supply the want of bread and being capable of Preservation for almost a Year, is often transported, and used upon Sea Voyages—another small root I found here *cocoes* which is known in Surinam by the name of *naapjes* and which is eat in the same manner as the Yams, but which is incomparably more delicious, while both the one and the other serve here for food such as Potatoes, Carrots, or Parsnips do in England—

In this Garden I also saw some Maize or Indian Wheat which grows on high perpendicular Stalks, with long Pale green leafs, where the Grain is produced, being of a Shining Yellow or Orange Colour, as

1774—APRIL 16, 18

large as Marrow Peas, regularly and closely set together, on ears that are the Size of the largest European Carrots; this Grain is not only Cultivated in great Quantitys in Surinam, to feed the Poultry of every Species, but often grinded into Meal of which the Creoles make excellent pudding and use it on many different Occasions—

With this they frequently eat the young Pods of the ocro or Althea plant, which grow on a very small Shrub with oblong leafs, and which are when boil'd /as Doctor Bancroft terms it/ of a Musilaginous, Slymy, and lubricative texture, which ropy or Glutinous Quality /However disgustful to appearance/ nevertheless makes a very good Sauce when properly Seasoned with Cayenne Pepper &c—

This Evening walking out with my Gun as usual I shot a bird that I have not yet mentioned cal'd here a *Sabacoo,* this was a Species of *Gray-Heron,* with the bill & Legs of a Greenish-black Colour, and very long, the last appearing like Jointed by large Scales of a hard and horny Substance, and the Claws on each middle toe dentulated, this Bird though the Size of a Common fowl to appearance, was so verry light, that an English House-Pidgeon would have easily Counterballanced it, and of a very fishy flavour—

I have of late said nothing on the subject of Cruelty, and am sorry at this time /while all seem'd harmony and peace/ obliged to relate some fresh instances of it, which I am Confident must inspire the most unfeeling Reader with Horror and resentment—

The first Object that attracted my Compassion was /while visiting in a neighbouring Estate/ tied up with both Arms to a tree, a truly beautiful *Samboe* Girl of about 18, as naked as she came to the World, and lacerated in such a shocking Condition by the Whips of two Negro Drivers, that she was from her neck to her Ancles literally died over with blood—It was after receiving 200 lashes that I perceived her with her head hanging downwards, a most miserable Spectacle, Thus turning to the overseer I implored that she might be untied from that moment, which seem'd to give her some Relief, but my Answer was from the humane Gentleman, that to prevent all Strangers from interfearing with his Government, he had made it an unalterable rule, in that Case always to redouble the Punishment, and which he instantaneously began to put in execution—I tried to stop him but in vain, he declaring the delay should not alter his determination but make him take vengeance with Interest upon Interest—Thus I had no other remedy left but to leap in my boat, and leave the detestable rascal like a beast of prey to enjoy his bloody-feast til he was Glutted, while from that Day I swore to break of[f] Communication with all overseers, and implored

Flagellation of a Female Samboe Slave

the curse of Heaven to be poured down upon the whole relentless fraternity—

On my having enquired since for the cause of such barbarity, I was too Credibly informed, that her only Crime had consisted in her firmly refusing to submit to the loathsome Embraces of her despisable Executioner, which his Jealousy having Construed to Disobedience, she was thus Skinned alive, and having hitherto not introduced the *Samboe* Cast, I take this opportunity, by here representing the miserable Young Woman to the Sympathysing reader as I found her—

A Samboe /as I have said/ is between a Mulatto and a black, being of a deep Copper-Colour'd Complexion, with dark hair that curls in large ringlets, those Slaves both Male and female are generally handsome, and mostly imploy'd as Menial Servants in the houses of the Planters &c—

At my return on the hope I was accosted by M.r *Ebbers* the Overseer of this Estate, who informed me /with a woeful Countenance/ that he had just been fined in the Sum of 1200 florins being about 100 Guineas, for having committed some time before the same diabolical Crime, with this difference that the victim had died during the execution and, which news of his distress /so far from giving him Consolation/ gave me the most inexpressible Satisfaction, and so I told him—

The Particulars of this Murder were as follows—During the time that Capt.n Tulling Commanded here, /and just before I came to the hope/ it happened that a fugitive Negro belonging to this Estate had been taken upon an Adjoining Plantation, and sent back guarded by 2 armed-Slaves to M.r Ebbers, which fugitive Negro while M.r Ebber was reading the letter that accompanied him, found means to Spring aside, and again escape in the forest–and which insensed the overseer so much, that he instantly took revenge upon the 2 poor Slaves that had brought him, whom having tied up in the Carpenters lodge, he keep'd on flogging at such an unmerciful Rate that Capt.n Tulling thought proper to interfere, and beg for Mercy–but this /as with me/ had just the opposite Effect, the Clang of the Whip mixed with their dismal Cries was heard to Continue for above an hour after, till one of them was absolutely flog'd to Death, and which ended the inhuman Catastrophe—A law Suit was instantly Commenced against M.r Ebber, for assasination, while paying the above Sum was his only Sentence and which price of *blood,* is always nearly divided between the Fiscal, and the Proprietor of the deceased Slave–it being a Rule in the Colony of Surinam that by paying a fine of 500 florins /not 50£/ per head you are at Liberty to kil as many Negro's as you please, with an additional price

1774—APRIL 18

of their value should they belong to any of your Neighbours, and then the Murder first requires to be properly proved, which is extremely difficult in this Country, where *no Slaves* evidence is admitted—

Such are the laws of the Legislature in Dutch Guiana; the above Mr Ebbers was indeed peculiarly tyranical, who tormented a boy of about 14, Call'd *Cadetty,* for the Space of a whole Year, by alternately flogging him one Month, keeping him lay'd flat on his back, with his feet in the Stocks for another, making him go with an iron triangel* about his neck Call'd a potthook to prevent him from escaping or Sleeping for a third Month, and chaining him to the landing place in a Dogs Collar Night and Day without Shelter, and orders to *bark* at every boat or Canoo that past for a fourth, &c &c. til the Youth was almost become insensible to his Sufferings, walked Crooked, and in a Manner degenerated into a brute—

The above Gentleman was nevertheless very proud of his handsomest Slaves, whom for fear of disfiguring their Skins, I have known him to forgive with 20 lashes, when by their roberies they had deserved, to get the Gallows.—

So much for publick and Private Justice in Surinam, to which I shall only add, that the above Gentleman having quitted the hope on this Occasion his next *humane* Successor Mr *Blenderman,* began his reign by one Morning flogging all the Slaves of the Estate, Male, & female, old, & Young without exception, for having out-Sleep'd their time about 15 Minutes—

And now what reader shall believe that the above inhumanitys can be exceeded, yet such they certainly were but very lately even by a female when a *Mrs Stolker* going to her Estate in a tent-barge, a Negro Woman with her sucking-Infant happened to be passengers, and seated on the bow, or fore part of the boat, but where the Child Crying /without it could possibly be hushd, and Mrs Stolker not delighting in such Musick/ She ordered the Mother to bring it aft, and deliver it in her own hands, with which forthwith, in the Presence of the Distracted Parent she thrust it out at one of the tilt-Windoes, and held it under water, til it *was drowned,* and while the fond Mother /being desperate for the loss of her helpless baby/ instantly leaped overboard in the same Stream where floated her beloved Offspring, and in Conjunction with which she was determined to end her miserable existance,—However in this she was prevented by the Care of the Negro Slaves, that rowed

* —these *Triangels* are frequently put upon the Negroes, which being formed with 3 long barbed Spikes like small Grapple's that project from an Iron Collar, prevent them from entering in the Woods, without entangling, and from Sleep except it be in a sitting Portion [position]—

the barge, and corrected by her Mistress for her unatural temerity—with three or four hundred lashes.—

Such was the Action of a hellish fiend, who had the figure and affected all the Softness of a Woman, Oh may such Shocking truths—

Teach Britain to resist tyrannic sway,
And drag her venal traitors to the Day?
                              enough

Now arrived Colonel Fourgeoud with all the Troops from Magdenbergh, preferring to establish his head Quarters rather nearer the Infirmary, for which indeed at this time he had great need, and thus pitched upon the Estate call'd *New-Rosenbeek,* situated between the Hope, and the Hospital,—to this place I now immediately repair'd, where I pay'd my Obeisances to the Chief, saw the remainder of his Miserable Army landed, and got the remaining news of this Campeign—

I have already mentioned Captn Fredereicy's being Shot through both his thighs, one Man terribly Wounded, and disarm'd, & another lost altogether by neglect, the Captives runaway with Chains and all, The Hero Scoft and laught at by his Sable Enemies, &c. to which I now shall add that a seek Marine was left behind, to die or recover as he could by himself, that one of the Slaves by bad usage got his arm broke, and that the Captive Negro Woman also was now lost /no more to return to her Conqueror/ who **NB** carrying back a big Belly got amongst the troops, had the opportunity of thus presenting a recruit to her dusky king &c—

These were the Particulars of the last 2 Months Campeign, while I must not omit to mention the Humanity of a poor Slave, who at every hazard had deserted Fourgeoud to attend the dying Marine, and with whom having remained alone til he expired, he returned to the troops to receive his Punishment, but where he was most miraculously *pardoned*—

Let me now do the Justice to Colonel Fourgeoud to say that upon such an expedition, and in such a Climate many of these little actidents could not well be prevented, & that while he kil'd his troops by Scores, without making any Captures on the Enemy, he nevertheless did the Colony an considerable deal of Good, by Constantly Disturbing, and hunting, and harassing them, and since independent of his destroying their fields with provisions, no Negroe will ever return to settle in those haunts, from which he has been drove, any more than a hare will to her firm, or a fox to the hole from which he has been unkenneld; to which I may add that his partaking personally in all the dangers & fatigues, and at his Age, can not but help to efface many of the other faults that stain'd his Character, and even serve in some Measure to establish his lasting Honour.—I wish from my Soul that I had nothing to write but in his praise, but equity requires it of me that for the general benefit of Mankind /while I display his shining Qualities/ I also point out those very great failings, which may serve in correcting others, and by which means even his *vices* may be made useful—for instance what could be more rediculous than paying the troops as I have said with *Silver* at Paramaribo, where Paper was just as good and now, while they were in the rivers, giving them *Cards* or *paper* for which they could not buy so much as a Yam, or a bunch of Plantains, and while he had whole Chists with Money in his keeping? without it was to reap the benefit indeed himself, and usurp the Profit of the whole Regiment at 10 Pr Cent by these proceedings, and with which Stigma, he was branded by the whole Corps in general—but I will proceed with my Journal—

I now entertained several Officers on a fish dinner who had come to visit me at the hope, amongst these fish were the *Kawiry,* the *Lamper,* and a Species call'd *Macrely*-fisy, which I will all briefly discribe—The Kawiry is a small fish without Scales, the head is large with two long Antheena, or Whiskers, projecting from the upper Jaw, and is very plentiful in all the Rivers—The *Lamper* is a Species of Lamprey, as are sometimes caught in the Thames[.] Those in Surinam are not large, but very fat, of a round Shape and Slymy or Glutinous aspect, their Colour is a blueish Green with Yellow Spots, except on the belly where they are white[.] this fish like the Salmon, frequents both the Sea, and the Rivers—As to the other fish, the only thing I can say about it is that it very much resembles a Mackerel in Sise and Shape, from which it has derived its name, but its Colour which is more blueish than green, is not nearly so splendid—all the above fish are most delicate eating, and taken in great Quantitys through all Guiana

However we had feasted so hearty, that one of the Officers was ill the same Evening, and next morning my poor Joana who had herself been the Cook, was attack'd with such a violent fever, that at her own request I instantly sent her to the Estate Fauquenbergh, to be attended there by one of her female relations, nevertheless she continued to grow worse, and in the Evening of the 25th was so extremely seek that I determined now to call upon her in person, but if possible without the knowledge of Colonel Fourgeoud /who was to come and visit me the next day, at the hope, and whose Satirical Jeers I could very well disperse with, while the most inoffensive and even laudable Motives, were no Guard at all against the Malice and inveteracy of his temper[/]—

However difficult this undertaking /being obliged to pass close by himself/ I nevertheless resolved to put it in execution at all Hazards, and as much as ever *Leander* had determined to visit Hero, by Swimming From *Sestos* to *abydos* across the *Hellespont*–Thus having told my friend Heneman where I was going, I set out at Eleven OClock at night, and row'd up the River with my own barge, til Comming before the Estate New-Rosenbeek, I heard Fourgeouds Voice distinctly, with one or two Officers walking upon the beach, and immediately after which, the Centinel challenged the boat, and ordered her to come on Shoare to be examined—I now thought all was over, But Still persisting to the last that he should not discover me, I desired one of my Negros to answer *Killestyn-Nova,* which was the name of an adjoining plantation, and they got leave to row up the river unmolested—Soon after this I landed at *Fauquenbergh,* and saw my truest friend /thank Heaven/ rather better & now thus far all was perfectly well, but next

🙠 Morning mistaking day-break for the Moon-Shine, I oversleep'd myself, and knew not possibly in what manner to return to the hope, since my barge and Negroes could *this time* not pass without being well known, to Colonel Fourgeoud and all the rest—In short delay was but loosing the battle, thus of[f] I set trusting for all recourse to the ingenuity of my Slaves, and I succeeded—they putting me ashoare just before we came in Sight of the Head Quarters, when one of them escorted me through the thickest part of the forest /as Flora Macdonald and Genny Cameron had done the pretender through the Mountains of Scotland/ til I arrived once more safe and Sound at the hope–but here my barge soon followed under a Guard, with every one of my Poor Negroes taken Prisoners, and an order from Fourgeoud, for me to flog them all, they being apprehended without a Pass, while their excuse was that they had been sent a fishing—

Their fidelity to me now was truly astonishing, declaring they sooner prefer'd to be all cut to Pieces, than to betray the Secret of so good a Master, but theyr hazard was not very great, since I did not only confirm what they had said, but added the fish had been intended to Regale the Hero himself, the whole Matter was thus ended to general Satisfaction and to which I join'd a donation of 2 Gallons of rum, for the benefit of my Sable privy-Counsellors; while this Passage however trifling in itself may serve as a Sample not only of European Weakness but of African firmness & resolution—

🙠 In short Colonel Fourgeoud came not this Day, but the next morn-

1774—APRIL 27, 28

ing arrived the Mulatto quite recovered, accompanied by a stout black, who was her uncle, and whose arm was decorated with a Silver band, on which were ingraved the words "true to the Europeans"—This Man who was named *Cojo,* having Voluntarily fought against the Rebels, before his Companions had been forced by the inhuman Mr D. Borde, to join them in the Woods, and of whom he now related to me the following Remarkable Circumstance—

>Having a little Girl by the hand Cal'd *Tamera*–This Childs father /say'd he/ is one of them whose Name is *Jolly Coeur,* the first Captain belonging to Barons Men* and not without a Cause one of the fiercest Rebels in the forest; which he has lately sho[w]ed on the Neighbouring Estate *New-Rosenbeek* w[h]ere now our Colonel Commands.
>
>Here one Mr Schults, a Jew, being the Manager at that time, who formerly was the Manager of Fauquenbergh, the Rebels suddenly appeared and took possession of the whole plantation—Having tied his hands and plundered the House, they next began to feasting and dancing, before they thought it proper yet, to end his miserable existance—
>
>In this deplorable Situation now lay the victim, only waiting Barons Signal for Death, when his Eyes chancing to fall on the *above* Captain, he address'd him nearly in the following words, "—O Joly Coeur, now remember *Mr Schults* who was once your Deputy-Master, remember the Dainties I gave you from my own table when you was but a child, and my favourite, my darling amongst so many others, remember this and now Spare my Life by your powerful intercession—" To which Jolly Ceur, "I remember it perfectly well, but you O Tirant, reccollect how you ravished my poor Mother, and flog'd my father for coming to her assistance, reccollect the Shameful Act was perpetrated in my infant presence, recollect this then die by my hands, and next be damn'd," Saying which he severed his head from his Body with a Hatchet at one blow, and with which having play'd at bowls upon the beech, he next cut the Skin with a knyfe from his back, which he spread over one of the Cannon to Stop the firing—

Here ended the History of Mr Schults, when Cojo with young Tamera departed, and left me to anticipate the Joyful news that I soon was to expect from Amsterdam, and when the deserving Joana should be unbound from all such Rascals—

And at last arrived about 10 O Clock, Colonel Fourgeoud with one of his Officers, and with the very Devil painted in his Countenance, which alarmed me much, however I instantly introduced him to my Cottage, where he no sooner saw my mate, than the Clouds /like a

---
* —as had before been told me by M.^r De Melly at Paramaribo—

vapour by the Sun/ were dispeld from his gloomy forehead, while I Confess that I never saw him behave with more Civility—

—Her heavenly form,
Angelic but more Soft & feminine,
Her Graceful innocense, her ev'ry Air
Of Gesture, or least Action, over aw'd
His Malice, and with rapine Sweet bereav'd
His fierceness of the fierce intent it brought—

Having entertained him in the best manner that we were able, and now related the Story of the hellispont he laugh'd heartily at the Stratagem and giving us both a Shake by the hand departed to New Rosenbeek in good Humour and perfectly contented and from all which Circumstances the above Chapter may be Stiled the Golden age of my West-India Expedition—

Chapter 14th

*Col: Fourgeoud to Paramaribo—Sample of ignorance in a Surgeon—
Example of Virtue in a Slave—Ferocity in a Commander—
The Troops reenter the Woods—Account of Loango Dancing—
Proof of the Force of Natural Affection*

Having delay'd his departure to this Day, Colonel Fourgeoud now finally row'd down for Paramaribo, accompanied by a few of his Officers to refresh themselves, and of which they had truly great need, while an arm'd barge keept floating up and down the river, and while the remaining amaciated troops /that were melted down to a very small number, and unfit/ til recruited in their Constitutions /for any further Military Service/ greatly required some rest—

Just before the Chiefs departure he sent me /who now Commanded the River/ the following very curious Instructions to observe, which as a proof of his generalship I can not be of from inserting; viz. amongst others "to ask the Planters if the Rebels were come to their Estates, in which Case to attack and drive them away, but not to follow, without I was sure that I certainly should Conquer them, and for which I should be called to an Account," which is in proper English that if I attacked the Enemy *without* success I must be punished, and if I do not attack them *at all,* ad idem—However Judicious the other Articles I had received, I could not help thinking the above so very absurd that imediately return'd them back with an Officer, and had the Good fortune /at my request/ to get them changed, into Common Sence—

Nor were the Provisions that he left for the troops /indiscriminately, the *healthy* and the *Seek*/ to be boasted of, which consisted weekly in Irish-horse, viz.

273

Salt beef	2 lb	besides one Spoonfull of Butter,
Salt pork	½ lb	One half Quart Bottle of Kildevil,
Salt fish	½ lb	1 Quarter of a pound of tobacco & a
barlay	4 lb	Pipe, This was by heavens the whole
rusk bisquit	6 lb	for 7 Days allowance—

and while the wheat flower, the Peas, cheese, Sugar, vinegar, beer, and Geneva, were kept back that had been so plentifully provided by the town of Amsterdam, as were also the many Cags of preserved vegetables, and Hogsheads of excellent Clerret sent for the Officers—

In Short not So much as a Candle being allowed for the Hospital, I now proposed to give in a request for the redressing of the above Grievances, to be Directed to Fourgeoud, and Sign'd by all the Officers in the River, but they being afraid to incur his displeasure, the Petition was lay'd aside and I may safely say *Starvation* Continued amongst the Soldiers, How happy was I at this time in particular, who wanted for nothing, and who had such an agreeable Partner for ever near me, whose Sweet Conversation was divine Musick to my Ears, and whose presence banished every Languor & hardships from my Ideas—

> Pone me pigris ubi nulla campis
> Arbor aestiva recreatur aura;
> Quod latus mundi nebulae malusque Jupiter urget:
> Pone sub curru nimium propinqui
> Solis, in terra domibus negata;
> Dulce ridentem Lalagen amabo, Dulce Loquentem

Painting, Musick, bathing, and Shooting, were now my principal amusements, in which my young Mulatto was my constant Companion–and who one Day straying with me through a watery Savanah, pointed to a bird which she desired me to shoot and which I did—

This was the Spur-wing'd Water-Hen of Edwards, and which may with truth, and reality, be call'd a beautifull Creature—

This Bird is supposed to be of the Plover kind, with the body about the Size of a Pidgeon, being of a deep Cinnamon Colour, viz between red, and a very rich Orange, The neck and belly are perfectly black, and the largest feathers of the Wings of a bright Yellow, being arm'd on each Pinion with a short and sharp horny Spur, that it uses for its defence, as game Cocks do use theirs in old England;

It has no tail, but a bill of near two inches in length, and long legs, which are as is the bill of a Yellowish Green Colour while its toes Especially the hinder-ones are of a remarkable length, and seem Calculated to support its Weight in the Mud, where it is most frequently seen, if not wading in the Water, to seek its food; these birds like Plov-

The Spur winged Water hen of Guiana.

The Red Curlew of Surinam.

London, Published Dec. 2, 1793, by J. Johnson, St. Paul's Church Yard.

ers never Swim, and have a scarlet-crest, and small Pearls /like those of the Muscovy Duck already discribed/ Seperating the bill from the Eyes, they are always seen in Pairs, and when they fly make an agreeable Whistling with their throats—The Spur-winged Water-hen, on account of its great Beauty, puts me in mind of another fine Bird, I lately saw upon one of the Neighbouring Estates, but which I had forgot to mention; This was the *Guiana-Curlew,* here call'd *Flamingo* from its great resemblance to the Famous bird of that name, seen in Canada, and many parts of North, & South America*–and which is supposed to be of the *crane* kind, with its body as large as that of an European Swan, while this bird is only the Size of a Small Heron—It has no tail, but a very long Neck and long Limbs, with 4 toes, the head is Small, and the bill also long, round, and arched—The *flamingo* or Curlew lays always 2 Eggs, which when hatched the Chickens appear black, next gray then white as they come nearer to Maturity, and finally the whole bird becomes a bright Scarlet, or Crimson, some not lighter than the Colour of Blood,—they live in Society like the Storks, and mostly on the banks of rivers, or near the Sea, where they are seen in such amazing Shoals or Quantities, that the Sands seem like died over with vermillion—these birds when Young, are reckoned very good eating, and are so tameable, that on the Plantations they are frequently seen Walking & feeding among the Poultry, though fish, and animal-food, is what they generally prefer—

Thus daily had I some new Object to discribe, and Spent the most agreeable hours, upon this Eligean-Plantation, but when all at once in the midst of my Glory My truly Halcion days were blasted, and I was almost plunged in despair, by receiving the fatal News, of the Death of Mr *Passelege* at Amsterdam, to whom I had wrote for to obtain my Mulatto's *Manumission,* and what could certainly not but redouble my distress, was the *Situation* in which now she proved to be, who promissed fair to become a Mother in the Space of a few Months—

It was now that I saw the wretchedness of my Situation, as much as Adam had done by tasting the forbidden fruit—

It was now that I saw thousand Horrors creep all at once upon my dejected Spirits, yet which I at first keept conseal'd from the Object that gave them birth, but which when she heard, she received with Calmness and with dignity—Heavens not only my *friend,* but my *Ofspring* to be a Slave, and a Slave under *such* Government—Mr Passelege my only recourse *buried*–and the whole Estate going to be sold

* —These are also known in Guiana by the name of *Phoenicoptherus,* but I never had the opportunity of seeing one myself—

to a *New*-Master—I could not bear it, and was totally distracted—nay must have died with grief, had the Mildness of her temper not supported me, by the fluttering hopes that *Lolkens* still would be our friend—

These were my Melancholy Reflections when on the Evening of the fourth, we heard the report of several alarm-Guns towards the North East—

Thus by Day break next morning I sent a detachement to Rio-Pirica, who returned about noon with the account, of the Rebels attacking the Estate *Merseille* in the River Cottica, but from which they had been beat back by the Plantation Slaves, as they had been before by those of Kortendeur—The other news was that they had ill treated a party of poor Indians, Suspecting them to have assisted the Estates, in making their defence,—Also that at Paramaribo an insurrection was discovered amongst the Negroes, who had determined to join the Rebels, after first having Massacred all the Inhabitants—However that they were detected, and the most Capital Ringleaders executed—

This Morning we again heard several Musquet Shot in the Woods, but which I apprehending to be some European Party that had lost their way, I made my Sentinel answer their Signals of distress, by firing his Piece alternately with theirs, Shot for Shot, to which I added 2 drums, that kept beating for several hours without intermission, when the report of their Arms gradually approached, and finally made their appearance, a Society Serjeant, and 6 emaciated Privates, that belonged to Reedwyk in Pirica, and had been lost in the forest for 3 Days, nearly Starved, without Hammocks, Meat, or Drink, excepting Water—Having refreshed them in the best manner I was able, they all recovered to my verry great Satisfaction, one of them being Stung perfectly blind for several hours, by a kind of Wasps, that go in this Country by the name of *Marobonso,* and of which the only thing that I can say is, that they are extremely large, live in hollow trees, are the Strongest of the bee kind, and Sting so Violently that besides the Pain, they always occasion a fever—

Having this forenoon Swim'd twice across the River Cottica, which is above half a Mile broad, I now came home in a Shiver, and next day had an intermitting fever, however by abstaining from annual [animal] food, and using plenty of Acid with my Drink, I had no doubts of my getting well in a few Days, the more so as Tamarinds grow'd here in profusion

> While I recline within the verdant Shade,
> Pluck me the Tamarind from yonder Glade:

1774—MAY 13, 16, 20, 21

That fever killing Pod that cools the Soul,
When to the Mouth we raise the Sparkling bowl:

- Indeed on the 16th I was almost perfectly recovered /weakness excepted/ when about 10 in the morning /as I was sitting with Joana before my Cottage/ I got an unexpected visit from a Mr *Steger,* who happened to be one of our Surgeons, and who having felt my Pulse, examined my Tongue, &c. declared without Ceremony, that I was to *be dead* before to morrow, without I made use of his immediate prescription—dead— I acknowledge the sentence staggered me so much that /while at other times I never used medicines at all/ I instantly Swallowed the dose, which he had prepared for me in a tumbler, without hesitation; but while almost as instantly I drop'd down on the Ground, like a Bullock that was struck on the head with A Butchers Hammer—

- In this manner did I lay till the 20th, being four Days before I came to my Sences, when I found myself Streached on a Mattrass in my little house, with Poor Joana sitting by me, all alone, and bathed in tears, who beg'd of me at that time to ask no Questions, for fear of hurting my Spirits but who next day related to me the dismal transaction— viz—That the moment I fell, 4 Strong negroes had taken me up, and

- by her direction put me where now I was—that the Surgeon having put blisters on several parts of my Body, had finally declared that I was dead, & had suddenly left the Plantation, when a Grave and Coffin were ordered to bury me on the 17th, which she had prevented by dropping upon her knees, that she had dispatched a black to her Aunt at Fauquenbergh for Wine-Vinegar, and a Bottle of old-Ranish [Rhenish = Rhine wine], with the first of which she had Constantly bathed my temples, wrists, and feet, by without Intermission keeping 5 Wet Handkerchiefs tied about them, while with a Silver Tea Spoon she had found means to make me swallow down a few drops of the Wine Muld, that I had lain motionless during all that time, while she had day and night by the help of *Quacoo,* and an old Negro, Attended me, still hoping for my recovery, for which she now thanked her God, to which I could only Answer by the Pearl of Simpathy that Started from my Eyes, and a feeble Squeese of Gratitude of my hand—

> Say not I died nor Shed a tear,
> Nor round my ashes mourn,
> Nor of my needless Obsequies take care;
> All Pomp and State is lost, upon an Empty urn.

However I had the good fortune to recover, but so slow, that /independent of that great care that was taken of me by that Heavenly Young

Woman, to whom alone I owed my life/ that it was the 15 of June, before I could walk by myself, during all which time I was carried on a Species of Chair by 2 Negroes, Supported on 2 Poles like a Sedan, and fed like an Infant, being so lame, and enervated, that I was not able to bring my hand to my Mouth, & while Poor Joana /who had suffered too much on my Account/ was for several days following, very poorly herself—In short great was the Change from what I had been but so shortly before,—Then the most healthy, and most happy in my body and my Mind, and now deprest to the lowest Ebb, in my fine Constitution, and my Spirits, which shows as Doctor Cotton observes—"T'is folly looks for cloudless days"—

My friend Heneman /who visited me every day/ now told me that upon information, he had discovered the Medicines which so nearly had kil'd me, to be nothing but *tartaremetick,* and *Epecacoana,* but in too great a Quantity viz. 4 Grains of the first, mixt with 40 Grams of the latter, the Surgeon having measured my Constitution by my Size which is above 6 feet[.] However I was so much incensed at this Piece of Stupidity that on the 4th of June, having drank his Britannick Majesties health in a rummer of Madeira, and the fatal Surgeon Comming to make me a bow, just at that time, he no sooner put his foot on the landing Place where I was sitting in my Palanquin or Chair, than having previously club'd one of the Poles that carried me upon my Shoulder, I let it drop down upon his guilty Pate, my Strength being as yet too feeble to aim a blow, and which the poor fellow no sooner felt upon his Pericraneum than he forgot the rest of his Compliments, and Skip'd back into his boat with all expedition, with which he row'd off as fast as the Negroes could trugg, to our no small entertainment, Who Saluted him with 3 Cheers—

About this time while the troops were doing nothing, two of the bravest Men in the Colony with the rangers entered the Woods, Viz. Capt.n *Fredereicy,* and the Militia Capt.n *Stoelman,* who kil'd 3 or 4 of the rebels, and took a few more Prisoners who were Starved for want of Subsistance, since Fourgeoud had ransack'd the surrounding forest—

In the Creek Pattamacca 2 Rebel Negroes were also Shott by M.r *Wines* Slaves, where they had tried to plunder some Provisions, and who had sent their heads barbacued to Paramaribo, as one of them was conjectured to be that of the famous Chief *bony,* but which afterwards proved to be a Mistake—

Being Still so Weak that I was unfit for any Duty, not even at the Hope, I now gave over the Command of that Post to the next Officer in Rank, and expecting the change of Air would do me good I /with

1774—JUNE 17

the previous knowledge of Colonel Fourgeoud/ went on a visit to a neighbouring Estate call'd *Egmond,* where the Planter Monsieur *de-Cachelieu* a French Gentleman had given me a most hearty invitation with Joana, my boy Quacoo, & a white Servant Jacobus van der Meer—

At this Place I was extremely Comfortable, and nothing could be better adapted for my Speedy recovery, than this Frenchmans good Humour, and his Frugality; eternally Singing, and feeding upon nothing—but which blessings were imbittered by his Severity and injustice to his Slaves—

For instance 2 *young* Negroes, who well deserved a flogging by breaking in, and robbing their Masters Storehouse, came off with a few lashes, while 2 Old ones, for a trifling dispute, were each condemned to receive no less than 300—On my asking for the cause of this Partiality, I was answer.d by Monsieur de Cachelieu, that the *Young* ones had Still a very good Skin, and might do much Work, Whereas the *old* ones had long been disfigured, worn out and almost unfit for any Service, nay that killing them altogether would be a Profit to the Estate—

At Arentlust a few Estates lower down, some Days ago a poor Negro being sent with a Letter, from his Proprietor to the Manager here, of which this last not liking the Contents, he gave the Messenger 400 lashes, telling the innocent Man at the same time to carry that for the answer to his Master; is not this a truly damnable usuage?—But to return to my french Host /who was in this alone excepted as Polite Hospitable, and Well bred a Man as ever I would wish to converse With/ I must mention some Particulars of his remarkable Œconomy, viz. a west-India-Rabbit Cal'd in Surinam Coney-Coney, and by the Indians *Puccarara,* but properly the *agouty,* I saw one Day come Roasted to the Table, of which he and I eat *one* Quarter—Next day it made its appearance a *la crapodine,* that is with Salt, & Pepper on the Gridiron,—The 3.d day the remaining half was entered by way of a french-fricasee—And the 4.th the last Quarter was Converted in what I call a Meagre Soup—

This I relate as a fact & while the Planter, his overseer, his Dog, and his two Cats, not weighing 14 Stone amongst them all, no family in Surinam could be more healthy, or Contented.—And could no one possess more Absteniousness, than did /in Particular/ the overseer M.r Bodewyn, who declared, that he never had *fought a Battle fired a Musquet, Mounted a horse,* or *kis'd a Woman,* while both were dress'd and Shaved by the Soft hand of a Young Negroe Wench—

Nothing could be better than the Oranges, and China-Apples, that I found on this Estate—The first I have already discribed, and though often Confounded with the latter are a very distinct fruit upon the whole—

The *China-apples* as they are usually cal'd, differ in this with the other Oranges, that they are still of a more lucid and Savoury taste, that the Shell is smoother, thinner, and not so deep Coloured, and particularly that while the Oranges may be eat in any Quantity, without pernicious Consequences, the immoderate use of the *China-Apples* is by long experience in this Colony, found out to produce very dangerous Effects—This fruit being here much the same as that which comes from Lisbon, it is supposed to be imported at first /as was the other/ by the Portegueese or the Spaniards—and it may well be conceived that in those Countrys where it drops ripe from the Trees in Golden clusters, it must be incomparably more delicious, than it can ever be tasted in great Britain, to where it is sent green, after which it indeed becomes *orange* but can never arive to its proper State of Maturity—As for the fine fragrance, that is diffused through all this Colony, by the many and perpetual Groves of orange blossom and other odoriferous fruits that it produces, it can more easily be conceived than described—I also found some fine *lemmons* on this Estate, which however are here generally thick sheld, but very large, viz. the Sower ones, there being also a Species of Sweet ones, that are Smaller and which have in my opinion a very insipid taste—

Having mentioned Monsieur de Cachelieu's fine fruit, I ought not forget his excellent french Wines, which were perfectly unadulterated, and truly delicious, particularly his Muscadell.—But in Spite of all these good things, I still Continued a Valetudenarian, being Oppress'd with Weakness, and indigestion—Thus in the hopes that exercise on *Horse-back* might do be good, I determined to take leave of my Hospitable French-friends, and ask a furlough to go for some time to Paramaribo—In Consequence on the 9th of August Colonel Fourgeoud arriving in the River at the Estate Crawassibo, expecting soon to reniew his Manoeuvres I on the 10th wrote him a letter for the above purpose, and also for above 6 Months pay that was due to me, but which was answered on the 12th not only with a negative to both my requests, and which had been granted to other Officers, but in such a truly impertinent Stile, as I could not from even himself have expected—Such as calling in Question my Zeal while I was Sick, and refusing me my own Money or even the proper means of recovering &c—which incensed me so much, that I now not only wished *him* in Hell, but *myself* also, to have the Satisfaction of seeing him burn; after which in a second Letter, I let him know, that I was incapable of doing, or asking any thing unbecoming my Character, but on the Contrary /ill as I was,/ ready to give him *such Proofs* of my Honour, as should leave him no further room to doubt of it, Should he be pleased to put it to the proof, which epistle /having drest myself/ I followed in person two Days after, with my french friend for my Companion, voucher, &c and who gave me the use of his tent boat and 8 Oars for the purpose—

At our Arrival on the Estate, I now expected no other, than to see him mad with resentment, put me under an arrest, and ask an Explanation of our last Correspondence, well knowing /particularly with him/ that

veritas audium parit—

But I dreaded not the Worst that he could do me, after the many trials to ruin me which he had already put in execution, and Death itself was almost preferable to his barbarity—

However, Monsieur de Cachelieu and I, were both disappointed—He not only took us Politely by the hand, but Solicited us to dine with him, as if nothing had passed between him and I—But this affectation I despised, and refused to accept Of his Invitation with Contempt, in which I was followed by my friend, when in my turn, I enquired for the Cause of this usuage, and to which this was the answer, viz that 30 or 40 of the ouca-Negroes, /who were our alies by treaty/ had deceived him in doing nothing, while they had been in the Woods, and during the time he had been at Paramaribo, that he was in Consequence determined, to push on the War with *double* vigour, on which account he had, not only forbid me to go to Town, but had since ordered even all the seek Officers, to come up & to follow the Enemy, while they had Strength or breath remaining, not so much as leaving one to keep the Colours, and the Regiments Chist, which had both been left to the Care of a Quartermaster, and this was literally so, but to which he might safely, and without hurting his Conscience have added, the inveteracy, and unforgivableness of his Disposition, with which he had Swore to persecute me, and some others to the last—NB It was only about this time, that he issued forth his orders to be observed on a March, and previous to which every thing was done in hurry and Confusion, and which indeed was to[o] often the Case, even since—

In Short, having now been near 2 Months on the Estate Egmond, where I could *not* recover, and not being permitted to go to Paramaribo, I prefer'd returning back again to take the Command at the hope, and where I having entertained Monsieur Cachelieu in the best manner I was able, this Gentleman in the Evening return'd to his Plantation—

Here I found my friend M:̣ Heneman, who was now made a Capt:̣ Seek with several others, but who were /the same as myself/ left without a Surgeon, Medicines, or Money, & while as I said before the many Hogsheads of Wine sent from Amsterdam, together with Scores of Cags Containing preserved Vegetables, and other fresh Provisions, were for ever kept invisible from the Poor, emaciated, and languishing Officers, for whom they had certainly been intended by that City—

In Short I made one more attempt to recover our Property, but to no purpose, Money, Medicines, Wine, and Refreshments were all keep'd back, while I now not received so much as an answer to my Letter—Thus did we continue to Pine, and loose Strength, instead of gaining it, Indeed I in particular had here the *least* Cause to Complain, being perfectly attended by Joanna, and my Servants, who the next day all arrived from Egmond at the Hope, besides receiving presents, which were as usual sent me from all Quarters—

However one new Inconveniency I had now again inherited, and that Consisted in one of my feet being infested with Chigoes, or Chiggers, which I partly impute to having during my Illness *wore* Stockings and Shoes with the good Frenchman—

Of this troublesome insect I have already made some mention, as being extremely numerous at Devils Harwar, but now shall Circumstantially discribe it—

The *Chigoe* is a kind of small Sand flea, that gets in between the Skin and the flesh, without its being felt, and most generally under the nails of the toes, where while it feeds it grows in proportion, till it becomes the Size of a large-Pea, Causing no other Pain than a disagreeable itching—At this Maturity it has the form and Consistency of a small bladder, in which are deposed thousands of Eggs or Nitts, which if it breaks, produce so many young Chigoes, and which in Course of time, by their Multiplicity create running ulcers, that are often of verry dangerous Consequence to the Patient—So much so, that I have known a Soldier, whose Soals of his feet were obliged to be cut away with a razor, before he could recover, and some Men have lost their limbs by amputation, nay even their lives by having neglected timely to root out this abominable vermin—Thus the moment one perceives a kind of itching-redness more than usual, especially about the feet it is time to begin extracting the Chigoe that occasions it, and which is done by the help of a Sharp-pointed-needle, at which operation the black Girls are extremely dexterous, taking every Care not to occasion unnecessary pain, and to prevent the Chigoe, or bladder, from breaking in the wound,—The Cure is to put Tobacco ashes in the Orifice, when in a little time thereafter it is perfectly healed—

🕬 I say'd I was infested with the Chigoes and on the 17th Joana with her needle, Picked 23 of those cursed Insects out of my left foot, which being all hatched under the nails, caused /as may be imagined/ the most excrusiating torments but which I bore without flinching with the resolution of an affrican Negroe—

🕬 I now received a Letter from the Commander in Chief, *not* an Answer to my last, but to send him up to the Estate *Crawassibo* /which was at present his head Quarters/ all the Provisions, Kettles, Axes &c that could be Spared at the Hope, he preparing to reenter the

🕬 Woods, which I accordingly dispatched the next day, and were not verry much, a whole barge with beef, and Pork, being Shipwreck'd in the River—

🕬 And now was discharged from the Regiment, /as incapable for his Office/ M.r *Steger,* the Surgeon who had so nearly poisoned me, and of which I could not yet get the better—Nevertheless /several Officers going to join Colonel Fourgeoud/ weak as I was, I entreated to be one

🕬 of the party—But on the morning of the 26th, his Adjutant, with another Surgeon visiting all the troops that were in Comewina, I was deem'd as yet incapable of supporting the fatigue—Indeed so much so,

🕬 that relapsing I on the 29th was even glad to be superceded, in the Command of the River by the Major M.r Medlar, & who arrived at the Hope this Day for that purpose—

But Still, I was condemned to linger at this Place, while one Months time at Paramaribo Might have perfectly recovered me—

I had now nothing earthly to do but to Continue my Drawings, for which the above Gentleman at that time offered me One hundred Crowns, but my Desire was if Possible to Compleat the Collection, and when I had the Strength, I walk'd round the Plantation with my

🕬 Gun, Amongst others I shot on the 3d of September a small bird Call'd *Kibry-fowlo,* on account of its being /in a manner/ for ever under Cover—It was about the size of a thrush and very much of the Colour of a Quail, which it also exactly resembled in its Shape, in the bill, and in the limbs only excepted, which were rather longer, and the first extremely Sharp pointed, this bird is very seldom seen on the Wing, but runs with an uncredible Swiftness through the Grass and Savanahs, where it hides itself the moment it is perceived, when dress'd it was as fat as a lump of Butter, and as delicious as an European Ortolan—

🕬 At last the Hero broke up from Crawassibo, and with all the able troops he could collect /which were now not much more than One hundred/ he once more launced into the forest after the Enemy—Having previously taken away the Post from the Jew Savanah, which he placed at the forsaken Estate *oranjebo* in the very upper Parts of Rio

1774—SEPTEMBER 11

Comewina, leaving the River Surinam to shift for itself, and having opened, and read all the letters that had been wrote to the deceased Officers from their friends on the old Continent—

It must certainly appear Singular in the Eyes of the World, that we did so tamely brook all this bad usuage and not officially Complain to his Serene Highness the Prince of Orange, whose Justice and Humanity are so Conspicuous and generally known, or to the late Duke of Brunswick-wolfenbuttel, field-Marshal of the Army in Holland, who was equally Benign, and indefatigable in fulfilling his Office, who was the father of the deserving Soldier, and the Scourge of those that dared to be neglectful in their Military Duty—But all things have a reason and so had this, our bearing Fourgeouds indignities /if we could/ without a Murmur, as shall perhaps be explained upon some other occasion—Suffice it to say for the present that neither of the two August Personages above mentioned, were supposed to be intirely ignorant of his barbarous Proceedings, But which theyr wisdom reserved to check at a More proper Opportunity, when the Good of a Colony should not be dependant on the Sufferings of an individual—While it would have been indelicate, if not presumptuous, to address the Court officially for what at the present Juncture, could not with Propriety be mended—

In short as I could *not* go to Paramaribo, I commissioned a fresh Supply of Provisions, and in a little time, *Fowler* my Serjeant arrived with the following Articles bought upon tick, I not having the value of one Shilling in my Pocket to pay for them viz—

Nº 1–Clerret	8–bacon hams	15–barlay	22–onions
2–Ranish	9–boulongue Sasages	16–rice	23–lemmons
3–Madeira	10–Bullocks tongues	17–curents	24–Salt
4–Rum	11–Salted Mackerel	18–raisins	25–Pepper
5–Coffee	12–butter	19–cheese	26–Mustard and
6–Tea	13–flower	20–Sweet Oil	27–Pipes and
7–Sugar	14–Boston Bisquit	21–vinegar	28–Tobacco

Thus did I want Still for nothing, while the Plantations furnished me with the rest, Happy for some of my helpless Companions who were now as little Stock'd with Money as myself, and some of whose *Credit,* was perhaps not so Good; even *Fowler* now shared of my Bounty, who related that at Paramaribo a Mʳˢ *van-der-Straten* had murdered a young Negro-Girl, by flogging her til she could not walk, and then Shutting her up in a room til she expired, which tragic account I shall diversify, by taking the liberty of producing a letter, that I at this time received-for the identical *Fowler* from his Mother in Holland, viz.

D.r Shony

I have releavd your Mistrus from the braytevel, and yoar holin Shits from the Pan-brocker. the baby is died, blesid be goat, while I hop you be living–yor lafing Mother til Death—

Magy Fowler—

Such was the State of Poor Fowlers Affairs, and such the epistle that made me laugh more hearty, than I had done before since I came to Surinam—

On the Hope happened this Day a most Singular Circumstance, and to[o] extraordinary almost to merit Credit.

A herd of Wild Swine cal'd *Pingo's,* and consisting in more than two hundred, having lost their Way in the forest, came galloping over the plantation in the fore noon, when above a Score of them were kil'd by the negroes, who knocked them down with their billhooks and axes—

In Surinam the Wild boar are of *three* Species, which I will take this opportunity to discribe—These are the *Pingo's or waree* above mentioned–the *Cras-Pinco*–and the *Mexicon-Hog* cal'd here *Pakeira*—

The *Pingo's* are about the Size of one of our English Small Hogs, they are black and have coarse bristles thinly Scatered, they live in herds of sometimes above 300 in the thickest parts of the forest, and run always in a line the one closely following the other—When the foremost or leader is Shott the line is instantly broke, and the whole herd in Confusion, for which reason the indians always take care /if possible/ to knock theyr Captain in the head before the rest, after this the others even often stand still, Stupidly looking the one at the other, and allowing themselves to be kild one by one, of which I have since more than once been a Witness—But they do not attack the Human Species, or make any resistance at all like the European Wild Boar when Wounded, as has been by some Authors Erroneously represented—As for their Attacking Dogs I can say nothing about it, never having had any with me in Company when I met them

The *Cras-Pingo**–are larger arm'd with strong tusks and their bristles still coarser than the former, This large Species indeed are very dangerous, by their Strength and ferocity attacking any thing that obstructs them in their way especially when Wounded,—They go in the same Manner, and in large Quantities as the former, but inhabit more the inland parts of the Country—both these Species when they hear the smallest noise in the forest, that indicates danger, Stop Short in their

• —The word Cras denotes Angry in Surinam

The Pingo Warree, or Wild Boar of Guiana.

The Pecary, or Mexican Hog.

Course, form in a Closs body, and crash their teeth at a most dreadfull Rate, preparing themselves for Defence against their Enemy, I think these are not natural to Guiana, but originally from Affrica, and Europe, their flesh is eat with avidity by the natives, and even esteem'd by the White Inhabitants, but is in my Opinion dry, hard, and unsavoury—

That Species cal'd the *Pakeira**–or Mexicon-Hog, is alone supposed to be the natural inhabitant of Guiana, and will not intermix with either the wild or domestic Hogs, this is particularly remarckable by having an Orifice on the back, which is vulgarly mistaken to be its navel, and which being about one inch deep contains a stinking foetid liquor, which some compare to the smell of Musk, but which is so very disagreeable, that the moment the Animal is kil'd, the natives take care to cut away this part with a knife to prevent its infecting the flesh, and which it makes disgusting, and uneatable, to a refined Palate—The length of this Animal is about 3 feet, it has no tail, fine limbs, short tusks, and Yellowish gray bristles, much resembling those of an English *Hedge-Hog*–on the back they are very long, but short on the Sides, and on the belly. The Pakeira is almost naked, they being both Short and so very thinly Scattered—It has a white band that comes down from the Shoulders on each Side to the breast—These kind of Hogs are more uncommon in the low and Marshy Countrys, than inland where they prefer feeding amongs'd the Mountains and dry Savanahs—The Pakeira is easily tamed, and in that State harmless, and inoffensive, but not so Stupid as is asserted by the Count de *Buffon,* where he says, "they know no person and have no attachement to those who take care of them" Since Major Medlar, had one at the Hope that followed him like a Dog, and showed the greatest Delight in being carest by its Master, to which I shall only add, that when iritated these Hogs are very wicked, go in large herds, produce many young at a time, and that their grunting is extremely lowd and disagreeable—

This morning we now again heard the report of several great-Guns towards the River-Cottica, where it since appeared the Rebels were a *Second time* beat back from the Plantation *Marseille,* by the fidelity, and bravery, of the Slaves belonging to that Estate—

Now came the news, that Colonel Fourgeoud having discovered and distroyed some fields belonging to the Enemy, who had again kept up a distant Conversation with him, and having found the Mangled Remains of poor Schmidt, who had been murdered by the Rebels, was once more come with his troops to Magdenbergh where he had en-

---

* —Mr Fermyn erroneously calls this the Pingo—

camp'd, til on the 11th when he reentred the forest again, previously sending the seek, and a young Officer under an arrest to the Hope, in order to be tried for not being able to undergo the fatigues as well as himself, that is having been ordered to watch 2 Days and 2 Nights, the Youth had been unequal to the task, and had dropt asleep under arms as he was sitting on the ground—The Climate indeed was such that even without these trials, nature was often overcome—

What kept Fourgeoud so stout hitherto, was his continually drinking a Medicine he cal'd *teasan* in large basons full, which had a taste sufficient to poison the Devil, and was composed of the *Jesuits-bark, Cremortartar,* and *Liquorish*-stick, boild together, which he drank as hot as he could bear it, and to which having used his Constitution, he could no more be without it, than a fish without water, in which however he was followed by none of the rest, well knowing that when this should once cease to operate, which it must at last, all other medicines in time of real need would be ineffectual—As for my own part I still continued to be so exceedingly weak; that I almost despaired ever more to recover, while my depres'd Mind on account of Joana's Critical, and helpless Situation, greatly Contributed to prevent the restoration of my health, particularly when on the 21st being visited by M.r & M.rs Lolkens at the Hope This Gentleman acquainted me that in Town it was the general Report that we had both been poison'd; that the whole Estate Fauquenbergh was again transfer'd, with its dependents, Since the Death of M.r Passalege; that the new Proprietor was a *M.r Lude* of Amsterdam, and with whom he had not the smallest interest—Yet which Sentence was greatly alleviated by the Civility of his Lady, who insisted that my young Mulatto Should accompany her to Paramaribo immediately, and where at her own house she should meet with every Care and attention, that *her* being present could bestow upon her, or her *delicate* Situation could require, so long til she should be perfectly recovered; to this I made a bow while poor Joana cried for Gratitude, and having Conducted them so far as their Estate *Killestyn-nova* /where we all dined/, I took my leave, and bid my last farewell /for the present time/ to that young Woman, to whom I was more indepted, than to all the universe besides—

At my return on the hope, my indignation was hardly supportable, where I was even upbraided for taking Care of my own offspring by my mesmates—"Do as we do /say'd they/ Stedman and never fear, if our Children are Slaves they are provided for, and if they die /for we/ may they be damn'd into the bargain, thus keep your Sighs in your Belly, and your Money in your Pocket my Boy that is all"—

Next morning awaking by Day break in my Hammock, the first

thing that I now saw when looking up, was a *Snake* about two Yards long, hanging with his head downwards like a rope, and streight above my face, from which he was not one foot distance, while his tail was twisted round the rafters under the thatch—Observing his Eyes bright as Stars, and his forked tongue in Agitation, I was so much distress'd that I Scarsely had Power to avoid him, which however I did, by running out; after which I heard a rusling in the dry thatch, where the Negroes attempted to kil him but in vain, he having escaped, thus can not say what Species he belonged to—

In Short being now by myself, and rather startled by this unwelcome Guest, I shut up House, and having sent my Cattle which was much encreasd to her Estate, I log'd and mes'd with my Friends the Major, Heneman, and Macdonald,—

Now on visiting my Boxes, great Depredations indeed were Committed by the *Ants,* which are throughout all Guiana so very numerous, and of so many different Species that on the Hope I have had a pair of New Cotton-Stockings, perfectly destroy'd by them only in one Night—Those frequenting the Estates are generally Small, but very troublesome—For instance the only way possibly to keep them from the refined Sugar, is by hanging the loaf to the Ceiling on a nail, and making a ring of Chalk around it very thick, which crumbels down the moment the Ants attempt to pass it—I imagined that Placing my Sugar-boxes in the middle of a tub, and on a Stone all surrounded with deep Water, would have kept back this formidable Enemy, but to no purpose, whole armies of the lightest Sort /to my astonishment/ marching over the Surface, while a few of them drowning the main body escaladed the rock, and in Spite of my teeth made their entry through the Key-Hole, after which the only way to clear the Garrison is, to expose it to a hot sun shine, which the invaders cannot bear, and all march of[f] in a very few Minutes—

That The ants provide for Winter, as not only Doctor *Bancroft,* and many others, but even King-*Solomon* supports, is found out to be an error by the most modern investigators—In Surinam indeed there is no Winter, but where there is, the Ants lie *dorment,* during which torpid State they want no food.

But my friend Captain van Coeverden /at this time marching in the Woods/ suffered a much worse depredation at Paramaribo, where not the Ants, but the Negro-Slaves, had broke in his boxes, and rob'd him of all his best effects, and near 20 Guineas in Money, and at which place lately another Society-Soldier was *Shot* by a Court Martial, this Ceremony happening there verry often, while on the Sixth one of our Men drown'd himself in a frenzy-fever, so very common in Guiana—Thus

1774—NOVEMBER 6, 8, 9, 13

went the Soldiers that were Spared by the Climate, or the Enemy,—

In Short having wrote to a Lawyer, a M*r* *Seyfke* to enquire whether it was not in the Power of the Governor and Counsel, to relieve a Gentlemans Child from bondage, providing he pay'd to its Master such ransom as their Wisdom should judge adequate?–I now received for Answer, that no Money or Interest, could purchase its *freedom,* without the Proprietors Consent, since according to Law, it was just as much a Slave as if it had been born in affrica, and imported from the Coast of Guinea—This news perfectly compleated my Misery, and I had at last recourse to drinking, which temporary relief, like a Spring tide only made my Spirits flow higher, to make them sink lower after its evaporation—

During this Conflict it happened now that I was invited with the Major to dine, at an Estate call'd *Knoppemonbo* in the Casawinica Creek, where a M:r De-*Graav* the proprietor, did every thing in his Power to amuse me, but to no purpose—

At last seeing me seated by myself on a small bridge that led to a Grove of Orange Trees, with a settled Gloom on my Countenance, he accoasted me, and taking me by the Hand, Said

> Sir I am acquainted by M:r Lolkens with the Cause of your distress, Heaven never left a good intention unrewarded, I have the Pleasure to acquaint you, that M:r *Lude* has now chosen *me* for his Administrator, and that from this Day I shall Pride in making it my business to render you every Service with that Gentleman, as well as the virtuous Joana, whose deserving Character has attracted the attention of so many People, while your laudable Motive redounds to your lasting Honour throughout this Colony—

No Angel descending from the Clouds could have brought me a more welcome Message, and no Criminal under Sentence of Death could have received a reprieve with greater Joy, the weight of a Millstone was removed from my labouring breast, and having made M:r De Graav repeat his Promise, I felt I should yet be happy—Soon after this I was surrounded by several Gentlemen, and Ladies, /to whom my Friend had Communicated this very romantic adventure/ Some of whom pleased to Call me *Tom Jones,* and others *Roderick Random*—They all indeed congratulated me on my Sensibility, and my having met with so valuable an Acquaintance, all seem'd to partake in the pleasure that I now felt, and the day being Spent in Mirth and Conviviality, I return'd to the Hope much better Pleased than I had left it, where next day the whole Company was entertained by Major Medlar, nor did we seperate, or Cease feasting up and down the River till the 13th when we once more Spent the Day at Knoppemonbo—

Here now M:r De Graav having bought some new Slaves, gave a Holy day to all the Negroes of his Estate, and there I had the opportunity of seeing the diversions peculiar to that People, but of which I must reserve the Particular Account til another Occasion, and only now say a Word or two of the *Loango-Dancing,* which was performed by the *Loango*-Negroes, Male and female, and not by any others, and consists from first to last in such a Scene of Wanton, and Lascivious gestures, as nothing but a heated imagination, and a Constant Practice could enable them to perform; these Dances which are to the Sound of a Drum, and to which they strike time by Clapping of hands, are more like a play, divided in so many Acts, which lasts hours together, and during which Pantomime, the Actors in place of being fatigued, become more and more Active and Animated, til they are bathed in a lather like Post Horses, and their Passions wound up to such a degree, that Nature being overcome they are ready to drop into Convultions—

However indelicate the above exhibitions Fashion, has rendered them no more so than any other divertions to the Europeans and Creole Ladies, who in Company with the Gentlemen crow'd about them without the least reserve, to enjoy /what they call here/ a hearty laugh, and there it ends, while they would cover an English Woman's face from white to Scarlet—

Custom is every thing, and Peculiar to every Country;—For instance, in the East-Indies /according to the Relation of an English Officer/ the Dancing Girls will act an amorous Adventure with Suppleness, dexterity, and Precision—Sometimes the actresses appear to be penetrated by soft emotions, seized with a flame never before experienced, and sometimes with the Powers of life apparently suspended, agitated and panting, they seem to sink under the Powers of an overpowerful Elusion—Thus by the most expressive Gestures and Positions, with Stifled Sighs, and languid looks, they express every Gradation of Passhion from the embarassment of Shame, through desire, fear, and hope, to the trepidations of enjoyment—These Girls, says the above Author, are almost the only females there, that are teached reading, writing, vocal, and instrumental Musick, while some of them Speak 3 or 4 languages—Their dress though light and Voluptuous, is yet more decent than that of the others of their Sex, and in few Countries social manners are purer and more respected, than amongst those gentoo Indians, scarce acquainted with the name of those harid Vices, that prevail in some other Countries, while sensual pleasures, are considered as a Religious Duty, and Celebrating the Praises of their

Gods—From which he concludes that thus amongst those gentoos, there is greater dencensy and reserve, than amongst the Europeans, into whom it is strenuously inculcated from their Infancy, that Simple incontinuance, is among Actions Subjected to the Divine Analthema; and amongst which Class I take the liberty to rank the Loango Dancers, who think that what they are doing is perfectly right, and look on European dancing as the height of incipidity—

The next morning I now returned again to the Hope, where I saw my Cottage unrooft by a Storm, but which now expecting no more to Inhabit, I let go to wreck, "The Cloud Capt towers, the Gorgeous Palases &c. shall desolve—" be that as it may, I had pass'd in it the most happy Days of my whole Life, and such as I can never expect to pass again—

Colonel Fourgeoud now being once more marched to the Wana-Creek after the Rebels, as I said after taking the Troops from the Jew Savanah they availd themselves of this absence, and not only pillaged a Plantation in the River Surinam, but burnt several Dwellings in the Creek *Caswinica*—From the above river they were however bravely pursued by a feeble Society-detachement that chanced to be there, but without Success, while 2 Soldiers were kild, and M:r Neagle their leader with several others wounded—

The Major now broke up the new Post that was at *orangibo,* which he also dispatch'd after the Enemy, but which having Cruised a Week in the forest also return'd without any manner of Success, which shows what a difficult thing it is for European troops, to wage War in the forests of South America—

This being the Aniversary of S:t Andrews, and now being in excellent Spirits, I roasted a whole Sheep with which I entertained all the Officers on the Hope, and with a Couple of Gallons of good Jamaica Rum in Punch, which we drank to the healths of all our friends on the old

Continent—And which Ceremony I repeated on Dec:r 4:th on receiving the tidings, that my Dear Joana was delivered of a Strong, and beautiful boy 27:th past having that very morning dispatched another letter to M:r *Lude* at Amsterdam, to obtain her Manumission, cooched [couched] much in the same terms as that which I had wrote to his Predecessor M:r *Passelege,* only praying for dispatch as I was now uncertain how much longer the expedition was to last, and in which request I was again seconded by My New Friend M:r De Graav, as I had been before by my old one M:r Lolkens, after which I entertained the Seek with a Dozen of old-Ranish, received from the former Gentleman, which had been in his Cellar since 1726—

Walking round the Plantation this Morning with my Gun, the whole

Slaves of the Estate were rose in a Mutiny, on account of the Cruel usuage inflicted by the Manager, but which however by the interfearance of the Military was presently Quel'd, to Mutual Satisfaction—

These frequent disturbances which I have at different times mentioned, plainly indicate the inclination of the Negroes to break out in an open rebellion, and which would Certainly have been often the attempt, had they not been awed at this Period by the Troops—

My Walk was however not fruitless, as I brought home 2 birds, the one Call'd *Toreman*, the other a Species of Grass Snipe—the *Toreman* or *Hanaquaw* is a shining black bird, as large as a Pullet, with gray legs, and a bill of a dark brown Colour, it is very good eating and easily discovered in the trees, where it perches on the highest branches, especially by its Noise repeating distinctly the Word *Hanaquaw, Hanaquaw*, at the approach of any Person in the forest, which has also occasioned the name of Toreman, and which Signifies in the Negro Language of Surinam a talebearer, or a Spy, on which account the Rebels in Particular have a Mortal Hatred towards it—

The *Grass-Snipe* was something less than a Woodcock, of a beautiful Silver-Gray Colour, and in Shape much like the Snipes of Europe, this bird is mostly found in the wet Savanahs, it is very plump and exquisitely delicate eating—I think I shall never have done with the great variety of beautiful Animals that are to be met with throughout Surinam, however I shall persevere in discribing them as I find them—

This Morning the Estate *Reetwyk* in Pirica, was attack'd, but the Enemy beat back by the Military—

Colonel Fourgeoud being now again arived at Magdenbergh, and I at last being perfectly recovered, after an illness of Seven Months, proposed by another letter that I might accompany him on his future excursions in the Woods, or go for some time to Paramaribo but neither the one or the other yet was granted—Mars and Venus were both deaf to my Prayers, and I was still doom'd to be keep'd at the Hope like a Prisoner of State—

In this Situation I now wrote a Letter to Town, to let them know that I was well, with which I went to the River Side, to look out for a boat; and towards noon haild the tent-barge belonging to Fauquenbergh which was rowing with the Overseer to Paramaribo—But this was a *new* Superintendent, and not knowing me refused to come ashoare for the Messuage—However I seeing the Negroes rest upon the Oars, took the Letter in my Teeth, and leapt instantly into the River to dispatch it, knowing they would put me on *Terra Firma* again—Having thus swimd with the Stream, in my Shirt and trowsers, till I came within 2 Oars length of the boat, I held up the Letter in my Hand, and Cal'd out, "who the Devil are you that refuses to take on board a piece of Paper," when being answered in French "Je Suit Jean Bearnee Paysan de Guascogne, a vot Service" I had the unutterable Mortification to see them pull away without I could possibly more *overtake them, or return*—In this distress I had now nothing left but to Perish it being impossible to Swim against the Stream, and as I was, incumbered with my Cloaths—However I struggled but sunk twice to the bottom in the attempt, and must inevitably have been drowned, had I not Caught hold of a projecting Paling that was in the River erected to catch fish—To this now was I sticking fast like a bur, when a Dutch Carpenter Spieing me from the top of the Sugar Mill, alarmd the whole Estate, and call'd out that the English Captain was trying to kill himself—On this news immediately a Dozen of Stout Negroes now leapt into the River, who having drag'd me safe ashoare, under the Direction of my Good Friend *Medlar,* and who believed the report, next loaded me upon their Shoulders to Carry me home—But *nemo homnibus horis Sapiit* the disappointment, the danger, In short Anger, vexation, and Shame, /for there was no Contradicting them/ had at this time so much wound up my Passions, and made such an Impression on my Spirits, that on Crossing over a small bridge, I actually gave a sudden twist, and from their Shoulders, through myself with a Jirk headlong over the balustrades, again into the Water—

Here a second time Miraculously I was pick'd up by the Negroes and now the Suspicion being Confirmed that I intended Suiside, I was put to bed and two Sentinels appointed to Guard me during the Night, while severals of my friends were shedding tears around me for my Safety, be that as it may having drank some Muld-Wine, I Sleep'd as sound as a Rock til the next morning, when seeing me Calm and perfectly Composed, My Words only began to gain Credit to my Joy, and idle apprehension did vanish accordingly—Such was the danger I escaped On Account of an upstart Rascal, who deserved the Gallows for this, amongst many other Actions of Unpresedented Brutality—

Next day however by one of my Negroes, and a small Canoo, I sent of[f] much the same Letter to Paramaribo with my Compliments—Seeing now about noon a *Molasses* boat before the Hope at Anchor, in which was broiling in the Sun an English Sailor, and 2 Negroes, I made the first Come ashoare, and entertained the Poor fellow to his great Surprize on a bowl of Punch, and a belly full of Eggs and bacon, he not having expected this kindness, or to be accosted in his *own* Country Language—What were this Mans gratefull Acknowledgements, whose Name was *Charles Macdonald* shall be seen in the Sequel of this Work—

A Molasses Boat is a barge row'd by 2 Oars that fetches the above Commodity in large Hogsheads from the Sugar Plantations, and delivers it on board the English American Vessels for transportation, to be distil'd in Rum, for which they pay the Dutch at an Average at about 3 Guineas per Hogshead—

Now arrived again an Officer sent from our Hero under an arrest, /the first was a Mr *Galquin*, and this was a Mr *Neys*/ for the Crime of disputing with the free Negro *Goasary* for a bunch of Plantains—Both these young Men were since sent to Europe by Fourgeoud to have them broke by Court Martial, but where after a very Short Confinement, however, they were Honorably acquitted to the Joy of the whole Corps and his unutterable Mortification—

Such was the inveteracy of this old Gentleman, who had not the Smallest Consideration for the foibles of Youth, who Constantly Saw the Splinder [splinter] in the Eye of his Neighbour forgetting the beam that appeared so Conspicuously in his own—When Speaking about *Plaintains* I think I will take this occasion to discribe a Production, which I ought to have mention'd sooner, it being as *useful* as it is *general* between the tropiks—

As for a very accurate, and botanical definition of this fruit, and indeed of most other Vegetables, I must refer the reader to *Doctor Bancroft*, thus suffice it to say that the *Plantain* tree is a native of America, and that it may With Propriety be call'd the Bread of this Country—It is rather a Plant than a tree, as the trunk has neither Wood or bark, but consists of a Stamen enwrapped by green vascular husks, succeeding each other in the manner of an onion, and above 10 Inches in Diameter, which husks diverge alternately at about 14 feet distance from the ground, and form not in branches, but in leafs, that Spread like an umbrella, about 12 or 14 in number, as large as to Cover the tallest Person each which lateral fibres of a Shining sea Green, and which fade, and hang down in tatters as their places are supplied by the Young Ones—From the Centre of all this, there grows a strong Stalk about 3 feet long, and also bending downwards, by the weight of a purple Spatha, Something resembling a Calves heart, and on this Stalk grows the fruit call'd Plantains, in the Shape of Cucumbers, and above One hundred in number, which is usually cal'd a Bunch—Each Tree or Plant bears but one of those bunches, when it is cut down, but incessantly supplied by the Young Shoots, that Spring from its bulbous root, and which in the Space of 10 Months time are ready to undergo the same Operation,–it requires a rich nourishing Soil to make it prosper, without which it never arives to proper Maturity—This fruit being divested of its tegument when Green, is inside of a Pale Yellow farinaceous Sub-

1774—DECEMBER 16, 18, 20

stance, and supplies /as I said/ the want of Bread, either boild or when roasted—It is besides of an agreeable taste and very wholesome—When the Shell becomes Yellow the inside is Soft, and then may be eat raw having much the taste of a very ripe Pear, at which Maturity it only is used by way of desert—

Another Species resembling this, is the *Banana,* which only differs with the Plantain, in its fruit being less, and more Oval, and that it is never eat til it is Yellow and fully ripe—The former is the most usefull in point of food, but this last which has a musky flavour is by far reckoned the most delicate—

> But what kind fruit so fair so rich appears,
> The Sweet Banana, mellower than the Pears
> That o'er their Winds or golden Honors Spread,
> And her green vales with greener umbrage Shade.

For a more Clear Idea than I am capable to give by Discription, I here refer the curious to the annex'd Plate where **A** is the Plantain Tree, with its fruit, **B** the Young Shoots that succeed it, **C** the fruit in its green tegument, **D** the same cut through the middle, and **E** the fruit cal'd Banana in its Maturity—In Surinam the *first* is known by the name of *Banana* and the 2nd by that of *Bacooba*—

Having now obtain'd my Friend Medlars Concurance I took a trip in *Cognito* to Paramaribo, where I found my Boy bathing in *Madeira* and Water*—and his Mother happy, and perfectly recovered—Having embraced them and presented Joana with a Gold-Medal, that my Father has given my Mother on the day of my Birth, and also thanked Mrs Lolkens for her great Civility, I immediately returned to the hope, where I again arrived on the 20th thus made extraordinary Expedition—

The Poor Negro whom I had sent before me with a Letter had been less fortunate than I, sinking with his Canoo** in the middle of the River Surinam, by the rufness of the Water—However having kept in an erect Posture /for this Man could not Swim/ the pressure of the boat against his feet, had enabled him just to keep his head above the Water, while the weight of his Body keep'd the Canoo sunk to his full length,—In this dangerous attitude he was picked up by a manowars boat, who taking away the Canoo for their trouble, put him on Shoare at Paramaribo, he having the letter, however Surprizing, still in his

---

* —This, however uncommon it may appear to an European, is often practised in Surinam by such as can afford it and amongst which Class was the Hospitable Mr Lolkens

** —A Canoo is a very small boat made of a hollow Tree by means of fire—

The Plantain Tree, and the Banana.

London, Published Dec.r 1.st 1791, by J. Johnson, St Paul's Church Yard.

Mouth—At this time being eagre to deliver it, he accidently run into a wrong house, where being taken for a thief /on refusing to let them read it/ he was tied up to receive 400 lashes, but Miraculously repriev'd by the intercession of an English Merchant named *Gordon* who was my Particular Friend, and knew the Negro.—Thus had the Poor Devil escaped Drowning, and being flog'd, having been rob'd of his Canoo into the bargain, either of which he would have underwent sooner, than to disclose what he cal'd the secrets of his Masera—Query, how many Europeans shall we find possess'd of so much firmness?—Answer none.

Having lately mentioned a *projecting-Paling,* erected to catch fish, and by which invention, having to day been plentifully Supplied, I will give a brief account of it—And consists simply in a kind of Square like a Garden, that juts out in the River, surrounded by long Palisades of the Manicole tree, tied very closs together, in this fence is a large door, which is left open with the flood, and Shut at high Water to prevent the inclosed fish from escaping, and by which means sometimes especially the Negroes and Indians catch very great Quantities—

Amongst those taken to day were the *logo-logo* and *Matuary*—The first is a Species of Eels, that are long sometimes 2 feet, and very thick, dark blue on the back and Sides, but whitish on the belley, they are extremely fat, and very good eating—The other is a small sweet fish without Scales, but one thing very remarkable is, that in Surinam most fishes, the moment they are out of the Water begin to make a noise, not unlike the grunting of Small-Piggs; and that fish have hearing /after many doubts & disputes/ has of late been clearly demonstrated by the most able Searches into Natural Philosophy*—

Having to day dined at the Estate Knoppemonbo, I will also mention two birds, which there attracted my Particular Attention—the one was on account of the very great Peculiarity of its nest, and is Cal'd in this Country lipee-banaw, as supposed to feed much on ripe bananas—Whether this is the mocking-bird of Doctor Bancroft, I know not but in some particulars it approaches his discription—

These Birds that I speak of had taken possession of a large tree near the Water Side, which the Negroes told me they had frequented undisturb'd for many Years, they were at least above One hundred in number, about the Size of English black-birds, some were a Shining black, with the tails and part of the Wings of a bright Crimson, the others were also black, but their tails and Wings were of a fine Yellow Colour—The first I was informed to be the Males, and the latter the fe-

---

* —vide. the account given to the Members of the Royal Society by John Hunter Esq! **F.R.S.**

males of the same Species, they indeed whistled a variety of Notes, but neither had that Melody, or imitation of other Songsters, which is so generally ascribed to the Mocking-bird, and of which besides I never heard make mention in all Surinam—These birds had their Nests /above 3 Score in number/ fixed to the extremity of the branches, where they were dangling in the Wind, resembling depending Eggnets that are Stuff'd with hay, and of which indeed they were built—About the Middle of these Cylindrical figures is a small hole where the birds go in and out, and in the bottom of which being perfectly round they hatch the Young ones, while the Spiral roof protects them from birds of Prey, and from the Weather—Also the Monkeys, that are so numerous in this Country are /by their Situation/ prevented to destroy them, since the branches, or twigs to which they are fix'd, though strong enough to support the nests and what is in them, are generally too weak, to bear the weight of Quadrupede invadors—To which I may add, that they are mostly depending over Water. See the nests in Plate 44 [45].

The other bird I shott in returning home, this was the Surinam *Falcon or Hawk,* its Size and Shape was like those of the same Species in England, its Colour light-brown, variegated on the breast and tail with Specks of Red, of black, and Yellow, its Tongue was cloven, its Eyes were remarcably bright, its legs a Citron Colour, and its Claws arm'd with long and Sharp pointed Nails—This bird is exceedingly destructive to the Plantations, committing great Ravages amongst the Poultry &c, it is say'd to have the Power of distending its head when either iritated or terrified—

But I must once more return to the Commander in Chief, who having drawn breath a few days at Magdenbergh, now again Marched with the remaining handfull of his Men to the Jew Savanah, from where he return'd /having seen nothing/ back to Magdenbergh, but with the new Title of being call'd the wandering Jew himself—

Be that as it may, the Major and I renew'd our Solicitations to accompany him in his peregrinations, but were prevented by his now going to Town, w[h]ere about this time a fresh supply of troops was hourly expected, to arrive from Europe, and be murdered as were the former, and where finally he gave me leave to follow him soon, with some other Officers, who were literally in want at a time, when fifteen hogsheads of fine Cleret, and fifteen thousand florins in Specy, were obeying his Commands at Paramaribo—

Chapter 15th

Description of the Aborigines of [or] Indians of Guiana—There Food [–] Arms–Ornaments–Employments–Diversions–Passions[–] Religion–Marriages–Funerals &c—Of the Charibee Indians in Particular —their Trade with the Europeans—

At last farwell to the hope, of which I am convinced the reader is by this time as tired as I—Thus rowing down I this night Sleep'd at the Estate Arentlust, and next day I dined at the beautiful Plantation Catwyk, where I had nearly ended all my travels, for M.r *Coetsee* the owner having lent me one of his horses to ride round the Estate, the Animal and I, both at once disappeared, not like the Roman-Soldier, that leap'd with his horse in an opening or cleft of the earth, to save his Country, but a wooden bridge over which we past /being rotten/ the part under us gave way, and we drop'd through it into the Canal—I however with much difficulty got ashoare, and having run to call some Negroes the Horse who stuck in the Mud, was just extricated alive and no more—

In the evening I now row'd to Paramaribo with the young-flood, which gave me an Opportunity to see the Mangroves that line the banks of the River Surinam, full of *Oisters* Stuck in the branches like fruit, from the Waters edge up to high Water Mark—

I acknowledge that to Speak of Oisters growing in Trees sounds very much of the Marvellous, yet if people will consider for a moment, they will find this no more extraordinary, than that they should be found Sticking upon Rocks, providing both be overflow'd by the tides—

These *Oisters* /which at some distance look like Mushrooms/ indeed are very small, and trifling, and of which one hundred are not Comparable to one Dozen that come from Colchester in old England; In

Surinam are also a kind of *Mussles,* but these are so small and insipid that they are scarsely worth to be mentioned—

Being now arrived in Town at my Friend *De-La-Mere's* House, I felt extremely happy, and more so seeing my little Boy and his Mother both well, whom I acquainted with my *second* Request being dispatched to the new Proprietor Mr Lude at Amsterdam, for their Manumission;

and the next day visited the Governor, Mr Kennedy, Mrs Lolkens, M.^{rs} De Melly, &c who all Congratulated me on my acquaintance with M.^r De-Graav, and highly Honor'd me, and approved of what I had done for so deserving a young Woman, and her Infant—

Our few remaining Troops being now mostly at Paramaribo, a Mr Van Eys gave an Entertainment to the whole Corps, but where I declined going scorning to dine at one Table with my Tirant Fourgeoud, while especially I had so many other valuable Friends—

And being now determined to be no longer without Cash, I next day went to the Head Quarters, where the Counting-House being open, I told the Quarter Master Mr *Gamb,* that *point d'argeant point de Swisse,* and that so he might report it to the *Grand Monarch* if he would while taking 2 Canvas bags of Silver, one under each arm, for which I left my Receipt, I march'd off with them unmolested to my Lodgings, and where I found their Contents to consist in 550 Florins dutch-Money, which without this Stratagem /like more others/ I might have wanted many months longer, and for which by the usurper, I was never call'd to an Account—

This day a great number of *Indians,* or Natives, being arrived at Paramaribo, and having now the time I shall with Pleasure discribe this People, who are the real aborigines of this Country—These Generations /who are in my Opinion the happiest Creatures under the Sun/ are divided in many Casts or tribes such as these the—

Caribbees—*	arrowouks—
Accawaus—	tawiras and—
Worrows—	Piannacotaws—

besides which there are a great many others, whose Manners are Unknown to us, and of which *6 Tribes* I will give a less or more Particular deffinition, after first observing that All these *Indians* in general, are of a *Copper-Colour,* while the *Negroes* of Africa that live under the same degree of lattitude are perfectly *black*—And which however inconceiveable at first, is easily accounted for, when one considers that the first, viz. the American-Indians in Guiana, are Constantly refresh'd by the

* —The 4 first are only mentioned by Doctor Bancroft

Cooling Sea-Breeze or easterly Wind that blows between the Tropicks, and that those who dwell in Tirra-Firma, and Peru, on the West Coast, enjoy that same Easterly breeze, still keep'd Cool, by the great Chains of inland Mountains, over which it Passes, and which have their Summits perpetually covered over with Snow*—While the 2nd viz the Inhabitant of Africa, that live South of the River Senegal, get the same **E** wind rather *heated* than Cool'd, by the Prodigious Quantity of inland burning Savanahs, and Sandy deserts, over which it passes—

These are the most Plausible Causes why the Americans are a Copper-Colour or Red, and the Inhabitants of Africa /cal'd Negroes/ are black, *viz*. The one being more burnt by the Suns heat than the other, and not because they are 2 distinct sort of People, there being in my Opinion, but 1 Set of People on the Globe, who differ with each other only according to the Soil and Climate in which they live—

As I hate Prolixity, I refer the Reader for a Clearer definition, to the Count de-*Buffon*, L'abe-Renald, &c, and shall only add, that these aborigines or Indian-Natives, will Still less be call'd a distinct People from those on the Old Continent, when one Considers the Proximity of Russia to N. America, from where by Appearance /however difficult/ the first have emigrated, and who have hitherto but thinly Peopled the New World, the Mexicons and a few others excepted til they were butchered by Spanish Avarice and Superstition—

A happy People I call them Still, whose Pease and Native Morals have not been Soild, with *mock* Christianity, and which are so beautifully, as truly discribed by the ingenious, and immortal Mr Pope—

> Lo the Poor Indian! whose untutored Mind,
> Sees God in Clowds, and hears him in the Wind;
> whose Soul, proud Science never taught to Stray,
> Far as the Solar Walk or Milky Way;
> Yet Simple Nature to his hope has given
> Behind the Clowd top'd Hill an humbler Heaven,
> Some safer World in depth of Woods embrac'd,
> Some happier Island in the Watery Waste,
> Where Slaves once more their native Land behold,
> No friends torment, no Christians thirst for Gold;
> To be Content's his natural desire,
> He asks no angels wing no Seraphs fire,
> But thinks admitted to that equal Sky,
> His faithful Dog shall bear him Company.
>   Go wiser thou &c—

* —It is well known by Men of literature, that in whatever Country either Cold or hot the high Mountains are always covered over with Snow—

1775—JANUARY 25

While I say with Socrates, that this kind of Poverty is alone the extremity of Riches, as those who want least approach nearest to the Gods, Who want nothing—This naturally leads me to the Speech of an Indian in reply to a Sermon preached by a Swedish Minister, at an Indian treaty held at Covestogue of which the principal Substance was as follows—

> Do you believe that our forefathers and we are all damnd, because we are not Christians—Are we not the Work of God?—And can the Almighty, not manifest his Will without the help of a Book—If this is true, and God is just, then how is it Consistant with his Justice to force life upon us, without our Consent and then to damn us all thereafter—We find the *Christians* more deprived in their Morals than we Indians Sir, and must judge of their Doctrines by the badness of their lives

—While this again can not but put me in Mind of M.[r] Pope—

> For modes of faith let graceless bigotts fight
> His can't be wrong whose life is in the right—

And one thing I perfectly well know, viz. that the native Indians of Guiana possess as few vises, as any Set of People existing under the Sun, and are in their Morals but little better for those Moravian Preachers, that are Settled amongst them on the banks of the *Serameca* River, w[h]ere they also try to Convert the Serameca Negroes—

All the Guiana Indians believe in God as the Author of all Good, and never inclined to do them an Injury—But they *Worship* the Devil whom they Call *Yawahoo*, to prevent his inflicting them with evil, and to whom they ascribe Pain, desease, Wounds, Death &c—So much so that where an Indian dies the whole family leave the Spot soon after as a residence—

All these Indians are a free People, that is not Governed by any Laws whatever, excepting that in most families the oldest acts as Captain, Priest, and Physitian, to whom they pay a reverential obedience,—These Men are Cal'd *Peii*, or *Pagayers*, and /like amongst Civilized Society/ live better than all the others—

Poligamy is admitted amongst them,* and every Indian is allowd to take as many Wives as he can provide for, though they generally take but one, of whom he is extremely Jealous, and whom he knocks on the head the Moment he has got a Proof of their inconstancy—

These Indians never beat their Children on any account Whatever, nor give them any Education excepting in hunting and fishing, run-

---

* —this is erroneously Contradicted by Doctor Fermyn—

ning, and Swiming, yet they never Call each other out of their Names, nor Steal, while a lie, is totally unknown amongst them.—To which I may add, that no People can be more Grateful when treated with Civility of which I shall in future relate one glaring Example, but I must not forget to say, that on the other hand they are extremely revengeful, especially when wrongfully injured

The only other vices with which to my knowledge they are acquainted /if such they may be call'd amongst them/ are their excessive drinking, when they have the opportunity and their very unaccountable indolence: an Indians only occupation when he is not out a hunting, or fishing, being to lay in his Hammock, picking his teeth, plucking the hairs out of his beard, or examining his face in a bit of broken Glass &c—

The Indians Still in General are an extremely cleanly people, bathing twice or thrice every day in the Rivers or in the Sea—

They have all black hair, and never become gray or bald, and both Sexes pluck out every vestige of hair in their body, that on the head only excepted, which is of a Shining black, and which the Men wear Short, but the Women very long hanging over their back and Shoulders to their Middle, as if they had studied the Scriptures, where it is say'd that long hair shall be an honour to a Woman, but a disgrace to a Man—

The Guiana Indians are neither tall, Strong, or Musculor, but they are Streight, active, and generally in a good State—Their faces have no expression whatever, that of good nature, and Content only excepted, and their features are beautifully regular, with small black Eyes, thin lips, and very white teeth—

However all the Guiana Indians disfigure themselves more or less by the use of *Arnotta,* or Roucou, by themselves cal'd *Cosowee,* and by the Dutch call'd *Orlean,* Which Seeds being Macerated in the Juice of Lemmons, mixed with Water, and Gum that Exudes from the Mawna tree, or with the Oil of Castor, Compose a Scarlet-Paint, with which all the Indians anoint their Bodies, and even the Men their hair which makes them look like boild-lobsters, they also rub their naked Bodies with *Caraba* or Crab Oil[•]—Nevertheless this is extremely usefull in a Scorching Climate, where the Inhabitants of both Sexes go almost Quite Naked and one day laughing at a Young fellow, who came from near *Cayenne,* he answered me in french, saying "My Skin Sir is kep'd Soft, my too strong Perspiration is prevented, and the Musquitoes dont

• —All these shall be discribed properly on another occasion—

Sting me as they do you, besides its beauty, this is the use of my Painting *Red,* now what is the reason of your painting white* excepting wasting your flower, dirtying your Coat, and making you look gray before your time?"—

These Indians also make use of deep purple blue, which they call *Tapouripa,* but this is purely for Ornament, and absolutely indelible for 9 Days—It consists of the Juice of a fruit in Sise like a small Apple, that grows on the *Lawna*-Tree, and which is bruised and Macerated in Water—With this, these People make figures on their faces, and all over their bodies, resembling herogliphiks, or those that were a few Years since call'd a *alagrecque* in Europe, and are Still cut in Coal Grates, fenders, &c While for a more correct Idea, I must refer the reader to the annex'd Plate, Where the Child alone is not painted—

So very fast Sticks this paint to the Skin, that one of our Officers who could not believe it, having by way of a frolick, made a pair of enormous Whiskers with it on his face, he was obliged /to our great Mirth/ to parade With them through Paramaribo, above a Week, When they gradually became Invisible—

The only dress Wore by these Indians consists in a Strip of black, or blew Cotton, worn by the Men to cover their Nakedness, and cal'd *Camisa,* as is that of the Negroes; being wound around their loins it passes through between their thighs, and the ends of which being very long, so they either throw them over their Shoulders, or negligently let them train over the Ground like a tail—

For the same purpose the Women wear an apron, of particolour'd Glass beads Strung upon Cotton, which they call *Queiou*—This Covering is large only about one foot in breadth, to 8 Inches in length, ornamented with fringes, and fastened round the Waste with Cotton Strings, but being heavy, answers all the Purposes for which it was intended, Many also wear a Girdle made of human Hair around their Waste, through which before, and behind, they fasten a Square broad Piece of black Cotton /but more tight and without a train/ like the Camisa of the Men, both Sexes wearing these belts or Girdles so low, that they almost Slide down over their Buttocks and make their Bodies appear Wonderfully long—In the inland Parts many indians Of both Sexes go perfectly naked without any Covering Whatsoever—The Indian Women also by way of ornament often cut small holes in their Ears, and their lips, In the first of which by raxing [= stretching] the orifice, they wear Corks, or small pieces of light Wood that are Shaped very like them, and through their lips they Stick thorns or all the Pins

---

* —Alluding to hair powder—

Indian Family of the Carribbee Nation.

London, Published Dec.r 1.st 1792, by J. Johnson, S.t Pauls Church Yard.

they can lay hold of, with the heads inside against the Gums, and the Points like a beard, dangling down upon their Chins—

Some still wear fethers through their cheeks, and through their noses though this is Seldom—

But the most unaccountable ornament in my Opinion, is that the girls at 10, or 12 Year old, work a kind of *Cotton Garters* round their ankles, and the same under their knees, which being very tight, and remaining for ever, occasions their Calves to Swell to an enormous degree, by the time they are grown Women, and gives their limbs a very odd and unnatural appearance, they also wear girdles, bands, and bracelets of various Colour'd Beads, Shells, or fish teeth, about their necks over across the Shoulders or round their Arms, but generally above the elbows;—Upon the Whole the Indian Women /already fat, and flabby, with their toes turn'd Inward like Ducks/ are still less attractable by their Ornaments, from which general discription, I exempt one Cast in Particular Cal'd *arawouks,* and which I will mention on another Opportunity, and while all their Girls may be call'd beautiful without exception—

The Embellishments of the Men consist in Crowns of various Colour'd feathers, or a Sash of boar or tiger teeth, across over one Shoulder, as tokens of their Valour and Activity—The Chiefs of Families sometimes wear the Skin of a tiger, and a Silver Plate resembling a croissant, cal'd by themselves a *Caracoly,* they also often are seen to have small Oval bits of Silver in the Cartilaginous seperation of their noses, which is sometimes supplied by a green, or a Yellow Colourd Stone—

All these Nations live in the forest viz. near Rivers, and along the Sea Coast, where they are Scattered in small Villages or Hamlets—

Their Houses or *wigwams,* which they Call *Carbets* are built as I have already discribed, but in place of being Cover'd with the leafs of the Manicole tree, they are Covered with the leafs of *Rattans,* or Jointed Canes here Cal'd *tas,* and which grow in Clusters in all Marshy places but mostly with *troolies,* viz. leaves that diverge emediately from the root, that are no less than 20 or 24 feet in length to 2 or 3 in breadth, and that will for Years effectually exclude all kinds of Weather—

Their furniture is very Simple but Sufficient for their Wants, consisting in a few black earthen Pots, of their own making, a few Calebasses or gourds, a few Baskets call'd *Pagala,* a Stone to Grind Call'd *Matta,* and another to bake their Cassava bread, a fan, a wooden Stool or *Moulee,* a Sieve they call *Manary,* a Press to Squeese the wet Casava calld *Matappy,* and a Cotton Hammock or Net for them to Sleep in—besides which /since their intercourse with the Europeans/ many of them are

1775—JANUARY 25

provided with a Hatchet and a knife &c. which last like a dagger the indians always wear by their Side, while I must not forget that every indian family is provided with a large boat or Canoo, to Cary all that they possess when they travel and which is not infrequent—

The only Vegetables cultivated by those People are, the Yams, Plantains, Bananas /already discribed/ and particularly *cassava* or Manioc, this last is a Shrub that grows about 3 feet high, of a gray Colour, and knotted, the leaves are digitated, and large, and supported by Cinnamon Colour'd foot-Stalks.—Of this Shrub there are two Species, distinguished by the Appellation of the Sweet and the bitter Cassava, and of which the roots alone are for use, which are Soft and farienaceous, and both in Colour, Sise, and Shape much resemble European Parsnips—The *Sweet* Cassava is roasted in warm ashes like the green Plantains, and eat with butter, when it is an agreeable and healthy food, tasting much like the English Chesnut—

But the *bitter* Casava, which when raw is the most fatal Poison for Men and beast, is however Strange nevertheless when prepared by fire, not only a very Safe food but the most natural bread, /as are the Plantains &c/ of the aborigines of this Country, as well as of several Europeans, and Negroes—

The Manner in which the Indians prepare it, is first by grinding or Grating these Roots, on the Matta or Ruff Stone; after which they put it in a press, to seperate the Juice from the Meal, and which Press consists in a kind of long tube made of *warimbo* or Reeds, which being hung to a Tree, and fild with grinded Casava, a heavy Stone or log of Wood is fixed to the bottom, the Weight of which gradually lengthening the tube, it is compress'd in Proportion, and the liquid Substance is Squeesed through the Crevices.

This done the Meal is baked upon a hot stone, in thin round Cakes, until it becomes brown and Crisp, when it is a wholesome food, that will preserve for half a Year yet while I must acknowledge, that the taste /which is become Sweetish/ is at the same time extremely insipid.—

The extracted Water of this root, if not Carefully prevented by the Negroes, is sometimes drank by Cattle, and Poultry, on the Estates, whom it instantaneously kils with Convulsive tortures, and Swelling*—yet this very Liquid if boild with Pepper and butchers Meat &c, is frequently made use of as Soup—

None should use the Casava Root for food—but such as are perfectly acquainted with it, many People having been poison'd to my Knowl-

* —for Experimental Proof taken of this Poison see Doctor Fermyns Description of Surinam—

1775—JANUARY 25

edge, by using the one for the other—The distinction between the two, consisting Principally in a tough ligneous fibre or Cord, running through the heart of the *Sweet or innocent* Cassava Root, Which the fatal or bitter is deprived of—

The Acajou Nuts are also used by the indians as a Vegetable, they Often bring them to Paramaribo, where they are Call'd *inginotto*, the Kernels of these Nuts are in Size and Shape very like Lambs Kidneys, are exceedingly delicate, and grow very far inland on high trees, which having never seen I shall say nothing more about them—

The other food of the Indians, consists in Sea and Land turtle, and Crabs call'd *Seereeca* which last are seen in great Quantitys in the Mud, all alongst the Coast of Guiana at low Water, and of which these People are extremely fond, as also the River Lobsters cal'd *Sara-Sara*, and which are here in great Plenty, but nothing pleases them so much as the *Leguana*, or wayamacca Lesards that I have already discribed while everything they eat, is so highly Seasoned with Cayenne Pepper, that the only tasting of their victuals, excoriates the mouth of an European, they use little or no Salt, but barbacue their Game and fish in the Smoak, which equally preserves it from Putrefaction, and if an Indian has neglected to provide food by hunting, or fishing, his hunger is aswaged by the Seeds of the green-heart, or the Eta-Tree &c—

Their Drink is made of Various Compositions, Such as the *Coumoo*[*]-fruit, dissolved and Macerated in boiling Water, which beveredge when mixed with Sugar and Cinnamon, is frequently used by the fair Inhabitants and tastes very much like Chocolate—

A Drink they Call *Piworree* is a Composition of Cassava Bread *chewed* by the females, and fermented with Water when it has something the taste of Ale, and will intoxicate—

Another drink nearly of the same kind they do make by the *Mais* or Indian-Corn, being first grinded and baked into bread, after which it is Crumbled, and Macerated with Water, til it ferments like the former, and this they call *Chiacoor*—

Still another Drink Call'd *Cassiree*, is much used by these Indians, being a Composition of Yams, Cassava, Sower Oranges, and Sugar, or Trekel, well macerated and fermented with Water—I shall only add that all these beveridges are inebriating, if used beyond Moderation, which is frequently the Case with both Males and females amongst the Copper Colour'd Generation I am Speaking of, and the only time at which they are unruly, and Quarrel amongst themselves—

* —The *Coumoo Tree* is one of the Smallest of the Palm Species its Seed consists in bunches of Purple blew berrys, resembling Grapes and the Pulp of which thinly adheres to a round, hard Stone like a Pistol Bullet—

In their accent the Indians in General have much of the Italion, their Words being Sonorous, and harmonious, and mostly terminating with a vowel, as may be observed in the few Speciments above—They have no Calculation for time, a string with some knots being the only Calendar they are acquainted with—

Their Musick Instruments consist in a kind of flute call'd *too-too,* and made of a Single piece of thick Reed, on which they make a Sound, no better than the lowing of a Bullock, or the barking of a Dog, without either Measure or Variety—Another Instrument is also used by them to blow upon cal'd *Quarta,* and Consists in Reeds of different lengths that are joined together, like the Pipes of an Organ, but even at the top, which they hold with both hands to the lips, and which by Shifting from Side to Side, occasions a warbling of clear but discordant Sounds, and agreeable to none but to themselves, nor can any thing better represent the *God Pan* playing on his Chaunter than a naked Indian amongst the verdant foliage, playing upon one of these Reedy-Pipes; they also make flutes of the *bones* of their Enemies, of which I have one now in my Possession viz. of a thigh bone—

Their Dancing /if such it may be cal'd/ Consists in Stamping the Ground, balancing on one foot, and Staggering round in different Attitudes for many hours, as if they were drunk, which as I have said is very frequently the Case—

The Indians are a Sociable People amongst themselves and frequently meet together in a large Wigwam, or Carbet, that is in every hamlet for the purpose; where if they dont play or dance, they amuse each other with fictitious Storys, generally about Ghosts, Whitches, or Dreams, and during which they frequently burst out in immoderate fits of laughter—

They greatly delight in bathing, which they do twice at least every day, Promiscuously Men, Women, boys, & Girls, who are all excellent Swimmers without Exception, and amongst which Parties, not the Smallest Indecensy is Committed by either Words or Actions—

The Imployments of the Men are /as I have said/ but very few, and Consist chiefly in hunting and fishing, at both of which exercises, they are indisputably more expert than any other Nation whatever—For the first they are provided with bows and Arrows, and of their own Manufacturing, and which *last* consist in different kinds, for different purposes—

The Indian bows are all made of the hardest, and tuffest kind of Wood, about 5 or 6 feet in length, and Wonderfully Well Polished, Which they do by the help of a Stone—In the Middle they are wound about with Cotton, and Strung with Cords made of *Silk-Grass*—

The Arrows are generally about 4 feet long, made of a very Streight and strong kind of Reed, to the end of which is fixed a thin Wooden Stick, long about one foot to ballance them, and arm'd with a Point made of Steel, or of a fish bone, generally barbed; Some of the Indians Arrows, are like a lance, others are doubly and triply barbed, and so Contrived as to stick in the Wound by the Wooden Stick giving way, when the reedy part of the Arrow is pul'd back, which though Sometimes not Mortal, incumbers the Game, and thus prevents it from making its Escape. at the Opposite Side these Arrows /like all others/ are stuck with feathers, 6 or 7 Inches long—Some arrows have blunted heads /in place of Points/ about the Size of a large Chesnut, with which they dont kill, but *stun* the Macaws, Parrots, and Small Monkeys, so that they can take them with their hands, Soon after which they recover and are sent alive to Paramaribo; the arrows for killing fish have something the appearance of a *tredant,* three and sometimes 5 barbed Sticks being fixed to the reed, in place of one, and which enables them to shoot fish even at Random, Some of the above Arrows are dip'd in the *woorara* poison*–which is instantaneously fatal—

But when intent on certain Distruction, this People make use of another kind of Arrows, that are not above 10 or 12 Inches long, extremely thin and made of the hard Splinters of the Palm-tree-bark, being in place of feathers, at one end wound round with a tuft of Raw Cotton, so as to fill up a hollow tube made of reed, near 8 feet in length while the points are dipt in the woorara poison and through which they blow by the lungs these little implements of Death to the amazing distance of near 40 Paces, and with so much certainty that the intended victim never escapes their fatality—

As an Instance of the dreadful Effects of this Poison, I shall only mention a *Negro-Woman* who during the late Rebellion in berbice, being Slightly Wounded by a Poison Arrow, not only instantly expired, but her sucking Infant also by using her Milk, though this last had not been touched by the Arrow at all—

The manner of their Catching fish is much as I have explained at the Hope, by inclosing the entry of Small Creeks, or Shoal Water with a Paling; shooting them with their *tridant* Arrows, or poisoning the Water by throwing in it the Roots of *Hiarree***–In Surinam call'd *tingee-Woodo*

* —The bark of a Tree *so* Call'd, mixd with others, but for a very particular Discription of this Accute Poison, viz of its Composition and of its dier Effects, I refer the reader to Do. Bancroft and the repeated experiments which that Gentleman has made to assertain its instant fatality

** —This tree is much Cultivated by the Indians who send Quantities of it to the Town & Plantations—

or konamee by which the fish come up in a Swoon, and are taken by the hand as they are floating upon the Surface.

These are the only Occupations of the Men, except making their furniture, ornaments, and Arms—

I must not forget that every Indian is possessed of a Club they call *apootoo* for their defence—These Clubs are made of the heaviest kind of Wood in the forest, they are long about 2 feet, flat at both ends, and Square, being heavier at one end than at the other, in the middle they are thin, so as to grasp them, and wound about with strong Cotton threads, having a loop to secure them round the wrist as the Sword tassles are used by some Cavalry—One blow of these Clubs Scatters the brains, and in which are frequently fixd a Sharp-Stone, which are used by the Guiana Indians, like the *toma-hawk* by the Cherokees, and on which besides other Hirogliphical-figures, they do paint the number of Slain by their effect—

The manner of fixing the above Stone in the Club or Apootoo, is by Striking it in the tree while it is yet growing, where it soon gets so fast, that it can no more be eradicated, after which the Wood is cut and Shaped according to fancy—

The Women are occupied in planting Cassava, Plantains, and other Roots, besides Yams, &c, in dressing the victuals, and in making earthen Pots, bracelets, baskets, or Cotton Hammocks—Their best Baskets are cal'd *Pagala,* and consist in a double Matting of Rushes, cal'd *Warimbo* some White, some brown, between which is a Seperation of tas, or trooly leaves to keep out the Wet—The Covering is usually larger and deeper than the basket itself, which it altogether envelopes, and thus makes Stronger, the whole, resting on two Cross Pieces of Wood fixt to the bottom—

Their Hammocks are wove with a Considerable deal of time, and trouble, by thread after thread traversing the *Warp,* in the manner that a hole is darnd in a Stoking after which they are stained with the juice of trees—

The Indian Girls are always come to the term of Puberty before 12 Years, indeed most times much sooner, when they are married, and which Ceremony consists Simply, in the Young Mans offering a Quantity of Game, and fish of his Catching which if she accepts of, he next proposes the Question "will you be my Wife," and to which if she Answers in the Affirmative, the Matter is Settled, and the Nuptuals celebrated in a Drunken feast when a house and furniture is also provided—

Their Women bear Children without any assistance or Inconveniency, in which they seem exempt from the Curse of Eve, even doing

1775—JANUARY 25

the Menial Services for their Husbands, the day after their Delivery; while /however ridiculous and incredible it may appear it is no less An absolute fact that/ these Gentlemen lay in their Hammocks, for above a Month Groaning and Grunting, as if themselves had been in labour and during which time all the Women must attend him with extraordinary Care, and the best of food, which he Calls enjoying himself, and resting from his fatigue—most of these People esteeming a *flat-forehead* a Mark of beauty, they Compress the Heads of their Children /it is sayd/ immediately after birth like the choctaws of N. America—

No Indian Woman eats with her Husband, whom she serves as a Slave, while they take very little Care of their Infants, which nevertheless are always healthy and undeformed, and which when they travel they Carry in small Hammocks Slung over the one Shoulder, in which sits the Child on its bottom, having one leg before and the other behind the Mother—

When the Indians are going to Die by Seekness, or by old Age, which is oftenest the Case, the Devil or *Yawahoo* is at Midnight exorted, by the *Peii or Priest,* by the means of Rattling a Calebas fil'd with Small Stones, Peas, and beads, accompanied by a long Speech—This Office is Hereditary, and by *these* Gentlemen no Animal food is tasted, but such as is Natural to their Country, while as I said before they live better than all the others—For an *emetick* the Indians make use frequently, of the Juice of Tobacco &c—

At the death of an Indian /being first washed and anointed/ he is buried naked, in a new Cotton bag, and in a Sitting Attitude, with his head resting in the Palms of his hands, and all his Implements of War, and hunting by his Side, during which time his Relations and Neighbours rend the Sky by their dismal Lamentations, but soon after which, by a general drunken riot they drown their Sorrow til the following Year*-at this time the body /being rotted/ is dug up, and the bones distributed to all the friends and acquaintances, during which the *former* Ceremony is the last time repeated, and the whole neighbourhood look out for another Settlement—

Some tribes of Indians having put their deceased friends in the above Posture, place them naked for a few Days under Water, where the bones being picked clean, by the Piree, and other fish, the *Sceleton* is dried in the Sun, and hung up to the Ceiling of their houses, or Wigwams, in Comemoration of the great regard for their dead acquaintance—

Whether these Indians travel by Sea or Land their Canoo which is

* —Has not this Passage some Affinity to Doctor Smollets discription of a burial in the High land Mountains of Scotland?

made of a large Hollow-Tree, by means of fire, is always Carried along with them, to transport their luggage, and which is like themselves all over tinktured and besmeared with Arnotta—

If they travel in the Rivers, they generally paddle against the tide, to have a better opportunity of shooting such Game as they may see in the trees, or on the banks whereas did they go with the Current, the rapidity of the Stream would make them often to run past *it*—

When travelling on the Coast, it often happens that these Canoos ship a Sea, which fils them, but never such a thing as a Ship wreck is heard off, both Sexes immediately leaping over board, where while Swimming with one hand they hang by the Canoo, and with the other by means of Calebasses through out the Water—

Notwithstanding the Guiana Indians are upon the whole a peaseable People, they sometimes go to War amongst themselves, purely for the Sake of Capturing Prisoners, to which they too much are encouraged by the Christians, who receive them for other Comodities, and make them Slaves*—

But these kind of Slaves are only for Show and Parade as they absolutely refuse to Work, and if at all illtreated, or especially beat, they Pine and languish like Caged Turtles, even refusing food, til by Heartbreak and Want they exaust to nothing but Skin and bone, and finally expire—

The Indians always take Midnight to fight their battles, which may with more Propriety be cal'd besieging as these broils consist only in surrounding the Hamlets of their Enemies, while they are asleep, and making prisoners of the Women, boys, and Girls, while they Shoot the Men with Poison Arrows, and with their Clubs or Apootoos divide their Sculs; they also Scalp them, and bring home some of their bones, with their hair, as trophes of War and presents to their Wives—In their open reencounters which happen very seldom, the bows and barb'd Arrows are their Principal Weapons of Offence—With these they often kill at a distance of 60 Paces—Nay the swiftest bird in its flight, providing it has the Magnitude of a Crow, Seldom escapes them—In Short such is the Skill of these People at this Manly exercise that the best Archers at *Cressi, Poictiers,* and *agincourt*** Must have Yielded to their Superiority, and even the Honourable Daines Barrington be lost in Amasement at beholding their Wonderfull dexterity—

* —this it is supposed to be as frequently as iniquitously practised on the Coast of Guinea—

** —Three famous battles fought with bows and arrows between the English and the french, the first in the beginning of the 12th Century and the other two Since in all of which the English were Victorious—

Now with full force the yielding bow he bends,
Drawn to an arch, and joins the doubling ends;
Close to his breast he strains the nerve below,
'Till the barb'd point approach the circling bow;
Th'impatient Weapon whizzes on the Wing,
Sounds the tough bow, & twangs the quivering String.

I only shall add further on this Subject that, when these Indians go to War, they at *that time* chuse one general Commander, whom they distinguish by the title of *Uill* probably from Don Antonio *Ulloa,* a Spaniard who formerly resided some time amongst them—

The Trade or traffic which the Indians of Guiana carry on with the Dutch, chiefly consists in Slaves, earthen-Jars, Canoos—Hamocks—baskets—Brazil-Wood, Hiarre-Roots—Macaws. Parots. Monkeys—Balsam-Capivi, arracocerra, Caraba or Crab oil, and Arnotta, for which they receive in Return Checker'd Cloth, fire-Arms, Gun-Powder; Hatchets, knives, Scissors, different-Coloured-Beads, looking-Glasses, fishhooks, Combs, Needles, Pins, &c—

The *Balsam-Capivi* exudes from the bark of a thick Tree that grows far inland with large pointed leaves, and bearing a fruit like a Cucumber, This Gum is Yellow, hard and transparent, resembling Amber, when Melted it has an agreeable Smell, and its uses are to varnish, Stop diaretick-Complaints &c—

The Gum cal'd *Arracocera,* exudes from an inland tree also, it is yellow as the former, but tenatious and Soft—it has the most fragrant Smell of all others, and is held in Great Esteem by the Europeans as well as Indians on account of its Efficacy in curing Wounds, and many other Complaints—

The *Caraba* or Crab Oil is made by bruising Macerating and boiling the Kernels that grow on the Crab-tree, in brown angular Nuts, much about the Size of a Large Chesnut—this Oil which is bitter, besides anointing the Indians, is used to many purposes by the Europeans, The Tree grows to near 50 feet high with leafs resembling those of the Laurel, but as I neither have seen this or the two former growing /to my knowledge/ I can say nothing more about them, and on which Account I prefer reserving the discription of the Arnotta or roucou Tree til I shall have met with it in the Course of my Travels—

The *Mawna*-Tree is high, Streight and light-brown-Colour'd, its leafs are Oval, and its Nuts resembling Nutmegs but without either taste, or flavour to attract—The Gum exuding from its trunk by insisions in the bark, is desolved by the Indians in Water, and as I have said mixd with Arnotta to anoint them—

The *Castor* or *Palma-Christi* Bush, by the Botanist cal'd the *Ricinus,* is a Shrub about 4 feet high, and jointed being covered with large digitated leafs, on long foot Stalks, viz. both the Stem and the branches—This Shrub consists of the *red* and the *White,* and produces triangular Nuts, inclosed in a green husk, which when Ripe turns to brown, and fals of[f]—from these Nuts are expressed the *Castor-Oil*[•]—which is very like that made of Olives, and /as I have mentioned before/ used Externally by the Indians to Paint, and internally by the Europeans for the dry Gripes—

Having thus far discribed the Aborigines of Guiana in General, I shall now Speak of a few Peculiarities belonging to their different tribes, or Casts, in Particular—

Amongst all these Nations the Caribbee indians are the most numerous, active, and brave,—These reside much near the *Spanish* Settlements, whom they often Harras, in immortal Revenge for the Inhuman Cruelties inflicted by them on their fore fathers at *Mexico,* and *Peru* &c. when they are Commanded by a Captain, and assemble by the blowing upon a Conch or Sea-Shell; with other Indians they have also frequent battles—But what disgraces them above all others in Terra-Firma, is that /however unnatural it may seem, and however much it has been Contradicted/ they are *Anthrophophages* or Canibals, at least they most certainly *feast on their Enemies,* whose flesh they tear and devour with the Avidity of Wolves, or Bull-Dogs, though this is generally supposed to be more from a Spirit of revenge than from any depravity in their taste—The *Occawow* Indians, are few in number, and live farther distant from the Sea than do the former—Though like those they live in friendship with the Dutch, they are both treacherous in administring Slow-Poison concealed under their Nails, and distrustful, palisading the Ground around their hamlets with Poisoned Spikes—

The *Warrows* Indians, if not the most Cruel, are the most despisable of any in Guiana, These are Settled alongst the Coast from the River Oronoque, to Surinam,—They are strong but dark Coloured, and extremely ugly, and with all so very lasy and indolent, that their poverty will scarse afford them a covering to hide their nuditys, which they often supply by the Web-like bark of the Palm-tree, and sometimes with nothing at all—They are also very timid, and pusilaminous, and Stinkingly dirty, while they live upon Crabs, and Water, for all Subsistence—Yet did our first parents not live more happy than do these Indians, whose Wishes are equally Confined to their Enjoyments—

The *Tairas* are settled also on the Sea Coast, between Surinam and the River Amasone—These are extremely numerous, being Computed

• —In Surinam this is Call'd *Carapat-oli*—

1775—JANUARY 25

in this Settlement alone, near 20 thousand—They are a very peaceable /but indolent/ People, and in many particulars resembling the Worrows—

The *Piannacotaws* live very far inland, and are enemies to the Europeans, with whom they refuse all Connections or dealings, and of which tribe the only thing I can say further, is that they wou'd murder all the Christians if they had the opportunity*—

The only Indian nation /of my acquaintance/ now remaining further to be mentioned in particular, are the *arrowwouks*—But as this Chapter is already sweld to a Considerable Length I must refer them to another opportunity thus for the present do I take my leave from this happy People—Who with the Divisions, of *Rank* or *Land* are unacquainted—Who know no evil but pain, and want, and with which they are so very seldom aflicted in this evergreen everblooming Climate, who while their Wishes are so few and Confined, possess all that they desire in this World, and most certainly are in my Opinion the happiest Generation existing on the Globe, while on futurity they all depend, but in such a manner, as not to give their minds the smallest uneasiness, nor do they indeed trouble their heads, about to *morrow*

For a better Idea of their furniture, ornaments, and Arms, I refer the Curious to the annex'd Plate, where N°—

1 is an Indian *Coriala* or Canoo, which is generally made of one Piece—

2 the Paddles in place of Oars—	9 arrows for shooting fish ----
3 a Sieve cal'd Manary----------	10 a blunted arrow for birds ---
4 an Indian fan ------------------	11 Common Arrows ----------
5 A stool Cal'd Mulee ---------	12 Poison Arrows---------------
6 a Pagala or Basket ------------	13 the Pipe or tube to blow them -----------------------
7 a Matappy or Casava Press---	14 a Crown of feathers ---------
8 an Indian Bow ----------------	15 an Apron call'd Queiou -----

16 An Indian earthen Pot--------------------------------------
17 A bow tow or Indian Club -------------------------------
18 An Indian Hammock ------------------------------------
19 A Sash of tigers teeth ------------------------------------
20 A Magik Shel or Goard ---------------------------------
21 An Indian flute ---
22 D:o of a Human bone----------------------------------
23 An Indian flute cal'd Quarta, Pans Chaunter ----------------
24 A Stone to rasp Cassava --------------------------------

• —Query are they in this to be blamed or to be Commended—

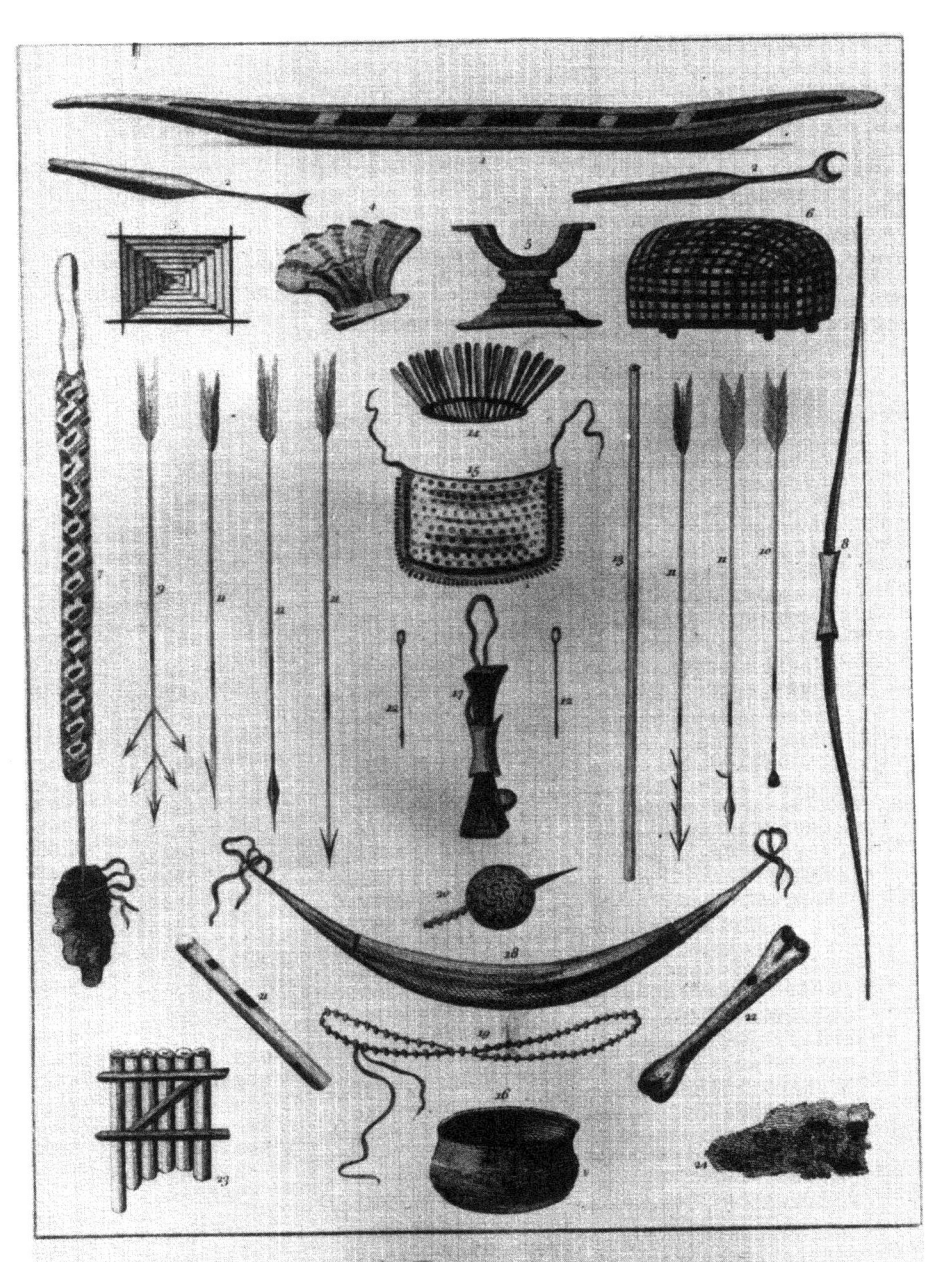

Arms, Ornaments & Furniture of the Indians.

And for a Clearer Discription than either my Capacity, or my Limits will allow, I Direct again the Reader to the Ingenious *Doctor Bancroft*, whose Merit in this particular, is perhaps known by too few—Who stands intitled to my highest Encomiums as an Individual, having lived so long in Guiana—And to the thanks of the World in General, for some of his fine Letters /as I have already Mentioned/ to Doctor *Pitcairn*, Fellow of the Royal College of Phisitians &c. in London, Published One thousand seven hundred and Sixty Six—

Chapter 16th

*Reenforcement of fresh Troops arrives from Holland—
Encampm.' on Mount Magdenbergh in Tempatee Creek—
Remarkable Instance of Lunacy in a Negroe—
Mountains—Beautiful view—the Sick are sent to Europe*

    Having thus far Dwelt on Natural History I shall now once more return to the Military Operations—I have before Mentioned that a Supply of fresh Troops was Expected to reinforce our Decayed little Army, and this very Day the news came to Paramaribo that the Transport Ship *Maastroom,* Cap.' *Eeg* was Arrived in the River Surinam and Came to an Anchor before the Fortress Amsterdam, with Colonel *Seybourgh* and two Divisions Consisting 120 Men together under his Command, two more Being Expected,—

    Next Day I went Down with a Row Boat to Welcome them and having dined with the new Come Gentlemen the Ship Weighed Anchor, and I Sailed with them up till Before the Fortress Zelandia where they Moored, and were Saluted by a few Guns—Amongst the Officers I reconoitred my old Shipmate poor Ensign *Hesseling,* whom we had left Behind us on the Helder, by appearance Dying with the small-Pox, when we Sailed from the Texel, the 24.'' December 1772,—This Young man who now Came with rank of Second Lieut.' had been Peculiarly Misfortunate, Since his Recovery, Soon After which taking a Passage on Board another Ship for Surinam, She was met by a Gale in the Bay of Biscay, where off Cape Finisterre her Quarter Gallery and Rudder Were Beat Away Besides Losing her Foremast and Maintopmast, in which dangerous Condition having the Wind a Head for Lisbon the Vessel ran with Difficulty into Plymouth, M.' Hesseling here took a Passage for France, on Board a small Sloop Loaded with Coals, with

1775—JANUARY 30, 31, FEBRUARY 1, 5

Which he had no Better Success for she run Unadvertently on the *Caskets,* which rocks went through her Bottom, and she Foundered Immediately. however Before the Vessel Sunk, he had time to Break open his Chest and take out a few Linens &c with which he Arrived /Covered over with Coal Dust/ in a Crazy Yol at Brest—He now took Shipping again for Amsterdam, on Board a Dutchman, who run the Ship Aground and he had Nearly been Wrecked another time—Nevertheless he arrived at the *Texel,* from Whence he had thus twice in Vain Attempted to set out for South America, and on this Last Passage it blew so Violently hard that all the Boats, the Sheep the Pigs, and Poultry, were washed Overboard, and by which he Inherited the Appellation of Jonah,—

Till this date I had been the Oldest Officer in the Corps, Colonel Fourgeoud alone Excepted—To Day this Gentleman gave a Dinner to the new Come Troops, which Consisted in *Irish Horse.*–Viz. Salt Beef. Pork, Barley, and hard Peas, at which I had the honor to Partake to my no small diversion, when Seeing the Significant Looks, Bestowed by these freshwater-Guests upon their Saltwater-Lord and Entertainer—In the Evening we Conducted them to the Playhouse where the *Death of Caesar* and *Crispin-Doctor* were Performed the *one* Exactly as Laughable as the other—I must however Confess that I was Better Amused the Next Day when the Governor gave to all a Superb Dinner and Supper, where the Strangers seemed to be as much Thunderstruck with its Magnificence, as they had been the Day Before, Amased at Col: Fourgeouds Scanty Production—Having met at this Table with some Excellent Preserved Fruits, Amongst which was the *Guava,* I will here Say something of it—The *Guaba* or *Guava-Tree* grows to about 24 Feet, with Leafs like those of a Plumbtree it is Light-Coloured, and the Wood of Little Consequence, but the Fruit which is Yellow Oval, and the Size of a Small Apple Incloses a Reddish Pulp, full of Small seeds, that is Very sweet, And may be Eaten raw or made in Marmalades, Jelly's &c when it is Delicious—There are two Species of Guava, that which is the Sweetest having the Smallest Quantity of Seeds—

To day the Troops that were so Lately Landed, were Already sent to the upper parts of the River-Comowina, to be Encamp'd /viz/ the private Marines while most of the Officers still Continued Feasting and dancing, as we had done in the Beginning, which of the two were really best off, was a difficult Matter to Determine, while nothing could be more Pompous, than in Particular was our grand Entertainment at the house of a M.r *Mercelius,* where to Crown the Banquet, a Half dozen Negroes, Kept on Blowing the Trumpett, and French horns in the

Room where we dined, till the Company Were Absolutely deafed, by discordancy, and noise, and I in Particular wished them Half a dozen times, to the Devil, here the Ball Continued till 6 OClock in the Morning, when we were all sent home to our Lodgings in Stately Carriages, never once reflecting on the Distressed Situation of the Poor Soldier in the forest. O ye Blind ones—

> Ye that put far away the Evil Day and Cause the Seat of Violence to Come near.—That lay upon Beds of Ivory, and Stretch themselves upon their Couches, that eat the Lambs out of the Flock, and the Calves out of the Stall.—That Chaunt to the Sound of the Viol and Invent to themselves Instruments of Musick like David—That Drink Wine in Bowls, and Anoint themselves with the Chief Ointment, but they are not Grieved for the Affliction of Joseph.—
>
> Amos 6 Chap.!–V. 3,4,5,&6

The Black Coachman not Knowing where to drive me and M.r Mercelius Insisting on me going home with his Chariot, I got Myself upon the Box, and like Sir John Lade or Lord Molesworth drove home to the no small Mirth, of all the Ladies and Gentlemen.—

And now we all got orders to leave Paramaribo together, to be Encamp'd at Magdenbergh /a Mountain in the *Tempatee* Creek in the upper parts of the River-Commowina/ to where /as I have Just mentioned/ the Reinforcement was Already Dispatched, thus having Prepared Myself to Set out on my *3.d Campeign* & taking Leave at M.rs Lolkens of my Little Family and Friends, I repaired to the watter Side, to set out in the same Barge with Col: Seighbourgh who Erroneously Supposing that the Troops Come with him from Holland, were a distinct Corps from those arrived with Fourgeoud in 1773, and in Consequence of which he took with him in his Barge, none but those he was Pleased to Call *his own* Officers and his *favourites* he made the Negroes shove of[f] the Boat in my presence, when I was not a Stonecast from it, and left me on the Beech to my Unspeakable Surprize and Mortification; while Fourgeoud having Swore he should dance Just as much to his pipes, as the Youngest Ensign in the Regiment, in which the old Trojan being Perfectly Right, I had Strenuously Supported him against his haughty Antagonist. However Setting off Immediately with a Sail-Boat, I soon overtook the *Polite* Col: Seigburgh, and we all sleep'd at the Estate *Vossenburgh* in the River Comowina—Next Day we came to the Estate Aurentrust having past the heavy Barges, that departed from Param.º on the 5.th, & to day—We made the *Hope,* where having spent so many Months I here present the reader with a View of that Estate, and of the Estate *Clarenbeek,* where still was Keept our Hospital—This day Col: Fourgeoud also Came up the River and Sleep'd at *Wajampibo.*—

On the Eleventh we arrived at the Plantation *Crawassibo,* where we passed the night, and when the Overseer a M^r *De Bruyn* was so very Impertinent that I /Already Hating the Fraternity of Overseers/ gave him such a d———nd Beating, that with his Bloody face he Suddenly decamped from the Estate in a Small Canoo With *one* Negroe, and in this Trim at 12 OClock at midnight appeared like *Banco the Ghost in Macbeth* before the Amased Fourgeoud, who thought proper to give

him no hearing, and to dismiss him with a hearty Curse—at Last we all arrived Safe at Magdenbergh viz Fourgeoud, the Officers, and the Barges with the privates—from the Hope the Estates begin to appear thinner, and after ones Passing *goet-accord,* about ten or 12 Miles more upwards, not a Cultivated Spot is to be seen, and where the Plantations were all Lay'd in Ashes by the Rebels in 1757, as I have already Mentioned, a Small place Excepted Just Below Magdenbergh, which is I think Called the *Jacob,* where a few Negroes are kept to Cut Timber—and does the River above Goat Accoord become also very Narrow, being Lined on each side with Inpenetrable bush Wood like the River Cottica, between Devils-Harwar and Pattamaca and while the Tempate creek becomes Still Narrower which may be look'd upon as the Source of the whole River Commewina.—Magdenburgh which is about a Hundred Miles from Paramaribo was formerly an Estate, but has now not a Vestige left to Show it, a poor old Orange Tree Excepted. It is at present, neither more or Less than a Barren Mountain.—here we found the Surface of the Earth in some places Cover'd with a Kind of Strata, that had the appearance of Mother of Pearl, and lay Scatter'd in Small Scales the Size of an English Shilling, in Many places of Surinam are found the marks of *Fossills* and *Minerals,* as I have Already hinted, Indeed *Ironore* is Frequent, and Leave no Doubt that *Gold* and *Silver* Mines Might be met with if the Dutch would be at the expence and Persevere in making the Discovery, I have Already Mentioned the Marawina *Diamond,* while white and red *Agate* are often Seen in the upper part of the River Surinam &c &c[.] in This Mountain we also found the Air more Cool and Pure, and of Course more Healthy than we had found in any other Part of the Colony.—

Now Come the News that the Transport Ship the *Maria-Helena* Capt *Jan Poort* with the remaining two Divisions of 120 Men, Commanded by one Capt *Hamel* were also arrived in the River Surinam the 14th Instant, thus the reinforcement Consisted in 240 Men together, and on

the Fifth Day of March they all Arrived in heavy Barges, at the Mag-

View of L'Esperance, or the Hope, on the Commewine.

View of Clarenbeek, on the River Commewine.

London, Published Dec.r 1.st 1791, by J. Johnson, St. Paul's Church Yard.

denbergh where I may now Say that Col: Fourgeouds whole Flock was Assembled, also here arrived to day one Hundred Negroe-Slaves to Carry the Loads, when we Marched &c &c one of the row Negroes Being Missed on Board a Military-Barge, and Marks of Blood Discover'd in it the Commanding Officers, a Mr *Chatteauview* and Sentinel, were both put under arrest to be tried for Murder, also a Complaint Come on *me* now from the Overseer of the Estate Crawassibo, for having Beat him, which however Ended in Nothing, and to day also two of our Captains fought a Duel, in which one of them got Wounded in the Head•—

- Col: Fourgeoud, this being the Prince of Oranges Anniversary treats all the Officers with a Glass of Wine. O the Wonder of Wonders, What a Wonder—

- A Barge with Provisions now Coming from Paramaribo /Shocking to relate/ found the Negroe that was Missed on the 5th at the Watters Edge Laying in the Brushwood, with his Throat Cut from Ear to Ear, but still alive, the knyfe having Missed the Wind Pipe, this Miserable Apparition of Skin and Bone, they took on Board, and Brought to Magdenbergh, where by a Skilful Surgeon /one Mr *Knollaard*/ the wound was all Sowed up, and the man Miracolously recovered, having Lain 9 days in that dreadful Condition without any Subsistance, or Covering whatever and Weltering in his own Blood, even without a Bandage. the

- week after I had nearly Lost my own Life by an Accident—two Negroes of the Estate *Goet-Accoord*, whom were Employed in Hunting and Fishing for Fourgeoud, one of them named *Philander* proposed to me to Accompany them in the Wood, where we might Chance to meet with some *Pingoes,* or *Powisa* which I have Both Already described, but a heavy Shower of Rain Coming on when we had only Walked about two Miles, we determined to Quit the Project, and repair to the Small spot Call'd the *Jacob* for Shelter, to Gain which we must pass through a deep March—having waded till under our Armpitts, Philander /who was the Finest Man without Exception that Ever I saw in all my Life,/ began to Swim, as did his Companion with one hand holding their Fowling pieces &c above the Watter with the other, while they desired Me to follow as they did, and this I Tried, having Nothing on but my Shirt and Trouzers, when after Swimming 2 or 3 Stroakes, I sunk to the Bottom like a Stone with the weight of my Musket, but which Relinquishing I Immediately rose to the Surface, and Begged that Philander would Dive for it who brought it up in a Moment—But we were Scarcely again Sat a Swimming when a Thundering Voice Called

• —Viz Capt Hamel by Capt Bolts.—

out through the Thisket "*Who som ma datty*" and another "*Sooto Sooto da Bony Kiry da Dago*"—who is there, Fire, Fire, it is Bony kill the Dogue[—]and Looking up we saw the Mussels of 6 Muskets Presented upon us, at a Very Little Distance, I instantly dived, but Philander Answering we Belong'd to Magdenbergh, we were Permitted to Come a Shoare, one by one, at the Jacob, where the Trusty Negroes having heard a Flouncing in the Water, and Seeing Three Armed Men in the Marsh, they took it for granted the rebels were Coming Headed by Bony Himself for when they had taken me, Being Almost quite Naked, and so Much Sunburned, besides my Hair Being Cut Short and Curly, that I Absoluetly Look'd like a Mulloto—Being here refreshed With some Rum, and dried Ourselves About a Good Fire, we now Returned Back to the Magdenbergh, where I congratulated Myself on my Escape though by the Loss of the Skin of one of my Shins.—

Colonel Fourgeoud now being Supplied with fresh Troops, Sent a whole Ship of Invalids to Holland, who Sail'd this day on Board the *Swan* Govert *Tunis* and on Feb.y 26th My d.r Friend *Heneman* had also Saild for Holland With Capt: *Michel-Cock* in an Extremely debilitated State—Amongst the Troops Saild this Day were Several Officers *not* Very Sick, but Justly disheartned, and disgusted at Fourgeouds Barbarous Usage, Particularly in having Stop'd the Prefermint as I have Sayed in the End of the 10th Chapt., And now Seeing Themselves Superceded by raw Youths, who were at School when some of the present Gentlemen had Been Lieutenants in 1772—With this Vessel Also went the Officers that he had put under an Arrest, See Dec.r 16th 74 but which Since were as I have Mentioned, Honourably Acquitted to our Joy and his Great Mortification—and never was an Hospital Ship so ill provided with refreshments—

> Let others brave the Flood in Quest of Gain—
> And Beat for Joyless Months the Gloomy Wave
> * * * * ─────
> Let some far distant from their Native Soil
> Urg'd on by want in harden'd Avarice.—
> Find other Lands, beneath another Sun—
> * * * * ─────
> While he from all the Stormy passions free,
> That restless man involve hears, & but hears,
> At distants safe, the human Tempest roar,
> Wrapt Close in Conscious peace.—

Now Fourgeoud reviewed with pleasure his revived Little Army, where I am sorry the *rangers* did not appear—and the 5 following days

1775—MARCH 21, 25

he sent out one Hundred Men on a Padrole to reconnoitre the Skirts of his new Encampment, of which Numb'r, I had the honour to be one, and During which Nothing Remarkable happened, except meeting with a Large Company of *Quarta's* which Being a Kind of the Most remarkable Monkeys In the World, from they'r Affinity to the Human Species I will here give an Account of them—It Was on The Twenty-fifth when in the evening walking with my Boy *Qwawco* without the Camp, they Came down so Low to Look at us, and throwing Small Sticks and Excrements at us, that we were Brought to a Stand, and I had an Opportunity Thoroughly to Examine Them, The *Quata* or *Quato* is very Large, with an Enormous Tail* thin Arms and Legs, and Being Covered over with Long Black Hair, makes indeed a Very Hideous Appearance, the More So as its face is Quite Naked and red, with deep Sunk Eyes, and which gives it much the Appearance of an Old Indian Woman—It has short Ears, and only 4 Fingers, without a Thumb on its hands, or fore feet but it has 5 Toes on the Hinder feet, All of which have Black Nails, and the Extremity of its Tail Which has a Spirall Turn Inwardly is Naked, and Callows, by its frequently hanging to the Branch, of the Trees, Serving the Animal like a 5.th Limb for that Purpose, Upon the whole the Quato S[e]ems to be that Link in the Chain of *Cercopethicus,* Which is Only divided by the *Ourangoutang,* from the Appearance of Man, and, in the Tail Excepted had much the make and Actions of that Species, Which I saw since at Haddington, in the Park of the duke of Baccleugh. most Wonderful is the Agility of these Animals in Swinging From One tree to Another, But I Never Saw them Leap.—Theyr throwing Short Sticks & Excrements, seems to be no more than a Humiliating Mock-Mimicry of the Human Actions, without any other Use, as they Neither have the Strength or the Dexterity to take any Aim, nor if they hit their Object, could they at all do it any hurt, Except in Nuisance, but what appears Peculiarly Remarkable, is that when one of them is hurted by a Musket. Arrow &c the Poor Animal instantly Claps his hand upon the Wound, Looks at the Blood, and with the most Piteous Lamentations, Ascends to the Extremity of the Top of the tree, in which he is Assisted by his Companions, and Where hanging by the Tail, he keeps on Bewailing his fate, till by the Loss of Blood he grows faint, and drops down dead at the Foot of his Adversary this was Asserted by one of our Officers, a Mr *Mathiew* Who Saw it after having Shot one of them Himself, In these Actions there Seems to be a Degree of Reason but is Certainly no more than Uncommon Instinct they being Even less fit to be taught,

* —here d.^r Bancroft is Egregiously Mistaken when he Asserts that this Animal is Divested of a Tail

than other Monkeys* For the rest they are Lascivious, and the females have regularly their Menstrua—They are in Short the most disgustfull, Dirty, Annimals, that I am Acquainted with, as I since Experienc'd By one, that was the Property of, and favourite of one of our Officers, I Shall here only add, that they kept on following of us till we returned to the Camp. doctor Bancroft Mentions An ourangoutang in Guiana, that will attack the Males, and ravish the females of the Human Species. and Such may Be Literally True, though I never heard of them while I was in that Country, but this I know, they will never Learn to *play upon the flute* as the Ourangoutang Mention'd by *Lord Munboddo,* I must however Mention another Monkey that I Saw at Col: Fourgeouds House, which is here Call'd the *Wanacoe,* and is Cover'd over with Long Black Hair like the Quato, but its Limbs are Shorter and more Hairy, while its face is a Kind of a Dirty-White—This Monkey is the only one of the Species that is not Sociable, Being for Ever found Alone And so Dispisable is this Solitary Animal, that he is Continually Beat, and robb'd of his Nourishment, by all the others, Whom he is too Lazy to Escape from and to[o] Cowardly to fight; of the Longhair'd Monkeys the *Saccawinkee* is the Smallest, and Indeed of all the Monkeys in Guiana if not in the World, Being not much Larger than a Norway-Rat—this is a Beautiful little Animal, with a Blackish-Gray frisled hair, a White face, and very Bright Shining Eyes, its Ears are Large and Naked, yet they are not very Perceivable, Being Cover'd by the very Long and white Whiskers, that Surround the whole Visage of this Little Creature, its 4 Feet are not Unlike those of a Squirrel, and its Tail is Bushy and Annulated—So very delicate is the Saccawinkee, and so Suceptable to Cold, that Scarcely one of them is Brought to Europe alive and if they are they verry soon pine and die—The Dutch Call them the *Shagarintee* from they'r Being Chagareend at the Very Smallest Trifle. in the Annexed Plate I have Delineated both these Monkeys, the Large *Quarto,* and the Small *Sacawinkee.* thus Trying to Correct with my Pencil the Deficiency that May Be in my Pen.—

And now I shall once more return to Magdenbergh, before where Arriving, I had nearly been Crushed to Death, by an Enormous Tree, it Dropping Just at my Heels by Age, which Frequently happens in the Forrest, and Slightly Wounded one or two of our Marines, During this Trip we had much rain and Crost over one or two small Creeks, which is Done by hewing Down one of the Palm Trees on the Watters Edge, and which Falling across the River, it forms a Temporary Bridge[.]

* —M: Hartzink says that they are Teached to fetch Water & to do other Menial Services, which I Deny & Without the Smallest Ceremony.—

༄ I now pay'd a Visit to the Miserable *Negroe* who had been found with his Throat-Cut & who was so Well as to be able to Converse, and having declared that he had done it with his *own* hands the Unhappy Officer and Centinel were Acquitted. I asked him what reason he had to Commit Suiside and he Said *None*—

> I have /Say'd he/ as good a Master and M^rs as I Could Wish, and a Family of my own that I much Love. I had Sleep'd Sound During the Whole night till About 4 OClock in the Morning, When Awaking I took my Knife to Pick my Teeth With it, and Instantaneously Cut my Throat without Knowing Why, and the Moment After repenting what I had Done; when Rising from my Hammock, I got in the Canoo to Wash myself and Try to Bind up the Wound but Stooping Over the Side, and bleeding very fast I turned Faint and fell into the River—Now no more Able to get on Board or to Cry for Assistance, I Still by Struggling made Shift to get on Shoar, Where I fell Down, and Helplessly Lay till I was Pick'd up by a Boat with Provisions Going to Magdenbergh, during all Which time of 9 Days I had my full Senses, And saw a *Tamannoir,* or *Antbear,* Come to Smell my Putrified Blood About my neck, who in Seeing me Move retired into the Forest—

I gave the poor Man some Boston Bisquit I had got from Paramaribo, and a Large Callebas with Barley /which we never Wanted/ to make Soop, & Also some Wine for which he was very Thankful. This Negroe Appear'd to be About Sixty Years of Age—And what is Extremely Unjust is that the Slaves are in General Obliged to Subsist on but half the Allowance of the Soldiers, Which I think I have Before hinted While they are forced to Do Double the Drudgery—

༄ I now to my Sorrow received a Letter from Mr Kenedy who was Preparing to go to Holland, that he desired my boy Qwacco might be
༄ returned to his Estate, whom I Accordingly Sent Down, but with a Letter offering to buy him from his Master as I had offered to buy *Joana* from Hers, While heaven knows I Was not master of a Shilling to pay
༄ the redemption Col: Fourgeoud now ordered all the Sick in the Colony to Magdenbergh, where he had Erected an Hospital and a Large Victualling Magazine. thus all the Scarecrows from Clarenbeek arrived here, with Surgeons, Apothecaries &c Where the Air was Certainly more Healthy. About this time the Old Gentleman was Peculiarly ill-natured and Abused his friends and Enenemies without Distinction—While he Swore not a Soul should be exempt from Duty providing they Could but Stand on theyr Legs, Scoffing at Agues and running Ulcers As Bagatels and Trifles, indeed he Neyther Posses'd Humanity or Religion.—

The Quato & Saccawinkee Monkeys.

London, Published Dec.r 2.d 1793 by J. Johnson, St. Paul's Church Yard.

I have Sent among you the Pestilence after the Manner of Egypt—your Young men have I Slain with the Sword and have taken away Your Horses, and I have Made the Stink of your Camps to come up unto your Nostrils yet have ye not returned unto me Saith the Lord.—

Amos 4 Chap! Verse 10th

About this time a Strong Detachment was Sent to the Estate *Bruyinsbergh* in Comowina where an Insurrection was Expected, the Slaves refusing to Work upon a Sunday to which however they Were Drove by the Lash of the Whip, is not this Barbarous?—
—It was now in the heart of the Rayny Weather which Fourgeoud declared he would henceforth Prefer to Scower the Woods, and in Consequence gave Orders for two Strong Columns to March next Day, The reason for Chusing this Season was, that by now disclosing the rebels they must Starve for Want, whereas in the dry Months the Forest is Overstock'd with fruits of every Kind—But this was in my Opinion a Very Vague piece of Generalship, when Considering on the other hand how the Wet weather Murdered his Troops Whom he killed I Suppose, 20 to the rate of one Negroe—Fourgeoud was himself of a very Strong Constitution having Been used to Hunting and Shooting the whole of his Lifetime, to which he Added Temperance and the daily Use of his *teasan,* his dress Consisted in nothing but a Waistcoat, through one of the Buttonholes of which he wore his Sword—on his head he wore a Cotton-Night Cap, with a White Beaver hat above it and in his hand a Cane But Seldom he Carried his Musket, or his Pistols—I have Seen him All in Rags and Even Barefooted. In short at 6 O'Clock this Morning the 2 Columns Set out upon their March—the one Commanded by Col: Seighbourgh the other by Fourgeoud to which Last I had the honour to Belong, and when I expected Soon to be put in Mind of my former many Grievances Our Poor men were now Loaded like Jack Asses—While they were Order'd to put their Fire Locks in Their *Napsacks* the Muzzels Excepted, and this was to Keep them Dry from the rain which now dayly Poured in a Torrent from the Heavens, our Course was **S.** by **E.** up Allongst the Banks of the *Tempatee* creek Where we Soon were in the Watter till above our Knees.—
This Day we met Some Very Pretty Squirls which are of Several kinds in this Colony—those that we Saw were Brown, with the Belly white, their Tails not so Bushy, nor Were they upon the Whole So Large as those of Europe—There are Also *White* Squirrels with red Eyes, and Also *Flying* Squirrels—These have no Wings but a Manbrane Between the Fore and Hinder Legs Being a part of theyr Skin, Which When they Leap Expands like the Wing of a Bat, And by Which like a Parachute

they rest upon the Wind and in these flights are Carried to a Considerable Distance.—

- We now marched again Course **S.** by **E** till 2 OClock When we Changed Course to **SSW.** and no rain—This Day we past by Piles of fire Timber that was Left there to rot, since 1757, When the Estates were Demolish'd by the Negroe-Slaves who rose in Rebellion, amongst this Wood was the *Purple-heart* Tree, the *Iron Wood* Tree, and the *Bourracourra,* Known in England by the name of Brazil—and in France By that of Bois De Lettres.—

The *Purple-heart Tree* grows Sometimes so high as 4 Score feet, and thick in Proportion, with a Smooth dark-Brown Bark. the Wood is of a Beautiful Purple Colour and Agreeable Smell, and much Esteem'd on Account of its Weight and Durability—The *Iron-Wood* Tree so called from the gravity and Everlasting Quality of its Timber, grows to About 60 Feet, with a Light Couloured Bark, & is much valued by the Natives as well as the Europeans on Account of Its hardness in Particular, resisting even the hatchet, and of its taking a Most Beautiful Bright Polish, this Wood will Sink in Water—The *Bourracourra* or Brazil grows between 30 and 40 Feet but not very Thick, with a reddish Bark, The heart only of this Tree is what people Value[.] After the White Sappy part is Cut away, and Though then But thin is as truly Beautiful, as it is Useful, the Colour Being a fine Crimson, Variegated with Irregular Hierogliphical Black Spots, and its Consistency heavy hard Durable, /though rather Brittle/ and is Susceptible of taking the Brightest Polish—This Last is very Scarce, but the others are more Plenty, Growing on the highest Grounds, where Also is found Ebony &c and which Trees Being Shaped first in Timber espescially for Sugar-Mills, are Sold to the English-West India Islands, often for the price of 50 Guin⁵ Each Piece which I recollect not if I have Mention'd Before—

- The Word of Command Being now again, *take up your Bed and Walk,* we Marched **SSE** and **S** by **E** through Deep Marshes, up till our Breast in Water, and in Very heavy rains, in which Resistless Situation we were Suddenly Alarmed, not by a Party of Rebels but by a Large Company of Monkeys Whom we Discovered in the tops of the Trees Knocking Large Nuts /of what Species I Know not/ Against the Branches of the Trees, to Break them in Quest of theyr Contents, with the greatest regularity, keeping time Alternately at Every Stroke While some of them threw Down their Burdens Which broke the Head of one of our Marines, and which Sound of *Tuck, Tuck, Tuck* we had Mistaken for the rebel negroes Cutting Wood with an Ax—In the Evening we Encamped near the Tempatee-creek where we had made Large Fires and Comfortable Hutts thus Sleep'd out of the Wet—Here I Drank the best

Watter ever I Tasted and in this Camp I saw two Remarkable *Lizards* the one Called the *Devil-of the-Woods* and the other *Agama* in this Country, the first is an Ugly Small Lizard of a deep Brown or Blackish Colour—Which runs with Amazing Swiftness up and Down the Trees—It has no Scales, a Large head and it is Said *to Bite,* Which is Uncommon in most all other Lizards—the Other is the *Mexican Cameleon* Which is as remarkable for its Dazling Beauty, and for its Brilliant Colours, as any Animal of that Species And of which I can say no More having never had the Opportunity of a Close Examination—In Surinam Also are Species of Lizards here known by the name of *Salamanders* but Which to my Knowledge I never Saw.—

We now marchd again keeping Due **W.** till 12 OClock through Very heavy Rains and deep Watter when we Changed our Course to the **N.** and Past over Very High Mountains Perhaps Pregnant with Treasure

>Rocks rich in Gems and Mountains big with Mines
That on the high Equator ridgy rise.—
Where many a Bursting stream Auriferous Plays
Majestic Woods of Ev'ry Vigourous Green
Stage Above Stage high Waving o'er the hills
>—Thompson

The two highest Mountains in South-America are that Peak of the Andes Call'd *Chimborazo* Which Measures 20,460 Geometrical Feet Above the Surface of the South Sea, having though under the Line 4000 Feet of its Summit Perpetually Covered With Snow—The other is that on which is Built the City of *Quito,* Being the height of 9370 Feet & The Highest Inhabited Land in South America if not in the World.—

We Still Continued Marching **N** Over Mountains, from Which we had to be sure the Most Enchanting Prospects by the Wildness of the Country and The Beautiful Verdure Display'd in so many Different Hues through the Forest—

>—But Chiefly the Gay Green
How smiling Natures Universal Robe.
United Light and Shade Where the Sight Dwells.
With Growing Strength and Ever new Delight.

Here I saw a Bird that is Called a *Wood-Cock* which Appears to have much the Colour of those in Europe but which flew very heavily, While I was told that it Can run with very Great Swiftness—But what mostly Attracted my Attention was the *Arnotta-Tree,* one of Which we here met With, and of Which I Coppied one of the Twigs with Great Exactness—This tree which is also Called the *Rowcow* and the *Orlean*-tree

Sprig of the Arnotta, or Roucon Tree.

London, Published Dec.r 1.st 1791, by J. Johnson, St. Paul's Church Yard.

and by the Indians *Cosowee,* may rather be Stiled a Shrub, Not Growing above 12 Feet in Height, the Leafs are Greener on one Side than on the other, and Divided by Ribs of a reddish-Brown Colour, as is Also the Stem, The Pods which are as Large as a Small hens Egg are *Echimated* or Bristled Like the outer-husk of a Chesnut—At first they are a Beautiful rose Colour Which as they ripen, Changes to Dark brown, When they Burst Open and Display a rich Crimson Pulp in Which are Contained Seeds that are Black, Like those of a Grape—The Uses of this Pulp I have Already Described See Page [305] When Speaking About the Aborigines, or Indians, and now I present the reader With a View of it, though on a Smaller Scale; Where **A.** is the Leaf Above, **B.** the Same Below, **C.** The Pod Before it is yet ripe **D.** The same ripe and Exposing the Crimson-Pulp, and **E.** the Black Seed Cover'd over with part of the Pulp—However Presumptuous I may Be thought I cannot help Observing the rowcow Plant Exhibited by the Celebrated *Miss Merion* is Perfectly Unlike the Original that I Saw, While She Also Says that it Grows on a *Large* Tree—We now having Crost an arm of the *Mapanee* Creek In the Evening once More returned to our Camp at Magdenbergh one of our Officers a M: *Noot* and Several others being so Ill, that they were Carried in they'r Hammocks, upon Poles by the Negroe Slaves, while a Great Number Were so Weak that they Could hardly Support the Weight of their Emaciated Bodies, but to Complain of Sickness Was to revolt, till they Drop'd down more Dead than Alive When they were Generally Allow'd to be Pick'd up. During this Expedition /on Which we Perceived nothing of the Enemy/ I was remarkably Good Fortunate–having Neither Suffered by the Fatigue, or been

- Persecuted by Particular bad Usage and the next Day Col: Seibourgh's Column Arrived having Seen as we had *Nothing.*—
- Now returned my Boy Qwacco from Paramaribo Where to my Great Joy his Master M: Walter Kenedy Sold him to me for the sum of 500 Duch Florins Amounting With other Expences to near £50 for which Col: Fourgeoud Civily gave me a Bill for his Agent with Which I Pay'd This faithful Servants ransom, Wishing to God My D: *Joana* and her Boy were also Mine, from whose new Master I had not yet Received an Answer.
- To Day a Negroe Brought to me A Beautiful Butterfly Which I Coppied with All the Correctness I Was Master of, and which I saw since in *Merian* Where it *also* is Coloured Very Ill—This Fly was a Dark Blue Ting'd with Green, and Variegated with Spots Like a Peacoks feathers, while on Each Wing it had Also a Spot of Pale Yellow,—The under part of the Wings were a Charming Crimson and Purple, the Body a Pale

The Blue & Crimson Butterfly of South America.

The Groo-groo, or Palm Tree Worms.

red, this Butter-fly Miss Merian Says she found on a Jasmine viz. the Catterpiller Which is Green, and Yellow, it is Crown'd with 8 Horns on the head and has 2 On the Tail—Cap.! Frederacy now returned Also from a Cruize in the Woods, who had a Corporal Drowned, by Slipping of[f] a Tree in Crossing over a Creek & which Accidents frequently happened, but the Men were Always Pick'd up while this Poor fellow sunk to the Bottom Instantly with all his Accoutrements—
This Evening another Negroe brought me a Regale of groegroe or *Cabbage-Worms,* as they are Called in Surinam This reptile /which is Produced in a Tree Called the *Mountain-Cabbage-Tree* and which is one of the Palm Species that I will Afterwards Describe,/ Grows to the Size and Thickness of a Man's Thumb from the Spawn of a Black Beetle and is Extremely Fat—However Disgusting to Appearance these Worms are a Delicious treat to many People, and regularly Sold at Paramaribo. the manner to Dress them is by frying them in a Pan with a very Little Butter and Salt, or Spitting them on a Wooden Skiver when in Taste they partake of all the Spices of India, as Mace, Sinnamon, Cloves, Nutmegs &c—Species of these Worms are Produced in all the Palm-trees Whatever, when they are Beginning to rot. Only some being Larger than others they are All of a Pale Yellow Colour With Black heads, and I acknowledge I never Made a Better Supper—In the Annex'd Plate are Represented the Above Mention'd fine *Butterfly* and the *Cabbage-Worms*—both Natural Size taken from the Life, of the Palm Tree Worms is made Mention in the Old Testament, but they must be of a Different kind,—

> I have Smitten you with the Blasting & Mildue when your Gardens and your Vineyards And your fig trees and your Olive Trees increas'd the *Palmtree Worm* Destroy'd them—
>
> Amos 4.th Chapt. Verse 9.th

By the Indians and Negroes they are Call'd *Toecoema*

- To Day departed a Command for La rochelle in Pattamaka—
- And this Day was Sent a Capt: with a few men Back to the *Hope* in Comowina, to protect the Estates in that River—Now the Miserable Old Negroe Who had Cut his Throat on the 5.th Day of March but had Since Recover'd, was seen by some Slaves to enter the Wood with a Knife, from which he no more return'd And where since he was found Stabb'd to Death. While it was Afterwards Discover'd by his Master, that two Months Past he had Attempted to Do the Same; thus regularly from Month to Month, Query Does not this Account for the Derivation or Etymology of the Word Lunatick.—

1775—APRIL 17, 19, 20, 22

- The Command returns from La Rochelle where the troops of the Society are all Sick.—
- The poor men Cruelly Beat by Lieut: Col: Seighbourgh for Complaining against the injustice of making them Cut Wood, Which he did 30 or 40 every Day only for his Amusement, Without the Least Necessity and Which Provoked Me and some others to treat him with Contempt.—
- Now Col: Fourgeoud treated me with the Greatest Politeness, Whom at his own request I Presented to day with a Painting of his own Figure Marching at the head of his Troops in a Deep Swamp and which picture he sent to the Prince of Orange, and the Duke of Brunswick as a Proof of What he and his Troops Underwent in Surinam, of Which however he was himself the Principal Cause, Be that as it may he gave me Leave for 14 Days to go to Town to wish M.̱ Kennedy a Good Voyage to Europe, And Availing my Self of his good Temper, I Left Magdenbergh Within one howr, And made such a Dispatch that I Came to
- Paramaribo the 22.ᵈ Where I found my Little family & friends all very Well, and Where I put up at the house of M.̱ *De Lamare,* to where they were Finally Sent from that of M.ͬˢ *Lolkens,* Who had During all my Absence Treated them with the Greatest Attention.—

Chapter 17th

New Samples of unprecedented Barbarity—
Occurrences on Mount Magdenburgh—Prices of Provisions at
Paramaribo—Discription of a new Animal—
Great Mortality amongst the Troops in Tempatee and Comewina River

The first Visit I now did was to Mr Kennedy to bid him farewell, and to Whom I Pay'd the 500 florins For the Black boy, for Which Gave me a Receipt And Qwacco was mine—About this time I got ill with a fever which however Did Last but a few Days, Walking out on the first Day of May I Observed a Croud of People About the Watter Side before the house of *Mr Stolkers,* where Appeared /dreadful to relate/ a Beautiful Young *Mullotta-Female* Floating on her Back With her hands tied Behind, her Throat Cut most Shockingly, And Stabb'd in the Breast with a Knife in more than 8 or 10 Different Places–Which was reported to be the Work of that Hellish Fiend Mrs Stolkers, from a Motive of Jealousy, Suspecting her Husband might fall in Love with this Poor Young Girl, and Which Develish Woman had Before Drown'd a Negroe infant for Crying as I have told the Reader—Nay *this Monster* Was Accused of Still Greater Barbarity, if Greater Barbarity Could be, viz. Arriving one day at her Estate to View some Newly Purchased Negroes, her Eye Chanc'd to Fall on a fine *Negroe* Girl About 15 Years of Age who Could not so much as Speak the Language of the Country, Still Observing her Such a Remarkable fine Figure, and Such a Sweet face, her Diabolical Jealousy Instantly Prompted her to Burn the Girl All over the Cheeks, Mouth, & Forehead with a red hot Iron, and Cut off the *tendon-Achilles* of one of her Limbs, which not only rendered her a Monster but Miserably Lame So Long as she Lived, Without the Victim knew what she had done to deserve such a Punishment—Some of the Negroes one day representing to this Lady the many Severities she Daily Inflicted and Supplicating her to be of a Milder disposition, She instantly Knock'd out the Brains of a *Quaderoon-Child,* And Caused 2 of the heads of its relations to be Chopped off, Being young Negroe Men who had Endeavoured to Oppose it—These heads &c when she had Left the Estate were Now tied in Silk Handkerchiefs, and by the Surviving Friends Carried to Paramaribo. Where they were Laid at the Governors Feet With the following Speech—

> This your Excellency is the head of my Son, and this is the head of my Brother, Struck off for Endeavouring to Prevent Murder by our Mistresses Command, we know our Evidence is Nothing in a State of Slavery, But if these Bloody heads &c are a Sufficient proof of What we Say, We only Beg that such may be Prevented in time to Come, When we Will all Cheerfully Spill our Blood and our Sweat, for the Preservation and Prosperity of our Master and Mistress—

To Which the Answer, was that they were all Inhumainly Flog'd round the Streets of Paramaribo for having told a Lie, till the Infernal fury was Glutted with Persecution—Had any one *White* Person Been Present at the above Carnage, the Evidence Would have been Good, but never that of a Negroe in the Colonies, and ever [even] then she would have Escaped by Paying a fine of £50 Each Murder—Enough, my Soul relents at Dwelling Longer on the Subject.—

- Being now again as well as Ever I took Leave from Joana and her *Johny* for thus he was named After Myself, though he Could not yet be Christned, and who both Continued at my friend De La Mares house, After which I once More did Set out for Magdenbergh in a tent Boat—
- I Call'd at Egmond on my French friend Monsieur Cachelieu and next
- Day Sleep'd at *Oranjebo* or *ornamibo* where I was heartily Entertained by my old Adversary Captain Meyland, with Whom I had fought the Duel at the Wana-Creek, and which Gentleman Swore he Loved me now Better than any man in the Colony, he was Just returned from a Cruize in the Woods of 12 Days—Amongst his men I reconnoitred one *Cordus* a *Gentlemans* Son from Hamborough in Which Character I had Known him but who had Been Trepand as a Common Soldier in the West-India Company Service Amongst Which Corps as I have Say'd are All Nations, Christians, Gentiles, and Jews, who Devoured Pork and Bacon as fast as the others When they Could Catch it—On this Spot Which had formerly been a Plantation but was now Choak'd with Weeds, I met with some herbs Which I Cannot Pass Unnoticed, while I have no other names for them but those Given me by the Negroes,

one Excepted that Which Doctor Bancroft Calls the *Siliqua Hirsuta* or *Cow Itch* /and Minutely Describes it/, and the Black People *Crassy-Weeree-Weeree,* While I shall only say that it is a flattish Pod Like a Green Pea, With Very small Purple-Beans—Which Grows on a Slender Creeping Vine And that it is Cover'd over (viz) the Pod With a Kind of Fine Elastick Hairs or Spicular, Which when touch'd Causes such a Confounded Itching that Nothing Can Exceed it—For the *Worms* Nothing Can Be Better, than this Hairy Coat Scraped from the Pod, and Used in a Teaspoon with Jelly &c—a Sort of Wood was here Also Shewed me by one of the slaves Which he Call'd *Crassy-Woodo,* and which had the same Itching Effect when Touched, but of Which I Can Absolutely say nothing Else—The other Shrubs Were what they Call'd *Consaca-Weeree-Weeree,* and Which Consists in Large green Leafs, Which the Negroes Use for the Cure of a Disorder in the Feet Call'd Consaca, When they Can have no Lemons or Limes, and Which I have Mention'd Dec.r 15th 1773—When Encamp'd at the Wana Creek—This Weed Also makes a Very Good Sallad—The *Dea Weeree-Weeree*—This is a fine Wholesome herb And very much Esteem'd—But the *Cutty Weeree-Weeree,* is Amongst the Cursedst Plagues in the Colony Being a Kind of Strong Sharp-Edged-Grass, which is in some Places very Plentiful, and /when Walking through which/ it Cuts ones Legs like a Rasor; So Much for Herbs Which are in this Country all Known by the name of *Weeree-Weeree.—*

I now arrived once More at Magdenbergh—here Col: Seighbourgh and What he Call'd his Officers Seem'd to be a Distinct Corps from those of Fourgeoud—Severals of whom Treated Each Other, With The Greatest Rudeness, While this Basha was Soverainly Hated by the Commander in Chief—this made things Still more Disagreeable,

While *I* however seemed to gain *his* Affection, But Which on the Eighth I had nearly again forfeited by an Accident, Viz. Col: Fourgeoud having bought from some Indians, a Couple Most Beautiful Parrots Call'd here *Cocatoos,* and Which were in a Cage ready to be Shipp'd off as a Present, to her royal highness the *Princess of Orange.* I Persuaded Monsieur Laurant /his Valet de Shambre/ to take one of them out, that I Might the Better Examine him, When it Gave a Shreek, and Disappear'd in an Instant, flying over the Tempate creek—The Poor Valet Stood perfectly Putrified–Who Could only Pronounce "*Voyer Vous*"– While I Betook to my Heels, to Avoid the Approaching Thunder But observed Fourgeouds Motions through the thick Underwood, Who no sooner was Informed of The *Dreadful Accident,* than he became Ramping Mad, Swore and Danc'd Like a Frantik, Killd a Poor Wadling duck by Kicking Belonging to one of our Officers, and at Last Trampled His

Wig under his Feet, /for he Wore one Sometimes/ while I stood trembling & All the rest were Laughing—having Continued in this Manner for half an hour, his Passion Gradually Abated, and When he had Recourse to a Stratagem Which Actually brought back his Parrot in his Possesion–Viz. he placed the Captive Bird tied by a Small Cord to its Claw on the Top of its Cage, Which he placed by himself in the Open Air, Putting a Ripe Banana Inside and the Door Open, So that any other Bird but the Prisoner Could Come at it, Who when getting Very Hungry made Such a Noise by his Shreeking that he Brought Back his Mate, and Who now Entering the Cage in Quest of Food Was thus once more Deprived of Its Freedom—At this time I Started from my Concealment and was Acquitted With a Gentle Reproof, While on Poor M.r Laurant he Bestow'd a Score of f——tu B——gres.—The *Cockatoes* are Less than the Parrots, and of a Green Colour Except the head, and a few Feathers in the Tail which are of a pale red—This Bird Derives its Name from a *Panash,* or Bunch of Feathers With which it is Crown'd, and which Generally Lay Backwards, but which it Erects at Pleasure, it is Supposed Mostly When its Iritated, or Afraid. I have Also seen in Surinam a Parrot of a Deep *Slate Blue* Colour, but not Like those that Come from the Coast of Guinea, which are rather of a Lead-gray. this Parrot is said to be very Scarce, as only inhabiting the Deepest recestes of the forest, from where it is bro.t to town by the Indians, this Bird is Less than the Common Parrot, but seems Extremely Strong and Lively, but the most Common Parrots in Guinea [Guiana] are those which Marcgrave Calls *Ajurucura*—these Birds are not Quite so Large as those that Come from Africa–they are Green with the Breast and Belly Pale-Yellow, on the top of the head they have a Blew Spott, and the feet are Gray, with 4 Toes, 2 Before and 2 Behind, in the Wings they have some Feathers of a Bright Blew, and some a deep Crimson, they are a Much Greater Nuisance than a pleasure in Surinam Where the /inprodigious flocks/ Perch Amongst the Coffee, Maiz, rice &c and Commit Great Devestations While even their Shreeking noise is Almost Insuportable—they Always fly in Pairs, and Very Swift, And I have Observ'd towards the East Meeting the Sun in the Morning, While toward the West they follow it at Night—they Generally Breed in remote places, and Lay 2 Eggs—I brought Down two of these Parrots at one Shot When I was at *Sporksgift* on M.r Mackneyls Plantation Who not Being Dead Scratched me Terribly with their Sharp Claws; they being very Strong and Tenatious of Life, We had them Dress'd and they made very Good Soop–they may Also do in a pie, as rooks in England, but any Other Way they must be tuff and Disagreeable—These green Parrots may be teached to speak, Laugh, Cry, Bark,

Whistle, or Mew but not nearly so well as those who Come from Africa—It is said that by the Seed of the Cotten Plant they are Intoxicated. Parrots are Also Subject to Fits, Perhaps by their Cholorick Disposition—Yet Longevity is peculiarly Ascrib'd to them by the Indians. these Birds have Strong hook'd Bills which Assist them in Climbing And with Which they Crack very hard Nuts, and Sometimes bite Very Severely, they Delight in Swinging, and Ballancing While hanging from the Branches And use one of their Claws Like a hand to take their Food—

In Surinam are Some Beautiful *Peroquets* which are of the Species of Parrots but Smaller, and they are not Less Common—the finest of these is the Size of a Very Small Pigeon—they are of a Lively Green on the Back and the tail, but the head & Neck is Auburn. The feathers on the Last being Edged with a Gold Colour. Which makes them Appear like rich Scolops or Scales—the Breast is of a Lead-Colour, the Belly Lilack the Wings Tipp'd with Orange and Azure and the Bill of a Very Dark Blue, the Eyes are Like fire, and the Feet are Quite Black—The other Species are perfectly Green, With a White Bill. and a Crimson Spot on the head, these make an Agreeable Chatter but are not Tameable like The Former.—

This very Eveining I was Presented by a Soldier With a Bird of a Quite Different Kind, And Which he had Actually Caught With his hands—This Was no other than the *Annamoe*-or Surinam-Partridge and a Finer Creature I never Saw—The Size of a Large Duck, it was fat as a Lump of Butter and of a Dark brown Colour on the Back and Wings And on the top of the head—the Underpart of Which, the Breast and the Belly and the Thighs Were of a fine Cream-Colour. Intermix'd with Orange Feathers, and Very small Transverse, Black Bars–The Body was Exactly the Shape of an Egg, having No Tail, the Neck was Long the bill not Long but very Sharp-Pointed, and a Little Arched, the Eyes were Bright, and as Black Jet. the Limbs short of the Colour of Vermillion with 3 Small toes on Each Foot—This Bird it [is] said runs with Amazing Swiftness hiding itself Amongst the Green but flies very Heavily, on Account of its Plumpness Which was the Cause of its being thus Overtaken by the Marine Before it Could Start—We had it roasted and indeed nothing Could be more Delicious—As I took a Correct drawing of it I refer the Readers to the Annex'd Plate Where they may See the *Parrot* of South America, as Describ'd Above, Besides a few Curious *Nests* of Which I have Given an Account, See Page [300], but Where I had no Opportunity to place them, and Which Besides their Curiosity may Show how the Publick is Imposed on When Comparing them, with those Exhibited in Goldsmiths Animated Nature Vol. 5 Page

The Anamoe & Green Parrots of Guiana.

London, Published Dec.1.1791, by J.Johnson St Pauls Church Yard.

253.–And Where that Author Yet Asserts that they Are Built on the Banana and Plantain Trees, Where Also the Monkeys and Numbers of Large Snakes Are Assembled, which I here Pronounce to be as False an Assertion as it Would be Ridiculous to put faith in it, and Unpardonable in Me to Let such Absurdities Pass by Unnoticed

Now an Accident had Nearly Befallen me Which Must have Broken my Heart—My Black boy Washing my Cotton Hammock in the Tempatee creek–it Was Suddenly Carried to the Bottom by the Rapidity of the Current, and himself Entangled in the Middle of it, So that both the One and the Other Disappear'd, however Luckily the boy Extricated Himself though With Difficulty And After being more than half Drowned Appear'd once More on Terra Firma, when he had the Presence of Mind instantly to Sink a Large *fish Hook* With Lead tied to a Strong Line on the very same Spott, With which he Actually bro! up the Hammock to All our Astonishment, the Stream running So Swift that rolling Over the Ground it Shiffled its Station Every Moment, the next Day Capt Hamel Angling on the Water Side his Tacle got fast to the Ground when I Diving to Clear it, Knock'd my Ancle With such Violence against a Rock that it Did not Recover in the Course of Several Months.—

At the Above Accidents Col: Seighbourgh Seem'd to be So much Entertained and they Seem'd to make him so Very happy that I in my turn treated him With that Contempt Which his Malice Deserved, and which Ingratiated me More in the Favour of Old Fourgeoud Who Already hated him than if I had Destroy'd half the Negroes in the Colony, During All this time Strong Padrols Cruised between Magdenbergh,

La Rochell and the Jew Savanah, and on the Seventeenth the Commander in Chief Marched to Pattamaka himself with nearly the Half of his Troops. Leaving me the Command of those that remained on the Mountain, not Being Able to Accompany him in Person, as having by this time a Dangerous Mortification in my Ancle—As I had now a Prospect of remaining some time at Anchor I Dispatched Qwacco to Paramaribo for Provisions—Whatever may be thought of Fourgeouds Manoeuvres, And his Not being Able to bring the rebels to a Pitched Battle it is no less true that he Exerted himself and his Troops to the Utmost, And that by his Constant Cruising about the Upper Parts of the Rivers /viz. the Skirts of the Colony/ he Prevented the frequent Depredations on the Estates that had been formerly—I now being here the Commander in Chief, the two Negroes formerly Mention'd /hunting and Fishing for me/ brought me one or 2 Pingoes—/Wild Boar/ every Day besides Fish Call'd *Newmara* some so Large as Codfish, that I will Afterwards Describe, With which Dainty's I regaled All the Officers Without Exception, and never was a Deputy Governor more respected, while I gave to the Hospital all the Plantains, bananas Oranges, and Lemons that were Occasionally Sent as Presents from the Jacob, and the nearest Adjoining plantations—Padrols were also Daily sent out to Every Quarter, and indeed though We Could not Expect to find the Enemy Within Several Days Marching—The Environs of Magdenbergh nevertheless were so Perfectly Scoured that no Invasion from the Rebels could be Practible & which was Perfectly Necessary, they having Besieged or rather taken by Storm or Surprise other Military Posts for the Sake allone of Carrying of[f] Ammunition fire Arms &c which is to them of the Greatest Value and to the Colony of the Most Pernicious Consequence, and in taking Which Precaution Col: Fourgeoud Show'd as much Generalship as he Did in Constant Marching, Which Last however was the Principal Part of his Duty and thus while we were Unsuccesful in taking the Rebels I Availed myself of Taking a Draft of Every Animal, reptile, or Shrub, that I thought Could Illustrate my Little Collection of Natural Curiosity, which I now began to form some Idea of Exhibiting one Day to the Publick if I was Spared to return to Europe. thus one of my Negroes this Day brought me two Curious Insects which though I had no Opportunity to Draw them, I will try to Describe them after my Way–The one Was What is here Generally Call'd *Spaanse-Juffer,* and Without Exception the most Singular Animal I saw in the Colony. It seem'd to have Some Affinity to the Grasshopper Kind but yet very Little—The Body of this Surprising Creature Which was no thicker than a Quil was no less than Seven inches and a half in Length Including the Tail, it had *no Wings,* and was Mounted like a Spider on 6 Legs, that were long near 6 inches, it had 4 Anthaena Projecting from its head 2 Being nearly 5 Inches, and 2 much Shorter, the head was Small the Eyes Large, Black and Prominent, & the Tail Articulated like most Insects, its Colour was a Brownish Green & Upon the Whole it Seem'd a Monster—This Creature is found near the Marshy places, where its Long legs Seems to Serve it in Wading through the Watter, but not to Swim, According to M.r *Farmines* Opinion and to Which its Feet are not Calculated, Which Terminate in two small Claws Like some of the Beetle Kind.—

The other Was a Large fly which Miss Merian /who Gives a Drawing of it/ Calls the *Vieleur* but Which I have Generally heard Mentiond the *Scaar-Sleep* while Both Names are Extremely Applicable from the noise it Makes towards the Evening, Which very much Resembles the Sound of the Above *Musical-Instrument* a Cimbal or that of a *Razor-Grinder* When he is at Work—This remarkable fly whose Grinding noise Always begins at Sun Set Viz. 6 OClock is Also Call'd the *Porte-Lanterne,* or *Lanthorne-Bearer* from the Light it Diffuses After that time, and Which is Much Stronger than any of the Fire fly Species, being Sufficient Almost for any Purpose.—These flies are Above 3 Inches Long, and very Thick, the body Green, and with 4 Transparent Wings, Variegated With light Marks of all Colours, particularly the Under ones, on Which are 2 Large roundish Spotts not Unlike those on the Tail-Feathers of a Peacock.—Under the head of this Insect is Seen an Inverted Straight Trump or Tube, Like a Needle, With which it is Said to Suck its Food from the Flowers and to Make that Disagreeable Grinding Noise though for my Own Part I Should rather Ascribe *that* to the Fluttering of its Transparent Wings like some flies in England—A Large Probucus or Snout Strip'd red and Yellow, And Shaped like the first Joint of a Man's Finger, Projects from the head, and makes one-third of the Whole Animal. Which Protuberance is Vulgarly Call'd its Lantern, and which Emits that Surprising Light from Which it takes its 2^d Name. I shall only Add that it is a Very Slow Creeper but that it flies with Extreme Velocity.—

Now arrived my boy Qwacco from Paramaribo with the Following List of a few Provisions &^{c} that he had Bo^t for me, and which to Give the Curious a real idea of the prices in Surinam I will here insert some Articles, as Stated on my Account in Dutch Currancy, Eleven florins make^g 1 Pound, and Which at this Juncture Were nothing like Extravagant—

	Flo. d.
2 Bacon hams 31 Lb at 15 Pence P^r Lb—	23. 5
A Small Cagg with Butter 10 Lb—	10. 0
A Small Cagg with Flour 100 Lb at 4^d P^r Lb	20. 0
A Dutch Cheese 11 Lb at 10^d P^r Lb—	5. 10
2 Quart Bottles with Vinegar—	2. 0
4 Lb Spermaceti Candles at 2 F. P^r Lb—	8. 0
2 Lb Dried Sassengers [sausages] at 30^d P^r Lb—	3. 0

The prices of Wine and Spirits &^{c} I have already Mention'd in the 12th Chapt^r of this Work.—He Also brought me a Goat With its Kid to Provide me in Milk for Which I pay'd 20 Florins being near £2 Which Prices are at Least Double and Some Tripple of What they are in England.—*Goats* are Extremely Common in All Guiana, they are not Large, but very Pretty Creatures, with Small horns, and very Short Sleek hair, Mostly of a *Dun* Colour, they are as Nimble as Stags, and kept on All the Estates, Where they Breed fast and give much Milk, and are Delicious eating When kill'd Young.—

1775—MAY 26, 28, 29

All this was very Well but I now was Sorry to be informed that All my European Letters were Sunk in the Texel roads on board *Cap:* *Visser* Who was Wreck'd Among the Ice. still more so that my Sincere and Very good Friend M:r Kennedy and his Lady & his Family had taken their final farewell from the Colony and Sail'd for Holland on board Capt. Mallenbergh, This Gentleman, M:r Rob:t Gordon, and a M:r Gourlay Were the Only Scotch inhabitants in the Colony one Burkland–one townshend and M:r Halfhide the only Englishmen, and Cap:t *Macneyl* the Only one that Came from Ireland.—

- Now returned Col: Fourgeoud with his Command from Pattamaca Much Ematiated himself, and all his People by Fatigue, Who left a Great Number Behind him in the Hospital at La Rochelle but no Account Whatsoever of the Rebels. Although he Varied his Route every time, thus it was Pretty Evident that they were Routed from this Quarter, if of Late. they had Been Settled there at All. but where to find them in this Unbounded Forrest was the Question, However he Never Dispared and Seem'd as Eager to Find the Ha[u]nts of the Rebel Negroes as he had been formerly in Discovering of a Covey of Partridges or a Nest of Black Badgers.—

- This Day a M:r Mathiew one of our Officers who had been out a Shooting Presented me with the taibo an Animal that is here Call'd a *Wood-Rat*—this Creature was the Size of a Young hare and of a *Reddish-Brown* Colour being remarkably thin with Long Limbs a Roundish head, and a Tail not Unlike that of a Sucking Pigg—the Claws were Exactly Like those of an Ordinary Rat, but Larger in Proportion and so was the head, viz. the Mouth Teeth and Whiskers, the ears were Short, and Naked and the Eyes Jet Black, and Prominent, With a White Iris, it is said to run very fast—We had it Dress'd, and Eat it, having been told that it was Very good, and so we found it, being Sweet tender and Even fat, Notwithstanding its thin and Skraggy Appearance—This Creature on Account of its Size puts me in Mind of Another Animal known in this Country by the name of *Crabbo-Dago* or the *Crabbed-Dogue*• for its Matchless Ferocity, killing and Devouring Every thing Comes in its Way, Without Exception, Whither Quadrupedes, fowls, Reptiles, or Snakes, and Seeming never to be Glutted with Blood it Murders All that it Can Vanquish, Which are not a few by its Courage, Activity & Strength & while it is not Larger than a Common Cat—from What I have read I think it Bears much of the *Ichnewman* but still More of that Animal Mention'd by M:r *Allamand* in the *Count-De-Bufon* See Vol. 4 Page 266. Which he there Calls the *Grisson* or *Gray-Weasel,* though this

• —Not Mangeur De Volaille According to M:r Farmin

1775—MAY 29

that I Mention was Larger, and Which he Says notwithstanding its Being an Inhabitant of Surinam, None of the People Coming from that Country Could give Any Account of it.—

If this is the Same Animal and Which I Doubt not, on Which Account I have given it the name of the *Crabbo-dago* or *Grisson* I am happy to have it in my Power to give the Above relation of it—As for its figure I shall Quote Literally the Counts own Words as Extracted from Mr *Allemand* Which Will be the best proof of its being the Same Animal When it is Compared to the Annex'd Plate, Where both the Wood ratt and the *Crabbo-dago* or *Grison* are represented, And had I seen this Account During the Count's Life I would Most Assuredly [have] taken the Liberty of Informing him by a Letter, what I now though in this Unconnected Method relate to the publick.—

> I receiv'd /says Mr *Allemand*/ the Small Animal represented in the Plate•
> in the Catalogue it was Call'd the Gray Weasal from Which Circumstance I Derived the name Grison, Because I know not how it is Denominated in the Country where it is Found—The Whole Upper Part of its Body is Cover'd with Deep brown hair having White Points, which Gives it a Grayish Brown Colour[.] Under the head and neck is a Bright gray because the hairs are Very Short, and the White part is of Equal Length With the Brown—The muzzle, the under Part of the Body and Legs, are Black; Which Singularly Contrasts With the Gray Colour on the head and Neck—
>
> The head of this Animal is Very Large in proportion to its Body; its Ears Almost form a Semicircle its Eyes are Large and its mouth is Armed with Strong Grinders, and Sharp Tusks—It has six Cutting teeth, in each Jaw four of them hardly rising above the Gums.—Both the fore and hindfeet have 5 Toes, with Yellowish Claws.—the Tail is pretty Long, and terminates in a point.—
>
> The Grison has a Greater resemblance to the Weasal than to any other Animal.—But it belongs not to the Weasal tribe, for its Body is not Long Enough, and its Legs are too Long.—It is not Mention'd by any Author or Traveller.—I Shewed it to Several Persons who had lived Long in Surinam; but none of them Knew it; hence it Either must be a rare Animal, Even in its Native Country or it must Live in Desert and Unfrequented places[.] the length of its Body is about 7 Inches I have not Been Able to learn any thing of its history.—

To this I shall only add further my *Surprise*. the Above Animal not Being so Extremely *Rare* in Surinam as Supposed by the Above Gentleman—and Which Probably Owes the Want of its not being Mentioned in History to its Extreme Ferocity, Which is Without Example, it being

• —Edition De Holande tome 15.—

The Wood-Rat of Surinam.

The Crabbodago, or Grisson.

London, Published Dec.r 1.st 1791, by J. Johnson, St. Paul's Church Yard.

indeed a very *Uncommon* thing when a *Crabbadago* or *Grison* is taken Alive—Thus Proov'd of having at Least Describ'd one Animal that was not known even to the Count De Buffon I will now once more proceed With my Journal.—

The *old Gentleman* and I were now Extreme friends at whose Board being Daily invited, he proposed to me to Paint his Figure at Large, in his bush Equipage, which Was to be Engraved at the Expence of the Town of Amsterdam, where he /to be Sure/ now thought himself as Great a Man as the Duke of Cumberland in England after the Battle of Culloden, and to this Performance I began on a Large Sheet of paper With China ink in his own hut, When one day looking him full in the face, to Examine the features of this Criterion of Wickedness, I burst out in an Immediate fit of Laughing to think how he & I now Sat staring at Each other, When all of a Sudden the Whole Mountain was Shoock by a Tremenduos Clap of Thunder, While the Lightning Actually Scorched Fourgeouds Forehead, and Broke all the Eggs under a Hen that was Breeding in a Corner of the Room, Where we Were Sitting.—

—Ille Flagranti.—
Aut Atho, Aut Khodopen, Aut Alta Ceraunia telo Dejicit—

The Above two Lines from *Virgil* being much Admired by Doctor Stedman in his *Laelius and Hortsenia,* and Which Gentlemans Nephew I have the honour to be I Quotted them from his Works as here not Unaplicable However Apprehending that the Next Thunder Bolt Might Mistake me for the *Old Hero,* I thought proper to Quit his Appartment, Which by the by was Exactly on the Summit of the Hill, and finish the picture in my Own hut Which I Did since to his great Satisfaction.—

About this time Died the Captive rebel-Negroe *September* of a Dropsy Who was taken on Nov.r 26.th 1773. Since Ever which time /When his Companion Was Shot/ being Near 2 Years and half this Poor fellow had followed by Fourgeoud like a Shepherds-Dog through All his ruf[?] Manoeuvres, the Colonel Always Expecting this Negroe Would One Day Surely Conduct him to the Haunt of the Rebels, but he was Mistaken. While the other Negro-Slaves Suspecting he had Actually given to Fourgeoud some Information, Attributed his Dreadful Death to a Punishment from God for his Want of trust & Fidelity to his Countrymen, to whom they had Conjectured he had Sworn to be True, While as I have Remarked in the 3.d Chap.t of this Book that it is an Unvariable Supposition Amongst the African Negroes that Whoever

Breaks his Oath Shall Die Miserably in this World, and is to be forever Damned in that to Come.—

The Hope in Comowina was now so Verry Unwholesome /in Regard to Cleanliness and Keeping of it Dry from Inundations, being Neglected by the New Come Troops, Who now Lay there/ that the Commanding Officer, and Most of his Men being Unfit for Duty, by Sickness /And Many of Whom Were Already Buried/ Col: Fourgeoud Sent down One Cap.! *Brant* to take the Command With a fresh Supply and Orders to Send *not to town,* but to Magdenbergh All the Invalids he Should relieve, which Orders he Gave in Such a Brutal Manner to the Above Gentleman /not so much as Allowing him time to Pack up his Things, While Col: *Seighbourgh* Shamefully Deprived him of his Servant, Whom he took to himself/ that M.!' Brand burst Out in Tears, and Declared he Wished no Longer to Survive his ill Treatment, and Departed to the Hope with a Truly broken heart, Where Arriving the Next Day he Could not Possibly Send Up the Late Commanding officer to Fourgeoud, whose Name was Cap.ᵗ *Brugh* and Whom he had found *dead* as a haring. This poor Man had done a few Padrols with Col: Fourgeoud in the Woods, but being Extremely fat, And Corpulent, he was no more Able to Support the fatigues, and Excessive heat, than Snow the Sunshine Which having Melted him Down Very fast helped to hasten his Desolution by a putrified fever—Col: Seibourgh Followed Capt. Brand to Inspect the Sick, and to Torment him more if Possible. I Shall now leave them together for Sometime and Describe two Fishes Which though Extremely Different in Size and Colour, Well merit a Particular Attention. the one Which I Saw Caught on the 5.ᵗʰ by an Angler & the only one that Ever I Saw, was About the Size of a Large Anchovy, and /the Dolphin Excepted/ had the Most Beautiful Colours that Can be Imagined, the Back and Sides being Divided in Longitudinal Bars of fine Yellow, and a Deep Blueish-Black, the Belly was Silver, the Eyes Were Black and Gold, and the Fins a Glowing Transparent Vermillion—its shape was not Unlike that of a Trout, and the Whole was Cover'd With Small Scales—it had one Dorsal Fin on the Middle of its Back With only the Vestige of Another near the Tail Which was Equally Biforcated—Under its Belly were 5 Fins, 2 Pectoral, 2 Ventral, and one Behind the Anus—the Under Jaw Projected before the Upper Jaw, & Made its Mouth Appear to be reversed—the Gills were Small; Having Enquired about the Little fish the only Information I Got from a Black-Man Was that it was Call'd *Dago-Fisee;* the other is that fine Large Fish Call'd by the English Rock Cod, by the Indians *Baroketta* and *New-Mara* by the Negro's Which I have Several

The Fresh-water Fish called Dago Fisee.

The Rock Cod, or Newmara.

times Mention'd but not Described, and is so Plentifully Caught in All the Upper Parts of the Rivers—This Fish is the Size of a Large *Cod-fish* but All over Scaly, and by Some Compar'd to a Salmon–the Back is a *Brown-Olive* Colour the Belly is White, the head is Strong With Small Eyes of Which the Pupil is Black, and the iris Gray, the Mouth is Very Large, and Beset With one Row of Sharp Teeth like those of a Pike fish, While it is no Less Voracious—the tail is Obtuse and Dark-Olive, as Also the Fins 6 in Number, Viz one Dorsil, 2 Pectoral, 2 Ventral and one Abdominal, This Fish is Extremely Delicious Eating, And Particularly Much Esteem'd at Paramaribo by the White Inhabitants but Where it is Very Scarce, Compared to the Upper Parts of the Rivers and Creeks Where, as I have Said, it is Caught in Great Abundance.—
Having Very Correctly Copied the Above 2 Fishes the Dago fisee Exactly in its own Size and the Newmara in Comparibly Less, I here Present them as a Feast to the reader's Eye, they having Been Honour'd in Surinam With the Epithets of a Masterly Performance and indeed they were Extremely like the Originals.—
About this time Several Officers Keeping Poultry and Hogs the *Last* All Died, in the Space of 2 Days, being Poison'd Probably by Eating *Duncane* Already Describ'd or some other fatal Weeds that Were Unknown—It is a General Observation that All Animals Know by Instinct to Distinguish their food from their poison And to this I have no Objection Viz. in their Own Country but the Sheep and hogs, being Exotics from Europe in Guiana Are an Exception to those Animals Who Naturally belong to a tropical Climate.—

◆ Now Returned Mr *Seybourgh* from the Hope, in Triumph With a Mr *Dederlin* /one of Col: Fourgeoud's Subaltern Officers/ As his Prisoner, Guarded by a Serjeant and 6 Marines With Screwed Bayonets, like the Worst of Criminals, for What was Call'd a Want of Subordination, but Which Proceeded Mostly from a private Peek When the Youth Exclaimed.—

> Si quoties peccant homines Sua fulmina Mittat.—
> Jupiter Exiguo tempore Inermis erit.—

◆ And Next Day arrived the Sick Officers and Soldiers from the hope in Barges, Some of Which Last being to[o] ill to be transported Died in the Passage Without Medicines or Assistance, While to day Also Died one of our Surgeons in the Camp, and Daily died a Great Number of the Privates, which were the fruits of having Marched So Much in the Wet Season.—

Chapter 18th

A Tyger taken in the Camp—
Fatal recountal of a party with the Rebels who kill several of the
Troops and force them back—
Description of a Planter of Surinam—Contagious distemper—
Suiside—Scene of primitive Nature

I have Mention'd that Several Officers Keeped Poultry &c Numbers of Which Were now taken Away Ev'ry Night Without Knowing by Whom, When one Capt.n *Bolts* /Was Suspecting the *Coati Mondi* or *Crabbodago*/ Made a Trap of an Empty Wine Chest, Only by Supporting the Lid With a Stick fix'd to a Long Cord, And into Which /having first Secured All the other Poultry/ he Put a Couple of fowls to Rust, Guarded by two Negroes at Some distance—they had not Been many hours on their Post When hearing the Fowls Shreek, one Pull'd the rope, and the other ran to Secure the Invader by Sitting on the Lid, And Who Proved to be no other than a Young *Tyger* Who Would Still have Clear'd his Way Out by Beating Against the Box, but Which being Immediately Secured by Strong Ropes, Was Dragged With the Prisoner in it, to the River, Where being held Under Watter he Was Drowned, Under the Most Amazing Efforts, by Beating, Still to Work his Escape. Cap.t Bolts Ordered the skin to be taken off, to be keeped as a Memorial of so Very Strange a Circumstance—Yet however fabulous it May appear that a Tyger Should be taken in a Wine Chest, Let the Reader Peruse Bankes's Sistem of Geography page 342 or Go to *Battersea* Near London, And the Marvel Will Cease, Where in the Church he May Read the following Words on a Very Elegant Monument.—

1775—JUNE 8

P. M. S
—Edwardi Wynter—
Equitius Qui Adhuc Impuber ex Patria
Proficiens in Orientalibus Indiis Mercaturam
Exercuit, Magnus Opus Comparavit, Majores Conflaturus
Si non Spevisset, ibidem Splendide vixit honorifice Post
Annos 42 Angliam revisit Uxoram Duxit Emmam filiam Ricardi
Howe Armigeri Norfolc decipit Martis 2º Anno ætatis 69 An Dom. 168 ⁶⁄₅

Posuit Marito Optime de se Merito
—Uxor Mastrissima—
Born to be Great in Fortune as in Mind,
Too Great to be Within an Isle Confin'd,
Young, helpless, friendless, Seas Unknown he Try'd.
But British Courage All those Things Supply'd.
A Pregnant Wit a Painful Diligence,
Care to Provide, and Bounty to dispense,
Join'd With a Soul Sincere, Plain, open, Just,
Procur'd him friends, and friends Procur'd him Trust.
Those Were his Fortunes rise: and then began
This Hardy Youth Rais'd to an happy man.
A rare Example, and Unknown to Most,
Where Wealth is Gain'd, and Conscience is not Lost,
Nor Less in Martial honour was his Name,
Witness his Actions of immortal fame,
Alone, Unarm'd, a *Tyger* he Opprest,
And Crush'd to Death the Monster of a Beast,
Thrice Twenty Mounted Moors he Overthrew,
Singly on foot, Some Wounded, Some he Slew,
Dispers'd the rest.—What more Could Sampson do?
True to his Friends, a Terror to his Foes.—
Here now in peace his honour'd Bones repose.
—Nita Peregrinatio.—

If this be true that Sir Edward Winter Drowned a Tyger Only With his hands for he kild him it is Sayd in the River Ganges and Which Seems to be perfectly Well Authenticated, besides his Other Amazing Actions Why Should not 2 Negroes Drown one in a Box.—

Having Mention'd these Anecdotes I Will here give an Account of All the *Tygers* that are Known in Surinam.—

The Count *De Buffon* Asserts that there are *no* Tygers in America, but Animals Much Resembling them, Which go by that Name.—Be that as it may, I Shall Describe them from Occular Demonstration, as I found them, and Leave to the Reader to Determine Whether they are Tygars or Not.—

The First and Largest is that Call'd the *Jaguar*, of Guiana—This Animal Which has by Some been Represented as a Despisable Little Creature, Not Larger than a Greyhound, is on the Contrary, Very fierce–Strong, and Dangerous, Some of them Measuring from the Muzzle to the Root of the Tail, Not Less than 6 Feet. Witness the Print of that Enormous tigers foot Seen by Myself in the Sand* Near Pattamaca, though Generally they are not So Large.—

The *Jaguar* is of a Tawny Orange Colour and the Belly White—on the Back it is Spotted with Longitudal Black bars—On the Sides With Irregular Rings, or Annular Marks, Light Coloured in the Center, and All Over the Rest of the Body, and the Tail, the Spotts are Smaller, And Perfectly black—Its Shape is in Every Sense like that of the *African* Tigers, though Rather more Slender, & being All of the *Cat* Kind, Need no Particular Definition, This Small Animal being Universally known—But their Size and Strength being so Much Greater, they Devour a Sheep, or a Goat, With the same Facility that a Cat Would Kill a Mouse, or a Rat, Nay Cows, and Horses, are not Protected from theyr Attacks, Whom they frequently Kill on the Plantations, And though they Cannot Carry them off in the Forrest, on Account of their Weight, Still Tear and Mangle Them in A Dreadful Manner, only for the Sake of the Blood, of Which this Ferocious Animal is Never Glutted—And it has Even Happened, that the *Jaguar* has Carried off Young Negro-Women at Work in the Field, And too Frequently their Children—This is the Contemptible Animal as it is Describ'd by some Authors** that Will Beat Down a Wild Boar With a Single Stroke of its Paw, and Seize by the Throat the strongest horse that ever was Mounted—Whose Savageness and Thirst After Blood is Such that it Cannot be Tamed, that it Will Bite the Very hand that Feeds it, and very Often Devours its own Offspring, Yet is this Formidable Creature no Match for the *Aboma-Snake* Which when it Comes Within its reach has the Unequalled Strength of Crushing it to a Jelly in a Moment*** As for a more Minute Description of the Jaguar, I refer the reader to Mr *Sonini De Manoncourt* in *Buffons* Natural history, But not to *himself,* Who seems in this to be but ill Informed.—

* —Vide Jany 7th 1774–Page [229]—

** —Mr Fermyn, While he Compares it to a *Dog* Strangely Affirms that it Cannot only Kill, but Carry off to the forest a *Cow* or *horse*—

*** —See August 26th 1774.—

The Next is the *Couguar,* Call'd in Surinam the *Red* Tiger—this Indeed may With More Propriety be Compar'd to a Grey-hound by its Shape, though not by its Size being Much Larger, While not in General So heavy as the Jaguar—The Colour of this Animal is a Reddish Brown the Breast and Belly are of a Dirty White, With Long hair, And *not* Spotted, the tail an Earthen Colour, the Extremity Black, the head is Small, the Body thin the Limbs Long With tremenduous whitish Claws The Teeth are Also Very Large, the Eyes Prominent, and Sparkling Like Stars.—This Creature is Equally ferocious With the Former.—

Another of the Same Species is the *Tiger-Cat,* Which is Extremely Beautiful, this is not Much Larger than I have seen some Cats in England, of a Yellow Colour With Small Anulated Black spotts, White Within, the Belly is a Light Colour, the Ears are Black With a White Spott on Each—The hair is Smooth and the Skin is Very Much Esteem'd—the Shape Like that of any other Tiger—The Tiger-Cat is a Very Lively Animal, With its Eyes Emitting flashes of Lightning;—But Ferocious, Mischievious, And not Tameable Like the Rest.—

In Guiana is Still Another of this Species Call'd the *Jaguaretta* of a Blackish Colour With Still Blacker Spotts &c but of this Last I Can Say Very Little, having Never seen one And Indeed the Others but Verry Seldom—however of the Jaguar, And the Tiger Cat I Present the Reader With a Drawing.—All these Animals have Long Whiskers like Common Cats, they Sometimes Climb Trees, but Generally Lay in Ambush Under the Verdure, from Whence they Bound With Uncommon Agility on theyr helpless Prey, Which when having Murdered they Drink the Blood Warm, and Never Cease to Tear And Devour till they are Gorged, but after Which they are Cowardly And Will take to flight for a Common Shepherds Dog. for *fire* Also they are Mortally Affraid, Which is the Best Bulwark to keep them at a Distance, and as Such Every Night Made Use of by the Indians in Guiana While more than Once it has been Observ'd, that Tigers had Enter'd our Camps for Want of these Precautions, but Luckily Without Committing any Depredations—

- I now Availing myself of Col: Fourgeouds good Temper not only Show'd the great Neglect towards Seybourg Whose Occassional Caresses I Scorn'd as indeed he Deserved, but Presented the Old Gentleman With a Plan, And Birds-Eye-View of All the Encampment of Magdenbergh, Which Pleased him so Much that he Also Sent this /as he had Done the first/ to the Prince of Orange and to the Duke of Brunswick, As a Proof of his Military Manoeuvres &c And Which had the Desired Effect, Since I not only now Became one of his Favourites, but he Declared his highest Esteem for the Scots and English—And Even Promised to Recommend me in Particular at Court—God; what a Change; I took at once the Blame of All former Animosity on Myself, And Could have Devoured the *Old Carl* With Caresses, But now all his Attention Was Suddenly Attracted by Affairs of More Consequence Since on the 14th Came the News that Some Rebels Huts Were Discover'd near the Sea Side that Capt. Meyland had Marched in Quest of the Enemy With 140 Men of the Society Troops Who had Actually found them Out, but /in Wading through a Deep Marsh/ had been first Attacked by the Negroes, Who had *Kill'd* Several of his Men /Amongst Whom was his Nephew a Young Volunteer/ Wounded More, and Beat back the Whole Detachment, After they had Already past the Marsh, And Were Mounting fast on the Opposite Beech to Storm the Village—This News Proved that the Sable foes Were not to be Triffled With, though they Were Discovered; In Consequence of Which Orders Were immediately issued for All the Troops that were Able to March, to keep in readiness Viz. Fourgeouds Marines, the Society Regiment, and My favourite Rangers, Who Wanted no Spur, and now hardly Could be keep'd Back till the Others were Prepared, And Which Troops Were to be Assembled at a Place of Rendezvous henceforth to be named, While Also a Detachment Marched to La Rochelle to Give information—Now All was Alive and in a flow of Spirits, Some in hopes that this Decisive Stroke Would End the War And theyr Misery Some from hoping to find a Little Plunder Amongst the Enemy, and some from a Motive of Revenge to these Poor Naked People, Who as I have Related before Originally Revolted on Account of Bad Usage and now took every Means to Retaliate Upon theyr Persecutors.—

> Some Afric Chief will rise, who Scorning Chains,
> Racks, tortures, flames—Excruciating Pains,
> Will Lead his injur'd friends to Bloody fight,
> And in the flooded Carnage take Delight;
> Then Dear repay us in some Vengeful War
> And Give us Blood for Blood, And Scar for Scar

However Let me Now do Col: Fourgeoud the Justice to Relate, till What Length Went his *Humanity* Against his Enemies, When in my Opinion, and in the Opinion of many Others he might have Attacked and Routed them with Advantage, Within a Fortnight After receiving the Intelligicence; but Which Vengeance he had the Good nature to Spin Out for no Less a Time than to the 20th August, being Above 2 Calendar Months After, And for Which Remarkable Generosity no Doubt, the Rebel Chief *Bony,* And All his *Black* Fraternity, Were Greatly Ob-

The Jaguar, or Tiger of Terra-Firma.

The Tiger-Cat of Surinam.

London, Published Dec.r 1.st 1798 by J. Johnson, S.t Paul's Church Yard.

lidged to him, Who thus had both the Time, And Advantage, of the Short Dry Season, to Look Out for a New Settlement, to Where they might retreat When they Should be Drove from theyr Present Habitation, by the Blood thirsty *Christians;* While to keep the Scales in Balance on the other hand Fourgeoud treated Many of his Friends With the greatest Barbarity—but I as mention'd Above Was now his Favourite And as Such Will Faithfully relate how the time Was Spent During the interval Without Partiality to Anyone Until the Day of the Grand Attack upon the Negroes.—

In the first place while one Cap.t *Perrett-Gentelly* had Nearly been Drown'd in One of the Neighbouring Creeks, the Account Come that *Cap.t Brand* Was Almost Dead with Sickness at the Hope, Which was at Present /viz where the troops were Quarter'd/ no better than a pest house And to this place As being one of his Favourites he Fourgeoud now Singled *me* Out. Declaring I might thank my Sound Constitution for Bestowing on me this honour—I now too Evidently Discover'd that All his Friendship Was only Flattery for my Paintings, &c And My Natural hatred having rekindled Against him Apace, for thus Sending me to be ingloriously Kil'd by Inches, When he had such a Fair Opportunity in View to see me Shot, I Departed instantly With this Salutary Consolation that I Should.—

> Curse him with my Last Departing Breath,
> And show the Vigour of my Life & Death,
> Then Boldly Venture to the World Unknown,
> Which Could not Use me Worse than he had Done

At my Arrival on the hope, my Orders Were to Send Poor Cap.t Brand *not Down,* but *up to* Magdenbergh but this Young Man Frustrated the Tyranical Command, Which he Suspecting had Sett out With a tent-Barge to Paramaribo before I Came, Where he Was no Sooner Carried to his Lodgings, than he expired of a Burning Fever, And a Broken heart; no one Could be More Regretted than Cap.t Brant nor ever Lost Fourgeod a Better Officer, or I a Better Friend, but he poor youth Was no More—

This being the Second Commander Dead in so short a time I Quietly took for my Motto.—

> Hodie tibi Cras Mihie

But I Was happily Mistaken, And Continued as Well as Ever I was in all my Life, following the Advice of Old *Caramaca,* And Bathing in the River twice ev'ry Day While I Despised Shoes and Stockings as Unnecessary Lumber—

I now Receiv'd a Visit from the Governor Mr *Nephew* on his Return from his Estate Appecappee to Paramaribo, With Whom I Condoled on the Loss of his Lady who was Lately Dead, I Also Received dayly Visits from Several Planters Who Complimented me With refreshments from theyr Plantations—Did Ever I Describe the Dress and Manner of Living of these West India Nabobs? if not here it is—A *Planter* in Surinam When he Lives on his Estate /Which is But Seldom, they Preferring the Society of Paramaribo/ Gets out of his Hammock With the rising Sun, viz. about 6 OClock in the Morning, When he Makes his Appearance Under the Piazza of his House, Where his Coffee is ready Waiting on him, Which is Generally Uses with his Pipe in place of toast And Butter, And Where he is Attended by half a Dozen of the Finest Young Slaves both Male and Female of the plantation to Serve him. At this *Sanctum Sanctorum* he Next is Accoasted by his *Overseer,* Who Regularly Every Morning Attends at his Levee, And having Made his Bows at Several Yards Distance, With the Deepest Respect, informs his Greatness What Work Was Done the day Before, What Negroes Deserted, Died, Fell Sick, Recover'd, Were bought, or Born, And Above All things Which of them Neglected their Work, Affected Sickness, had been Drunk, or Absent &c. Who are Generally presented, being Secur'd by the Bastias or Negro Drivers, And instantly tied Up to the Beams of the Piazza, or a Tree, Without so Much as being heard, When the Flogging begins, Men, Women, or Children, Without Exception, on theyr Naked Bodies, by Long hempin Whips that Cut round at Every Lash, and Crack like a Pistol, During which they Alternately repeat *Dankee Massera,* /Thank you Master/ but While he Stalks up and Down With his Overseer, Affecting not so Much as to hear theyr Cries, till they are Sufficiently Mangled, When they are Emediately Untied and Order'd to Return to theyr Work. Without Even a Dressing—This Ceremony over, the *Dressy Negro* /a black Surgeon/ Comes to Make his Report, Who being Dismissed With a hearty Curse, Makes her Appearance a Superannuated Matron, With All the Young Negro Children of the Estate, Over Whom She is Governess, Who being Clean Washed in the River, Clap their hands, and Cheer in Chorus, When they are Sent Away to Breakfast And the Levee Ends with a Low Bow from the Overseer—Now his Worship Sa[u]nters Out in his Morning Dress Which Consists in a pair of the Finest holland Trowsers, White Silk Stockings, and red or Yellow Morocco Slippers, the Neck of his Shirt open & Nothing Over it, A Loose flowing Night-Gown of the Finest India Chintz Excepted—on his head is a Cotton Night Cap, As thin as a Cobweb, and Over that an Enormous Beaver Hat, to Keep Coverd his Meagre Visage from the Sun, Which is Al-

1775—JUNE 20

ready the Colour of Mahogany, While his Whole Carcase Seldom Weigh'd above 8, or 10 Stone, being Generally Exausted to the Climate and Dicipation, And to Give a better idea of this fine Gentleman, I here Represent him to the Reader, With a pipe in his Cheek / Which Almost Every Where keeps him Company/ And receiving a Glass of Madeira and Watter, from a female Quaderoon Slave to Refresh him During his Walk—

Having Loitred About his Estate, or Sometimes rode a horseback to his fields, to View his Encreasing Stores, he returns About Eight OClock, When, if he Goes Abroad, he Dresses, but if not, remains just as he is—Should the *first* take place, having Only Exchang'd his Trowsers for a Pair of thin Linnen or Silk Breeches, he Sits Down and holding out one Foot After Another, Like a horse going to be Shod, A Negro Boy puts on his Stockings And Shoes, Which he also Buckles &c, While Another Dresses his hair, his Wigg, or Shaves him; and a third is fanning him to keep off the gnatts or Musqueto's—Having now Shifted, he puts on a Very thin Coat and Waistcoat All White, when Under the Shade of an Umbrella Carried by a Black boy, he is Conducted to his Barge Which is Waiting him With 6 or 8 Oars, Well provided With fruit, Wine, And Watter, and Tobacco, by his Overseer, And who no Sooner has Seen him Depart than he Resumes the Command With a Vengeance—But Should this Nabob Remain on his Estate, in that Case he remains as he is, And Goes to Breakfast About ten OClock, for which A Table is Spread in the large hall, Provided With a Bacon ham, hung-Beef, fowls, or pigeons broil'd hot from the Gridiron; plantains, & Sweet-Cassavas, roasted; Bread, Butter, Cheese &c to Which he Drinks Strong-Beer, such as Ale, & Porter And a Glass of Madeira Ranish to Mozel wine And while the Cringing Overseer Sits at the further end keeping his Proper Distance, both being Served by the most beautiful Slaves that Could ever be pick'd out; And this is Call'd Breaking the Poor Gentlemans fast. After this he takes a Book, Plays at Chess, or Billards–Entertains himself With Musick &c, till the heat of the Day forces him to Return to his Cotton-hammock to enjoy his Meridian nap With Which he would no More Dispense than a Spaniard With his *Siesto,* and in Which he rocks to and fro, like a Performer on the Slack rope, till he falls Asleep, Without Either bed or Covering, & during Which time he is fan'd by a Couple of his black Attendants, to keep him Cool &c—

About 3 OClock he Awakes by Natural instinct When having Washed, And Perform'd himself he sits Down to Dinner, Attended as at Breakfast by his *Deputy Governor,* And Sable pages, Where nothing is Wanting that the World Can Afford, in a Western Climate, of Meat, fowls,

A Surinam Planter in his Morning Dress.

Venisons—fish, Vegetables, Fruits &c. While the Most exquisite Wines are often Squander'd Away in Profusion; After this a Cup of Strong Coffee, and A Liqueur finish the repast. at 6 OClock he is Again Waited on by his Overseer, Attended as in the Morning by Negro Drivers, and Prisoners, When the flogging once more having Continued for some time, and the Necessary Orders being Given for the Next Days Work, the Assembly is Dismissed, and the Eveining Spent With weak punch, Sangaree, Cards and Tobacco—His Worship, Generally begins to Yawn About 10 or 11 OClock—When he Withdraws, And being Undressed by his sooty pages, he retires to rest, where he passes the Night in the Arms of one or other of his Sable Sultanas, for he Always keeps a Seraglio, till about 6 OClock in the Morning When he Again is Reparing to his piazza Walk, Where his Pipe and Coffee are waiting his Commands, And Where /With the Rising Sun/ he begins his Round of Dicipation like a little king, Despotick, Absolute And Without Controlle, And Which Cannot but have the Greater Relish to a Man, Who in his Own Country viz. Europe was ten to one a—Nothing—Which in *this* Colony is too frequently the Case, Where Plantations Are Sold Upon Credit, And Which is Left /by the Absent Proprietor/ to the Sworn Apprisers, Who by Selling them Cheap find theyr Accompt in the Buyer, And Which while he Lives at the Above Rate, Under Pretence of bad Crops, Mortality Amongst the Slaves &^{c}, like an Upstart Rascal as he is, Massacres the Negroes by Double Labour, Ruins, And Pillages the Estate of All its Productions, Which he Sells Clandestinely for Ready Money, Makes a Purse, and Goes to the Devil—However Exceptions take place in Every Circumstance, And I have known as many Good Gentlemen that were planters in Surinam As I ever Would Desire to be Acquainted With as I have Already Mention'd—As for the *Ladies* they indulge themselves as Much after the Same Manner I have Describ'd Above, as their Distinction of Sex Will Admit of, While Decency and Decorum, /Nay Even Compassion, I am Sorry to say it/ Are With them too Often terms totally Unknown—I Say too Often, Yet, While Such a Heavenly Woman as Mrs Elizth Danforth now Godefrooy And a Few more, Whose Characters shine With treeple lustre, Draw a Veil Over All the Other Imperfections too Common to theyr Sex in this Climate—

A few Words More and I take my leave, Which is that Hospitality is in no Country Practised, With Less Ceremony, and Greater Diffusion; a Stranger being Every Where at home, And finding his Table And his bed at Whatever Estate he Chuses to Step Ashore, Which is the More Convenient, no inns being Ever Met With in Any of the Surinam Rivers.—

Should the reader be Surprised at the Above Account of a Surinam planters Manner of Living, let him peruse M\[r\] *Smiths* tour through the United States, Where he Will find that of a Virginia Planter little Different, though a M\[r\] *Glen's* Act of Barbarity to his Wife in publick /as described by that Gentleman/ is Unknown in Surinam, Perhaps not from Want of Inclination, but from Want of Vigour And bodily Capacity—And now farewell to *the Nabobs,* having first Mentioned a few kinds of fish With Which I Entertained them, viz. the *Sunfish,* the *Snakefish,* and the *Spotted-Cat.*—

The *Sun fish* frequents both the Salt and fresh Watter Like the Salmon, it is About 18 or 20 inches Long, Shaped Not Unlike a Kite, And being Covered Over With Scales of a Golden Colour, Darts forth Very Bright Beams as it Swims in Clean Water, from Which it has derived its Name.—The *Snake-fish* takes its Name from its Resemblance to that reptile, this is a Black Eel, With a White Belly, it is not Large, And Very Common in All the Rivers[.] *The Spotted-Cat* is Call'd So from its Taby Colour, And Long Antennae, or Whiskers, this fish is form'd not Unlike a Pike With Very Sharp teeth, but it has no Scales; it is Extremely Fat, Weighing Sometimes Above 70 Pound, but its Flesh is Yellow And not at All Esteemed as Delicate Eating, however here Excellent fish is Never Wanting, Such as the Newmara, Passassee, Warrappa, Jackee &c &c—

The Hope With All this Was now Truly a Most Shocking Place of residence, Where I Much Lamented my *Former* Cottage, and Sweet *Companion* the one in the Ruins, the other at Paramaribo, and Where at preasent not a Man Was to be Seen Without Agues, Fevers, Rotten Limbs &c And Where the Bloody Flux also began to Make its Discovery, While they had Neyther Surgeon, Medicines, or as Much as a Light, & Verry little Bread left. thus I Distributed All my Boston Bisquit, Lemons, Oranges, Sugar, Wine, Ducks And Fowls Amongst the Unhappy Sufferers—With a few Spermacety Candles, While I sent up to the hospital at Magdenbergh to Day, two Sick Officers, *Orleigh* and *Fransen,* With All the Privates that Could bear to be Transported, And my Humble Entreaties to be Soon Relieved from so Very Disagreeable Situation, for Which indeed there was not the Smallest glimpse of Necessity. And to be one of the Party to March Against the Rebels—

In Short While the Accounts Came from below that Fresh Nests of Negroes Were Discovered, Even Close to Paramaribo, the News Came from Above that the Troops there Were Dying Away to No Manner of Purpose, Where Amongst Others Were Expired on the 22\[d\] A Cap\[t\] *Seybourgh* brother to the Noted Colonel, thus *the 3\[rd\]* Cap\[t\] in one Month.—

🙞 And from Where now Arrived two fine Young Officers, /one of Whom had been page to the prince of Orange/ Ruined for theyr Lives, by having Got Ruptures, And Which all Was Occasiond by Fourgeouds Unaccountably Persisting to Cruize through the Woods in the Rayny Season—when it is so Very Slip'ry and he Could Do Nothing, while Now it Was so Dry he Scorn'd to Stirr & When he so Well knew Where the Enemy Was to be Met With—But as I have Said Before he Gave for Reasons, that in the Wet Season the Enemy Might easier be Starved—how Much he gain'd by these Measures Shall be Seen in the Sequel.—

🙞 This Evening one of our Marines one *Spanknevel* was Missing Without Any Conjecture Could be Formed What Was Come of him, till the twenty ninth when one of the Negroes having been Out hunting, his Dogs brot him to a Tree, Where Was Suspended by the neck to one of the Branches /With a Nebee/ the Unfortunate Man, as Naked as he Was Born, Exhibiting a Dreadful Spectacle, being Swell'd like a Drown'd Carion, by the heat of the Climate and Already Swarming in Corruption—he Was a Germain, And had hang'd himself Utterly from Despair, but What Appear'd Singular was that not one of his Comrades Would so Much as Cut him Down to be Buried in Spite of What I Could Say, Alledging that to touch him Was Becoming as Infamous as he Was himself.—However the Negroes Were Exempt from this Prejudice And by my orders he Was Interr'd.—

Now Came at Last to my Great Satisfaction an order for my Relief, And Another Capt having taken the Command in my place I Left the Miserable Situation Almost instantly, and that Very Evening Arrived at *Goed-Accoord* In Company With Capt Bolts Who had been Down, and Where the Planter Mr *De Lange* With his Lady happened to be, We Were received With Much hospitality—This Sugar Estate is as I Said the Last that is Cultivated in *Comowina*. Where the Negroes are Allow'd to do just as they please for fear of an Insurrection And Which indeed Was Very Little—here We Saw Which to Us hetherto had been a Novelty Viz that the Young Negro Women Who Attended as Servants at Table &c And Who Were Come to the Age of Puberty Should all be Stark-Naked, Without so much as a fig Leaf—Had in my Cheeks at this time been left Any Blood, I must have Blushed—however Asking the Cause of this Strange Phenomen I Was Answered by the Lady that it Was intended so by their Mothers and Matrons to Promote their Growth, by thus being Detected in theyr too Early Cohabitations With the Other Sex, that other Wise took place.—And indeed finer figures I never beheld, Who Were a Treat to Every spectator of a real Taste, Let prudes and Coquets Say What they Will, Nature Will be Nature Still, And no Stays, Gowns or Petticoats Can Ever Correct the Cimetry and

Native Graces of a Well Proportion'd Young Woman, but indeed may serve to hide theyr Defects—While the Strength, livelyness & Agility Anex'd to a Natural State, are Great Inducements to Plead in its favour. And While even in the Black Women theyr Sparkling Eyes.—Ivory Teeth, and remarkable Cleanliness All over, fully Compensates for the Silk Ribbonds, Gold lace, and Borrow'd Feathers that Grace the to[o] many Languid Looks, Sallow Complexions, deform'd Bodies, And Broken Constitutions, of our European Contriwomen—

At Goet Acoord the Men Were no Less Fine, Witness *Philander* /as I have Said/ And Which Was All Owing to the Negroes here Living After theyr own Way Without being Crushed Under the Yoke, And Mangled by the the Lash of a Relentless European, And Which Proves that the *Africans* in a State of nature, Are not that Wretched People Which they are by too Many ignorant European Wretches Represented—

❧ Having here dined next day and Drank a hearty Glass of Wine We Departed for Magdenbergh, An hour before Sun Set, Greatly Against the advice of M.^r and M.^{rs} De Lange, in a Small Barge with 6 oars, and Covered with a Loose Awning—We had not rowed above 2 Miles When not Only Night Came on, but We were Overtaken by Such a Show'r of Rayn as had nearly Sunk us, the Boats Gunnel not being more than 2 inches Above the Watter, however by the help of our hats We kept her Swimming, While a Negro Sit upon the Bow, With both his Arms Streight out Before him to Prevent Us from being Overset by Unadvertantly running Against the roots of Mangroves &^c Which thickly line both the Banks of the rivers All upwards—in this pickle and Hels Darkness, at 10 OClock at Night We Came to the *Jacob* being Just afloat and no More, Where Bolts and I no Sooner Step'd ashoar like Drown'd Cats that the Boat Sunk with All the rest that was in her, /the Slaves Swimming Ashoare/, And Amongst Which Was My Box With my Whole Journal, And All my Paintings that had cost me Above 2 Years so Much labour Care and Attention.—I Was truly Distracted at this Loss, When a Skilful Negroe having Dived Several Times to the Bottom before 12 OClock brought up my Little Treasure, Which, though thoroughly Soaked I Was happy to have Again in My hands, Which ended our Shipwreck. And We fell all Asleep round a Swinging fire by which I Made Shift to Dry Myself, and my Poor papers—

❧ Next Morning we Again Set Out & row'd for Magdenbergh When Coming About half way, our Voyage Was Obstructed by an enormous Tree that Was Accidently fallen Across the Creek, So that we Could Neither Drag the Boat over or under it, thus We Were Obliged to return to the Jacob Again, from Whence We now Proceeded to Magdenbergh on Foot, through thorns roots, Brambles, and briers, And Where We Finally Arrived torn, and Bloody by the Scratches &c, While My Ancle Which had been Nearly Recover'd Was Now wounded Afresh to the Bone, the Skin And Flesh being quite torn Away by the Numberless inconveniences that Obstructed our Passage—

There we Were now Acquainted that Mr. *Orleigh* /one of the two Officers that I had Sent up to Magdenbergh from the Hope on the 23d Ult/ Was Also no more—Thus Died Most all our Gentlemen that had been During the Last Month Upon the Hope, from Whome Scarcely one Single Private Returned in Health, And Which I Will Maintain Was Greatly owing to the Dry & Burning hot Month of June, When the *Sun* Suddenly Scorched them After Marching, And even Sleeping in Cool Wat'ry Swomps, And heavy Rayns, During the whole Wet Season—But Col: Fourgeoud Consoled himself with Declaring /as he had Done before/ that the Greater his List of Mortality the Greater Should be his Fame When he return'd to Europe, but his People thought Otherwise, Some of Whom Seeing themselves thus Sacrificed to no Purpose, even *Cried* aloud With Despair.

> And the Songs of the Temple shall be howlings in that Day Saith the Lord God there Shall be many Dead Bodies in every Place they Shall Cast them forth With Silence—Amos 8 Chat v. 3

However I Still Escaped this Ceremony by my fine Constitution & great flow of Spirits, Which God Forgive me I Determin'd now Forcibly to keep up from Sinking, by Laughing, Singing Damming, and Sinking [singing] While All the Rest were Crying and Dying, around me—

CHAPTER 19th

*The Troops march to Barbacoeba in Rio Cottica—Frensy Fever[—]
Gratitude in a English Sailor—
Discription of the Government of Surinam—Some account of a
Noted American during the late War—
Scene of unprecedented Generosity*

The rayny Season being now Again at hand, & Colonel Fourgeoud having Pick'd out All the remaining healthy People, Who Amounted to About 180 in Number, he this Morning Set out upon his March for *Barbacoeba,* in the River Cottica, Which Spot he Appointed as the General Rendezvous before the Grand Attack on the Rebels–And at Which Place Were to Join him the troops of the Society And the Corps of free Negroes or Black Rangers—Of this Party I had the honor to be one. but on the Surgeons Declaring I Run the Hazard of Loosing my Foot by Amputation if I March'd in the Woods I Was Order'd to remain at Magdenbergh, With Liberty if I Soon Recover'd to Joyn Fourgeoud the Best Way I Could at Barbacoeba. My Limb Was Now indeed So Sweld And my Wound so Black by the Gangrene or Mortification that I Could hardly Stand Without Pain And of Which I Shall bear the Mark While I Live—During this confinement I received Dayly Presents from Philander, And the Other Negroes I being Always Extremely kind to them, Amongst Which Was a Dish of *Mountain-Cabbage*—This Grows As I have Mentioned Formerly in All the Palm Trees Whatev'r But that Growing in the *Mountain-Cabbage-Tree* is Preferable to All the Rest— this tree is High Sometimes Near to 60 Feet, the Trunk of a Brown Colour, hard, Ligneous, Divided in Short Joynts, And Pithy Within like the Elder; it is thick in Proportion. Streight And Tapering like the Mast of a Ship—Near the Top the Tree takes a Fluted Green form, Occasion'd by the husky Tegument, that forms the Branches, And

1775—JULY 3

Which near the Summit Diverges in a Horizontal Direction, like the Crown of a Pineapple or Ananas, & Which Branches are Covered Over on both Sides With Strong Pennated Leaves About 3 Feet Long, of a Deep Green Colour And Sharp pointed, but Which are Folded And Confusely intermix'd, not Dropping in that Graceful form like those of the Manicole, or Coco-nut Tree, Already Described, the Seed is inclosed in a brownish kind of Spatha that Arises from the Center of the Branches, And hanging Downwards Consists in Small Roundish Nuts not Unlike a Bunch of Dried Grapes, but Much Longer in Proportion to their Circumference—if the Cabbage is Wanted the Whole tree Must be Cut Down When it is Divested first of its Branches. And next of that fluted Green husky Tegument that forms them. After this the heart or Cabbage is taken out, White, long About 2 or 3 Feet, and round Resembling a Polish'd ivory Cylinder, Which is no other than a Kind of Tender Longitudinal White Flakes like Silk Ribbands Ready to form the Succeeding Green Tegument, but so Close that they make a Crisp Solid Body—this When eat raw tastes Something like the Kernel of an Almond but is More tender and More Delicious—When Cut in Pieces and Boil'd, it Eats like Cole-flower—it may be Also Peel'd in the Above long thin Flakes When it makes an Excellent Sallad, but too Much of it Either Raw or Dress'd, is Unwholesome, being Apt to Occasion diaretick Complaints—It is in this Cavity /after the Cabbage is Removed from it/ that a Black Beetle deposits its Spawn, from Which the *Palm-tree-Worm* is produced /as I have Say'd/ And Which feed on the Remaining tender Substance. When it Begins to rot, till they Acquire the Size Already Mention'd•–Though those in the Manicole, and Other Trees of the Palm Species grow not so Large, and Are Also Differently Shaped—The *Maureecee Tree* by the French Call'd Latanie is Certainly the highest of All the Palm tree Species or indeed of any Species in the Forrest of Guiana, And I do Aver to have Seen Some of these Trees Whose Lofty Summits Appeared to Rise no Less than a hundred feet from the Surface of the Earth, While the Circumference of their Trunks Was 10 or 12 Feet—The trunk of this Tree is Largest at About one fourth Part from its Root from Whence it Tapers, not only Upwards, but Downwards. Also, And Which Singularity has perhaps Escaped All other Writers—it is of a Light brown or Gray Colour and divided in Joynts all the way upwards to its branches, while the inside is a pithy Substance like all others—at the top it diverges in long green arched boughs, naked til near theyr extremity when these again diverge or digitate, in long broad leafs of a pale green Colour and Disposed in

• —See Page [338]—

an Orbicular Manner with great regularity not Unlike Sun Beams, or as a Lady fan Expanded—As the Young Branches Spring up from the Center in the Summit, the Old ones fade at the Bottom, and hang Downward, Shrevel'd, and Dangling in the Wind—From the heart of the green Leaves the Indians Extract long White Fibres or Threads, as they Do from the Silk Grass Plant*—& which being Equally as Strong, Serve as Cords When twisted to String their Boughs [bows], Make nets &c—from the Middle of the Branches Appears the seed, hanging Down Also in the form of a large Truss of Onions, I have Seen many Prints Representing palm trees But take the Liberty to Say that Most of Them are impostures on the Publick, Which have Either been done from fancy, or from a Very Bad Description While All those that I represent to the Reader, Where taken from Nature on the Spot—viz the *Cocoa-nut* Tree, the *Manicole,* the *Mountain Cabbage,* And the *Maureecee* Trees, Whose Branches And Leaves, Are All Extremely Different from Each other And not Confounded, as they are in two Many paultry Publications—The two First the reader has Already Seen And the 2 Others I now Offer to his View Where **A** is the trunk of the Mountain Cabbage Tree, **B** one of its Branches, Separated from the Rest, And **C** the Seed or Husky Spatha inclosing it—**D** is the trunk of the Maureecee tree, and **E** one of its Branches Dropping Down—**F** is the Beetle that Produces The Mountain Cabbage, and Maureecee Worms **G,** And Which are not so Large or So Delicious as the former—

Having had no Opportunity to Show in What Manner the indians, and African Blacks Assend Trees. There by Letter **H** represent a Negroe Climbing a Young Maureecee tree, to Which they Dont Cling with Arms and Legs, but taking the Trunk between their hands, they place the Soals of their Feet Against it, And thus Walk up in a Most Astonishing Manner, by Which they save their Skin from the Bark, Which Certainly must require Verry great Strength and Activity—

Having thus far Dwelt on the Palm tree Species &c I must now once More Return to Domestick Occurances—I have Say'd that all the Officers And Most of the Privates that had been Station'd at the Hope Lately had Died, or Were Sent up dangerously Ill, While I had Escaped the Contagion, but Alas now it Became my Turn having only had a Reprieve And no more Since on the Ninth I was Ceised With the Same Burning Fever, that had Carried off the rest, What happened from that time till the Morning of the Twelfth I know not, When I Was a Little Better, And one of our Officers a Mr *Luck* put a paper in my hand, being my own Epitaph as I had repeated it in the Frensy Fever & Which

* —Dr Bancroft I think Calls this the Silk Cotton tree —

The Mountain-Cabbage & Maureecee Tree.

London, Published Dec.r 1.st 1791, by J. Johnson, St Pauls Church Yard.

he had Wrote Down While he Was Sitting on his Chest Under my Hammock, And Which to be Sure Was a Masterly Performance here it is.—But Yet before I Presume to Transcribe it to the Publick Who may Doom it as Savouring of the Marvellous, let me Ask them the Question, how often have it not Been Remark'd, that the Effects of Enebriation have been Indusive to the Composition of Poetry or Musick, And Why May not then the Effects of a fever be the Same? Thus here it Goes

Under this Stone,
Lays the Skin and the Bone,
While the Flesh was Long gone of *poor Stedman*

Who Still took up his Pen,
And Exousted his Brain,
In the Hopes these Last Lines Might be red Man,

Of his Life he was tir'd,
At no more he Aspir'd,
D——nd the rogues, Shut his Eyes & Went Quietly to bed man

It has been Remark'd [a]lso that *Such Frensys* Are Very Bad Omans, be that as it may, but being Come a Little to Myself again I determin'd to Confute *this* Pretty Elegy, at least at Magdenbergh, from Which I took my Congee Without Any Ceremony, Fourgeoud &c. being Absent, and Attended by my Poor Black Boy /Who was now Also Sick from Day and Night Watching at my Hammock/ Got Myself Transported in a Crazy Canoo, So far as *Oranjebo* on my Way to Paramaribo after giving over the command to another officer—in Going Down I Met a Barge Again Crowded With Seek Officers & Men from the Hope, Which Was by this time as Dangerous as Smirna—

Next Day I Was Excessively ill, And *Qwacco* Also–thus that While We Could have no help or Refreshment at Oranjebo /Which Cap.t Meyland had left/ We were too Seek both to be Transported any Further—I now thought myself in Hell by the Burning Heat of the Climate and my Fever, Still With this Consolation that While Providence Will Allow one to be so Cursed in this World, he Will Certainly not Permit Them to be Again Damn'd in the Other, Where he Promises that "Should their Sins be as Scarlet, they Shall be White as Snow & though they be red like Crimson that they Shall be as Wool"—

In Short on the 14.th once More farewell to this Unhospitable Spot–and now

Bear me Pomona! to thy Citron Groves,
To Where the Lemon and the piercing Lime,
With the deep Orange glowing thro' the Green,
Their Lighter Glories Blend—Lay me reclin'd
Beneath the Spreading tamarind that shakes,
Fann'd by the Breeze, its fever-Cooling fruit.

However I Could Reach no further than Goet Accoord here on the fifteenth I Was Expected to Die, Where an old negro Woman found Means to Make me partake of Some Buttermilk boild with some Barley and Molasses, Which Was the first food I had tasted Since the 9th And which Certainly did me a great Deal of Good so that the day following I was Again Able to be transported And the Black boy was much Better—This Evening I Reached Fauquenbergh Where I was met by a Packet of 6 or 8 Letters from Different Friends Accompanied With Presents of Hung Beef, Bullocks Tongues, Madeira, Porter, rum And 2 Gallons with Excellent Shrub, besides a fine Bacon Ham, And a Beautiful *Pointer* from the identical Chas *Macdonald,* the English Sailor, Which he had brought for me from Virginia, in Return for the Little Civility I had formerly Showed him so unexpectedly at the hope, And Which Mark of this poor fellows Gratitude, and Generosity /the true Characteristic of a British Tar/ Gave me Greater Pleasure than All the other things I received Put together, two Letters Excepted, the one from Mr *Lude* at Amsterdam, And the other from Mr *Degraff* his Administrator at Paramaribo, Acquainting me finally, And to my Heartfelt Satisfaction, that the Amiable *Joana* and her *Little Boy* Were at my Disposal But at no Less a Price than 2,000 Florins, Amounting With Other Expences to near £200, a Soom Which I Was no more Able to pay than to fly, And While I Already Owed the £50 that I had Borrowed for the Black boy *Qwacco's* Redemption—indeed She Joanna was a Charming Young Woman, And though Apprized at one Twentieth Share of the Whole Estate, Which had been Sold for 40000 Florins, no Price Could be too Dear for one that Was so Valuable to me—King Solomon Well Observes that "as Cold Water is to a thirsty Soul so is Good News from a far Country." And this News had the Same Effect on Me, Without ever once Reflecting how I should raise so much Money, Since from that Moment I found like the weight a Milstone removed from my Breast, And While I Gave All the Presents I received, except the *Ham* and the *Dog* to Joanas Relations at Fauquenbergh, Who Loaded me With Adorations and Caresses—Oh that I Could have rose a Sum to Purchas Every one of them—I now Found Myself though Exceedingly Weak so much Better that on the next Day I went down so far as the Estate *Bergshove* from Whence the Administrator–a M^r

Gourlay humanely Caused me to be Transported to Paramaribo in a Decent tent Boat With 6 Oars, and Where relapsing I arrived Just alive and no More on the Evening of the Nineteenth having Past the Last night at the Estate Called the *Jalosee*—

I Will not leave the River Comowina Without Presenting to the reader a View of *Magdenbergh* from the tempatee creek, and a Peep of *Calais* from the Hope, at the Mouth of the Casaweenica—

Being now in a Comfortable Lodging at M:̲ De la Mares, And Attended by so Good a Nurse as Joana, I Recovered apace, and Was so Well that on the 25th I Was Able to Scramble Out for the First time, And Dine With M:̲s Godefrooy, M:̲ De Graaff not being in Town, to Finish Matters Concerning *Joanas* Emancipation, Who had now Once more Literally Saved my Life—At this Table was never Wanting All the healthy and Refreshing Nourishment that I Stood in need of With the best of Fruits—Among the Articles Condusive to restore health Are Reckond in this Country All the different kind of Pepper, Which it Affords, And the Acid Particularly of Limes—amongst the First are the *Cica* Pepper, the *Lattacaca,* and the *Dago peepee* as they are Call'd in Surinam, the Negroes Denominating Every thing from its Resemblance to Another, but Which Are known in Europe by the Appellations of *Cayenne Piment,* and *Capsicum*—the first And indeed most all is Call'd *Cayenne,* from the *french* Settlement of that Name in Guiana, but *Cica-Pepper* from its round Shape, And Size, being Much like the insect Call'd Chigoe Already Describ'd; the Next resembles Rats Excrements &c &c—All the Above Species Besides some Others Grow on low Green Shrubs, And are Equally as hot as fire & Ready to Excoriate ones Mouth, to Which they With more Propriety may be Compared from theyr high Scarlet Colour—The Europeans Seldom eat Anything Without it, but the Blacks, And Especially the indians, Swallow it by Handfuls both as a Relish And a Certain Cure Almost in every Distemper—

The Limes Grow on Beautiful Trees like Lemons, While the Leaf and the fruit is a great Deal Less—The Limes have a fine thin Shell And are Extremely full of the Richest, Acid that I know, Which is a Great Blessing to the Sick Soldiers & Sailors in this Colony who have them for the Picking—The Last returning Daily With Large Hampers full on Board their Vessels—In Surinam are Made whole hedges of Lime-Trees, And All Round Paramaribo they Grow Wild—It is a Pity this Fruit Cannot be Transported to Europe, but Whole Casks, of its Juice Are frequently Sent over, While they are Also pickled and Preserved in Large Jars by the inhabitants—The Limes are rather a Brighter Yellow than the Lemons And have a Particular fine flavour—

View of Magdenbergh, on Tempate Creek.

View of Calays & the Creek Cawinica.

London, Published Dec.r 1.st 1791, by J. Johnson, St. Paul's Church Yard.

1775—JULY 25

At the Des[s]ert /Amongst many other Excellent fruits/ I Observed one Call'd here the *Mammee*-Apple and Some Very Good Nuts; The Mammee Apple grows on a Tree the Sise of an Orange Tree, With a Grey Coloured Bark, the Wood is Whiteish and Coarse The Leaf verry thick, Polished And of a Triangular form Without Fibres—This fruit is nearly Round and the Size of a Small Shadeck, viz 5 or 6 inches in Diameter, Covered With a Russet Coarce Skin—The pulp has the Colour and Consistancy of a Carrot, Enclosing two Large Stones With Bitter Kernels, And is in the Same Manner Cut in Slices, but is of a Delicious Taste, Sweet Mixed With Acid, And a Smell Superior in fragrance to Almost any Other Fruit in the Colony—

The Nuts were two Species Usually Call'd *Pistachio,* but by the Negroes Pinda, one kind of them Resembles Small Chesnuts, And Grow by Bunches upon a Tree—the Others Belong to a *Shrub* and Grow Under Ground, Both have Sweet Oily Kernels the Last 2 in One Pod, And Are an Agreeable Eating, More so When roasted in hot Ashes— To illustrate the Above Description I Present the Reader With the Plate here Annex'd, where

- **A.** is a Sprig of Limes in full Ripeness,
- **B.** the Cayenne or Cica Pepper,
- **C.** the Pimento Pepper or Lattacaca,
- **D.** the Capsicum Call'd Dago Peepee,
- **E** the Mammee-Apple When it is fully ripe
- **F.** the Leaf Above of a Beautiful Green
- **G.** the Leaf Below of a Yellowish Green
- **H.** the Pistacho nut in the Husk
- **I.** the Ground Pistachio in its Dried State
- **K.** one of the Kernels belonging to the Latter

The Whole of the Above Was taken from Nature though on a Smaller Scale, Yet I will Maintain, more Like the Originals than Some of Miss *Merions* With all the Boasted Reputations, for instance Who will Dispute me that the Leaf of her Lime Tree is not too Round—and if by her *Palisade-Branch* in Plate Eleven She means the *Manicole-Tree* I am Quite Confounded Never having Discovered Such a Leaf Amongst the many Thousands I have helped to Cut Down;—her Cotton *Twig,* And Especially the *Pod* Containing the Cotton Are Also, no more like that Growing in Surinam, than an Egg is like an Oyster—in another place, she Declares that *grapes* are Common in Guiana, Which I Also Contradict, While it is well known that no thin Shell'd fruits Can Ever Come to Perfection in a Tropical Climate, Such as Cherries, Currents, Strawberries, Plumbs, Apricocks, or Peaches, not even Common Apples or Pears, nay even the Oranges Lemons Shaddock, Mammee, And Anana

Limes, Capsicums, Mammy Apple &c.

or Pine Apple are Exoticks, And have been imported from Other Countries—From the Above Observations I take the Liberty to say that independent to Miss Merions beautiful and Valuable Performance, She has been Liable to Verry Notable Mistakes, Which is the Less to be Wondered at When one Considers that it is an Hundred Years Ago, since she Presented her Discoveries to the World. And since Which time Mankind in every Science has been more Enlightened—

Being now once more at Paramaribo I will in Place of the Animal and Vegetable Productions, try to give some Account of the *Government* of this fine Colony, Which I am Persuaded Some of the readers have Long ago Expected, but having not before now had the Opportunity to Gratify their Curiosity on this Subject, Was the Occasion of my Silence—

This Day Dining with his Excellency *Governor Nepvew* he Gave the following Information—

I have Already Mention'd the Charter, And that at Present Surinam belongs, *two Thirds* to the Town of Amsterdam, And *one third* to the west india Company Also that it is Governed by Several Courts of Judicature, thus I shall now proceed to Describe them in their proper order, as he Gave me the Relations, in the first place the Court of *Polity,* and *Criminal* Justice—This Consists of 13 Members Chosen by the Votes of All the Inhabitants, Each Member Continuing for Life And of Which the Governor is President, and the Commandant or Deputy Governor first Counsellor Viz—

> The Governor
> The Commandant
> The Fiscal
> The Town Clark and
> 9 Counsellors

To this Court Belongs the Decision of All *Criminal* Matters, viz *Capital* Offences only, While the Governor has the Power of Reprieving from Death & Pardoning any Convict, Without farther Ceremony Whatever—

The Court of *Civil Justice* Consists Also in 13 Members but these are Chose by the Above Court only, And renewed every 4 Years, While the Governor is Also President, viz—

> The Governor
> The Fiscal
> The Town Clark and
> 10 Counsellors

1775—JULY 26

By this Court are Decided all Capital *Law-Soots* and petty offences—

The next is the Subaltern College of Eleven Members Chosen Also by the Governor, and Court of Polity, and as the Other Renewed every 4 Years, the *Town Clerk* Excepted Who Sits for Life—The Members are one of the Late Counsellors of Justice as

Deputy President
The Town Clark and
9 Counsellors

The Above Court Supervises the publick Buildings Streets, Canaals, Orange Trees &c and Desides All Money Disputes that are Under 25 Guineas–any Sum Above that Going to the Court of Justice—

Besides these there is an Orphan And insolvent Debtors Colledge Consisting of

The Commissarys
The Town Clerk
The Book Keeper
The Treasurer and
a Sworn Secretary

The Publick revenue officers are—

The office of importation and Exportation duties,
The office of Excise and small imposts
The office for head Money, or Tax upon heads
The office for publick Sales and Vendues
The office for Retaking Negroe Deserters &c

But these I Will more Amply explain, When I Shall Speak of the General Revenue of this fine Colony, And for the Present only touch upon its Government—I have formerly Mention'd that the Governor is at the head /not only of the Civil but/ of the Military Law, the other Publick employments are Principally—

The Secretary to his Excellency the Governor
The Commisarys of the Victualling offices
4 inspectors of the Exportation Sugars
1 inspector of the Molasses Hogsheads
1 Supervisor of All the N: American Vessels
2 Publick Auctioneers
2 Sergeants or Messengers of the Court
2 Sworn Land Surveyors
3 Measurers of the Square timber
1 inspector of the Black Cattle &c

1 Sworn Overseer of Weights and Measures
3 Low Dutch Clergimen
1 French Clergiman
1 Lutherian Clergiman
3 Publick Schoolmasters &c.

The Militia Con[s]ists in Eleven Companys, With one Captain, one Lieu! one Second-Lieut, one Ensign one Secretary, and one Cashier each—And which Capt? are Generally the Sworn Apprisers of the Estates for Sale, in the Different Rivers Where they Chance to have theyr Department—

These are the Principal Functions in the Government of Surinam, and though thus Unconnectedly inserted, Are Sufficient to Give an idea of the Civil Department of this Colony, Which is not Upon a Bad Establishment at all were it not Corrupted by Sordid Avarice to the Great Detriment of this Beautiful Settlement in General, And to that of its inhabitants in Particular Especially the Miserable Negro Slaves, the *first* being no Other at Present than a Rotten Constitution, And the *Second* the Bleeding Victims to Prevent it from totally Expiring, While by Proper Management this Spot Might be made the Garden of Eden not only for the European Settlers, but Also for their African Domesticks. as I Shall Clearly Demonstrate before I finish this Work /According to my Promise Already Made/ When I Will Clearly Point out Where the Cancer lies, and Perscribe the Means of Scopping it Out *no more to Return,* thus if I Cannot like the *Good Samaritan* Pour the Balm in the Wound of any one, At Least leaving the *Perscription* to Cure the Deadly Wounds of many Thousands—

I have just said that at Present by the desperate means of *Blood* Was Prevented its total Annihilation, how much more Glorious Will it be /by those Who have it in Theyr Pow'r not only to Save this Country but many Other Valuable West india Settlements/ by the Balm of a Well Plann'd Justice and Benovelence. thus much for the Political Government of Surinam Which I Will not Leave Without Describing its *Motto* so verry Contrary to What they Profess being, "Justitia—Pietas—Fides"

The Arms are Tripartite, Which I Apprehend to be some of those of the House of Somelsdyk, the West india Company and the town of Amsterdam, Crown'd and Supported by two Lions Rampant, And With these are Stamp'd All their Card Money formerly Mentioned &c—But to proceed—

❧ I now met the Poor Sailor *Charles Macdonald* And having just Bought 30 Gallons of Grenada Rum, I Gave him a Handsome Return for his

Bacon ham, and *his Dog* besides a Fine *Bottle Screw,* Mother of Pearl set in Silver, as a Keep Sake, he Sailing the Day Following for Virginia on Board the Peggy Capt: *Lewis* Who Promised me to Make him his Mate at my Recommendentation—Speaking About *Dogs* I must make two General Remarks on *those* Animals in Guinana, viz that here, they Lose the Faculty of *Barking* if imported, While the Native Dogs Never Bark at All, And that in this Country it is Observed Also that Dogs are never Ceized With the Hidrophobiae, at least I don't Remember Ever to have Seen, or to have Heard of a Mad Dogue in Surinam, And this is the More Strange, that Dreadful distemper Being generally Occasioned in other Countries by the *Great heat* from Which even the *Canicules,* or Dog Days, have Denied that Appellation—The indians or Natives of Guiana All keep dogs which they use in Hunting, they are of a dirty White Colour, Meagre & Small With Short hair, a Sharp Mussle, and erect ears, All these are Verry Dextrous in Discovering All sorts of game While they Posess all the Wickedness of a Terrier*—I ought not to Forget that, if Dogs here don't Bark they are very fond of Howling, &c, of Which my Virginia Dog was such a Lover that he got his Brains knock'd out by the Neighbours Within a Fortnight After he Was in my Possession—

It Was now, that Several *American* Families Arrived at Paramaribo on Account of the Enmity that Was at Present Broke out to a high Pitch Between the Mother Country and her Colonies, And for Whom I felt very Much While I Shall ever Declare that no People Could have a Better heart or greater friendship for a British individual than they had And Which Particularly they Showed to me on many different Occasions—I have heard an American Sailor /While he was Cleaving hard Wood/ Wish from the Bottom of his Soul, that the Head of *Lord North* Was under his Hatchet, While *Isaac Hopkins* /Who was Since one of theyr Admirals/ has hug'd me to his Breast—at this time both the Above Gentlemen and his son *John* frequented Surinam Where they traded with the inhabitants for Molasses—

Now M.r De Graaff being Arrived in Town, Who had finally Settled Affairs With *M.r Lolkens,* the Late Administrator of Fauquenbergh, I thought I Would take the first Opportunity to Settle Matters With him, by Proposing to Give me *Credit* till I should have it in my Power to Pay the Money for Which Joana and Johnny had been sold to me, And which I was Determined to save Out of my pay if I Should exist till

• —M.r Hartzink Says that the dogs in Gui[a]na Get Mad by eating the bones of the Powessa or wild Turkys—D.r Bancroft that theyr ears are pendulent, the nose Blunt, And the hair Long—And M.r Fermyn says the Dogs are of three Species—Viz the Common dog—the Crabbodago *or Grisson*—and the Watter dog *or Otter*

then, on Bread and Salt And Nothing Else, And Which even then, I Could not Do in Less time than Between 2 or 3 Years—But Heaven interceded and Prevented my Penurious Resolution, by Sending that Angelick Woman M:^{rs} Godefrooy to my Assistance, for no Sooner was she Acquainted with my Strugling Situation than She sent for me to dine With her, When she Address'd me in the following terms—

> I know good Stedman too well the present Feelings of your tender heart, And the incapacity of an Officers income to Alleviate your Distress But know that even in Surinam, Virtue will meet with friends—Your Man'ly Sensibility for that Deserving young Woman and her Child Must Claim the Esteem of all well thinking people in Spite of Groveling, Malice, and folly, And so much have these Actions Recommended you to my Attention in Particular, that I should think myself Blameable in not Patronising your Laudable endeavours—Permit me then to Participate in Your Happiness And in the prosperous Prospects of the Virtuous *Joana* and her Little Boy, by y^r Accepting the sum of two thousand Florins, or any sum you Stand in need of, With Which Money go Immediately, Stedman, go and redeem Innocence, good Sense, and Beauty, from the Jaws of Tiranny—insult, and Oppression—

Seeing me Like thunder Struck And Gazing upon her in a State of Stupefaction Without Speaking She Continued with a Heavenly Smile—

> Let not your Delicacy Stedman take the Alarm, and here interfere. Soldiers ought ever to be the Men of fewest Compliments, and Rectitude of Mind Supply an incoherent Chain of Empty Words—This I Expect from you thus say not one Word on the Subject—

Being now Come to myself I however Replied, that I Was at a Loss how most to Express my Admiration of Such Benevolence—I Say'd that

> Joana had Certainly merited my eternal Affection, Who had so frequently Preserved my life but that my Gratitude Could not be of Less duration to one Who had so Generously put me upon the way to Redeem that inestimable Woman from Slavery—And Concluded with Observing that I Could not now touch a Shilling of the Money but Should have the honour to Call upon her the next Day When I retired—

I Was no Sooner Come home than I Acquainted Joana With all that had happened, Who Bursting in Tears Call'd out,

> *Gado Sa Blesse da Woma,* And insisted on *She herself* to be Mortgaged to M:^{rs} Godefrooy till every Farthing Should be paid, While She indeed

Wish'd to see the Emancipation of her Child but till which time She absolutely refused to Accept of her own Liberty—

Without here Endeavouring to Paint the Struggle that I felt Between *Love* and *Honour,* I Shall Bluntly say that I Yielded to the Last, And pressing this Fine Woman to my Bosom, Whose Sentiments Endeared her to Me Still, I instantly Drew up a Paper, Declaring my Joana according to her wish to be the Property of M.rs Godefrooy, till the Last farthing of the Money she Lent me Should be Reimbursed—And on the next Day—With the Consent of her Relations• I Conducted her to M.rs Godefrooys house in person Where Throwing herself at the Feet of that Divine Woman, She herself put the Paper into her hands—But this Lady /having Raised her up/ no Sooner had Read the Contents than She Exclaimed,

> Must it be so, then Come here my Joana, I have a Spirit to Accept of you, *not as my Slave,* but more as my Companion, you shall have a house built in my Orange Garden, With my own Slaves to Attend you till providence Shall Call me Away, When you shall be Free as indeed you are now the Moment you Shall Wish to Posess your Manmonition [manumission], And Which Perogative you Claim both by your Extraction and Behaviour••—

on these terms, and no other I Accepted of the Money on the fifth, Which Carrying in my hat to M.rs De Graaffs I emptied the Contents on his Table for a Receipt in full and Joana Was transferr'd from the wretched estate Fauquenbergh, in[to] the Possession of the first woman in the Colony for which she thanked me With a Look thatt Can only be Expressed in the Countenance of an Angel—

M.r De Graaff on Counting the Money Address me in the Following Short Speech—

> Two hundred Florins of this Sum belongs to me as Administrator, permit me Also to have a Small Share in this very Joyful Circumstance, By not Accepting of this Dividend, While I find myself Amply Paid by the Pleasure of having been instrumental in bringing About, What Seems so much to Contribute to the Happiness of two Deserving people.

—I Thankd my Disinterested friend With an Affectionate shake by the Hand, Immediately Returned the 200 Florins to M.rs Godefrooy, and all

---

• —Without the Consent of Parents, Brothers, & Sisters, no Respectable Slaves are *individually* Sold in Surinam.

•• —I have Already Mention'd that *Joana* Was by Birth a *Gentlemans* Daughter from Holland, While her Mothers Family were Distinguished people on the Coast of Africa—

was Happy, While next Day my Praises Rung Through the Town of Paramaribo And I Was Crown'd for What I Had thus far Finished, With Praises, and Congratulations, Particularly by M! & M!ˢ *De Melly,* and M! and Mʳˢ *Gordon* this Being indeed the third Person /including *Qwacco*/ that I had Rescued /Within a little more than 3 Months/ from the Jaws of the Monster Persecutor, Yet to see Matters so Happily Concluded Was What I Could never have Expected, nor was ever the Proverb so happily Verrified as on this Event—

Accidit in Puncto Quod non Speratur in Anno.

I ought not to forget as a further Proof of Mʳˢ Godefrooys Humaine Character, that hearing of the Dejected Situation of the Sick at Magdenbergh, She Sent them in a Present of a Whole Barge Loaded With Fruit, Vegetables, and refreshments of every Kind that the Colony Could afforded—

Matters being thus far Settled, I now Wrote a Letter to M! *Lude* at Amsterdam, to give him intelligence & to thank him for having parted With the Most Valuable Property of his Estate, And now My Ancle being Pretty Well recover'd I Wrote to Col: Fourgeoud at Barbacoeba that I Should have the Honour to Joyn him in a Few Days for there he was Still, While the intrepid And Active Militia Captain *Stoeleman* Was Beating up the Woods With a Few Rangers at Another Quarter, Who this Day Sent in four Captured Rebel Negro's to Paramaribo•—

I now being ready once More to enter the Forest, Again took Farewell from my Little Family, and friends, Leaving the first Still at M! De La Mares at theyr Request, and Voluntarily Set off With a Tent Barge on my 5ᵗʰ *Campaign,* in the hopes of Accompanying Fourgeoud, who having Receiv'd all his Remaining forces About him, With every other Arangement to Attack the Enemy Was now Determined to March in a Very few Days—

In Short I Arrived on the 14.ᵗʰ at *Barbacoeba* in the Upper Part of the *River Cottica,* Where formerly I was & I had Formerly kill'd the *Aboma* Snake, leaving my boxes at Mocha an Estate—I found here the old Gentleman /Who Civilly Welcomed me/ Ready to Start the verry Day Following, While I do declare I never saw the troops in Such fine Spirits, Proceeding from different Motives as I had said before, Some in the hopes of Plunder, Some from Revenge, & some from Wishing to see the War at an end, While I Believe in my Soul that others were tired of

---

• —it is a Maxim With the Rangers to Chop off the *right* hand of Ev'ry Rebel Negroe they Kill, for which they Receive 25 Florins, & for every one they Send in Alive 50 Florins [/]also for finding a town or village 1000 Flor[/] being a Premium of About £5 Sterling.

their Existance by Continual Illness, and Bad Usage, And heartily Wished for a Glorious End of All their Miseries, as in general nothing Can be more Wretched than a Military Life in a Tropical Climate More so under a Relentless Commander, as *old Fourgeoud* Was thought to be even by his Friends

    If as Philosophy doth often muse
    A State of War is Natural State to Man
    Battles the Sickness Bravery Would Choose
    Noblest Decease in Natures Various plan

    Let Vulgar Souls Stoop to the fevers rage
    Or Slow Beneath Pale Atrophy Depart
    With Gout and Scrophola Weak Variance Wage
    Or Sink With Sorrow Cankering at the Heart

    These be to Common minds the Unwish'd Decree
    The firm Select an illness more Sublime
    By Languid pains Scorn their high Souls to free
    But Seek the Swords Swift Edge and Spurn at time
          —From Ana Matilda's Poems

Chapter 20th

*A Rebel Negroe described—Bush fighting—Sentimental Expressions
of the African Blacks—The Town of Gado Saby
taken by Col: Fourgeoud—Superstition
wonderful Shifts—and great Generalship in the Enemy*

The *Rebels* Flush'd with their Late Victory over Cap.! *Meyland* And his Party, Whether to Dare Fourgeoud, or to intimidate his Troops, being Well Apprised by their Spies that he was at Barbacoeba, had the Assurance lately to set fire to all the huts in two Different Camps Which had been left Standing by his Circumbulating Padrols—and While they were Shouting And Hallowing all the night, but this however proved rather a Spur to Rouze him than otherwise, and enraged the Old man so much that he now Swore he would be revenged of them *Coute qui Coute*

> Though they Dig into hell there shall mine hand take them; Though they Climb up into Heaven thence will I Bring them Down

I think I Shall by and by have Quotted no Less than the whole book of Amos—In short an hour before day Break, Col: Fourgeoud with his Troops were ready to March, & enter the Woods Exactly 200 Europeans, the others being ill but no Rangers were as yet Arrived, who had been however Expected, but were so much Disgusted with being Under Fourgeouds Command that they Delayed Appearing at all, Which gave the Vitron Commander an Opportunity to Call them, a pack of Pussilanimous Rascals, And indeed I myself Was Extremely Surprised at this Wilful Absence of my Black Favourites, Who were at other times so eager & Keen to fall Upon the Enemy, And had Declared their utmost Satisfaction in the hopes of having a Stout Brush With

their Sable Countrimen—Last night a large Tiger alarmd the Camp & this Morning Just before Marching /I having the Van Guard/ Colonel *Seybourgh* now took the Opportunity to show me every insult before the Men, by Declaring they were not Properly dress'd in a Line, that they Did not Carry their heads, or their Arms, as they Ought to do; that they did not Stand still, and Look to the right &c—According to the Military Reglement lately Published by the Order of the Prince of Orange—While no Body Else followed this Etiquet in a Wild Forrest, I However Determined to Show him, that I was Acquainted with Military Obedience, And with great Difficulty Accomplished his Wonderful Command except in Keeping the Men silent, who one and All burst out in a *Loud Laugh,* which Attracted the notice of Fourgeoud & who heartily Joyn'd them; this made the *Drill-master* Perfectly Mad, Who swore now that "if I Persisted with my European Tactics, in such a Climate, And on such a Spot, where no Ceremony Could, or ought to be Look'd after, he Would instantly put me in Arrest, And have me Tried for Disobedience"—At this I Could hold no Longer, but before Fourgeoud desired him to Proceed, Swearing in my Turn, that "D——nation itself Could not be Much Worse, than to be Longer *Hagrid* by such a Mercyless Tyrant, Who from Private Resentment, Publickly found Fault, first for *not* Doing his Will, and then for *Doing* it, And Which Could only be Reconciled to a Diabolical Disposition, or to insanity, Which was Equally as Troublesome"—He was now Like a fury, Swell'd and Ready to Burst with inward Rage—However Before he Could retort my Sarcasm, the old Hero Enterfear'd with a smile, and Ended the Despute, by ordering the Whole to face the Right and March—The Sun beginning just to Appear Glittering Amongst the Foliage—This Whole Day our Course was due **E** And having Proceeded About 8 Miles /Which is a Great Deal in this Country, Where the *Pioneers* With Billhooks must Constantly open a Path/ We erected huts and Encamped; Having frequently Mentioned the *Rebel* Negro's, With whom we were now Certain to Have a Recounter, I here Present the Reader With the figure of one of these People upon his Guard, As Alarmed by Supposing to hear a Rusling Amongst the Bushes, And a Couple of rangers at a Distance Ready to take him by Surprise—
The first is Armed With a firelock, and a Hatchet, his hair /though Woolly/ may be Observ'd to be Plaited Close to his head, by way of Distinction from the *Rangers* or any other Stragling Negroes, who are not Accepted yet Amongst them, And his beard is Grown to a Point, like that of All the Africans when they have no opportunity to Shave—The Whole dress of this Man Consists in a Cotton Sheet Negligently tied Across his Shoulders, Which Protects him against the Rayn, And

A Rebel Negro armed & on his guard.

London, Published Dec.r 1st 1794, by J.Johnson, St Pauls Church Yard.

Serves him as a Bed to lay Down, and Sleep, in the most Obscure Places he Can find; the Rest are his Camisa, his Pouch w.h is made of Some Animals Skin—A few Cotton Strings for Orament Around his Ancles and Wrists, and a Superstitious *Obia or Amulet* tied About his Neck, in Which case he Places all his hope and Confidence—

The Scull and Ribbs are Supposed to be Some of his enemies Scattered upon a Sandy Savannah. This Figure, and a few others Belonging to this Collection, Viz The *female Mullotto* Slave, the negro-Woman in Chains, the Arowacca indian Maid, &c had the Honor to be inspected by Sir *John Reynolds* who Signalized it With a verry high Compliment as Verry Expressive, And upon the whole an Excellent Performance— While it was Also highly Approved of by Mess.rs *Cossway, Rigaud, Cross, Humphreys,* and many others—

Such Were the Enemies we had to Engage, Who never gave any Quarter, And thirsted for the Blood of the Europeans; A Country Farmer /a M.r Wright/ Humourously Observing, that the *above* Figure Look'd not Unlike that of the Devil in Miltons Paradise Lost—

The two *Rangers* Who make theyr Appearance at a Distance may be Distinguished by their *Red* Caps, While I must Observe that the Rebels many times have Avail'd themselves of Capturing one of these Scarlet Distinctions, Which by Clapping on their own heads, in an Engagement, has not only saved their lives, but given them an Opportunity to Shoot their Enemies—

Another Stratagem of theirs has Sometimes been Discovered, Viz that Fire Arms being Scarce Amongst them Numbers have intermix'd in the Crow'd, With only a *Crooked Stick* Shaped Something like a Musket to Supply it in Appearance, Which has even more than once had the Effect of Preventing a proper Defence by The Plantation Slaves, When they Came to Ransack the Estates, who were thus Struck With a Panick, And Whose Courage Dampt, with the Show of Such Superiors in Number, Allow'd the Rebels Calmly /after Burning the Houses/ to Carry Away even their Own Wives, and their daughters—

We now Continued Again Marching Due **E** Upon a *Ridge or Elevated Ground,* Which if I Mistake it not Run in this Country Generally **E** and **W,** as do Also most of the Marches or Swamps—Having Advanced Rather less than we had Done the Day Before We were ordered early to Sling our hammocks, And to Sleep Without any Covering to Prevent the Enemy from hearing us Cut the Timber nor were any Fires Allow'd to be Lighted, nor Speaking While a Strict Watch was Kept Round the Camp and which were all verry Necessary Precautions, but if we Were not Discovered by the Enemy We were almost Devoured alive by Such a Cloud of Gnats or Musqueto's in this place, as I Vow to God I had not even met With on Board the Fatal Barges in Upper Cottica, And Which arose from a Neighbouring Marsh, While we Could Make no Smoak to Drive them Away—In this Situation I Saw the Poor Men Dig holes With theyr Bayonets in the Earth, into Which they Thrust their heads Stopping the Entry and Covering their Necks With their Hammocks, While they Lay with their bellys on the Ground—In any Other Possession [position] to Sleep was Absolutely impossible however by the Advice of a Negroe Slave I Enjoyed my Rest. "Climb /said he/ Massera With your Hammock to the Top of the Highest Tree that is in the Camp, and there go Sleep, not a Single Musqueto Will Disturb you, the Swarm being to[o] much Engaged by the Smell of the Sweating Multitude that is at the Bottom"—And this I Tried being near a Hundred feet Above my Companions, Whom I Could neyther see by the Mist of Musqueto's below me, Rolling like the Clouds under Blanchards Balloon, nor hear them by the Sound of Theyr Infernal Singing Musick—

This Cursed Company was the more Distressing Since During our Days March we had frequently been Attack'd by Whole Armies of Small *Emmits* Called here *firy-Ants* from their inveterate Biting—These insects are Black, and Verry Diminutive, but Live in Such Amasing Multitudes together that their hillocks have Sometimes Obstructed our Passage by their Size, over which if one Chances to Pass the feet and Legs are instantly Covered over with them, When these Small Creatures take such hold of the Skin with their Pincers that they Sooner let the head be Parted from their Body, than let go their Grip—Yet the Burning Pain Which they Occasion Can in my Opinion not Proceed from the Sharpness of theyr Pincers only, but must be owing to some Venemous Liquid Which they infuse, or the Wound imbibes from theyr Fangs—be that as it may I have seen a Whole Company hop About as if they had been Scalded with Boiling water or Possest by the Devil—

We now March Again **E** till 9 OClock when we Altered our Course to the **N** and had to Scramble through great Quantities of those Mataky Roots or Trumpetters already Describ'd, Which Proved that the Ground began to be Lower, And indeed at Last it Became verry Marshy—but Luckily though now in the Wet Season We had as Yet verry Little or no Rayn—This Evening We Encamped About 4 OClock Col: Fourgeoud being ill with a Cold fit of the Ague—

As I have Undertaken to Describe All I Could of the innumerable Curious Animals & Vegetables that one Perpetually meets with in this Country—I am Determined Strenuously to Proceed with the Difficult Task, that is According to my Abilities, let me be in Whatever Situation I may, Fire, Watter, or the Clouds, no matter What, Providing I Can only keep above the Ground—Slinging now my hammock Between two Large Branches /but not so high as the Proceeding Night, here Being though a much Lower Situation, no Musqueto's at all Compared to Yesterday/ my Eye Chanced to fall upon the *Leaf* of a Tree, Which Seemed to move by Crawling up Against the Bark—I Called Several Officers to See it, When a Gentleman of the Society exclaimed in French *Cest la foeille Ambulante,* that is the Ambulatory or walking Leaf. And Which upon Closer Examination Proved no Other than an insect, Whose Wings Perfectly Represent the Above Deception— Nothing Can be more Wonderfull indeed than this strange fly, Which has Absolutely by many been Mistaken as the Production of a Vegetable—It seemed a Species of Grashopper, but Covered over with 4 Wings of an Oval form and About 3 inches in Length, the two uppermost so folded together as to appear like a *Brown Leaf* With all the Fibres thereto Belonging.—

This must seem verry strange to many People, but let those who doubt the Resemblance, and even the existance of Zoophiles viz the Affinity between the Animal & Vegetable Creation Peruse an Extract, from an unpublished Pamphlet, entitled *an Essay on the Subject of Chimistry and their General Division by D: Richard Watson Lord Bishop of Llandaff,* which they may See in the European Magazine for Nov: 1784, And they will meet With more Persuasive Arguments than Either my Time, or my Capacity, Will permit me to Afford—

I now turned into my Hammock, Where Reflecting on all the Wonders, and Wonderful Bussel of this World, while the Silver moon Glittering through the Verdure of the Trees, Added Beauty to the Quietness, and Solemnity of the Scene. I fell most perfoundly Asleep; but not Longer than till About Midnight when we All awaked in hells Darkness, and a heavy Shower of Rayn, by the Hallooing, and Shouting of the Rebel Negroes, who also Discharged Several Musket shot, but not any at our Camp, at Which we were Extremely Astonish'd, but Could not in the Least understand the Meaning—This Disturbance Continued till near Day Break having Expected ev'ry Moment to be Surrounded When we unlask'd [unlashed] our Hammocks and Proceeded on our March Due **N** toward the Place, where by Conjecture the Hallooing noise had Come from, While we were Extremely fatigued for want of Sleep, Especially Colonel Fourgeoud who Could hardly Support himself by the Ague—We had not Marched 2 Miles when I having the Van Guard, a Rebel Negro Sprung up at my feet, from under a Shrub, Where he had been Conceal'd Asleep, But who /while we were forbid to fire upon Straglers, and Without he firing at me/ Disappeared like a Stag Amongst the Underwood—of this I no

Sooner made Report to the Old Hero, than Swearing he was a Spy, Which I Believe was true, he Shook off his illness and Redoubled his Pace with Double Vigour. /Col: *Seibourgh* Damming me for Marching too fast/ but our Pursuit was to no Purpose at least this day, Since About 1 OClock we were Led in a Bogue, that we Could hardly get out of, And thus oblidged to return back to our Last nights Lodgings, having lost 2 Private Men of the Society who were missing—to day we saw great Quantities of *Arnotta* Trees, With Which this Part of the forest seem'd to Abound, And this evening a Slave Presented me with a *Bush-Spider* of such a Magnitude, that Putting him into an empty Case Bottle, high about *8 inches*, he Actually Reach'd with some of his hideous Claws upon the Surface While the others were Resting upon the Bottom—No Creature Can be more Dreadfully Ugly than this Enormous Spider, which the Surinamers Sometimes /though Erroneously/ Call the *Tarentular*—the Body is divided in two, the Posterior Part Oval, and the Size of an Orlean-Plumb, the fore Part Square and Tabulated, with a kind of Star upon it, this Monster has 5 Pair of Thick Legs, With 4 Joynts in each, is entirely Black or Dark Brown, and Cover'd over /Legs and all/ with thick and Long Black hair, like some Catterpilers, while each Leg is Armed with a Crooked Yellow nail, And from the head Project two Long Teeth with inverted Pincers, Resembling the Claw of a Crab, with which it seises its Prey and the bite of Which is fatal by the Venemous Liquid it infuses in the Wound—it has 8 Eyes like most Spiders, and feeds on other insects of Every Species, nay it is even Asserted, that young birds do not Escape it, out of Which this Spider sucks the Blood; its Web is small but very Strong; upon the Whole this is Such An Abominable Looking Creature, that the verry sight of it Alone, is Sufficient to inflict a Tremor in the most Audacious—Innumerable indeed are the many Plagues and Dangers, one is hourly Exposed to in the Woods of this Tropical Climate—And /While I only make mention of such few as must appear new to the reader/ Most of us were Perpetually tormented, with all those others that now I Pass over with Silence, as being Already Described—Yet a Recapitulation only of theyr Names, may not be Amiss to Refresh the memory of Those, who have a Heart to Simpathize with our Sad Sufferings—I have Already Mentioned the *Musqueto's, Monpieras Patat* and *Scrapat Lice, Chigoes, Cockroaches Common ants, fire-Ants, Horse flies wild Bees & Spiders*—besides the *Prickly heat–Ringworm Dry-Gripes, Putrid fevers, Boyls, Consaca, Bloody-flux*— *Thorns, Briars–Alligators, Snakes* and *Tigers* &c But I have Say'd nothing yet of the *Bush-worms, Large Ants, Locusts Centipedes, Scorpions Bats & flying lice*, the *Crassy-Crassy Yaws, Lethargy, Leprosy,* and *Dropsy*, besides a Thousand other Grievances, that no Less, for ever Keep'd us Company, and the Description of Which I must delay till the most Suitable opportunity for inserting them in this Narrative—

Such were the Torments that had to Struggle with a Parcel of Poor, ematiated, forlorn, and I may say half Starved Creatures, in a Strange Country, who were Dying by Dozens, And Scores, without Assistance, or Pity, frequently with not so much as a friend to shut their Eye Lids, and Always Without a Coffin or Shell to receive their bones, being for the most Part Promiscuously thrown together in one Pit, no Better than I have Seen a heap of Carrion thrown for the Dogs—

We now Again broke up, And after Keeping a little to the South, Marched East till 10 OClock, when we were overtaken and Joyn'd by a party of one Hundred Rangers, With theyr Conductor a Mr *Vinsack* which made us now Just 300—however Little Colon'l Fourgeoud Affected to Care for these Black Soldiers at other times, he seem'd verry far from Displeased With their Company at this time, When he knew he was fast approaching an Enemy, Whom Certainly the Rangers knew Better how to Engage than Marines; and it will ever be my Opinion that *one* of these free negroes, was Preferable to half a Dozen White men in the *Woods* of Guiana, which Seemed their natural Element, While it was the bane of the Europeans—Col: Fourgeoud now gave out orders to march in three Columns, Viz his own Regiment in the Center, the Society Troops on the Right, And the Rangers or Black Soldiers on the Left, all Within hearing of each other, and to have a few *flancqueurs* or Riflemen, dispers'd Without the whole; thus Aranged we Advancd forwards till about Midday When we Changed our Course from **E** to **N E** And Again Continued our March over a *Biree-Biree* swamp or *Quabmire,* Which are very Common and Dangerous in this Country, being a Deep soft Miry Marsh, only Covered over with a thin Crust of Verdure, Strong Sufficient in most Places to Carry the Weight of a Man, and trembling if Walked over it, like the head of a *Devonshire* Creampot When a fly Crawls over the Surface; yet Should this Crust give Way, whoever Breaks it is Swallowed up in the Chasm Where he must in[e]vitably Perish, if not Extricated by immediate help, thus it has happened that men have Sunk in to it over head and Ears, Who have never more been heard of—Quick sands are Quite Different from this yet only by their gradual Succion, Whereas the Effects of Quabmires are instantaneous—to avoid these Accidents We Crowded as Little together as Possible, Which indeed occasion'd a verry Long Rear, Yet Could we not get over, Without several men Sunk through it, as if the ice had broke under their feet & Some in my Presence were up to theyr Armpits But they were all happily Extricated—In the Afternoon we Passed through two old fields Where formerly Cassava Seem'd to [have] been Planted, which indicated our Certain Approach to the Rebel Settlement, and next falling in With Cap.? Meylands old Path /which we knew by the Marks Cut upon the Trees, as Explained/ that we were sure of it but this Evening being too Late to engage the Enemy we encamped a few miles from the Swamp in which Cap.? Meyland with his Party had been defeated—

Having had a verry Long March and the Men being much fatigued Col: Fourgeoud allowed both huts, and fires, Which indeed Surprised me being so near the Rebels, While at other times he Prevented these Comforts, When he was Sure to be a Hundred Miles from them—However I Availed myself of his Bounty, & having got some *Pidgeon-Peas* from my Serj.? Fowler, which he had Pick'd up in the old Cassava Grounds, And Caught hold of one of the Kettles. I invited him and a Cap.? of the Black Corps Call'd *Hannibal* to a Share Who having Conjunctly with me thrown their Salt Beef and Rusk bisquet in the Mash, And Stirr'd it round with a Bayonet, we made a Verry Excellent Supper but in a Confounded Dark Gloomy Night and heavy rayn—

> Now Black and Deep the night begins to fall
> A Shade immense. Sunk in the Quenching gloom
> Magnificent and vast are heaven and earth,
> Order Confounded lies: All Beauty Void;
> Distinction Lost and gay Variety
> One universal Blot.

Nevertheless before I fall asleep I must Shortly describe the above peas, and Give some Account of a Conversation that I kept with *Hanibal* While I lay in my Hammock and he Sit smoking under it—

The *Pigeon or Angola Peas* grow on a Shrub about 8 or 10 Feet high—5 or 6 of these Pease are Contained in a Pod, Which are flat and of a Reddish brown Colour; All the Negroes are Extremely fond of them, and Cultivate them in their Gardens without Expense or Trouble; But now for Hanibal, Who Observeing that we Should Certainly see the Enemy to morrow Asked me, if I knew in What Manner Negroe Engaged Against Negroe, having Answered in the Negative he gave me the following Relation—

> Massera /Said he/ Both Parties are Divided in small Companys of 8 or 10 Men & Commanded by one Captain With a horn Such as this /he Showing me his/ By that they do every Thing I Want, and either fight or Run Away, but if they go to fight they Seperate immediately, lay down on the Ground, And keep firing at The flash of each others Pans through the Green—While each Warrior is Supported by two Negroes *unarm'd,*

the one to fill in his Place if he is kill'd, And the other to Carry Away the Dead Body, And Prevent it from falling in the hands of the Adversary•—

From this discourse I Perfectly Understood his meaning, Which I have since seen Put in Practice and which for the Clearer Conception of the Reader I have now illustrated, with the following plan And where the Whole Engagement is seen at one View—
In this, the 2 Blew Columns **E** and **F** Are Supposed to be first engaged, where N.° 1 in the Column **E** Commences the Attack by firing at Random in the Opposite Bushes, and instantly Retires by Shifting his Place to N.° 1 in the Yellow Column **C** Where he Reloades; While N.° 2 in the Column **F** fires at the flush of his Pan, and Advances in the Same Manner shifting his Station to N.° 2, to reload in the Yellow Column **D**; And at the flash of Whose Pan is fired by N° 3 in **E**; And again at his by N° 4 in **F**; &ᶜ &ᶜ this Continuing in a See Saw Manner, through both Lines, till N° 8 has fired in **F**, When the whole have Shifted their Stations; and the same Manoeuvre is Continued With the Yellow Column **C** and **D**; beginning Again by the identical Numbers 1, 2, 3. &c at the top; and these Lines having Shifted their Places, Still the firing is Repeated by the Red Lines **A** and **B**, And thus add infinitum, till by Sounding *the horn* one of the Parties gives Way by flight & the Battle is over—I Shall only Add that When the forest is Thick in Place of Laying on their Bellies, or kneeling, each negroe Sculks at the back of a Thick tree, which serves him as a Bulwark, & from Which he fires at his Adversary with more Certainty•• and less Danger, like the Shawanese and Delaware indians, According to M.ʳ Smiths tour through the united States of America, in that Passage Where Major Lewis was kill'd near the River Ohio—

Capt: Hanibal having Mention'd to me Also, that *Bony* was Supposed to be Present in Person Amongst the Adjoining Rebels, Who was born in the forrest amongst them, Notwithstanding his being a Mullato, but Which was Occasion'd by his Mother Escaping to the Woods from the ill treatment of her Master, by whom she was Pregnant—And I having so often Mention'd the Different *Shades* between a Black and White, do in the same Plate Represent them to the Reader at one View, Where from the two Above Colours is Produced the *Mullato*, from that, with Black, the *Samboo* And with white the *Quaderoon* &ᶜ—

• —All the negroes have a Savage Custom of in a Shocking manner Mangling and tearing the bodys of their Slain adversarys, even some devouring Part of them With their teeth like Chareebee indians who are Certainly Canibals

•• —Usually resting their Pieces against the trunk or in the fork'd branches

Manner of Bush-fighting by the African Negroes.

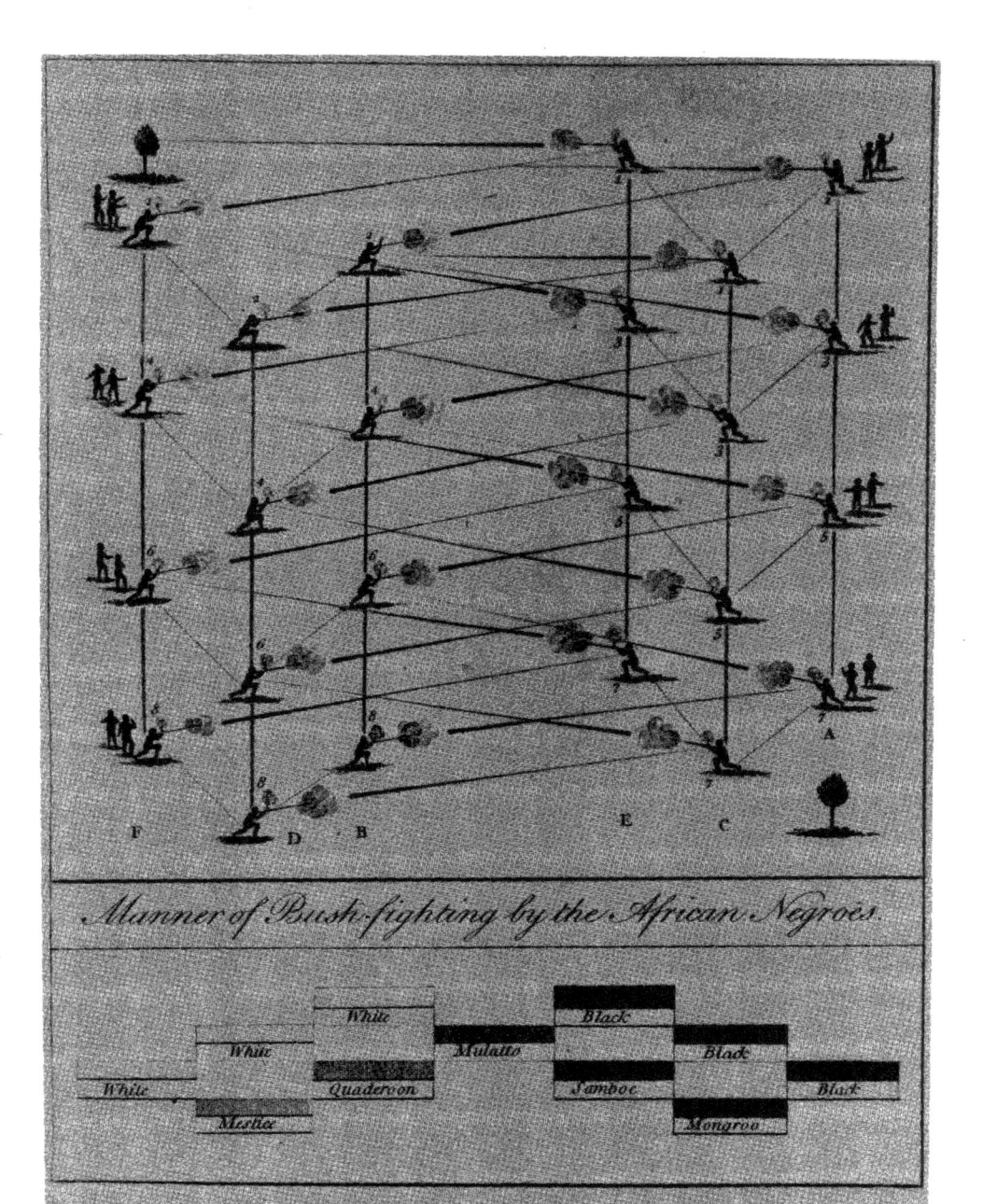

Gradation of Shades between Europe & Africa.

This Sable Warrior further made me Acquainted With the names of Several Rebel Commanders, besides bony, And Against whom he had frequently Battled for the Europeans Such as *Quammy* Who was the Chief of a Seperate Gang, and had no Connection with any Others—*Coro-Mantyn Cojo–Arico–*And *Joly Coeur*–the two Last being Celebrated Captains, Whose revenge was insatiable Against the Christians, Particularly *Joly Coeur* & who had great reason indeed•–he Also mention'd the noted Rebel Negroe Chief *Baron* Whom he Believed was now Serving under the great Bony—

The names of the Capital Rebel Settlements he Said were the following, Viz Some Already Destroyed, some in View, And some of Which only the Appellation was Discovered, but all which I thought so verry *Sentimental* that /as helping to illusidate our ideas of the Negro Nation/ I have thought Proper to give them a Place in this Narrative together with their translations and Meaning into English Viz—

    Boucoo—It shall moulder before it Shall be taken,
    Gado Saby—God alone knows it & no Person else—
    Cofaay—Come try me–if you be men—
    Tessee See—Take a tasting–if you have a liking—
    Mele me—Do disturb me–if you Dare—
    Boosy Cray—The Woods Lament—
    Me Salasy—I Shall be Taken—
    Kebree me—Hide me O ye Surrounding Verdure—

The others were—

    Quami Condre—From the name of the Chief
    Pinenburgh—From the Pins [palisades?] which formerly Surrounded it
    Caro Condre—From the indian Corn or Maiz it Produced
    Reisee Condre—From the Quantity of Rice it afforded

Such were the names of the African Warriors And their Settlements, And now in the hopes of a Glorious Victory—viz to do good without Committing Cruelties I Shaked hands with the Black Captain Hanibal, and fell most Profoundly Asleep by fatigue, /as I have said/ in a Dark Gloomy night With heavy Rayn, during Which Time I Dreamt of nothing but blood and Goare fire and Smoak &c—

    But yonder Comes the powerful King of Day
    Rejoicing in the East. the Lessening Cloud
    The kindling Azure, and the Mountains brow

• —See May 1st 73 And April 27th 74—

1775—AUGUST 19, 20

> Illum'd with fluid gold, his near Approach
> Betoken glad—
>
> —Thomson

Now no one Could be better in Spirits than Poor Stedman, till they Were again Damp'd by the Relentless Colonel Seybourgh, Who even the Moment before an Engagement must try to Distress them, nor was it I, alone; he tiranized indeed over All Except Fourgeoud who was the only one Above him, And Whose Cruelty I Believe upon my Soul, he would have Overpass'd had he been invested with equal Power—While such Characters may serve as a Warning for Princes, And Ministers, never to invest persons with Superior Authority over so many individuals, Especially in a Foreign Country, Without being as Well Acquainted with their feelings, as With their Flatteries, no man being fit to Command but Such as know what it is to be Commanded, and Whose Valour is tempered with Humanity, Since Bravery is ever incompatible with a hard Heart—in Short we set out, Stil **NE** towards the Swamp, While my Melancholy Evaporated with the rising Sun, And Which Swamp we Entered About 8 OClock, when we soon found ourselves in the Watter till Above our Middle, & Expected /as Captain *Meyland* had met with/ a verry Warm Reception on the Opposite Shoar; however having waded through this March /Which was broad Above half a Mile/ the Van Rappelly mounted the Beach with Cock'd firelocks and, Screwed Bayonets, the whole Body Close following, Without meeting with the smallest opposition—But here was a Spectacle Almost Sufficient to Damp the Spirits of the most intrepid Soldier, Viz, the ground being Strew'd with the Sculls, bones, and Ribs, Still Covered with Part of the flesh, and Besmeared with the Blood, of those unhappy men kill'd with Cap.! Meyland, Which that Gentleman indeed had found means to Bury, but which had Since by the Rebel Negroes been Dug up, for the Sake of their Cloaths, And Mangling the Bodies, by tearing them limb from Limb Like Savage Brutes—Amongst these the Fate of Milands Nephew, that Promising young Man was Peculiarly to be Lamented, Who Came all the way from the Mountains of Switserland, in hopes of Preferment to be shot in a Marsh in Surinam, and whose Bravery was Equal to that of his Uncle, but whose intrepidity in voluntarily exposing himself, had been too often without any Bounds—Such is the Enthusiasm of Ambition—

> And 'tis most True while times Relentless hand
> With Sickly Grasp Drags others to the Tomb,
> The Soldier Scorns to Wait the Dull Command
> But Springs impatient to a Nobler Doom.

Tho' on the plain he Lies Outstretch'd and Pale
Without one friend his Stedfast eyes to Close,
Yet on his Honour'd Corpse shall many a Gale
Waft the Moist Fragrance of the weeping Rose.

O'er the Dread spot the Melancholy Moon
Shall pause a While a Sadder Beam to Shade
And Starry Night amidst her Awful Noon
Sprinkle Light Dews upon his hallowed head

There too the Solitary bird Shall Swell
With Long Drawn Melody her Plaintive Throat
While Distant Echo from Responsive Cell
Shall oft With fading force Return the Note

Such Recompense be Values Due Alone
* * * * * *____
—Della Crusca

However this being the Second, or third Group of Human bones, we met with During our Peregrination I Frankly Acknowledge, they were no Stimulative for me to Engage with negroes, While those Relikts Seem'd rather to Spur upon the Common Soldiers, with a View of taking revenge for the Loss of theyr Massa[c]red Companions—
Having so often Spoke of Marching through a Swamp, I think it will not be Amiss to illustrate the Description by the Annex'd Drawing, Where the First Figure Represents *Col: Fourgeoud* Preseded by a negro Slave as a Guide, to give Notice when the watter is too Deep, And followed by some of his Officers and Private Marines, Wading through the Marsh in a heavy shower of Rayn till Above Their Middles, and Carrying their Ammonition & their Accoutrements Above their Heads as they Can, to Prevent them from Dragging through the Swamp While in the Offing may be seen how the Slaves Carry the Burdens, And in What manner sometimes the rebel Negroes fire on the Troops, out of the Palm trees &c And which Situation of Marching is Certainly the most Dangerous in Surinam where they may be Attacked from under the Surrounding Bushes, without being Able to Return the fire more than once, Since in such a Depth of Watter no Soldier Can Load his Musquet Without Wetting the Lock, And Who generally is Already too much Animated by the heat of the Action•—But to Proceed—
Being now Come in a Kind of a Foot Path made by the Enemy, we had only to follow it, And which Led us /after a Little Turning/ in a due **W** Direction—At this time Serj! Fowler who Proceeded the van Guard

---

• —See June 15th And July 8th 1773—

March thro' a swamp or Marsh, in Terra-firma.

Came to me Declaring that the Sight of the Sculls &c had made him terribly Sick, And that he at this Moment felt himself the Greatest Coward in the Party, being Fascinated to the Ground without he Could Absoutely Advance one Single Step—or knew what to do with himself to Conceal it, & And I only having time to D——n him for a Pityful Scoundrel he Lag'd astern—at 10 OClock we met a small Party of the Rebels, with each, a Green Hamper on his Back, Who having fired at us, Without we Returned it, let drop Down their Bundles And took to their Heels, back towards their Village, And whom we since Learned were Transporting *Rice* to Another Settlement to Subsist *Boneys* People, When they Should be Drove from this Call'd *Gado-Saby* & which they Dayly expected since they had been Discovered by Capt Meyland—The Green Hampers /which were most Curiously Plaited with the Manicole Leafs and which they Call *Warimbo's*/ Our men Cut open With their Sabres, from which Actually burst forth the most Beautiful Clean'd Rice, that ever I Saw, Which was Scattered and trampled under Foot, we having no Opportunity to Carry it Along—A Little After this we Saw an empty shade Where an out guard had been kept to give intelligence of the Approach of an Enemy, but Which Deserted theyr Post—We now Vigourously redoubled our Pace till About 12, OClock when two more Musquet Shot were Fired by an Advance Guard of the Enemy as a Signal to *Bony* of our Approach—& A Little again after w^h we Came to a fine field with Rice india Corn &c—Viz, Major Medler, and Myself, with the Van Guard, and a Party of the Rangers; We here made a Halt for the *two* Colonels, And to Let up the Long rear some of Whom were at Least 2 Miles Behind us; However in About half an hour we all got together, and we on[c]e more Proceeded by Cutting through a Small Defile of Wood, into Which we no sooner had Entered, than /Ding Dang/ the firing at last Commenced from every Side, the Rebels retiring and we Advancing till finally we Arrived, in the most beautiful Oblong Square field with Rice in full ripeness that ever I saw in my Life, And in Which Appear'd to our View the Rebel Town at a Distance in the form of an Amphitheatre Shelterd by the foliage of a few Ranks of Lofty Trees, Which they had left Standing, the whole Presenting a truly Romantick and Enchanting *Coup Doeuil* to the Unconcerned Spectator—In this field the firing now lasted like one Continued Peal of Thunder for near 40 Minutes, During Which time the Rangers Acted with Wonderful Skill, And Gallantry, While the White Soldiers were too much Animated, the one firing over the other at Random, Yet a few of Which I Saw with the Greatest Deliberation imitate the Blacks, & Amongst whom was now the *Daunted Fowler* Who being Rouzed by the Popping in the Beginning of the onset, had Rush'd to the front, And fully reestablished his *tarnished* Character, by fighting the Enemy at my Side like a Brave Fellow, till the Muzzle of his Gun was Splitt by a Shot from the Rebels, which Prevented him from reChargeing—I Received myself a Ball through between the Shirt And the Skin, And my Lieutenant M:̲ *Decabanes* had the Sling of his Fusee Shot Away, While Severals were Wounded, some Mortally, but I Saw not a Single man Drop *dead* at my Feet to my Great Astonishment, And for Which I Will Presently Account—The Stratagem of the Enemy in Surrounding and interspearcing the field by the Large Trunks, and the Roots of Fallen Trees we met with made our Advancing verry Different and Dangerous & at the Back of Which Fortifications they lay Lurking, and firing upon us Without themselves Could be Materially hurted, And over Numbers of which Timbers we had to Scramble before we Could Come to the Town; However we keept Advancing, and While I thought this excellent Generalship in them their Superstitious Simplicity Surprised me much of Which I'l only Relate one instance—A poor Fellow trusting in his *Amulet* or *Charm,* by Which he thought himself invulnerable Advanced frequently on one of these trees, till very near us, And having Discharg'd his Piece Walk'd off the Way he Came, to Reload With the Greatest Confidence and Deliberation, till at Last one of my men—/an intrepid Walloon named *Valet*/ With a Ball Broke the bone of his Thigh, And down he Came, now Crawling for Shelter Under the Same Tree which had Suported him but the Soldier Went up to him instantly and Placing the Muzzle of his Musket in his Mouth, blew out his Brains & in Which manner Severals of his Countrymen were Knock'd Down—So much for *Priest Craft* in every Country, While I honestly Acknowledge that in Place of like M:̲ *Sparman* who kill'd 5 or 6 Hottentots at one Shot•—Even at this Moment my Sensibility Got so much the Better of my Duty, And my Pity for these poor miserable, illtreated People Was such, that I Was rather induced to fire with Eyes Shut, like *Gill Blas* when he was amongst the Robbers, than to take a Proper Aim, of Which I had Frequent Opportunities—

In Short being now about to Enter the Town, a Rebel Captain wearing a Tarnish'd Gold Laced hat, & Carrying a Wisp of flaming Straw in his hand Seeing Their Ruin inevitable, frustrated the Storm in our Presence by Setting the town on fire, And which by the Dryness of the Houses instantly Occasion'd One General Conflagration, When the Popping from the Wood immediately Seized [ceased]; And Which *Masterly Manoeuvre* not only Prevented that Carnage to Which the Common Soldier is too Prone in the heat of Victory, but gave them The Opportunity of

• —Vide Clarksons essay on the Slave trade

1775—AUGUST 20

Retreating With their Wives & Children, and Carrying off their Best Lumber; While our Pursuit, And even our Falling on any of the Spoil, was at once also frustrated by the Ascending flames, And the Unfathomable Marsh Which we soon found to Surround them—Upon the Whole, to Draw this Picture Were a fruitless attempt, thus I Shall only say that the incessant Noise of the Firing, Mixed With a Confused Roaring, Hallooing, Damming and Sinking, the Shrill Sound of the Negro Horns, the Crackling of the Burning houses, the Dead & Wounded all Weltering in Blood, the Clowd of Dust in Which we were involved—And flames and Smoak Assending; Were such a Scene of Beautiful Horror /if I may use the Expression/ as would not be unworthy of the Pencil of Hogarth—And Which I have faintly tried to Represent in the Frontispiece, Where I may be seen After the Heat of the Action Dejectedly Looking on the Body of an Unfortunate Rebel Negro Stretch'd at my feet—

I have just Say'd the Battle was Ended; and now made their Appearance the Two Chiefs—Fourgeoud having Lag'd astern to Drink a Bason of his *Teazan*, being Seiz'd With a Violent Griping in his Bowels from the time the firing Began—Which he Call'd *un Shoc* or *Coup De Main* And Col: *Seybourgh* having been Employed in Beating up the Rear With his Cane, And Thus Preventing them to hang an A———e—

At this time After Congratulating each Other with this Glorious Victory, /though not a Prisoner was taken/ Washed off the Dust, Sweat, and Blood, and Refreshed ourselves with a Dram and a bit of Bread, /The Fatigues of the Day Which was so Scorchingly Hot having nearly Exhausted us/ We went to inspect the Smoking Ruins of the Town /While the Dead were Buried, and the Wounded were Dressing by the Surgeons/ And which we soon discovered to have Consisted in near one Hundred Houses, or Huts, Some With 2 Stories high—

Here Amongst the Glowing Ashes were pickd up now a few trifles that were Saved from the flames, Such as, a Silver spoon and fork, With the mark of **B·W***—Some knives, Earthen Potts &c—Amongst Which *one* with *rice & Palm tree-Worms* Came to my Share, Which /having Wanted no fire to Dress the Contents, & I no Appetite/ I Emptied it in five Minutes And Seldom have made a Better Meal, though /Since/ some were Afraid it had been Left behind, with a view to Poison us, but Which however proved to be Without foundation—For the Plate I Well Rewarded the men who Pickd it up, Which I Determined to Carry off as a Trophy, And have made use of it ever Since—But here we Also found Something of a Different Nature. Viz. 3 Sculls upon Stakes

---

* —Formerly pillaged from the Estate Brunswick in Cottica—

Which were part of the Relicts of our own People formerly kill'd,—& What Surprised us 2 Negro heads Which had the Appearance to be fresh Cutt off, And which We Since heard had been Executed During the Night Of the 17.th When we heard the Shouting and the firing—

Having buried them in one pit We now Returned to Sling our Hammocks, Under those fine and lofty trees Which I have before Mentioned. Where I am Sorry to Relate, We Shokingly Saw the Rangers Employ'd Playing at Bowls with those *heads* they had Chop'd of[f] from their Enemies—And who Related that on Reconnoitring the Surrounding Skirts of the Wood they had found Much Scattered Blood of Which the Bodies had been Carried Away by the Other Rebels—To Stop or Reprimand them from the Above Inhuman Diversion Was to no Purpose, of Which they Seemed as fond as Blood Hounds of Carion, telling us it Was Negro fashion. And Which festival they Crown'd, After Mangling, And Kicking the Heads, by Cutting of[f] their Lips, Cheeks–Ears and Noses; they Even took out the Jaw Bones all Which they next *Barbacued* or Smoakedried, together With the right hands, to Carry home as Trophies of their Victory to their Wives and Relations; That the Above Custom Generally Prevails amongst Barbarous Nations is a Well known fact, Proceeding from a Motive of Unsatiable Revenge, And is no small Proof that *man* the Boasted Lord of the Creation, is in his Natural State nearer Connected to the Brute, than Civilisation /Which in Other Words only is Polity/ shall be ever Able to Contradict—Indeed in this one instance, Col: Fourgeoud Might have prevented their Proceeding by his Authority, but Which in my Opinion he Sensibly Avoided, Observing that as he Could not Do it by Persuasion, it Would be breaking their Native Spirit to Do it by his Power—So much for Barbarous Customs—

It was now About 3 OClock **PM** And we as I said Were Busied Slinging our Hammocks, When we were Suddenly Surprised by an Attack from the Enemy but Who After Exchanging a few Shot Were soon Repulsed—This unexpected Visit however Put us upon our Guard During the Whole night, by Allowing no fires to be Lighted And Doubling the Sentinels All around the Camp—Thus Situated I being Excessively fatigued /besides Several Others/ Ventured in my hammock, Where I soon fell asleep; but not Longer than the Space of an Hour; When my Faithful black Boy Qwacco Awaked me in pitch Darkness Crying, *Massera Massera Boosee Negro, Boosee Negro,* And hearing at the Same time a brisk firing, While the Balls Russled through the Branches About me, I imagined no other than that the Enemy Was in The Middle of our Camp—in this Surprise, and not perfectly Awaked, I Started up With my fusee Cock'd, and /I not knowing where I Run/ Overset

Qwacco, And next fell myself over two or three Bodies that lay on the Ground & Which I took to be Shot. but one of Which Damming me for a Son of a Bitch, told me if *I moved I was a Dead Man;* Col: Fourgeoud with all his Troops laying flat on their Bellies, & Who had issued orders no more to fire, the Men having Spent most of theyr Ammonition the Preceeding Day—I took his Advice and soon Discovered him to be one of our Granadeers, Call'd Thompson—In this Situation we Continued to Lay Prostrate on our Arms till next morning, When the Sun Rose and During Which time a Most Abusive Dialogue Ensued, between the Rebels, and the Rangers, both Parties Cursing And menacing each other at a Terrible Rate, the *first* Reproaching the others as being Poltroons, and Betrayers of their Countrimen, Whom they Challenged the Next Day to Single Combat, Swearing they only Wanted to Wash their hands in the Blood of Such Scoundrels Who had been the Capital hands in Destroying their fine Settlement, While the *Rangers* Dam'd the Rebels for a Parcel of Pityful Skulking Rascals Whom they Would fight one to two in the Open field, if they Dared to Show theyr Ugly faces, that they had Deserted theyr Masters being too Lazy to Do theyr Work, While they /the Rangers/ Would Stand by the Europeans till they Died; After which they insulted each other by a kind of War hoop, then Sung Victorious Songs, And Sounded their Horns in Defiance; After Which once more the Popping Begun; And thus *Add Perpetuem* the Whole night till Break of Day, the Musick of their Manly Voices &^{c} resounding Amidst the Echoing Solitude and Surrounding woods with Redoubled force; And Which being Already dark and Gloomy Added Much to an Awful Scene of Pleasing dreadfulness; While According to me the *tout ensemble* Could not but inspire the Brave With thoughts of Fortitude and Heroism And Stamp the Trembling Coward for What he is—

At last Poor Fourgeoud Entered in The Conversation, by the help of myself, And Sergeant Fowler, Who spoke the Language, as his interpreters but Which Created more Mirth than I before heard in the Colony—

He Promised them Life, Liberty, Meat, Drink, and All they Wanted, but they Replied With a Loud Laugh, that they Wanted Nothing from him Who seemed a Half Starved Frenchman, Already Run Away from his own Country, that if he Would Venture to give them a Visit in Person, he Should not be Hurted, And might Depend on not Returning With an Empty Belly—They Call'd to us that we were more to be Pitied than themselves, Who were only a Parcel of White Slaves, hired to be shot at, & Starved for 4 Pence a Day, And that they Scorned to Expand much of theyr Powder Upon such Scarcrows, Who had not been the Agressors by Driving them in the Forest & Only Obeying the Command of their Masters; but if the Planters and Overseers Dared to Enter the Woods themselves not a Soul of such Scoundrels should ever Return, no more than the *Rangers,* Some of Whom Might Depend on being Massacred that Very Day, or the Next, And Concluded by Swearing that *Bony* Should soon be the Governor of All the Colony—After this they Tinkled their Billhooks, fired a Volly gave three Cheers Which were Answered by the Rangers, And all Dispearsed With the Rising Sun, to our great Satisfaction, being heartily tired of Such Company—Whatever small our Loss, While our Fatigues were Such that only The Hardships suffered since by the British Troops at Gibraltar, Could be Compared to them, Where Also /Notwithstanding the Contest Lasted such a Length of Time/ the Loss of Men by the Enemies fire was but verry inconsiderate; However the Mysterie of our Escape /Which in Gibraltar was Owing to fortification/ was this Morning unrevel'd by the Surgeons, Who Dressing the Wounded Extracted in Place of Lead Bullets only *Pebbles* Coat *Buttons,* and *Silver* Coin, Which Could do us Little harm, Penetrating Scarce more than Skin Deep, While even Gold Could do themselves as Little Good in a Wild Forrest where they had nothing to buy for it—We Also Observed that Several of the Poor Rebel Negroes who had been shot, had their Pieces Supplied, only with the *Shard* of a Spa Watter Can in Place of a Flint Which Could not so Well answer the Effect &*^c*—And this must Account for theyr Little Execution on the Bodies of their Cruel Beseigers, who never the Less were Pretty well Pepper'd with small Scars, and Contusions—Inconceivable are the many Shifts Which these People make in the Woods—

> Inventas qui Vitam Excoluere Per Artes;
> Who by invented arts have Life improved

& Where in a State of *Tranquility* they Seemed as they had Said to us Want for Nothing—Being Plump and Fat at Least Such we found those that had been Shot—For instance *Game* and *fish* they Catch in Great Abundance by Artificial Traps and Springs, And Which they Preserve by Barbacuing, While with *Rice, Cassava, Yams, Plantains,* and so on, theyr fields are ever over Stoked—*Salt* they make with the Ashes of the Palm trees like the *Gentoos* in the East indies*—Or Use Red Pepper. We even Discovered Concealed near the Trunk of an Old Tree a Case *Bottle* With Excellent *Butter* Which they the Rangers told me they Made by melting and Clarifying the fat of the Palm-tree Worms And Which

• —See Guthry Page 685

1775—AUGUST 21

fully Supplied the Above ingredient While I absolutely found it more Delicious—The *Pistachio* or pinda nuts they Also Convert in Butter, by their Oily Substance & Frequently use them in their Broths—The *Palm tree Wine* they are never in Want of, And which they make by Cutting Deep insitions of a Foot Over Square in the fallen trunk, where the Joice being Gathered it soon ferments by the Heat of the Sun, When it is not only a Cool and Agreeable Beveridge but Strong Sufficient to intoxicate—and Soap they have from the dwarf[?] aloes. To Build their *Houses* the Manicole or Pinda Tree Answers the Purpose, theyr *Pots* they Fabricate with Clay found near their Dwellings While the *Gourd* or Calebas tree gives them Cups &c. the Silk Grass Plant and Maureecee tree Provides them in *Hammocks* And even a kind of *Caps* Grow Natural upon the Palm trees as Well as *Brooms*—The Various kinds of Nebees Supply the Want of *Ropes, fuel* for fire they have for the Cutting, While a Wood call'd *Bee Bee* Serves for Tinder to Light it by Rubbing two Pieces on each Other, And Which by its Elasticity Makes *Excellent* Corks—Neyther Do they Want *Candles,* being well Provided with Fat and Oil While the Bees Also Afford them *Wax,* And a Great Deal of Excellent *Honey,* as for Cloaths they Scorn to Wear them Preferring to go naked in a Climate Where the Mildness of The Weather Protects them from that Cursed incumbrance—

The Rebel Negroes might Breed Hogs, And Fowls &c for their Supply And keep Dogs for Hunting And Watching them, but this they Decline from the Apprehension of Being Discovered by Their Noise, even the Crowing of a Cock being heard in the Forest at a Considerable Distance; After this Digression I shall return once more to my Journal—

Col: Fourgeoud now made it his next Business to Destroy the Surrounding Harvest, When I was Ordered this Morning to Begin the Devastation With 80 Marines, and 20 Rangers by Cutting all the Rice &c. that /as I have said/ was plentifully Growing in the two Above Fields, Which I did and during Which time I Discovered a third Field **S** from the First, When I Also Demolish[ed] and made report of to Fourgeoud to his Great Satisfaction—

—In the Afternoon was Detached Capt: Hamel, with 50 Marines, and 30 Rangers to Reconnoitre behind the Village, And find out if Possible how the Rebels alone found Means to Pass to and fro' through an Unfathomable Marsh, while we Could not Pursue them—When this Gentleman Discovered a Kind of a Floating Bridge made of Maureecee Trees, so fastned that but one man Could Pass a Breast, on Which were then Seated a few Rebel Negroes to Defend the Communication, And who instantly fired on the Party, but were Repulsed by the Rangers, who brought down one of them but who was Carried away by his Companions—

🙞 It being now too Late, Our Commander order'd the next Morning a Detachment to Cross the Bridge on Discovery at all Hazards—Of this Party I Led the Van, When we took the Pass without Oposition, and having All marched or rather Scrambled over this Defile of Floating trees We found ourselves in a Very Large field of Cassava and Yams, And in Which were About 30 Houses but Forsaken, being the Remains of the Old Settlement Call'd *Cofaay*—In this field we Seperated in 3 Divisions to Reconnoitre Viz one Marching **N** one **NW,** And the Other **W,** When the Mystery Again Was Unrevell'd, Why the Rebels had Kept Shouting Singing, and Firing Round us the whole night of 20th, Viz, Not only to Cover the Retreat of their Friends by Cutting of[f] the Pass, but by theyr Unintermitting *Noise* to Prevent us from hearing them, Who were the Whole night imployed men, Women, and Children, in Preparing Hampers or Warimboes With the Finest Rice, Yams, Cassava, &c for theyr Subsistance During their Escape & of Which they had only Left us the Chaff, and Dregs for our Contemplation And to our Great And inconceiveable Astonishment—And which most Certainly was Such a piece of Generalship in a Savage People Whom we Affect to Despise as must have Done Honour to an European Prince & Even *Frederick the Great* himself Needed not to have been Ashamed of, With which Remark I beg Leave to end this Long Chapter—

Chapter 21st

Spirited Conduct of the Rangers and Rebels—A Skirmish— fine scene of Brotherly affection—the Troops return to Barbacoeba—Plan of the Field of Action &c—A Slave kill'd by the Ooroocooko Snake

Col: Fourgeoud thus Seeing himself *Fool'd* by a *naked* Negro, was Ramping Mad And Swore he would Pursue Bony to the Worlds End, but his Ammonitions and Provisions were Expanded for the present, While if they were not, it was the most Don Quixot Scene that Could be invented to think now of Overtaking them—However the Hero Persevered in this inpracticable Project, Which he Began by Dispatching Capt Bolts With one Hundred Men and 30 Rangers, besides a Number of Slaves, to Fetch a Quantity of Shot And a Weeks provisions from Barbacoeba, and from which time he Gave out Orders to Subsist on half Allowance, Which he bid the poor Men Supply by Picking Rice &^c And prepare it the Best Way they Could for theyr Subsistance Which was Also the Lot of Most of the Officers & of which Number I was one, While it was no bad Scene to See 10 or 20 of us, with heavy Wooden Pestles beating the Rice, Like so many Apothecarys, in a Species Of Mortar, Cut All Along the trunk of a Level'd Purper hart Tree for that purpose, Viz by the Rebels before they had Expected to be Honour'd by our Visit, This Exercise was nevertheless Very Painful & Verified the Sentence Propounced on the Decendants of *Adam* that they Should Eat Bread by the sweat of their Brow, Which trickled Down my Forehead in Particular like a Deluge, Yet Which Profusion of Fluid, we were at Liberty Plentifully to Supply by *Watter*, but nothing Else, this being at Present the only Beveridge in the Camp.—
Amongst other Vegetables we had the Good Fortune to find here a

Great Quantity of Wild *Purslana* which only Differs from the Common in Growing nearer the Ground, the Leafs being Less, and more of a Blackish Green Colour, this vegetable grows wild in the Woods of Guiana, And may be eyther eat as a Salad or Stew'd, Without Reserve, being not only a Cooling Agreeable Food, but Reckond an Excellent Antidote Against the Scurvey—

We Saw here Also a Great Quantity of *Gourd,* or *Calebas Trees,* Which are verry Useful to the Negroes and Natives of the Country—This tree grows the Height of a Common Apple Tree, With Large thick pointed Leafs—The Gourds it Produces are of Different Forms and Dimensions, Some being Oval, some Conical, & some Round, Growing often to 10 or 12 inches in Diameter, the Shell is thin, Hard, and Verry Smooth being Cover'd over with a Shining green Skin or Epidermis, Which Becomes Brown when the Gourd is Dry and fit for use—the Heart or Pulp is a Pithy or Spungy Substance Which is Easily extricated by the Help of a Knife—Various are the Uses to which these Gourds are imploy'd, Such as Bottles, powder horns, Cups, Basons, Dishes &c While I myself Seldom Travelled Without one, Which Served me by the Way of a Plate in the forrest, And Which the Negroes Generally Adorn by Carving on the Outer Skin All Sorts Of Fantastical Figures, filling up the Vacancies With Chalk-Dust, When some of them Are Verry Pretty.—

The Rangers having been out to Reconnoitre Returned this Afternoon With the news that they had Discovered Still Another Field of Rice in the **NE** Which they had Destroy'd, And this pleased Col: Fourgeoud Verry Well, but When I in the Dusk of the Evening now Observed to him that I saw several *Arm'd Negroes* Approach at a Distance, he turned Pale Exclaiming "*I am Undone*" And Orderd the whole Camp to turn Out Immediately for their Defence—in a Few Seconds these Negroes were sufficiently near however to Discern that Severals Amongst them were Carried on Poles in Hammocks when Fourgeoud Again Call'd out "*we Still are Totally Ruined this is no Enemy but Captain Bolts beat Back With All his Party*" And so it Was, which Unlucky Gentleman /having Delivered the Wounded to the Surgeons/ Made his Report that having Entered the Cursed Swamp Where Cap:t Meyland was Defeated, he was Attack'd by the enemy on the Opposite Side & Who had made a Dreadful Havock Amongst his Rangers, Without hurting at this time one Single European[.] Amongst these was a Valiant Fellow Call'd Captain *Valentine* Who while Sounding his Horn, to Animate his Companions, it was not only Shot Away, with his Pouch also, but himself Dreadfully Wounded in 5 Different Parts of his Body—This Man when met by his Brother named Captain *Avantaje* Who seeing him Mortally

Wounded, a Scene of Such Real fraternal Affection Ensued as one Seldom meets with in a Civilized Country—Kneeling at his Side he Sucked out the Blood and Gore from his Bloated Breast & Cherished him by the Manly Promise that he Should fight his Foes until himself was killed & he should meet him Again—Let Christians here in Savages—

> Behold how good a thing it is
> And how Becoming Well
> Together such as Brethren are
> In Unity to Dwell—

In Short Col: Fourgeoud now saw that the Rebels had kept theyr Promise, of Massacreing the Rangers, /Some of which first Cap:t Bolts had declared openly fired from the Tops of the Palm trees On his Men, After Which Sliding Down with Agility, they Disappeard/ While the Later were forming for Revenge on their Haughty Adversarys & Could hardly be Restrained from an Immediate Pursuit—

Thus our Mighty Hero now Perceiving his Mad Sc[h]eme Frustrated of Following the Enemy And even in Danger of Total Destruction, being Cut Off from every Supply, While he had Neyther Ammunition, or Provisions Left in his Camp, And Little else but Sick and Wounded to Defend it, he began Seriously to Consider of a Safe Retreat to Which he was Urged besides by The incessant Murmurring of the Troops in General, Who were not only Starved but Harrass'd to Death by Dayly Fatigues & Nightly Watches—

> They Wandered in the Wilderness in a Solitary Way they Found no City to Dwell in—
> Hungry and thirsty their Soul Fainted within them—
>   Psalm 107 V: 4 & 5.

Thus having the next Day Detached 140 Men Commanded by two Field Officers to Destroy the Old Settlement, and Field, Call'd *Cofaay*, And Of Which Party I Again had the Honour to be one, the Camp *Broke up* in the Afternoon Immediately after our Returning, During Which Last trip we had Pick'd up out of the Marsh Some Utensils Such as Tea Kettles, iron potts &c Which the Rebels had formerly pillaged from the Estates and had now thrown in the Watter, to Conceal them from us with a view to Return and Fish them up When we Should have Left Gado Saby—

If During this Last Expedition we Neyther made Captives nor Buty [booty] We nevertheless Did the Colony a Material Piece of Service by Rooting out this Concealed nest of their Enemies, Who Being once

Discovered and drove away from their Capital Settlements /As I have Remark'd Already/ never more to Think of Returning to Live near the Same Spot—Indeed I may say more, And Almost Pronounce this Last Victory as Decisive, I say Almost since Except Demolishing a few Plantations for Immediate Subsistance, and from a Spirit of Revenge the Rebels were by this Discovery, Struck with such a Panick, that from the Present Period not only their Depredations were Less, but they Soon after Retired So inaccessibly deep in the Forest that they Could neyther do any material Damage, or be Joined by Deserters—
But now I must Relate an Act at Least of impolicy in Fourgeoud, Which in the Opinion of Many Deserves a Worse Epithet, Viz This Evening on our Way home when We Entered the Noted Marsh he Snatched up one of the Empty *Bread Boxes* Which having Stuft with a Hammock he Carried it before him Crying *Sauve Qui Peut*—At this Moment a Walloon Named *Mattow* Stept up to him Who Reply'd "Mon Colonel, but few Can, and I Hope fewer will follow your Example, Drop your Shield, and Don't intimidate your Soldiers, one Brave Fellow Creates Others, thus Follow thy *Mattow* and fear for nothing—" Saying Which he instantly threw open his Bosom And Charging his Bayonet Was the first Man that Mounted the Oposite Beech With intrepidity, When the Rest Soon followed, but Meeting no Oposition, We a Little after Encamped where We had Pass'd the Night before the Action, for the Above Act of Heroism this Private Marine was Since Promoted to be a Serjeant, While I Should think myself Deficient, in not Paying the Walloon Soldiers the Compliment in General of Being a Parcel of Verry Gallant Fellows—

On the Morning of the twenty fifth We Again Set Out Early and having now a Beaten path before us, we Reached our General place of Rendezvous Barbacoeba on the Afternoon of the Following Day, but in Such a Shocking Situation that had the Rebel Negroes seen us they must not only Claimed the Victory on theyr Side, but Absolutely have Pitied us in The Bargain—Almost the Whole of the Detachment Were Knockd up, the Others Starved While ev'ry Soul of the Slaves were imploy'd in Carrying the Sick and Wounded many Mortally in their Hammocks on Long Poles While they Could Hardly Support themselves Which was the End of Taking Gado Saby—

> Hic Labor. haec requiem multorum pugna Dierum
> Attulit: & Positis Pars utraque substitit armis

In the hopes it Will not be Disagreeable to the Reader and to Shoe the Masterly Manoeuvres of our *Sable* Foes to more Advantage I here Present him With a plan of this Extraordinary Settlement, together with our Different Stages After Leaving our encampment on the Borders of the River Cottica Viz

Nº 1 2 & 3. is Supposed to be the General Rendezvous at Barbacoeba And the two Succeeding days Marches—
4. The Spot where we heard the firing & Shouting of the Rebel Negroes on the night of the 17th—
5. The Latitude where the troops were Joined by the Rangers—
6. The Last nights Encampment before the Engagement—
7. The Beech on the Opposite side of the Marsh Where Capt: Meyland With his troops had been Defeated—
8. The Advanced Post of the Rebels Where the First Shot were fired at the Troops—
9. The field with rice and indian Corn entered Without Opposition—
10. The Pass or Defile in which the firing Commenced—
11. The Beautiful field with rice in Which the Action Continued 40 Minutes—
12. The Town of *Gado Saby* in flames at a Distance
13. The Spot from where the Rebels fired on the Camp And held the Conversation With them on the night between the 20th & 21st—
14. The Ground of the Old Settlement Cofaay With the Floating Bridge that Covered the Retreat of the Rebels—
15. The Different Fields With Cassava Yams Plantains &c that Were Discovered and Demolished Since—
16. The field of Rice Destroyed by Myself on the 21st—
17. A Field Demolished by the Rangers on the 23d—
18. The Swamp or Marsh Surrounded the Settlement—
19. The Quab Mire or Biree Biree Adjoining it &
20. The Forrest—

Having before Mentioned how we Erected *Our Huts* I Will here Also Add a Small Plan of the Manner of Aranging them During Our Encampment in the Woods of Guiana, Which Was Generally in the form of a Triangle As the Most Secure Way of Defence in Case of Being Surprized but this was only when the Situation of the Ground Would Permit it Which was Wide Distant from being Always the Consequence; in this plan—

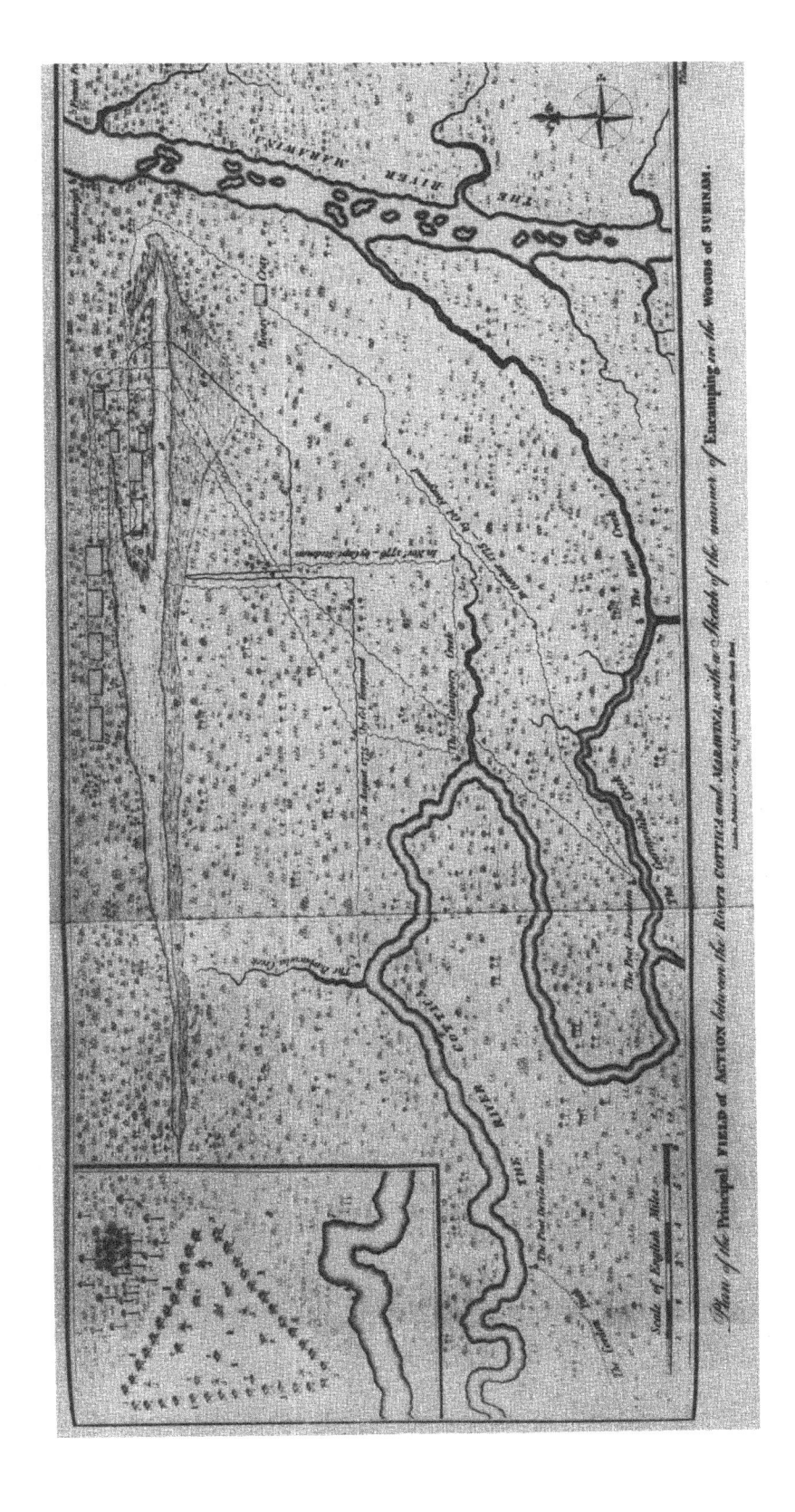

Plan of the Principal FIELD of ACTION between the Rivers COTTICA and MARAWINA; with a Sketch of the manner of Encamping in the WOODS of SURINAM.

1775—AUGUST 26

    N° 1 is the Hut of Colonel Fourgeoud or the Commanding Officer in the Center with a Centinel—
    2 The huts of all the Other Officers in a Small Triangel Surrounding the Commander in Chief—
    3 The Angels of the outer Triangel being the Huts of the Privates in 3 Divisions—Viz the main Body the Van and the Rear Guard With Centinels at Proper Distances to Cover the Front—
    4 Powder Chists, Provisions, Medicines &c &c With a Centinel—
    5 The fires in the Rear of Each Division to Dress the Victuals and round which the Negro Slaves are Lodged on the Ground—
    6 A Copice of Manicole Trees to Erect the Huts &c—
    7 A rivulet or Creek to Provide the Troops in Watter, and
    8 The Surrounding Forrest—

I Shall Now once More Return to my Narrative, by Observing for The Honour of Col: Fourgeouds *Perspicacity,* that in place of Barbacoeba being in a State of Sending him Provisions at Gado Saby as he had Wished, it Could hardly Afford dayly Bread to his Ematiated Troops that Came from it, Who having So many Days Lived on Rice, Cassava, Yams, indian Corn &c Were Soon after Attack'd by the Flux, for While the Above nourishment Will keep the indians and Negroes as Strong as Horses the Europeans Cannot Long Subsist upon it Without Animal Food, And Which was so Scarce that Even the Jew Soldiers of the Society Troops eat Salt Pork when they Could Catch it, for my own Part I Was Still Amongst the few that Were Healthy Which Was a Miracle having indeed Fared verry hard for Want of my Private Provisions Which as I have Mentioned I had Left at the Neighbouring Estate *Mocha,* However Expecting now to go and Fetch them in Person I Was in Good Spirits also—But I was Disappointed Col: Fourgeoud Declaring he Could not Spare me a moment While I was Well Thus I Waited Patiently for Some Opportunity to send for them, During which time I Existed, /Sharing With my Black Boy/ on the Pityful Allowance of a Private Soldier, Some mountain Cabbage, and Palm-tree Worms Excepted, & a few Warrappa fish, and During which time Col: Seybourgh treated All the Captains With a Roasted Sheep Excepting me Alone. at the Same time hinting some Reports not to my Credit Relating to the time When I Left Magdenbergh, which Last insolence Exasperated me so much that I Swore that he his Sheep and his Reflection might go be D——nd together Concluding that in a Little it Would be ten to One but I Would have a piece Even off his Tongue, And instantly wrote for a Certification from the Surgeon of the Regiment—

This Sarcasm Extremely Pleased most of the Officers, Whose hatred for him was as Strong as theyr Regard for me, And Who Generously

Offered to Supply me With some wine, And Share of their provisions, of Which I however Declined partaking, While themselves who Enjoyed Less Health Stood verry much in need of Them—Yet so famished was I at this time that I Vow to God I Could Almost have Wished myself in an English Kennel, Where I might feed plentifully with my Brother Hounds on a piece of Carrion While indeed the Irish Beef that was Left Amongst us was Little Better from Which when a Worm Deserted I Caught him back not to Diminish the Quantity—As for the Miserable Slaves they were now so Starved that having kill'd a *Coata* Monkey /the Lord knows how/ they Broild it With the Skin, hair, Guts and all Which they Devoured with theyr teeth before it was half Dress'd like a Parcel of Canibals Offering me a Limb. Which however hungry as I Was I thought proper to Refuse—Upon the Whole had I not at this time been Posses'd of Sterling health And Spirits I must have Sunk under the Load of Oppression—In Short such were the Hardships, that the Rangers Again All Left the Camp With theyr Conductor Mr *Vinsack* who instantly threw up his Employment, as Mr Mangel had done before During Fourgeoud's first Campeign While a more brave and Active Little Fellow never entered the Forrest—

And on the first of September the Bloody Flux Raging in the Camp to a high Degree he sent off All the Sick Officers and Privates, Without Exception, not to be Recovered in the Grand Hospital at Paramaribo, but to Linger and Die in the Rivers Where they were to Relieve others to undergo the Same Misery, Viz his Own Sick to *Magdenbergh* in Commowina, And those of the Society to *Vreedenbergh* in Cottica—So Severe was Col: Fourgeoud to the Officers that even those who were Past recovery Could not have a Servant of The Troops to Attend them, Whatever Price they Offered, Some of Whom I have Seen Expanded Between two trees, While the Filth for Want of Assistance was Dreeping through their Hammocks—Of this Number was Ensign *Strows*, yet Whom he Nevertheless in this Dreadful Situation ordered to be Transported to Devels Harwar—

At Last Col: Fourgeoud himself Was Seised With the flux When his Beloved *Teasan* Could Little more Avail, yet he soon Recovered by the Plentiful use of Clerret and Spices, Which his Companion Seybourgh made use of as a Preservative Against the Loss of his Health But Which by Swallowing in overplentiful Doses Rather Promoted the Loss of the Little he had Remaining of his Reason—

In such a Situation and in Such a Despisable Encampment, the Old Gentleman had Nevertheless the Vanity to Expect a Deputation from the Court at Paramaribo with Congratulations on his Victory, in Con-

1775—SEPTEMBER 1, 5, 6, 8, 9

sequence of Which he had Built an Excellent Shade, and Sent for a few
Sheep, and Hogs, to Entertain them but the Deputies never Arriving he Cut their Throats for the poor Soldiers to Whom for the first time in his Life he Distributed one Pound Each—

Indeed theyr Number Was at Present Verry Small Which was however
Recruited the Day Following by a Hundred Men from Magdenbergh in Comowina And from the Society Post Vreedenbergh in Cottica nearly as many, Who brought the Account that M[r] *Strows* at Devels Harwar was Dead besides a Great Number of Privates Who had Assisted at the Taking of *Gado-Saby* and who had Expired While they were Transporting From Barbacoeba—The intelligence now Also Arrived that the Defeated Rebels Had Cross'd the River Cottica below Pattamacca intent on Mischief and Marching Westward. in Consequence of Which a Capt: and 50 Men Were Immediately Detached by Watter to Reconnoitre the Banks near the Pinenbergh Creek Who Returnd the Eigth And Confirmed the Unhappy intelligence—However our indefatiguable Chief again Determined to Pursue them, but having no Slaves to Carry the Ammunition and provisions And who were Sent home to their Masters Estates Nothing but Skin and Bone I Shall Relate what happened the 2 Days Following till the Arrival of the fresh ones Viz—

On the Ninth Were Sold to the best Bidder and on Credit the Goods of the Deceased Ensign Strows When the Poor Soldiers Regardless of any Price And Only Wishing to Come at Some Cloaths & Refreshments to keep Soul and Body Together Actually Paid at the Rate of 700 P[r] Cent, Which is Equally True as it is infamous And Which Debt Accordingly was Stated to their Accounts For instance I have Seen a Private Marine Pay 5 Shillings for a Pound of Mouldered Tobacco that was worth Sixpence, And Double the Prime Value for a pair of Old Stockings or Shoes—A Sick Man Paid for a Couple of Meagre Chickens one Guinea, And for a Broken Bottle Case to keep his Lumber Another pay'd the same Sum—This Were a parcel of Poor Dying Wretches Robb'd even of that Little income Which they so Dearly Earned at the expence of their Sweat And Blood And Which might have So easily been Prevented by Only Supplying them With What was their Due, but this Was a Perquisite in a Certain Somebodies Pocket With Whom I am Almost Ashamed to own that I had even any Concerns, and I have known a private Marine Call'd Sem Swear in his Passion that he Would Certainly Shoot Fourgeoud Whenever he had a Proper Opportunity Which being Overheard I Bribed the Evidence on Condition of his Repentance not to inform Against him which Literally Saved the poor rash fellow from the Gallows—

420

1775—SEPTEMBER 10, 12, 13

🙵 However All the world did not Possess this Chiefs insensibility Since the Day Following the Good Mrs Godefrooy Again sent up a flat Bottom'd Barge with a fat Ox, Oranges Plantains &c for the Private Soldiers Who was Accordingly knock'd in the Head And With the Vegetables Distributed Amongst Them—The Same Evening some Little Provisions Also Arrived for me from *Joana* With a few Bottles of wine though Part was Stole And part was Damaged on the Way Which Nevertheless made me Extremely Happy—When we talk of Provisions in the Woods We only mean Such as Rum, Sugar, Limes Joice, Coffee, Tea, Boston Bisquit and Cheese & Sometimes a Bacon ham or a Cag of Sassengers Since not much else Can be Carried through the Forrest by a Single Negroe Slave We being Allow'd no more—indeed Shirts Stockings, and Shoes Are Generally necessary But of the two Last Articles I never made any use Being Accustomed as I have Said before to Walk Barefooted Which I had now practised for Above two Years With Considerable Benefit to my Limbs When Compared to the Ulcered and Rotten Shanks of my Companions. The Fresh Supply of our Negro Slaves now being Arrived the necessary Preparations Were made to

🙵 pursue the Rebels the verry next Day Directing our first Course toward the Spot formerly Call'd Jerusalem of Which I have made mention in 1773 When I Commanded the fatal Cruise in Upper Cottica—However before Starting my Late Adversary having got Drunk once more took the Opportunity of Showing me his spleen in a Very Singular Manner indeed Viz—Observing his Surgeon's Mate Who Was shaving me and who was the Only Tonsor in the Camp he Allowed him to Finish the half of his Operation and then Call'd him Back forbidding him on pain of Losing his Place ever more from that Moment to touch my face with a Razor Which threw me in such a Violent Passion, that Oversetting the Little Barber Whose name was Remeling With all his Apparatis I run up to the Lieut. Colonel With my Face full of Sudds "Sir Said I Damn your Mate With his Rusty Knife but here is a Letter from his Master which may prove Sufficiently Sharp to Cut your Throat." which being a Certificate I Just Received from Mr. *Knollaert* the Surgeon at Magdenbergh Confuting all his Late Malice made him Swell like a Turkey and Leave me Without Speaking—Nevertheless he kept Thundering near my Hammock So verry Loud and Long that he "*even*

🙵 *Robb'd me of the Last of Comforts sleep*" till the Next Morning when the Sun rose—

At Last being Prepared to Leave Barbacoeba the Provisions &c Were sent before us by Water to *Jerusalem* Escorted by the Sick Officers and Private men While Several Others Already Unfit for Duty Went to Recover in the Rivers, and 3 of the Last Come Slaves Deserted to Return to their Masters—Indeed so verry Scarce were men at Present Fourgeouds Whole Army being a 2^d time mostly Knock'd up that till Further Orders not any of the Sick Gentleman Were Allow'd a Servant to Attend them. While the poor Slaves were Oblidged to do Double drudgery And who were Persecuted in the most Barbarous Manner by Beating them Starving them and Fatiguing them To Death—For instance I saw the free Negroe *Gousary* this Morning knock down a Poor Black Man for not Taking up his Load and Fourgeoud knock him down a Second time for Doing it too Soon, While the Wretch not knowing What to Do Call'd out for Mercy in the name of *Jesus Christus* And was Actually knock'd down a Third time by an Enthusiast for daring to use a name to Which he had not the Smallest Pretentions—I have Before Remark'd that the Above *Gousary* With his Companion *Ackera* had been Rebel Captains in the Colony Berbice Where before they Surrendered they had Committed the most Diabolical Murders[.] These were the Men Whom now Fourgeoud employ'd to Manage the Slaves And with Whom they had no more Compassion than if they Had been beating on tann'd Leather—

   In Short, the Camp broke up When Bidding Farewell to Barbacoeba We entred the Woods keeping Course **SE** And Past the Night on the Opposite Beech of the Cassiporee Creek—During this Days March a Large Drove of *Warree Hogs* or *Wild-Boars* broke through our Line Severals of Whom Were Cut down by the men with their Sabers, And Stabb'd by theyr Bayonets but none Shot[,] firing at game being forbid by the Commander in Chief—These were Cut in Pieces and Divided Amongst the whole to Whom they Proved a Verry Seasonable Dainty—It is Verry Strange that if the first Wild Boar or Leader Passes through Whatever Danger, All the Others Stupidly follow in hopes Of the same escape, Which on the Contrary is the Cause of their Destruction—

   We now having Marched **SW** till About Noon Arrived at *Jerusalem,* Where the Van had Got an Hour Before us being All Thoroughly Soaked by the heavy Rayns, and one or two Men With Ruptures in the Groyn by falling Over Roots Large Stones &c—

Here to my Great Astonishment We Again found the Identical Mr *Vinsack* With a hundred fresh Rangers Who having heard of the Rebels Passing Upper Cottica had been Prevailed on to Resume his Office, And now once More Offered his Service to Col: Fourgeoud Who was Happy to Accept of it—

Just as We Entred the Above Camp Which was much Overgrown With Long Grass, One of The Slaves unfortunately Was Bit in the foot by a Small Serpent Called here the *Oroccoco Snake* from its Colour Resembling the Bird of that name /to wit the Owl•/—In Less than a Minute The Mans Leg began to Swell while he Was Seized With the most excruciating Pains and Soon After got Convulsions—At this time one of his Companions having kill'd the Snake made the Patient Drink its Gall mixt with half a Glass of Spirits Which I Gave him And he semed /Perhaps from imagination/ to Bear his Misfortune With more Temper however not Long When the Fits Rather Encreasing than not he Was instantly Sent to his Masters Plantation where he Died—

That the Gall of Adders Externally Applied is Efficacious I have often heard, and Read Accounts of–And Amongst others in the Grand Magazine for April 1758 may be seen a Letter Dated March 24. Signed **IH** Which Systematically enters in the Definition of Applying Gall, but these investigations I must Leave to the more Learned, And Only Observe in General that the Smaller the Snake /at Least in Guiana/ the more fatal seems to be the Consequence of its Bite as it is both Justly and Beautifully Observed in Thomson's Seasons—

> —But still more Direfull he
> The small Close-Lurking Minister of fate
> Whose high Concocted Venum through the Veins
> A Rapid Lightning Darts Arresting Swift
> The Vital Current—

In this Grassy Wilderness one of the Rangers kill'd Also to Day /What they here Call/ the *Whip Snake* from its Resemblance to that Rod of Correction—this was About 5 Feet in Length And not much Thicker than a Swans Quill, the Belly White and the Back a Lead Colour, of its Bite I Can Say Nothing at All—I Was informed by the Negroes that with its tail it has the Power of giving a Very Severe Smack like the instrument it so Very much Resembles—

Let me Still make mention of an Amphibeous Animal Which some of the Blacks kill'd here this Evening and which they Call'd the *Cabiay*[.] This is a kind of Watter Hog About the Sise of a Pig two years Old—it is Covered with Gray Brissles, is Arm'd with a Number of very Strong Teeth, and has no Tail, its Toes were 3 on each Foot and Web'd like those of a Duck to Assist it in Swimming[.] this Animal is Said to go Ashore During the Night only, Where it Feeds on young Grass and Other Vegetables[.] I have been told it is no Bad Eating but Never did Taste it myself—

Having here Rested one day Col: Fourgeoud Detached two Strong Parties to Reconnoitre Viz. Lieut: Col: De Borgnes With 100 Men to

•—This is the Snake I Apprehend Which Dᵒ Bancroft Calls the Small Labora and Which he mentions having kill'd a Negro in Less than 5 Minutes when he was at Demarary

the Wana Creek in Upper Coermoetibo, and Col: Seybourgh with an Equal Number to the Creek Pinenbergh in Upper Cottica, Which Last Returned Just Before Midnight With two Canoos he had found Haul'd Ashore on the Opposite Side, and not far Below the mouth of the Claas Creek—This Immediately Confirmed that the Rebels were gone Westward intent on Mischief, and Who had Brought the Empty Canoos down the Claas Creek from the Rice Country, to Send them Back Loaded with Booty from the Estates they had in View to Pillage—

In Consequence of this News the Proper Preparations Were Immediately Made to Pursue them With Vigour And the fruits of Which Expedition I intend to make the Subject of the following Chapter—

Chapter 22nd

Allarm in the Pirica River—A Detachment marches to its Relief—Ambuscade—Wonderful effect of the Biting of a Bat—Scene in a Quabmire—Sketch of the inquisition—and return of the troops to Coermoetibo Creek

Now Marched Col: Seybourgh With 100 Marines and 40 Rangers, Who did me the Honour to Pitch on me for one of his Party and Was Upon the Whole so Civil & so Polite in Opposition to What he had been Lately that I knew not at all how to Account for it—In Short having Crost the Coermoetibo Creek we keep'd Course **SW** and by **S** till we Came near the River Cottica, When we Encamped–Having met with nothing this Day worth my Discription, Except a kind of *Ants* which were no Less than one inch in Length and Perfectly Black—These Monsters Pillage a Tree of All its Leaves in a Short time, Which they Cut in Small Pieces the Sise of a Sixpence, and Carry under Ground while it is not Unentertaining to see a Whole Army of these insects Crawling Perpetually the same Way With each his Green Leaf in a Perpendicular Direction—Some have Vulgarly imagined that this Devastation was to Feed a Blind Serpent Under Ground, but the truth is that it Serves for Nourishment to the young Brood Who Cannot help themselves And are Sometimes Lodged Eight Feet Deep—Miss Merian Says they form themselves in Chains from one Branch to Another, When All the Others Pass Over this Temporary Bridge, And that once a Year their Formidable Armies travel from one House in Another Killing all the Vermin &c that Comes in their Way; neither of Which Curiosities ever Came Within the Limits of my Observation but that they Can Bite Confoundedly I have found by Experience Which is however Nothing Like so Painful as the Bite of that Diminutive insect the Fire

Ant Already Described—Having beg'd Pardon for this Long intruding on the Readers Patience I Shall Proceed—

We now Followed Along the Banks of the River Cottica till near the *Claas-Creek* Which I Formerly Swimmed Across With my Sabre in my Teeth*, And Early Slung our Hammocks While I Was Detached With a few Rangers to Lay an Ambuscade in the Mouth till it was Dark—here however I Discovered Nothing at All Except that the Rangers Were Possess'd of the Same Superstition As the Rebels With Regard to their *Amulet or Obia's* Making them invulnerable—Which they told me as the Latter got it from their Priest**, so they Bought it from their *Gramans Qwacy*, A Celebrated And Cunning Old Negro Whom I Will in Proper Place Circumstantially Describe[.] "D——n you fool Said I how Come any of you or them to be Shott?" When I Was Answered "Because Like you Massera they had no faith in the Amulet or Obia"— This piece of Policy in M: Qwacy, however had the Virtue of making all his Free Countrymen brave Fellows Whose Undaunted Valour had so often Surprised me, Besides it Was no small Accumulation to his own Wealth And Which for a Blackman in Surinam Was not a Trifle— in the mouth of this Creek I Again Saw Several Nuts Float on the Surface of the Watter Such as I have Mention'd See Page [132], When I was informed that they Were the Real *Acajou* or *Cashew Nuts* which I Partly Described page [310] To Which I now Shall add that they Grow on the End of a Pulpy Substance Like a Very Large Pear Which is Produced on a Middle Sised Tree with a Gray Bark And Large Thick Leafs, and that this Excellent Nut Will bear to Be Transported to any Part of the Globe, And keep Good for a Considerable Time—It is by Some Called the Anacardium Ocsidentalis—from the Tree Exudes a Transparent Gum Which When Dissolved in Watter has the Consistancy of Glue—

I here Also tasted the *Eta-Tree Apples* of Which the Rangers Seemed Verry Fond—This Tree is of the Palm Species With Large Leafs, but is Less in Sise than the Maureecee or the Mountain Cabbage Tree, and on Which the Above Fruit Which is Round grows in Verry Large Clusters Resembling Grape Shot—in the Middle of Each Apple is a hard Nut and Kernel Which is Covered near half an Inch Thick With an Orange Coloured Pulp that has a Most Agreeable Acid Taste—It is Seldom Used till the Apples by Ripeness Drop from the Tree When the Indians Steep them in Watter, And by Masseration Convert them in a most Healthy and Agreeable Beveridge—But to Proceed—

* —See Jan 6–1774

** —And According to M: *Bruce*, the *moors* get it from the Koran—

1775—SEPTEMBER 21, 22

🙥 An Express now Arriving by Watter from Col: Fourgeoud that the Alarm Guns* had been Fired in the River Pirica. We instantly Cross'd to the Opposite or **W** Shore of the River Cottica, Where the Rangers With a Party of Marines were again Ordered to lay Concealed in Ambuscade, in hopes of Cutting of[f] the Rebels or theyr Retreat, When they Should Return to Cross Cottica With the Booty—in the Afternoon a Rebel Negro Was seen With a Green Hamper, Who Allarm'd by the Smell of Tobacco /Some of the Rangers Smoking/ Stopt Short, of his Own Accord, he was instantly Fired at by me, and a Ranger, And the Warimbo or Hamper Dropt, but himself Escaped, This Bundle we found Stuft With a Dozen of the finest Table Linnen a Cocked Gold Lace Hat, And a Couple Superb India Chintz Petticoats Which I Gave All to my Black Companions The two Last Articles Excepted Reserving them as a Present for Joana—The Free Negroes or Rangers Now Rushing forward Like Hounds to meet the Enemy, I Ask'd Liberty to Follow them And Calling for Volunteers A Great Number Presented themselves Which however Col: Seybourgh Reduced to 4 Only, With which he Sent me off, and having Scrambled through Thorns and Briers /Wove together Like a Net/ Which tore one of my Legs in a Terrible Manner I Overtook them. Shortly after Which we Discovered 13 Fresh Huts Where the Rebels by Conjecture had Sleep'd but a few Nights Before—In Consequence of this I now Dispached a Ranger back to Colonel Seybourgh to Give him the intelligence & Ask Permission for the Rangers and myself to March Forwards to Pirica Without Delay, But the Answer Was for us instantly to Rejoyn him Without Omission—We now Returned to the Camp, the Rangers in Particular were Verry Discontented, And Making Wonderful Remarks, Where we found a Reinforcement Just arrived from Jerusalem of 60 Men Black and White, With Positive Orders for us to Break up And March Early the next Morning for Pirica River, While this Whole Night a Strong Party Again Lay in Ambush—

🙥 Accordingly at 6 O'Clock all Was Ready but Some Unaccountable Dilly Dally taking place it Was Very Late Before we Left the Camp– During Which time We were informed that a Canoo Was Seen Crossing the River With one Single Negro in it, Who was no Doubt the poor Fellow on Whom we had Fired the Day Before—

I Cannot here be of Relating a Singular Circumstance Respecting myself Viz that on Waking About 4 OClock in my Hammock, I Was Extremely Alarmed at Finding Myself /Like a Cold Fowl in Gelly/

---

* —By this are Meant Minute Guns Which Are Fired on those Estates Which are in Danger & Which Being Regularly Answered by The Neighbouring Plantations soon Alarm the Whole River, and Bring Assistance—

Weltering in Congealed Blood And Without Finding any Pain Whatever—I instantly Started up When my Appearance Was infinitely more Frightful than that of Tom Jones Where Mr. Fieldings Represents him as a Ghost frightning the Centinel—This Young Gentlemans Bones being at Least Covered over with Flesh, and that Again With Decent Cloaths, but Behold in poor Stedman an Apparition Divested of Both—The first being Melted Away by Hardships and Fatigues, and the Latter Reduced to an Old Check Shirt, and Tattered Pair of Trowsers—Barefooted & Bare Headed The Remains of an Old Straw Hat Excepted, my Hair Cut Shorter than my Ears, With my Face most Horrible Pale and Ghastly–My Sword and Pistol Slung Across my Meagre Shoulders, My Whole Carcass all over Besmeared with Clotted Blood and a Fire Brand in my Hand to Seek the Surgeon I might Well have been Ask'd the Question—

> Be thou a Spirit of Health or Goblin Damn'd
> Bring with the[e] Airs of Heav'n or Blasts from Hell

In Short the Mystery Was that I had Been Bit by the *Vampier* or *Spectre of Guiana* Also Call'd the *Flying Dog* of New Spain Which is no Other than a Monstrous Large Bat, that Sucks the Blood from Men and Cattle When they are a Sleep Sometimes till they Die; and as the Manner in Which they Proceed is Truly Wonderful I Will give an Account of it—Knowing by instinct that the Person they intend to Attack is in a verry Sound Slumber they Pitch Generally near the Feet, Where While they keep Fanning /with theyr Enormous Wings to keep them Cool/ they Bite a Small Piece out of The Tip of the Great Toe, Which Orifice is so Very Small that the Head of a Pin Could not be Received into it, And Consequently not painful, yet through which Opening they keep on Sucking Blood till they Degorge it. then begin Again and thus Continue Sucking And Degorging till they are Scarce Able to Fly & the Sufferer Sometimes Sleeps from time into Eternity—Cattle they Generally Bite in the Ears, but Always in Such Places where the Blood Flows Spentaneously perhaps in An Artery but for this I must Leave the Faculty to Account—Having now got the Wound fill'd With Tobacco Ashes as the Best Cure and Washed the Goar from myself and Also from My Hammock I Observed Several Small heaps of Congeal'd Blood All Around the place Where I had Lain Upon the Ground, the Surgeon Judging by Conjecture I had Lost at Least 12 or 14 Ozs During the Night—

As I have since had the Opportunity to knock down one of these Damnable Bats, I Cut off its Head, Which I present to the Reader in a Natural Sise as a Great Curiosity, With itself flying on a Smaller Scale

1775—SEPTEMBER 22

And Which having Measured Between the Tips of the Wings I found to be 32 inches and a Half, While some are Above 3 Feet—The Colour was a Dark Brown, next to a Black, but Lighter, under the Belly; its Aspects was truly Hideous upon the whole, but Particularly the *head,* Which had an Erect Shining Membrane Above the nose, Terminating in a Shrevel'd Point, the ears were Long, Round, and Transparent. the Cutting Teeth Were 4 Above, and 6 Below—I Saw no Tail But, a Skin Divided in the Middle by a Tendon—it had 4 Toes on each Wing with Sharp nails, Divided like the Web Foot of a Duck•—And on the Extremity of Each Pinion Where the Toes are Join'd, was a Nail, or Claw to Assist it in Crawling like those of its hind Feet, by Which it Hangs Suspended When Asleep to Trees Rocks &c—

One of the Marines having this Morning taken a *Murine, or Mouse Oppossum,* I Will here Also Describe it, And Represent it to the Reader as I Designed it from the Life, But Which Differed Certainly in Some particulars Mention'd by Buffon—for instance it Was much Swifter than any of the Oppossums he Speaks of, And had the Whole Tail Covered Over With Hair in place of Scales to the Best of my Remembrance, However if my Sight Deceived me, I am not the Only Erroneous Writer on the Subject of this Animal, *Linaeus, Seba,* and Mr *Vosmeer* /With Which Last I am Acquainted/ Ascribing it to Both the Old and New Continent, Whereas All its Species are Most Assuredly inhabitants of America only Linaeus is also mistaken When he Speaks About All Bats having 4 Cutting Teeth in each Jaw See Buffon Volume 5 Page 282—But to Proceed—This Murine Oppossum Was not More than the Sise of a Verry Large Mouse—It was Perfectly Black except the Belly—The Feet and the Extremity of the Tail Which were All Buff Coloured, with a Ditto Spott Above Each Eye & Which Resembled those of a Rat. the Ears were Long, Roundish, and Transparent—its Toes were 20 in Number, one on Each Foot being Placed Behind, and Serving as a Thumb—it had 10 or 12 Paps to Which the Young Ones Stuck fast. it is Said so soon as they are produced, And When they are not Larger than Small Beetles; but it Wanted that Pouch Which is so Common to All Other Oppossums, in place of Which were two Longitudinal Folds inside each Thigh, Equally Adapted to preserve its Offspring from every injury & Which no Tortures Whatever not even fire Will make it forsake Having Only Added that it Burrows in the Ground, and often Climbs Trees, While it Feeds Like a mouse on Grain, Fruits & Roots, I Shall Defer the Description of its Other Species till Chance gives me

• —In Vol: 4 Plate 83 By the Count De Buffon a Bat is Represented With only but 3 Toes on each of its Wings—

The Murine Oppossum of Terra-Firma.

The Vampire or Spectre of Guiana.

London, Published Dec.r 1.st 1791, by J. Johnson, S.t Paul's Church Yard.

the proper Opportunity—Miss Merion Mentions one kind of them that Should in Time of Dangers Carry its Young ones upon its Back, But Which Animal I Acknowledge never to have heard of in Surinam, & now once more to the Soldiers—

I have Said Already that it Was Verry Late Before we Left the Camp by Some Unaccountable Dilly Dally, however we Started at Last /I having the Van Guard/ With the Rangers, And the Poor Marines Loaded, NB With 9 Days Provisions on their Backs; in this Condition we had not Proceeded Long When one of the Rangers Sounding his Horn, they Spread /I Amongst them/ And fell flat down on the Ground, With Fire Locks Cock'd & Ready to Engage, but which proving to be a false Alarm by a Stag Rushing through the Foliage We All Soon Rose and Rejoyn'd—At this Moment Stept up to me Lieut: Col: Seybourgh from the Rear With his Fusee in one hand, And an open Cartridge in the Other, Who while he was Spilling All the Powder by Shaking with Canvass and in Vain Attempting to Load his piece Ask'd me three Different Times Distinctly, If I thought *he Was Afraid* to face his Enemy, to Which I Making no Reply, he instantly Retired /Muttering Some Words/ to the Place he had Come from & Leaving me Stamp'd /upon my Soul/ With No greater impression of his Valour than I Ought to have—in short having Marched Plumpety Plump the Whole Day through the Watter and Mud, we at 3 **PM** encampt on a high Ridge Where not a Drop of it was to be met With. till we had Dug a Hole for the Same Purpose, When it was so Thick that we Were Obligded to Drink it through a Cloath; here I Was Again Accoasted by the Lieut: Col, Who invited me to Some Supper in his hut And Treated me upon the Whole with verry Uncommon Civility—

We now Again Marched Course **W** and **NW** While it Rayn'd Verry Hard And we Entered in a Quabmire that Lasted 3 Hours; to me Who had the Rear to Day it was peculiarly Distressing. The Negro Slaves with their Burdens Sinking Under the Surface every Moment, While the Loaded Marines had Enough to do to Mind Themselves, and I Was to[o] Weak by the Late loss of Blood &c to Give them any Assistance—Coming near the Beach I Perceived Several *Dead* Negroes Scattered on the Ground With their heads and Right hands Chopped off, While the Bodies were fresh Which made me Conclude they must have been Rebels Verry Lately kill'd in some Engagement by the Troops and Rangers Stationed in the Pirica River, While had we been Allowed to Pursue on the 21st When we Were Ordered back The Enemy must have Been between two fires in Which Case few Could have Escaped, And All the Plundered Spoil must have been Retaken Just so it was 2 Year's Before When I was Stationed at Devels Harware. had I been at Such Times

Provided With Men and Ammunition to Pursue, I Might have Done the Colony a Material Piece of Service, & Which two *Capital Blunders* I am Sorry to Relate, But Adherance to Truth and impartiality Obliges me to it—Let these Remarks not Brand me With the name of Cruel, Since no one Could have a Greater feeling at Seeing such Manly Youths Stretch'd Dead Amongst the Shading Foliage as now I Saw And finer Bodies than were two of them in Particular Were never Beheld in any Country—

> So two Young Mountain Lions nurs'd with Blood
> In Deep Recesses of the Gloomy Wood.
> Rush Fearless, to the plains, and Uncontroul'd,
> Depopulate the Stalls, and Waste the fold;
> Till pierc'd at Distance from their native Den
> O'erpower'd they fall, Beneath the force of Men
> Prostrate on Earth their Beauteous Bodies Lay
> Like Mountain Firs, as Tall, and Straight as they.

Such is the Fate of War Which however Dreadful through all its Different Stages, is no Less a Necessary Evil, And Which Can no more by Man, than by the other Links of the Creation be Avoided—

> But Sure 'tis Heavens immutable Decree,
> For Thousands ev'ry Age in fight to fall
> Some Nat'ral Cause prevails we Cannot see
> And that is Fate which we Ambition Call
>   Written on the Plain of Fontenoy by *Della Crusca*

Enfine, During my making the Above Remark's My Poor Loaded Slaves Remained Still entangled And Struggling in the Quabmire, While the Commanding Officer With all the Other Troops /having got on a Dry Ridge/, Were fairly out of Sight, and out of Hearing, by Which Separation the Rear Guard with all the Provisions &c And in such a Situation Particularly, not Only Run the Hazard of Losing All the Baggage but of Being Cut to Pieces in the Bargain—Having not a Single European that had Strength Remaining, I now Gave Over the Command to my Lieutenant, And Rushed Forward Myself through the Wood till I Overtook the Party, When Reporting the Situation of the Rear Guard to Col: Seybourgh, I beg'd he Would Slacken his Pace till they were Able to Extricate Themselves and Come up from the Marsh, Without which I Could not be Accountable for the Consequence—to this the Reply was that he Would make Camp When he met With Good Watter, And I return'd instantly to the Rear—Having now Struggled till it was *Pitch Dark,* in a Most Distressed and Dangerous Situation the Last Man was Dragg'd finally out of the Mud, and we Proceeded on till we Entered the Camp; at Which Moment I was met by the Adjutant, And put Under an Arrest by the Commanders Orders to be tried by a Court Martial Under Pretence of having quitted the Rear Guard Without his orders, but the Truth of Which was my having Convicted him of an Error, Which Besides Savouring Much of his Pusilanimity, in Case of an Accident he Could never have been Accountable for—I was now Distracted and Shed Tears with Rage When Reflecting that I was in a Strange Country, Without a Real friend to Counsel Who were mostly Dead & Where After being So Exausted by Fatigue, Starved Wounded & Nearly Poisoned, Deprived of All my Rest, my Pay, and even my Provisions, I was next going to be Robb'd of my Character Also, the Only thing I had Left Remaining and thus, Dropping on one knee, implored the Vengeance of Heaven to Fall on my Head, if I should ever forgive this Last injury in Case I suffered by it—Which much Alleviating my Grief, I Went to my Hammock, Pittied by All the Officers While my infamous Foe was Universally Despised for whose Late Civility to me was now Accounted Viz he having Like Judas Iscariot only Carrest me to effect my Future Ruin—

All Europeans in this Climate are impatient And Cross, but Col: Fourgeoud, Lieut: Col: Seybourgh & Myself by this Time so Effectually hated each Other that no Triumvirate was ever more Compleat, While indeed the Same Distemper Raged With Almost equal force Amongst the inferiors,

> Dependants, friends, relations Love himself
> Savag'd by Woe forget the Tender Tie
> The Sweet Engagement of the feeling Heart

As for myself—"O Dier revenge Come haste to my Assistance, Or Let me Gloriously be free"—"O were I to Curse the man I hate"—but no—"Damnations Selfs' too Good for such a Wrech," these were my Ejaculations—

&. We now Again March'd the next day early Course **S** And **S** by **W** When we Pass'd Close by Pinenbergh A forsaken Rebel Village formerly Mentioned—I must here not Omit that /though a Prisoner/ I Was Ordered to Carry my Arms and Accoutrements till further Orders this was /I Believe/ Unprecedented—

&. March'd Again keep'd Course **SW** through a Mataky or Trumpetter Moras that was Verry Deep, And Which we entered when we were All in a Violent Sweat by Advancing too fast Upon the Ridge; but mens healths we here [were] not Look'd After, and What Possess'd us to Proceed in this *Sig Sag* Manner /by Changing Course every Day in Place of Going Forwards/ it was never Yet in my Power to Discover,

Without it was a Spirit to kill the Europeans in place of the Rebels—
We now having got again upon a Ridge, An Accident had nearly Befallen me uncomparably Greater than All my former Misfortunes Put together, And which was no Less than having got into a Deep Revery While I followed the Rear Guard, I insensibly Wandered Away from the Troops till I was entirely Lost and by Myself in an Unbounded forrest—Qwacco no sooner had Missed me than poor Fellow at every Hazard he Rush'd through the Wood to Recover his Master, & by a Miracle saw me While I was Sitting Under a Tree in the most Dejected State of Mind that is Describable, Sunk in Grief And having Abandoned Myself Utterly to Despair—I had that Morning thought Myself Perfectly Unhappy, but now would have given the World once more to be in the Same State—Good God–entirely Cut off from Society, Solitary–and in a Wilderness Surrounded by Relentless Savages, While a Deluge of Rain Poured down from the Heavens; in Short Tigers, famine & Every Woe Stared me full in the Face—"Farewell forever Joana"—Such was the Picture, When /Seeing the Boy/ I Started up from the Ground, And a new Life instantly Diffused itself through all my Frame—Having now Straggled some time Backwards and Forwards I Called to the Lad I saw a Pool through Which the Troops seemed to have Past the watter being fresh Clouded with Mud—But he Observing that this Puddle was only Occasion'd by a Tapira[*] Who had been in it /Showing me the Print of the Animals foot in the Surrounding Mud/ We were Again Miserably Disappointed—At this time the Boy Shed Tears Crying "Massera we Dede we are Dede"—However in the Middle of this Distress Recollecting that by the Map the River Pirica was due **W** from us I Determined to Lose no more Time but to Set forward Without Delay; thus having fresh Primed my Fusee I Bid Qwacco to Follow me, but Again to no Purpose my Compass being With the Troops, and not a Glimpse of Sun Shine Owing to the heavy Rayn till the Black Boy Put me in Mind that on the **S** Side, the Barck of the Trees Was Smoothest—This Was a Luckie Hint and off we Set through Thick and Thin, til Overcome by Fatigue and Hunger, we Sat down, & look'd at Each other again, Exactly Like two Victims going to be Executed—During this mournful Silence we now heard Coughing and the Rustling of Arms, which /thank Heaven/ at Last Proved to be our own Troops Miraculously Resting near an Old Encampment, where the Pursuing Party from the River Pirica had Lately Lodged—at this Moment notwithstanding my Present Situation of being a Prisoner &^{c} no Mortal

• —This is the Hipopotamus of S: America Which I Will Describe in Proper place—

Enjoyed an Equal Degree of Mental Happiness, Which Proves how much all Good and Evil are only such by Comparison to Better or Worse—Having been Heartily Welcom'd by the Other Officers & Partaken of Some Cold Beef and Bread, With a Gourd full of Grog, As Also the Poor Black Boy—The Party Rose and Pursuing our March We once more Entered a Quabmire or Rather a Mud Pool, the Surface being too Thin to Carry us & through Which having Woddled till it was Dark We were Oblidged to Encamp in the Middle of it, The Troops by Slinging their Hammocks in the Trees and the Slaves on Temporary Rafts made Above the Surface of the Watter on which were Placed the Powder, Victuals &^{c}—

The Good Colonel now having Drunk his Coffee in his hammock, /While he kept the Troops Standing round it in Watter Above their Middles for an Hour Before Day Light/ we Again Scrambled forward keeping Course first **W** And Afterwards **NW,** When the Road was so Verry Bad that Several of the Slaves Let fall their Loads, Breaking, and Spoiling every thing that was in them—At Last /having past through a 2^d Camp of the Pursuers/ we made Halt to Pass the night on the Old Cordon or Path of Communication on which I Formerly Discovered the Track of the Rebels When I Commanded at Devels Harware; At this Place a Small Quadrupede Running with incredible Swiftness through the Camp it was Cut down by one of our Rangers with his Sabre; this was the *Paca* or *Spotted Caviay* Called in Surinam the *Aquatic Hare.* this Animal is the Size of a Sucking Pig and Extremely Fat—The Under Jaw is Short, The Nostrils Large, The Eyes Black, & the Ears small & Naked—it has 5 Toes on each Foot, a Tail like the first Joynt of a Mans Thumb, and Whiskers like a Cat–The Colour is an Earthen Brown, with Longitudinal Rows of Buff Coloured Spotts, The Belly is a Dirty White the hair being all Over Course and Short—

The *Paca* is an Amphibeous Animal, on Land it Burrows in the Earth Like the Hog in Quest of Food, And When in Danger flies to the Watter for its Safety—

Notwithstanding this Animals being so Verry Plump and Heavy I Repeat that it Runs Swifter than most Other Animals of its Sise in S: America Contradicting the Account Given of it in the Supplement to the Count De Buffons Definition[*] Where it is Said not to be Nimble, to Run but Seldom, and then With a Bad Grace, Which may All be true in a Domestic State /for the Paca Will Tame/ but not in a State of Nature, And this I know to be true by Occular Demonstrations—We had

---

* —See Buffons Natural History Vol: 5 Page 398

this Animal Dress'd for Supper, Which is Still more Delicious than the Wood Rat, or even the Warra-Bosena, indeed nothing Can be better Eating than the Pacca or Spotted Caviay.—

The Long *Nosed Caviay* More known by the name of the *Agouti* Pacarara or *Indian Coney* is Also verry Common in Surinam. this is the Sise of a Large Rabbit, its Colour is an Orange Brown, the Belly Yellow its Legs Are Black And Slender with 4 Toes on the fore feet and 3 on those Behind, the Ears small, the eyes a Bright Black, the Upper Lip Divided With Whiskers, and its Tail is Short Like that of the Paca— This Animal Breeds verry fast And Suckles its Young 3 or 4 in Number in Conceal'd holes of Old Trees &c Where it Also Retires for Shelter if Pursued; but it does not burrow in the earth like the Former—the Agouti is easily Tamed and feeds on fruits Roots Nuts &c but i[t]s flesh though verry Good is Nothing Like so Delicious as the Other—In Surinam I have been told there is Still Another Species of the Agouti Call'd the *indian-Rat-Coney* on Account of its having a Long Tail—This I never saw, Without it is the Same Animal /And Which I Apprehend it to be/ that I have Described Under the name of the *Bush-Rat* See Plate 45 [46] &c—

On the Morning of the Twenty Seventh, we now once more finally Broke up, And Arrived at the Estate *Soribo* in the River Pirica in the fore Noon to Defend the Plantations, but Which was Already Compleated, as I Supposed it would be, before we made our Appearance, having been 6 days Cruising upon a March, Which by going straight Forwards Might have been Performed in three—

No Sooner Was I Sat Down at this Place /where was Also kept a Post of the Society Troops/ than I was Accoasted by Several deputies sent me from Col: Seybourgh With an Offer of being set at Liberty Providing I Would Acknowledge before two Commissarys, that I had been Justly arrested Which I Refused—An hour After Several Gentlemen Came to me Again, /even the Planters/ And beg'd of me

> to Comply in only Avowing on a Piece of paper /for the Colonels Satisfaction/ that I had been Wrong. When All should be Forgot, & While if I did not, I Was Henceforth to be Look'd on as a Criminal, And Guarded by a File of Marines With Screw'd Bayonets

to Which I Replied,

> that if at this Moment a Halter was Tied About my Neck, & All the Trees in the Forrest were so many Gallowses 'nay that if it were Possible to hang me so many Different Times Still would I Persevere Despising all Threats and Promises, in not Complying to Acknowledge a Crime of Which I knew myself not Guilty, At Which I Spurn'd as an infamous

The Agouti, or Indian Coney.

The Paca, or Spotted Cavey.

Request While my Honour should be equally Vindicated, even with Applause for what I had done Which was Neyther more or Less than a Virtue Construed into a Vice, that this Message and no Other should ever by my Answer

When /thanking the Gentlemen for their good Natured Intentions, but Begging they would Spare Themselves such Unnecessary Trouble for the future/ I made a Bow and they Retired—So Inveterate now was this Temporary Chief, that /having broke a Serjeants Arm in his Fury with a Stick/ he ordered my Fusee, Sabre and Pistol, to be taken from me, And to be Close Guarded by a Centinel as a Malefactor, Swearing he should do *for me* in a Little time, Which gave me not the smallest Uneasiness but on the Contrary my Melancholy hourly Abated. At this time the Marines trusting to Colonel Fourgeoud Were on the eve of a Mutiny on my Account, And this I Acknowledge gave me new Concern, till by my Declaring to have the Ringleaders instantly Discovered it was happily Qwel'd And every thing was quiet—

The River Pirica by its many Windings is thought to be Long About Three Score Miles,—it is Verry Deep but Narrow and has its Banks like all the Others Lined with fine Coffee and Sugar Plantations—its General Course is from **SE** to **NW**—

Col: Seybourgh Who was now Convinced of his Blunder but Did not know how to Extricate himself Without Shame at Last bribed 3 Officers /or rather Scoundrels/ 2 of Which whom had formerly been Private Soldiers, to ensnare me by Cross Examination—in Consequence on the Morning of the Twenty Eight, I was Drag'd to the inquisition before these 3 Judges, & in a Private Room, Where I Was Ordered to answer, to no Less than to 21 Different Articles Without being Allow'd to Sit, to ask the Meaning of Any Question, or the Assistance of Pen & ink to make Anotitions, And on which infamous interrogations, having refused to make any Reply Whatever, /Which I Call'd a *Voxet Pretera Nihil*/ the Court was Dismissed, and I Remitted to my Prison, With the new title of the English Bull Dog for What they pleased to Call Unplyable Stubborness, While I Stampd them in my Turn to be 3 Jack Asses—

During this time Col: Seybourgh With the Other Officers Went to Dine And Carouse at the Other Post, Call'd *Bellair,* where the whole Was invited & Which Party Returned in the Evening with 2 Live Sheep Which I alone never Tasted, and the Pirica News Viz that on the 20th the Estates Schornhove and Altena had been Pillaged by the Rebels, Whom we had Rooted at Gado-Saby, & Who had Also Pay'd a Visit to the Plantation *Poelwyk,* but been beat back by the Slaves—That the

Rangers Station'd at an Estate Call'd *Hagenbos* had Pursued them on the 21.ʳᵗ Overtaken them on the 23, kill'd Severals And brought back most of the Booty—Also that on that Very Day Another Party of the Rebels had made an Attempt to Seize the Powder Magazine at Hagenbos, While the Rangers were in Pursuit of theyr Associates, /which was Extremely Cunning/ but been Repulsed by the Manly Behaviour of a few Arm'd Slaves, One of Whom /belonging to the Estate Timotibo/ took an Arm'd Rebel by himself, And Next Discovered theyr Camp at the Back of his Masters Plantation for Which he was handsomely Rewarded—& from all Which I And a few other Gentlemen Made up the Conclusion, that if Seybourghs Party on the 16ᵗʰ had marched Forwards in Place of Retiring /Which however were then his Orders/ The Above whole mischief that Happened since at Pirica Might have been Prevented, And the Retaliation of the Rebels Frustrated, that the Fellow we fired at on the 21ˢᵗ Was Certainly one of the Plunderers on the 20.ᵗʰ• And that the Bodies found Dead on the 23.ᵈ had been shot that verry same Day—

During my Confinement Amongst other Fruits were sent to me some *dates* by a Society Officer—This Tree is Also of the Palmeto Species but not Extremely high, its Leafs Diverge from its Summit Verry Thick hanging Down in the form of an Umbrella—The dates appear in great Clusters being an oblong thin Fruit, Like a Man's Thumb, & of a Yellow Colour The Pulp which is Fat Firm and Sweet Adhering to a hard Greyish Oblong stone with Longitudinal Furrows—

🙠 Now Mynheer Seybourgh With all his Gentry Going to Feast at the Estate *Lamarouge* I Wrote the following Letter to Colonel Fourgeoud—

> Sir—
>
> Being Persecuted till I am weary of my Existance, by imprisonment insult &ᶜ for Crimes I have never Committed, I hope you will soon put a Period to my Misery one way or other, as nothing on earth except the decision of a Court Martial, & for Which I Pray, shall be ever Able to Persuade me that I am Wrong, I Humbly entreat of you still to Hasten my Fate, since no man of Honour Can much Longer Brook the Verry Disgraceful Usage so Undeservedly inflicted Upon me by y.ʳ Lieut: Colonel Seybourg Whom Pray Order Immediately to give in the Accusation—I am &ᶜ

Having Seal'd and Directed this Letter I Gave it in with other Papers

• —If this Loaded Negro Could Walk from Pirica to Cottica in 2 days Qwere Why Could not M.ʳ Seybourgh have Marched it in 3—

—NB: 6 was the Number

Ready to be dispatched to the Commander in Chief, & Determined to Wait the Event With Resignation—

I ought not to Forget that this day 60 Rangers going to Reconnoitre, Discovered the Old Rebel Camp at the Back of Timotibo, Which Seemed to have Contained about 60 Armed men—

In short, every thing being ended in Pirica, we now Prepared to Leave this River, And Return Back to Jerusalem, When I got Another Proposal for to Comply, Brought me by an Officer, Accompanied With the Colonels Servant, but to Which first the Verbal Answer was that, "D——nation should Seize me first." And the Second /Treating me With the Greatest Disrespect/ I Trampled Under my Feet, And next kick'd him out of Doors, Desiring him to Carry this Message with my Compliments to his Master—A Little After this We Left Soribo, at Which place Numbers of our Sick were put in the Hospital And then Marched, Steering first for Devels Harware in the River Cottica, While a M.r Jacot And Several Other Gentlemen Shook me by the Hand, And Pitying me /While they Approved of my Firmness, and Resolution/ Entertained me With Madeira Wine And Bisquits—

On the first of October we Came to Devels Harware, much Fatigued, nothing Remarkable having Happened on our March, Except that I had been Shut up During the Night with a Centinel to Guard me in one of the old Ruins on the Cordon Call'd *Seldom-Rest,* When one of the Rangers named Captain Qwaci Exclaimed, "if in this Manner one European Can Torture another how is it to be Wondered at to see them Dayly Torment the Poor African Slaves"—I Was now Ordered to be Lodged in the Common Guard Room at Devels Harwar Amongst the Private Soldiers as his Last Recourse of Persecution, However not Long /When the other Officers enterfearing/ I Was Permitted to Sling my Hammock Amongst Themselves—To Complain to *the Court* I have Already Remark'd was out of Season—To Fourgeoud I had Wrote a Letter it is true but Whether to trust more to him than I already did to Seybourgh, was the Question—Thus Situated between Scilla and Charibdes I Relied on the Court Martial as my Sheet Anchor, And only hope, While I Reconciled my Mind to the Worst that Could Befall Me—

However the Day Following my Stormy Voyage Was brought to a Conclusion by my Adversary Himself, Who being Conscious he must Lose the Battle if it Came to a fair Trial, & Seeing that All his Brutality and Threat'nings were to no Effect now had Recourse to Flattery, & Ask'd me With an Affected Smile If I had a Heart to Forget and Forgive All that was Past—to Which I Sternly Answered, "*I had not*" And Desiring him to do Worse if Worse was in his Power I instantly Prepared to Leave him—But he Again Asked the Question "Would I forget and Forgive it," Adding "on my Side the Affair shall never more be Mentioned"—Sir Said I "you have by infamous Usage tried to Compel me to ensnare myself you have by God twisted a Virtue in a Vice and endeavoured to Ruin me in ev'ry Shape but to no Purpose My Character Defies your Malice to Hurt it My Health you may—But Sooner shall this Body rot in Irons than shamefully Confess a Guilt it never Committed—No Sir–to the Supreme being itself would I not make this Vile Concession much Less to You—And if—" Here he Grip'd me by the Hand in Presence of All the Officers, And Begging of me to be Pacified Declared that he Would make Peace on any Terms "Sir say'd I, am I a Man of Honour?" He Answered I Certainly Was—"then as Such Sir" Continued I Pulling back my Hand, "I Reject every Proposal till you have Acknowledged y.e Error here in Publick, and in my Presence tear out of y.e Journal every Word, Respecting Myself on the March to Pirica, if you are Col: Seybourgh my name is Cap.t Stedman—

> Take back the Unjust Reproach Behold me stand
> Stretch'd in bright arms & but expect Command
> If Glorious deeds Afford thy Soul Delight
> Behold me plunging in the Thickest Fight
> Then Give thy Warrior Chief a Warriors Due
> Who Dares to Act What'eer thou dares to View.

The Journal Book now was instantly Produced And I was Crown'd With Honourable Satisfaction, When I Actually *gave the Col:* my hand of Reconciliation, And All the Officers Wish'd us Joy, After which we Dined together Seybourg Giving a Feast on the Occasion, While I was Seated at his Right Hand & the Champain & Burgundy Sparkled in the Glasses•—

But if the Tragedy was, the farce Was not Yet Ended for when a M.r *Gibhart* an Upstart Ensign who acted as Adjutant And Spy to Seybourgh Returned my Arms All Rust, And told me With a Jesuitical Grin that he had been verry Sorry for me, Which I knew Well to be False I instantly bid him and his Compliments go be D———nd before All the Troops, and told him at the same time that if he did not in the space of an Hour Produce my Pistol, Fusee, &.c as Bright and Clear as he had Received them From me, he might Depend I Should Put him Without Ceremony in that verry inquisition Where I Was Convinced he had Gloried to see me Just Before; Such Fellows Deserve indeed only such treatment Who too Often

• —in Case these Delicasies should seem strange in our Famish'd State the Reader ought to know that Several Gentlemen keept theyr Provisions in the Magazine at Devels Harware—

> Forget the Dunghill Where they Grow
> And think themselves the Lord knows Who

In a Little time my Arms were Returned in Perfect Order by Mr Gibhart, When to my unutterable Surprise his Master Put in my hand the Letter I had Wrote to Col: Fourgeoud Requesting a Court Martial, And which he Acknowledged to have intercepted to Prevent a Trial—

In short So Compleat was now my Triumph As had been my Disgrace by the Wickedness of my Enemies, While the News of my Coming off With Flying Colours Against the Lieut: Colonel Resounded to my Honour through the Camp, And Gave that Pleasure to every individual /Black and White, without Exception/ Which was best Exprest Upon theyr Countenances—Col: Seybourg now Also Acquainted me that Col: Fourgeoud was Encampt at the Wana Creek in place of Lieut: Col: De Borgnes Who went Down Sick—

❧ Every thing being now Adjusted And the Troops having had some Rest We set out for the Head Quarters at Jerusalem, I Leaving Qwacco at Devels Harwar ill with the Surgeon, And that Evening Encampt Opposite the Mouth of the Coermoetibo Creek, Where I Found my name Cut on one of the Trees Since I had Commanded the Barges in 1773—

❧ Next Morning having Cross'd Cottica River I Marched the Troops once more to Jerusalem /where Col: Seybourgh was Gone Before me by Watter/ Never having Past a More Disagreeable fortnight, Since I Can Remember my Existance—

However much I Suffered, Still I Suffered not the Most, finding here Amongst others a newly Arrived Acquaintance, a Mr *Pater* Who having Squandered Away in Europe Above £30,000, And Whose Beautiful Wife was Eloped from him, now Reduced to the Income of an Ensigns Pay in the Troops of the Honourable Society—This Man having Formerly Possess'd great Properties in this Verry Colony, his Situation at Present Must Assuredly be the more galling on that Account—

> Prive de tout mes biens
> dans un Climat funeste
> Je t'adore et te perds
> Le Poignard seul me Reste
> Mais Oh Je Suis Pater
> Reserve pour Souffrir
> Je Sourois Vivre encore
> Et faire Plus que Mourir

These were his Words which he Exclaimed from Voltaire on seeing me: Throwing at the same time the last money he had left Amongst the

Slaves, And indeed Nothing Could be more applicable on himself, or more Pityfull than Was now the Appearance of this poor Spouting devil, Who /God Forgive me/ Created in me no more than a loud and immoderate fit of Laughter—

Chapter 23rd

*Second march to Gado Saby—Account of a living Skelaton—
Enchanting Landscapes—Devastation—the Commander in chief
fallsick and leaves the Camp—some Rebels taken—
discourse on the Existance of Mermaids—heavy rains—deasease—
Famine—Misery*

- Col: Fourgeoud now Returned from the Wana Creek, having Sent
- down the half of his Party Sick by the Barges, and who the day Following /they being Greatly Augmented by the invalides of Jerusalem/ were All Transported to Receive the *Coup De Grace* in the Hospital at Devels-Harwar, & While all the Rangers took theyr Leave and March'd with theyr Conductor M.r Vinsack to Pirica-River—Fourgeouds News was having found during his Cruise a Hundred Empty Houses, and Seen a few Stragling Rebels but taken none—he also found a Scalp fix'd to the Branch of a Tree Which we Conjectured to be the Remains of the Unfortunate Schmidt Who was Lost, and Which is here verry Uncommon as no *Tommohawk* is ever to be seen in All this Country—This Gentleman being informed by the Ranger Qwaci /Who it seems had left Seybourgh at Devels Harwar for the Purpose/, how inhumainly I had been Treated on the March to Pirica, Did now his Utmost Endeavour to Urge me to Give in a Complaint Against him, When *Biter Bite Biter* would have been Acted Immediately but this I Scorn'd having Past my Word to say nothing About it and Which independant of every Consideration ought to be ever kept Sacred—
- Three Days After this Came up Qwacco /Who was Recovered/ And the News that Cap.t Stoelman With some Rangers had Espied a Fresh Nest of Rebels /by a Large Smoak in the Forrest Appearing at a Distance/ but had not Yet Attack'd them—That Cap.t Frederecy With a Party of Sable Volunteers was Ranging the Lee Shore Below Paramar-

ibo—that the 2 Men we had Lost on the 18th of August had Miraculously found their way to the Post at the Marawina River and that no less than 12 fine Negro Slaves were Just Deserted from the Estate the *Gold-Mine* to Join the Rebels Which so Animated Col: Fourgeoud that this indefatiguable Man /being determined to Persevere to the last Drop/ Again entered the Woods Early on the Morning of the Fifteenth, Although he and his Little Army were now Reduced Next to Nothing, And having but the Evening before buried one of his own Countrymen a Volunteer Call'd Matthew brother to the Ensign—but death was so Common to us on this Expedition that after Losing our Dearest Friend or Relation the first Question ask'd Generally was "has he left any Rum, Brandy or Tobacco—" "*Pauvre Laurant,*" Said I to his Shrivel'd Valet de Shambre /for I was again Selected as being still Healthy to be one of this Party/ "The brave Fourgeoud is like fire, he is to the Colony an Excellent Servant, but I think both to You and I a d——nd bad Master." the Man Shugg'd up his Shoulders, Reply'd "oui *Foutre*" With a Heavy Sigh And entertained me with a Pinch of Snuff—However we Set out Exactly **NE** When Just a Little before Starting 7 Negro Slaves again Ran away to their Masters And About an hour After my Box With All my Bottles was dash'd to Pieces by falling from the Head of Another, to such a Rate were these Wretches Disgusted and Fatigued—this Evening we Encamp Unknown to us near the Cassiporee Creek, thus having no Watter we dug a Pit for it as we had done Before & no more Huts were Allow'd to be Built till Further Orders, Which indeed was now of Little Consequence the Dry Season being Fairly Set in—

The Day Following we again Marched **NE** When we Arrived where Fourgeoud had Discovered the Hundred Houses, And which was no Other than a Temporary Settlement Erected by the Rebels as a Shelter or asilum on their *Expected Retreat,* before they were Dislodged by us at Gado Saby, and to which they had Given the name of *Boosy Cray* the Woods Lament; on this Spot we Encamped and took Particular Notice of Bonys House, Which was built like a Wattering Machine Elevated from the Ground and with 2 Doors that he might the Better see Around him, And Prevent a Surprise Also to keep him more healthy he having in some Action received a dangerous Wound in the Groyn Which we knew since by a Prisoner—Near Bonys House were the Private Baths here being no River Where his Women wash'd Themselves Morning and Evening—

One of our Slaves here Presented Me with a *Land Turtle* Which indeed we had met with several Times Before but having never Described this Animal I Will here give some Account of it—The *Land Turtle* of Surinam is not more than 18 or 20 inches in Length & of an Oval form—

The shell is more Convex than that of the Sea Turtles And Mark'd with 13 Elevated Regangular Shields, Dark Brown and Yellow being so hard that it will bear any Weight almost Without Breaking—The Under Shell is a Little Concave and of a Light Yellow Colour the head of this Animal Resembles much that of other Turtles, the Tail is Naked, and Short but in Place of Fins or Swimmers it has four Feet Covered with Scales, And Arm'd With Sharp Claws to Assist it in Crawling over the Ground, When this Poor Creature is in Danger it instantly Shrinks Within its Shell in Which Situation the Indians put it on the Fire where they keep it Broiling Until it is Drest When the under Shell Seperates from the Upper which serves for a Dish to eat the Contents—but a less Barbarous Way And which I always Followed is only to Provoke the Animal by the Gradual Heat of the Embers to Run Away, when Stretching out its head, Neck &c. it is easily Chop'd off, and the Food Extracted without Additional torture, of Which I was verry fond being in my Opinion Excellent eating—I have known Mr. De Graaff keep 3 or 4 of these Land Turtles for Above 4 Months for Transportation During All Which time they Lived Without any Nourishment Whatever Notwithstanding Which they were Vigourous and even Prone to Propagation, Another kind of Land Turtle Call'd here the *Arlacacca*, I have often Seen, but this is less in Circumference and Extremely Flat of an Ugly Greenish Colour & Nothing like so Good as the Former—

- The Seventeenth We Still keept Marching **E & NE** in hopes of more Discoveries but Without Success[.] This Day we past some *Ants Hillocks* of about 6 Feet high And Which I am Persuaded were Without Exageration Above one Hundred feet in Circumference, We Also saw Quantities of Valuable Timber, Amongst the Rest What they Call'd the *Black Cabbage* Tree, the Wood of Which is a deep Brown And Excellent for the use of Carpenters and Joyners—The *Sandkooker* Tree was Also show'd to me, thus Call'd from the fruit Which being divested of its Seed &c and having the Shape of a Large Onion With Small holes in the Surface, is Used as a Compleat Box for holding Sand, to Wryters; the Seed itself is both a Laxative and An Emetick but the Joice of the Pulp is a Fatal Poison—More than this I know not About them, having neyther the time or Capacity to investigate With that Accuracy Which is Peculiar to a Bottanist only—

- Having Again Marched the same Course for a few Hours We fell in With a Beaten Path Which /though in a Round About Way/ Seemed to be a Communication Between Gado-Saby, and Boosy-Cray, And having Followed this Which now led us due **W** for a few Hours, We found a Miserable Rebel Negro, Just Alive & no more, Covered over with Manicole Branches he was Nothing but Skin and Bone, And had one eye nearly knock'd Out of the Socket—I put my Bottle to his Mouth. he Swallowed a few Drops of Rum and Watter When he Say'd with a Low Voice *Dank ye me Massera* but Could say Nothing more—Fourgeoud having ordered him to be Carried With us in a Hammock, We Encampt near a Biree-Biree or Quabmire—

I Ought not to Forget that this Day we Saw a Small Number of fine *Locust Trees,* some as high as Four Score feet, And Prodigiously thick, While very Streight; the trunk is Gray and divested of Branches till near the Top on Which the Leaves are Disposed two and two to one Stem— But What made us more Particularly Notice this Tree was its Seed being like beams 3 or 4 in Number enclosed in a broad light brown Pod that lay Scattered on the ground below it, and which tasted very much like some kinds of Dutch Ginger Bread—No finer Tree than this /Which is Justly Call'd the King of the Forrest/ Can any Where be met With, the timber is of a Beautiful Cinnamon Colour, And Possesses every quality of Gravity, Polish, Grain and Durability, that Can be Wish'd for While from its Root Exudes a Gum, which by Proper Preparation Affords a Varnish hetherto Unequalled in brightness and Goodness by any Other Whatever

Innumerable indeed are the Various fine trees that are dayly met with in this Country, And where they may be had for the Cutting. yet when one Considers the Distance Some grow from the Rivers, the Great Labour in Falling and Working them, the Number of Slaves Required to drag them through the Forrest & Where no horses Can be employed— The many Dangers, and Loss of Time &c the enormous Price for best Timber in Guiana will be Easily Accounted for.—

I am well Persuaded that While some of my Readers wish me in Greenland for these Degressions, others wish me at the Devel for dwelling at All on the Expeditions &c but I have Read the Fable of the Man the Boy And the Ass, And While I am well Convinced that I Cannot please All the World I Will at Least by those Varieties have a Chance to Gratify a few of every Denomination Without Exception, this is my Plan & Assuredly a Better one than to be tied down to the Whims of one Particular Set of People—Thus I Will ever /Gentle Criticks/ Proceed in my own Way—

Most Enchanting Were some Parts of the Forrest which we Past during this March to Which the dry Season much Contributed And Where Simple Nature greatly out Shone and Overpast the most Strenuous Endeavours of Art, Such as Open green Savannah's interspear[s]e'd with Meandring brooks of Limpid Watter, the Borders Adorn'd with Rural flowers, While here and there Small Clumps of Elegant Shrubs, or a Single Beautiful Tree Scorn'd to be left Growing Designedly to

Enrich the Scene, The Whole Surrounded by a Vast Wood of Lofty Palmetos, Waving their Sea-Green Foliage above the Variegated Copses of Never-fading Verdure, blossom, & Fruit, as if to invite the Panting Wanderer Under its Cooling Shades While

> —Flaming Up the Heav'ns the Potant Sun
> Melts into Limpid Air the high Rais'd Clouds
> * * * * *
> And Tirant heat Dispreading through the Sky
> With Rapid Ray his burning influence Darts
> On Man and Beast & Herb and tepid Stream

Till in the Cooler Hours he may Return to enjoy the Bracing pleasures of the Cristal Flood, and Contemplate Natures Beauties Undisturbed! One Universal Silence Reigning All Around—How Often now did I think on *Joana* And Wish with herself Alone to Swim through Life in These Elisian Fields While as Oftentimes I thought on the Primitive Bless Enjoyed by our first Parents in the Guarden of Eden—How happy happy he

> —Who far from Publick Rage
> Deep in the Vale With a Choice Friend Retir'd
> Drinks the pure pleasures of the Rural Life, and
> Where human Felicity is ever Crown'd With
> —Simple truth plain innocence
> Unsullied beauty; Sound Unbroken Youth,
> Patient of Labour, With a Little pleas'd
> Health ever Blooming; Unambitious toil
> Calm Contemplation and Poetic Ease—

We now fell in With our own old Path, & which We followed Leading Directly to the Fields of Gado-Saby, Where quantities of Rice &ᶜ Appeared again in full Bloom, And /Which we having Cut down and Burnt/ the Poor Rebel-Negro Was Ordered /Neyther Seeming to die or Recover/ to be buried Alive, And so he was; however not Covered Up With Earth but by my Care With Green Boughs, After Which we Slung our Hammocks being Almost Choak'd with Smoak—In these Fields I saw a *Lizard* Above 2 feet Long Which the Negro Slaves kill'd and eat it & to Which they Gave the name of *Sapagala,* it was of a Brownish Green Colour, but did not Resemble the Leguana—While Amongst the Ruins of the Consumed Town We Discovered Some *Scolopendras* or *Centipedes* of no Less than 8 or 10 Inches in Length, this Enormous Reptile is of a Yellowish Brown Colour, Walks verry fast Backwards or forwards And bites to Such a Degree that the Venum it infuses /though not deemed Fatal/ Generally Occasions a fever—Dʳ

Bancroft Says they have 20 Pair of Legs, And Dr Fermyn Asserts that the Pairs are 40, but as I never Counted them, I shall only Observe that they Appeard to me Exactly Shaped like the Centipedes in Europe; Some of our Gentlemen form'd Large Collections of these Curiosities Which were very Valuable, but Which I Neglected Contenting myself with the Drawings and Descriptions only—

On the Twentieth we Marched to Visit Cofiay When I Observing the Unhappy Captive Negro Still Alive After Removing the Branches, he was by my intercession once More Transported With us, While the Slaves being Discontented With such a Load took every Opportunity in my Absence to torture him by Bouncing him Against Stones Roots &.^c as they went Along, And Dragging him through Mud and Watter &.^c—Here different Patrols Went out to Reconnoitre While the Rest Encamped in the **W** Part of Cofiaay Who besides Several Carcasses /being the Relicts of our Late Engagement/ Also Discovered no less than 4 Beautiful Fields in one Chain, Still due **W** from Cofiay & Stock'd With Cassava, Yams, Plantains, Maise, Pistachio Nuts, And Pidgeon Peas•—We found here Also a Species of *Medlars* of a Crimson Colour, and a Taste verry much Like Strawberries, this Fruit Grows on a Large kind of Green Shrub, and is Cultivated in many Gardens at Paramaribo &.^c—

A kind of Wild Plumb tree Call'd *Monpe* We here yet met with—The fruit is yellow Small and Oblong, the Stone is Large the Pulp thin, and as Sour as Vinegar but of an Agreeable Flavour—

All Which the Morning Following Were again Cut Down and Destroyed by Fire, After Which Returning to our Last Nights Camp, we found it in flames, and in Consequence Slung our Hammocks **E** in the Skirts of the Woods—I now Recollecting that the Poor Rebel Black Was Left All Alone, I Ran Back by miself to the Burning Camp to Afford him some Assistance but Where having Sought him in Vain for a Considerable time, through a thick Clow'd of Smoak, I Was Glad to Save Myself from being Lost or made a Captive by Returning to my Companions before it was Dark, who only Laught at me and Blamed me much for my Temerity.—Thus was this Miserable Object Consumed by the Flames Who but the day before had Escaped from being buried before he was Dead.—

Having now Compleated the Devastation we Marched back to Jerusalem, Where we arrived Perfectly Exausted on the Twenty fourth, And the Old *Gentleman* at Last so ill himself With a Frensy fever, that he was Confined to his Hammock And not Expected to Live through the

---

• —The Situation of the above Fields are Mark'd in the plan, Plate 55 [56] by N.º 15—

night, Which indeed was the Sincere Wish of all the Camp, however Wicked.

 But Still he Persisted in Commanding, And the Following Morning Shewed his Authority by Ordering a Private Marine to Run the Gauntlope, Viz to be flog'd through the Ranks With Leather Slings till Within an inch of his Life, for having dared to Cough /he being bad with a Cold/ Within his hearing—And by *BastonnAdding* another who was Barefooted for asking Shoes; A Captain was Also Dispersed from the Service and Confined in Fort Zelandia for having Married Without Asking his Consent &c &c &c—

In Short Sickness and Death Again Rag'd through the Camp, And every thing Was in the Greatest Confusion, While on the first of Nov!

25 Negro Slaves Again Run Away, and on the third Came the News that no less than 50 Arm'd Rebels Were Seen swimming Across the River Cottica, About a Musket shot Above Barbacoeba; in Consequence of Which Seybourgh With the few Remaining Healthy Men were Sent out on a Padrol & Who were Almost Ready to Attack their own Officers for Hunger, and Distress, Smoking Gray-paper, and Chewing Leafs and Leather to Supply the Want of Tobacco•—As for myself few People at this time Could be more Wretched having hetherto neyther Received my Provisions, or Cloaths from Mocha—thus Was I Almost Naked as Well as Starved, with a Running Ulcer in my left Foot, Since the Ambuscade in Pirica; And not a Friend that Could give me any Assistance, While to Make my Misery Compleat, My Remaining blood was two following Nights Suck'd away by the Vampier Bat or Spectre, till I Fainted in my Hammock, And was Almost Sorry to Recover Particularly When being informed by a Letter that Joana and her Boy Were Dying With a Putrid fever at Paramaribo—

At Last Arrived one of my Boxes from the Estate Mocha With Serjeant Fowler, Which Fellow /independant of my Situation/ Made me Laugh Alloud When Producing now a Letter from his Mistress in Europe, Wrote *in Rhime* And Copied from an Old Almanack Without eyther Sense or Meaning, Yet it made him happy—My Box did me the Same though three fourths of my Things were Rotted and Devoured by the Cockroaches &c—This Evening Also Col: Seybourgh's Party Returned having Seen Nothing and two Days After this Col: Fourgeoud Was so Dangerously ill, that at Last he Determined the next day Following to Relinquish his Command, and go to Town for his Recovery; While I Going my Round to Recommend Quietness Got some Words With a

• —Without this Engredient All Sailors, Soldiers & Negroes are here Perfectly Miserable Which they say keeps up theyr Spirits & some Prefer Almost to Bread

1775—NOVEMBER 14, 15, 19

Capt: P—— and no Sooner was I Returned to my Hammock than I Distinctly heard Ensign M—— Make him Solemnly Promise With his Sword to Run me through the body by Break of Day—Having Understood this Sentence of Murder Pronounced Against Me I Could not Sleep but Getting up An hour before the Plot was to be Executed I Went up to my intended Assasins, Arm'd; Whom having Call'd two infamous Scoundrels, I Challenged one by one to fight a duel but to Which they both Declined declaring they had been Drunk And begging my Pardon which Ended the Affray—What had made me more Circumspect was that my foes Were from the Borders of Italy, Whose Sanguinary Characters are no Mystery to Englishmen, though with what Degree of Justice I will not Pretend to Determine—
Now went Down Sick to Paramaribo Col: Fourgeoud, /and a Whole Barge full of others to Devils Harwar in the Hospital/, who having Sacrificed All his Troops, was at last fallen himself a Victim to his Unbounded Ambition and Avarice, for he and they might have Toild much less, and Lived much better had this Poor man but Chused it, 'While Just Equally as much Service for the Colony might have been Performed—in Short had he Possess'd All the Military Virtues of Caesar, or Alexander, they must have been Despisable While he Wanted the Feelings of a man, And these no one Stood in need of in more Superlative Degree /Perhaps *Nero*, or *Seybourgh* Excepted/ than did the identical Col: *Louis Henry Fourgeoud*—
The Command of the Remaining Scarcrows now Devolved on the Good Lieutenant Colonel, Who Strange to tell that very Evening inherited the Distemper With the Supremity, for no Sooner Was the Barge with the Old hero Row'd out of Sight, than this Gentleman was Attack'd in the Same Manner with a frensy Fever, And Which indeed now were very Common Amongst all Ranks, Broiling at Jerusalem under a Burning Sun /for it was now in the dry Season/ When we ought to have been in the Woods but for Which Excursions as I have Said Before the Heavy Rains Were most Unhappily Preferred—

At this time, and Before now Several Officers Would have thrown up their Commissions, And they had Reason, but During an Expedition or being on Actual Service this Favour is never Granted nor do I think it Ought Without the Highest Necessity, to be Ask'd for—

Nevertheless I as one who Could have Wish'd to go for some time to Paramaribo, but this Favour not being Offered to me, While all the Others /and even the Slaves/ were Relieved I Scorn'd to Give in a Petition as Long as I Could Stand—

On the Nineteenth However my Foot became so Bad, that I was Re-

1775—NOVEMBER 19, 20, DECEMBER 3

ported unfit for Duty by the Surgeon, but I Still Remained in the Camp like a Prisoner of State—

🙢 The fresh Troops, Slaves, and Provisions now being Arrived Major Medlar Marched with 150 Men to Make Discoveries—
Amongst other Plagues the Whole Camp at this time was over run with *Locusts* Who appeard every Where in dreadful Quantities devouring every thing they Could Come at Without it was Watch'd, indeed the Curse of Heaven seem'd to Attend us in ev'ry Respect Common *Lice* being so plentiful now that in Spite of ev'ry Exertion no one Could be Perfectly free, & on Which Cursed insect I here made the Singular Remark, /however indelicate, Viz./ that being put on a Sheet of White paper &c Whatever way this may be turned it always Marches Back to the Person they Come from at Least so we found it, Which made some Call out they were Condemned to be eat Alive at Last by Vermin—

The Above *Locusts* were brown, two inches in Length and Shaped like a Grasshopper, they Did not Fly but Constantly kept Crawling by Dozens, and Scores, on the Verry Tables and Boxes Where we Sat down to take our Dinners, and by night they Run over our Faces—I do not Remember that anyone Was *Bit* or *Stung* by them, However they were Vigourously *so* by Col: Seybourgh Who Continued Still in his Frensy Fever And Flogg'd the Men dayly by Mere Capreece—
The only thing good at Jerusalem was that we never Wanted Plenty of Fine fish, particularly Newmara, and Warrappa, Amongst Others were the *Patakee,* And *Ouriwifee,* both Verry Excellent; the 1st is About 2 Foot Long Shaped like a Whiting, the other is the Sise of a Large Pearch, but more Roundish and Flat—A kind of Needle fish Call'd *Naaynaay Fisee* swarm'd here Also in Great Abundance, these were Extremely thin, And About one foot in Length, Besides a kind of *Dungfish* the Bigness of a Small Herring though the two Last were only used by the Negroes—

🙢 Now Returned After 14 Days Absence Major Medlars Party With a Captive Rebel Woman And her Boy About 8 Years Old, taken in a Small Field with Bitter Cassava; the Poor Woman was Pregnant and under very Great Alarms but tenderly treated by Medlar Who was Always a humane Well thinking Gentleman—but most Unluckily he had Lost two of his best Men one *Schoelar* a Corporal, And the other Call'd *Philip Van de Bos* a Private Marine Who /having Unadvertantly meant to Refresh themselves With a few Roots of the Above Cassava/ Were both Poisoned and died during the Night With Excrutiating Pains and Convulsions; the Antidote is Said to be Cayenne Pepper and Spirits Neyther of Which were at that time to be had—

The Woman Confirm'd that Bony was Wounded, Besides the Names of *Gado-Saby* & *Boosy-Cray*—She Say'd the Poor negro we had found was Call'd Isaac & Who had been left for Dead; And that one *Captain Arico* had a New Settlement near the Sea Called fishee hollo—Nothing Could Equal She assured us the Discipline that Bony kept up Amongst the Rebels, Who was Absolutely Dispotick, and had Executed 2 of his People but 3 days before we took Gado-Saby, Only on Suspicion of having hinted a few Words in favour of the Europeans*—She say'd none of his People were trusted with Arms Except such as had first served him some years as Slaves, and had Given him unquestionable Proofs of theyr Bravery and Fidelity And which were but few in Number Compared to the others who were his Vassals, And bound to do /Without Murmuring/ Just exactly as he thought Proper but that he was Still more Beloved than he was Feared on Account of his inflexible Justice, And Great Courage—

The following Day the Poor Woman and her Boy were sent to Paramaribo With Ensign De Cabains Who had Seized them, and had nearly taken a Young Girl About 15 but Which through her Great Agility and being Stark naked Slipt through his hands—

> Visa fugit Nimphe: Veluti perterrita fulvum
> Cerva Lupim—
> —Fugit Ochior Aura
> Illa levi: Neque ad haec Revocantis verba Resistit
> Nimpha, Precor, Peneia, Mane: non insequor hostis,
> Nimpha, Mane—
>   *Ovid*—

It being Proved at the Court that the Above Woman had been forcibly Carried off by the Rebels /though many years Before/ the Poor thing was pardoned, and Joyfully Returned to her Masters Plantation—it was verry Remarkable that When the boy saw the first Cow or Horse he Nearly fell into Convulsions With Terror, nor Could he bear to be Approached by any White Person, he never having seen one Before, and Whom in his Language he Call'd Yorica Signifying the Devil—

About this time Floated by the post of Jerusalem a Dead *Sea-Cow* or *Manatee* When the Negro Slaves fell on it like so many Crows on a Piece of Carrion Swimming round it, and round it, Some with a Rusty knife, some with a Bill Hook, & each Carrying off a piece for his Dinner or Supper, at Last they Drag'd the Stinking Animal on Shoare of Which I instantly took a Drawing—

This *Manatee* was Long Exactly 16 Foot Without any Shape being an

---

* —During the night of the 17th of August When we heard the frequent firing And Hallooing and Which were the 2 heads we found on the 20th Placed upon Stakes—

enormous Lump of Fat, Tapering Backwards Without Fins and a Fleshy broad Horizontal Tail—it had no Neck And a thick Round head Resembling I don't know What, With a Flattish Snout Large Nostrils, and Bristles, both on it[s] Nose and its Chin—It had Small Eyes and Auditory Holes in Place of Ears that Open & Shut—in Place of Feet it had two Excressences or Fleshy fins like those of the Sea Turtle, Projecting from near its neck, With which it swims and moves Awkwardly on Land to eat the Grass on the Banks of the Rivers, being an Amphibeous Animal—the Colour Was All over a Greenish Black, With a hard uneven Skin by Large Knobs and Circular Wrinkles, & Was Scattered Over with a Verry few Stiff Hairs, it had Teeth in its Jaws but none before and a Verry short Tongue—The Sea Cow or Manatee is like the Whale a Viviperous Animal, the Female Sucking its Young by the Help of its Swimmers—They are Extremely Numerous in the River Amazon And theyr Flesh is Said When Fresh to be like Veal, and Verry Good, but this was too far Gone for me to taste it, it had the Marks of being twice Shot Which it Certainly was by the Rebels on the 27th When we heard at a Distance the Report of two Musquets—This Creature by the french is Call'd the Lamantyn—

Another Amphibeous Animal Peculiar to Guiana is the *Hipopotamous* or *River Horse* Also Call'd the *Tapira,* And Which bears a Great Resemblance to the Hipopotamus of the Nile on the Old Continant Except that it is a Great Deal Less in Size, This Creature is About the Size of a Small ass but much more Clumsy in ev'ry Shape—the Head is not Unlike that of a Horse, but the Upper Lip much Longer Projecting Something Like the Proboscis of an Elephant, And is Also Moveable, the ears are Short, the Tusks are Strong and sometimes Visible, the Mane is Brisly and Erect the Limbs Low and Strong, With a kind of Hoof Divided in 4 Claws, And the tail is Stumpy Like that of the Elephant—The Skin of this Creature is Excessively Thick, of a Brown Colour And When Young Mark'd with White Spotts Disposed Like those of the Stag, and the Paca, in Longitudinal Rows, it Feeds on Grass & Other Herbs that Grow in Wat'ry Places And is so Shy that When Alarm'd by the Smallest Noise it Plunges Under Watter /Also like the Paca/ for its Security, And Where it Often Remains a Considerable time—The Flesh of this Hipopotamus or Tapira is Delicate, being Reckon'd even Superior to the Best Ox Beef—See both the Above Amphibeous Animals in the Annex'd Plate

A M.r *Selefelder* of the Society Service Assured me he Saw a Quite Different Sea Horse in the River Marawina, in Which Nevertheless I Apprehend he is Mistaken While Major Abercrumby of the Same Service Declared that a *Mairmaid* was Lately Seen in the River Surinam—

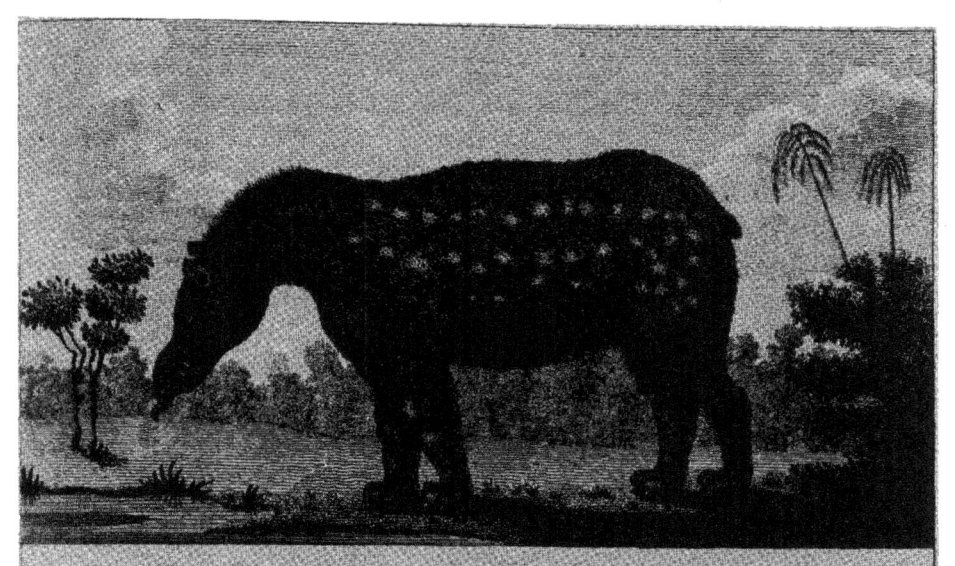

The Tapir, or Hippopotamus of South America.

The Manati, or Sea Cow of Guiana.

London, Published Dec.r 1.st 1791, by J. Johnson, St Paul's Church Yard.

Lord Munbodo Also Possitively Affirms the Existence of Sea Women, and Sea Men Who Supports they were Seen so Late as 1720—And Homer Mentions the Wat'ry train Comforting Achilles after the Death of Patroclus

> Far in the Deep Abysses of the Main
> With Hoary Nereus and the Wat'ry train
> The Mother Goddess from her Crystal Throne
> Heard his Loud Cries and Answer'd Groan for Groan
> The Circling Nereids with their Mistress weep
> And All the Sea Green Sisters of the Deep

By Horace they were Sung in Company with Latona, Diana and Venus—

> Nos Cantabimus invicem
>   Neptunum, & virides Nereidium Comas;
> Te Curva Recines Lyra
>   Latonam, & Celeris Spicula Cynthiae
> Summo Carmine &c—

In *Virgils Eeclogs* they are introduced in many places, And Ovid as Frequently Speaks of Them in his Metamorphouses

> Nais an ut Cantu, nimiumque Potentibus herbis,
> Verterit in Tacitos juvenilia Corpora Pisces
> Donec idem Passa est—
> —&c &c &c

While who has not Read of the Mariners being Changed into Dolphins, by the Alluring Charms, and Singing of the Sirinis—

In Short However Good the Above Gentlemans Veracity, And Beautiful the Poetical Descriptions of the Classic Authors they Differ Widely from the Originals, So far as I have been Able to investigate—But the Truth is this, that in many Rivers between the Tropicks both on the Coast of Guinea and South America Appear Sometimes half Above Watter, a Fish, that has Some Distant Resemblance to the Human Species, but is Less, And of a Blackish Green Colour, the head is Round with a Deformed kind of Face, And a Strong Fin from near the Eyes to the Middle of the Back, in Place of flowing Hair—the two Quandum Arms are no Other than two Fleshy fins, or Digitated Swimmers, the Female has Breasts Assuredly like a Womans, being a Viviparous Animal While the Tail is Exactly like that of a Fish, All in which it Agrees much with the Seal, this Last having no Fin Along the Back Excepted, being infinitely Larger, And never Appearing Erect Above the Watter &c—

The Above information I had from Several Old Negroes and Indians, Who all Agreed Perfectly in the Description, they added further that they Sung /Which I Apprehend to be no Other than a Grunting Noise Like many other Tropical Fishes,/ and Concluded by Assuring me that though they were Scarce, Nothing was more Dreaded by their Wives And Children than the Watra Mama, Which Signifies the Mother of the Watters—So much for the Monsters of the Deep, And now once more for those infesting Terra Firma—

I have Just Mention'd that on Account of a very Bad Foot I was Given in Sick by the Surgeon Viz on Ultimo 19th, And Who Shall Believe that this Day were Sent to me, and to Capt Perret, /Who was Also Sick/ Another Surgeon With the Adjutant and 2 Captains to inspect us, When the First gave his Declaration upon Oath of Our incapacity to Undergo Fatigue, but Seybourgh Who was Still in his Frensy Fever Swore we Should instantly enter the Woods if he Should Order us to be Drag'd in a Wheel Barrow, when Perret Complied though he Could hardly Stand, and I Swore in my Turn to Blow out the first Mans Brains who Dared Disrespectfully to Touch me; the Consequence of which was—my being Close Confined in my Hut, till I Should be Recovered Without the Benefit of Eyther Air or Exercise. Query what man of Spirit Would not Become Desperate by Such Usage? but to Proceed—

On the Eleventh Came now the News that a Number of Arm'd Rebels Were Just Seen Opposite to Devils Harwar, Who proved since to be on their Retreat from the River Comowina, Where on the 5th they had Burnt the Dwelling house of the Estate *Killestyn-Nova* With Mr *Slighter* the Overseer in it, Ramsackt the Whole Plantation, kill'd and Carried off 33 Negro Women With a Sabre Chopt off the Limb of a Mullotto Child in Revenge to its Father, And that the Rangers from Pirica were in the Woods for theyr Pursuit; the Same Day Arrived Capt Fredercy Who was now Entered from the Society Troops into Fourgeouds Regiment, And who Confirmed to us the Above Reap of the Sabines &^{c}—While finally /After Starving 4 Months/ I Received All my things from Mocha, Three Parts Rotted and Devoured by the Cockroaches And the Rest of Which I Distributed Amongst the Sick Marines. Also the Cheering Account that my Little Family were Past Danger and Recovering at Paramaribo Which so much rais'd my Spirits that the Following Morning I Reported myself fit for Duty, Which heaven knows I Was not but to Which I was Also much induced for Want of Air And Exercise in my Confinement; this Evening a Boat full of Charibee Indians Row'd up Coermoetibo for the River Marawina by the Communication of the Wana Creek—

🙰 Being now in Reality Recovered of the Wound in my Foot, And Seybourgh of his Frensy Fever I and Another Officer Determined to play him a Trick for his former bad Usage Which We Executed as Follows, Viz. having invited him With his Adjutant &c. to See us Act a Comedy by Candle Light, I Perform'd the Part of a Drunken Sailor, And the other my Wife, with Whom Quarreling, And Fighting, we next Affected to go to it in Good Earnest, And having kick'd out the Candle the Door being well Secur'd, we Laid on our Blows With Such Success in the Dark by a Wilful Mistake on the Shoulders of a Certain Gentleman, that Calling out Murder he was the First in Leaping out a Window—

Nothing ever gave me Greater Pleasure than did this Farce at Which however Col: Seybourgh Declared he would never more be a Spectator While we both Seem'd Sorry he Should have been Hurted, And Again affected to be with Each other Perfectly Reconciled—

Orders now being Arrived From Col: Fourgeoud /Who was much Better/ to Break up our Camp at Jerusalem, and March to the Wana Creek—The Sick were Sent down in Large, Barges to Devils-Harwar Which was Choak Full, And Severals of Whom were at this time Labouring Under a Disease Something Like the Timpany Calld here the *Kook* being a Prodigious hardness And Swelling in the Belly Occasion'd /it is Said/ by Drinking Bad Watter Without any Spirits Which

🙰 With us was the Dayly and General Beveridge, And on the Twenty Second We All Decampt from this Spott at 6 OClock in the Morning Marching up Alongst the Banks of the Coermoetibo Creek, through a Perfect Bogue, in Which an Old Slave sticking fast with his Burden got his Head Terribly Cut by a Soldier and Was Left where he was—Another Negroe was Knock'd Overboard one of the Baggage Boats that kept us Company and was Drowned—We to Day Again saw great Quantities of Pingoes or Warree Hogs, Which Breaking as Usual through our Little army Severals were Saber'd Down and Stabb'd while some Run off With the Bayonet Sticking in their Hams

This March was Peculiarly Disagreeable since /though out of Season/ the Heavy Rains Fell down in Torrents and so Cold were the Mornings by the Damps &c. in Opposition to the Warm Days, that they Frequently set us a Shiv'ring in our verry Hammocks, and put us in Mind of Frost particularly when Sleeping in Wet Cloaths—

🙰 This However I prevented for the Future by Marching in my Buff, like a Negro, and Putting my Shirt in one of the Empty Kettles While it Rayn'd, my Skin soon drying When the shower Was over, When Again I put it on, And found myself more Comfortable than any of my Trembling Ghastly Looking Companions—This Evening We Encampt near a Rivulet Call'd the Caaymans or Alligator Creek, Where a Tree Call'd *Monbiara* Afforded some Excellent Fruit but Which was entirely Strip'd by the Slaves before I Could eyther taste it or even see it in Perfection—

- The Rains Continuing to Pour down in a deluge I thus Again March'd Stript, when we now slung our Hammocks near a Brook Call'd *Yorica* or the Devils Creek, And made Huts or at Least Shades to Cover us—

- Having now once more Flounced through Deep Mud, and Heavy Showrs Like Amphibious Animals we Encampt at Another Small Brook Call'd the *Java Creek* 3 Miles Below Wana & in Such a Trim that most Assuredly we were more worth Seeing than the Lions in the Tower—Here now All Rested—While I Alone with a Small Party was

- Selected the next Day to go And Reconnoitre the Old Camps at Wana Creek; in the Evening we Returned having seen Exactly Nothing but Mud and Watter, through Which we had Waded till up Above our Middles, Except Some Birds, and Curious Trees Which I will not Pass Unoticed—

The Birds were Call'd the *Cromback,* the *Camawerry* and the *Crocro*—the First is a kind of Large Snipe With a Crooked Bill, Which Seem'd the Sise of a Wood Cock, the other is Also a Watter Bird but About Three times as Large, both of Which /on Account of their Swiftness, and Disappearing in a Moment/ I Can give no Other Description—The *Crocro* is Something Less than our Ravens, And I Believe of the Same Species, it is one of the most Canevorous Birds in Surinam of a Blueish Black Colour, With a Strong Bill and Limbs, And its Croaking Excessively Loud and Disagreeable Espescially by Night—

The Trees were What the Negroes Call'd the *Matakee* And the *Markoory*—The first is Extremely Remarkable for its Roots Which are Spread Above Ground in Such a Manner that they will Conceal a Score of Men from each Other, Nay so Large are they Sometimes that a Horseman Can ride through Between the Crevises, And one Single piece is Sufficient to make a Table for Holding Twelve People With the Greatest Conveniency*—to Give the Curious a Better Idea of this Wonderful Tree I Refer him to the Annex'd Plate Where I have Placed it on the Opposite Shore of the Encampment at Jerusalem, While he is Presented on the Same Plate with a fair-Weather View of the Camp at Java Creek—

The Other Tree Call'd the Markoory** is as Equally Dreadfull for its Poisones Qualities Which are of Such a Subtle Nature, that the Verry

* —If I mistake it not I saw a Piece of the Root at S.r Jos: Bankes's in 1788—

** —I Apprehend this not to be the Hiaree but the Hearee of D.r Bancrofts—

Smoak of this Wood When set on fire is Fatal to those Animals Who Receive it in their Lungs, And it is Always on that account seen to Grow by itself, Killing every thing Around it, Nay even the Slaves Refuse to Cut it Down on the Plantations so much Afraid are they of Touching it With any Tools. This Tree is Low and Ugly being Uneven With a verry few Branches and a pale Verdure—I have been told Some Indians make theyr Arrows Fatal by Dipping them in its Sap—

On the Twenty Seventh Another Padrol was Sent out to no Purpose—

I have Say'd that my Foot Was Recovered but now out of my Right Arm I Extracted two Abominable insects Which Left verry Deep Sores—They are here Call'd the *Bush-Worms* And are Shaped and Sised Like the Aurelia of a Common Butterfly, With a Pointed Tail and Black Head—They Stuck Extremely Fast before they Could be Extricated, With a Launcet from my Skin, and are got by Marching in Stagnated Watters, as we had Done, Where they Naturally Breed—My Heart at Last began to Come Sick with Accumulated Torments—Even my Mind Began to Flag by too Constant Misfortunes to Which I Saw no End and I turn'd Wearied of Life

> *Life* makes the Soul Dependant on the Dust
> Death gives her Wings to mount Above the Spheres
> Thro' Chinks, Stil'd Organs Dim *Life* Peeps at Light
> *Death bursts* the involving Cloud and all is Day
> All eye, All Ear, the Disembody'd power
> *Death* has Feign'd Evils, nature shall not feel.
> *Life,* ills Substantial, Wisdom Cannot Shun
> Is not the Mighty *mind,* that son of Heaven!
> By Tyrant *Life* Dethron'd imprison'd, pain'd?
> By *Death* enlarg'd, enobl'd, Deify'd?
>   *young*

One thing However I Certainly Did Viz upon my Naked Knees I invoked the Malediction of God to fall on me, If I did not Seperate myself from this Regiment, and Service, the first Honourable Opportunity that Should be Offered me, And in Which I Faithfully have kept my Word as shall be Seen in the Sequel—

So Dreadfully ill were we now encampt /While at the Wana it was totally inpracticable/ that all the Arrived Ammunition and Provisions Were Oblidged to be supported on Wooden Rafters, & While we Could never Stept out of our Hammocks Without being in Watter at Least Above our Knees, in Consequence of Which a Whole barge full of Sick Soldiers was Again sent down the Coermoetibo Creek, Amongst

View of the Camp at the Java Creek.

View of the Encampment at Jerusalem.

London, Published Dec.r 1.st 1791, by J. Johnson, St Paul's Church Yard.

whom the Poor old Negro with his Fractur'd Scull, Who had found Means Yesterday to Rejoyn us, even in his Shocking Condition, And Which Floating Charnel-House Weigh'd Anchor—on the Last day of the Year With which I shall beg Leave to end this Dreary Chapter—

Chapter 24th

*Two Volunteers Companies erected of free Mulatoes & Negroes—
discription of the Arowowka Indian Nation—
Col: Fourgeoud's Regiment receives order to sail for Europe—
Countermanded—Reenter ye Woods—trade of ye Colony—
discription of a Cacow Estate—Sample of sable Heroism*

- To What Good Star I was Oblidged this Day in the Middle of All the Above Bustle I know not, but true it is, that the Colonel having Sent for me he not only Solicited my Future Friendship, /And Declaring he was Sorry for all the ill he had ever done me, for which he Principly Blamed Gibhart his Adjutant and Spy/ but Taking me by the Hand as a proof of his Real Regard Permitted me from that Moment to go to Paramaribo, or to where I pleased to Refresh till Further Orders, And Which had Such an Effect on my Side, that having Converted every Drop of my Rum into Grog We Sit down together With two more Officers And Drown'd All Former Animosity in Eternal Ob[l]ivion, till we Could Hardly see, or Stand in Which Condition I took my Leave that Verry Evening of my *new* Friend and the Camp at Java Creek—
- Having Slept During most of the Passage, in The Morning I Breakfasted at Devils Harwar, where the Wretch *Gibhart* had Just died to my Great Satisfaction, and Arrived in the Evening at the Estate Beekslied, for my Negroes had made Extraordinary Dispatch *Fumming Watra* all the Time* to Encourage each Other
- On the Third I Arrived at The Fortress Amsterdam Where I was Entertained with an Excellent Fish Dinner; And Where I must Again Stop to Describe the Different Species Viz. The *Passasy–Prare-Prare–Provost–*

  • —That is, one of the Rowers Beating the Watter with his Oar at every Stroke in Such a Manner, that it Sounds Different from the Rest to Which the Others sing a Chorus—

and *Curema*—The *Passasy* is Above 2 Feet Long Weighing Sometimes 20 Pound—The Head is Broad and Flat it has two Long Barbs and no Scales. this Fish is Verry Delicate Eating—The *Prare-Prare* is about the Same Sise and Equally Good—The Provost is Large Often 5 Feet and of a Yellowish Colour—The Food of this is Less Agreeable but the Oil it Produces Comes to Good Amount—As for the *Curema* this is a Species of Mulet Sometimes Long Above 2 Feet, With Large Silver Eyes and the Under Jaw Longer than the Upper—Near this Place are Also Found a Kind of *Sea Snails* of Which Miss Merian makes mention & the Fore Part of Which Exactly Resembles that of a Shrimp—

And now for Paramaribo Where I Arrived this Evening at 6 O Clock and Found Joana With her Boy Perfectly Recovered, After having both been blind &c for Above 3 Weeks, and With whom being invited to Lodge at the House of my Friend Degraaf, I Was Perfectly Happy—

The next Day I Dined with Col: Fourgeoud who now was as well as Ever, and Who gave me a verry indifferent meal of Salt Provisions* but an uncommon Hearty Welcome—He Acquainted me that 2 New Companys of Free Mullatto's and 2 Ditto of Free Negroes All Volunteers had Just been Rais'd, that the Serameca and Ouca Negroes were Deceitful Rascals, that a few Rebels had been Kill'd in Cassiwinica Creek, that he Was in Hopes to Root up *Fissy-Hollo*—That Bony with his People were Almost Starving in the Forrest /Notwithstanding theyr Late Depredations Which Could not Last much Longer,[/] And that he Was Fully Determined if he Should Lose his Last Man to make this Rebel Foe Surrender, or Harrass him, till he and his Gangs by Hunger and distress Should be Obliged to Quit the Colony, to all Which I Answered *Bravo*—His Other News, Was that a Frenchman had Escaped Hanging for Betraying the State of the Fortification &c to the Governor of Cayenne, that he had Pardoned Cap.t Fulling for his Clandestine Marriage, And that Lieu.t Col: De Borgnes Was just entered into Matrimony with a M.rs Crawford, in short he was Quite the Reverse of What he had been Before, And upon the whole so verry Verry Agreeable in his Manners that I would never wish to spend my Time in Better Company, While how I should become at Once the Favourite of *Both* these Colonels Was a Secret I Could never yet Discover without it was Owing to Remorce of Conscience for past Barbarous Usage, or Spring from a Motive only of Jealousy to gain me from each other Who were Still Mutual Enemies; Be that as it may I Henceforth kept the most inflexible Neutrality, which I also did between them and the Governor,

* —This he Absolutely held as the best Regimen for Health Notwithstanding he had Brought Several Cooks from Europe—

where I was invited next Day, not on Salt Beef, but on a Truly Magnificent Entertainment—

Thus I kept on Dayly Visiting my Friends viz M:rs Godefrooy, the Demellys, the Gordons, and the Macneyls, I even spent a Verry Agreeable Day With the Black M:rs Sampson or Zubly, who was now a Widow•—And was Present at a Mullatto-Ball Who were All Free independant Settlers, Where the Musick, the Lights, the Country Dances the Supper, and Above all the Dresses were so Supberb And their Behaviour so decent and Genteel that the *tout Ensamble* might Serve as Model for Decorum and Etiquet to the more Fair and Polished inhabitants—

On the Twentieth Seeing a Number of Indians and Black People of Both Sexes Swimming at the back of Fort Zelandia, Young Donald Macneyl & Myself Compleated the Group by Stripping and Getting in among them and never did I See Greater Feats of Activity in the Watter, the Negroes Fighting a Sham Battle by Plunging, or rather Tumblng like Porposes, When they Strike each other with their Legs at a Wonderful Rate, but never use their Hands, & while the Indians who were of the *Arowaka Nation* Swam and dived like Amphibeous Animals— Being Sufficiently Refreshed we sat Down upon the beach near the 21 Gun Battery Where I had the Opportunity to Examine the Features and Figure of one of their Young Females as She like Venus Rising out of the Sea Came to us out of the Watter, And Which people being so Widely Different from all the other Indian-Nations, that I have Already Describ'd I will here According to my Promise give a Particular Account of Them—In the first Place her Skin which was now Emerging Clean from the River & Divested of Arnotta-Paint, Appeared much Fairer than the Copper Colour of the other Indians, Neyther were her Limbs Deformed by those Strait Laced Bracelets, or Cotton Bands, so Peculiar to the Rest, nor did her Hair hang down, Which was Neatly Plaited Closs round the Crown of her Head, and fastned in the Center with a Broad Silver Plate••—Her only Dress Consisted /both During the time she Bathed, and now/ in a Small square apron made of Beads as I have Mention'd Before, in every other Respect she was Perfectly Naked, nor Could a Finer Figure be imagined–Erect–Vigourous– Active–Young–& Healthy Which Help'd much to Convince me that when the Body is Exposed /as it Certainly Was Ordain'd by Nature/ how Little the Face is Taken Notice of, Yet, While in her Feauture, was

• —See who she was Page [79]—

•• —This at other Times they Supply by a Shell or the Tooth of a Tiger—

to be Seen that Beautiful Simplicity, that native unsuspecting Innocence, Which Cannot be put, on where even Guilt is only Known—Nor is the Olive Colour Incompatible with Beauty Which is Certainly the Standard Complexion of the Human Race, While the Black and White are only Degenerations Occasion'd by the Extremities of Heat and Cold—As this Indian Girl was Perfectly Handsome, so she seem'd to be Perfectly Happy, Which as the *Abe Renald* wisely Observes is more Frequently found in a Pure State of Nature than in that of the most Refined Civilisation—to be sure an European Woman would Blush to her Finger ends, at the verry Idea of appearing Publickly Stark Naked, but Education and Prejudice is everything Since it is an Axiome that where there is no Conscious Guilt, there Can Assuredly be no shame Thus Hail thou Primitive State

> —Such as Arcadian Sung
> Transmits from Ancient Uncorrupted Times
> When tyrant Custom had not Shackled Man
> But Free to follow Nature was the Mode.

Yet do I not Conclude from this but that is Right to be Cloathed in those Countries where the Rigour of the Climate makes it Necessary but most Certainly the Less the Better—

I Remember to have Seen an Indian Youth whose Name Was *Weekee* at Bergen up Zoom, where he Was Brought over from the Colony Berbice with General Desalve, Who Cloathed and Partly Civilized him—Amongst other things he Learnt Cookery and to be Something of a Taylor, at his Own Request that he might be enabled to Provide both for his Back and his Belly—After Sometime however Expressing a Desire to see the Colony, he no Sooner Touch'd American Ground than Stripping himself of his Lumber, he Launch'd Naked into his Native Woods, where he ended his Happy days As he had begun them Amongst his Beloved Countrymen—But to Return to the Girl she had a Live parrot Which She had *Stunn'd* with a Blunt Arrow from her Bow and for Which I gave her a Double Bladed Knyfe*—So Wonderfully Expert are the Arowaka Indians at this Exercise that they Frequently Bring down a Macaw in full Flight or even a Pidgeon,

---

* —The General Traffick Carried on between all the indian Nations, and the Europeans, Consists in Balsam, Capaiva, Arrococerra, Oil of Carrabba, Arnotta, & Bees Wax besides peces of Brazil & Ebony, the roots of Hiaree & Varnillas, Canoos, Hammocks, Slaves, Monkeys, Parrots and Peroquets for which they Receive fire Arms Knives, Hatchets, fish hooks, Combs, Coral & Glass Beads Blue Cotton Looking Glasses &c—

Indian Female of the Arrowauka Nation.

London, Published Dec.r 1.st 1792, by J. Johnson, S.t Pauls Church Yard.

1776—JANUARY 20

She takes the Bow Directs the Shaft Above
And Following With her Eye the Soaring Dove
Implores her God to speed it thro' the Skies
* * * * * * *
The Dove in Airy Circles as the Wheels
Amid the Clouds the Piercing Arrow Feels
Quite through and through the Point its passage found
And at her feet fell Bloody to the Ground
    Parody from Homers Ilead.

I Shall now Say something of the Unspotted Moral Character of these People, who not only Live in Peace with the other Indian Nations but are Peculiarly Attached to the Europeans in Particular, & Who on their Side Esteem then verry much—

As a Proof of their Gratitude, I Will only Relate one Glaring Instance—Some Years ago an Indian Woman being at Paramaribo in the Critical State of Just Going to be Delivered a M.ʳ *van Der Mey* Humanely Ordered his Servants to Conduct her with her Husband into his House, Where giving them a Private Apartment and every other Conveniency wish'd them Good Night—Before the next Morning the Woman was Delivered but When the Servants went in to Renew their offers of Friendship neyther man wife or Child were to be found, who had before Day Break Quietly march'd into the Forrest•—Various were at this time the Conjectures Concerning the Boasted integrity of the *Arowaka* Indians till no Less than 18 Months After the same Indian Returned to M.ʳ Van Der Mey With a Charming Captive Lad of the Accawaw Nation that he had taken in Battle•• And Which Presenting to his Benefactor, he only said *"thats for you"* And Without waiting for an Answer instantly Disappeared—For this Slave the Above Gentleman was offered £200 Which he Refused, and Treated him as well as if he had been free—

Here we View the Purest Gratitude Divested of every Ceremony With all her Beauties, as Want of Cloaths Reveals their native Charms in the fullest Perfection of Such as Really Possess them—I must Repeat it Again and again how Preferable to Contemptible Artifice are both the one and the other, of these divine Gifts When Beheld by those that Can see as they Ought to be Naked and Without a Veil—

The Education these Happy People Receive in their infancy being the Dictates only of Simple Nature theyr Minds or theyr Bodies are Verry Seldom Deformed While a too Nice Attention to Eyther is

• —I have Mention'd Before that the indian Women are Exempt from Pain in Labour—

•• —This is However Extremely Uncommon no peaceabler People Existing in the Universe—

468

Equally as Detrimental as a Total Neglect—The ingenious Dr Bancroft is of the Same Opinion Which he illustrates by a Quotation from Quintilian, Book 1.st Chap. 3.rd—"Mollis illa educatio quam indulgentiam Vocamus, nervos omnes et Mentis et Corporis Frigit—"

Though the Arrowaka Indians live in perfect Friendship and Harmony With us, and indeed with all the World in General, they still sometimes go to War as I have Say'd with others of the Indian Nations When Provoked in which Combats they use Bows and Arrows And the Club Call'd Abowtow*—but they do not eat their Prisoners like the Chareebee Indians, Which Last even Devoured the Negroes whom they kill'd at the insurrection in Berbice—

Notwithstanding these people live at more distance from the Sea than the Warrows &.^c Yet they have Canoos /in Which they Come down the Rivers/ Sometimes so Long as 4 Score Feet—The Arrowaka Indians particularly are Great Herba Lists And for all External Accident have Recourse to Simples with which the Woods of all Terra Firma Abound—Having only Added that of all the Indian Tribes they are the most timid, and that not an immodest word or Action Escapes from either Sex I shall once more Return to my Journal—

☙ On the Twenty fifth I was Ill with a fever and Bled in the foot, in Which the Orifice being Struck too Deep /for Struck it was, as they bleed the horses/ I Again become Lame & During which time Colonel Seybourgh Arrived from the Java Creek to recover Who was at Last Also Sick—

Now Col: Fourgeoud while he was Just Ready to renew his Operations /having Already sent a Small Detachment to the Jew Savanah for intelligence/ Receiv'd Letters from the Hague With Orders to break up the Expedition Immediately, And with his few Remaining Troops to Sail
☙ for Holland Without delay in Consequence of Which on the Twenty Seventh the Transport Ships were put in Commission and all the Officers and Privates Receiv'd their Clearance Which made them verry happy While All at Paramaribo was Alive except myself Alas—Alas Poor Joana—

☙ However on the Fourteenth of February /ill as I was with a Bad Foot, A Sore Arm, the Prickly Heat, and all my Teeth Loose with the Scurvey/ I found Means to Scramble out with a Thousand Florins in my Pocket which having Divided between Fourgeoud and Mrs Godefrooy for the Redemption of the Black Boy Qwacco and my Mullatto I Returned home without a Shilling in my Pocket, Yet by this small

* —The new Zealanders Call their Clubs Pato Patoo Which Affinity is Remarkable on account of their Great Distance—

sum of 500 Florins though not Adequate to 1800 Which I owed that Lady, she was enduced Generously to Renew here Persuasions of Carrying Joana and the Boy with me to Holland, but Which the other as Nobly as Firmly Refused, declaring that independant of all other Considerations she Could never think of Sacrificing one Benefactor to the Interest of Another, and that her own happiness or even mine Which was Dearer to her than Life, Should never have any Weight, till the Debt of her Liberty should be Pay'd by me or by her own industry to the Last Farthing, and Which she did not Despair to see one Day Compleated—She added, our Separation Should only be for a time, And that the Greatest Proof I Could ever Show her of my Real Esteem, was now to undergo this Little Trial of Fortune, like a Man, Without so much as Heaving a Sigh in her Presence, Which Last she Spoke with a Smile, next Embraced her infant, then turned Suddenly About & Wept Bitterly—

At this Moment I was Call'd to M.r *De La Mares* Who had Just Died, & by which Joanna's Sister was Also become a Widow but Left a Slave with 2 Beautiful Children in the Bargain—
In Short I Determined to Weather one or two dreadful Years in her Absence and Began to Prepare for the Voyage, During which I Sometimes went to Dicipate my mind at M.r Roux's Cabinet of Curiosity, where as my eye in Particular Fell on a *Rattle-Snake* I will Before I Leave the Colony Describe this Dangerous Reptile—
The *Rattle Snake* of Surinam is Sometimes no Less than 8 or 10 Feet in Length, and very thick about the Middle Tapering towards the neck and Tail—The Head is Dreadfully Ugly, being Flat and Broad And With two Large Nostrils near the Snout, and a Large Scale or Knob Like the Alligator Above each eye, Which are Jet Black and Sparkling—at the Extremity of the Tail are Several thin horny Shells Joined together, which are verry Dry and which when Iritated the Animal Shakes, Sounding much Like a Rattle from which it Derides its name, And Which Shells augment it is Said one Yearly by which it is Supposed its Age may be Known—This Whole Snake is Covered over with Scales Which on the Ridge of the Back it erects and Appear Dentulated to make it more Hideous—The Colour is a Dirty Orange mixed with Dark Brown and Black Spotts, which Last are Also in its Head, Appearing Like Velvet And Mark'd in a Verry Conspicuous Manner, the Belly is Ash Coloured With Transverse Scales like most other Serpents—When this Animal is intent on Mischief it Lays Coil'd like a Rope, With the Tail a Little in motion Which having Rattled it Launches forth upon its Pray Making no Further Reach than it is Long this Done

it Coils a 2ⁿᵈ Time And so forth—The Bite of the Rattle-Snakes is Reckon'd Fatal at Least is thought verry Dangerous Over All America but in Regard to the Fascinating Qualities of its eyes, Such as making mice Squirls and Birds Run into its Mouth I Believe them not, And Reject them as Fallacious Errors; the Supposed Charm Consisting in Nothing more, than that the Poor Animals finding themselves Surprised by the impending Danger are Seized with Such a Trepidation by Fear that even the use of theyr members Forsakes them, And they are Rivetted to the Place till they die or till exerting their Remaining Strength in trying to Escape, they Rush on Certain Death, being Seized During their Leaping by the Foe; And which System is Elegantly Supported by a Gentleman Who is of my Opinion in a Letter to the Editors of the new Universal Magazine for October 1787 Where he Proves that most Animals become a Prey to others During the time of Motion only, Such as Frogs, Mice &c Nay that even a man might Escape the Jaws of a Lion, or a Tiger by Laying Perfectly Still; to Which he might have Added that a Hare is more Seldom Chop'd in the Form than taken in the Chase—Thus the Supposed Fasination or Charm is found out only to be Existant in the Tremor of the Captive—the Last Rattle-Snake I saw was in Piccadilly 1788 Which I Was Told Refused Food for Several Months, Still the poor Animal was Alive but Reduced to Almost a Perfect State of Skin and Bone only—

In this Cabinet I also saw the *Blue Dipsas* of Surinam, Which had Almost the Colour of Ultramarin on its Back, the Sides were Lighter And the Belly nearly White—I was not informed that the Bite of this Reptile is *Fatal,* but that it Occasions immoderate thirst in the Patient, from which it took its Name the word *Dipsa* Signifying thirst in the Greek Language—

Another Snake I here Still Observed About 3 Feet Long, being Annulated with Different Colours And Call'd *Amphisboenoe* from the Supposition of its Having 2 Heads—but the Truth is that from its Sylindrical Figure the Head and Tail so much Resemble each other that the Error is almost Forgiveable, besides the Eyes are Almost imperseptible—This is the Snake Which being Supposed blind And fed by the Large Ants Already Describ'd is Here Honourd with the name of the King of the Emmets•—

Amongst Mr Roux numerous Collection of fine *Butterflies* one of a middle Size I thought Peculiarly Beautiful all its Wings both above and

---

• —How Miss Merian Should Call this Reptile an *Oviparus Viper* I Acknowledge Surpasses my Comprehension—

Below being Elegantly Streaked with Transverse Bars of a Velvet Black and a Variegated Bright Green—The Amazing Height and Great Velocity with which these insects fly make them so Rare being Very ill to take—The Caterpillar is a Sea Green & all Cover'd Over With hard Feelars not unlike Feathers—

For a Better Idea of the Above Snakes, & this Fly See the Plate Annex'd where the Last was Improved from Miss Merians Collection—So much for Reptiles—

I have Said that we were Ordered to Leave the Colony And that all was Alive myself alone Excepted, but now by Letters from Holland our Dereliction Was Again Countremanded for 6 Months Longer, And every one was Damp'd, while I Again Suddenly was Revived Determined to Live on Bread and Salt, till Joanna's Redemption should be Fully Accomplished—But What Grieved me to the Heart Was alas the other News from Europe, Viz that the *Scots-Brigade* had been Ask'd to Come to Britain by his Britannic Majesty, Without I Could Possibly be one of the Number, While in the Other Hand an *American* Company was put Into my Offer, but Which I Refused without Hesitation And With Contempt—

In short the poor Dispirited men were again Sent up to Magdenbergh, a Large Party Still Remaining at the Java Creek, While the Humour of the Officers Were become so Cross that a M.r Fisher of our Corps fought no Less than two Duels in two Succeeding Days Dangerously Wounding both his Antagonists who were of the Society Regiment—

I not being yet Recover'd now Stay'd some time Longer at Paramaribo where /at the house of a M.r Reynsdorp/ I saw a Portuguese *Jew* teaching his Children the *Christian Religion,* While the pious Mother of the Charity-House Nephariously Kept Flogging the Poor Slaves dayly because they were She said Unbelievers—to One Black Woman in Particular She wantonly gave 400 Lashes, Who bore Them Without a Complaint, While the Men she Always Strip'd *Perfectly* Naked, that not a *Single* Part of theyr Body might Escape her Attention—to what is Religion Come at Last?—But Let me leave such Brutes, And while I have the Leisure Give some Account of the Trade and intrinsick Value of this Blood Spilling Colony, which might be still more Rich did they not Follow the Example of The Woman with her Golden Eg, in the Fable; who Cut up the Useful Fowl all at once to Come at the Treasure, and whose Recompence in the End was nought but Dung—

In the first place in Surinam are Computed to be About Six or Eight Hundred Plantations, producing Sugar, Coffee, Cacao & Cotton, besides some Indigo & Valuable Timbers &c. The Exportation of which

The Green Butterfly of South America.

The Rattle Snake & Dypsas of Guiana.

1776—FEBRUARY 18

four First Articles Only, and theyr Value, may be seen at one View in the Following Table for 4 Successive Years

Anno	Sugar	Coffee	Cacaou	Cotton
1771	19,494	11,135,132	416,821	203,945
1772	19,260	12,267,134	354,935	90,035
1773	15,741	15,427,298	332,229	135,047
1774	15,111	11,016,518	506,610	105,126
Total	69,606	49,846,082	1,610,595	534,153

69,606 Barrels of Sugar at 60 florins Pr Barrel make ————————————	f 4176360	—	—
49846082 lb of Coffee at 8^{d½} P^r Lb make ——	21184584	17	—
1610595 Lb of Cacao at 6^{d½} P^r Lb make———	523443	7	8
534153 Lb of Cotton at 8^d P^r Lb makes————	212661	4	—
Sum Total——	f 26097049	8	8
But this as I have Said is the Avaridge Produce of 4 Successive Years & was Ship'd for Amsterdam Alone— Which makes in one Year Exactly ———————	6524262	5	0
If I now Add what Goes to Rotterdam & to Zealand besides the home Consumption & the Return of the Rum and Molasses, the indigo at 4f P^r Lb & the Timber from 5^d to 5 florins Pr Cubic Foot it will Amount to so much more ————————————	6524262	5	0
Thus Altogether ————————————	f 13,048,524	10	0

Which Supposing it was but 11,000,000 f makes a Yearly income of neat one Million in Sterling Money-

How the Above Sum is Divided between the Republick of Holland and this Colony Shall now be my Second Observation-

1776—FEBRUARY 18

The Town of Amsterdam Affords About 50 Ships of at an Avarige 400 Ton burthen Each, which Receive for importation freight of Various Commodities the Sum of ————————————	f 6000	
And for Exportation d.° of the Above Productions which grow in the Colony* ————————	32000	
Thus each Vessal gets for freight –	f 38000	
Which Multiplied by Vessels ———— 50		
Makes Exactly ————————		1,900,000
For Rotterdam & Zealand I Calculate together About 30 Vessels more of different burdens thus ————————		1,200,000
And for the Brick that serves for Ballast Passengers &c ————————		80,000
Each Guinea Ship importing yearly from 250 to 300 Negroes is Valued at Least at ————————	f 120,000	
thus Supposing Vessels in Number ————————	6**	
Amounts to ————————		720,000
Now to All this I shall add the Merchandise imported from Holland Such as Wine Spirits, Beer Salt-Beef, Pork & Flour, Silk, Cotton, and Linnen Manufactures, Cloaths Hats, Shoes, Gold Silver & Steel Ornaments.— Yron work Arms, and Ammunition even masons & Carpenters tools &.c &.c Which Profit all at an Avarige About 50 P.r Cent Besides Correspondants Charges, insurance Duty, Storehouse Expence, Porters Fees, Wharfage & Package, which Last Articles Cost the Inhabitants 10 P.r Cent more—		
Thus Altogether————————		1,100,000 — —
Makes already the Soom of————		5,000,000 — —

* —Sugar pays About £3 P.r Barrel & Coffee About as much P.r £1000 Other Commodites in Proportion
NB. this I insert unauthenticated thus Errors Excepted—
** —These are Some Years but 4 & Some Years 10 &c—

1776—FEBRUARY 18

Brought Forward ----------------------	f 5,000,000	–	–
Still Let me Mention the interest of 6 P.r Cent for the National Debt of 5 Million Sterling due by the Colony And what they are Defrauded of by Userers, in Holland, where Prodigious other Charges are brought in And where those who have made theyr Fortunes go to Spend it And the Amount will be found to Produce at Least-------------	1,000,000	–	–
The whole of which Items Added together Produce no Less a Sum Yearly than ------	f 6,000,000	–	–
Which is Clear Profit to the Republick Viz Principally for Amsterdam Rotterdam & Zealand—Thus the inhabitants of Surinam get for theyr share of the Above Treasure only ----------------------------	f 5,000,000	–	–
Which makes together as I Said 1 Mill.on Sterling or ----------------------	f 11,000,000	–	–

My 3.rd Observation now shall be to Show in what Manner the internal Expence of the Society of Surinam is Kept up by Taxes Which Amount to no Trifle as Shall be Seen—

Having Already mention'd when Speaking of the Government that the Publick Revenue Offices were Five in Number, I Will now Point out how they Collect the Cash Respectively Each for the Support of the Above Expences—

The first of these is that of Importation & Exportation duties

To this is Pay'd Viz

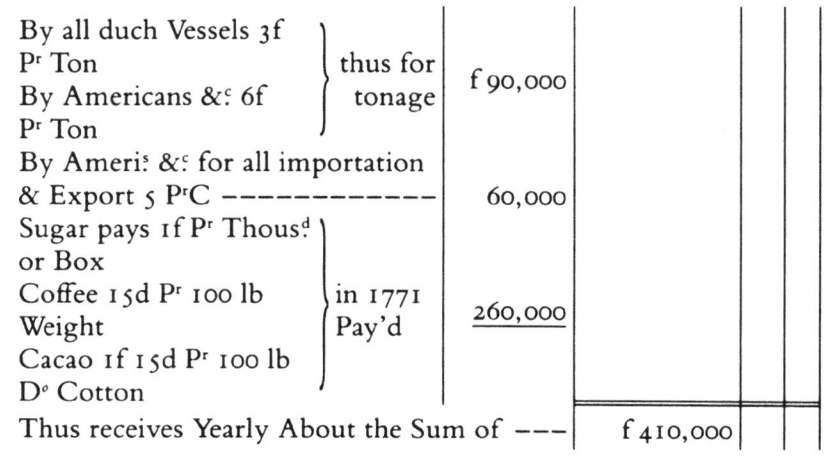

By all duch Vessels 3f P.r Ton By Americans &.c 6f P.r Ton	} thus for tonage	f 90,000
By Ameri.s &.c for all importation & Export 5 P.rC ------------		60,000
Sugar pays 1f P.r Thous.d or Box Coffee 15d P.r 100 lb Weight Cacao 1f 15d P.r 100 lb D.o Cotton	} in 1771 Pay'd	260,000
Thus receives Yearly About the Sum of ---		f 410,000

476

1776—FEBRUARY 18

Brought Forward -------------------------	f 410,000
The Second is the Office of Excise & Small Duties	
To this is Pay'd Viz	
For a Barrel of Beer --- f 3.0.0 ⎫	
A D.º of Clerret -------- 12.0.0 ⎪	
A pipe of Madeira ----- 23.10.0 ⎪	
All Spirits P.r Gall.n ----- 0.0.6 ⎪	
All Wines P.r Quart ⎬	
Bottle ------------ 0.0.1 ⎪	
The Tax on Publicans ⎪	
is -------------- 600.0.0 ⎪	
d.º on small Retailers -- 300.0.0 ⎭	
And which Amounts to a yearly Produce of at Least -------------------------	100,000
Then follows 3.rdly the Office for Taxation on Heads Which Receives for all inhabitants Black & White Without Exception Viz	
for men and Women f 2.10 ⎫	
For boys & Girls Under 12 f 1.5 ⎭	
this Produces Yearly about ------------	150,000
Next Comes the Offices for sales & Slaves which gets Viz	
For Selling Dead Stock including Estates &.c 5 P.r Cent ---------- ⎫ thus --	130,000
For Selling newly Arrived or imported Negro Slaves 2½ P.r Cent -- ⎭	
And Finally the Office for retaking negro Deserters Which was the Last Erected the other taxes not being Sufficient, which Produces Yearly Viz:	
by an Additional tax on Heads Black & White 1 f is ----------- 80,000	
by 4 P Cent of ev'ry Profit got during the Year, upon Oath is ------- 400,000	
Which makes Exactly ---------------	480,000

477

Still let me now Forget what is Yearly Pay'd for what is Call'd the Support of the Common, or Grass Fields Viz
For a House According to its Size
For a Coach---------- f 20.0.0
For a Whiskey &c ------- 10.0.0
For a Saddle Horse ------10.10.0

Which Add to the Above impositions Again ------------------------- 12,000

And then if sumon'd together Makes A Yearly Revenue of no Less than --------- f 1,282,000

Which Dreadful Taxations are Levied upon the publick to Defray the Necessary Expence And Support them from Sinking in that Whirlpool Where they are Already up to the Ears, And in Which they were Plunged by the Unprecedented Tirany and Barbarity of a Rotten Constitution—But to Proceed—

Having now Clearly Demonstrated Partly by the Assistance of Dr Fermyns *Tableau de la Colonie De Surinam,* and Partly by my own Experience that the intrinsick Value of this Settlement is worth Yearly one Million of Stirling Money And Which Riches by Proper Management might be Still Encreased, Also that the Greatest share of it Goes to the Republick, While the People are thus Crushed on theyr Estates by Almost insupportable Taxations, Which induces many to be Rogues who would Perhaps Otherwise be Honest—I shall by way of Appendix give some short Account of the Trade Carried on in this Colony by the *N: Americans.* These People Arrive /as I have Mention'd/ with Small Brigs, Sloops, & Scooners from Virginia, Rode Island, N: York, Boston, Jamaica, Grenada, Antago, Barbadoes &c from which Places they import Flour, Beef, Pork, Herrings, Salt-Mackrel, and Leaf-Tobacco for the Negroes. Fir, Boards, English Rum And other Spirits. Loaf Sugar• Spermacety Candles Onions &c besides each Vessel is bound to bring in one Horse•• Which they often Supply by a Head only, Alledging he Died on the Passage—For the Above Commodities the American Traders Export all the *Molasses* of this Colony to distil Rum at Home, & Frequently Ship Loads of other Productions And Merchandise though this is done in a Clandestine Manner, Yet by which both the Seller & Buyer find Good Account, being Ready Cash for the one, and a Cheap

• —I have Said they Can here make no Rum neyther do they Refine Sugar—

•• —Mr Hartzink Mentions 4 Horses but this is a Mistake being only one—

Bargain for the Other; From the Leeward Islands these Vessals also import Private Mullatto and Quaderoon Slaves for Sale, which being Generally Young and Handsome, Whatever may be theyr Morals go of[f] at a Considerable Price, And are Always much Esteem'd till the Purchaser Generally Perceives that he has Caught a Tartar—

Having thus Fully and Clearly Demonstrated According to my Abilities in What Consists the Commerce and intrinsick Wealth of this Fine Colony, I will now take my Leave of these Matters and Continue with my Narrative—

- On the Twenty First M.ʳ Reynsdorp the Son in Law of M.ʳˢ Godefrooy now took me with his Sail Barge for Change of Air to *Nuten-Schadelyk* one of his own Coffee Estates, Where I Saw a white Man who had Lately Lost both his Eyes in one Night by the Bats or Spectres, and
- Next day Sailing up Comewina River, he Accompanied me to the Delightful *Cacao* Plantation *Alkmaar* the Property of the Above Lady where the Negro Slaves are Treated like Children by the Mistress, And whom they all Look up to as theyr Common Parent—here were no Groans to be Heard, no Fetters to be met with, or no marks of Severity to be Seen—but all was Harmony and Content—The Superb House and Other Offices of this Charming Estate /Where Pleasure and Hospitality ever Reigns/ I have Already Represented in Plate N.º X While the Fields and Gardens, nay even the Negro Houses bore all the Marks of Perfect Peace and Plenty, And now having a Proper Opportunity I will Describe Also its Productions—

The *Cacao Trees* are Supplied from Nurceries for the Purpose like Orchards in England, And Planted verry Regularly at 10 or 12 Foot Distance from Each other Where they Grow the Height of our English Cherry Trees—but these Plantations must be well Shelter'd both from the Hard Wind And Scorching Sun, When Young the Roots not Entering Deep in the Ground, to Succour them, nor Can they at that time bear Extraordinary heat on Which Account the Groves are Fill'd up with Cassava Shrubs, or Plantain Trees for theyr Shelter, and at the Same time to kill the weed Which Grows so Luxuriously in all Tropical Climates—by these Cares the Trees will bear Fruit before they are Three Years Old, When they Afford two Crops Annually but they are best at the age of 12 or 14—The Leaf of the Cacao Tree is Above 8 inches Long, and near 3 Broad, thick, Rib'd like the Cherry Leaf, Pointed, And of a Bright Green Colour—The Fruit is about the Same Sise, And when Young like a Cucumber, but when Ripe it becomes yellow like a Large Lemmon, with Ribs like the Melon, and Tubercles Which inclose the Seed or Nuts, near 30 in Number, Longitudinally; & which when fit for Use are the Sise of Olives, and Purple Coloured—

1776—FEBRUARY 22, 27, 28, MARCH 6

The Trees are Supposed to bear at each Crop from Thirty to Three Hundred Pods each and About 300 Nuts weighing one Pound from which a Calculation may be made how much will be the produce of Each Harvest—After a few days the above Nuts are Extracted from the Pods and dried in the Shade During which time they Undergo a verry Strong Perspiration, When they are put into Barrels And fit for Transportation to be Converted into that Well known and Agreeable Beveridge Call'd Chocolate—it is Said the Cacao Trees are Natives to Guiana, And Grow wild in Large Quantities near the River Amazon, be that as it may, Governor Chattilons Son Planted the First Tree in Surinam, in 1684, And the first Crop was Exported to Holland in 1733—

A Great Advantage in Cultivating Cacao Trees is that *fewer* Slaves are Required than in any other Branch of the Planting Business, Notwithstanding which the profit is immense, Witness the Year 1774 When 506,610 lb were exported to Amsterdam Alone, Which Produced 202,614 f Dutch Money being Equal to 18,419 Pound Sterlng—The prices have been Fluctuating from 4^d to 9^d P^r lb the Avaridge being About 6^{d}½ the best Estates of Which *Alkmaar* is one Produce Yearly Above 80,000 lb Weight—In the Plate Annex'd **A** is the Leaf Above, **B** below*, **C** the Wood, **D** the Flower, **E** the Young Pulp, **F** the Same in Perfection, And **G** the seeds or nuts to make the Chocolate—

- On the Twenty Seventh we Return'd to town Where the Day before a Society Soldier was Shot for Mutiny—
- The day Following a Ship was burnt in the Roads[.] At this time the Celebrated Free Negro Qwaci who was the Prophet, Priest & King of
- the Rangers &^{c} Went to Holland on a Visit to the Prince of Orange with Letters of Recommendation from Fourgeoud, whose Praises he was to Resound and Complain on the Governor for not Treating him with due Respect, And now this being the Period of the Sessions Another Negroes Leg was Cut off for Sculking from a Task to Which he was Unable, while two more were Condemned to be hang'd for Running Away Altogether—The Heroic Behaviour of one of these Men before the Court deserves Particularly to be Quotted, he Beg'd only to be Heard for a few Moments Which being Granted he Proceeded thus—

I Was born in Africa Where Defending my Prince during an Engagement, I was made a Captive, and Sold for a Slave on the Coast by *my* own Countrimen—One of y^r Countrimen who is now to be my Judge became then my Purchaser, in whose Service I was treated so Cruelly by

---

* —Dr Bancroft & Brooks say the Leaf is light Above & Dark Below which in my Original Drawing is Quite Reverse Also in Dr Fermyn—

A Sprig of the Cocao, or Chocolate Tree.

his Overseer, that I deserted, and Joyn'd the Rebels in the Woods—Here again I was Condemned to be a Slave to *Bony* their Chief, who treated me with twice the Severity I had Experienced from the Europeans till I was once more Forced to Elope Determined to Shun mankind forever, And inoffencibly to end my days by miself in an Unbounded Forrest—Two Years had I Persevered in this Manner, Quite Alone, Undergoing the greatest Hardships and Anxiety of mind, mostly for my Dear Family who are Perhaps Starving on my Account in my own Country, I say two miserable Years had Just Elapsed when I was discovered by the Rangers, taken, and Brought before this Tribunal who are now Acquainted with the truth of my Wretched Life, And from whom the only Favour I have to Ask, is that I may be *Executed* next Saturday or so soon as it Possibly will be Convenient—

Which Speech was Uttered with the utmost Moderation by one of the finest Looking Negroes that was Perhaps ever seen, And to which his Former Master whom as he Observed was now one of the Judges made the following Laconick Reply—"Rascal, that is not what we want to Know, But the *Torture* this Moment shall make you Confess Crimes as Black as Yourself, as well as those of your Hateful Accomplices"—to Which the Negroe, who now Swel'd in every Vain with Rage, And eneffable Contempt "Massera, The verry Tigers have Trembled for these Hands" holding them up "And Dare you think to threaten me with your wreched instrument, no I despise the Greatest Tortures you Can now invent, as much as I do the Pityful wrech who is Going to inflict them," Saying which he threw himself down on the Rack, where Amidst the most Excruciating Tortures he Remain'd with a Smile & Without they were Able to make him utter a Syllable, Nor did he ever Speak again till he ended his Unhappy days at the Gallows—

I now having Dined with Col: Fourgeoud where we Celebrated the Prince of Oranges' Anaversary, /& while Mr Reyndorp gave a treat to all the Soldiers,/ he Acquainted me that the Rangers were alone Encamp'd at the Wana Creek, that the Pestilential Spot *Devils-Harwar* was entirely Forsaken at Last, And that the 2 Lately raised Companies of Sable Volunteers had taken a few Prisoners and kill'd others on the Wana Path behind Paramaribo—

I was at this time a good Deal Better but Still not being Quite Recovered—he who had formerly Treated me so severely now even insisted on my Staying some time Longer at Paramaribo, nay Gave me an Offer to Return to Europe but which I Absolutely Refused, in Short, about the Middle of the month, I was as Well as ever I was in all my Life, when I with Fourgeoud dayly went a Visiting the Ladies, but at some of whose Company no man Could help being Disgusted—So Languid were theyr Looks, and so Unrestrain'd theyr Conversation, that a M.̲̲ʳˢ N—— even Ask'd me Sans ceremonie to Supply the place of her Husband while she might as well have Ask'd me to Drink for a Relish, a Tumbler of Salts—However on the Seventeenth, at Least my Eyes were Better Feasted, When Going to Dine with *Col: Texier* of the Society Troops I first took a Walk in the Orange Grove and the Governors Gardens—Here Peeping through Amongst the Foliage I Soon Spied two most Elegant female Figures indeed, the one a fine Young *Samboo,* the other a *Blooming Quaderoon,* which Last was so verry Fair Complexion'd, that She might have past for a Native of Greece, While the Roses that Glow'd in her Cheek were Equal to those that blow'd in the Shrubries*—they were both as they Came to the World Walking Hand in Hand, And Conversing With Smiles on a Flowery Bank that Adorn'd the Side of a Crystal Brook, & in Which they Plunged the Moment they Heard me Rusling Amongst the Verdure—

> Then to the Flood they Rush'd; the parted Flood
> Its Lovely Guests with Closing Waves Receiv'd;
> And ev'ry Beauty Softening, Every Grace
> Flushing Anew, a Mellow Lustre Shed.

I Could not help being Riveted to the place for Some Time; And True it is, Again and Again, that where the Whole shapes are exposed to View, the Features Attract the Smallest Attention, While it is Equally as true that the Human Figure of Eyther Sex, whether white Black, Copper-Colour'd, or Olive when Naked Particularly Amongst the Green or Verdure, Exibits a verry Beautiful Creature to Which the most Splendid apparel Cannot Give any Additional Elegance—

However, though these were but *Slaves,* I Discretely Retired, by which I Escaped perhaps Actions Fate inflicted by Diana, And Leaving them to Enjoy their innocent & Healthful Amusement of Bathing, I Spent the Remaining Hour before Dinner Amongst the Shading Fruit Trees, flowery bowers, and Meandring Gravel Walks—Where indeed I Saw Greater Variety of European Plants than I Imagined were Produced in a Tropical Climate—Such as mint, Fennel, Sage, Rosemary, Golden-Rod, and Jesmin, The Sensative plant, Pomegranets, Roses, Figs, and even some Grapes—Of the Pomegranet Flowers a Specimen may be seen in Plate N.º 28 [29] the Figs are both without and within of a Beautiful Crimson Colour, but the Roses are Rather Pale—Here were some beautiful Pine Apples and Melons Which though they are so Generally

---

* —it is to be Remark'd that though Europeans look Pale under the Torrid Zone the native Inhabitants have Often a Freshness Peculiarly engaging Particularly Mullattos and Quaderoons—

known, I will Nevertheless give some Account of—

The Imperial Fruit Call'd the *Annana* or Pine-Apple Grows in the Centre of an Elegant Sea Green Plant, on a Stalk of the same Hue About 8 inches in Length, its Leaves Diverging near the Surface of the Earth, which are Smooth, Long, Strong, Pointed and Dentulated with hard Prickles—The Shape of this Fruit is nearly Oval, the Sise of a Sugar Loaf, All over Checkered, and of a most Beautiful Orange or Golden Colour, being Crowned with a Sea Green Tuft of the same Leafs as the mother Plant, and which when put in the Ground Produces Another Pine Apple, in the Space of About 18 Months. The Delicious taste and Flavour of this Fruit Can only be Expressed by the taste of it Which is a Mixture of Rich and Agreeable Acid, And the most Lucid Sweet—So Spontaneously Grow Pine Apples in this Climate, & of different kinds Without Any Cultivating, that on many Estates /as I have Said/ they Serve as a Common Nourishment for Hogs—

The *Musk* and *Watter-Melons* Grow Also Plentifully in this Country— The first is of a Globular form, Large like the Crown of a Small Hat, Rib'd, buff, Orange and Green, the Pulp is Yellow, firm, Sweet, and Succulant Still it is eat with Sugar, but most often with Black Pepper and Salt, the Smell of this Fruit is Excellent—The *Watter-Melon* is of an Oval or Cilindrical Shape[.] Its Colour is a Bright Polished Green and Partly Verry Pale Buff—The Pulp of this Fruit is a pink Colour, And of a Mellow Watt'ry Substance—its taste is Sweet Exceedingly Cooling and of most Agreeable Flavour—Both the Above Melons are of the Cucumber kind, Growing on Ruff Stalks With Large Leafs that Creep along the Ground while it is Remarkable that the Watter Melon which may be Freely eat in all Distempers Without the Least Pernicious Consequence, Thrives best in Verry Dry and Sandy Places—

> O thou fair Melon Sweet Distilling Child
> Of Torrid Suns nurs'd in Some Sandy Wild
> But yet more Cool than founts Secret from day
> Or Murmuring Rills thro' flood worn Rocks that Stray

In the Annex'd Plate may be seen the *Annana* or *Pine-Apple* with the *Musk* And *Watter-Melon* besides the Seed from which this Last is Produced—

❧ I now Sent to a M.ʳ Reygersman in Holland A most Elegant Collection of Surinam *Butterflies* Which are here in unnumerable Varieties, And by which even Some People make Small Fortunes, but the Verry Idea of Pricking them Alive to a Sheet of Paper, was Sufficient to Prevent me from becoming a fly Catcher—

The Musk Melon, Water Melon & Pine Apple.

London, Published Dec.r 1.st 1798, by J. Johnson, S.t Paul's Church Yard.

1776—MARCH 19, 20, 22, 26

>Lo the poor Beetle that we tread upon—
>Feels just a Pang as when a Giant Falls

- I Conducted Fourgeoud now to view M:̣ Scootens Superb Collection of Prints, Paintings, and Drawings, which Highly entertained him,
- while on the Twenty Second Cap:ṣ *Van Geurick,* and *Frederecy* with Serjeant Fowler all were Sent on an Embassy to the *Ouca,* and Sarameca Free Negroes, if Possible to implore their Assistance Against the Rebels Which they always Continued to Promise, while Colonel Fourgeoud gave them Presents; but never yet Perform'd—A few of the other officers Still Stay'd with me, Gallanting at Paramaribo, Amongst Whom Major Medler and Cap:̣ Hamel* Who had both been with General Desalves Regim:̣ in the Colony Berbice, And before that the first was in the Prussian Service—It was no bad Caricature to see us who had but so little time since Appeared like wild men now Strut through Paramaribo dressed like french Marquis—I have seen Hamel in Particular while he Carried his *Cane* in one hand, his *Umbrella* in the Other his *Hat* under his Arm and his *Sword* Dangling by his Side. Such are the Different Customs that Prevail in diffrent Countries, but to Proceed—
- Being a Particular Favourite of Governor Nepveus, I one day took it in my Head to Ask him a piece of Uncultivated Forest Ground, to Cut down and thus begin a plantation. When he immediately Offered me 400 Acres near *Wanica* but Which being in a Dangerous Situation, And Requiring a Number of Hands to Clear it as it ought to be, I Dropt the Scheme of Becoming a Planter, and once more Prepared to set out on my Duty, yet had this Plan been eyther safe or practicable, the Climate Should have been no Obstruction

>Should fate Command me to the farthest Verge
>Of the Green Earth to distant barbarous Climes
>Rivers unknown to Song, where first the Sun
>Gilds indian Mountains, or his Setting Beam
>Flames on the Atlantic isles tis nought to me
>Since God is Ever present Ever felt
>In the Void waste as in the City full

In Short having Saved a Poor Black Woman from 200 Lashes by replacing a Dozen of China which she had Broke by Accident, While Another was kill'd this day by a Frenchman who Cut his own throat from Remorce, his Companion Director hanging himself—And having Vis-

---

* —This Gentleman Sail'd Since in the Year 1783 from the Texel to the Molucco Islands where as Commander in Chief he kill'd the King of Pongar, with his 3 Sons & 600 Men And Dethron'd Also the King of Salangoor whose Land he Captured for the East India Company besides 127 Pieces of Cannon &c—

ited the Poor Negro Who had Lately Lost his Limb, I Pack'd up my Boxes, to Set out the verry next Morning on my 6th Champaign & a 2^{d} Time to take the Command of the Hope in Comowina River, Just Before which Arrived at my Lodgings 6 Loaded negro Slaves with Presents from my friends of every kind that was Valuable in the Colony—

Chapter 25th

Singular Method of detecting a Thief—A Strange escape of a Frog—Rencounter between the Rangers and Rebels—Amazonian fate in a negroe female slave—Wonderful segasity in Wild Bees—the Regiment recieves a second order to return to Europe

- Adieu then once more Paramaribo And my Dear Joana who had by this time made great Proficiency in her Learning &c, And farewell my Sweet little Johnny, Who for the Present Absorbd All her Attention—Just Before Starting I Saw M:r *D'Halbergh* terribly bit by a Large Leguana or Lizard, at the Moment he was Pressing me /And others who were Going with me/ to Stay but 2 Days Longer, when he was to Celebrate his Silver Wedding Viz a Feast on the 25 Anaversary of his Marriage–but to no Purpose, and off we went in a Chance tent boat and Came that Evening at the Estate Sporksgift, where Overtaking our own Boat /which had given us the Slip/ I Gave the Pilot a most Confounded Drubbing—Here Cap:t Macneyl entertained us a Couple of Days. During which time having Slung my Hammock Above Some Green Coffee in the Lodge, I was Nearly kill'd by its Evaporating Steams, Which I was Since told are Extremely Pernicious but with which Danger I had been Unacquainted—
- On the Twenty ninth late in the Evening we made the *Gold-mine* Where Seeing a Negro boy and a Girl Suspended from a high beam with a Rope tied to theyr Hands which were Behind them /thus in the most Agonising Tortures, and with theyr Shoulders half out of Joint,/ I Without the Smallest Ceremony Cut them Down, Swearing to Demolish the Overseer for inflicting this New mode of torture Without he Promis'd to forgive them which Miraculously did—
- On the day following we Arrived at the *Hope* where I immediately took

1776—MARCH 27, 29, 30, APRIL 1, 4

the command of the whole River; An Hour before our Landing at this Place I had Discovered a little Theft by means of a verry Singular Experiment* Which I must relate, Viz finding all my Sugar gone with most of my Rum, I told the Negroes 6 in Number, that this was not Ship Ship Bristol-Fashion, and I was Determined to find out the Plunderer by making a *Parrots-Feather* Grow on the tip of his Nose; After Which Pronouncing a few incoherent Words and making 2 or 3 Circles with my Sabre on the Tilt, I Crept under it and Shut both the half Doors After me—Here I Continued my Ejaculations Again, Peeping through the Crevises to the Rowers with Great Attention, And without theyr Knowledge, when I Soon Observing *one* of them /as Regularly as he Tugg'd at his Oar/, bring up one of his hands to his Nose, I Stept up to him, Crying "I see the Parrotts Feather thou art the Thief thou Rascal," To which the Poor Superstitious fellow instantly answered *jaw me Massera* When being Seconded by the Rest, and Kneeling for Mercy to the *Sorcerer,* he was Pardoned with all his Accomplices, who /for theyr Confession/ got a Dinner of Salt Beef and a Gourd full of Groats in the Bargin

Being now once more the Prince of Comewina, I Built a High Palace on 12 Stakes in imitation of *Bonys* the Prince of the Rebels, in *Bossy-Cray,* And which Aereal Habitation was Verry Necessary, the whole post being inundated by others Neglect, & Become a Compleat Mirepool, while my former Cottage was Long since Demolished—I here Also found the Greatest Misery amongst the Marines who were Almost naked, having sold even theyr verry Shoes, for fresh Provisions, but this is nothing to they who were the Cause of it, we Exult Say they

> That we may buy the poor for Silver, & the needy for a pair of Shoes, yea and Sell the Refuge of the wheat—
>
> Amos 8 Chap. 6 Verse

But which Grievances I however Speedily Redress'd by my Labour and intercession with Fourgeoud, whose Favourite I Became more and more, thus that the hope in a Little time was a Paradise—

Shooting was now as formerly one of my favourite Diversions, and on the fourth I brought home a kind of *Plover* a Couple *Red-Breasts* and near a dozen *grass-Sparrows*—The *plover* of Guiana is fully as Large as a Pidgeon, its Colour is a Dark brown and White with Transverse Bars on the Tail—The Wet Savannahs are Full of them And they are a Delicate Eating—The *red-breast* is a kind of Large bull Finch, with the upper

---

* —NB: this was no invention of my own, I having Read Something like it however it Answered the Same Purpose as shall be seen—

1776—APRIL 4

Part of its Body a deep Chesnut, and all the rest of a blood Colour—This is Reckon'd as Good as an Ortolan and verry frequent on all the Estates—The *Grass-Sparrow* which I think is by some Call'd the *Anaca* is a Beautiful Little Creature like a Small Perroquet, these birds are Perfectly Green with a White Bill and Red Eyes—they do much damage amongst the Rice and indian Corn flying in prodigious flocks on the Plantations.—

On the Hope the *Trochilus* or *Humming-birds* also were so thick, among the Tamarind Trees, that they Resembled a swarm of bees, Severals of Which a Lieut. Swildens brought down by Blowing Peas or indian Corn through a Hollow Reed—of All of the Tropical Birds, this Little Bird is particularly worth Attention, not only on Account of its Beauty, but Also on that of its Diminutive Sise, being not Larger than the Joynt of a Man's Finger, And when deprived of its feathers than a Large blue Bottle Fly—However they are of different Species, and Some twice as Large—These Birds varie much in theyr Colour, which is Generally a Deep Shining Green, Reflecting Purple, brown, Azure &^{c} As they fly in the Sun—The head is Cressed with a Small tuft of Green, Black, and Gold Colour;—The tail and prime feathers of the Wings are a Glossy Black—The Bill is not much thicker than a pin, long in the same Proportion, black and Crooked at the end, the Tongue being Forked like a Divided Red Silk thread with which they drink the Nectar or Honey due from the Flowers while they are Flying, during which time they are Stationary Exactly as Bees, and which Joyce Seems to be of these little Creatures the only Nourishment—They often make theyr nest on the Leaf of a wild pine Apple Dwarf Aloes &^{c}—Which is Constructed mostly of Cotton, and not Larger than the Husk of a Walnut, while theyr Eggs 2 in Number* are the Sise of Peas—In the Annex'd Plate both they and theyr little Habitation may be Seen, while it was impossible for me to draw them more Properly upon the Wing, theyr Motion being so verry Rapid that the Feathers are Hardly Perceptible, and which Occasions that Humming noise Which gave the name to this Unparraleled Delicate Creature—**

* —Miss Merian says the humming bird sits on 4 Eggs in which Again she is Mistaken I never Remembering to have Seen or heard of more than a Couple—

** —I Had almost forgot that one day going out a Shooting more than two Hundred *Monkeys* were assembled in the Sugar Cane fields leaving centinels all around to give the necessary allarm—one of these perceiving Me instantly Shriek'd, and Set all the others a running away with theyr Plunder while him Self nearly had lost his life my full Shot lodging in the trunk of the tree at the back of which he Sculk'd—after which chattering aloud he Made a precipitate retreat and followd his Companions—The above Scene appearing to Me So verry Sagasious I thought it worth inserting—

The Humming Bird, with its nest &c.

Swimming was Another of my Great Amusements which from first to Last Contributed to keep me Stronger than the Rest of my Companions—

This is the purest Exercise of Health,
The kind Refresher of the Summer Heats:
—Hence the Limbs
Knit into Force, and the Same Roman Arm:
That rose Victorious o'er the Conquer'd Earth
First Learn'd when Tender to Subdue the Wave
     Thomson—

- On the Fourteenth I Shot an Alligator, from which Excursion Returning in a Boat, a Packet of Letters was Reached over to me Comming from Col: Fourgeoud Which Unluckily fell in the Watter, and Sunk immediately—
- However the next Day I was informed of the Principal Contents by Some Officers passing by the Hope Viz. that Col: Fourgeoud going to Renew his peregrinations he Wanted me to Send up all my Spare men, Provisions, &c to Magdenbergh, And the Society troops which were now at Oranjebo to the River *Pirica* and Which I Performed Henceforth keeping only 12 Crippled Soldiers without a Surgeon or Medicines at the Hope, and as many at Clarenbeek, with which Small number Notwithstanding I did dayly Padrols by Land and by Watter—the other news was that one Ensign *Van Halm* was dead and that Another ship *with Sick* was Going to Holland while the Old Gentleman still kept Snug at Paramaribo. However he Attentively Continued to Command,
- And on the twenty third ordered a Hundred men to march from Magdenbergh to the Wana Creek & Marawina River, but who saw nothing—
During all this /Forseeing I was to be Station'd some time on the Hope,/ I Commission'd my sheep, which had Greatly encreased, together with my fowls, Ducks &c from the Estate where I had left them, of Which first I Gave a Ram and Yew for a Breed to Mr Gourley; being as I have said Before a kind Superior to any in the Colony—
- About this time one of my men brought me a Snake he had kill'd which was Long About 4 feet, and not thicker than the Barrel of a Musket, yet perceiving a Knob Larger than my fist near his Middle, I Cut it open for Curiosity, when made its Appearance an Enormous *Frog* who was Still alive And Entire, a Part Excepted on the Back of his head and Neck, which was blue and Slimy as if beginning to Putrify— However /by way of Experiment, having fastned a String to his foot/ I placed him on a Grass Plot near the River for 3 Days When finding the

1776—APRIL 26, 28, 29, MAY 6, 9

poor Devil hearty and Well I gave him his Liberty with a Caution to Give a Better Look out for the Future—

 I now pay'd a Visit to the Honble Thos *Palmer* at his Estate *Fairfield* which Gentleman was Late Kings Counsellor at Masachusets Bay, And where I Saw both the Planter and his Negro Slaves happy and Contented under his Carefull Administration, indeed few Estates in the West indies Could perhaps brag of Greater Prosperity eyther in *Productions,* or *Population,* While the Courtesy and Hospitality of the Proprietor to Strangers was Conspicuous throughout the Colony–Returning from

this Plantation to the Hope, I was now Acquainted by Col: Fourgeoud in a Letter that Mr Vinsack with his Rangers had taken Eleven Rebels besides killing Several Others, yet, that Another Party of Rangers had been *Attack'd* by the Rebels A few of whom had Unluckily been Shot Dead in theyr Hammocks while Asleep—During these Skirmishes one Remarkable Presence of Mind was Exhibited by a Rebel Negro, Viz, a Ranger having Leveled his firelock was just going to Shoot him, when the Rebel Call'd out holding up his Hand, "What Sir do you mean to kill one of your own Party," which the other Believing to be true Replied, "*God forbid*" and dropping the Muzzle of his Piece, instantly Receive a Ball through the Body from his Adversary who being Safe, disappear'd like Lightning. One of the Captive Negroes Related that the evening before they were taken, a Rebel /formerly Deserted from Fauquenbergh/ was Sabred to Pieces, as had been the other two before we took the town of Gado Saby—

 It now blew a Hurrican so Violent, Accompanied with Thunder and Light'ning, that most Houses on the hope were Unrooft, and Trees unrooted, yet my Aereal Habitation had the Good fortune to Remain Standing, in Which with Pleasure on the Eighth, I introduced both my dear Joana with her Boy who were Come once More to live with me, thus I bid fair to be again as Happy as I had been before in 1774 the more so, Since my Family, my Sheep, and my Poultry were twice the Number to Which if Added that I had begun to Plant a beautiful Garden, I might with some Degree of Justice /if not that of a Planter/ at least Claim the name of a Little Farmer.—

 in Short on the Ninth we were all Invited by M^r De Graaff to Dine at his Beautiful Plantation *Cnoppemombo,* where this Good man had Foretold to Me before my boy Being Born that he and his mother one Day Should be Free—At this Estate I saw the following Roots and Plants of which I have Said Nothing, Viz *Tayars* which are the Heart of a Farinatious Green Shrub, Growing like the Trunk of the Bannana tree, but not Above 2 or 3 Feet High, with Remarkable Large Leafs, in the form of a Heart—This Plant being Cut Down and with a Knyfe and Divested of its Outer Tegument has the Appearance and Consistancy of a Yam or Potatoe, but is better Eating being a much finer Grain—the Teyers are of Different kinds the Smallest being Preferred and made Use of in the verry Same manner as the Above Roots—A kind of real Potatoes, I here Also found in Great Quantities, but Which were only used by the Negroes being inferior even to Pigs Potatoes in Old England—

The Tobacco Plants grows here in Large hairy Leaves, that are full of feebres, its flowrs Almost forever, and will last for 12 or 14 Years but is so inferior to the *Virginia Tobacco* that it is only used by the Slaves, this Plant derived its name from the Island of *Tobago* where it was first Discovered in 1560.—Here I saw Also a kind of wild *Tea* which they Reckon verry Wholesome, but which in my Opinion was no better than English Ground Ivy—Next I found plenty of *Tomate* which being Rear'd in many British Gardens I will not further Describe, than by Observing that the Jews in Particular are here verry verry fond of it Who Stew it with Butcher meat in place of Onions—The *Physick nut Tree* I here Also met with—This is a Knotty Shrub that Grows About 10 or 12 Feet in Height and verry Slinder, the Nut that it Produces has a kernel like an Almond and tastes as Well Providing it is Deprived of a Thin white Skin or follicle, that Adheres to it; without, which a Violent Vomiting & purging is the Immediate Consequence—Next were Shown me Several kinds of Peas, and Beans, Such as the *Cassia* being hard Shining Yellowish Seeds, inclosed in a Woody Shell near 16 Inches Long, and verry Small with a black soft pulp as Sweet as Honey, which is Reckon'd a verry Safe Laxative &^{c} the Cassia Grows on a Tree verry Common in Guiana, they are I think Call'd here *Soete Boonties* and *Cotiawn*—Another kind of Pod Call'd *Sevejaars boontie* has its name from being Said to be in blossom 7 Years before it produces—A shrub they Call'd the *Snakee Weeree Weeree* Was next Showed me, Which they told me was a Sovereign Remedy in Fevers And Which I Suppose to be what is Named the *Serpentaria-Virginiana* or *Virginian Snake Root*—Besides Still Another Vegetable, or Flower, Call'd *Seven boom* Which is too Frequently Used by the Young negro Wenches to promote Abortion, As are Also the *Green pine* Apples which are said to have the same Effect—

Thus Having spent not only an Agreeable but instructive Day at Cnoppomombo we took our leave from our Good friend M^r De Graaff and in the evening Row'd Contented back to the Hope—I had Almost forgot to Say that amongst other Presents wth wch he loaded us were a

1776—MAY 9, 13, 18

few *Cocoa nuts*—These one of his Negroes After Walking• not Climbing up the Tree fetched down in my Presence, yet Not without first /on the Summit/ having had an Engagement with a Serpent, which /by the help of a Knife/ he Vanquished And to Every ones Astonishment made Drop down dead at our Feet—

On the Thirteenth the Slaves of the Hope & Fauquenbergh testified their Respect for Joana & her Boy by bringing in presents of Fowls, fruit, Eggs, Venison and Fish, while to day Mr Palmer handsomely Complimented Us, With a Large Quantity of *Maiz* &^{c} to feed our Poultry—Thus every thing Contributed to our Happiness Which was however Much Damp'd at the Disagreeable News that my Dear Friend *Kennedy had died* just after his Arrival in Holland, And that the Dutch had refused the *Scots-Bregade* to his Britannic Majesty, which indeed Surpassed my Comprehension they being his Lawful Troops, besides which it was Breaking theyr Treaty; in Short to Diversify my mind I Went on a Short visit to my French Acquaintance Monsieur Cacheliew, at his Plantation Egmond—Here I found amongst Other Company a Planter named *d'Onis* who was an Italian And had but one Arm, with which however he took up a knife at Table, and Without the Smallest provocation made a back thrust at me as I sat next him to the Surprise of All that were Present—having Luckily Parried the blow by beating up his hand with my Elbow, Which made the knife pass over my Shoulder, I Started up & was going to Massacre him in my Fury, Yet this was Prevented, when I Offered to fight him with one hand tied to my Back, at eyther fist, Bludgeon, Sword Pistol or Fusee, but this he Refusing to Accept of in a Cowardly Manner, was kick'd out Amongst the Company and Sent home to his Estate *Hazard*—So Violent was this Unhappy mans Disposition that he Lately Ordered a Negro Woman to be Flogg'd, Who was Advanc'd 8 Months in her Pregnancy till /it was Said that/ her very intestines Appear'd through her Body And all this for having broke a Cristal Tumbler—one of his Male Slaves Trying to evade his Severity Another time, was Shot dead during his Elopement, and not a Slave belong'd to his Estate Who Was not Cut and Carved by the Lash of his Whip from the Neck to the Heels—

Having now Received by Col: Fourgeoud's Orders a Proper Supply of men with a Surgeon, and Medecines, the Hope got a more Agreeable Aspect And health and Content began to be Visible in every Countenance, Amongst other things I Encouraged the men in Catching fish

• —See page [373]—plate 49 [50]—

which were here in Great Plenty and for which Purpose the negroes had taught them to make Proper Traps, Amongst which were the *Spring Hook,* and *Mansoa or Spring Basket*—Of both these I have Given a Representation in the Plate adjoy[n]ing, where the *Spring-Hook* is Express'd by Letter **A** being a Long Elastick Pole like a Strong Fishing Rod, Stuck in the Ground under Watter, at the Other end of which is fix'd a Double Line, the Shortest having Fastned to it a Stick 10 inches Long, Like the beam of a Ballance, And the Other the Same a Little Lower, while at the Extremity of *this* is Hook'd a *Small Fish* through the back fins, So that it may Swim to and fro to serve as a Bate for its Larger Species—two long Sticks being next placed in the Ground So as to Appear Above Watter, a 3.^d one that is much Shorter forms them in a Gallows—Above this Gallows is bended the Large Pole by means of the double Line, With its Beams; but in so Verry Subtle a manner that upon the Slightest touch the whole Apparatis Gives way, when the Elastick Pole Erects itself and the fish that Occasion'd it /by taking the bate/ is Suspended to the Hook in the Open Air, as it is Exibited by Letter **B**—

The *Mansoa* or *Spring Basket,* is much upon the same Construction, and may be Seen by Letter **C** Where it is Represented Open, and Under Watter, with the bate Swimming in it—this Basket is made of Reeds Call'd Warimbo, in the form of a Sugar loaf the Above Aparatis being fix'd to the Middle, and in the Small end of Which the Elastick Pole is fastned, While at the other end is an open trap door, the whole being Supported in an Erect Position by a Fork'd Stick—No Sooner has a Large fish entered, and taken the Bate, than this Pole as the former erects itself with a Jirk and the Snap or trap dorr being Shut up the invader is taken, as may be Seen by the Representation of Letter **D** And with this Difference from the former that here no Hook of any kind is Necessary—by the two Above Constructions the Genious of the Negroes is Prettily Displayed The more so Since this Manner of Catching Fish, Requires no Attendance, but the Snaps being Set at Night, the fish is found taken in the Morning, Which is Generally the *Newmara* or *Barracota* Already Described

Amongst the other fish taken by the men were the *Siliba* being a small Oval fish Checker'd, not Unlike a Pine Apple; And that cald *Sokay* which is a Large Fish & Extremely good eating[.] Also were taken here a Fish Call'd *Torro-Torro* and Another Call'd *Tarpoon,* the first as Long as three foot, the Other Which is White About the Sise of 2 feet and 6 Inches—

On the Twenty Sixth I Saw a most Surprising Performance of Activity, Strength, and Courage, in a Young negro Female /Call'd *Clardina*/

Manner of catching Fish by the Spring-Hook.

Manner of catching Fish by the Spring-Basket.

London, Published Dec.r 5.th 1791, by J. Johnson, S.t Paul's Church Yard.

at the Hope where a *Wild Stag* Having Stray'd from the Rest, at the moment it Came Galloping over the foot Path, She Seiz'd it in full Speed by the hinder Leg, and not being Able to Stop it, Allow'd herself to be Drag'd several Yards till she was terribly Wounded before she would Let go Her Gripe—Show me such a Woman on the whole European Continent—

The Hope was now Again truly become A Charming habitation being Perfectly dry, even in Spring floods, And wash'd by Pleasing Canals that Let in the fresh Watter Every Side, While the Surrounding Hedges were neatly Cut inclosing Gardens that Afforded fruit & Vegetables of every Species, Also the Houses, bridges &c Were Repair'd And finally the Stricktest Adherance to Cleanliness Amongst the men Recommended by Which Precautions not one Seek person out of 50 was found on the Twenty Eighth, where Sloth, Stink Disease, and Mortality had so Lately before Swaid its Destructive Sceptre, And in Which both the Land, and Sea Scurvey, besides the Venerial Disease had no Small Share; the *Above* Scurbutick Complaint Differing in the One Covering the whole Body With Bloaches, And the other Affecting the Teeth and Gums—As for myself I now Enjoy'd the Greatest flow of Health and Spirits, while most of my Old Shipmates were dead or return'd to Europe, Nay *not a Single* Officer was at this time in Rank Above me, Except Such as had formerly been inured to the West India Climate.

But to return to my Garden;—here were at present Exibited Carrots, Cabbages, Onions, Cucumbers, Lattices, Reddises & Pepper Cresses &c All prospering as well as in Europe Besides Some of two Kinds Viz the Common and the Red, which Last grows upon a Shrub And is Excellent to make Jam or Marmalade—the *Jesmin* Also is of Different Species, that Growing on a Small tree being most Admired, Which is of a Beautiful Pale red Colour and a most Agreeable Smel, the Leaves are thick Shining & fild with milky Joyce—One kind of a Sensative Shrub they Call'd *Shame-Shame* still Grows here as Does the Sleeping Plant—So Call'd from its Leaves which are Set in pairs Clapping Close together from sun set, to Sun Rise, and Appearing as if the two were but one, After which they Open and Resume their Duplicate Form— All the Above Shrubs were Dispearsed through my hedges besides *Pomegranets,* and *Indian Roses,* which blow fresh every Day while a few Elegant *Red Lillies* Adorn'd the Banks of my Canaals which also Grow wild in the Savannahs; the Leafs of this Flower being a verry Bright and Beautiful Green Polish; thus Situated we were Amongst Others Visited by a Madame de *Zoele* in Company with her brother, and a Mr Schadts who were Lately all Arrived from Holland and which Lady was the finest Woman that ever Europe Produced, and the most Accomplished, Speaking Every Language, and being Perfectly mistress of Vocal and instrumental Musick, Painting &c. She danced Elegantly and mounted well on Horseback nay she even excelled at Shooting and Fencing, while I Could not Help offering her my Assistance in learning to Swim, which however /with a Smile/ She Thought Proper to Refuse—in Short my Verry Soldiers and Negroes were Compleatly Happy, amongst Whom the most Perfect Harmony Consisted, while I frequently indulged them with a merry evening and a Gray beard of Rum—One night in the middle of this Festivity I Secretly Ordered the Sentinel to fire his Piece, and made a false Alarm, as if the Enemy was on the Estate; when I had the Satisfaction to See them Seize their Arms, and rush out with the Greatest order and intrepidity, which Experiment I was induced the Reader[?] to put in Practice—as it was Reported that the Rebels intended to Pay a Visit to the River Comowina—However this Joy and festivity Lasted not Long by the Setting in of the Dry Season, when Mortality once more began to Rage, 10 or 12 Men Dying dayly at the Java Creek, and Magdenbergh, while those under my Command &c. at the Hope diminished Hourly, Amongst others on the third my Surgeon made me Report that my Ensign Mr. De Cabains had his Anchor a Peek, and would Certainly Set Sail for the Other World at the Ebb tide, Which was the Case for he Died that verry Evening, and Which Grieved me the more he having Got his Commission through my Interest, And the next Day With the Spring flood My Dams Broke through, which put the whole post Under Watter and Created such a Confusion, that to drink the Kings Health was Quite out of our Memory while the Overseer a Mr. *Blenderman* Refusing me every Assistance, So hot a Quarrel at Last ensued, that he was fain to make his Escape from the Plantation—I have frequently mention'd the insolence of those brutes, but I must Compleat their Character by Saying that most of them, are the Scum of the Earth, and having been brought up in Germany, or else where, Under the Cane of Some Corporal, now Distribute theyr Sause & Barbarities with double interest where they Dare—"Well" said one of these Rascals ironically to an old free Negro "don't you believe that the monkeys are a Parcel of Damn'd Christians that have been thus transform'd for Showing so much Lenity to Such as you?"—"No Sir /Replied the Black man/ we think not that the Monkeys are Damn'd Christians, but I and all of us Believe that many Christians are a Parcel of Damn'd Monkeys" nor Did ever any Repartee Give me Greater Satisfaction. of the Administrators I shall say nothing nor of the Appraisors of Estates having I think Already Mention'd that the first get 10 Pr. Cent of All the Produce & the 2d

Riches for the Purchasers & themselves by Selling under Value What is intrusted to theyr Care—

🙵 I now being informed that a M.ʳ Morym the Administrator of the Hope was on the Opposite Shore, in a piece of new Cultivated Ground, with the impertinent Blenderman, I row'd over to th.ᵐ Arm'd with a Bludgeon, and Ask'd for immediate Satisfaction from the Later that is to beg my Pardon or take a Broken Head in his masters Presence, he Chose the first and having Promised to Repair my Dams, I broke my Stick which I threw at his feet, when a Reconciliation Was again Reestablished—

Walking through these new fields, where Already a neat new [house] had been built &.ͨ I saw some Beautiful Birds, Amongst which a Wood Pecker & which indeed I ought Formerly to have Described M.ʳ Mathew having shot one, besides Another unknown bird, when I was at Magdenbergh, of which nevertheless I had both taken the Copy; the above *Wood pecker* which is the Size of a Thrush is of an elegant Cinnamon Colour, Specked with Dark brown and Yellow, near the Rump it is Perfectly Yellow, the head is Crested with a fine Crown of Small Feathers like the body, the Tail is long and Black, the bill is Streight and of a Sea Green Colour, as are the Legs and the iris of the Eye, under which on each Side are two Spots of Beautiful Crimson—the *Anominus* bird /which However the Negroes Call'd *Woodo-Louso fowlo* as feeding they say'd on Wood Lice/ is Larger than the Former but uncommonly Brilliant in its Plumage, the head and upper part of its Body being of a Rich Grass Green, the breast and belly Crimson, divided by an Ash Coloured Bar—the Tail is long and dark Blue, as are the Prime Feathers in the Wings, which are Also divided from the Green by an Ash Coloured Bar, the Bill is Yellow and hooked, being Surrounded by a Number of Small black feathers, as are the eyes the iris of which is of a Blood Colour—

In the Annex'd Plate both the Above birds may be Seen but as I said however beautiful the Plumage the Melodious Song is here Verry Scarce*

On this Spot were Also Several Tame *Gelenies* or Guinea Hens in Surinam Call'd *Tokay* but as these are So well known in England I will Say nothing About them—Amongst the Plants I here Saw the *American*

---

* —For Natures hand
  That with a Sportive vanity has deck'd
  The plumy nations, there her gayest hues
  Profusely pour. But if She bids them Shine
  Array'd in all the beauteous beams of day
  Yet frugal Still She humbles them in Song—

The Yellow Woodpecker & Wood-louse fowl.

Aloes Tree being Above half a Foot in Thickness, and Above 20 Feet in Length, for ever Green, Pithy within; and without Covered with Sharp Pointed Follicles which grow less as they Approach near the Summit, this Tree has numerous thick Leaves Diverging as its Base like the Pine Apple plant, Which are verry Long Broad Pointed & Dentulated with Strong Prickles—On the top of it Grows a Cluster of Yellow Flowers, Whose Pedicles Contain the Seed of future Aloes and which never Fail to Come to Perfection in 2 Months—In the Skirts of the Surrounding Woods I was also Shoed the *Vanillas* or *Bannilla,* which is a Shrub that Climbs up Alongst the trunk of Other Trees Adhereing Close to the bark like Nebees, or ivy, by the help of its tendrils—The Leaves are Prodigiously thick and Dark Green, As Also the Fruit Consisting in a triangular Pod of 6 or 8 inches long, and fill'd with Small black polished Seeds—these pods having Dried a fortnight in the Sun become brown, having a Fattish Aromatick Taste, and most agreeable Flavour, on Which Account they are Used to Scent the Chocolate—there are 3 Different Kinds of Vanilla, that being extremely the best Which has its Pods most Long and Most Slender

A Small sweetish Seed was here Also Shown me by the Negroes which they Call'd *Bonjera* & eat with Sugar—On Returning to the Hope I met Joanas Uncle, Who had Shot one of the *Howling Baboons* & Which he Brought to Show me, being of no Less a Size than a Small bull Dog, the Colour of these Animals is a Reddish Brown With Long hair they have a beard, And are upon the Whole Extremely Ugly, but what mostly Distinguishes them from Other Monkeys, is theyr Abominable *Howling* which they do in Chorus, and is So Loud that it Can be Heard at Above 1 Miles Distance, which Discordant Concerts the negroes told me they Generally Repeat both night and Day at the Period of high Watter, and which they know by instinct; they are Also verry Lascivious and will sometimes Attack the female of the Human Species—

Being again entered into the Discriptive Parts, I must not omit one most Singular Remark Viz On the Sixteenth being Visited by a Neighbouring Gentleman I had no Sooner Conducted him to the top of my ladder, than in place of entering my Areal Habitation, he leap'd down to the bottom roaring with Agony, and instantly Plunged his head into the river; Looking up I Soon Discovered the Cause of his Distress Which was no other than an enormous Nest of *Wassee-wassee,* or *Wild bees,* Just Above my head as now I Stood in my door, when I, Suddingly took to my Heels as he had Done, and Ordered them without Delay to be demolished[.] A Tar Mop was Brought in Consequence, and the Devastation just going to begin, but Which Was prevented by an old Negro Who Stept up to me Offering to Receive any Punishment if a Single bee Should *ever Sting me* in person, "Massera" Said he "they would have Stung you long before now had you been a Stranger to them, but they being your tenants, that is Gradually Allow'd to build upon your territories, they Assuredly know you and Yours, and will never hurt eyther you or them["]—Done said I, and tying the black man to a Tree I made Qwacco Assend the Ladder Quite Naked, but he was not hurted—I now Ventured to follow and Declare upon my Honour, that even after Shaking the Nest which made the inhabitants all buz About my Ears not a Single bee Attempted to Sting me for which Discovery I Recompensed the old Negro with a Gallon of Rum—This Swarm of Bees I Since kept unhurted as my Guards who have made many Overseeers take to this Desperate Leap, and which Rascals I never faild to Send up my Ladder with Some frivolous Message When I owed them any Revenge which was not Seldom—Nay the Above Negro declared to me that on his Masters Estate was an Ancient Tree, in Which had been Lodged since ever he Could Remember one Society of *Birds,* and Another of these *Bees* who lived in the Greatest Harmony together While should any Strange birds Come to disturb or Feed on the Bees, they were instantly Repulsed by their Feather'd Allies, and if Strange bees Dared to Come near the Birds nests, the native Swarm instantly Stung the invaders to Death, Adding that his masters family had so much Regard for the Above Association, that the Tree was forbid to be touched by a Hatchet till it Should drop down by Old Age, But now of Something else—

A Padrol Arriving from Rietwyk in Pirica brought the news that Col: Fourgeouds Troops were Just Return'd /from a Cruize to the Marawina/ at the Java Creek, and that between them and the Rangers Several Rebel fields had been Destroyed during this Campeign, which sable Allies for theyr faithful Services were now Complimented by the Society with new Arms, and had been Cloathed for the first time in Green Liv'ry—but the other news of more importance was that the Ambassadors were Returned the 15.th Instant from the Ouca and Sarameca-Negroes, having made a fruitless Journey there, Since neyther of these Gangs would Lend the Smallest Assistance, in Consequence of Which /Col: Fourgeoud being tired himself, and having Perfectly Exausted his troops While indeed most of the Rebel Settlements were Destroyed/ he At Last Determined to break up the Whole Expedition, & of Which he Previously Acquainted the Prince of Orange—

thus on the following Day I Received an Order, to Leave the River Comowina on the 15th Current, And with All the troops under my Command to Row down to Paramaribo, Where the Transport Ships for our Departure were put in Commission Which order I instantly read to all the men to theyr great & unspeakable Joy, and next began to make the Preparations, yet while my breast laboured with heavy Sighs.

O my Dr Joana, O my Boy, who at this time became so verry ill the one with a Fever, the other with Convulsions, that no Life in eyther was expected, while during All this Hurry I Ran a Nail Quite through my Foot which Complications of Sorrow had nearly Deprived me of Hope, though at the Hope itself—

—Even so a Gentle Pair—
By fortune sunk, but form'd of Gen'rous Mold—
And Charm'd with Cares beyond the Vulgar breast
In some lone Cot Amid the Distant Woods
Sustain'd alone by providential Heaven,
* * * * * *

During this Distress the *Strix or Night Owl* of Guiana did never Miss his Nocturnal Visits even in the Apartment where we Lay, Pouring out his Melancholy Not[e] till kill'd by one of my black Attendants, this bird is here Call'd *Orococoo* from its Sound to which this word has some Affinity—it is the Size of a Pidgeon* the bill is Yellow, and hooked like that of a Sparrow hawk, the eyes are Also yellow, the tongue is Cloven, the ears verry Visible, the head large, the Legs Strong, Short, and Arm'd with sharp Claws, while the Whole hue of the bird is a pale brown except the breast and Belly which are white with Spots of Amber Colour—the most Superstitious of the negroes generally believe that where the Strix, or night Owl, makes his Appearance, mortality must Follow, which is the more Excusable this Creature only frequenting the Apartments of Sick People, but which in my Opinion proceeds eyther from the Lights that on those Occasions Generally are kept Burning all Night, or from the morbid air by which the Creature is Prepossess'd in Expectation of Meeting with Carrion—perhaps from both—

In Short an Indian Woman /of Joana's Acquaintance/ being sent for to the Hope, I was soon Recovered but my Little Family Continued so ill that I thought it Proper to Send them to town under a Physician, &

On the Tenth I Sent all my Sheep and Poultry to Fauquenbergh, one Couple of fat Yews Excepted Which I Kill'd And with which I entertained in two days twenty four Gentlemen of the River, having Received white bread, fruit & Spanish wine to help out the Feast in a Present from Mr Gourley, while the Villanous Overseer at the Hope

---

* —Dr Bancroft Calls it the Size of a Small Thrush

even Refusing me the fuel to Dress the Victuals /which having Got out of the Forrest/ he was Deservedly hunted out from Amongst the Company—

- On the Thirteenth I ordered down the troops from Clarenbeek where lately an Hospital had /a Second time/ been Erected and who this Evening Anchord off the Hope—
- Next day an Officer of the Honourable Society Arriv'd to *relieve me,* and whose men from that moment began to Do the Duty—When I removed my Flag from the Hope to the Barges; and in the evening took my Last Farewell from Fauquenbergh And Joana's Relations who Crowding round me Exprest theyr Sorrow at my Departure, and invoked the Protection of Heaven for my Safe and Prosperous Voyage—
- On the fifteenth we finally left the hope and /at 10 O Clock, having marched my Troops on Board,/ I fired my Pistol at 12 as a Signal to Weigh Anchor After which we immediately row'd down the River Commowina—

Chapter 26th

*The Troops on Board—still order'd to disembark—great dejection—
Mutiny—Insolent conduct of an Ouca Negroe Captain—
near two hundred sick to Holland—General Discription of the
African Negroes—Of Unhappy and happy Slaves*

- Having Anchor'd last evening off the Estate Bergshoven where I Spent the night Ashore with my Good friend M:̲ Gourley, we Now Continued to Row Down When I took farewell from the Hon.̲ᵇˡᵉ Tho:̲ Palmer—
- The day following I Past the evening with Cap.̲ᵗ Macneyl And on the
- Eighteenth my fleet Arrived Safe /in Conjunction with the Barges from Magdenbergh and Cottica/ at Anchor in the Roads before Paramaribo, Where 3 Transport Ships lay ready to Receive us, and on board of Which /an Hour After/ I Embark'd the troops that had been under my Command—I next Stept Ashore myself where having made my Report to Col: Fourgeoud I had the Pleasure to find Joana With her Boy Perfectly Recovered—
- The next day I was Again Sent on board to make Proper Arangements
- for the Voyage, and on the Twentieth was Entertained with no Contemptible Dinner by the Old Gentleman Fourgeoud, where Amongst the Rest were two kinds of Fish I have never mention'd Before, the one Call'd the *Haddock* being much like ours, but Rather Larger and whiter Coloured—The other the *Separee,* which had no bad Resemblance to the Skate—On the Desert was a fruit they in Surinam Call'd *Zurzack,* but which I believe in English is named the Sour-Sap—it Grows on a Tree of a moderate Size with a Gray Bark and Leaves like the Orange Tree but Set in Pairs, this fruit is of a Pyramidical Form heavier than the Largest Pear Perfectly green and all Covered over with inoffensive

1776—JULY 16-21, 23

Prickles, the Skin is Extremely Thin the pulp a Soft pithy Substance as white as milk, and of a sweet taste mix'd with a most Agreeable Acid, in which are Seeds like large kernels of an Apple—

> Their Joice Combin'd emits a Grateful Steam
> Like Hibla's Honey mixts with Devons Cream.

The above lines were wrot on the *Star apple* of Jamaica while I think them equally applicable on the Sour Sap.—Another Sort of *Small Zurzack* Grows in this Country Something Resembling Hops, but this is not of any Use Whatever—the other fruit I here saw was the *Sapadilla* which Grows on a Large Tree the Leaves Resembling Laurel—this fruit is the Sise of a peach verry Round brown and Covered with a Soft Down being Cut in two the Pulp is not Unlike Marmalade, in which are found the Seeds & Which is such a lucid Sweet that it is to many Palates even Disagreeable—

We now once more Received our Clearance, NB in Card money, by which we lost Considerably, where I instantly went to M:rs Godefrooy And Again, gave her *All* that was in my Pocket, being no more than £40. this Excellent Woman Renewing her Entreaties that I ought to Carry *Joana* and her Boy with me to Holland, but to no Purpose, Joana was unmoveable even up to Heroism, no Persuasion making the Smallest impression on her till She said we should be Able to *Redeem her* by Paying the Last farthing that we owed—Thus Situated we both Affected to bear our Fate with Resignation while both were Equally Tormented with the Agonies of Death—

In Short the Colours were Put on Board with Great State /which Put a Final end to the Expedition/ but without Receiving any *Honours* from Fort Zelandia Which did not Salute them with a Single Gun, nor even hoisted a Flag to the mortification and Surprise of Fourgeoud, but of nobody Else, he never so much as having given the Governor any Official Notice of his Departure—this day the Baggage was also sent on Board, and the Marines entertained with 300 Bottles of Wine by a Gentleman named *Van Eys*—while I Received from Different Families Various Presents to Refresh me on the Voyage, Amongst the Presents were the *Female* Papau, /the males bearing no Fruit/ which Grows on a Gray Trunk near 20 Feet high Streight and Pithy within, the Summit being Covered with a Crown with only 14 or 16 Diverging Leaves extremely Large & Digitated—This fruit Call'd here *Papaya* grows Close to the Trunk, the flower or Blossom having a delitious Fragrance—When Ripe it is the Sise and Shape of a Watter Melon, & becomes from Green to Yellow, while its Pulp is much the Same but more Firm, the inner Pulp is Soft and Slymy, which is Fill'd with innumerable Small Seeds—this Fruit at full Maturity is Cut in pieces and Boil'd when it eats like English Turnips, but when Young both itself and the Blossom are used for Confections and Sweet meats, Which are Extremely Delicate—the Other not yet Mention'd was *Preserved Ginger*—this is the Root of a Kind of Reedy Stalk, that never Exceeds 2 Feet in Height, with Long narrow Pointed Leaves, these Roots are tuberose, flatish, Small, and Cluster'd in many different Shapes, not unlike Pig Potatoes, & inside they are nearly the Same Colour, but feebrous, Acid, hot and Aromatick to the taste, while the Smell is Extremely fragrant, this is not only an Agreeable Preserve but an excellent Medicine in many Cases—

But to Proceed, the Sails being bent to the Yards we now went in Corps to take leave of his Excellency the Governor of the Colony, who, while he was verry polite gave our *Hero* Satirically to Understand that were his Colums a *Second time* to be Sent on Board they would now Certainly be Saluted with those Honours that were their Due, After which he sent the whole Corps of Society Officers to the Head Quarters to wish us a prosperous Voyage in form, & in which Contest of Etiquetts he most Assuredly Got the Better, which I hinting to Fourgeouds Favourites had nearly entangled me in a 2ᵈ verry Serious Quarrel—Our men having been embark'd Since the 18ᵗʰ the Officers now Joyn'd them thus the poor Remains of this Fine Regiment were finally embark'd to Weigh Anchor, and Proceed to Holland the next Day, while all were Jovial and Happy, *one* only Excepted who Suffered Excessively—& who this *one* was that Reader who Possesses Sensibility Can easily Discern without Giving me the Pain to enter on Particulars—Adieu then Paramaribo, Adieu my Friends, and Adieu thou who art Dearer to me than my life itself—I say Farewell once more

> Thou Land of Wonders which the Sun Still Eyes
> With Ray Direct as of the Lovely Realm
> Inamourd and Delighting there to dwell
> —Thompson

I have just Said that nothing Could Exceed the happiness of the few Remaining Troops, Especially when the Orders were Given to Weigh Anchor, But it was Ordain'd by fate that their Ardent Hopes Should be once more Blasted, Since on the verry —moment of their Departure a Ship entered the River Surinam with orders for the Regiment to Reenter the Woods again immediately, till they Should be Relieved by a Fresh Party Sent from Holland for the Purpose, When the will of his Serene Highness the Prince of Orange was instantly Read to the men from the Quarter Deck of Each Vessel, together with his most Sincere

Thanks for the Manly And Spirited Conduct they had Supported During so long a Trial, and so many Great and imprecedented Hardships, and which news however Struck such a Damp upon their Spirits that in my Life I never Saw People more Distressed, I being in my Turn the *only* happy Person now who had but just before been the most Compleatly Miserable—In the middle of this Gloomy Scene the poor men were now Ordered to Give *3 Cheers* which those on Board one of the Vessels Absolutely Refused But Colonel Seybourgh, and most unluckily I, Were Ordered to Compel them to it—When he with a Cane in one hand, & a Cock'd Pistol in the Other, like a frantick first began by beating, and next Calling them upon the Quarter deck by threatning with bitter Oaths instantly to blow out the brains of all those who Should now Disobey his Orders—knowing his Temper to be Firy and Irascible, Good God what my Heart Felt at this Moment? however I Suddenly Leaped in the Boat that Lay Along Side, Where After Haranging those Few that Lean'd over the Ships Gunnel and Promising the Crew 20 Gallons of Hollands Gin to Joyn in the Melancholy Chorus, I Again mounted the Quarter Deck Acquainting the Colonel that all were now Ready an[d] Willing to obey his Commands when we Reentered the Boat a 2ᵈ Time, and in Shoving it of[f] I had the Satisfaction to give 3 Hearty Cheers in which Joyn'd a few Marines /with Languid Looks and Such Verry Countenances as I have Seen Sing Psalms at Tiburn, when the Halter was Already tied about their neck/ by which was Prevented Perhaps a Wreched Catastrophy the Proverb *Vox Populy Vox Day* not being known in Surinam—At this time the Prince of Oranges Goodness of Heart was Seen in a Conspicuous Manner, whom we all knew to be Sorry for the Lot of his Soldiers, but which he Could not Remedy, while he Ordered all Private Surgeons & Physicians Accounts due by the Troops, to be Paid at the Expence only of the Nation, Which however trifling it may Appear it was no Trifle to Some of the Officers, and Showed in his Serene Highness that Attention Which is wide Distant from being Always found in Princes—If the troops were Sorry the Colonists were extremely Glad as this our Second Debarcation in the Town of Paramaribo, where indeed a Petition Signed by the Principal inhabitants had but two Days before Presented to Col: Fourgeoud, through a Mʳ Jacott, imploring our Regiment if it was at all Possible to Stay Some Longer, and Give the Finishing Stroke to the Rebels which we had so Gloriously Persevered in Rooting and Harrassing, and this was Certainly true, for though we had not made many Captives we had in Conjunction with the other Troops & Rangers Demolished /Perhaps/ every Settlement of any Consequence they had been Posses'd of Within the bounds of the Colony, and Drove them to such a Considerable Distance that /by a few of their Detached Parties Excepted/ both the Depredation & Deserting of Slaves, were incomparably less than at our First Arrival, and which was better than making with them a Shameful Peace as had been made before With the Rebels of the *Ouca* and *Sarameca* Settlements and which /without our Coming to Guiana/ would have again most Probably been the Consequence— As a Sample of what these fellows are when independant I must Relate what Happened between one of them, and Myself at Paramaribo, where the Troops had leave to Refresh before they were /once more/ to Reenter the Forrest—

- Dining at Cap.! Macneyls the Day after our Debarcation /who was now Come to Town from his Estate/ a Captain of the Owca Rebel Negroes /at Present our Allies/ Came in to Ask money from his Lady and was very importune, Seeing which I desired her in English to *give him a Dram, and* he would be gone, but which the fellow understanding Call'd me without to the door, and then Lifting his Silver Pummel'd Cane, Ask'd me if that was my House, and What Business I had to interfere, "I am Said he with a Thundering Voice Captain *Fortune Dago Sow,* and if I had you in my Country at Owca I would make the earth Drink up your Blood Sir"—to which I Reply'd /drawing my Sword/ that my name was *Stedman* and if he Spoke one Syllable more I would make the Dogs Run away with his Guts, when he Snapt his Fingers, and went off leaving me in a Verry Disagreeable State of mind & Cursing Fourgeoud for Ever Showing to those Rascals So much indulgence—Returning from Dinner in the Evening to go home I now Again met the identical black bully, who instantly Stept up to me Saying, "Massera you are a Verry Brave and Gallant Fellow, Wont you give some Money to the Owca Captain," which I Sternly Refusing for the Present, he kis'd my Hand and Shoed his Teeth in token of *Reconciliation* he Said and let me Go Promising to Send me a Present of Pistachio Nuts, which by the by never Came nor if they had Should I have tasted—Such were these Overbearing fellows, whom as Pomfrid Says tis better

> To put up with an injury
> Than be a plague to he
> Who Can be a Greater plague to me.

While I must Acknowledge that they are unfairly Dealt with, the Society of Surinam not Sending the Yearly *Presents* According to their Shameful Capitulation & they disregarding Fourgeouds *Flattery* as a paultry trifle, without Which Perhaps they would be more true & faithful Allies than they have been at least Since we Came to this Colony—

Although we now Continued to Stay in Surinam, I must Observe that Surely our future Service Could but Little Avail for its Prosperity being so very few in Number, and out of Which Number /small as it was/ were on the first of August Sent Sick and incurable to Holland, no Less than 9 Officers, and Above *one Hundred and Sixty* Private men; I myself was at this time verry ill with an Ague And Offered to be one of the Party, but Refused to go, being Determined to see out the Expedition Which it was Evident Could Last but a few months Longer, However I Avail'd myself of this Opportunity to send some Presents to my European Friends Amongst Which were a Couple of Beautiful parrots two Curious Monkeys, An Elegant Collection of fine Butterflies, and three Chests with Preserved Sweetmeats, Pickles, Confections &c Which I put all on board the *Ship Paramaribo* under the Care of Poor Serjeant Fowler, who happened to be one of the invalides bound for Europe—

This Vessal being Sail'd down & of Which Major Medler had the Command, his Office now had in turn Devolved upon me, thus I Acted as Major, and began to entertain some hopes of one Day bringing home the Regiment in Quality as Chief, so verry fast were our Officers Diminishing, while Amongst those that Remained a Couple still had the Courage to be married to two Creole Ladies.—

Every thing being now Settled in Peace & Quietness I got so well on the tenth that I walked to Mrs Godefrooy to Acquaint her, that I now Wished to Emancipate at Least *Johnny Stedman,* and begg'd her to become bail before the Court for the usual Sum of £300 that he Should never become a Charge to the Colony of Surinam; but which she firmly *Declined* to my utter Astonishment as she Run no Risk, till I was Acquainted that She had Refused the verry Same favour to her own son, what Could I do—My boy was Oblidged still to Remain in Servitude till I Could find bail for his free Manumition & While I had not the Smallest Cause to blame his Excellent new Propriator—

When Speaking About Slavery I think it will here not at all be out of Character to give a General Account of this Set of People who are so Verry Little known in Europe, I have Already mention'd the mode of theyr being Purchased, imported, and Sold, thus Shall now Confine myself to theyr Manners both Natural, and as Dependants, in Which I Flatter Myself to bring some truth to Light that have Hetherto been burie'd in Obscurity, at Least to the Generality of Mankind—

In the first place as to the *Complexion* of a Negro or his being Black, this is /as I have Said before/ entirely owing to the burning Climate in which he lives, Which is Still more Heated by the Sandy Deserts over which the trade Winds Pass before they Come to him, Since the indians of America existing under the same Degree of Latitude, but who get this Wind Refresh'd by the Atlantick Ocean are Copper Coloured, and the inhabitants of Abassina &c who Receive it Cool'd by the Arabian and indian Seas, are intirely Olive, thus North of the Great River Senegal, the Complexion Changes from Black to Brown Amongst the moors, as it does towards the South Amongst the Caffers & Hotentots, And am I of Opinion that the Wooly Texture of the Hair, is the Derived Effect, Proceeding from the Verry Same Cause—the *Epidermis* or Cuticle of the Negroes I have Seen Dissected more than once, this is very Clear and Transparent, but between which and the Real Skin lies a thin Follicle which is perfectly Black, and when Removed by verry Severe Scalding or Flaggelation, Exposes a Complexion not inferior to that of the European—

On the Estate *Vossenbergh* in Surinam were even born two *White Negroes* whose Parents were yet both black as others, the one was a Female sent to Paris in 1734 the other a boy born in March 1738 but these were Monsters, such as lately one was Exibited in England, whose Skin was not a Natural White, but Resembling Chalk, nay even theyr hair on every part was the Same, while theyr Eyes were a Perfect Blood Colour* And with which they Saw verry Little in the Sun Shine, Neyther were they fit for any kind of Labour, While theyr Mental Faculties Corresponded with the incapacity of their Bodys—

With Regard to the *Shape* of the African Negro's it is from head to Foot Absolutely Different from the European mould, though not in any Degree inferior in my Opinion when prejudice is Laid Aside— Theyr Features indeed with high Cheek Bones, flat Noses, and Thick Lips Appear to us Deformities Which Amongst themselves are esteem'd perhaps quite the Reverse, but even with us theyr black Eyes, And white teeth are Deem'd Oramental, & one Certain Advantage in a Black Complexion, is that all those Languid, Pale, Sickly Looking Countenance[s] so Common in Europe, are never Exibited amongst them, nor are the Wrinkles and Ravages of Age, nearly so Conspicuous, though I must Acknowledge that when a Negro is Verry *ill* his Black Changes to a Disagreeable Sallow Olive—

As for great *Strength* and *Activity,* their Shape is Assuredly Preferable to ours, being Generally Sturdy, And Muscular near the Trunk, and Slender towards the Extremities, such as for Instance, they have mostly a Remarkable fine Chest, but are Small About the Hips, while theyr Buttocks are Round and Prominent—their Necks are Thicker than

---

* —this is well known Also to be the Case with many Animals such as Rabbits mice &c that are Perfectly white to have theyr Eyes Perfectly Red.—

Ours, and their Genitels Conspicuously Larger, A Negro is Verry Stout About the Thighs, so are his Arms Above the Elbow, but both his Legs & Wrists are verry Slender, in which Description much of the Herculanean make of M.ʳ *Broughton* the Late Famous Boxer may be Traced— & as for the Deformity of their Limbs, this is entirely Accidental, Owing to the Manner in which they as infants are Carried on the Mothers Back, with their tender Legs tied Close Round each Side of her waste, this mode of Nurcing Alone Creates the Unnatural Bend with which they are not born—Nor are theyr Children ever learn'd to Walk, but left to Creep amongst the Sand and Verdure where they please till Gradually they Acquire Strength, And inclination to Erect Themselves, which they do verry Soon, but by which Method the Position of theyr feet is much Neglected, yet by which means /and Dayly Bathing/ they Acquire that Native Strength And Agility for Which According to me they are so verry Remarkable, While it derides the dispute so often Resumed, And proves that man was Sure born to walk upon two Legs—Another Cause of this *bend* in their limbs may be Partly Accounted for, Which is, that during 2 Whole Years that they Suck, After the Mother had made them drink a Large Quantity of Watter, She shakes them twice a Day by every Limb with so much Violence that all the infants Joynts Crack, & after which with a Leg or Arm they are tost in the River to be Outwardly Scrub'd, but this deformity is fully Compensated by the health and Vigour which is Annex'd to such an Education, and from which benefit theyr female Race not being Exempt, makes *them* a Generation not inferior to the Men in Size alone Excepted, While Some of them in Point of Running, Swimming, Climbing, and Dancing, if not in Wrestling are Even their Superiors*—Nor are these hardy daughters of the Torrid Zone less Remarkable for Propogation, I knowing a Female Servant at M.ʳ Degraafs House, Call'd *Lesperanza* who bore Actually 9 *Children* in the Course of 3 Years, first 4, next 2, and then 3, Which they bring to the World without Pain like the indian Women, Resuming theyr Domestick Employment even the Same Day While theyr infants are as fair as any Europeans, the first Week; from which they are only Distinguished, by the boys having the Parts of Generation Partly Black—After which theyr Whole body Gradually becomes the same Colour—

Theyr Women Also Come Early to the age of Maturity, but in this it may be Said as with their Fruit, soon Ripe, soon Decay'd, yet those People live a Considerable time, I having Seen one or two that were

* —that it depends on Education to breed an Amasonean Race of Females After many Disputes has been Proved by the Soundest Philosophers—

Past a Hundred Years, and in the London Chronicle for Oct. 5th 1780 is even made mention of a Negress Call'd *Louisa Truxo* who was then living at Tucomea in South America at the Surprising Age of 175 Years—in what Tables of Longevity is to be found Such an European? While this Venerable Person Probably had Spent most of her Youth in hard Labour as Other Slaves, Which though a Negro Can bear it in a Tropical Climate better than a European, this is both unnatural on the Coast of Guinea, and in Guiana, Where without Toil the Necessaries of Life are Spontaneously Produced and Vegetation flourishes for ever— One Singular Remark I have made on the *Constitution* of the Negroes, which is that while they Can bear the Heat, they Can Also bear moderate Cold better than at Least I Could do, for I have seen them Sleep in the Dewy Moon Shine, Nay in the wet Grass Perfectly Naked without any Hurt, while I was Glad /Especially in the Early Mornings/ to have a fire Under my Hammock—And in Regard to hunger and Thirst, and even Pain in Sickness &c no People Can be more Patient— This Short Sample Sufficiently ought to Show that the African Negroes though by Some Stupid Europeans treated as Brutes* Are made of no Inferior Clay but in every one Particular are our Equals—

> Alba ligustra Caducit Vaccinnia nigra legunter
> —Virg. Ec. 2 Verse 18

I have formerly Mention'd the Names of above a Dozen Negro Tribes, All these know each other from the different Marks And insisions made on theyr Bodies; for instance the *Coromantyn* Negroes /Who are the most Esteem'd/ Cut 3 or 4 Long Slashes on each of their Cheeks as I have Represented in the face of the Arm'd free Negro or Ranger See plate **VII**—And the *Loango* Negroes /who are Reckon'd the Worst/ Distinguish themselves by Puckering, or making the Skin of their Arms Thighs &c With Square Elevated Figures like Large Dice, See Plate **LXVII** [68] these Also Sharp point the foreteeth which makes them look frightful & like those of a Shark, while all the Males are Circumcised in the manner of the Jews—but the most Remarkable thing is that the Females of the *Papaw* Nation have Actually the same Excressence on the Pudenda which is Said to be Conspicuous in the female Hottentots at the Cape of Good Hope—

Amongst the Strange Productions Of Nature deserves highly to be Noticed a kind of People who are known by the Name of *Accorees* or *two fingers,* And live Amongst the Saremeca Negroes in the verry upper

---

• —by Linaeus the Whole human Race, the whole human Race together is Classed amongst the Monkeys

1776—AUGUST 10

Parts of the River of that name—this Hetoregeneus tribe being so much Deformed on hands and Feet, that while some have but 3, or 4 fingers, and toes, on each, the Greatest number have Absolutely but 2 fingers and 2 Toes on each hand and foot Which are Hideous to Look at, Resembling the Claws of a Lobster, or rather limbs that have been Cured After Mutilation by fire, or some other Accident—This Deformity in one Person would be nothing verry Uncommon, but that a Whole Community should be inflicted with this Singularity is a Phenomenon that I think Cannot be Accounted for, Without it be perhaps Owing to their Mingled Blood, for they are neyther Negroes, nor indians—yet they Partake of both Without the Smallest Resemblance to *Samboes*— in Short /however Strange/ Such People there Assuredly are and 2 of Which were Shoed me at Paramaribo, but at too great a distance to make the proper Occular Observations, While as a further Proof of their Existance, an Engraved Copper Plate, With one of their Figures was Presented by the Society of Surinam to the Society of Arts and Sciences at Haarlam in Holland—Nay I was even Assured that Some men with the Rudiments of a Tail Existed in Guiana, before ever I Read Lord Munbodo's *Ancient Metaphisiks,* but Which however Wanted Confirmation to insert here as a Truth—When I Acquainted his Lordship with the Above Lucis Natura the *Accoorees,* he Seem'd highly Delighted with the Subject which he did not Discredit, yet testifying his Surprise that it Should be a Whole Community[•]—I Shall Now quit this Subject to Prevent my being Suspected of Dealing in the Marvellous, And Continue With what will seem Better to Quadrate with Nature—

With the Languages of the African Negroes I am very Little Acquainted however as a Specimen I will Repeat just a Few Words for that Call'd the *Coromantyn* if I must Credit my Boy Qwaccoo, Who belong to that Nation; for instance—
"Go to the River & fetch me Some water."
Co fa ansyo na baramon bra.
"my Wife, I am Hungry"
Me Yeree, Nacomeda mee
But as for that Spoke by the Black People in Surinam, I pretend to be Perfectly well Acquainted with it, being a Composition of Dutch, French, Spanish, Portuges & mostly English, Which last they liked best and have retained Since the English Nation were Possessors of the Colony—this mixt speech /in Which I have even Seen a Printed Grammar/ ends mostly With a Vowel like the Italion and is so sweet, & Son-

[•] —Query why Should it appear more Surprising to see a Race of these People than a race of men with one leg one Eye Dogs heads long tails &c—

orous that even Amongst the Genteelest European Companies, nothing Else is Spoke in Surinam; it is also extremely Expressive and Sentimental such as, "Good Eating," *Sweety muffo,* "Gunpowder," *Mansanny*–"I will Love you with All my Heart so long as I Live"–*Mee Saloby you langa alla Mee Hatty so langa mee leeby*–"A pleasing Tale," *Ananasy tory*–"Live long, so long till your Hair Comes as White as Cotton"–*leebee langa tay, tay, ta-y, you Weeree weree tan witty likee Catoo*–"Small" *Pekeen* "verry Small" *Peekeeneenee*–"farewell Good by I am Dying and Going to my God"–*Adiosso Crobooy Mee de go dede me de go Na mee Gado*—In this Sample may be Perceived many Corrupt English Words, Which however begin to Wear out near the Capital Town, but are Retain'd Near the Distant Plantations—At the Estate *Goet Accoord,* I have heard an Old Negro Woman Say, *we lobee fo lebee togeddere,* by Which she Meant we Love to live together—At Paramaribo to Express the Same they tell you, *we Do looko for tanna Macandera.*—but what is Extremely Surprising, is that Some of their Expressions are Perfectly as those at *Liege* in Germany Viz *Looco* "to see" *me Cotto* "my Peticoat" &c. While *Camisa* and *Yam* which in the Gipsy Language denotes "a Shirt" and "food" or "Victuals," is the same in the Negro dialect of Surinam—

 Their Vocal Musick is like that of some birds, melodious but without Time; in Other respects it is not unlike that of some Clarks reading to the Congregation, One Person Pronouncing a Sentence Extemporary, which he nexts hums or Whistles, when all the others Repeat the Same in Chorus, another sentence is then Spoke and the Chorus is Renew'd a Second time & So ad perpetuum. as a Specimen of it I Will try to Put the following Not[e]s to Musick Supposing a Soldier going to battle taking leave of his Mistress

one bus adiosi - o daso adiosso me dego me loby fo fighty me man o na inny da boosy amimba o daso adiosso me dego—

Such is theyr Vocal Musick, While that of theyr Dancing and instrumental Musick /Which is Perfectly to time/ I will Speak of in the future having Already hinted that of the Loango Negroes—

 However that these People are not Divested of a Good Ear, and Even of a Poetical Genious, has been frequently discovered when they had the Advan[ta]ge of Education Witness Amongst Others a black Girl

1776—AUGUST 10

Call'd *Phillis Wheatly* who was a Slave at Boston in New England, She even learn'd the *Latin Language* And Wrote 38 Elegant Pieces of Poetry on different Subjects, which were Published in 1773—From these I Shall here only Repeat part of that Extracted by the Rev:d M:r Clarkson, intitled *thoughts on Imagination*—

> Now here now their the Roving fancy flies
> Till some lov'd Object Strikes her Wand'ring Eyes,
> Whose Silken Fetters All the Senses bind
> And soft Captivity involves the Mind,
>
> ———
>
> Imagination! Who Can Sing thy Force
> Or where describe the Swiftness of thy Course,
> Soaring through Air to find the bright abode
> The imperial palace of the Thundering God;
>
> ———
>
> We on thy pinions Can Surpass the Wind
> And leave the Rolling Universe behind.
> From Star to Star the Mental Opticks Rove
> Measure the Skies and Range the Realms Above
> There in one View we Grasp the mighty whole
> Or with new World's Amaze th' unbounded Soul.

What Can be more beautiful than the Above Lines Come forth from such a Pen, While who has not heard of that Wonderful Negro *Ignatius Sancho* whose verry Sublime Letters and Sound Philosophy would even add Luster to the brightest European Genious of the Age[*]—And with Regard to memory and Calculation I Shall only Produce *Tho:s Fuller* a Negro Slave the Property of a M:rs Cox, in Maryland N: America Who was Living so late as the Year 1788—And to Gratify the Reader Verbally Copy one of his Anecdotes as Related to a Gentleman at Manchester in a Letter by Doctor Rush of Philadelphia; being once Ask'd by a *Respectable Company* of the Above Town, Who were Travelling through Maryland And had heard of his Amazing Powers, how many Seconds a man of Seventy Years and some Odd Months, weeks, and Days had lived, he told the Compleat Number in a Minute And a half, the Gentleman who had Put the Question /took up his Pen And having Calculated the same Sum by means of Figures/ told the negro he was mistaken as the Number he had Declared was Certainly too Great. "Top Massera /said the Slave/ you have forgot the Leap Years," And having included the Seconds they Contained their Sums were Exactly found to be the Same, this Same man multiplied 9 figures by 9 from

[*] —his Letters & are Printed in 2 Volumes Avo: by Dilly London Price 6 Shillings in Boards—

Memory before Another Company—Now that such Amazing mental Faculties Should be Posses'd by an African Black Who Could neyther Read or Write must Appear Astonishing Yet Such they were Without the Smallest manner of Doubt*—Before I Quit the Above Subject I Cannot help making one More Remark on *Philis Wheatly's Poetry,* Which is that it bears so Great a Resemblance to that of a Civilized Nation, While ever the pen of a *British Subject* Can have so much Affinity to the Writing of a *Cherokee-Indian*—to Prove best What I Say I will insert, first a few Lines from *Carloc and Orra* translated from the *Erse* by the Rev.d W. F. Mavot master of the Academy at Wood Stock, which I think verry fine And After that part of an *American Eclogue* Translated from the Cherokee Language, found in the Fragments by *Leo* who is exactly of the Same Opinion in Which I make no Doubt of our being join'd by many readers the Poem, in Earse ends as Follows—

> No Sooner *Irvan* met his Eyes
>   Than *Carloc* Hurl'd the well pois'd Spear
> The Hostile Shield the Stroke Defies
>   And Countless Foes Surround his Rear,
>
> ———
>
> Brave Carlocs troops ill fated Strove,
>   To break the Phalanx firm & Strong
> The Chief himself inspir'd by love,
>   Nor less by Rage Resisted long.—
>
> ———
>
> With many a Shout he Calls his Bands
> Alas no Cheering Shout Returns;
> While like the Mountain Rock he Stands,
> And Circling Hosts intrepid Spurns,
>
> ———
>
> At length, by Irvan's hand Opprest
>   He fell, and falling, Stabb'd his foe,
> A mutual wound Tansfix'd each breast
>   Nor ebb'd each Vital Current flow.
>
> ———
>
> The Dismal News to Orra Came!
>   No frantick Grief her face Deforms
> She neither Wails nor Weeps her flame
> Nor with a Woman's Weakness Storms,
>
> ———
>
> But /Rushing on the Ensanguin'd Plain/

* —See the Supplement to the town and Country Magazine for 1788.—Negroes however in General keep no time Calculating even their Age by the Growth of a Tree —

1776—AUGUST 10

    She found the Place where Carloc lay,
With Dauntless Soul Explor'd the Slain
    To find her ill Starr'd lovers Clay.

    She found him Gash'd with many a Wound
        She kiss'd his Gore Distained Face
Then Rais'd his Cold Corse from the Ground
And Grasp'd him in a last embrace.

The *indian* Eclogue finished thus *Zornbaxathwit* Recounting his Victory over *Dano* to the Lovely *Bulldermuller,* Mark the Striking Singularity.

Last Morn Proud Dano dared me to the fight
And on Carpanto Stood with Dawning light
"Zornbaxathwit!" loud as the Storm, he Cried,
"Zornbaxathwit!" the hills & Dales Replied
Fierce as a Blast he thundered down the Hill
Fixt as a Rock I in the Vale stood Still,
Bright as the Lightning both our Armours Shone,
Our Shields beneath our thundering Falchions groan,
Our blows tho' Strong our Armour will not Pierce
At last I fling the Hero on his ——:
He with a Voice like distant Thunder Cried,
Dont Slay me fall'n great Son of Walderskide,
Away my Shiel'd and Giant Sword I threw
And Breast to Breast in equal Combat flew,
The Caves of Rodkir echoed back our Noise
The Shepherd's View'd us from the top of Droise,
At our Fierce Tramplings the high mountains shook
The Rocks were Tumbled & Calascars brook–
/Affrighted at our Feet/ its Course forsook–
At last beneath mine Arm fierce Dano's head
I Got—& by my Soul I Squeez'd him dead,
So spoke the Youth, & pale as Ashes Grew
The Lovely Daughter of Mardancarew,
The Love of Dano to her breast Return'd
And to Revenge his Death the Virgin Burn'd,
Give me the Sword fair Buldermuller Said
That Yet with Cruel Dano's Blood is Red
He gave the Sword She Plung'd it in her Breast
And While the blood gush'd out made this Request,
O raise my Tomb Zornbaxathwit she Cried
O Raise my Tomb by Lovely Dano's Side,
Then Shall the Hunter as he Passes by
Our Moss Clad graves say here two Lovers lie—

1776—AUGUST 10

After this Whole Admiration will not be Raised Still Higher in favour of *Philis Wheatly's* Soft and Elegant Manner of Writing—

To what I have said I Shall now add that all Negroes Believe firmly on a God Whose Goodness they Trusts more than Many Whining Christians, nor have they any fear for Death. Confident they will See Again Some of their Friends & Relations in another World but not that if they die Abroad they will Rise in theyr Own Country /as Good Mr *Clarkson* Miss *Merion* & many Others Erroneously were taught to Believe/—that no Negro ever Breaks an Oath I have Already in the beginning of this Work Clearly Demonstrated to the Shame and infamy of those Europeans, Who *Break it Dayly,* and treat with Contempt this Race of People more Religious than themselves—Neither does a Negro ever eat or Drink Without Offering a Libation—

> Stay till I bring the Cup with Bacchus Crown'd
> In Joves high name to Sprinkle on the Ground,
> And pay due Vows to All the Gods Around—
> Then with a Plenteous Draught Refresh thy Soul
> And draw new Spirits from the Generous Bowl.

And as in Thomsons Favourite Tragedy *Sophronisba* Expresses before She takes the Poison

> Add hither had he Come I Could have taught
> Him how to die—I Linger not Remember,
> I Stand not Shivering on the brink of Life,
> And /but these Votive drops which Grateful thus
> To Jove the high Deliverer I Shed/
> Assure him that I Drank it, drank it all
> With an Undaunted, Smile Away—

Such are the Oblations of the African Negroes—

They Also bring their Offerings to the *Wild Cotton tree*• Which they Adore With high Reverence,

> this Proceeds /Said an Old Black Man to Me/ from the following Juditious Cause, having no Churches on the Coast of Guinea and this Tree being the largest and most beautiful Growing there. Our People Assembling often under its branches to keep free from the Heavy Show'rs of

---

• —this tree Which the Negroes Call *Cot-tan teeree* Grows to a Considerable Height & thickness it is Verry Streight & Covered with a Strong gray prickly Bark, the boughs spread to a Considerable Circumference with Small Digitated leaves. The Cotton /which it Produces Triennally/ is not verry white & being neither verry plentiful, is little Sought for. Upon the whole this tree bears Some Resemblance to the British Oak yet the Largest of Which in this Island it Surpasses both in Elegance and Magnitude—

rain and Schorching Sun Shine, when they Are Going to be instructed; do not You Christians Pay the Same homage to Your bibles &c We well know that our tree is but A Wooden Logg Covered With Leaves of Green, Nor is your book Assuredly any more than a Piece of Lumber Composed of Leaves of Paper—Under this tree the Gadoman or Priest Delivers his Lectures and for which the Vulgar Negroes have much Veneration, that they Will not Cut it down upon any Consideration Whatever—

Indeed nothing Can be more Superstitious than the Common Class of these People, While they are Still more kept in darkness by their Pretended *Loco-men* or *Prophets* & who find theyr interest in their Blindness, by Selling them *Obias,* or *Amulets* as I have Already mention'd, With Other Charms, not Unlike those Hypocrites Who even Sell Absolution for a Comfortable Living—Nor are a kind of *Sibils* wanting Amongst them who deal in Oracles, these Sage Matrons Dancing And Whirling Round in the Middle of an Audience, till Absolutely they froath at the mouth And drop down in the middle of them; Whatever She says to be done during this fit of Madness is Sacredly Performed by the Surrounding Multitude, which makes these meetings Exceedingly dangerous Amongst the Slaves, who are often told to murder their Masters or Desert to The Woods, & on which Account the Excessive of this piece of Fanatism, is forbid in the Colony of Surinam on Pain of the Most Rigourous Punishment, Yet it is often Put in Execution in Private Places, And Verry Common Amongst the Owca, & Sarameca Negroes, Where Captains Frederecy & Van Geurick told me they Saw it Performed—this is Called here *Winty Play* or the Dance of the *Mairmaid,* and takes its Origin from time immemorial the Classick Authors Making frequent mention of this Unaccountable Practice.—

Virgil in his liber Sixtus when Speaking of Æneas Visiting the Sibil Of *Cuma* Says—

Talibus affatta Ænean /nec Sacra Morantur
Jussa viri/ Teucros Vocat Alta intempla Sacerdos
Excisum Euboicae latus ingens Rupis in Antrum;
Quo lati ducunt aditus centum Ostia centum;
Unde: ruunt tolidem voces, Responsa Sibillae
Ventum erat ad Limen, cum virgo, poscere fata
Tempus, Ait: Deus, ecce, Deus? Cui talia fanti
Ante Sorus, Subito non vullus non Color unus,
Non Comptae mansere Comae; Sed pectus anhelum
Et rabie fera Corda tument, majorque videri,
Nec mortale sonans, afflata Est numine Quando
Jam propiore Dei. "Cessas in Vota Precesque,

1776—AUGUST 10

> Tros. Ait Ænea? Cessas? neque enim ante dehiscent
> Altonitae Magna ora domus." Et talia fata,
> Conticuit.—

Again after the prayer of Æneas—

> —Finem dedit ore loquendi
> At Phoebi nondum Patiens immanis in Antro
> Bacchatur Vates. magnum si Pectore Possit
> Exussisse Deum: tantum magis illi fagitat
> Os Rabidum. fera Corda domans fingitique Premendo

And after the Phrophecie he Continues—

> Talibus ex adyto dictis Cumae Sybilla
> Horrendis Canit ambages Antroque Remugit
> Obscuris vera involvens: ea fraena furenti
> Concutit et stimulos sub pectore vertit Apollo
> Ut primum cessit furor et Rabida era quierunt
> Incipit Æneas heros:—

Ovid also mentions the same Subject Particularly in his XIVth Book where Ænea wishes to visit the Ghost of his father

> Has ubi Praeteriit. & Parthenopeia dextra
> Maenia deseruit; laeva de Parte Canori
> Æolidae tumulum, & Loca foeta Palustribus ulvis
> Littora Cumarum. vivacisque antra Sybillae
> Intrat: &. ut manes adeat per Averna Paternos,
> Orat. At illa diu vultus tellure morratas
> Erexit: tandemque Deo furibunda Recepto
> Magna petis, Dexit, Vir factis maxime, Cujus
> Dextera per ferrum, Pietas Spectata per ignes
> Pone tamen, Trojane, metum; potiere Petitis
> Elysias que domos, & Regna novissima mundi
> Me duce Cognosces. Simulachraque Chara Parentis
> Invia virtuti nulla est via.—

But What is Still more Strange is that these Unaccountable Women by their Voice know how to Charm the *Ammodytes* or Papaw Serpent down from the trees• this is an Absolute fact; nor is the Above Snake ever kill'd, or Hurted by the Negroes, who on the Contrary adore it as their friend and Guardian, and are even happy to see it enter in their Huts—Nay when the above Sibyls have Call'd or Conjur'd down the

---

• —this Creature is from 3 to 5 Feet long, and being Perfectly Harmless it has not the Smallest Apprehension to be hurted, even by *man* while the Undescribable Brillancy of its Colours are Perhaps another inducement for the Adoration of the negroes—

Ammodytes Serpent from the Tree, it is even Common to see the Reptile twine and Wreathe About theyr Arms, neck, and Breast, as if the Creature took delight in hearing her Vocal musick, while the Woman Stroakes and Caresses it with her hand—All I Shall now say further in this Subject, is that those who doubt of it I Refer to the *Holy Writings* as I have done the former to the Classick Authors & from which I shall only Quote the following Passages—Then should my Account meet with Discredit it matters me not—In the 58th Psalm verses 3^d, 4th & 5th we Read thus

> The Wicked are Estranged from the Womb they go Astray as soon as they are Born Speaking Lies.—Theyr Poison is like the Poison of a Serpent they are like the Deaf Adder that stoppeth her Ear.—Which will not Hearken to the voice of the Charmer Charming never so Wisely—

And in Jeremiah 8th Chapt: Verse 17th as follows

> For behold I will send Serpents and Cockatrices Among you which will not be Charmed they shall bite you saith the Lord—

Still in the Book of Ecclesiastes 10 Chapt: Verse 11

> Surely the Serpent will bite without Enchantment

Thus I have Described Some strange Peculiarities which however Absurd are not so much so, as those of the Vulgar Europeans believing in the Apparition of Ghosts, and the incantations of Witches, Some of Which Poor Creatures /or at Least Supposed to be so/ were Inhumanly Burnt Amongst us so Late as the Middle of the Last Century—
One more Glaring instance of Superstition Amongst the negroes I must relate, & I have Done on this Subject, Which is, that every Family is distinctly Prohibited, from Father to Son, to Eat of one Particular kind of Animal Food, this may be eyther Fowl, fish or Quadrupede, but Whatever it is, no negro will Touch this, While I have seen Some Good Roman Catholicks eat Roast Beef in Lent, and a Religious Jew devouring a Slice of a fat flich of Bacon.—However Ridiculous some of the above Rites of Devotion Amongst the African Blacks they are Certainly Necessary to keep the Rabble in Subjection, and their Gadomen or Priests know this as Well as do our Clergimen in England—And in one thing these illiterate mortals have Assuredly the Advantage of the Modern Europeans–Viz that Whatever they Believe they *Believe it Firmly* Which is more than the Generality of the Former Can Boast of—And as for the Good Works of the negroes, or indeed of the Indians being better or Worse, I Will not Pretend to Determine, but this I know, that their faith is never Staggered, on Which delicate point, they

thus are never Troubled With the Qualms of a Guilty Conscience—
Upon the Whole I think them a happy People and who Possess so much
friendship Amongst each other, that they need not to be told to Love
their brethren, as theirselves, Since the Poorest negro Amongst them
having but an Egg Scorns to eat it Alone, but were 12 Others Present
& every one of them a Stranger, he Would Cut or Break it in as many
Shares•—While Should one Single Dram of Rum be Divided amongst
Such a Number, Still is this not done, as I have Said, Without first
Spilling a few drops on the Ground as an Oblation to the Gods—Come
here now thou Hypocrite, And take an Example from thy Sable
Brother: but Alas I am afraid it is too true, "that no more than the
Ethiopian Can Change his Skin or the Leopard his Spots, no more is it
in thy Power to do Good who art Accustomed to do Evil," thus keep
thy Canting Meravians at Home••—And try not to Lead a People from
the Paths of Innocence into a Mystery which is too Frequently Abused,
and is too intricate as well as too Sacred even for thyself Well to Understand it—a Name /which to[o] often only Cloaked with Godliness,/
has been for Ages Dyed in Scarlet & Reeking with the Warms Streams
of Human Blood, Nay at which Three Quarters of the World Still
Shudder and hear Pronounced With Contempt & Abhorrance—
What Racks and Tortures have not been invented by thee Gold Thirsty
Enthusiast, Particularly on the American Indians, and Poor Negroes
transported from the Coast of Africa their Native Home, who only
Struggle to Relieve their Lost Liberty—

> *What Good man Can* Reflect the tear Stain'd Eye,
> When blood attests even Slaves for freedom die?
> On Cruel Gibbets high disclosed they Rest,
> And Scarce one Groan escapes one bloated Breast.—
> Here Sable *Caesars*••• feel the Christian Rod:
> There Afric *Platos,* tortur'd hope a God:
> While Jetty *Brutus* for his Country Sighs,
> And Sooty *Cato* with his freedom Dies!

But by what I have Advanced, let it however not be Understood that

- • —this proves that the word *negroish* is verry ill applied when meant to discribe greediness or Self interest.—

- •• —Moravian Preachers have been sent Over & I am Persuaded with their best intentions to Convert the Indians & Sarameca Negro's but hetherto without the Smallest Good Effect.—

- ••• —The Above names are Generally given to Imported Negro Slaves, with Such as *Nero Pluto Charon Cerberous Procersmina Medusa* &c—in Exchange for *Qwaccoo Qwacy, Qwamy, Qwamina Qwaciba & Adjuba.* Which Assuredly have not a Less Agreeable Sound—

I am an Enemy to Christianity as I have Said before, God Forbid, nor an Enemy to any Religious Sect Whatever, but most Undoubtedly the Greatest friend to those Whose Actions I know best to Correspond With their Morals—

Let us now Proceed to take a Cursory view of the *Natural* Character of the *African* Negroes—this I Will first Represent Under its Blackest Colours, Contrary to the Rules of Painters, & Next introduce those fair Shades to Which I know they are intitled—

In the first place no People have Greater thirst for *Revenging An injury*, even biting their verry Lice with their Teeth, because they first bit them indeed I never Yet saw an Negro forgive Another Person Who had Wilfully Offended him, & for which the only Apology I Can make is the Strength of their Passion they being equally Grateful on the Other Hand & next the Old Grecian Adage which Says that—

A Generous Friendship no Cold Medium knows
But with one Love, with one Resentment Glows.

However theyr Abominable Cruelties, as those of all Barbarous Nations are truly Shocking, Witness the Colony *Berbice* Where during the late Revolt they made no Scruple to Cut up Alive theyr European Mistresses Who were with Child in the Presence of their Husbands, besides many Other Horrors too dreadful to Relate, And in the Art of *Poisoning* not even the *Accawau* Indians are more Expert, which some of these Wretches Carry under their Nails, and by only Dipping the Thumb in a Tumbler of Watter which they Carry as a Beveridge* to the Objects of their Hatred, infuse a Slow but no less Certain Death—Nay whole Estates as well as Private Families have become the Victims of their Wrath & Experienced their fatality, putting even to Death Scores of their Own friends and Relations, with the Double View of Depriving their Proprietors of their best possessions And at once Delivering those Negroes Slaves whom they love best from Under the lash of their Tiranny

These unhappy monsters are Distinguished by the name of *Wissy men* Perhaps derived from *wise,* or *Knowing-men,* and by their Subtle Genious sometimes Carry their Destruction to a most Dreadfull Length before they are Detected—the other Vices of this Nation Consist in theyr being Thieves by Nature, Generally Stealing what they Can Come at with impunity, and in Regard to intemperance in Drinking they are without Any Bounds, I have Seen even a *Negro-Wench*

• —this is an Absolute fact of which I only Would be Convinced, After the most Scrupulous information & Occular Demonstrations

empty a China bowl at one Draught With *two bottles* of Clerrett, which I Myself had given her to Make the Experiment—

I ought not to forget that the *Gango* Negroes are Reckon'd Anthropophagi or Canibals, Just as are the Chareebee Indians, that is from an Unsatiated Retaliation on their Enemies, Amongst this Class of Rebels After the taking of Boucou some Pots have been found on the fire with human flesh in them, Such as hands, feet, &c. Which one of the Officers had the Curiosity to taste declaring it was not inferior to Other Meat—

Since this time a Mr. *Vangills* an American Assured me that having travelled up alongst the banks of the River Ganges in Africa for a Great number of miles, he Actually Came to a Place where Human Arms, Legs, thighs &c. hung on Wooden Shambells, And was Exposed for Sale like butchers Meat in Any other Country—

I shall now Only Observe that black & heneous as are the Above Crimes they are the Natural Effects of Revenge and Avarice Alone, but how many Crimes are known amongst us that are unnatural—Over the one and the Other, let me Quickly Spread a Sable Veil, and dispel this Gloomy Cloud by the Sun Shine of theyr Virtues—

Theyr *Genious* has been Already Conspicuously Observ'd, so has their *Gratitude* Which they will even Carry to Such a Length that, they would *die* for those who have Showed them any Particular Favour, While nothing but the faithfulness of a dog Can equal that *Fidelity,* And Attachment they have for those Masters who use them Well & Which Shows that theyr Affection is As Strong as is their Hatred. the Negroes are Naturally *good Temper'd* Particularly the *Coromantyn* & these of *Nago,* While of the Passion of *Love* they are not Unsusceptible witness the Jealousy of their Wives, to whom their Resentment for incontinancy is Absolutely implacable, but as for what they did before they bear that Title, it Gives them no Uneasiness; and Such is the Delicacy of these People, that I dont Remember ever /Amongst the many Thousands that I did live With/ to have Seen one Offer a Kiss in public to a Woman, While the maternal tenderness of the Mothers is Such for their Children, that /during the 2 Years While they are at the breast/ none Cohabit with their Husbands, thus it Seldom happens to See one of them Pregnant Again, which they deem both unnatural, and Prejudicial to the Sucking infant, the Case of Lesperanza being no Exception, whose babies died Almost so soon as they Came to the World—

As for the Exemplary *Cleanliness* of the Negro Nation, it is Peculiarly Remarkable they being at least three times a Day over head in the Watter, & in *which the Congo tribe* Are Still distinguished from the Rest being the verry next thing to Amphibeous Animals—

the Negroes are *Spirited, brave & patient* in Adversity while theyr Undaunted fortitude in Going to Death through ev'ry torture Approaches even to *Heroism*, no negro ever Sighs or Complains though he is Expiring in the middle of Surrounding Flames. indeed on no Occasion Whatever Can I Remember to have Seen an African Shed a Tear, Yet to Beg for mercy they never fail When they are Ordered to be Flogg'd, while if they are Punished, Without Deserving it /in their Own Opinion/ Emediate Suiside is too often the fatal Consequence, Especially Amongst the Coromantyn Negroes, Who frequently even during the Act of Castigation throw back their Head, And by doubling the Tongue have got a Method of Swallowing it down, by Which it Swells, when they Choak themselves upon the Spot, And drop down dead in the Presence of their Masters; yet when they are Sensible of having deserved Correction no People Can be more Humble or go through their Unhappy fate with so much Resignation—Others have got a Practice of eating Common Earth, by Which the Stomach being Prevented from the Ordinary digestion they dispatch themselves Without any immediate Pain, yet by which they linger Perhaps for a Whole twelve month in the most Wretched Condition—

The Swallowing of the Tongue which Always takes place during the verry moment of Discipline has of late been Prevented in Surinam, by the humaine method of Clapping a *Fire Brand* or Burning Stick to the Victims face, Which Serves for the Double Purpose of Singing his Lips, and Suffocation; & by which means he is Divested /for the Present/ from Putting in Execution his Fatal Determination—

Against the *Ground Eaters* Who are Verry Common the Severest Punishments are Decreed by the Laws but Without much Effect, they Being but Seldom Detected in the Commission of this Act of Desperation—

Having thus far Described the Mental and Bodily Faculties of the African Negroes in a *Natural Condition*—We will now *Doubly* View them in a State of *Bondage*, first under all the *Oppressions* that they are Exposed to under a Rod, of Barbarous Tiranny, & Next as Protected by the mild hand of Justice And Humanity—While the *one* Picture /I am Almost Afraid/ will Occasion Such a Shudder, that any further Perusal of this Work will be dropt & Laid Aside, but I pledge my Word that the *Other* will make full and Ample Compensation, & in which State of *Servitude* I Will finish to Delineate the Striking Peculiarities of the Negro Character, Which I have thus far brought to a Conclusion—

That Slaves have been from the Earliest times /Witness Philemon & Onesima/ need no Comment, indeed we are all Dependants in a Less or more Degree, but how to treat those Whom fate has Subjected to our Commands that is the Question, & how they are Treated in the Colony of Surinam Shall Presently be Seen—

The Reader may Remember that I have introduced them in the 9th Chapter as Landing from the Coast of Guinea in a Lamentable State of Skin and bone, when

> Their Visage is Blacker than a Coal they are not known in the Streets, their Skin Cleaveth to their bones it is Withered it is become like a Stick
> —Lament. 4th Chapt.—Verse 8—

I have there Say'd that under the Care of Other Old Negro Slaves, they Soon become verry Fat & Sleek, learn the Language of the Colony, &c, When they are next Sent to Work in the Fields, to Which at first they Cheerfully Submit, but I have known Newly imported negroes to my Surprise Absolutely Refused to do any work *at all,* eyther by Good or by bad Words, Promises or threats nay even Rewards, or blows, till the Wonder Ceased, by being informed by the Others, that these unhappy People had been *Princes,* or People of the First Rank and Condition in their own Country, who by some Misfortunes in War &c, had Come to this infamous State, but whose Pride & Heroick Sentiments, Prefered even instant death to Vile Servitude, & upon which Occasions the Rest of the Slaves have Dropt down upon their Knees imploring the Masters, to Allow themselves to do the Work Required, Which Generally being Granted, the same Homage & Respect is Showed to the *Captive-Prince* that he was Accustomed to in his own Country—I Remember to have had a Charming Looking new Negro Call'd William, to Attend Me, whose Wrists and Ancles being Gall'd by the tying of a Rope, I enquired for the Cause,

> my father Said he was a King, and treacherously Murdered by the Sons of a Neighbouring Prince—I to Revenge his Death went dayly out a Hunting with some men, in hopes to Retaliate on the Assasins, but I was Surprised, taken tied and Sold to your European Countrimen on the Coast of Guinea, Which was deemed a *Greater* Punishment than killing me at Once—

The History of *Qwacoo* my Black boy was still more Strange,

> my Parents said he lived by Hunting and Fishing, from whom I was Stolen with two little Brothers when we were all verry young & Playing in the Sands, being Carried /Alone/ Some Miles in a Bag, I became the Slave of a King on the Coast of Guinea with many hundred more, who when our Master died, had all their heads Chopt off to be buried Along with him, Miself Alone Excepted, with other Children of my Age, And

who being Bestow'd As Presents to the Different Captains of his Army, My *new* Master again Sold me to the Captain of a Dutch Ship for some Powder & a Musquet—

How hard must this not be Already, to be *Drag'd* over a Turbulent Sea to a *Strange Country* never more to Repatriate, let them be Used As well as even it is Possible—

> The naked Negro Panting at the Line
> Boasts of his Golden sands & Palmy wine,
> Basks in the Glare or Stems the tepid wave,
> And thanks his Gods for all the Good they gave,
> Such is the patriots boast where e'er we Roam
> His first best Country ever is at home.

In Short no sooner do these Wretches begin to flag in their Work, than *Whips, Cow-skin, bamboo-Canes, Ropes, fetters,* and *Chains,* are introduced till they are Ready to Sink under toil and Oppression, nor Can with some Masters theyr Tasks ever be fulfilled, Making them fag on Day and Night even Sundays not Excepted—Nay I Recollect A Strong young negro Call'd *Marquis,* who having a Wife he Loved and two fine Children, Generally finished his Task /which was to Delve 500 Feet According to the Usual Custom/ before 4 OClock in the Afternoon, that he might thus have some time to Cultivate his little Garden & fish or Fowl for his family; hard, hard, did Marquis Labour to earn this Additional Pittance, close by him Working his Juliana, who

> —While he delv'd the Stubborn Soil
> And When he Sunk beneath the Sultry Toil,
> Fetch'd the Cold Beveridge & with Gentle Hand,
> Wip'd from his Pallid front faint Natures dew.

This Humaine Master however Apprised of his industry, for his Encouragement, now told him, that if he Could Delve 500 feet by *4 OClock* he Could Assuredly finish *600 Before Sun set,* to Which from that Day the Unfortunate man was Absolutely Condemned *for ever After,* Add to this that in Surinam they are next to being keept perfectly *Naked,* while theyr Chief food Consists in little more than a bunch of Plantains, indeed About twice a Year they Receive a Scanty allowance of Salt-fish, with a few Leaves of Tobacco, which goes by the name of *Sweety Muffo*—Still more Provoking it is, that if a negro and his wife have never so great an Attachment to each other the woman if handsome must yield to the Loathsome embraces of a Rascally Manager, or see her Husband Cut to Pieces by the Whip for daring to think of Preventing it, which truly drives them to Distraction—By these and many other Complicated evels Severals eyther kill themselves, Run away to the Woods, or become Spiritless and Languish under Various Diseases the Effects of the Above bad Usage, Such as the *Lota* which is a White Scurbutick Spot that Externally Covers the Body, the *Crassy-Crassy* or *Itch* from top to Bottom the *Yaws* Which is a most Disagreeable Disorder by Which the Patient is all over Covered with yellow Ulcers, and is a most disgusting Spectacle, this Disease most Negroes have once in theyr Life, yet only once—Some people have Compared it to the French Pox; While it is so infexious that if a Fly has been feeding on one of the *Above martyrs,* /& Who are Generally Covered with them/ Pick on an open Scratch of any Healthy Person, he is Almost Sure to be inflicted with the Cursed Malady, & which Continues for Several Months together—the General Cure in Surinam is to put them under a Salivation, to Which may be Added a Spare Diet & Uninterrupted Exercise to Promote Perspiration, when the Poor Devils Absolutely Look like decay'd & Corrupted Carcasses—Still more dreadful than this is the *boassy or Leprosy* which is incurable for Ever. this Consists in a Swelling of the Face Limbs &c. While the whole body is Covered over with Scales & Ulcers, the breath Stinks, the hair falls out, and the fingers and Toes becoming Putrid drop off Joynt after Joynt, till they Expire, which is often not Under the Course of many Years—The *Lepers* are naturally Lascivious, and Apt to Convey the Disease to Whoever Comes within their Reach On Which Account /at the Plantations/ they are Separted from every Other Society—

Another Disorder Call'd the *Clabba Yaws* or *Tubboes* I had nearly forgot, which is verry Troublesome and often Lasts a verry long time—this Consists in Painful Sores About the Feet, and mostly under the Soles, Which /being between the Skin and the flesh/ must Generally be Cured by being burnt with a Red hot Iron, or Cut up with a Launcet when the warm Joyce of Roasted Limes, with Success is Squeez'd in the Wound—

To *Worms* the African Negroes are also Subject of many Species both Subcutaneous, & internal, Owing to the Wading in Stagnate Watters & to the Crudity of theyr Diet &c, Amongst the Former is one Call'd the *Guinea* or Lint Worm, Which Exists between the Skin & the Flesh & is Sometimes two Yards in Length, While it is not Thicker than the 2d String of a Base-Viol, Shining, & as White as Silver; this insect Occasions verry Dangerous, & Painful Swellings in those Places Where it Coils itself, Which is Most Usually about the Legs; the Method of Cure is to Seize the Head, when it appears Above the Skin, & Gently to Extract the Worm by Winding it about a Stick, Which Operation Cannot be Done too Carefully, for Should it Break /Which often Happens/

not only the loss of the Limb but the Loss of life itself is frequently the Fatal Consequence. Some are infested With Six, or Eight of those Worms at one time—

Besides the Above Dreadful Worms & Calamities the negroes are Subject to every other Complaint Peculiar to the *Europeans,* who are not free in Guiana from the Loathsome and Dangerous distempers I have just decribed in the African Blacks—

After what I have said, it is little Wonder to See some estates Crowded with miserable Objects who are mostly Left under the Care of the *Dressing Negro* only by the Overseer, and whose Skill Consists in Giving a Doze of Physick or Spreading a Plaister only as for the Numbers whose bodies are Raw from neck to Heel by Constant Whipping, these are Left to Cure themselv's or Continue to do theyr Work *Without a Skin,* if they think proper—I Shall now Regularly Continue the links of this black Chain—

By the Above Complicated Oppressions from Nature & a Drunken Rascal of a Manager, it must follow that numerous Slaves become unfit to do any Work, Some being to[o] Weak, others Sculking from it from fear, & others becoming Old before their time, but for *all these* Desperate Evils, this *Dispotick Basha* nevertheless finds a Cure, which is no Other than to *kill them* outright Which loss Devolves /not on him but/ on his Master to Whom to be Sure he is Proud of Showing none but Such Slaves as are hardy & Able to do the Work, telling him at the Same time, that the Others died by the Venerial Disease & for Which the Villains Word only is Sufficient, the others Negroes not being tolerated to give Evidence in any Case Whatever—

Dictio testimonii non est servo homini—

Yet Should by some inforsean Accident an European Chance to prove the Murder, the Delinquent pays as /I have say'd/ about £50 only as a Fine, besides the price of the Slave if his Master Requires it, and for which Price of blood he may Butcher on from January to december, and this he does Assuredly whenever his Passion or bloody inclination Leads him to it, having Such frequent Opportunities to evade the Penalty Should even the Magistrates be Present, & Some of Which Stratagems I will Relate—For instance I have known it to Happen that Such a Brute being tired of an Old Negro, When wishing to get Rid of, he Only took him out a Fowling, when Desiring him to Discover the Game, the first Bird that Started he Shot the Poor Man dead Upon the Spot, which is Call'd an *Accident* without any Further Enquiry is made About it—Others to get Rid of them have been kill'd in the Following Manner, a Strong Stake being Fastned in the Ground the Slave was

Chain'd to it in the Middle of an Open Plain & burning Sun Shine, Where *one* Gill of Watter, with *one* Single Plantain, was brought every day till he was Starved to death—but this is not Call'd dying with Famine by his Master, who declaring he had Wanted neither Meat or Drink till he expired, is *Honourably Acquitted.* Still Another method of Murdering with impunity has often been Put in Practice—this is to tie them Stark naked with arms and Legs expanded to a Tree in the Forrest under Pretence of Streaching their Limbs, but where they Remain /being Regularly Fed/ Till they are Absolutely *Stung to death by the Gnats* or Musquetos, which is, to be Sure a most infernal Punishment & Child of the most Diabolical invention—Nay Kicking them Over board, with a Weight Chain'd to their Heels by Which they are Drown'd inevitably, is Call'd Accidental Death, while even by the orders of a Woman Negro Slaves have been Privately *burn'd* to Death, Miserably Chain'd in a Surrounding pile of Flaming Faggots—As to the Breaking out of their *Teeth* for Tasting the Sugar Cane Cultivated by themselves, or Slitting up their nose & Cutting off theyr Ears from private Peek, these are Look'd upon as Laughable Trifles, not Worth so much as to be Mention'd or to Come in to Consideration—

Such are the Damnable inventions, in *Modern* times inflicted, with impunity /though more than Savage Rage/ by man on man—

> From Egypt first the Ethiop Traffic Came,
> But dawn'd so mild that Slav'ry was not Shame,
> While nature yet Preserved some Genrous Right
> The Yoke was Easy & the Burthen Light,
> And here the Patriarch law each wrong Restrain'd,
> And eye for eye & Tooth for tooth ordain'd—

Till at Last—

> Detested Hawkins arm'd his Pirate Host,
> And Wolf-like Prowl'd on Guineas fated Coast,
> Force, Brib'ry, Stratagem, were all employ'd,
> O! Shame till twice ten Millions were Destroy'd;
> The Work of *Christians* this—

In Short to Such a Pich of Desperation has this Unhappy race of Men Sometimes been Drove, that from spite to end theyr days, and to be Relieved from Bondage they have even Leaped in a Chaldron of Boiling Sugar, thus at one Blow depriving the tyrant of his *Crop,* and his *Servant.*—

> All! All is Lost, but with a Gen'rous Pride,
> Ev'n Slaves Spurn life when freedom is Deny'd.

The Above *Skeaches,* together with those Acts of Barbarity I have so frequently Related through out this Work, are Assuredly Sufficient to melt the Heart of the most Unfeeling with Compassion, nor is it to be Wondered that Armies of Rebels at every Hazard Assemble in the Forrest to Seek Revenge & Liberty

I Shall now end the Dreadful Scenery by a General Remark on the Effect Which this Diabolical Usage has on Population—

In Surinam are Supposed to be at an Avarige about 75,000 Negro Slaves, but out of Which number if we Extract the Children, and the Superannuated Men & Women, I am Confident no more than 50,000 are Able Bodied, and Calculated to do any Work, thus 2 out of 3 Which is a Large Allowance—

The Guinea Ships that import Slaves from Africa being from 4 to 10 in Number, & having on board each Vessel a Cargo of from 250 to 300 Slaves, We Will Suppose the Yearly importation to be About 2500 to Supply and Compleat the Above 50,000, And then we will find the mortality to be just 5 Pr Cent Viz *more dead than born,* Notwithstanding each Negro has a Wife or two if he Chuses, by Which it is Proved that the Compleat number of negro Slaves Consisting in 50,000 Healthy people is Exactly Extinct one every 20 Years Which is truly Shocking to Human Nature, & more so when one Reflects that this is but in one Colony—What must the mortality be throughout the whole American Settlements—The Calculation is 100,000 Pr Annum thus in 20 Years two millions of People are murdered to Provide us with Coffee & Sugar—

> But Hark! the Afric' Genius Clanks his Chains,
> And Damns the Race that Robs his native Plains!

Not only *Robb'd* they are, but the Produce is infamously *Squandered*

> O Slavery! thou Fiend of Hells Recess,
> Profuse of Woes and pregnant with Distress;
> Eternal Horrors in thy Presence Reign.
> And meagre Famine leads thy Doleful train.
> To each Curst Load Subjection Adds more Weight,
> And pain is Doubled in the Vassals Fate.
> O'er natures Sprightly Face thou Spread'st a Gloom,
> And to the Grave dost ev'ry Pleasure doom.

Now O Fie be to thee, *Wretch* Who art the Cause of the Above Complicated Miseries, Yet which /bad as they Are/ Heaven hath Compassionately Prevented From being universal, as I Shall /by impartialy Reversing the Picture/ make Appear, And not /like the Rever^d Gentlemen

1776—AUGUST 10

Ramsay & Clarkson/ only Show the Darkest Shades through a Glass, Carefully preserving and Concealing the most Elegant Touches from the Public investigation. No; in a Manly manner Will I Bring Truth to Light, and Fairly expose the *Good* as well as the Bad to the Eye of a Candid World—That is to Say the *Good* when the negro Slaves are Treated as they Ought to be Treated, Which at some Estates they are, & might be Always if the Cancer was once Eradicated from the Root Where it Lies, Viz from the laws which are deaf to the cry of the Afflicted Dependants, While the Master is invested With that unbounded depotism Which ever ends in a Tirannical Usurpation, and Shall I ever Honour the Result of a Late Process in London, where a Negro Slave being Supported /by the Rod of Justice And Humanity/ Against his Master, enjoy'd that Liberty to Which in a Free Country he had a Right by the Laws of Nature—Now to Proceed—

In the first place I Will introduce a Negro Family in that State of Tranquil Happiness to Which they are all entitled When they are Well treated by their Owners; they are Supposed to be of the *Loango Nation* by the marks on the man's Body, while on his Breast may also be seen the letters **J.G.S.** being the enitials of my name, And Supposed to be the Cypher by which each master knows his Property—he Carrys a Basket with Small Fish on his Head & a net, While a large Fish is in his Hand, All Caught by Himself; & While his Wife /who is Pregnant/ is employ'd in Carrying Different kinds of Fruit, Spinning a Thread of Cotton and Comfortably Smoking her pipe of Tobacco—Still besides All Which She has a boy on her back And another Playing by her Side•—

Under Such a mild Government no Negroes work is more than a Healthy Exercise, which ends with the Setting sun, Viz at 6. O'Clock & When the Rest of the time is his Own, Which he employs in Hunting, And Fishing, Cultivating his Little Garden, or making Baskets, Fishnets &c for Sale; With Which Money he buys a Hog, Sometimes a Couple, or a Quantity of Fowls or Ducks, All Which he Fattens with the Spontaneous Growth of the Soyl, Without they Cost him eyther Cash, or much Trouble & which in the End Afford him Considerable Profit—

Thus Pleasantly Situated he is Exempt from every Anxiety, And looks up to his Master as the Common Protector of him and his Family, Whom he Adores not from Fear or Flattery but from a Conviction of his being the Object of his Care and Attention—He Breathes in a Luxorious Warm Climate like his Own, thus Wants no Cloaths besides

• —For the Above Picture I Was Offered 50 Florins by Mr A. Reynsdorp at Amsterdam—

Family of Negro Slaves from Loango.

Which incumberance & Expence, he Saves the Time of dressing, Undressing, Washing &c, & enjoys much more Health and Pleasure by Going naked*

His *house* he Can Build After his Fancy, the forrest Affording him All that he wants to make it Comfortable for the Cutting—his bed is a Hammock or a mat Call'd *Papaya,* and his Elbow his Pillow, if he is Wearied Standing he sits Sqwat upon his Hams Which he is Teached by Nature—his Pots he makes himself, And his Dishes or Gourds Grow in his Garden—he never lives With a wife he does not Love Exchanging her for another the Moment he, or She is Tired, Yet which more Seldom Happens here than in an European state of Matrimony—Besides his Masters Allowance of Plantains &c Which are two Bunches a Week, his Female friend has the Way to make him many Savoury Dishes; Such as *Braff* being a Hoch poch of Plantains & Yams boild With salt meat, Barbacued Fish, and Cayenne Pepper—*Tom-Tom* is a verry good Pudding Composed with the Flour of Indian Corn, and boild with Flesh, Fish, Cayenne pepper and the Young Pods of the *Ocro* or *Althea* Plant—*Pepper-pot* is a Dish of Boil'd Fish and Capsicum eat with Roasted Plantains—*Gangotay* is made of Dried, and Afo foo of Green Plantains—*Acanara* and Doquenoo are Composed of the Flour of Maiz, the last eat with Molasses &c—his General Drink is the Limpid Stream Sometimes Sweetened, and Corrected with a Dram of New Rum—If he is Indisposed he is Cured for Nothing, Yet but Seldom Troubles the Faculty being Perfectly Skill'd in the Knowledge of Herbs or Samples, besides Which Scarifying and Puckering the Skin, are a Constant Practice, Which serves for a Bleeding; even the inconveniency of Vermin he Removes Without a Comb by Pushing up all his Hair in Clay, Which being Dried on his Pate, And then Wash'd With Soap and Watter makes him Clean beyond every Conception—indeed in Regard to Cleanliness no People Can Surpass Some Negro Slaves, Particularly their Teeth are for Ever kept as White as Ivory, for which they use Nothing more than A Sprig of Orange, Which /being bit to the Consistancy of a Small Brush/ they are for ever Rubbing their gums with, nor is any Negro /male or Female/ ever Seen without this Little Green Tool, Which besides has the Virtue of Sweetening the Breath—So much for the *Body,* and in Regard to the *Soul* he is Seldom Troubled with any Qualms of Conscience or Fear of Death being Firm and unshaken in What he was

* —How Preferable this is to his Modernized Countrymen, Who walk the Streets of London with their Hair Combed & Powdered in a tail which makes them look like Monkeys, the Young Women However in Surinam are mostly Supplied With Chintz Petticoats, Generally of Ten Breadths, Gold ear Drops, Granat-Bracelets &c–While a Silk handkerchief tied Round the Head is Verry Common—

taught to Believe, and when he is no more his Companions or Relations Carry him to Some Grove of Orange Trees, Where he is interred With uncommon Expence for those People, being Put in a Coffin of the best Wood & Workmanship—While the Cries & Lamentations of his Surviving Friends pierce the Sky—the Grave Being Fill'd up & Green Turf neatly Spread over it, a Couple of Large Gourds are Put by the Side of it, the one with Watter the Other with Boil'd Fowls Pork, Cassava &c. as a Libation, not from a Superstition /as some D———nd idiots/ Believe that he will eat or Drink it, but as a Testimony of that Regard Which they have for his Memory, while Some even Add their Little Furniture that he left Behind, Breaking it in Pieces Over the Grave, this Done every one takes his Last Farewell Speaking to him as if he lived, by testifying their Sorrow at his Departure, However that they hope to See him in a Better Place, Where he now Enjoys the Pleasant Company of his Parents, dearest Friends And Ancestors, When Another dismal yell ends the Ceremony, and All Return home Where /a fat Hog being kill'd with Fowls Ducks &c./ a General Feast is Given by his Relations to All the Other negroes, & Which ends not till the Following day—Now those who Were his Nearest Connections Cut out their Hair and Shave the head both Male & Female, round which having tied a Dark blue Handkerchief they Wear this Mourning for a Whole Year, After which once more Visiting the Grave, Offering a Libation, and taking their Final Farewell, Another Hog &^{c} is Kill'd, & the Funeral Rites are quite Ended by a Second Feast, Which Finishes with a Joyful Dance & Songs of Praise in memory of their Dr Relation—

No People Can more Esteem or have a Greater Friendship for each other than the negro Slaves who enjoy each others Company With an unbounded Pleasure—During which they are not Destitute of Diversions Such as *Soesa,* which Consists in Dancing Opposite to each other and Clapping With their Hands on their Sides to keep in time, When each With Pleasure throws out one Foot—if they meet Across the Party Wins one Point, if Sides it is for the Other till one or the Other has got Twelve Sometimes 20 Points Who Gets the Game—So verry Eager are they at this Play in Which Sometimes Six or Eight Couple are Engaged at once, that the Violent Exercise having kill'd Some of the Negroes, it is Forbid by the magistrates at Paramaribo—*Awaree* is an innocent Amusement Consisting in Piching With a large kind of Marbles in Defect of Which they use the Awaree nuts—The men also Cudgel, and Wrestle, Yet at this I think them inferior to eyther those of Cornwall or Devon—

But Swimming is theyr Favourite Diversion Which they Practice every day at least Twice or Thrice, Promiscuously in Groops of Boys and Girls, without Distinction like the Indians, when both Sexes show Astonishing feats of Courage Strength and Activity—Nay I Have not only Seen a Negro Girl beat a Hardy Youth in Swimming Across the River Comowina /While I Was one of the Party/ but on Landing Challenge him & beat him Stark naked at a two miles Race, While every Idea of Shame on the one Side & of insult on the other Are totally unknown—

I Shall now Say Something of their musick and Dancing—I have Already mention'd that of the Loango Tribe in Particular, thus will now decribe that Practis'd by the other nations in General—first their instruments of Sound /Which are not a Little in Genious/ are All made by themselves, And Consist of those Represented in the Annex'd Plate Where—

No 1. /Which is Call'd *Qua-Qua*/ is a hard Sounding board elevated on one Side like a boot Jack, on Which they beat or Drum time With two pieces of Iron, or two bones—

2. Is the *Kiemba toetoe* or hollow Reed, Which is blown thro' the Nostrils, like the nasal flute of Otaheytee, it has but two Holes one at each end, the first Serving to Sound it the Other to be Touched by the Finger—

3. Is the *Ansokko bania* Which is a Hard board Supported on both Sides like a low Seat, on which are Placed Small blocks of Different Sises, which being Struck with two Small Sticks like a Dulcimar gives different Sounds that are not at All disagreeable—

4. is the Great *Creole Drum* being a Hollow Tree open at one end and Covered on the Other with a Sheep Skin, on Which they Sit Astride & So beat time with the palm of their Hands Answering the Effect of a Base Viol to the *Qua Qua* board—

5. Is the Great *Loango Drum* being Covered at both ends & Serves to the Same Purpose—

6. Is the *Papa Drum* beat as the others—

7. Is the Small *Loango Drum* beat together with the Great one—

8. The Small Creole drum for the same Use—

9. In Call'd *Coeroema* this is a Wood Cup ingeniously made and Covered Also with a Sheep Skin, When it is beat with two Small Rods or Drum Sticks After the Manner of the Qwa Qwa board—

10. The *Loango bania*—this I thought Exceedingly Curious being a Dry board on which are Laced, & kept Closs by a Transverse Bar, different Sized Elastick Splinders of the Palm Tree, in Such a manner that both ends are elevated by other Transverse Bars that are Fix'd under them and the Above Apparatis being placed on number—

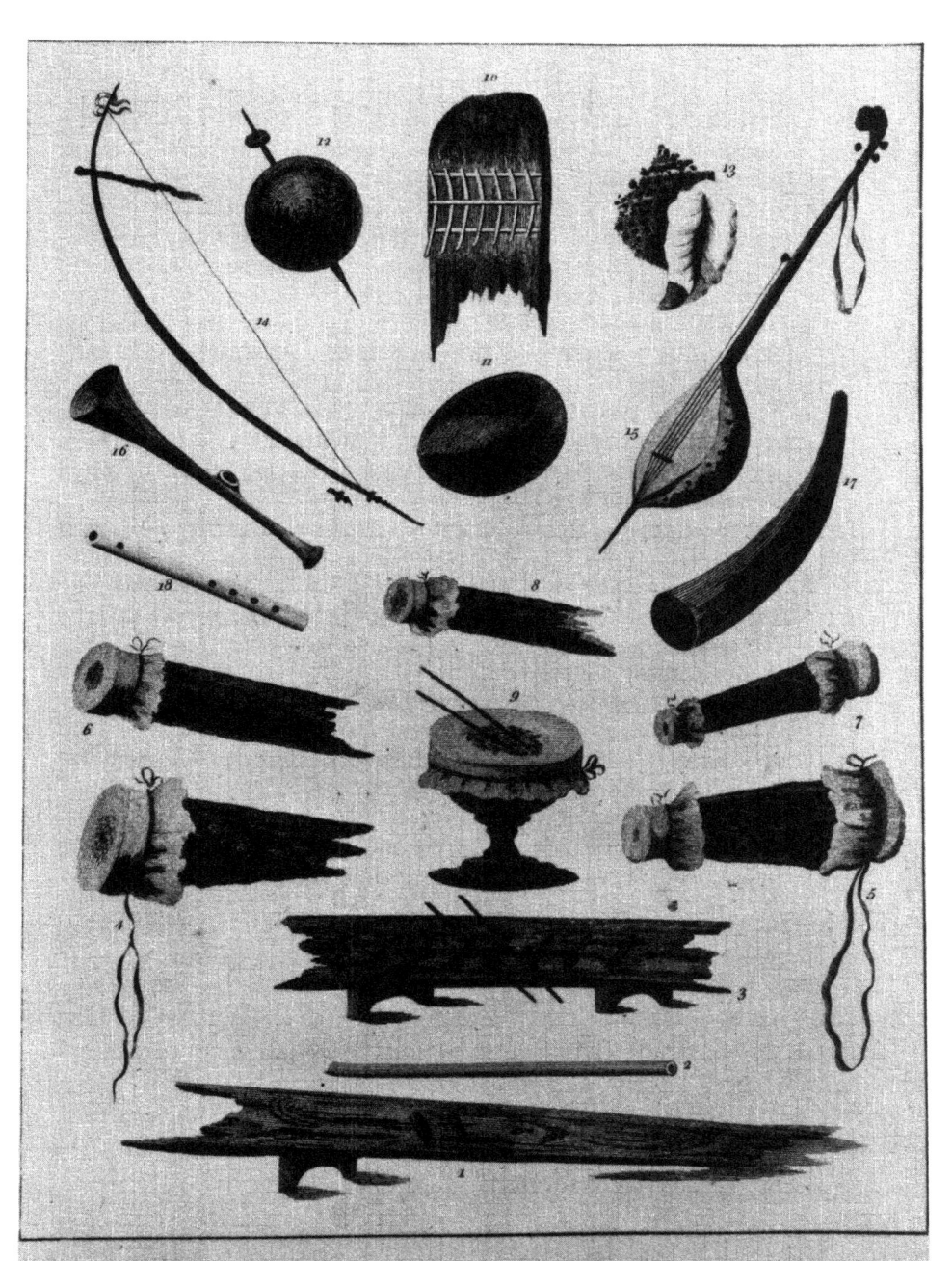

Musical Instruments of the African Negroes.

London, Published Dec.r 1.st 1791, by J. Johnson St Pauls Church Yard.

11. /which is a Large *empty Gourd* to promote the Sound/ the extremities of the Splinders are Snapt by the Fingers, Something in the manner of a piano Forto & have the same Effect—
12. is Call'd by the Negroes *Saka Saka* being a hollow Gourd With a Stick & handle fix'd through it, & fill'd with Small pebles /not Unlike the Magick Shell of the Indians/ this they hold Above theyr Head and Rattle it to Measure While they Dance—
13. this is *a Conch or Sea Shell* Which /by the Lungs/ they Sound for Pleasure, or to Cause An Alarm &c but is not Relative to their Dancing—
14. The name of this is *Benta* being a Branch bent like a Bow, by means of a Slip of dry Reed, or Warimbo, Which when held to the Teeth the String is Beat on with a Short Stick, and being Shifted back and Forwards Sounds not Unlike a Jew's Harp—
15. The *Creole-Bania,* this is like a Mandoline or Guitar, being made of a Gourd Covered With a Sheep-Skin, to Which is Fixed a Verry Long Neck or Handle—This instrument has but 4 Strings, 3 Long, and one Short, Which is thick and Serves for a Bace, it is play'd by the Fingers, and has a Verry Agreeable Sound more so when Accompanied With a Song—
16. Is the *Trumpet* of War to Command Advancing, Retreating &c—and is cald the *too too*—
17. A *Horn* used to Supply the other, or on the Plantations to Call the Slaves to Work—
18. is the *Loango Tootoo* or Flute Which they Blow /as the Europeans do/ After the Common way it has but 4 Holes for the Fingers, yet independant of which they make it Produce a Variety of Sounds—

Such are the *musical Instruments* of our African Brethren, to Which they *Dance* With more Spirit than we do to the best band in Europe—

To What I have Said I will only Add that they always Use *full,* or *half Measure* but never *Treeple* time in their Dancing Musick, which not Unlike a Bakers Bunt /When he Seperates the Flour from the Bran/ Sound *Tuckety Tuck,* and *Tuckety Tuck,* ad Perpetuum—

To this Noise However they Dance With Uncommon Pleasure And Sometimes Foot it Away With Great Art and Dexterity—

Saltantes Satyros imitabitur Alphisiboeus—

But to Proceed With my Description of a happy Slave, every Saturday Evening he shuts up the Week with an Entertainment of this Kind, and at Least Once a Quarter is indulged with a Grand Ball, At Which the Neighbouring Slaves are invited, And Where the Master often Contributes to the Happiness by his Presence, or at Least by Sending a Present of a few Jugs of *kill devil* or new Rum, At these Grand-balls the Slaves are Remarkably neat the Women Appearing in their best Chintz Petticoats, and many of the Men in fine Holland Trowsers, and so infatiguable are they at this Diversion that I have known the drums to Continue Beating without intermission from Sun Set on Saturday Night, till that Celestial Orb Again made its Appearance on the Monday Morning following, being mostly Accompanied by Cheering, Hallooing, & Clapping of Hands—the Negroes dance Always in Couples, the men Figuring & Footing, While the Women turn Round like a Top, and their Petticoats Expand like a Circle which they Call *Waey Cotto*—

During this the Bystanding Youths fill about the Liquour, While the Girls Encourage the Performers And Wipe the Lather from the Brows And Sides of the Unwearied Musitians—

It is indeed upon the Whole Astonishing to See With What Good nature and even with a Degree of Good Manners* these Dancing Societys are kept up, of Which I Still Repeat they are so verry fond, that I have known a Newly imported Negro /for want of a Partner/ Figure & Foot for near the Space of 2 Hours to his Shadow Against the Wall—

All that I have now Said Above in Regard to their being Happy is Still but a Trifle When Compared to that Felicity of Living till they die With their Parents and Nearest Relations, while theyr Children are for ever near Them, and Provided for, to the end of theyr Lives, Nay Some have the Satisfaction to See their Offspring About them to the 3^d or 4th Generation—

How Wide Different is not this from the Generality of Europeans who spend /under the name of Liberty/ a Wretched Existance Enveloped in a Turbulent Sea of Care & Anxiety, While theyr Decendants are even Happy if by being Wafted to all the Different Corners of the Earth, And being torn to all Eternity from theyr Presence they Can only Get Bread, though Steep'd in Bitterness & the Sweat of their Forehead—Good God, What are our Soldiers & Sailors, are they not Dependant under the Verry Severest Laws, do they not Sell theyr Liberty for a Precarious Subsistance, And to Serve as Marks to be Shot at; Away Destestable prejudice Which Cannot See its own Chains on Account of theyr Guilding—And Hail; thou Happy People, Who under the Name of Slavery enjoy often the Purest Bliss—Which is to Say in

* —the Negroes Generally Salute each other by Shaking hands, When they meet the tops of the Middle Fingers Snap them 3 times and make a bow Saying how dee Matee, how are you Friend—

Other Words, that the African Negroe Slaves, Who have the Good Fortune to be Under a Master Who is Really a man, Enjoy that State of Felicity, that is Superior to most, & even inferior to None•—This to be Sure is too Seldom the Consequence at Present, Heaven knows it, but Such may be the General Case in time to Come, When good Sence and Humanity Shall have Dictated Such Laws for the Government of the African Negro-Slaves, as Shall be Proved to be for the Permanent Good Of Both the Ruler & the Subject, and that Such Laws Can Exist I Will give a Hint of as I have Promised, before I Leave these Pages—

As a further Proof of What I have Said in Regard to the Happiness of Some Slaves /I Say only Some/ I Refer the reader to a Work Intitled "Cursory Remarks upon the Reverend Mr Ramsays Essay on the Treatment and Conversion of the African Slaves in the Sugar Colonies, by a Friend to the West India Colonies And their inhabitants, Printed in 1785," Where the Author after Comparatively Styling the Peasantry and Labouring People in England as *the Devoted Sons & Daughters of Wretchedness* draws the Picture most Surprisingly Similar to What I have done—

I Also Refer him back to what I have Said in this Narrative Jan.y 28.th 1774—And after Still Attesting that I was Acquainted With a free Negro Woman /at Deventar in Holland/ Who since Voluntarily gave up her Liberty, & again Preferred to be a Slave in Surinam /in Which State I also knew her/ I Will take my Final Farewell of the African Negroes, and put an end to this verry Long and Tedious Chapter by the Old & Juditious remark that all Sublunary Happiness Con[s]ists in imagination only, when *health of Body* and *Peace of mind* are not interrupted by Oppression—

• —Such is the Confidence Some Planters have in theyr Slaves that they Even trust their infants to a Negro *wet nurse*, who to be Sure treats them Generally with the Greatest Tenderness and Affection—

Chapter 27th

The rape of the sabines—Shoaking Execution and African Fortitude—Discription of an Indigo Plantation—the spanso Bocco—a Punishment—Troops again reenter the Woods—the Expedition draws to a Conclusion

Now Came the news to Paramaribo that though the Rebels had Desisted of Late from Cruelties and insurrections, they had Still Ventured a Second *Rape of the Sabines* by taking Away all the Women at the Estate Bergendal on the *Blue-Bergh,* Call'd also mount *Parnassus* in the Higher parts of the River Surinam, Notwithstanding a Military Post was Station'd at the Above place—In Consequence a Party of the Rangers was instantly Detached thither to Assist in Pursuing them &c And About the Same Time, the long Projected Cordon or Path of Circumvolation was also begun to be Cut by 700 Negro Slaves Around the Colony, which Path Was Henceforth to be man'd with Military piquets at Proper Distances to Defend the Estates Against any Further insurrections from Without, And prevent Desertion to the Enemy from Within—

The Above Mount Parnassus is Situated on the **W** Side of the River Surinam & distant from Paramaribo /if one includes the Windings of the River/ Above one Hundred miles—it being a Pleasant Situation I Present the Reader with a View of it in the Plate Annex'd, As also of the Village Call'd Jews Savannah with [which] is Distant from Town /in Ligna Recta, as I have Said/ Something more than 40 but by Watter Above 60. Miles—Here the Jews have a Beautiful Synagogue & keep theyr Solemn Feasts & Festivals—here they also have theyr Capital Schools & Seminaries while at this Village Reside some verry Respectable Jewish Families—these People possessing Particular Rights & Priviledges in this Colony, With which they were endow'd by king Cha: the II.ᵈ, when this Settlement was English, & Which I never yet knew Jews to Possess in any Part of the World Whatsoever—

From Paramaribo, or indeed from the Fortress New Amsterdam—the River Surinam /like Cottica and Comowina/ is Beautifully Lined with Sugar and Coffee Plantations, as are Also Several Creeks or Small Rivers that Communicate With it, Such as the *Powlus, Para, Cropina & Paracac* Creeks &.ᶜ but Above mount Parnassus not a Single Estate /that may be so Call'd/ is to be found, neyther is the River any Longer Navigable, not even for Small Craft, on Account of the Prodigious Rocks & Cascades or Watter Falls, with which is Obstructed Winding through between Excessive high Mountains And an inpenetrable Forrest, which form a Enchantingly Romantick *Coup Doeuil* indeed, but Debar the Possessors of the Colony from making Such Discoveries, as might perhaps Reward theyr Labour with verry Considerable Riches—but to Proceed—

If /as I have Just mention'd/ Cruelties Were become less Common in the Rivers by the Rebels, Barbarities Still Continued in a Shocking degree in the Metropolis, Where my Ears were deaf'd With the Clang of the Whip, & the Shreeks of the Negroes—Particularly a Missy *Spaan* Who lived next door to M.ʳ Degraaffs—I Saw with Horror from my Window, Order a Black young Woman to be Flogged Across *the Breasts* and no where Else till She was Cut to Pieces—infernal b——ch Could I have Disciplined thee at this Moment What would have been thy Portion? I now got in a Whiskey And Rode out to Dissipate my Self, When the first thing I Saw Was a Negro Girl Call'd *Europa* fall naked from a Garret Window, on a heap of Broken Bottles, this Was indeed an Accident but Mangled her /though not Dead/ in Such a Condition that I Cannot Describe it—Damning my unlucky fate I turn'd the Horses, and drove to the Beech as the only place to Avoid every Scene of Cruelty but here I had the mortification to See two Philadelphia Sailors, While Fighting on the Fore Castle of their Vessel both fell over their Ships Bow & be Drown'd, While on Board Another American Brig I Discovered a Little Tar, Defending himself from the Cross Trees with a Hatchet Against a Sergeant & 4 Arm'd men for a Considerable time—having Threatned to Shoot him out of the Rigging he at Last Surrendered & being brought Ashore, Was Drag'd to Fort Zelandia in Company with two more by a File Of Musqueteers, where for having been Drunk on Duty they Received a *Fire Cant* Each at the Captains Request, that is Bastonaded or beat on the Shoulders by two Corporals With bamboo Sticks, till theyr backs were Swell'd like a Cushion; However Arbitrary this mode of Correction the Captains fully Ex-

View of the Settlement called the Jew's Savannah.

View of the Blue Bergh called Mount Parnassus.

London, Published Dec.r 1.st 1791, by J. Johnson, St Paul's Church Yard.

plain'd the Necessity of it, the Private American Sailors being of a Turbulent Spirit, indeed when in Liquor, While if Sober they may Fairly be Class'd amongst the best Seamen in the World—

The next morning early /While musing on all the different Dangers and Chastisements that the Lower Class of People are Subjected to/ I Heard a Crow'd pass under my Window—Curiosity made me Start up, Dress in a hurry, & Follow them When I discovered 3 Negroes in Chains Surrounded by a Guard going to be Executed in the Savannah—their Undaunted look however Averse to Cruelty's fassinated my Attention and determined me to see the Result, Which was Viz, that the Sentence being Read /in Low dutch which they did not understand/ one was Condemned to have his head Chop'd Off With an Ax for having Shot a Slave who had Come to Steal Plantains on the Estate of his Mistress, While his Accomplice was Flogg'd below the Gallows—the Truth Was However that this had been done by the mistresses Absolute Command, but who being detected & Preferring the Loss of the Negro to the Penalty of 500 Florins, Allow'd the Poor man to be Sacrificed; he laid down his Head on the Block With uncommon Deliberation & even Streached out his Neck when with one blow it was Severed from his Body—

The third negro whose name was *Neptune* was no Slave, but his own Master, & a Carpenter by Trade, he was Young and handsome—But having kill'd the Overseer of the Estate Altona in the Para Creek in Consequence of some Despute he Justly Lost his Life with his Liberty. —However the *particulars* are Worth Relating, which Briefly were that he having Stole a Sheep to Entertain some Favourite Women, the Overseer had Determined to See him Hang'd, Which to Prevent he Shot him dead Amongst the Sugar Canes—this man being Sentenced to be brook *Alive* upon the Rack, without the benefit of the *Coup de Grace,* or mercy Stroke, laid himself down Deliberately on his Back upon a Strong Cross, on which with Arms & Legs Expanded he was Fastned by Ropes—The Executioner /also a Black/ having now with a Hatchet Chop'd off his Left hand, next took up a heavy Iron Crow or Bar, with Which Blow After Blow he Broke to Shivers every Bone in his Body till the Splinters Blood and Marrow Flew About the Field, but the Prisoner never Uttered a Groan, or a Sigh—the Roaps being now Unlashed I imagined him dead & Felt happy till the Magistrates moving to Depart he Wreathed from the Cross till he Fell in the Grass, and Damn'd them all for a Pack of Barbarous Rascals, at the Same time Removing his Right hand by the help of his Teeth, he Rested his Head on Part of the timber and ask'd the by Standers for a Pipe of Tobacco Which was infamously Answered by kicking & Spitting on him, till I With some Americans thought Proper to Prevent it—

he then begg'd that his head might be Chopt off, but to no Purpose, at Last Seeing no end to his Misery, he declared that though he had Deserved death, he had not Expected to die So many Deaths, "However you Christians /Said he/ have mis'd your Aim, and I now Care not were I to lay here Alive a month Longer," After Which he Sung two Extempore Songs, With a Clear Voice taking leave from his Living Friends & Acquainting his Deceased Relations that in a Little time more he Should be with them to enjoy their Company for ever—this done he Entered in Conversation With two Gentlemen Concerning his Process Relating every one Particular with Uncommon tranquility, but Said he Abruptly, "by the Sun it must be Eight OClock, & by any Longer discourse I Should be Sorry to be the Cause of your Loosing y:r Breakfast" then turning his Eyes to a Jew whose name was *De Vries,* "Appropo Sir said he Won't you please to pay me the 5 Shillings you owe me"—*for what to do*—"to buy meat & Drink to be Sure: don't you perceive that I am to be kept Alive" Which /Seeing the Jew look like a Fool/ he Accompanied With a Loud and Hearty Laugh—Next Observing the Soldier Who stood Sentinel over him biting Occasionally on a piece of Dry Bread he asked him, "how it Came that he a *White Man* Should have no meat to eat along with it" *Because I am not So rich* said the Soldier. "then I will make you a Present first pick my Hand that was Chopt of[f] Clean to the Bones Sir—Next begin to myself till you be Glutted & you'l have both Bread and Meat which best becomes you" & Which piece of Humour was Followed by a 2.d Laugh & thus he Continued when I left him which was about 3 Hours After the Execution but to dwelt more on this Subject my Heart

—Disdains
Lo! tortures, Racks, whips, Famine, Gibbets, Chains
Rise on my mind, Appall my Tear Stain'd Eye
Attract my Rage, & Draw a Soul felt Sigh,
I Blush, I Shudder, at the Bloody theme,

In the Adjoyning Plate See the Above Dreadfull Chastisment—

Now How in the name of Heaven Human nature Can go through so much Torture, With So much Fortitude, is truly Astonishing, Without it be a mixture of Rage, Contempt, pride, And hopes of Going to a Better place or at Least to be Relieved from this, & Worse than Which I Verrily Believe Some Africans know no Other Hell—Nay even So late as 1789 On October 30 & 31 /at Demerary/ Thirty two Wretches

The Execution of Breaking on the Rack.

were Executed, Sixteen of Whom in the Above Shocking Manner, Without So much as a Single Complaint was Heard Amongst them, & Which days of Martyr are Absolutely a Feast to many Planters—thus in Place of Applying M.r Humphries Rhymes to Britain Alone, are they not more Suitable to the European Race in General—

> Why *Christians* Rag'd thine Insolence & Scorn
> Why Burst thy Vengeance on the Wretch forlorn
> The Cheerless Captive to Slow death Consign'd
> *Weigh'd down With Chains* in Prison Glooms Confin'd
> Of hope Bereft by thy Vile minions Curs'd
> With hunger Famish'd & Consum'd with thirst
> Without one Friend, when Death's last Horror stung
> Roll'd the wild eye & Gnaw'd the Anguish'd Tongue

I Should be Rather inclin'd to think That Britain is the Standard of humanity, by being the first nation /Whether Politically or not/ that Attempted the Abolition of the Slave Trade, how Applicable are the Following Passages from Daniel to this Subject—

> And in those times there Shall many Stand up Against the King of the South, Also the Robbers of Thy People shall exalt Themselves &.c

Then Follows—

> After this Shall he turn his Face to the isles And Shall take many —but a *Prince* for his Own Behalf Shall Cause the Reproach offered By him to Cease, without his own Reproach he Shall Cause it to Turn upon him—

I must now once more Return to the Savannah where one of the Strangest Circumstances took place that ever Befel me in my Life, the Effects of which might have been not a Little Prejudicial to a weak mind, had I not Chanced emediately to find out the Cause from Whence they proceeded—

 Being desirous to know if the unhappy *Executed negro* Was Still Existing I Walk'd by myself about 3 in the Afternoon to the Spot of his Sufferings, where while I was Ruminating on his miserable Fate, the first thing I saw was his Head at Some Distance placed on a Stake nodding to me Backwards & Forwards, as if he had been Really Alive—I instantly Stopt Short, & Seeing no Person in the Savannah, nor a Breath of Wind up Sufficient to move a leaf or a Feather, I Acknowledge that my Resolution of advancing Further had Almost Faild me till Reflecting that I must be mad indeed not to Approach this Head, And find out the Wonderful Phenomenon if Possible, thus I Stept Forward & Instantly Discovered the Natural Cause by A *Vultures* Perching Upon the Gallows as if he meant to dispute with me for this Feast of Carrion, Which bird having Already pick'd out one of the Eyes had Apparently Fled at my First Reproach & by kicking the Scull with its Talons as it took its Sudden Flight, Occasion'd the motion already Described—I Shall now only add that After Living near 6 Hours the Poor Wretch had been knock'd in the Head by the Commiserating Sentinel the marks of Whose Musket were Perfectly Visible by a Tremenduous Fracture in The Scull—

Vultures are Compared by Some to the Eagle though those of Surinam Posess the verry Reverse Qualifications—they are indeed a Bird of Prey, but in place of feeding on What they kill like the Other noble Animal, they Exist entirely upon Carion, And Generally Attend Burials places of Execution &c. Which they Discover by the most Accute Smell, So much so that by the negroes they are Call'd *Tingee-Fowlo* or Stinking Fowl; the Guiana Vultures are the Sise of a Common *Turkey,* of a Dark Gray Colour, With Black Wings & Tail, the Bill is Streight With a Crooked Point, and Verry Strong the Tongue is Cloven, the Neck without Feathers, and the Legs verry Short—Besides Carrion these Birds eat Serpent, & indeed every thing that is Obnoctious, till they are so much Gorged that they can Hardly Fly—

The Bird Call'd the *King of the Vultures,* Is not verry Common in Surinam though Sometimes the indians Bring one or two to Paramaribo for Sale on Account of its Great Beauty, this is Larger than any Turkey Cock With a naked Head and Neck, the Skin of Which is Partly brown Yellow Scarlet &c. And Round Which Last it has a Dusky long Feathered Colour, in Which it Can at Pleasure Withdraw both the one And the Other, till nothing but Part of the Head is Perceptible, Notwithstanding these Distinctions it equally Feeds on Carrion, Serpents Rats, Toads and even Excrements, and is upon the whole /like the other/ a Cowardly indolent Stinking Animal.

In the Forrest of Surinam is Also found amongst Others the *Crested Eagle* being a verry fierce Bird, & Verry Strong, the Back is Black but yellowish at the Base, the Breast & Belly white With Black Spots, so are its Thighs, and even the Feathers of the Legs, the rest of the Body is brown all over and its Feet are Perfectly Yellow—the head of this Bird is Flat, ornamented with 4 Feathers 2 Long and 2 Short which it Can erect or not erect at Pleasure—

About this Time the *Hind* an English Frigate with her Tender were on the Coast looking out for American Prizes—

It now Being the *Heridatary Prince of Orange* his Birth day, the whole Corps were Entertained with Salt Beef, Salt Pork, Barley, Pudding & hard Peas—And this day /Poor Joana being inflexible in her Resolutions/ I Ratified the Agreement with the Good Mrs Godefrooy in Presence of her mother & Other Relations, Whereby the Above Lady bound herself never to Part with her to myself alone Excepted until she died, and in Which Case not only her Liberty, but a Spot of Ground for Cultivation, besides a neat House built upon it &c. Should be her Portion forever to Dispose of as she Pleas'd, After which She Return'd my Remaining bond of 900 Florins & gave Joana a Present of a purse wth Gold Containing *near 20 Ducats,* besides a Couple of Elegant pieces of *East-India Chintz,* advising me at the Same time to give in a Request to the Court for Little Johnnys immediate Manumition, which She Observed was a Necessary Form Whether I Should Be able to Get the Bail Usually Required or not, and Without which Formality, even if I had the Bail Ready to Appear nothing Should be done to his Advantage—having both thank'd this Heavenly Woman, I went to Sup with his Excellency the Governor transported with Joy, to whom giving in my Request in full form, he Coolly Put it in his Pocket with one hand, while he gave me a Hearty Squeese with the other, and Shaking his head told me frankly that he would lay it before the Court, but at the Same time was Perfectly Convinced my boy must die a Slave, Without I Could find the necessary Bail, which /he was At the same time Well Persuaded/ verry few People would wish to Appear for—

Thus had I after Spending so much time & Labour, besides the Expense of above a Hundred Guineas Already Pay'd, Still the Heartfelt mortification to See this dear little Fellow, of whom I was both the Father And the master Exposed to Perhaps Eternal Servitude—As for Joana She was now Perfectly Safe but Alas! Poor Johnny, who feels not for this infant While Assuredly I alone was the only Cause of all these Complicated Evils that Threatned his early Youth, and as such with Justice I take the Whole Blame upon myself—However one Consolation Still Presented itself, /viz/, that the Famous negro *Graman-Qwacy* formerly mention'd, & who was Just return'd from Holland, brought the news that Partly by his interest, a Law was there enacted by which All Slaves were to be free 6 Months After theyr Landing at the Texel, which indeed on Application of theyr masters Might be Stretched to 12, but not a Single day Longer on any Account Whatsoever—

By this being Persuaded I Should one day Joyfully Fetch both him & his Mother, over the Atlantick, my heart was Relieved from the weight of a Milstone—

Who the Above *Graman Qwacy* was, I will more Sufficiently Explain before I take Farewell from the Reader, Suffice it to Say for the Present that the Prince of Orange besides Paying his Out & Home Passage, & Giving him Several Presents Such as a large Gold meddal &c. Sent him back to Surinam dress'd in a Suit of Blue and Scarlet, Trim'd with broad Gold lace, While on his Hat he wears a White Feather & Looks upon the whole not unlike one of the dutch Generals, which made this King of the negroes very proud & even Sausy—

The Governor of the Colony now giving a large Feast to Several of his Friends at *his indigo* Plantation, which was Situated but a few miles at the Back of his Palace I had the Honour to be invited as one of the party & the pleasure to inspect the Process of making indigo—

In the First place I will Present the Curious with a drawing of the *indigo Plant* which is a Knotty Shrub, growing from seed about 2 feet from Ground, and that Comes to Perfection in the Space of two Months, while it requires a Verry Rich Soil & which besides ought to be Kept perfectly Clean from weeds—in the Plate **A** is the Colour of the Sprig; **B,** the leafs above, **C** the Same below, **D** the Seeds inclosed in Small Brown Pods—**E** the Sise of the leaf as it grows, & **F** the Piece of indigo Ready made for use—

The Above Sprig was Design'd from nature on the Spot, but on a Smaller Scale.—it has Something of the Tamarind branch Viz in the Size of the Leaf, which also Grows in Pairs, and is Darker above than Below, but at the extremity of each Shoot in this Shrub *one* Leaf Grows Single—The young Shoots in the tamarind Trees also appear at the extremity of the Branches, here they Spring Forth as may be Seen from the base which is quite the Reverse—

I Will now Proceed to Explain in which Manner the above indigo plant is Converted to indigo Viz having Cut off all the Verdure, the whole Crop is Tied in Bundles, and put into a very Large Tub with Watter, Covered over with very heavy Logs of Wood by way of Pressers—thus Steept it begins to Ferment in less than 18 Hours, when the Watter Seems to Boil, and becomes of a Violet or Garter Blue Colour, Extracting all the Grain from the Plant—in this Situation it is tapt off into *Another Tub,* which is Something less & the Remaining Trash is Carefully pickd up & thrown away, And Which *Stinking* Abominably, Occasions the Peculiar unhealthiness annex'd to this Business—Being now in the *Second* tub the mash is Agitated by Paddles for the Purpose, till by a Skilful masseration, the Grain all Seperates from the Watter; the First Sinking like mud to the Bottom, While the later appears Clean and transparent on the Surface—this Water being Cautiously Removed till near *the Body* the Remaining Liquid is Still Tapt into a *Third Tub* to Let what Grains it may Contain Settle in the Bottom, When these Last drops being also Removed the indigo is put in Proper Vessels to Dry where being Divested of its Last Remaining moisture & Shaped into

Sprig of the Indigo Plant.

London, Published Dec.r 1.st 1791, by J. Johnson, St Pauls Church Yard.

Small Oblong Square Pieces, it is become a Beautiful Dark blue & fit for Transportation—

The best indigo ought to be Light, hard & Sparkling, indeed in Surinam but little of it is Cultivated, for what Reason this is I know not Since 1 Pound is Sold for about 4 Florins, which is above Seven Shillings in Sterling money. It is Said this Article was first introduced by one *Destrades* who Call'd himself a French Officer & Should have Brought it from the Island of S.t Domingo, so late that I myself was well Acquainted with this poor Fellow, & who Since shot himself with a Pistol through the head at Demerary—

The Cause of his Death being verry Notorious indeed I must Relate it—Having involved himself in debt he made to Ready money his Remaining Effects & Fled from Surinam, when next Setting up in the Spanish Countreband Trade, his all was taken—Deprived of every thing, he now Applied for Protection to a Friend at Demerary, who humanely gave him Shelter; at this time an Abscess gathering in his Shoulder every Assistance was Offered but in Vain, M.r Destrades refused to let it so much as be Examined—his Shoulder grew worse & even Dangerous, but he Persevered in not Allowing it to be uncovered, till one day having Dress'd himself in his Best Apparel the family was Alarm'd by the Report of Fire Arms, When they found him Weltering in his Blood, And /Strange to tell having Stript him/, the Mark of **V** for *Voleur* or Thief on the Verry Shoulder he had Strived to Conceal—thus ended the Life of this Poor Wretch who had for Years Supported the Character at Paramaribo of a polite Well Bred Gentleman—

Dinner being Over at the Governors indigo Plantation, I now departed with his Excellencys Coach to the watter Side Where a Tent Barge & 8 Oars lay in waiting to Row me down to the Estate Catwyk in Rio Comowina & where I was invited by M.r *Goetzee,* a Sea Officer, who was the Proprietor of this beautiful Country Seat—here no Amusements of every kind were Wanting—Such as Carriages, Saddle-Horses, Sail Boats, Billard Tables &c.—but what imbittered the Pleasure was the inhuman disposition of M.r Goetzee's Lady, Who Flogg'd her Negro Slaves for everry Little Trifle—for instance one of her Foot Boys Call'd *Jacky* /lately not having Rinced the Glasses According to her mind/ She ordered him to be Whip'd the next day morning, but the lad gave her the Slip for having taken Farewell from the other negroes of the Estate he went up Stairs, laid himself down upon his masters own Bed, Where Placing the mussle of a Fowling Piece in his Mouth, by the help of his Toe he drew the Trigger, and blew out his Existance—A Couple of Stout Negroes were instantly Sent up to See what was the matter, who /finding the bed bespattered with blood

& Brains/ threw the Body out over the window for the dogs While the master and mistress were so verry much Alarm'd, that they have not got the better of it to this day*—nor would any One lay in the Same Apartment, till I Chose it by Preference being Assuredly the most pleasant Room And the Best bed in the House—

What added much to the Alarm of the Family was the Circumstance of a favourite Child laying Fast asleep in the Same Apartment where the Catastrophy Happened till Such time as they were informed it had not Received the Smallest Damage—

I had not been 14 days on this Plantation when a Female mullatto Slave Call'd *Yettee* for having Jocosely Said her mistress had some debt as well as herself, Was Stript Stark naked And in a verry undecent as well as unhuman manner flogg'd by two Stout negroes before the dwelling house door, /While both her Feet were lock'd to an iron Bolt/ till hardly any Skin was left upon her Thighs &c—

Five days after this only I had the Good Fortune to get her Relieved from the Billoes or Iron Bolt that was Across her Shins—but a Mrs *Van Eys* Alleging she had Affronted her Only by her Looks, Prevail'd on Mrs Goetzee to Renew the Execution the Same Week—When She was so Cruelly beat that I Expected Upon my Soul She Could never more Recover.

Tire'd with this Barbarity I left the Estate Catwyk, determined no more to Return to it, but Still Accompanying Mr Goetzee to visit Some of his Other Plantations in Cottica, and Pirica[.] on one of these Call'd the Alia a new Born Female Child Was Presented me by Way of Compliment to Give it a Name, which I Call'd *Charlotte*, but the next morning during Breakfast 7 Negroes were Again tied up and Flogg'd here some with a Cowskin which is Verry Terrible**—from here Also I made my Retreat to the Estate *Sgraven-Hague* & there Meeting a Mullatto youth in Chains, whose name was *Douglas*, I With Horror Recollected his Unhappy Father who had been Oblidged to leave him a Slave & now was dead—In Short being Heartily tired with my Jaunt, I was Glad to make haste back to Paramaribo—

Here the news was that Fourgeouds *Valet de Shambre* had given up the Ghost, & Who was Reported to have been Actually Buried before he was Yet quiet Dead—Such was at last the end of *Pauvre, Pauvre Monsieur Laurant*—

Also that /having been drunk in an Alehouse/ no less than 13 of our Poor men had Severely Run the Gauntlyre and as many were terribly

* —The Above unhappy People were Since Poisoned by the Slaves though more than 6 Years After

** —the name given to the Dried Penous of a Bull

bastonaded, the Greatest number of Whom since died in the Colony—A poor Recompense for the many dangers & Hardships they had Sustained in helping to Protect it—Also a Quaderoon Youth, and a Duch Sailor were found murdered on the Beech—Going now to take a Walk on this Plain or esplanade I was Call'd in by M.̲ Stolkers, who next Conducting me 3 Storys High—

> From this Window /Said he/ Leap'd one of my Boys lately to Escape a Gentle Flogging—However being only fainted We soon brought him to Life Again by a Hearty Scouring on the Ribs, thus he did not Escape —& After which for having Risk'd himself /that is to Say his Masters Property/ and Frightned my Wife, She ordered him to be sent to Forto Zelandia where he Receiv'd a most Confounded Spanso Bocko—

The Punishment Call'd a Spanso bocco is Extremely Severe, & Executed in the following Manner, the Prisoners hands being lash'd together he is laid down on the Ground, When both his knees are Thrust through between his Arms, & Separated from them by a Strong stick as he Lays on his Side, the End of Which being Placed in the Earth or held Perpendicular, he Can no more move than if he was dead—in this Lock'd Position he is Beat on one Breach by a Strong negro With a Handful of Knotty Tamarind Branches, till the Verry Flesh is Cut Away—he is then Turn'd over on the Other Side Where the Same Dreadful Flagelation is inflicted till not a Bit of Skin is Left, and the Spot of Execution is died over With his Blood & After which the Raw Lacerated Wound is Wash'd with Lemon Joice & Gunpowder to Prevent a mortification & when he is sent home to Recover as he Can—

The Above Punishment is Sometimes Repeated at every Street in the town of Paramaribo Which is a Severity Absolutely beyond Conception, However never *thus* inflicted without a Condemnation from the Court, While a Single *Spanso bocco* may be Ordered by any Proprietor eyther at home or by Sending the Victim to the Fortress, With a Line to the Publick Executioner & to whom is Paid some Trifle in money for taking the Trouble—

Neyther Age or Sex are a Protection from this inhuman Castigation as may be Seen in the Plate Annex'd, where a miserable woman is Represented to undergo the dreadful discipline, while her Irons &c are Scattered on the Ground—

I next was Address'd by a monsieur *Rochetaux* whose Coromantyn Cook having Spoil'd his *Ragoo,* had Just Cut his Own Throat To Prevent A Whipping, M.̲ Cha.̲ˢ Reynsdorps negro lately did the Same, &c. &c.—

Now is it to be Wondered at that the negro Slaves Rise up in Rebellion against their masters, & Commit the Enormities I have so Frequently mention'd? Assuredly it is not—

Not Recollecting if I have ever Described in what manner they Generally Attack the Estates, this naturally Leads me to it—having Lain during the night Lurking in the Adjoyning Bushes that Surround the Estate, they Always Appear & do instant Execution About the break of day, when it is most Difficult to Repulse them,—At this moment massacring the Europeans, they Plunder the Dwelling house, which they next Set on fire & then Carry off the negro women Which they load with the Spoil, and Treat Verry Rudely Should they make Opposition; For minute Particulars I Cannot do Better than Refer the Curious to M:r *Belknaps History* of New Hampshire where he describes the insurrections of the American Indians Which are Almost Perfectly Similar to those of the African negroes—

And now Farewell ye Wretched Objects who have made not the Least Conspicuous Figure in these Bloody Pages, & for Which I Should be more Ready to Apologise to the Reader had I not been induced to make Vice Ashamed of itself, & humanity Gain Ground—that at Least in some measure my Plan may be Crown'd with Success is my earliest & Latest Prayer to Heaven, despising Gloomy Cruelty from the verry bottom of my Heart, thus

> Hence ev'ry Harsher Sight for now the Day
> O'er heaven & Earth diffused Grows Warm & Light
> Infinite Splendor! Wide Investing all—

I have Said that on the 24.:th of August I gave in a Hopeless request to the Governor for my Boys Emancipation, & on the eight Instant I Saw /with Joy and Surprise/ an Advertisement Patch'd up Containing, "that if any one Could Give in a Lawful Objection why John Stedman a Quaderoon infant the Son of Capt: Stedman Should not be Gifted with the Blessing of Freedom &c. Such Person or Persons to appear before Jan:y 1:st 1777—"

I no Sooner Read it than I ran with the Good News to my Friend the Hon:ble *Tho:s Palmer* Whom I not only had the mortification to find ill, but who Assured me that the Above was no more than a form Put in Practice on Supposition of my Producing the Bail Required, which Undoubtedly they Expected from my So Boldly Giving in my Request to the Governor of the Colony—I now thought the Blood Would have Sprung from my nose With Astonishment And without being Able to Utter one Syllable Retired to the Company of Sweet Joana, Who bid me never to Despair, that Johnny Certainly one day Should be free—She never fail'd to give me some Consolation—

1776—NOVEMBER 1, 7, 9

About this time only Arrived the News that *Long Island & New York* were taken by the King's Troops, Where the Havock was nearly equal to that at *Bunkers-Hill,* Also appeared in the Utretcht Paper a Libel against the Good Fourgeoud Ridiculing him with his Embassy to *the Ouca* And *Saremeca negroes*—Which Gentleman getting no Assistance from those Allies /and the relief from Holland being Still at Some Distance/ however Scorn'd to keep us idle, but having Provided the few Remaining Private marines With new Cloaths, /NB, the first Since 1772/ besides bought new Sabres, Bil hooks &c. he Sent them all up Again Accompanied by the Subalterns only, to Encamp once more at the mouth of the Cassiporee Creek in the higher Parts of the River Cottica, the Staff Officers & Captains being soon to Follow—

Thus I who was now Perfectly well, /Amongst others/ Prepared to Set out upon my 7.th *Campaign* Carefully Sealing all my Papers with a direction to the Honble Gen! Stewart in Case of my Decease, to be Delivered to my Relations Advised—Being fully Determined they Should never fall in the hands of Col: Fourgeoud Who had even intercepted many Private Letters of Which he had not Made at Last the Smallest Secret, while he Shaped the Character of the *Authors* at Court &c. According as he was pleas'd or not Pleas'd with theyr Contents—

On the Seventh I Was Surprised, /While I dined with him/ to See a fine Surloin of fresh Roast beef upon the Table, till I was informed it had been Sent him Ready done from Amsterdam in the Manner I have Formerly Described—

Here on the Des[s]ert was a kind of Fruit Call'd in Surinam *Pomme de Canelle*—or Cinnamon Apple—it Grows on a Shrub in most Gardens at Paramaribo, & has Something the Appearance of an Artichoke being Covered With a kind of Green Scales—the Skin of this Fruit is half an Inch thick, & the Pulp like Clotted Cream mixt with brown Sugar, thus verry Sweet but not much Esteem'd by many Palates, being Rather too Luscious—the Seeds which are Black, hard, and Large are Contained in the Pulp or Creamy Substance—

Having now made a Present to M.r Goetzee of all his Estates in watter Colours, & Received a Profusion of Wine, Spirits, & Refreshments to Carry With me to the Woods from Different friends at Paramaribo, I left my D.r Family once more to the Care of M.rs Godefrooy, in Order the following day to Renew my duty as an Officer for the good of *the Colony*—

Chapter 28th

The Rebels fly for protection to Cayenne—third march to Gado-saby—a second reenforcement of Troops arrived from Holland—Shipwreck of the Transport Paramaribo—March to Rio Comewina—dismal picture of distress & of Mortality—the Colony restored

Every thing being Ready I now once more left the metropolis, & in Company with Several other Gentleman set out in a Tent Barge for the Encampment at the *Casseeporee Creek,* this day the whole Colony being full of Smoak, the woods having taken fire near the Sea Side by some Unknown Accident—

On our Passage we met Col: *Texier* who Came from the Post at the Marawina with a detachment and Assured us that Since the Blow we Gave the Rebels at *Gado-Saby,* they were mostly Fled to the other Side of the Above Great River, where they got Refuge amongst the French, who were Settled in Cayenne; he had however taken a Woman, And a Lieutenant Keen took 2 Men and kill'd 2 more, While the 2 New Sable *Volunteer Companies,* Supported the honor of theyr Colours /which they had Received with so much Ceremony from the Governor,/ by Occasionally bringing in a few Captives from the Lee Shoar behind Paramaribo, in Which they were Assisted by the Indians Who had Voluntarily Fought & Defeated the Enemy there more than once—thus every thing bid Fair to See our Expedition draw to an end & the Colony Soon Reestablished to its former Grandeur and Tranquility—

On our Passage we Stop'd at the estate *Scaardan,* the Proprietor of Which is /Since his Late Marriage/ our Lieut: Col De Borgnes.—Seeing here An American Sailor who Came to Load Molasses, I Undertook to try the Skill of the Above new Planter and his Overseer in *Rum* thus Having desired the Tar to Colour a Couple of Gallons of *Kill devil* made at the Verry same Plantation, he brought them Ashore, and declaring it to be new Rum brought from Antigua, they Gave him in Exchange for it a 6 Gallon Cagg of the same Spirits & /Swearing it was much Better than theyr Own/ drank the Contents in Punch to my verry great Entertainment—the Sailor Said, he Should Colour the 6 Gallons Also, & did not doubt of Loading his Boat to the Watters edge before he Reach'd Paramar⁰, such is the Force of Prejudice—

☙ Having been Verry well entertain'd at the Estate Scaardan, we set forwards & Arrived Safe in the Encampment at the Casseeporee Creek, where I no Sooner set my Foot Ashore than I Escaped from being bit by a Land Scorpion•—This Insect which is the Size of a Small Cray-Fish, or River Lobster, & has an Oval Body, the Colour is like that of Soot, and it is Cut Across in moveable Rings, it has 8 Legs divided by Joynts, And two Joynted Claws Projecting from the Head much Resembling those of a Lobster, there is no neck to be seen, the head Appearing like Part of the Body, with Such small Eyes that they are Hardly Perceptible, the Tail is Divided in Seven Globular Divisions like beads which terminate in a *Double Sting,* and which it bends not Downwards but over its Back to Protect its Young ones by its Sting or Prickles, & to Where they Resort, after being hach'd from Eggs like pin Heads in a Small Portable Web, Spun by the Female••—The Sting of the Land Scorpion is not Reckon'd Fatal, but occasioning a Violent Pain, & throws the Patient in a Burning Fever—

Several Of our Officers however for Amusement have iritated one of these Animals by Touching it with a Small Stick, till it has Finally Stung itself to Death, to be Delivered—it is Said they Change theyr Skin as Crabs do theyr Shells; the *Scorpions* Generally haunt Old Trees, Old Furniture & are frequently found Amongst Dry Rubbish—

The Next thing I here Saw was a Poor Fellow, a Marine going to Bathe in the River who was instantly Snapt away by a Large Alligator••• I no Sooner beheld him Disappear than having Stript I *div'd* After him by the help of a Long Oar Which a man held Perpendicular under Watter for the Purpose, I keeping it Always in Motion—However I found ☙ him not, & Tugging the Oar as a Signal to Pull it up, the Fellow by miscomprehension Push'd both myself & it down with Such Violence that we did not Come to the Surface till in the middle of the Stream—

• —Still Continuing as I had begun to walk barefooted by Preference

•• —Aristotle Calls the Scorpion *Viviparus* in which amongst many others he was ill informed—

••• —this was the Second or 3ᵈ man we had lost in the same Manner—

560

🙾 I now being Ordered to march on Discovery to Gado Saby &c. Set out on the Twentieth with 2 Subaltern officers 3 Sergeants 7 Corporals & 50 men besides a Surgeon & the noted Free Negro *Gousary* And a Box with 800 Ball Catrtridges, Which when afterwards I Examined Proved to be no more than 480—In Short having lost Gousary for the Space of 4 Hours, we Encamp'd near on the Banks of the *same Creek* not having Advanced Above 6 Miles due **W** from its mouth—I Acknowledge that After the Long and many distresses I had Already undergone during this Cursed Expedition, I was tired of it from the bottom of my Soul but Consoled myself with the following Latin Line—

Live Sit quod bene ferta omnes—

🙾 The next day we march'd 7 or 8 miles Streight **N** Without finding a drop of Watter the whole day this being in the heart of the dry Season, which was this Year Extremely Schorching & the Poor Loaded men being Scarcely able to Get Forwards at all—

All Conquering Heat, oh intermit thy Wrath!
And on my Throbby Temples potent thus
Beam not so Fierce! Incessant still you Flow,
And Still Another fervent flood Succeeds
Pour'd on the Head profuse. In vain I Sigh
And Restless Turn and Look around for night
Night is far off & Hotter hours Approach

🙾 Having now Chang'd my Course to the **NE** & Past the Quab mire we About noon marched Dry through the late Fatal Marsh, & an Hour After Which, Again we Kept due **W,** When falling in with a large Field of Yams &c. I Demolished it; then Continuing forward, I Encamp'd in the Old Settlement Cofiaay Almost Choak'd for want of Watter, Not having met as Yesterday With a Single drop of Watter from the moment We Set out—However here the Negro Slaves found means to Procure us some to keep us from Starving, though Stagnated & Stinking like a Dirty Kennel & Which we Drank through our shirt Sleeves, During this march I Still took Notice of the Following Trees not Yet Describ'd Viz the *Canavatepy* & the *Berklack* Which are Extremely Fit for Carpenters Use—The first is beautifully Striped Black & Brown, & has much the Appearance of that Usually Call'd Brazil, while it diffuses a Smell in Working, not inferior to that of a Carnation—

The Second is of a Pale Red or Pink Colour & is equally Good for everry kind of Use—I Was to day Also Presented with a Singular kind of Fruit Call'd here the *Marmalade Box* being about the Size of a Large

Apple Rather Oval & all Covered Over with down—this Fruit in the Beginning is Green & being Ripe it turns to a Brown Colour—The Husk is Hard & by a Certain Movement Opens in two Halfs like a Box when the Pulp Appears like that of a Medler, being a Sweet brown Substance & Adhering to Large Kernels Which the inhabitants Suck off them with Avidity, on Which Account they Gave it the Above Name— As I took no Particular notice of the Tree I am Sorry not to be Able to give any Verry Exact Account of it—

The next day I marched East from Cofiaay to try for Some fresh Account of the Rebels by a Path of Communication, Cultivated fields And so Forth; but fell in with Nothing Some Delightful Views & a Large Herd of Warree Hogs excepted, which by Gnashing their Teeth & Stamping the Ground before we Saw them, we had Actually mistaken for the Enemy, And in Consequence fresh Primed & Prepared for an Engagement—About noon we Return'd to Gado Saby, where Sitting down to Rest from our Fatigue, An Old & Tall Rebel Negro Appear'd Suddingly in the middle of us, With a Long White Beard, a White Cotten Sheet tied About his Shoulders & a broken Cutlass under his arm; Seeing this Venerable Apparition I instantly Started up and Desired him to Approach Swearing no one under my Command Should dare to Hurt him, but that he Should get every thing for his Relief that I Could Afford—He Answer'd *no no Massera* With the Greatest deliberation & Shaking his Head in an instant disappear'd like a Shot, While 2 of my men /Contrary to my Orders/ fired After him at the distance of Perhaps 6 Paces only, Yet both Missing theyr Object to my Satisfaction, he being a poor forsaken Creature that had been Left behind by the Rest Gleaning his Precarious Subsistance from the Ravag'd fields we had formerly destroy'd—What makes the negroes so ill to hit with a ball is that they never run Streight forwards from it, but *See Saw or Zig Zag* like the Forked Lightning in the Elements—I now to Compleat my Orders once more Ransack'd Cofiaay with its Adjoyning Plains though with a Sore heart on Account of the Poor old Lonely Rebel negro, in Which having Cut down Several *Cotton & Plantain Trees, Okero or Althea, Pidgeon-peas, Maiz, Pine-Apples & Some Rice* /All Which Was Again Spontaneously Sprung up since our Last Devastation/ I Could not help leaving him a Few Rusk bisquits & a Piece of Salt beef, as Also a Bottle of Kill devil in Return After Which we once more Encamp'd in the fields of Cofiaay—

Having so often mention'd *Rice* I think I will here say something of its Growth Which is high About 4 Feet, With Furrow'd Stalks, & not unlike to Wheat, but they are Knotted by intervals & Stronger, the Leaves are like those of Reeds, but not so Dry—. The Seeds are Produced Somewhat like Barley & Placed on each Side of the Branches Alternately—

The *Oryza* or *Rice* is Cultivated in a Warm & Marshy Soil—the Grains are Oval & if Good ought to be White hard & Transparent—As for the Use of this Commodity for Food it is so well known that I will say no More About it—

Without *this* Grain, our Poor marines must Formerly have been Starved Viz in August 1775, When for All Allowance they Got Pr Day, *one Rusk Bisquit & 3 Spikes of Maiz or indian Corn* for 5 Men, *Rice* Supplying as I have Said the Rest of theyr Allowance—

Having now fully Compleated my Commission I march'd back with my Detachment for the Casseeporee Creek, Shaping my Course through the Ruin'd Field of *Gado-Saby* Which was at Present Choak'd up to a Perfect Wilderness—from here we kept first to the **S:W,** And then due **S** After Which we Slung our Hammocks near a Former Encampment—it is to be Observed that at this time All the Marshes Were next to being dry on Account of the Hottest Season I ever Remember, While the Fetid Smell Occasiond by the miriads of dead *Warrapa* Fish, that had been deserted by the Watter, Stunk worse than Billingsgate, being Sufficient to Poison the devil Himself—Out amongst these Putrid Finny Tribes our marines & Negro Slaves nevertheless Selected the Best Which they fryed in the evening, & Caused to Serve them for a delicate morsel—

The morning Following we again marched **S:W** by **W** & Slung our Hammocks not above 4 Miles from the Cassepoeree Creek And on the

Twenty Sixth /Keeping **SS:W**/ We Arrived in our Camp much Fatigued and Ematiated /myself with a Swell'd Face or the *Eresipellis*/ where I Gave in my Journal to Lieu^t Col: De Borgnes*—I Believe upon my Honour that had we been ordered to Remain 20 Years on this Expedition With a Possibility of Saving our Lives, the Different diseases, Plagues & Torments Would Still have Accumulated to Which there was no end—

A Command of 50 men was next sent Out to Reconnoitre *Jerusalem* &c. And finally on the 6:^{h} of December Arrived in the River Surinam from Holland the long expected relief Consisting in 350 men, After a Voyage of 9 Weeks & 3 days, of Which they Spent A Fortnight at Plymouth in England—by these Came now the Unfortunate Account, that Capt *Jocham Meyer* /Who had on Board A Considerable Sum of Money for our Troops/ Was taken by the Moors & Carried With his Crew to Morocco, Where they Were Condemned to be Slaves to the Em-

* —The whole *Route* of the Above march may be seen in Plate LV [56] Where the former marches are Also Distinctly Delineated—

peror*—& that the Ship *Paramaribo Cap.*ᵗ Spruyt /being one of the Vessals that Carried Over the Sick, in the Beginning of August/ Was Wreck'd in the Channel on the rocks of Ushant & entirely Lost, but that by some Fishing Boats the Crew & Troops had been Saved, & Who were Carried into Brest, from whence they had taken a Fresh Passage for the Texel, After Which his *Serene Highness the Prince of Orange* /Who is for ever doing good And Humane Actions/ Ordered, the Officers And Private men /Above a hundred in number/ to Receive the Following Sums by way of Defraying theyr Loss on this Occasion Viz Each marine to Receive About 4, The Subalterns 30, the Captains 40, & Major Medler that Commanded the Marines 50 Pound Sterling, but I poor Fellow, by the Shipwreck lost 3 chests of Valuable Preserved Sweetmeats & Pickles besides all my Monkey's, Parrots & Butterflies intended as Presents to my Friends in Europe; What Could I do there was no Remedy but Patience—

Having now Above a month being Lodged in a poultry Hut beat by the Wind & Rain /Which set in Unexpectedly/ & being informed that /independant of the Arrived Relief/ we were to Stay Still Some months Longer in the Woods Which broke many Hearts I Set about Building for my Self a Comfortable House, & Which was Finished Without eyther Nail or Hammer in less than 6 days, though it had 2 Rooms, a Piaza with Rails, & a Small Kitchen, besides a Species of Garden, in Which I sow'd in Pepper Cresses the Sweet Names *Joana & John,* While my next door Neighbour being my Friend Cap.ᵗ Bolts, Who made Shift to keep a Goat, We Lived Extremely Comfortably—Others kept Hens, but not a Cock, Was to be Seen; Who having Barbarously had all theyr tongues cut out to Prevent theyr Crowing to no Purpose, had been Since Condemn'd to lose theyr Heads—In Short Our Gentlemen built a Row of Verry Curious Houses indeed, Projecting from the Beech, While on the Opposite Side Above a Hundred huts being Constructed to Receive the new Come Troops, the Whole together Form'd no Contemptible Street, Whatever Contemptible Scarcrows its inhabitants—What was most Remarkable in my Own Habitation Consisted in its *Entry,* Which was not by the door, nor yet by the Window, by *the Roof* only, Where I Creep'd in and out having Absolutely no other door, & by Which I Was Effectually Prevented from those frequent Visitors Who Used to make too Free with my Eggs & Bacon, besides interrupting me While I Was Drawing, Writing, Reading &c. Upon the Whole I must Acknowledge that this Encampment was Agreeable enough More So being on elevated Ground had it not been for these

---

* —The Above Capt: & his Crew were Since Set at Liberty—

Pestilential damps & Sulpherous vapours that Exale Constantly from the Earth & Already had Occasion'd numbers to depart for the Other World—

During this Short space of Tranquility I Constructed in *Miniature* my Cottage /in Which I Lived at the Hope/ on an Oblong Board About 18 inches in Length which being entirely made of the manicole tree & Branches like the Original, it Was a master piece & Which I Sent in a Present to my Friend M.̱ Degraaff at Paramaribo, Who Since Placed it in a Cabinet of Natural Curiosity's at Amsterdam—Speaking so much About Huts & Houses, I Cannot help Gratyfying the Reader with a View of Each; the *one* that at the Hope Above Mention'd Where I Spent such Happy days, & the *Other* temporary, Such as we Constructed to be Sheltered from the Rain &c.—in the first may be seen the Emblem of Domestick Felicity—in the 2ᵈ that of Rustick Hardship & Fatigue—

I Will now Proceed with my Narrative—The Troops of the Society of Surinam Who had been encamp'd at the Wana Creek /Perceiving the Rainy Season thus Prematurely Setting in/ Wisely broke up & on the 26ᵗʰ Passing us Row'd down the River Cottica on theyr Way to the Plantations in the Pirica Creek, but as for us we were Condemned to Linger at Cassiporee Creek, while Fourgeoud Still kept at Param? as Snug as a Bug in a Rug—With the Above Officers We Received intelligence that a Few more Rebels had been taken at the Marawina while we Ourselves dayly Continued to send out Padrols to Right & Left—

At Last on the Twenty Ninth Came to Anchor before our Encampment 6 Barges with Part of the Fresh Troops that were Arrived from Holland for our Relief Which I Could not Help Eying With Compassion, & not without a Cause many of them being Already Attack'd with the Scurvey & other Diseases—We Sent for Bricks & Built them an Oven to Bake fresh Bread &c. & did all that we Could to Comfort them but to Little Purpose, it being Determined by Fourgeoud they Should no more Return to Paramaribo where heaven Knows but Few of them Since made theyr Appearance, As Shall soon be Seen—I in Particular /having Received a Supply of *wine* from The town/ Gave a Hearty Welcome to All the Officers to Cheer theyr Spirits. when Perret one of our Captains on Account of some Misunderstanding Challenged me to Fight Him instantaneously—

Having Retired at some distance from the Camp and Drawn our Sabers, he burst out in an immoderate Fit of Laughter, & throwing away his Weapon Desired me to Cut away, but that for his Part he had such a Real Regard for me that he Felt it Was impossible for him to make any Resistance*—After Which Catching me in both his Arms he

---

* —This was the Gentleman Who had formerly been Advised to Run me through the Body—

Manner of Sleeping &c. in the Forest.

Rural Retreat — The Cottage —

London, Published Dec.r 1st 1791, by J. Johnson, St Paul's Church Yard.

Gave me so hearty an Embrace that I Could not Without the Greatest Difficulty get Disentangled—Being Recovered from my Surprise I Could not help Smiling in my turn And After a Friendly Reprimand Reconducted my Valliant Opponent to the Company's where we Shut up the Year with the Greatest mirth & Conviviality—

A Confounded tumble through my Hammock having Ushered on the morning of 1777 We now Went *en Corps* to pay the Compliments of the Season to The Commanding Officer in the Camp, When I Was Show'd the *Philander or* Mexican Oppossum, here Call'd *Awaree* that had been Just Taken Quite Alive and With All its Young—I have Already mentioned the Murine Oppossum See page [429],—thus Shall now only Describe Such Peculiarities as Distinguished this from the Other & Which were indeed but few in Number, The Animal being in the Bottom of An Empty Hogshead When I Saw it, & not in my Hand—in the First Place, it was much Larger being the Sise of an Overgrown Norway Rat—The Colour was a yellowish Gray All over, and the Belly & Limbs a Dirty White, the mussle was more blunt than the murine Oppossum with long Whiskers, its eyes not Black but Transparent with a black Ring, the taile Extremely long thick & hairy Particularly near the Root, & its Smell was verry Offensive—This Oppossum had a pouch under its Belly formed by the Folding of the Skin, Which is Said to be hairy within as Without—from this pouch I saw the young ones /5 or 6 in number/ Several times Run out When the mother was *not* Disturbed, but as often Run into it upon the Smallest noise or shaking of the Hogshead—Pitying the poor Creature at Last After it had long enough been Tormented, I Suddingly kick'd over the Hogshead, When the Oppossum with all its young escaped & Ran Swiftly up a verry high tree before Col: Seybourghs Cottage & Where it hung by the Tail to one of the Branches, but /besides eating every thing Else/ being a Dreadful destroyer of Poultry, & the Colonel Swearing that it would kill every one of his Fowls he ordered it to be Shot down immediately—The *Virginian* Oppossum I never Saw and my only further Remark on *this* Shall be that its Activity verry much Astonished me being Contradicted by every Other Author I have Read on the Subject, While for further Particulars I Refer the Reader to the *murine* or mouse Oppossum Above mention'd, the one & the other Agreeing in every other Circumstance—

Speaking of Poultry Destroyers I am naturally led to say something of Another Animal in this Country known by the name of *Qwacy-Qwacy* but which properly is the *Coati-Mondi* or Brasilian Weasal though many People /With Small Degree of Propriety/ Compare it to a Fox, it being often able to Carry away a Goose or a Turkey, While it

1777—JANUARY 1

is extremely Cunning & Artful—This Creature is Long Sometimes near 2 Foot, the Body Shaped like that of a Dog, & Black, or Rather dark brown, though many others are of a bright bay Colour—The Tail is long, Hairy & Amulated Black & light brown—The breast and belly are a dirty white–the head is a Light Brown, With long Jaws & a Black Snout that Projects upwards for near 2 inches and is moveable like that of the Tapira, the Eyes are Small the ears Short, & rounded, While on each Side a Black Curved Stripe Corresponds between them And the Muzzle—The Legs of the Coati are Short, Espessially the Foremost the Feet are verry Long & Callous, with 5 Toes on each, While the Animal like the bear Always walks on the Heel And Stands on those Behind—No Quadrupedes /the monkey's not Excepted/ Are Better Climbers on the Trees, Where they Commit dreadful Ravages Amongst Birds nest, every Small Animal Which they Can Conquer becoming theyr prey & Particularly in the Poultry Yards they Commit Great Devastations, on which Account every thing that Can be invented is put in Practice to destroy them*—

Having mention'd this Poultry Thief before I leave the woods, [I] must still describe another Animal *inhabiting* them, which /though more than twice its Sise/ lives Chiefly on *ants*. This is the Great Ant eater or Ant bear Also Call'd the *tamanoir* or *Tamandua Guaca* & by Some *Osa Palmera*, the Body of this Creature is Covered over with a Verry Long Shag or Hair—On the Back & belly it is Black, And on the neck or Sides a Gray or Yellowish White, the head is Extremely Long and Slender of a light bay Colour With Verry Small eyes—The Ears are Short & Round And the mouth /which has no Teeth/ not much Larger than to admit of its Tongue, Which is Always Double, Respiring by the nostrils. The tail is of an Enormous Size With verry Long Black Hair, Something like that of a Horse, But With which when Asleep /Which is Generally through the day time, or during a hard Show'r of Rayn &c/ the Animal Covers itself like a Squirl, at Other times he trails it Along, & Sweeps the Ground—

The limbs are Slender, but Covered with Long Hair, the hindmost being Shortest, & Black With 5 Claws, While those before are Of a Dirty white with but 4 Claws the 2 Middle most being of an Extraordinary Length—the great Ant eater is a Very Bad Walker Resting Always on the heel of his Awkward long Feet like the Coati & Bear, but he is a better Climber & so good a Fighter that no dogs will hunt him, Since Whatever Animal he Catches between his Fore Claws /nay even

* —Some Authors have Compared this Coati to the Sow badger, & Others to the Racoon, though in my Opinion to the last with most Propriety—

the Jaguar or Tiger/ it Can no more be Extricated till it is dead—his Food as I have Said Consists in Ants or Pismires Which he takes as Follows—Coming to an ants-Hillock, he unfolds his Slender tongue which is Above 20 inches Long—this /being Covered with a Viscuous Clammy Matter or Salisva/, the Ants Get upon, till it is Perfectly Black, when by Contracting it he Swallows them all Alive And Renews the Operation till no more are to be found, When he Marches in Quest of Another Mountain & in the Same manner Destroys the Unguarded inhabitants, he Also Climbs the Trees in Quest of Wood-lice, & Wild Honey, but Should he meet with Little Success in his Devastations he is able to fast a Considerable time Without the Smallest inconvenience. it is Said that the Great Ant bear is Tameable, when he will pick Crumbs of bread & Small Pieces of Flesh, & that When kill'd Affords good food to the indians & Negroes, the last of Which I have Seen Devouring his Flesh with Pleasure. Some measure from the middle to the tip of the Tail no less than 8 Feet—See the two last Describ'd Animals in the Plate Annex'd—

A Small Species of Antbear Call'd the *Tamandua* is Also found in Surinam though not Verry Common—this differs with former in having 20 Toes, the head being thicker in Proportion. & the tail Smaller Which is Variegated with bands of Black And Yellowish white—A Lesser Species Still is Call'd the *Four-Miller* & is Said to be Sometimes met with, Which however never Came Within my Observation; All those 3 Kinds indiscriminately Produce but one Young one at a time•—And Are Extremely Tenatious Of Life—

Now Arrived 6 more barges with troops from Paramaribo /having lost a man Who fell over board And Turn'd Another Out of the Ranks who was Discovered to be Branded on the Back for being a Thief/ Which Compleated the number of 350 last Arrived from Holland, to be murdered by a Combination of misery & an Unhealthy Climate—Amongst these being informed there Was one Captain *Small,* Who /having Exchanged with Poor Ens: *Macdonald* & who went over Sick/ Came from the Scots Bregade; I instantly Scul'd down the River in a Canoo to meet him And Offer him any Assistance the more so as he Was my friend & Acquaintance—I had no Sooner got on board his Barge, Where I found him Suspended in a Hammock With a Burning Fever, then *not* knowing me on Account of my Dress which was no Better than that of the most Ragged Sailor he Ask'd me what I Wanted, but when he Reconnoitred his Poor friend Stedman Changed from a Good looking Sprightly young Fellow to a miserable Debilitated Tat-

• —M.˙ Fermyn Says they Produce many more but he has been Assuredly misinformed—

The Tamandua, & Coati-Mondi.

ter'd Scarcrow, he Grip'd me by the Hand without Uttering a Word & burst Out in Such a flood of Tears as much increas'd his illness & Show'd the Goodness of his Heart to me, more than any Thing he Could have Utter'd on the Subject—

"Da———n you Blubbering Charles Said, I turn out of this Stinking Cockle Shell I'll Presently Cure thee" & Getting him hoisted in my Canoo, brought him Ashore in my Own Habitation With the Greatest Difficulty, being Oblidged to thrust him through a Window, as the *hole in* the Roof was uncalculated even for Any Healthy Person myself Excepted—Having here Slung His hammock, near to my Own & Boil'd Some Watter I treat him with Warm Grog, & a Toasted Bisquit, when upon my Soul he became much Better from that Verry moment—He now Acquainted me that Col: Fourgeoud having entertained them with a Ball After theyr Landing, at Which his Cook & a Couple of *meagre* marines had been the Fidlers, he Nevertheless Concluded his illness to be the Consequence of his dancing too much—A Little after this Col: *Fourgeoud* himself Appearing in Person in the Camp Amongst us, he Soon made us Prick up our ears With musick of a Different kind, Which was no less than the disconsolating news that by the newly Arrived Corps of Officers, Severals of us poor Fellows lost our *Rank both in the Regiment & in the Army, who* had been melting Above 4 Years under a burning Sun, And toil'd ourselves to Death for the Satisfaction of Eating Stinking Beef and Black Rusk—So Violent Was this Stroke of fortune to Some /of Which this Chief himself was the Principal Cause/ that they gave themselves Over to Utter Despair invoking Publickly, one malefaction to fall Above Another, on the author of theyr hard fate And Disgrace, but Without Effect or Redress while Miraculously myself for one had the Good fortune to Weather this Storm of unprecedented unjustice, Which had it taken me Amongst the Rest, I must inevitably have had the Recourse to a halter—

To add to the Above Grievance we were in place of being Relieved, Ordered to Stay Still in the Woods & teach the others that duty by which they usurp'd our Preferment; Which is in other Language we were Sentenced to put the Tools in theyr Hands with which they Broke our own Heads—

During the Above Unpleasing Manoeuvres the Majors duty Came to my Share which was Extremely disagreeable being Oblidged dayly to Chastise the men who Stole for Hunger; Amongst Others a Poor Fellow was Nearly flogg'd to Death for Borrowing one of the Colonels Sasages, While NB They had Already Wanted the Article of Bread for 7 Days the Oven being Fall'n to Rubish

> Strength is Derived from Spirits & from Blood,
> And those Augment by Gen'rous Wine & food:
> What boastful Son of War, Without that Stay,
> Can last a Hero thro' a Single day?
> Courage may prompt, but Ebbing out his Strength,
> Mere Unsupported man must Yield at length;
> Shrunk with Dry Famine, & with toils declin'd,
> The Droopping body will Desert the mind:
> But built Anew with Strength conferring fare,
> With Limbs and Soul untam'd he tires a war.

> At Last not only Arrived a Barge with a Supply of Rusk but a Bullock & 2 Hoggs in a Present from M.r Felman who Accompanied them with his Lady & her maids on a Visit to Fourgeoud—

The Above Animals being kill'd they now Were Distributed Amongst above 400 people thus the Shares were verry Small, After which the Company Walk'd about to View our Different Habitations—being Arrived at my Dwelling Fourgeoud led them Round and round but Seeing no Door to get in he Call'd, *No body at home,* When I instantly thrust my head out through the Thatch & Offered to hawl in the Ladies but who politely Refused it—Nor did I ever See Fourgeoud burst into Such a Fit of Laughing which when beginning to moderate he exclaim'd, *Sacredieu il faut etre Original Comme lui,* And Reconducted the Company back to his Own Apartment,—

Nay even when Small & I Went out We Spent our Moments without the Camp Where in a Beautiful Savannah We erected a Green Shade, to be free in Conversation & Call'd it *Ranelah*—here we Carous'd And Crack'd a Bottle in Private till we Could Crack no Longer, having lived so Well that in Little more than a week my Cheese & Bacon hams quite Disappear'd While the Devil a drop of Wine or Rum was left in the flasks. After this he, as well as I, were Oblidged to live on Short Allowance, While Small had the Satisfaction however to see *his* Shipmates do the Same, Who not being Acquainted with that Oeconomy necessary in a Forrest made All theyr flour in Pan Cakes & were Already Oblidged to break theyr teeth on a piece of Rusk—

> So early as the twelfth, 150 of these newly Arrived People, were now already Ordered to march When the Strange Fourgeoud to Augment theyr Hardships /Besides heavy Accoutrements & Hammocks/ made each Carry a Stuf'd knapsack on his Back & of Which Party my Friend *Small* was one, Who being as Corpulent As Sir John Falstaff & I having Accoutred him in the Above Manner—I Vow to God, the Poor Lad Could Hardly Walk at All, till Declaring to Fourgeoud that I must Roll him Along like a Hogshead he Got Leave to be Debarrassed of Part of

his Appendages—Every thing being Ready, the Loaded Detachment now made face to the Right & Set out with Fourgeoud to the River Marawina—

Indeed /while I must Acknowledge that this Chief was become to *myself* as Civil as I Could desire/ Equity Requires of me to Say that to All others, he Remained Just as Great a Tyrant as Ever I had known him.

During theyr Absence I hew'd down a *Cabbage Tree* on the other Side of the River Cottica, not only for the food but for the *Groe Groe Worms* with which I knew it Would Swarm in About a Fortnight—Straying here through the Woods with my black boy Qwaccoo, I met with the following Trees Still left for Discription Viz the *Cedar,* the *Brownheart* & the *bullet-Tree*—

The first though it bears that name is Different from the *Cedars of Lebanon* which grow in a Pyramidical Form, While this does not, though at the same time to a verry Uncommon height—What makes the Surinam *Cedar tree* Principally esteem'd is, that the Wood is never Exposed to be eat by the Worms or other insects on Account of its Great Bitterness.—it has besides a most Charming Flavour in Working it And is used Preferably to most others for making Chests, Cubboards, Lockers and all Sorts of Joynery, besides which it makes most Excellent Tent-Barges & Boats.—The Colour of the Timber is a Pale Orange it is both hard & Light, & from the Trunk Exudes a Gum not unlike the Arabic which is Transparent & Diffuses a most Agreeable Smell—

The *Brown Heart* is in Hardness of the Consistancy as the Purple Heart & the Green Heart Already Mention'd, & Shaped in Heavy Timber for the Same Purpose Such as Constructing Sugar mills &c. the Colour of this wood is A Beautiful Brown—

The other is *the bullet Tree*—this Tree Grows Sometimes to three Score Foot, but is not So thick in Proportion as many Others—The Bark is Gray and Smooth, the timber brown Variegated or Powdered with white Speaks—no Wood in the Forrest is equal to this in Gravity, being Heavier than Sea Watter, And so very durable that when exposed to the open Air neyther Rain or Sun Shine have Any Effect on it—for this Reason /besides Shaping it in Large Blocks for Various Uses/ it is Split in Small boards, Call'd *Shingles* to Roof the Houses in Place of Slates or Tiles which /as I Formerly mention'd/ would be too heavy, & too Hot, & Which Shingles are Sold for £4 P.r Thous.d at Paramaribo And Continue Sometimes 24 Years Without once being Renew'd—I here Still ought to mention a kind of Mahogany that is found in the Woods of Guiana Call'd the *Ducolla Bolla* but Rather of a Superior

Quality, being as D:̲ Bancroft Says of a Deeper Red Colour, of a finer, more equal and Compact Grain, of Greater Hardness & Weight & Capable of Receiving a more Elegant Polish

About this Time the Whole Camp Was infested /Amongst all the Other Plagues/ with a kind of insect in Surinam Call'd *Wood Lice* but Which with more Propriety might be term'd White Ants, or Pismires, Resembling them Almost in every Particular except that the *first* dwell in the Ground, & the Others build on Trees—the Nest or Habitation of the Wood Lice Appears Externally upon the trunk, being Black, Round, & irregular, not unlike the Woolly head of a Negro, but Sometimes as Large as the Half of a Hogshead, & Composed of a Rust Coloured incrustated Earth Which is Extremely hard & invulnerable to the Weather—in this Mass /Which internally Consists of innumerable Cross Roads like the Quill of a Goose/ they live together by miriads, And from which they Sally forth to Commit theyr Depredations, Unequal'd by any other insects in Guiana, Pearcing through the hardest Wood, Leather, Linnen Woollen or Whatever Comes in their Way— they also Frequently get into the houses by an incrusted Barrel Road made against the Wall like the half of a Sliding Pencil, which is with its Windings Sometimes Several hundred Feet Long; & by neglecting timely to Destroy them /which must be done by Arsenack, or the Oil of Turpentine/ Some dwellings have been entirely Rotted & Come down to Rubish—these insects /Notwithstanding theyr Fety'd Abominable Smell/ Are an exquisite Food for Poultry on Which it is Said they thrive better than on indian Corn—I Ought not to Forget theyr Extreme industry in Repairing theyr habitation When injured, & theyr Wonderful Propogation Which /let ever Such numbers be Destroy'd/ brings them in a verry Short time to their former Unaccountable Multiplicity—

Still Another Plague we were in the Camp often Subjected to though not so frequent, Viz Clouds of *Flying-lice* Which Covered our *Cloaths* Sometimes So thick that they Absolutely Appeared all of a Gray Colour—however this Was much Owing to the Shedding Of theyr Wings, Which being 4 in Number they Generally left them behind them After they Alighted While Also they were thus prevented from Quickly Retiring—besides thus Covering us all over, they Caused us however no other inconveniency While I am of D:̲ Brooks Opinion that these *flying lice* are nothing else than the Above Mention'd *Wood lice* Which when they become Old Get Wings, leave theyr nests & fly About like Some other Ants both in Europe & America—

So Strict was the Discipline at Present in our Camp that Whoever made the Smallest Noise was Severely Punished, nay even Sentinels were Ordered to Challenge Rounds & Padrols by no Other Sound than Whistling which was Answered in the Same manner & on the Eighteenth one of these being Ordered to be Flogg'd for his misbehaviour I found means /Fourgeoud not being yet Returned/ to Get him Pardoned After he was Already Strip'd—the following day However, I Show'd that I Could Punish when things went too far, for Seeing a Large Piece of Boil'd pork /About 2 Pound Weight/ flying past me like a Bolt Shot, And finding it was thrown by one Marine to Another, While they had a Quarrel, I instantly ordered them to Pick it up & /having Cut it in two halves/ Stood over them till they Swallowed every bit of it in my Presence Sand & All Without eyther Bread Drink or any thing else, Which they Since declared to me was Such a Punished, as Surpassed my Conception & they Should Remember it the Longest day they lived.—

Now Arrived for me from town a Well Tim'd Supply of Wine & fresh Provisions & the Same day Col: Fourgeoud with His Detachment from the Marawina, While poor Small was melted down by Appearance at Least a Dozen of Pounds, during this trip our Commander had Again discovered & Destroyed 59 Houses, besides 3 Fields of Provisions Which Absolutely Gave the *Finishing Stroke* to the Rebel Negroes, Since having no more Supply on this Side the Watter, they Finally went to Settle in the French Colony Cayenne; but his men had Suffered Prodigiously especially those newly Arrived who were Carried in Hammocks by Scores, while near 30 were left Sick at the Marawina—at this time in the Camp Hospital were Above a 100 Dangerously ill, While the Above Poor men Died Dayly by half Dozens, nothing being Heard but Sighs, Complaints, & the dismal Shreeking of the Strix or Guiana Owl, Which forever kept them Company during the night—the *Amor Patriæ* the *Spleen, & Cramp* so Common in Surinam having also infected those that did the Duty, it may be said there was not a happy Person Amongst them all.—

> But vain theyr Selfish Care: the Circling Sky,
> The Wide enliv'ning air is full of fate;
> And, Struck by turns, in Solitary pangs
> They Fall, untended & Unmourn'd.

In Short here Appear'd one Covered with *blood-Boyls* from top to Bottom, there Another led along by two of his Comrades in a *Deep Lethargy,* who in Spite of Pinching & Pricking him, Sleep'd into Eternity, & there a Third Swell'd like a Hogshead by the *Dropsy* implored the Surgeon in Vain to tap off the Watter, Who Generally being Answered that it was too Late, got leave to Choak, or burst the best way they Could; in the Hospital, Some were Seen Clasping their Hands & Praying Aloud to God to be Relieved, While Others lay at their Side in a Frensy Fever, tearing their Hair, Blaspheming their Maker, & Cursing the day that they first drew Breath &c—in Short All was dreadful beyond Discription—

> ——Sad Noisome Dark
> A Lazar House it Seem'd wherein were laid
> Numbers of All Diseas'd, all Maladies
> Of Ghastly Spasm, or Racking torture Qualms
> Of heart-Sick Agony, all fevourous kinds
> Convulsions, Epilepsies, fierce Catarrhs
> Intestine Stone & Ulcers Cholic Pangs
> Demoniac Frensy, moping Melancholy
> And Moon Struck madness, pinning atrophy
> Marasmus, and Wide Wasting Pestilence,
> Dropsies and Astmahs, And joint Racking Rheums.
> Dire was the tossing, deep the Groans; Despair
> Tended the Sick, Busiest from Couch to Couch
> And over them Triumphant Death his dart
> Shook, but Delay'd to Strike, though oft invok'd
> With Vows as their Chief Good & Final hope
> Sight to Deform what heart of Rock Could Long
> Dry ey'd Behold.—

On the Twenty Sixth mortality Still Gain'd Ground While by Some Accident the Camp got in Fire also but was luckily Extinguish'd Without material bad Consequence by the Activity of the negro Slaves—& this Same day /O Strange to Tell/ Without I ask'd it, Col: Fourgeoud gave me the Offer of a Fourlough to Accompany him in Person to Paramaribo Which I most Greedily Accepted—

Thus farewell thou Cursed forrest where I Escaped so many Deaths & Underwent Such misery as Nothing Can be Compared to but the *Ten Plagues of Egypt alone*—

> In the first place did not our verry Rivers in a manner *Change in Blood* by the Devouring Alligators the flux & other Diseases Which dayly they Received—

2.^{ndly} Were we not overun in the *Place of Frogs with* tigers Serpents Centipedes, Lizards, bats & Scorpions &c. &c.—

3.dly Was not our verry Earth Covered with *Chigoes,* & we devoured by Common Wood, flying, Pattat & Scrappat Lice—

4.^{thly} Could any thing Exceed *the Swarms of Gnats* Mawkers, monpiera & flies of ev'ry Kind that forever keep'd us Company—

5.^{thly} Where no *flocks of Cattle were* to be had at all it Was Assuredly equal to Seeing them Kill'd by Mortality—

1777—JANUARY 26, 27

6.^{thly} Did a Single man of us Escape from being Cover'd over with Scars, wounds, boyls & *Running ulcers* from head to foot—

7.^{thly} May not the dreadful Rayny Seasons Always Accompanied by Loud Peals of Thunder & Flashes of Light'ning be Compared to *Showers of Hail & Fire* that Fell from Heaven—

8.^{thly} Did not the Worms, Ants, Cockroaches, & Locusts that destroy'd & Gnaw'd thro' both our Food & Apparrell fully overbalance the worst that Could be Effected by *Grashoppers*—

9.^{thly} In place of *3 days darkness* were we not often for 3 months together Shut up in an Obscure Forrest from the light of the Sun & all Mankind And—

10.^{thly} Not only our *First born were* Condemn'd to die but both first & Last Promiscuously were drag'd to an Untimely Grave Without Exception—

> Ah Little think the Gay Licentious Proud,
> Whom Pleasure, Power, And Affluence Surround;
> They, who theyr Thoughtless Hours in Giddy Mirth,
> And Wanton, often Cruel Riot Waste,
> Ah, little think they While they dance Along,
> How many Feels this verry moment, Death
> And all the Sad Variety of Pain.
> ——How many Stand
> Around the death-bed of their Dearest friends
> And Point the parting Anguish——.

Enough of Horrors;—Having now made my Friend Capt Small a Compliment of my *Ranelah* my house & my Fresh Provisions—having Sup'd on a dish of my fried Cabbage or *Groe Groe Worms* that were just Come to Perfection—And nearly Got my Throat Cut by my Other Friend Capt: Bolts for depriving him of this Delicacy, & having entertained them both & Some Others /Whom *I never Saw Again*/ with a hearty Glass of Clerrett, I took my last Farewell of them and On the morning of the Twenty Seventh at Half Past twelve OClock, And Row'd down the River Cottica with an Elegant Barge & 8 Oars, in Company with my Chief Colonel Fourgeoud And two more Officers, Who now Declared to Us that having Ransack'd the Forrest in every Direction, & drove the Rebels over the Marawina, he was now Determined no more to Return to the Woods, but in a few weeks to draw the Long & Painful Expedition to a final Conclusion, At which indeed nature Shrunk & even Heaven itself must be Offended—

> And he Shall Judge among many Peoples, & Rebuke strong Nations afar off, and they Shall beat theyr Swords into Plough Shares, & their Spears

into Pruning Hooks; nation Shall not Lift up Sword against nation neyther Shall they Learn War any more—

But they Shall Sit ev'ry man under his Vineyard & under his Fig tree, & none shall make them afraid for the mouth of the Lord of Hosts hath Spoken it—

—Micah 4.th Chap: Verses 3rd & 4th

Now Reader it Remains for You to Say that I have *not led you About the Bush,* but through it & without Contradiction with indefatiguable Perseverence, the more so when it is to be Considered that in the middle of the Above Hurry & Distress, Under which So many have Sunk, I have Often been Deprived of Pen, ink & Paper to make proper Anotitions & which last Defect I have even more than once, Supplied by With a Pencil Writing on my *Cartridges,* or on a *Bleached bone*—had this not been the Unavoidable Case, many more, & perhaps more Consequential Should have been the Remarks I would now Lay Before thee, which one need never be at a Loss to make in a Country so Replete with Speculation, & where the Different Species of the Animal & Vegetable world are never to be ennumerated—

Having now Row'd all night & breakfasted at the *new Cordon* /which was begun to be Cut not far from the Quandum Post Devils Harwar/ we Came About noon to the Estate Lapaix, where we dined with the Planter Monsieur *Rivieres,* After Which Fourgeoud with his Adjutant Pursued their Voyage to town, while I with another Officer Went to the *Sea Side* at the Back of the Plantation to Shoot *Snipes & Curliews*— On our March there, & back Again, Passing two Post of the Society, The flag was Hoisted & Every other Civility Shown us that was in the Power of the Commanding Officers—in the Shooting Way However we had verry Little Sport Except that of Killing Some *Snipes* Which flew in Such Clouds, that they in a manner darkened the Sky, thus by only firing from time to time Above our Heads we brought down Scores at Every Single Shot, but they were of Such a Diminutive Species indeed, that they were Scarcely Worth the Trouble of Picking them up—

We might here have kill'd Birds of Greater Consequence Such as Spoon Bills, Cranes, Red-Carliews & Wild ducks of many Kinds had we not unluckily been Cut off from the Banks on Which they were Scattered by the Sea overflowing the Quick Sands, Betwixt us & Them—

They Affoarded nevertheless a most delightful View, the Banks Appearing at a Distance like a Sheet of Scarlet Embroidered with every other Colour—

The *Shoveler* or *Spoon Bill* /which has some Affinity to the Crane/ is About the Size of a Goose, the Legs are not Verry Long nor is it but Little web footed, the Feathers are a Beautiful Rose Colour though white when they are Young—but the Bill is truly Remarkable in this Bird, being flat, much Broader before than at any other Part & Circular not ill Resembling a Spoon, from which it takes its Denomination—they are Said to feed on Frogs Rats & Lizards, yet I Believe Fish to be theyr Principal Nourishment both from frequenting the Sea Side & having a Fishy taste when they are kill'd—

The *Crane of Surinam,* or *Jabiru,* I Can best Compare to a Stork, of Which it has much the Appearance but is Larger—the Body of this Bird is milk White,[*] but the Prime feathers of the Wings & Tail are Black—the Limbs & Toes are Excessively Long, in which I observed one *Peculiarity,* Common in no Other Birds Viz that it Frequently Sits upon the Heel—the neck & bil are of an uncommon Length, the Last being Strong, & a Little Hook'd at the Point, but it is Said to have no Tongue—the head of the Crane or Jabiru is Perfectly Black; for Which by the duch it has Got the Appellation of *negro Cap,* it Frequents the Coast like the others Above mention'd and lives entirely upon Fish—this bird is verry Tameable I having Seen a Couple of them, in the Poultry Yard belonging to Col: Fourgeoud—See both these Species of Sea fowls in the Plate Annex'd, where the Last is Represented Sitting as I have Discrib'd—

To Describe the different kinds of *Wild ducks* that are in Surinam with any Degree of Propriety is a task which I acknowledge to be far beyond my Reach, thus Suffice it to Say that in General they are not verry Large but Adorned with the most Splendid Tints & beautiful plumage, Particularly those that they Call the *Cowereekee,* the *Sookooroorkee,* And the *Amakee,* Which last are the Smallest, While no Watter fowl of any kind Without Exception Can be more Delicate Eating than all those I have just mentioned—As for Swans Wild Geese or Divers /indeed never meeting With any/ I will Say nothing About them, nor Can I Tell if the two first are to be found in all Guiana—

Having the Following day Got the Opportunity of a Boat I now pursued my Voyage down the Cottica River to Param°, Where in a flow of Spirits & *Perfect Health* /however Strange/ I arrived that Verry Same Evening, which was the End of my 7.ᵗʰ & *Last* Campeign, & made me Repeat with Exultation on Landing, the Poets words—

Acti Labores Jocundi Sunt—

[*] —M.ʳ Fermyn is Wrong when he Says this Bird is all Cover'd over with Black Feathers—

The Spoon Bill or Shoveler.

The Jabiru, or Crane of Guiana.

London, Published Dec.r 1.st 1791, by J. Johnson, St Pauls Church Yard.

Chapter 29th

Some account of a remarkable negroe—the Troops prepare for Europe—discription of a Coffee Plantation—plan of reform for the encrease of population, and Universal happiness— one more sample of Hellish Barbarity, and Example of Humanity— the Regiment embarks

Being now once more Arrived in town And Wishing to be no Longer Troublesome to Any Body I hired a Verry neat Small House of my own at the Watter Side in Which we Lived nearly as happy as we had done at the *Hope* but Without the Smallest marks of the Emancipation of Sweet Johnny Stedman Which I had not a Little flatter'd myself to have Seen Accomplished towards the new Year—What Could I do— Here the first Person that Visited me was the American *Captain Lewis,* of the Peggy, Who to my Great Vexation told me that Poor *Macdonald* the Grateful Sailor had died on the Home Passage after being 12 Days at Sea, And Desired him in his Last Words to Return me /with his Welwishes/ the mother of *Pearl Bottle Screw* I had formerly Given him, of Which I now made a Present to his Captain, Who further Acquainted me /Also to my Sorrow/ that 3 English Vessals had been Captured by the American *Revenue* Privatteer Sloop which lay at this time with her Prises in the Roads before Paramaribo one of which belonging to Ireland Was Valued at above 50,000 P: Sterling—

Having been further waited on by a number of Planters, Apprisors, & Administrators /Amongst whom were most Assuredly some Verry Pretty Gentlemen/ with Felicitations on our Victory over the Rebels; The next who Pay'd me a visit was no Other than the Celebrated *Graman Qwacy* Who Came to Show me his Coat, Gold meddal, &c. Which he had got in a Present from the Prince of Orange—

This Being one of the most Extraordinary Black men in Surinam or

1777—JANUARY 28

Perhaps in the World I Cannot Proceed without Giving Some further Account of him; the more So as he has made his Appearance once or twice already Throughout this History—

In the first place by his insinnuating temper and industry this negro not only Obtained his Freedom from a State of Slavery time out of mind, but by his Wonderful artifice & ingenuity has found the means of Acquiring a verry Competant Subsistance—

For instance having got the name of a *Loocoman,* or *Sorcerer* among the vulgar Slaves, no Crime of any Consequence is Committed at the Plantations but *Graman* Quacy /which Signifies *Greatman* Qwacy/ is Sent for to Discover the Perpetrator, & Which he so verry Seldom misses by their Faith in his Conjurations, & looking them Steadily in the Face, that he has not only often Prevented further mischief to their masters, but Come home with very Capital rewards to himself—The Corps of Rangers & all fighting free negroes are next under his Command, to Whom by Selling his *Obias or Amulets* to make them invulnerable, /they under the Power of this Superstition fearing no danger & fighting like bull dogs/ he not only has done a Deal of Good to the Colony but fill'd his Pockets with no inconsiderable Profits Also, while his Person is Adored & Respected like a God & the above trash Cost himself nothing, being neyther more or less than a Composition of Small Pebles, Egg Shells, Cut-hair, Fish bones &c. the whole Sew'd up together in Small Packets which are tied in a String of Cotton Around Some part of theyr Body—But besides these & many other Artful Contrivances he had the Good Fortune to find out the Valuable Root known Under the name of *Qwacy Bitter* of Which this man Was Absolutely the first Discoverer in 1730, & Which Notwithstanding its being less in Repute in England than formerly is Highly Esteem'd in many other Parts of the World for its Efficacy in strength'ning the stomach, Restoring the Appetite &c—in 1761 it was made known to *Linæus* by M.^r D'Halberg Formerly Mention'd which Swedish Virtuoso has Since wrote a Treatise upon it, And by Which Qwacy might have even Amassed Riches were he not in other Respects an indolent dicipating Blockhead, whereby Which he at last Fell into a Complication of Loathsome disorders of Which the Leprosy is one & which is as I have Said Already incurable for ever—

Nevertheless his Age /though he Could not Exactly Ascertain it/ must have been verry Great, Since he used often to Repeat that he Acted as Drummer & Beat the Alarm on his Masters Estate when the French Commodore Jacques Cassard Put the Colony under Contribution Which was in the Year 1712—

The celebrated Graman Quacy.

London, Published Dec.r 1.st 1793, by J. Johnson, St Paul's Church Yard.

Having taken a Portrait of this Extraordinary man with his Gray Head of Hair, & Dress'd in his Blew & Scarlet with Gold Lace, I here take the Liberty in the Annex'd Plate to Represent him to the Curious Reader—

This very Same week we Again Saw the Efficacy of Graman Qwacy's Obias or Amulets, a Captain of the Rangers named *Hanibal* bringing in the Barbacued hands of Two Stragling Rebel negroes which he had Shot himself, & one of Which hands was that of the noted Rebel *Cupido* formerly taken in 1774 but who Since Escaped from Fourgeoud in the Forrest Chains & all—

I now went out in my turn to Visit Some friends amongst others Mr And.^w *Reynsdorp,* Who Show'd me the Loop & Button of his Hat Which being Diamonds had Cost him about 200 Guineas, Such is the Luxury of Surinam—Being enter'd on that Article I Cannot Help Also mentioning the Above M.^r *D'Halbergh* Which Gentleman when I waited on him /besides a Gold Snuff Box Surrounded in Brillants Value 600 Pound Sterling/ made me Remark two *Silver Bits* Set in Gold and Surrounded With Diamonds with the inscriptions *Soli deo Gloria, Fortuna Boeticum* &c. Having Signified my Surprise at this Last adoration of two Sixpences, he declared to me they were all the money he had in the World when he Came to Surinam from his own Country Sweden; *did you Work* Say'd I—"no"—*did you beg*—"no"—*you didn't Steal Sir*—"no"—"but enter nos I Whined & Acted the Hypocrite which is Sometimes Necessary & Preferable to the other three," to Which I answered "Sir your Confession is Confirmed by the Usage to your negro Slave Baron after having Promised his Manumission in Amsterdam"*—one Sample more of the Extravagance and Folly of the Surinamers & I have done–two of them Quarrelling About a most Elegant Carriage that was imported from Holland, a Law Suit ensued emediately to determine who was to have it during which time the Coach was left uncovered in the middle of the Street till it Lately fell to Rubish—

Most of our Officers now being Arrived from the Camp at Paramaribo Colonel Fourgeoud entertain'd us with a feast as he pleased to Call'd it /an Old Stable Lanthorn with broken panes of Glass hanging over our Heads which I Expected a Thousand Times would have dropt into the Soop/—here he Acquainted us that he had at Last put a Final End, to the Expedition having notwithstanding So Little Blood Shed Accomplished his Aim in Rooting out the Rebels, by Destroying *21 Towns* or Villages & Demolished *Above 200 Fields* of the Vegetable Productions of every kind & whom /he had got Confirm'd intelligence/

—See Page [85]—

Were now to a man fled Over the River Marawina, Where they & theyr Friends were Settled and protected by the *French* Colony Cayenne, who not only Gave them Shelter, but French like Supplied them with every thing they wanted—Thus, *Finis Coronant opus,* With which Good news we all Gave him Joy, & Drank further Prosperity in a bumper to the Colony of Surinam of Which the future Safety now alone depended on the new *Cordon* or Path of Circumvallation, defended by the troops of the Society and the Corps of Black Soldiers or Rangers—In D!" *Fermyns works* Col: Fourgeoud & his Troops are twice mention'd as the Saviours of the Colony, A Compliment to Which both he & they are with truth entitled, And what Cannot but Reflect to his Honour is that in the middle of his Hurry, & the Severity to his own Troops his humanity never would Permit him deliberately to Put a Captive Rebel Negro to death, nor even if he Could avoid it deliver them in the hands of Justice—Well knowing that While it was his duty to Extirpate them, nothing but the most Barbarous Usage & Tiranny had drove these poor People to this Last Extremity of Sculking in the Forrest—

Indeed myself whom during the first *Three* Years he Persecuted with unremitting ferocity must do to him the Justice to Say, that he was indefatiguable in doing his Duty & that I believe him at Bottom /in Spite of a few unaccountable Blunders/ a verry brave Old Fellow—He further Acquainted us that the Vessals with a fresh Supply of Provisions for our Departure to Holland, had been Cast on the Lee Shoare in Texel Roads, one of them having her Upper Cabbin wash'd away with the 2nd mate, & 3 of the Hands, however that Part of the Stores had been Saved & Loaded on board two Bilanders, Who Were this Verry day Arrived in the River Surinam—in Short So much in Particular Was I now become *his Favourite* that he even made me his *Confident,* and told me that the last Come troops /however fast they were dying Away, and Who had Lately Lost *a man* by Straying in the Forrest/ must Stay still Several months Longer in the Colony—Which officers were Worthy of Preferment, and which he intended to hurt as much as he Could; while here I took the Liberty to Cut him Short, Declaring upon my Honour to apprise those Gentlemen /whom he Probably mistook/ of theyr impending danger if he Continued & Which Effectually Stop'd his Career at Least from Going on at this Strain—"Sir Said I Permit me further to Put you in mind of these very Troops you just Mention'd in Regard to theyr truly Distress'd Situation at the Casseeporee Creek, While theyr Surgeon Major M! *Neyzeous* is Gaining Gold Watches & diamond Rings by Curing fashionable Diseases among the Gentry at Paramaribo"; to Which he Reply'd *Vous etes un brave Guarcon,* & Promis'd to take my hints into emediate Consideration, Such Were the Leading Features in the Character of this Verry Strange man, the inpenetrable the Unaccountable Col: Fourgeoud—

Being now invited once more by Capt: Macneyl to Spend a few days on his Coffee Estate Sporksgift /from which I was Prevented/ I will however not Quit the Colony Without amongst the Rest describing that Useful Berry, & Which not being natural to Guiana, it is Said Was first planted in Surinam by the Count *De Neale* though others A[s]cribe it to one Hansbarch a Silversmith in 1720—in the Island of Jamaica it was introduced by Sir *Nicholas Laws* in 1728•—*The Coffee berry* is the Produce of an Elegant Tree which is Seldom Allow'd to Grow Higher than a man Can Reach, in order to facilitate the negroes in Picking it—the bark of this tree is a Light brown, and the Leaves like Lawrel a bright green Polish, with which it is thinly[?] Covered, the Branches diverging from near the Surface of the earth to the Summit, & forming it into a Beautiful kind of Pyramid—The Berrys /Which are Oval/ are first Green, & Gradually Change their Colour till when Ripe they become a fine Crimson Colour like that of a Cherry—in each of these berrys are 2 Kernels or Coffee Beans Laying Flat Upon each other, of Which a Good Tree is Said to Produce 3 or 4 Pounds weight at each Crop, & Which like most other Vegetable Productions in this Luxorious Climate are Yearly two—

To Give the Curious a better Idea of this useful Commoditie I Present him with a Sprig of it Coppied from Nature, in the Annex'd Plate; though like most of my other Plants & Shrubs on a Smaller Scale for Conveniency—in the Letter **A** is the Colour of the Wood where it was Cut off, –**B** the Colour of the Leaf Above, & **C** that of the same Below, **D** is the Coffee Berry just beginning to Change, **E** the Same in its full Perfection being of a beautiful Crimson, & **F** the Kernels or Coffee Beans as they Appear When First they are divested of the Husk, & Ready for Transportation—

Thus have I in Point of Vegetation Compleated those Observations which by a Prodigious Labour & Constant Perseverance I was enabled to make, though neyther my time or indeed my Capacity would Permit me to Discribe any thing like the Thousands of Different Trees, Plants, & Shrubs that the Colony of Surinam So Spontaneously Produces And most of Which /I may Safely Say the greatest number/ are not only unknown to me, but to the oldest inhabitants of this Settlement & all *the World* Besides—

Few years ago one Count Gentilly an ingenious nobleman travelled

---

• —In 1554, it first came to Constantinople from Arabia—And about the middle of the Sixteenth Century it Come to London—

Sprig of the Coffee Tree.

London, Published Dec.r 1.st 1791, by J. Johnson, S.t Paul's Church Yard.

on Purpose thro: the Desarts of Guiana with some Indians, & having Already Amassed Considerable Knowledge in this his Favourite Study, Promised fair to be of material Benefit to the Botanical Society & to mankind in General, When by Excess of Labour & Fatigue he took a fever & died in the middle of his Useful Researches at the River Correntine—

Having once more Repeated that the different Shrubs, Spices, Gums, & Perfumes Are Absolutely innumerable as they are /though unknown Perhaps/ Excellent, I will Close this Subject by a General Explanation of the Process Relating to a *Coffee Estate,* which will Compleat the Account of those Productions to which the Colony is principally indepted for its Riches, Viz the *Cotton, Sugar, Cacao, indigo, Coffee* &c. And if I have not excel'd in the Discriptive Parts I have at least adheard to truth, & to my knowledge not Presumed to Write at Random, of Which fault I am sorry to say too many Authors, & even men of Character have lately been Convicted,—Nevertheless that the *best may err* is incontradictable—

The buildings on a Coffee Plantation are the *Dwelling house* Which being Pleasantly Situated not far from the banks of the River, is thereby for the Pleasure & Conveniency of the Proprietor; adjoyned to this are the *Outhouses* for the *Overseer,* Book keeper &c. the *Kitchen,* the *Store house* & Small offices—the other Necessary Buildings are a *Carpenters-Loge,* a Dock or *Boathouse* And two Capital *Coffee Loges,* the one to Bruise the Pulp from the berries, the other to dry them &c—The Rest Consist in the *negro-Houses,* the *Stables,* the *Hospital,* the *wach House,* and a few others, which Altogether Appear like a Small Village, While often the Coffee-Lodges Alone, Cost above 5 Thous.^{d} Pound Sterling—

Being extremely desirous to please those friends who have advised me to Accomplish this Work, I Still present them with a Plan in the Plate Adjoyning w[h]ere all the Buildings, fields, Paths, Gardens, flood Gates, & Canaals are mark'd, & Explain'd by the necessary References, & Which Plan is Contrived at the Same time for Elegance, Conveniency, and Safety from the Enemies Devastations—*Elegant* as being Perfectly Regular without any Omissions or Additions—*Convenient* as Having every thing at hand Viz, within the planters own inspection, without eyther the noise or nuissance at some estates unavoidable—& *Safe* being Surrounded by a Broad Canaal which by Flood Gates lets in the Watter fresh from the River besides a draw Bridge which during the night Cuts off All Outward Communication—

I will now Proceed to the Planting Ground Which is Divided in Large Square Pieces, Supplied Sometimes *each* with two Thousand

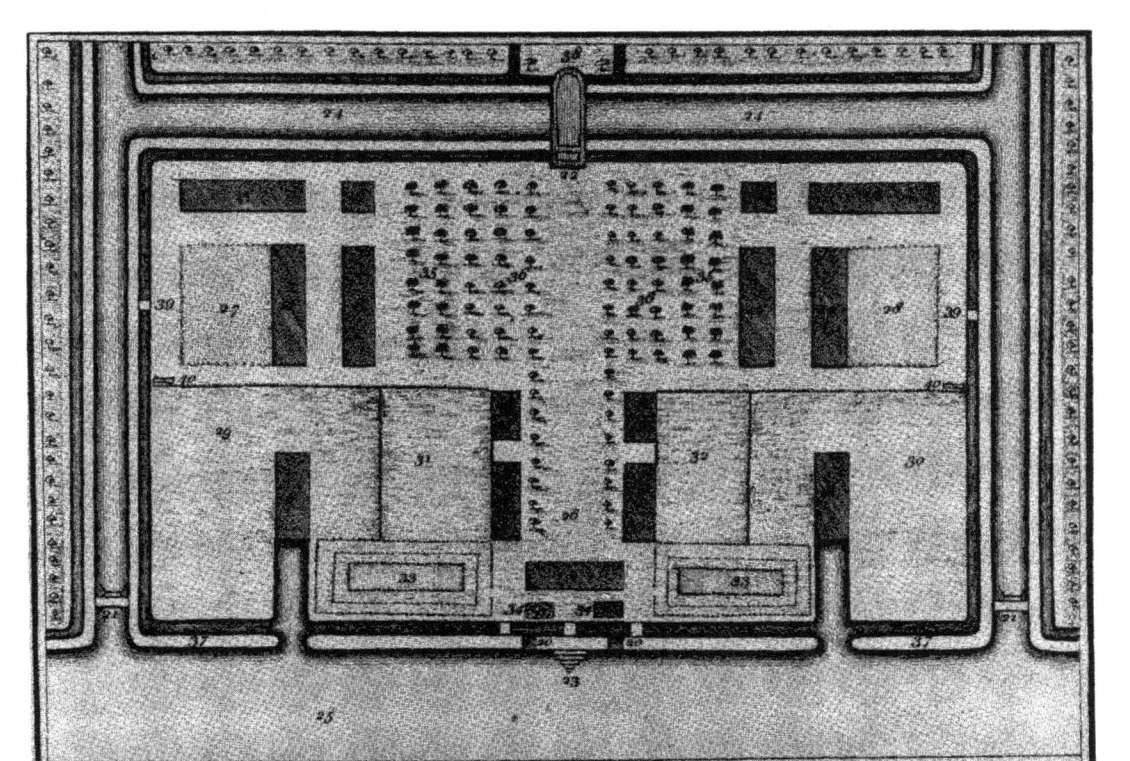

References to the Plan.

1. The Dwelling House
2. The Overseers Dwelling
3. The Book-keepers Office
4. The Kitchen
5. The Storehouse
6. The Poultry-house
7. The Hogs-sty
8. The Boat-house or small Dock
9. The Carpenters & Coopers Lodge
10. The Drying Lodge for the Coffee
11. The Bruising Lodge for do
12. The Negro-houses
13. The Horse Stables
14. The Fold for Sheep & Bullocks
15. The Great Guard house
16. The Hospital
17. The Pigeon-house
18. The Corn-house or Granary
19. The Necessary houses
20. The Sentry Boxes for Watchmen
21. The Floodgates
22. The Great Draw-bridge
23. The Landing Place
24. The Great Canals
25. The River or Creek
26. The Gravel walks
27. The Drying Floor for Coffee
28. The Negro Gardens
29. The Pasture for the Horses
30. The Pasture for the Sheep & Bullocks
31. The Poultry-yard
32. The Hogs-yard
33. The Kitchen Gardens
34. The Flower do
35. The Plantain Trees
36. The Groves of Orange Trees
37. The Dams & Gutters for Draining
38. The Path to enter the Fields
39. The Bridges over the Gutters
40. The Gates, Barriers &c.

Plan of a regular Coffee Plantation.

T. Conder Sculpsit

London, Published Dec.r 1.st 1791, by J. Johnson S.t Pauls Church Yard.

beautiful Coffee Trees, growing at 8 or 10 Feet distance from each other—These Trees which begin to bear About 3 years Old, are in theyr Prime at 6, And Continue to Produce fruit till 30. The manner of Supplying them being from Good Nurceries, which on no Coffee Estates are ever Wanting—having Already mention'd, that they Afford two Crops every Year, Which Generally are home before Midsummer, And Christmas, And at which times of Harvast it is not Unpleasing to See the negroes Picking the Crimson Coffee Berries Amongst the polished Green When All Ages & sexes are employ'd to fulfil theyr task with ardour, and when the youth who having first fil'd theyr baskets wantonly run naked & play, shining like Ebony Amongst the Luxorious foliage—

I will now Conduct them before the Overseers presence Where all the baskets being Inspected /& while the *whips are unlashing*/ the flogging begins regularly every evening Without the Smallest lenity on all those who have eyther from idleness, or incapacity neglected to do theyr duty,—After this Ceremony the Coffee Berries are Carried home in *the Bruising* Loge, & the negro Slaves Return home to theyr Houses—

The Berrys being bruised in A Mill /for the Same Purpose, in the Above Loge/ to Seperate the Kernel from the husk or Pulp, they are next Steep'd a night in watter to Cleanse them, and then Spread on the Drying Floor Which is in the Open Air made of Flags or Flat Stones, After which they are Spread on Garrats made for the Purpose to let them evaporate & dry internally, & during which time they must be moved every day With timber shovels—this done they are once more dried in Large *Coolers or Drawers* that Run on Rollers out from the Windoes*—When they still are put in timber mortars Which are Cut All Along in a Couple of verry Large Trees, And beat /by Candle Light/ with heavy Wooden Pestles like the Rice at Gado Saby to Divest them of a Thin Coat or Pellicle, that unites the two Kernels in the Pulp**—being next Seperated from the Chaff through a bunt-mill, once more thoroughly dried on the Coolers, & Pick'd /Viz the whole beans from the Bruised which are Consumed in the Colony/ they are finally put in Barrels About 3 or 400^{lb} W$^:$ for Transportation—

I will now only further Observe that in Surinam Some Coffee Plantations make above 150,000 Lb. Weight Pr Annum, and that /as I have Already Mention'd/ in the Year before our Arrival Viz 1772 no less was

• —To Prevent them from being Overtaken by Showers of Rain &c.—

•• —At this Exercise the Negroes Wonderfully Keep time & Always Sing a Chorus—

Transported to *Amsterdam Alone* than 12,267,134 Lb. of this ingredient, the Prices of Which have fluctuated from 3½ to 1/6ᵈ—but Which Calculated at the Avarige price 8ᵈ½ Produces a yearly income of no Less than 400,000£ Which is no despisable Revenue, besides what Goes to Rotterdam & Zealand, And Shows that the Cultivating of Coffee is Highly worth the Attention of the Surinam Planters—As for the Virtuous Qualities of this Excellent berry Without entering in Particulars, I will only Refer the Reader to that Highly Approved Pamphlet entitled "a Treatise Concerning the Properties and Effects of Coffee by Benjamin Mosely, **M:D** Author of Observations in the Dyssentery of the West Indies" from Which I Cannot but Extract the following passage *Bacon Sais*—"Coffee Comforts the head & heart, & helps digestion" Dʳ *Willis* Says, "being dayly drank, it Wonderfully Clears & enlivens each Part of the Soul, And Disperses all the Clouds of every Function." The Celebrated Dʳ *Harvey* used it Often; *Voltaire* lived Almost on it, & the Learned & Sedentary of Every Country have Recourse to it, to Refresh the brain Oppressed by Study & Contemplation—
Having now According to my Abilities /& the help of some other Authors Particular Dʳ *Fermyn* which Gentleman is highly Correct & Preferable to All that I have read in Point of Calculation/ Clearly demonstrated the Production & Management Relative to the Different Estates and the work of the negroes

I will next try to fulfil my Promise /however Vain & Ostentatious I may be deem'd for my Labour/ and Point out those means by which not only Surinam but all the West india Colonies will Accumulate wealth to *themselves,* & Permanent happiness to The *Slaves* that are under them, Without having recourse to the coast of guinea to Supply theyr Number which will be *fully,* & *ever* Compleated by the means of Population alone—To Accomplish this Arduous undertaking I will begin by Showing how, & in What manner the negro Slaves are *divided* & *Treated* by the Laws in this Settlement only, without entering in the *Division* or *Government* of them in other Colonies, yet by Which those that are Guilty may take the hint—& then I will finish by Pointing out how in my Opinion they ought to be *divided* & *treated* According to the Laws not only of humanity, but of Common Sence, when a Thousand to one but my Plan if ever Executed, will have a Salutary Effect & a General felicity will be Accomplished—

I have before Observed that in Surinam are Supposed to be at an Avarige About 75,000 negro Slaves of All denominations, which Allowing them for the *Sake of Calculation* to be 80,000, are here divided in the following Extraordinary manner Viz The Plantations being About 800 in number /which though some have but 24 negroes, &

others 400/ we will suppose to Possess one Hundred Slaves each Which Compleats Exactly the Above number of 80,000 people—These are employ'd in this Settlement nearly as follows—

Imployments	on one Estate	on 800 Estates
Foot boys or male Servants to Attend about the house	4	3200
Maids or *Female Serv.ts* to Wash Sow iron &c.	4	3200
Cook for the Planter & the Overseer &c	1	800
Fowler or Huntsman to Provide Game for the Table	1	800
Fishing negro to Provide fish for do.	1	800
Gardners to Provide the Table & Flower Garden	1	800
To Attend *the Bullocks & Horses* on the Estate	1	800
To Attend *the Sheep* on the Estate	1	800
To Attend *The Hogs* on the Estate	1	800
To Attend *the Poultry* that is on the Estate	1	800
Carpenter negroes to build Houses Boats &c.	6	4800
Cooper negroes to make & Repair the Hogsheads	2	1600
Masons to Build & Repair the Brick foundations &c	1	800
At Param.o Some *to trades* others *for Show* or doing nothing	15	12000
A negro *Surgeon* to Attend the Sick negroes	1	800
Sick & incurable that are in the Hospital	10	8000
A *nurse* for the negro Children that Cannot be with theyr Parents	1	800
Children under age that Can do no work of any kind	16	12800
Superannuated negroes wore out by Slavery	7	5600
To work *in the Field* no more than 25 miserable Wreches	25	20000
Total, or Compleet number of Slaves in the Colony	100	80000

From this it Appears that but 20,000 /Viz, *one fourth* of the Compleat Number/ are Condemn'd to do all the Labour of the Fields, on whom it may be said falls *Alone* the Dreadful Lot of untimely mortality that I have formerly mention'd, Whereas did the 50,000 Able bodied negro Slaves that are in the Colony of Surinam do *equal Drudgery*, it evidently must follow that the Above mortality which is now 5 P.r Cent would then encrease to at Least the number of 12 out of every Hund.d & Compleatly Extirpate the whole in Little more than *Eight Years time*

Having thus at an Avaridge demonstrated how they are *divided,* I will

Briefly Observe that while full 30,000 live Better than the Common people in England, & near 30,000 are incapacitated to do any Work att all the Remaining 20,000 may be truly Classed /that is in General/ Amongst the most miserable Wretches that the earth Can Produce, who are *work'd Starved, insulted,* & flog'd to death without being so much allow'd as to Complain for Redress, without being heard at all, or ever Righted, thus dead Alive Since Cut off from the most Common Privileges of Human Society—

I will now Proceed by Candidly Asking the World if the Above is not an infamous misapplication, not only of Wealth, but of Human Flesh, which by a Proper *Division & management* might so much Accumulate the One & Facilitate the other—then be it Said that by Abandoning *Pride & Luxury,* only in a moderate Degree, at Least 20,000 Negroes Could be Added to those now Labouring in the Fields, which would at the same time keep the Above Superfluous number of *Idlers* employ'd, & by *helping* The others in the necessary Accupation, greatly Prevent that Shocking mortality to Which they are at Present Exposed by ill usage, & which Reflects eternal Shame & infamy on those who have it in theyr Power to Prevent it, & do it not—

The Other Shocking Causes of *mortality* & of Depopulation are next the manner of Government to which I will now point out the grand ways of *Reform* by first beginning at the fountain head Viz the *Legislator*—That Sovereign Power then which Alone is invested with the Authority of *making* Laws and *Breaking* them ought in the first place to make it a Sacred Rule, never to allow eyther the Governor or the magistrates of a Colony to be the *Proprietors* of more Slaves, than only those required to Attend on their Persons; & for this Fundamental Reason, that whatever Laws & Regulations Such People may enact for the Prosperity of the Settlement & the good of the Slaves, & from whatever Good Designs or motives, they will never See them inforced & Supported Longer than Such time as they begin to Clash with their own *Private* interest, while even more than once to my Knowledge it has happened, that Such Lawmakers have been the First that broke them for the Paultry benefit of Causing their negroes to Work on a Sunday or following the bent of their unbounded Passions, by Which Sordid Example from the magistrate the Contagion soon must Spread Amongst the individuals, & next fall on the Poor ill Treated Slaves till it at Last Redounds back With Doubled force against the Blind & Guilty Forehead, from which it Originally Sprung, and had its Blasting Birth: No;—Let the Governor & Principal magistrates be Chosen in Europe, let them be Gentlemen of Fortune & Education, & above All, men of liberal ideas, men that are firm & Proof to the Tempting Allurements of Cursed Gold, & whose Passions are bridled by Sentiment & manly feelings—Let these men be handsomely Rewarded from that Nation whom they So materially Serve, and the Colony whom they so Conspicuously Protect, but let their Salaries be Stipulated, without depending on the *blood* & Sweat of the miserable Africans—then let Such men enact impartial Laws by which the negro slaves are to work no more than theyr fair task, by which they are not to be Rack'd, tormented, wantonly murdered, & infamously Rob'd of all that is dear next to their Life /Viz/ their wives & Daughters &c., Laws by which they are to be Properly fed, & Attended when Sick or indisposed, & Above all Laws that will Permit them to get a Hearing—Permit them to Complain, & enable them to Prove by witness the Grievances to which they Allude, & that will Right them by a Judge & impartial Jury even partly Composed of their own Sable Countrymen—By a Judge & Jury that will give Eye for eye & tooth for Tooth, that will not only Protect the innocent & Punish the Guilty, but even Reward Virtue & merit in a Slave—In those days nations will feel the benefit of their Colonies, then Planters will Grow rich, & overseers Grow Honest—in those days *Slavery* will only Consist in the name, when the Subjects will with Pleasure fulfil theyr Limited Task—then & not till then will Population encrease Sufficiently for the necessary work, & the Cursed Coast of Guinea Trade be totally Abolished, that *now* Assuredly is Carried on with Barbarity, & unbounded usurpation, Then the *master* will with Pleasure look on his Sable Subjects as on his Children, & the Principal Source of his Happiness; while the *negroes* will bless the day that their Ancestors first Set foot on American Ground—

Having thus Pointed out the Ways & the only way if well Considered to Redress the Colony of *Surinam,* at least, I would now Recommend All Planters & Overseers in General to Peruse with attention a Small work entitled, "letters to a young planter or observations on the management of a Sugar Plantation, to which is added the Planters kalender, written on the Island of Grenada by an Old planter, Publish'd in London in 1785, 8Vo. price 1/6^d & Sold by Strachan—"

Let them next take an example by that divine woman Mrs *Godefrooy* Whose other is so Seldom to be found who looks upon her Slaves as her equals without Paying the Smallest regard to eyther theyr Complexion or theyr not being Christians—

No *holy Fury* thou, blaspheming Heaven,
With Consecrated Steel to Stab their Peace,
And thro' the land, yet red from Civil wounds,
To Spread the Purple tiranny of Rome.
Thou, like the harmless bee, may'st freely Range

From mead to mead, bright with Exalted flow'rs,
From Jasmine Grove to Grove may'st wander Gay.

As for the moravian missionary's that are Settled Amongst them to Promote theyr faith &c. I have no Objections, Providing their morals go hand in hand with theyr Precepts, but without Which they ought /like a Pack of Canting Hypocritical Rascals deserve/ to be Strip'd naked, then tar'd & Feathered by the negroes, & flog'd out of the Colony—I will now Proceed with my Narrative which draws fast towards a Conclusion—

On the Sixteenth being invited to dine with his Excellency the Governor I now laid before him my Collection of *Drawings & Remarks* on the Colony of Surinam, Which I had the Satisfaction to See him Honour with the highest Approbation, while I Return'd him my Sincere thanks, not only for the material Assistance he Afforded me in Completing this Work, but for the unlimited marks of Friendship & Distinction with which he had treated me from first to Last during the time that I Resided in Guiana—

Availing miself of his Protestations in wishing to be of further Service to me, I Ventured two days After to give him the following verry *uncommon* request, to lay before the Court, which with a smile on *my private Account* /however Strange/ he Promised to Perform—

> I undersubscribed do pledge my word & my Honour /being *all that I Possess* for the present in this world,/ as bail, that if my last ardent Request for the emancipation of my D:r boy John Stedman be Granted, the Said boy will never to the end of his Life become a Charge to the Colony of Surinam—was Signd J.G.S.—

Having now done the utmost that Lay in my power I waited the Result with Anxiety, but without the smallest appearance of Success, thus with a Broken heart I was Oblidged at Last to give him /Sweet Fellow/ over for Lost or take him with me to Europe which must have been plunging a dagger in his mothers bosom—

In this Situation on the Twenty Sixth the Transport Ships were put in Commission for our Departure & I myself ordered as one of the Commissarys to see them Wooded & Wattered—While the officers were Clear'd theyr Arrears & 13 men Discharged at theyr own desire to push theyr Fortune at Param?—

I ought here not to Forget that the industrious Fourgeoud Again Pay'd us all in *Paper* by which /as usual/ we Lost *10* P:r Cent, but which equivalent /by letting the Jews have the Gold & Silver/ he Carefully Lodged it in his own private Pockett—the many hundreds of Florins Allow'd us by Government to Defray Excise duties, Taxes &c. were

Also never brought to Account, or Rather we were forbid to Enquire after them, but these were trifles when divided amongst so many—yet while in one hard Lump they were no Contemptible Picking—

🙵 A Sergeant now Arriving from the *Casseporee Creek* /where the Last Come troops were fast dying away/ brought the almost incredible Account that the man I mention'd to be lost in the Woods on Feby 10.th was Actually Return'd after having been missing *exactly 26 Days,* 9 of which he Subsisted on a few Pounds of Rusk Biskquit & 17 on nothing at all but Watter—he added that he had entirely Lost his Voice & was Reduced to a Perfect Sceleton, however that by the Care Show'd him by the Officers he Promised to Live—Should any one Scruple to Believe this Extraordinary fact, let them Read *Monsieur Godins* well Authenticated Letter to his friend Monsieur *de la Candamine,* Wherein he gives an Account of the dreadful Sufferings of his Lady, during her Route from *Riohamba* to *Laguna* through the woods of South America in October 1769, & where a poor weak woman, after being deserted by the Indian Guides, after both her Brothers had Already died by misery, & Living ten days alone in a Wild Forrest, without food, without knowing where she was & Surrounded with Tigers, Serpents, & Hazards of ev'ry kind, is still seen to survive the Complicated Dangers Notwithstanding the Delicacy of her Sex. I Say let them only read the Narrative of *this Ladys* Sufferings, and theyr Credulity will not Longer be Stagger'd at what I myself have Related Above—

I have even omitted truths which /on Account of theyr Strange Singularity/ must in the eyes of the Vulgar & illiterate Seem to border on the Marvellous yet while Almighty God knows, that in the Forrest of South America are to be met with, the Verry Strangest occurrences, without being Oblidged to have Recourse to Exagerations—

For instance who shall believe that near a whole Detachment of 80 marines one day marching through a thick Wood, all imagined they were Stepping one by one, over an Enormous *Tree* that obstructed theyr Way /as is very Common in Guiana/, till finally it began to move & Proved to be no other than a full Grown Serpent of the *Aboma* Species, measuring by Col: Fourgeouds Computation betwixt 30 & *40 Feet* in Length, yet such is a Truth as Sacred as the truth of my Existance—the above Animal was neyther Kil'd or hunted, the Colonel ordering the Remaining Party to March Round it in forming a Half Circle, in order that themselves at the same time might escape ev'ry Danger—

Another Circumstance I Cannot help inserting, which was that one morning Col: Fourgeoud Resting in his Hammock with one hand Carelessly Leaning over the Side, a *Large Rattle Snake* /that lay Coild among the Long Grass that was under it/ was Actually Severed in two by the Sentinel, during the verry moment of *Action* that it made its Leap to bite him & of Which the Soldier whose name was *Kieshaber* had been Apprised first by the Sound of his Rattle & next by seeing the Snakes head erected while it was Playing with its forked Tongue—

While on this Subject I must Still take notice of a *Mr Francis Rowe* of Philadelphia a venerable old man, who informed me that Riding out one morning to visit a Friend, his horse Refused to go Forwards, being frightned at a Great Rattle Snake that lay across the Road, Mr Rowe having heard of its Power of Fasination in which he Believed Alighted to Lead the Animal Around it, but during which time the snake having Coil'd itself, Sounded its Rattle & Stared him so full in the Face & with such fire in his eyes, that the Cold Sweat broke out upon him, and /whilst he dared not Retreat/ he imagined him Gradually Rivetting to the Spot, however Continued he "my Resolution at once getting the Better of my alarm, I Suddenly advanced upon him & with one Stroke of my Cudgel knock'd out his Brains"; but to Proceed—

On the third of March now my Friend de Graaff Sail'd for Holland but first for St Eustatia where his Brother was Governor, And to my Great Satisfaction took with him Joanas youngest Brother *Henry* for whom he Also Since Obtained his free Manumission—I /having Sail'd with them down the River as far as Bramspoint, And wish'd them a Successful Voyage/, now went Ashore with a Fishing Boat, when having Stript I Leap'd into the Sea & enjoy'd the Cooling & Healthy, Pleasure, of Swimming in the *Atlantick Ocean*—The Fishermen having Caught a Quantity of Large Fish I discovered one amongst them not yet mention'd in my Narrative, this was the *Yellow Back* long between 2 & 3 Feet & thus Call'd from its Colour which is Almost like that of a Lemmon, but the belly is White, the head is Verry Large with two Long Barbs but the Body is Small, & Without Scales like the Cod—it is however not nearly so Good being at the same time Coarse & incipid—two other Smaller Fish I also saw in the Boat, the one Call'd here *Weepee* Resembling a Whip, the other *Waracoo* a Very delicate Eating, but which /besides a few others whose names I did not Ask/ I thought not worthy a Particular discription—

On the Eigth the Prince of Oranges birth day Was Celebrated at the head Quarters, where after dinner hearing Capt.ⁿ Bolts very Grossly abused by the Colonels Adjutant, for Recommending one of the young *Volunteers,* of an Excellent Character but who had no friends to Support him[•]—I broak through the Ring that Surrounded them in the Court,

---

[•] —A Mr *Sheffer* Already named who had Served with Honour from first to last on the pay of a Private Soldier, During this painful Expedition—

& not being able to Restrain myself publicly insulted the Agressor /even in Fourgeouds own Presence/ whom I next Challenged to fight me at whatever weapon he should Chuse—

Next morning the Consequence was, that at Sun Rise we Walked to the Savannah without Seconds, where we drew our Swords—And After making a few Lounges at each other Capt: V. Geuricks Point met my Skell which having nearly Pearced his Blade Snapt in two, & the fortune of War Put him entirely in my Power—Scorning however to take Such a mean advantage I instantly drop'd my Sword & desired him to Step home, & Replace his Own, when we Should Renew the Battle—this Proposal in his oppinion now he was pleased to Call so Genrous, that taking me by the hand, he Requested a Renewal of Friendship & when /Acknowledging we had been Rather too hasty on *both* sides/ we went to Visit poor Bolts who knew nothing About the matter & whom I persuading to enter also in the Amity treaty, a Second Rancounter was happily Prevented And a General Reconciliation took place—

The tenth /having now spent most of the Day with his Excellency the Governor/ I in the Evening went on board the Vessels with Captain Bolts to inspect the Preparations for the Voyage, & where the mice & Rats had made Such Havock Amongst our Provisions with which we were Already not Overstock'd that I was under the necessity of Procuring half a Dozen of Cats to Destroy them, And which Useful Animals are in Surinam neyther so Plenty or so Good as in Europe, being Lazy and indolent on Account of the Heat, I Observed they were Also Less, & Ranker with wonderful long mussles & Sharp ears—

The following day I was almost Struck dead with Astonishment, at Seeing *Miss Jettee* one of the Deceased Mr *de Lamares* daughters, a Lovely mullatto girl Aged 14, who had been Christned in 1775, & educated like a young Lady. I say at seeing her drag'd to Court in *Chains* with her mother* and a few more of her Relations, & Surrounded by a military Guard; having suddingly enquired for the Cause, And Almost attempted a Rescue, she Call'd out to me herself, Crying most Bitterly, that she was going to be tried by Mr *Schouten* her mothers master for Refusing to do the work of a Common negro Slave, neyther which she had ever Expected, or to which indeed she had at all been brought up— The Result however Proved /O shame to be mention'd/ that According to the Laws of the Country she was not only Oblidged to Submit but /at his insisting/ Condemned for Disobedience to be Privately Flog'd, together with her poor mother & All her Relations who had Dared to

• —This was not Joana's Sister but a former blackwoman

Support her—Nevertheless /by the humanity & to the immortal Honor of his Excellency the Present Governor Mr *Wighers* who was at that time the Fiscal or Town Clark/, the Sentence was never put in Execution, but forced was the unfortunate Miss Jettee de Lamare notwithstanding to Stoop henceforth to the tiranny of her unmanly Lord & Master, Pittied & Lamented by all her Acquaintances & ev'ry stranger that saw her—Such were the dreadful Consequences of not having been timely emancipated & made me tremble—

Let me now Relate, Strange to tell what instantly follow'd & what was of greater Consequence to me than all that had happened hetherto in the Colony—this Reader was no Less than a Polite message from the Governor & the Court, Acquainting me that /having taken my former Services into Consideration, together with my *Gallantry & Humanity* in offering my honour as bail to see my Child timely made a free Citizen of the World,/ they had Presumed without further Ceremony or Expence to Compliment me with a Letter of his *Free Emancipation* from that day forever after, which was Henceforth officially Presented to me by the Principal Clark of the town hall, to Whom I gave 5 Guineas— No man Could be more Suddingly Transported from Woe to happiness than I this day, while his Mother Shed tears for Joy & Gratitude, the more so as we have given over all hopes, And it was so Perfectly unexpected, while near 40 beautiful boys & Girls were Left to Perpetual Slavery by theyr Parents of my Acquaintance, many of Whom without being so much as once enquired After, nay /while the well thinking few highly Applauded my Sensibility/ many not only blamed me but even publickly derided me from my Paternal Affection which was Call'd a whim, a Weakness &c. &c. be that as it may I Shall be Thankful for it to Providence & Proud the verry Longest day that I live—

> What Conscience dictates to be done,
> Or warns me not to do;
> Thus teach me more than hell to Shun.
> That more than heav'n Pursue.

So Great indeed was my Joy this day at having Acted the Counter part of *Incle & Yarico* that I become like one Frantic with Pleasure—I not only made my Will in his Favour while I had nothing to dispose of, but Appointed my Friends Mr Robt *Gordon* & Mr Ja.^s *Gourlay* to be my Executors & his Guardians during my Absence, in whose hands I Left all my Papers Seal'd till I Should ask for them again or they shoul'd be informed of my Death—

I then Ordered All my Sheep Poultry &c. which had Prodigiously encreas'd to be transported, & put under theyr Care, While making a

Spleet new Suit of Blue trim'd with Silver for the Occasion & which Cost me 20 Guineas I waited on a M:̣ *Snyderhans* one of the Clergymen at Param:̣ to Appoint a day when the boy was to be Christned—

Next getting tipsy with some of my Companions my irascible temper involved me in Another Despute—Out I & one of Them marched again to the Savannah where nearly under the Gallows we drew our Swords & fought in our Shirts, when I was Deservedly run through the Right Arm & which Ended the fracas—

Now Came down at last on the Eighteenth our Remaining troops from the Encampment at Casseeporee Creek & every Preparation was fast making for our Embarkation—At the Same time the extacy of the few going home Marines was now so Great /& who also Received Part of theyr Clearance,/ that /besides Drunkenness & the venereal Disease/ the Greatest Riots & disorders ensued & even a Civil War broak out between them & the Troops of the Society till some being wounded & some being Flog'd the peace was Finally though with difficulty Reestablished—A poor Sailor was Also drown'd in my Presence, who fell over board with an Anchor that had been neglected to be lashed—I instantly leap'd in a Boat to save him but Could only get his hat the man went down to the bottom—

The day of our departure now approaching, from hour to hour, I about this time gave up my house, & at M:̣ Godefrooys pressing invitation spent the few Remaining moments in that she had Prepared for the reception of Joana & her boy in her beautiful Garden, Charmingly situated under the shade of fine Tamarinds & Oranges which she also neatly furnished with every Accomodation that Could be necessary, besides Allowing her an old negro woman & a girl to Attend on them for ever—thus Situated how bless'd should I have been to end with her the Rest of my days but fate ordained it otherwise—

In Short, on the Twenty Second I waited with Capt: Small on Parson Snyderhaus, According to Appointment, but who to both our Surprise, now Peremptorily Refused to Christen the Boy—he Said going to Holland, I Could not Account for his Christian education—We Replied he was under two Proper Guardians—the blacksmiths son /for such he was/ Persisted—& we Remonstrated but to no purpose, he was as deaf as his fathers anvil, & I believe upon my Soul quite as empty as his Bellisis [bellows], till finally tired out with his Fanatical impertinance, I Swore that I would sooner see him die a heathen than allow him to be Christned by such a Pityfull Blockhead, while my friend Small Could not help bestowing on him a hearty Curse, & Slapping the door with a vengeance we departed—Now Coming to Joana who had him dancing on her Lap, she Ask'd us with a smile if we Really thought herself the worse for the omission of the Ceremony to which we both Replied no—then Continued she say no more on the Subject & Leave the Rest to Providence, to which we Agreed, at least for the Present & having Cut out a Lock of his hair• to Carry with me, we spent the evening verry heartily over a bowl of Punch—

Now feasting & Joviality once more went round at Param? as it did at our Arrival—Grand Dinners, Suppers & Balls were heard of every where, but at none did I at Present Chuse to Partake, at Governor Nepveu's Alone Excepted where for the Last time I made one of the Company at a truly magnificent entertainment, which ended the Scene of Philanthrophy & Hospitality for which the Polite inhabitants of Surinam are so verry Conspicuous, & on the Twenty fifth the baggage was Shipt on board the Vessals—Various indeed were the Presents for the Voyage with which I in Particular now was Overstock'd from every Quarter, thus that with my Provisions Of Live Cattle–Poultry–Wine–Rum &c. &c. they were almost Sufficient to Carry me Round the Globe—amongst the Rest in a small bottle Case Containing liquours, I found a Crystal viol Containing *essential Orange oil,* & a parcel of what they Call'd here *Tonquin beans*—the *first* is extracted from the Rind or peel of the Oranges, which is done here by the tedious method of Squeesing it betwixt the finger & Thumb And this must be the work of a Prodigeous deal of time & Patience—a few drops of this on a small Piece of Canary Sugar is an excellent Remedy to Strengthen the Stomach, Create an Appetite & help digestion while an Single drop smells so Strong that it is Sufficient to Perfume a whole Apartment—The *Tonquin* Beans are said to Grow in a thick pulp something like a Walnut & on a Large Tree—I never Saw them but dried, when they bear some Resemblance to a Prune or dried Plumb & are made use of to Scent snuff & Tobacco, to which they Convey a most odoriferous flavour—

On the Twenty Sixth we took leave at last from his Excellency the Governor en Corps, after which all the officers of the Society waited on Col: Fourgeoud at the Head Quarters to wish us a Prosperous Voyage to Holland, & where the day was Spent by a Regale en Militaire, Viz a Dinner as usual of Salt provisions but I must Acknowledge as much good drink of Every kind as Coul'd be Swallow'd—I do Believe near a hundred times did Fourgeoud now shake me my the hand Declaring there was not a Young Fellow he Loved better in the world, that had he Commanded me to march through fire, as well as watter, he was Convinced I Should never have Left it without first Receiving his

---

• —it is to be Remark'd that this infants hair which was now as fair as flax Since Gradually Changed its Colour till it become as black as Ebony—

order, many other Lavish Compliments were Paid me on this Occasion, but though I had a Heart to Forgive, my mind would never Permit me to Forget the many & unnecessary dangers & miseries to which I had been too wilfully exposed under his Barbarous Authority—at the same time as he now informed me that he did not depart with us, but intended to follow the Regiment soon with the Remains of the last come Relief, I was wicked enough to Suspect that his Politeness proceeded from fear only of my informing against him in Person, when I Should be introduced to the Prince—Be that as it may, few people now were better Friends, than were the Old Col: Fourgeoud & Capt: Stedman—

In the evening I now went to take a Short Leave of my valuable acquaintances, Such as M.rs *Godefrooy* M.r & M.rs *Demelly* M.r & M.rs *Lolkens* M.r & M.rs *Gordon*, M.r *Gourlay* Captain *Macneyl*, Doctor *Kissam*, &ct who had all /besides M.r *Kennedy* and M.r *De Graaf* who were gone to Holland/ treated me with the most distinguish'd Civility Since I had been in the Colony, but my soul was too full of a Friend that was Still nearer to be impressed with that sensibility on Separating from them, that it must have felt on another Occasion—O my dearest *Joana*, O my *Johnny*, Consider for a moment the bitter Circumstance of Perhaps going to be tore from you both for ever—But I must forsake you at Least for a Time, I must forsake you,—my duty Commands me, And I must obey—

——Si possem, senior essem,
Sed trahit invitam nova vis,——

And well may I say with *orosmane* in the Tragedy of Zara by Voltaire—

Zaire il est trop vray que l'Honneur me L'Ordonne
Que Je vous adoray—que Je vous abandone
Que Je renonce a vous, que vous le desirer,
Que sous un Autre loix.—Zaire vous pleurer.

Yet while my Conscience ubbraids me with the following just Reproof—

Atque ope nescio quis servabitur advena nostra,
Ut, per me sospes, sine me det lintea ventis,
Virque sit alterius? poenae Medea relinquar?
Si facere hoc, aliamue potest praeponere nobis,
Occidat ingratus.——

But no,—nothing like this did ever escape from my Joanas lips whose good sence even Check'd the tear to start in my Afflicted Presence; no—even now while offering her still to accompany me, & while seconded by the inestimable M.ʳˢ Godefrooy and all her friends she was equally inflexible & her steady answer was as before Viz,

> that dreadful as appeared the fatal separation, which she forbode was for the Last time never to meet again, yet she Could not but Prefer the Remaining in Surinam, first from a Conciousness that with propriety she had not the disposal of herself—& Secondly from pride, wishing in her Present Condition Rather to be one of the first amongst her own Class in America, than as she was well Convinced to be the last in Europe at least till such time as fortune should enable me to establish her above dependance—

Not knowing in What Respect most to adore this unhappy young woman /for that she was Perfectly at this Period/ or indeed what to say at all, I determined Calmly to Resign myself to my trying destiny & exchanging a Ringlet Of her hair, Prepared for the Fatal moment of by all Appearance an Eternal Adieu—

Being ordered at 7 O'Clock next morning all to wait en Corps on Col: Fourgeoud at the head Quarters, who was to Conduct us on board the Transports, I now was Perfectly drest at 6, not having shut my eyes during the night by watching her distracted Sleep, then Calling my name, & then Starting Alternatively

Thus Situated my heart relented at the thought of Awaking her in so Critical a moment—I then most tenderly embraced my Joana & my boy—then stole away—Good God stole away no more to return—Farewell both—Reader forgive my saying any more on the Subject—Perhaps I say'd too much—

No Sooner did we Assemble at Col: Fourgeouds than he now instantly walk'd us to the beach where the boats Lay in waiting & we were Row'd on board in a Salute of 9 Guns from each Vessal, I having knock'd down the 2ᵈ mate of a dutch ship at the watter side for obstructing my Passage, of whom at another time I should not have taken the smallest notice—

The Troops now being all embark'd to sail under the Command of Lieut: Col: De Borgnes the Staff Ship to which I belong'd immediately fired a Single gun to weigh Anchor when both Ships drop'd down with the Last of the Ebb tide, the drums beating the Granadiers march & each Vessel saluting Param? with 3 Cheers—

About a Cables Length below Fort Zelandia which had *now* the Colours Flying, & with which we Exchanged the Compliment of firing 9 Guns Still we once more Came to an Anchor on account of the young Flood—

Here /after all the Officers had dined on board the Staff Ship/ the old Gentleman *Fourgeoud* took his *Final Leave* & wishing us all a prosperous Voyage was Row'd back to town under another Salute of 9 Guns from each Vessal—He was escorted by both his Adjutants & on departing Politely asked me to Accompany him till to morrow, which in spite of my depres'd spirits I nevertheless thought proper Civilly to decline— at this time *Qwaccoo* poor fellow was the only Soul on board that I Could Converse with and this Chiefly from a kind of Apology for having since the Last 3 Days Absolutely forgot that such a Person existed at all—

At 12 at midnight a double signal being now again fired the 2 Ships drop'd down till before the fortress *Amsterdam*, once more Came to an Anchor, & with which fortress they also Exchanged a Salute of 9 Guns each—here my D:r Friends Gordon & Small Affectionately Coming too see me after the Hospitable Col: Seybourgh /for that he Certainly was/ had entertained them on board his Vessel, did no less than prevail on me to Accompany them back to Paramaribo—my heart Could not Resist this Second invitation of once more beholding all that was dear to me in this World—Away then I went & /must I say it/—found Joana who had show'd so much fortitude in my Presence now almost desolved to nothing by weeping since my Departure—She had neyther eat, drank Slept, or spoke to a living soul, nor had she indeed Stir'd from her apartment at all—

The Ships not being Ready to go to Sea till two days After I now a little longer Could keep her Company, which seem'd to Cheer her— But alas too dear did we pay for the Short Reprieve, Since finally I Got an Abrupt message that a Second boat was waiting to Carry me on board without Delay—At that instant O! Heavens what were my feelings! Joanas mother Suddenly took the infant from my Arms while the Alworthy M:rs Danforth supported her trembling self—At the same time her Brothers & Sisters hung around me Crying & invoking Heaven for my Health & for my Safety, but she the unfortunate Joana holding me by the hand, & who look'd a thousand times more dejected than *Sterns Maria* spoke not one word—I perceived she was Perfectly distracted I was the same—the hour was Come, I finally prest them both to my Bosom—the Power of Accent now forsook me, my heart invoked the protection of Providence to befriend them—I Gave them my Last embrace with my blessing—here the beauteous Joana now but 19 years of Age shut her tear-bedued eyes; the Colour of her Lips became the Colour of death, she bowd her head & motionless sunk in her Chair—

The Scene was now too Distressing to bear it any longer—I Roused my Remaining fortitude & Leaving them Surrounded by every Care, & Attention Walk'd accompanied by my friends to the watter side— The Boat delaying a few moments I at this time Still stept up to poor Fourgeoud gripping whose veteron hand, I Could not for my Soul but forgive him every injury he had ever done me—he was affected— this was a debt he owed me—I wished him every Good & finally departed—

>Ne'er did my heart, before this Hour,
>Such sad emotions know;
>Yet ne'er so little felt the pow'r
>In words to paint its woe.

>Could all the efforts of the muse
>   Make half my Grief Appear,
>Thy Gentle nature Could not Chuse
>   But drop one pitying tear.

>The deep that gently glides below,
>   To others smooth and Clear,
>Appears in stormy rage to flow—
>   Wafts *me* from all that's dear,—

>The hated Vessals full in sight,
>   In which I must remove
>Far from Whatever gave delight—
>   Far, Far! from all I Love!

>We seek not, when the soul's in pain,
>   The Beauteous & Refin'd:
>Perhaps as well this Artless strain;
>   Displays my troubled mind.
>   —Majoribanks—

I now found both the Ships Come to an Anchor at Branspoint where Mr *Texier* the deputy governor still Come on board to wish us a good voyage, & who after Dinner under a Salute of 7 Guns together with Capt.^{ns} Small & Fredercy who had Accompanied me here, Return'd back to Param.^o—

>By my Sad Follies Learn to shun my Fate
>How wretched is the youth who's wise too late

Chapter 30th

The Ships weigh anchor and put to Sea—review of the Troops—
Account of the Voyage—the arrival in the Texel—
discription of the Pampus near Amsterdam—final debarkation in
the Town of Bois le duck—the Death of Col: Fourgeoud—
End of the Expedition—Short History of the late Scotch Brigade,
Conclusion

Every thing being at Last perfectly adjusted for our departure both Vessals weigh'd Anchor on the morning of the first April when with a fresh breese at **E** We put to sea Course **NW** taking our Final leave of Surinam & all Guiana—

Having still dispached a Letter to Messrs Gordon & Gourlay the Guardians of my late delight I now fell in Such a fit of Despondency as nothing Could Equal, & of which it was universally thought I Should hardly get the Better—motionless and Speechless did I look over the Ships Stern heaving Sigh after Sigh, till the Land quite disappeared out of my Languid Sight, after which—

But why should I torment the Reader longer with what I Could not help feeling upon this Occasion both in mind & Body—Suffice it to say that in a few days Reason so far Prevail'd again as almost to make me Ashamed of my too Great Sensibility /*not of my love*/ And that I Gradually became once more a man like the Rest of my Shipmates, that is, I got the better of my *Passion*, but not of my *Affections*, which Heaven knows never more Can Forsake me while I Live—

What Could not but Greatly Contribute in Restoring my tranquility was the happy Reflexion that /if I had in some measure hurted myself/ I had at least done material good to a few others by Relieving 3 Deserving people from a State of Bondage—nor had I enter'd 1 Farthing into Debt notwithstanding, while my Constitution was Perfectly sound, & my Character unspotted with the smallest blemish, favours of Fortune that too many of my Friends Could not boast of, Severals of whom had left Slaves behind them too nearly Connected, while others were Ruin'd both in the frame of theyr *Body & mind* past all Recovery; for instance no less than 4 of the handsomest Young Officers in the Corps went to Europe with incurable Ruptures, while others Lost the use of *all theyr Limbs* & some theyr memory Nay one or two were entirely deprived of theyr *mental* faculties, & Continued in a state of *insanety* for ever. in Short out of a number of near twelve hundred Able bodied men, now not one hundred did return to theyr Friends at home Amongst whom Perhaps not 20 were to be found in perfect health, all the others /a verry few of the Remaining Relief Excepted,/ being Repatriated, sick; discharged, past all Remedy; Lost; kill'd; & murdered by the Climate, while no less than 10 or 12 were drown'd & Snapt away by the Alligators—Amongst the dead were including the Surgeons betwixt 20 & 30 Officers, three of which number were Colonels, & one a Major, which were the Fruits of this Long & Disagreeable expedition in the marshes & woods of Surinam—

One or two Remarks I must still make before I leave this Subject, which first are that amongst the Officers & Private men who had *formerly* been in the West indies, none died at all, while amongst the whole number of near 1200 together I Can only Recollect one Single marine who Escaped from Sickness—& next that of the few belonging to the Corps that now were on theyr Voyage for the Texel, I myself was the only Officers who had sail'd out with the Regiment in 1772 those Gentlemen Excepted Alone who now belong'd to the Staff or Head Quarters—Reflexions which Assuredly Could not miss to make me very thankful Since 'tis most true that

> Of all things in this World health is the best
> And is most valued when 'tis Least Possest

On the 14.th having now met with some hard squals of Wind & heavy showers of Rayn we Past the Tropics & Changed Course towards the **NNE** & **NE** After which we were overtaken by a dead Calm that Lasted several days—

I ought not to Omit /at about 15 degrees **N** Latitude/ our Sailing through what is Vulgarly Call'd the *Grass Sea* from its being Covered over with a fleating [floating] kind of Grass, or Green Weeds, some of which when dried in the Sun and Spread betwixt two sheets of Paper are verry Curious, Resembling Trees, flowers Shrubs &c. and in which are Harboured small Crustaceous fish Scollups Maseles & Shells of many Thous.d different Species—Amongst the Last is often found that Wonderful Sea Reptile Cal'd the *Hippocampus* or *Sea Horse,* which I Can

Compare to nothing better than the Chevailler of a Chesboard though it is Generally Larger And Sometimes 8 or 9 inches in Length, the body is Composed of Cartilaginous Rings—the head Snout and mane are incrusted all over, And the Tail which is Curvated upwards in the figure of an **8** terminates in a Point—The way to Preserve them is by Submerging them in Spirits—

On the 19.th the Calm still Continuing we were dayly entertained by swarms of Flying-Fish, & Several Dolphins, & *Grampusses.* Swimming & Tumbling before and after the Ships as if delighting in keeping us Company—The *Grampus* is a fish of the Cetaceous kind, Something Resembling a Dolphin but much Larger, being near 20 Feet in Length and Prodigiously Fat, this fish has 40 Strong Teeth, is of a dark brown Colour, and spouts watter with a Considerable Force—We also saw at some distance from the Vessals Severals times Above the watter a Large *North-Caper*—This fish which very much Resembles the Greenland Whale, is more Dangerous On Account of its being more Active, & which Proceeds from the body's being smaller & more flat than the former—the Jaw is also shorter with very small barbs,—the Skin is white and the produce of its blubber Amounts Seldom to more than Thirty ton—

About the Twenty Second the weather began to Change Considerably & the whole ships Company were Attack'd with a Severe Cold & a Cough many also took fits of the Ague—

On the 30.th the Crew were so weak, as to be hardly Able to do theyr duty, two of whom and one marine were Already dead & thrown overboard—Col: De Borgnes also was at this time so much indisposed, that the Command of the Vessal Devolved upon *me* for a few days during his illness, when Observing the other ship a head & almost out of Sight, I hoisted a pinnet from the main top, and fired a Gun to Windward to bring her to which she Observed—

A Large *Shark* now Swimming Alongst the Ship's Side we did all that Lay in our power to Catch him but to no purpose—Sharks are in these Seas of different kinds, but what is Generally Call'd the *white Shark,* is the most Tremenduous of its Species on Account of its Size weighing often one Thousand pounds, and measuring sometimes 16 or 18 Feet in Length—The head which is somewhat depress'd is very Large with an Oblong Snout, 2 Spouting Holes & prominent Eyes, which it Can turn in every Direction to look for prey & Which speak the Malignity of its all Devouring Nature, behind which are seen the Gil holes; nearly under these frightful Looking *Globes* is Placed the mouth and Throat, of such an enormous size that it will sometimes swallow a whole Dog, if by Accident wash'd Overboard—while the teeth /which are Aranged in 5 or 6 Rows/ are said to be 144 in number, Triangular, sharp & so strong that they will Almost snap through any thing, and with the Greatest ease Cut off a man's Arm or a Leg which too frequently happens in the Tropical Seas when they are bathing &c. the body of the Shark is round like the dog Fish, with a Slymy Rough Strong skin which when prepared is what we usually Call Shagareen—it has Remarkable Large fins, one dorsal–two Ventral–two abdominal and one Above & under the Tail which is Bifurcated, the upper part being Considerable Longer than the other—this formidable Monster which may Justly be deem'd the Terror of the watters Swims with the most astonishing velocity & is seen playing at ease Around the Swiftest Sailing Vessels, where with undaunted Boldness it Looks about for pray, yet which /on Account of the position of its mouth/ it Can never Seise without first turning on one Side, by which Smaller fish Occasionally Escape its Voracity—the manner of taking sharks is by Striking a Barb'd instrument Call'd a *Fizgig* into theyr bodies, or by a strong hook fix'd to a Chain at the end of a Rope bated with a piece of Salt-Beef or Pork which they verry Greedily Seise—And when drag'd on board they Still flouncing & Striking most Violently with theyr Strong tail to begin by Cutting it off with a Hatchet—

It is said that a Certain small Fish often Swims before the Shark to direct him to his Prey & which also feeds upon his Gill holes on which Account it is generally Call'd the *Pilot Fish*—

Another Cal'd the *Remora* or Sucking Fish is also frequently found sticking to Sharks, or even to the bottom of a ship—this Fish which is of an ash Colour is Long sometimes near 20 inches—the body is roundish and Tapering towards the Tail, the Fins are placed nearly like those of the Shark & the under Jaw is much Longer than the upper—But what renders the Remora most Remarkable is its *Sucker,* being an Oval Grisly plate long about 6 inches & Furrow'd with Transverse Ridges like the Palate of a Sheep*—which is placed above the head & gives it the Power of Attraction to such a degree that not the Beating of the largest waves Can make it quit its hold—

Having seen neyther the shark or Remora out of the Watter I Coppied the head of the First from that Elegant Print entitled the Boy & shark & Design'd the Rest from perusing the best Descriptions yet which I venture both to Present to the Reader with a View not only of pursuing my plan but of Compleating my Collection—

* —M.ʳ Fermyn here differs with almost ev'ry other Author & very Conspicuously when he declares that he saw one or two of these *fish* who had the above Attracting quality not on the ⌐op of the head but under the Body, whose lower Jaws were Shortest &c.—

The Shark, & Remora.

Being now exactly one month at sea during which time /by way of making a Trial/ I had Continued Barefooted & Bareheaded, I this day for the first time drest like my other Ship mates, without feeling the Smallest inconveniency from the Experiment—About this time a Mr *Neyseous* one of our Surgeons having on Board a *Crabbodago* or Grisson to Carry home as a Curiosity, & whose Ferocity I have already described, the Cursed Creature broke Loose, and in one night murdered all the other Animals & Poultry that were on board the Vessal, while he Drove most of the Crew who had the Watch down the Hach way till Luckily one of them with a Hand spike knock'd out his Brains—

On the Third of May we had hard Gusts & heavy Showrs at **SE** Latitude about 40—From this time the Gale daily encreased till the Ninth when the weather began to moderate—we now saw Several *Porpuses, Herring-Gulls* &c. the First is a Fish about 5 or 6 Feet Long Excessively Fat, of a Blueish black Colour & without Scales—the head has Small Eyes & no Gills but a Long snout & Sharp Teeth the Fins are but one dorsal & two Ventral, & the Tail is Horisontal to enable it in Leaping above the watter which it does Frequently to Blow or Breathe when its uncouth Snorting may be heard at a great distance—the Flesh of the Porpus when Kil'd is red & Looks like Pork—The *Herring Gull* is a Bird as Large as a Tame Duck Perfectly White part of the Back & Prime Feathers Excepted which are of a Dark Ash Colour—The eyes are Gray the Bill & Feet are Yellow the Claws are Black & the Length of its Wings is between 4 & 5 Feet from the Extremity of the one to the other—

On the Thirteenth in the Morning watch being not far from the *Azores or Western isles* the Vessal was nearly Laid on her beam ends, [/] sailing then under Double Reeft Topsails/ by a sudden Squal at **E**—

The Fourteenth the wind was violent Carrying away our Fore Gallant mast & spliting the main sail while the other vessel lost her Boltsprit &c. and on the evening of the Fifteenth it Blew a Perfect storm Accompanied by Thunder & Lightning with very heavy Rains which Continued during the night & brought our Maintopmast by the Board, while the ships Crew were so very much reduced as hardly to be able to Clear the wreck in which I Assisted by Cutting away with a Hatchet—The two following days we kept Sounding before the Wind with a Reef in the Fore sail the Sea then running mountains high and Constantly Breaking over the Vessal—pumps going day & night—I now with Astonishment Observed those tremenduous Surges or bodies of Watter that by intervals Came Rolling a Stern & Seem'd to threaten emediate destruction by Swallowing up the Ship—by ovid they are Taken notice of in his beautiful description of a tempest as follows—

> Sic ubi pucsarant acres latera ardua fluctus,
> Vastius insurgens decimae ruit impetus undae:
> Nec prius absistit sessam oppugnare carinam,
> Quam velut in Captae descendat moenia navis,
> Pars igutar tentabat adhuc invadere pinum,
> Pars maris intus erat.———

At this time a Broken top Gallant mast, a new Handspike &c. Floated past the Vessal the Melancholy Remains of a Shipwreck which we since were informed to be a duch homeward bound East India man that had foundred with all the Crew near the Island of *Terceira*—In Short the wind once more becoming fair we were Carried within Soundings on the 19th when we heaved the Lead at 90 Fathom Watter—but it then Shifting to the **NE** with fowl Weather we beat about in the Chops of the Channel till the morning of the 21st when at half past one we fired a Gun as a Signal; to the other Vessal, that we saw the Light of Scilly & at 4 OClock **PM** got the Pilot on board, immediately after which we saluted the *Alarm* Frigate of 24 Guns Captn. Van Braam from Holland who return'd the Compliment—

On the 27th only we saw the Duch Coast & not sooner having been becalmed two days off Dover.—here purchasing from a boat that Came along side a prodigious quantity of fine fish we made a Delicious Feast & wash'd it down Accordingly with good Clerret, when a serious dispute Arising between a Certain Commander & Myself, The Company was no sooner withdrawn than I Challenged him to fight me with a Brace of Pistols across the Cabbin Table—he Gallantly accepted the Offer and took his Distance but being Overheard Friends suddingly enterfear'd & the difference was Amicably made up to mutual Satisfaction*—

Having kept off Shoar during the night, we at Last doubled *keykduyn* & the *Helder* with flying Colours Jack and Pendant & on the twenty Eight at 3 O'Clock **PM** both ships under a discharge of 9 Guns each happily dropt anchor in the Texel Roads—

On the thirtieth having past the small island of *Urk* in the Zuydersea, & which is the only rock in the Province of Holland both Vessals Running before the wind with a fine Breese premeditately stuck fast

---

* —The Above dispute having been Chiefly kindled by the Captain of the Vessal, I must do him the Justice to declare, that he *Jan Yonker* on this, as on all other Occasions during the Voyage, proved himself to be a dirty dog & no Sailor, while Captn. *Jan Riems* with whom I sailed from the Texel behaved to every officer & private marine in the Character of a Gentleman—

upon the *pampus* which is a bank of soft mud Covered with shoal watter not far from amsterdam & which naturally protects it like a Barier from all foreign invaders, since all Ships whatever must eyther be Lifted or drag'd over this Strange Fortification—the first is done by Sinking two Concave vessals Cal'd *Camels* which being Chain'd together under the Bottom of an India man, or man of War of whatever burthen the watter is in equalbriam Pump'd out Of them when they Gradually are seen to rise to the Surface with theyr Burthen, & Carrying it to where there is sufficient depth to keep it afloat without the Smallest Danger—The Second method is Practised on Smaller Vessals & Consists in half a Dozen Sail Boats Cal'd *watter Manakins* towing them through the mud, which Can never be done but when the Wind is streight abaft & when not only the Ship but the Boats that have her in tow must Crow'd all the Sail they Possibly Can Carry—

On the Thirty first having been Becalm'd all night a fresh breese at E Again Sprung up in the Morning when we fired a Gun as a Signal & 5 or 6 Watter manakins instantly Came off, with which team we were drag'd over pampus, not at the Rate of 14 Miles an hour, but at that of 14 *Hours a mile* Since we did not get Clear of it in less than 3 Days Sailing, the two last of Which however I must Confess we had Scarcely any wind at all—

During this tedious Passage it was no bad entertainment to see the Contrast between some just arrived *Norway-men* and us, those people sitting upon Deck in theyr Shirts & Rubbing down the sweat, while we were Struting in great Coats & fur Caps to keep us from the Cold though at this Season—

Having at this time Received a Considerable present of Refreshments from the Grateful Amsterdamers for having saved their favourite Colony, & being so near Revisiting our old Friends & Acquaintances, all on board was in the highest flow of Spirits & Exulting with Gladness, myself alone & individually excepted—

In vain we Strove our Sufferings to Conceal
When worn with Sorrows or with Cares Opprest
The unbidden pang insensibly will Steal
And paint the Struggling tortures of the Breast,

O! thou *Joana,* who hast so often saved my Life, & thou *sweet infant* who wast the Darling of my soul what is your Fate at Present?–yet surely you are Happy—

But where am I? ah! where indeed! declare
Ye Pitying powers to whom my woes are known,

By Oceans parted, tortured with despair
And doom'd to Anguish endless as her own

Again thou Virtuous Slave why didst thou love me so?—Perhaps like *desdemona* loved the moor of Venis for the many dangers he had Past—but I Can never be *Othello*—Kind Reader forgive me this Ejaculation—

Now every thing being Ready the Troops were put on board 6 Lighters appointed to transport them to *Bois le Duck:* in which town they were next to be Compleated & do duty as part of the Garrison—

On Leaving the Vessals we were once more saluted with 9 Guns from each ship Which we Return'd with 3 Cheers & Set sail immediately for the fortified place Above mention'd—It is to be Remark'd that during the whole Course of our home Voyage which had lasted two months two of the Officers Continued to be Sea Sick from first to Last which is verry uncommon this disease generally Continuing but a very few days—

My next Remark on board the Lighters was that when passing through the inland towns such as *Scaardam, Haarlem,* & *Tergow* I thought them truly magnificent particularly the *Glass painting* in the Great Church of the Latter, but theyr *inhabitants* who Crowded About us for Curiosity to see us appeared a Pack of the uglyest & nastyest tatterdemallions that I ever Behel'd, Since I had been Accustomed to live amongst the indians & Blacks—

Theyr Eyes seem'd to be like those of a pig—theyr Complexion like that of Foul Linnen, they seem'd to have no Teeth & to be Cover'd over with Rags Dirt & Vermin—This prejudice however was not against these people only but against all Europeans in General when Compared to the Sparkling eyes ivory Teeth, the Shining skin and Remarkable Cleanliness of those I had left Behind—But the most Laughable was, that during all this we never Considered the truly Contemptible Figure that we exibited *our selves* our Dress Excepted being in other respects so much Sunburnt, so Pale that we look'd exactly like tann'd Leather or dried Parchment, while our hair was mostly become Gray by heat and Fatigue & we were so thin that our Backs seem'd to Stick fast to our Bellies yet besides All which /having been so long in the Woods and unaccustomed to frequent polite Company/ we had perfectly the appearance of Wild people & myself amongst others very Deservedly inherited the distinguish'd name of *Le Sanvage Anglois,* or the English Savage—

In this pickle having Still Passed by *dordrecht, Gorcum,* & *Louvesteyn*

Which last is the Place of Confinement for Prisoners of State, we finally arrived & the troops march'd ashore in the town of Bois le Duck—

> Hail Source of being! Universal Soul
> Of Heaven & Earth! Essential presence hail!
> To thee I bend the knee; to thee my Thoughts,
> Continual Climb; who with a masters hand

hast Brought us back after so many Perils—

Thus ended Perhaps one of the most Extraordinary expeditions that was ever undertaken by European troops & to which only the exploits of the American Buccaneers Can have a verry Distant Resemblance—Be that as it may, having saved my Life, it has afforded me in the end not only much instruction but a pleasing entertainment also, to Recollect the very great Hardships I have so luckily gone through & the many Hazards I have so happily escaped—it has teach'd me in place of idle modes & Fashions to know more about men & manners, & enables me now to look on those gifts of Providence with great thankfulness, which I formerly deem'd no good Sufficient for the meanest of my fathers Domesticks—thus it has Accumulated on me a *store of Riches,* if it is true That riches Consist in Content—And what gives me above all a peculiar Satisfaction, is that by having so Constantly employed my spare moments, to drawing & Writing, I have it now in my power to lay before my friends the History of a Country so little explored & hetherto so very little known Particularly to the English nation, a Nation which ever delights in new & useful discoveries, & never did I recollect the Latin Adage with more Satisfaction Viz. that

> Vox andita perit, Litera scripta manet—

I had once made a plan of Giving some Account of the other duch West india islands, Viz *Berbice, demarary,* & *Essequebo* besides the islands of *Curacao* & *S. Eustatia* but all these being sufficiently known & Describ'd espescially since the late war with Holland I will say nothing about them, except that *Surinam* is the largest and most valuable possession in theyr high & mightinesses transatlantick dominions—but to proceed—

Lieut: Col: *Westerlo* /who went sick to Europe in 1773 but was not yet Recovered—& who Acquainted me that one or two of the Privates also sent over indisposed had since Cut theyr Throats in deliriom/ now invited me in Company with some others to dine with him at the Publick mess, where, while some duch Gentlemen Complain'd that the Soop was smoaky & the Beef was old, We Surinamers declared never

1777—JUNE, 9, 10, 18, JULY 10

to have tasted a more delicious Repast, And at the same time while they Rung out in Praises of the Strawberries, Cherrys, &c we thought them exceedingly inferior to the *Avigato Pear Watter-Melon* & *Pine-Apple* which shows that everything in this world is only good or bad by

🙦 Comparison to Better or to Worse—in Short on the Following day we were introduced on the parade to the Lieut: Governor General *Hardenbrook* and Spent the evening at his Lady's Card Assembly Where I must acknowledge that I was Charm'd with some verry sweet Faces fresh as the Rose & the Lilly & where we Lost our money with a good Grace like Sailors, while they were no less entertained with our grotesque Appearance independant of our Powder & Pomatum; Another Risible thing was that while all the Company Complain'd of the Warm weather we Sat Chattering our teeth like so many Baboons—indeed so little Could I in particular bear the Cold that though in the month of June I kept burning a Constant Coal Fire in my Apartment & when walking, always sought the *Sun* while others were happy to retire in the Cooling shade—

🙦 On the Eighteenth the Troops were finally Clear'd off their remaining arrears, and those who Chose it permitted to Return to theyr *old* Regiments when some of the privates had 30 or £40 to Receive and which /sailor like/ having won it like Horses they spent it like Asses— Amongst others a young Fellow named Jack *Keefhaber* & whose former Regiment was inquarter'd in the Same town hired 3 Coaches to Carry him the length of *one* Street only, ordering a Couple of Drunken Fidlers in the first—his knapsack in the Second, & himself in the 3.ᵈ Supported by a Couple of hungry whores—he nevertheless was shipwreck'd being run Foul of by the place Major who having broke the Fiddles, & Set the Ladies a Dreft tow'd himself safe to the Quarter-Guard after a hard Struggle, where he Came to an Anchor in the Bilboes, till the Gale of his Dicipation was quite Spent & he had got rid of all his Ballast. & while in a Similar manner now went most of the money that had been earned with so much danger sweat and hardships—At last it became my turn to keep *my long made promise* & bid a lasting farewell

🙦 to Colonel Fourgeoud's Regiment from which I on the tenth day of August [July] /in Consequence/ obtained my free *dismission* having requested it immediately after my debarcation from the Prince of Orange, & who at the same time honour'd me with a new Captains Commission to Reenter in the Hon.ᵇˡᵉ Gen.ˡ *Stuarts* Regiment which I had left in Spt.ʳ 1772, while for this long & painful Service Viz to this verry day, my pay had amounted to little more than £450 having been Stop'd near 200 Guineas for the Putrify'd beef, Rusk-bread, & hard peas that so miraculously had kept my Soul & Body together. And now before the God of Heaven do I Solemnly declare that sooner than to undergo my former miseries again, for whatever Reward, I would even embrace the fate of poor *Madan Blanchard* the Sailor & end my days amongst the Savages at Pelew—When Tirany Commands the post of Honour is a private Station—Let me however not utter this as a Reproach to the Duch nation in General, who indeed Omitted nothing for our Preservation & encouragement, a people whose Gallantry has been for ages as Conspicuous as theyr Courage, witness the Admirals *Van-Tromp, Peet-Heyn, Obdam* & *DeRuyter,* not Forgetting the Hero *Zoutman* who so lately as nobly Signalized himself against the Valiant Parker on the Dogger bank—Neyther let me Reflect Against the *Corps* in which I Served so long whose Perseverance & Bravery without exception ought ever to make them Notable in History while the Patience firmness & Resolution of the *Scotch Swich* & *Waloon* Private Soldiers, well deserves to be Recorded for theyr Lasting honour, but *Fourgeoud* the Hapless *Fourgeoud* Alone is the Object not now of my Revenge, but of my unceasing Reproach Whose unmanly want of Feelings was the death of so many Worthy men, while the Sovereign was infamously imposed upon by those who Recommended this man to Such a distinguished Rank, & Office, as I myself have taken the Liberty to tell them since my Return, but which Recommendation to Court proceeded from self interest Alone to be Reinburs'd the money that he Was in theyr debt & not from a Contientiousness of his merit—while Strength of Constitution & indefatiguable Perseverance were Assuredly his Due. such, & such alone were the Causes of our Hero's preferment which I have formerly promis'd once to devulge, while should any one ask, how Came the Court to be blinded & deceived? my Answer is because it is the *Fashion* all over Europe, nor Can the Prince Avoid it, whose high & Elevated Situation in Life let him be never so well inclined too often prevents him to see otherwise than with *borrow'd* eyes or through a *Cloud*—Should now the next Question be why do I Reveal the above *poor man's* Weaknesses to the world! I Candidly Reply because it is Already too much the Custom Also to trumpet nothing but praise & adulation, & as I am not a man of the fashion; espescially since I liv'd so long amongst the uncivilized, I delight in like them openly, & equally, to Sound a man's vices as well as his virtues, which Character I adopt not only as being more manly but more Suitable for the General benefit of mankind—But Should any of my Friends throughout this narrative think themselves hurt or too Rufly treated they may depend that while I have the Severity to unmask vice & folly I at the Same time possess the Generosity to give ev'ry Gentleman that Satisfaction to which I reasonably think he stands intitled—

1777—JULY 10, 29, 30, AUGUST 25

Having now once more exchanged my *blue* Coat for a *Scarlet* uniform, bought a Verry handsome English horse & put my Black boy Qwaccoo in a Brillant Livery, I entertained for the Last evening my Dearest Shipmates with whom *without Exception at all* I drank an Everlasting Friendship, then taking my final Farewell from them all, I the next morning Departed & Set out to Rejoin the old Scots Regiment where I was Since Received with those true marks of unfeigned friendship, as Can only flow from the tenderest Regard & warmest affection, while my heart felt no less glad to be again amongst them than they unanimously proved to be happy at my Safe Return—

Per Varios Casus & tot descrimina Rerum
Pervenimus ad Latium——
——Olim Meminisse Jubabit—

—Virgil—

Amongst the Trifles I brought over to disperse among my Acquaintances such as *Cocoa-nut punch spoons* trim'd with Silver, and Macaw Rings with theyr Sifres set in Gold, I Cannot Omit making mention of a Supper of Surinam *hens* Eggs which by way of Experiment I had preserved fresh in douce notwithstanding they were Actually 4 Months Old—the Fowls eggs in Guiana are Smaller & more Sharp Pointed than any I ever saw in Europe—

Going now to take my last Leave of *Surinam* after all the Horrors & Cruelties with which I must have hurt both the *Eye* & the *heart* of the Feeling reader, I will Close the Scene with an Emblematical Picture of *Europe* Supported by *Africa* & *America* Accompanied by an Ardent Wish that in the friendly manner as they are Represented they may henceforth & to all Eternity be the Prop of each other; I might have included *Asia* but this I omitted as having no Connection with the Present Narrative—we All only differ in the Colour but we are Certainly Created by the same hand & After the Same Mould thus if it has not pleas'd fortune to make us equal in Authority, let us at Least use that Superiority With Moderation & not only Profer that Happiness which we have to bestow on our Superiors & Equals, but with Cheerfulness to the very Lowest of our dependants—

I now on the twenty fifth of Aug.t went to the palace of Loo in Gelderland, where by the Colonel of Gen.l Stuarts Reg.t I was introduced to his Serene Highness the *Statholder* & which illustrious Prince not only was pleas'd to give me a gracious Reception Remarking I must have Suffer'd very much by my Looks, but was soon after pleas'd to promote me to the Rank of *Major* in the above Scotch Reg.t thus was

Europe supported by Africa & America.

London, Published Dec.r 1.st 1792, by J. Johnson, St Paul's Church Yard.

1777—AUGUST 25, SEPTEMBER 24, OCTOBER 8, 28

both I & all with whom I was Concern'd happy in the end[.] Deer-Deer however did I earn this mark of distinction, nor Could ever *Lord Cutt's* Motto be inapplicable to myself who was made a British Peer by Army Services alone—

Per Sanguine et Sudore
By Blood & Sweat—

& Which heavens knows was as much my Case as any Mans—

I might have *now* with some Degree of propriety mention'd our former bad usage but I had given my hand to old Fourgeoud, besides which I was Convinced it Could give the Court but little pleasure to hear him mention'd any more, Such Was Nevertheless my Consolation that truth did prevail & every Enormity Came Gradually to Light—

Magna est veritas et prevalebit

While my Pleasure lay in my Triumph Alone, & not in that punishment by Which his Guilt So Justly deserv'd to be Overtaken—

On the twenty fourth of September I next went to the Hague, where I Complimented his Serene highness With 18 Figures in Wax made by myself for his Musaem, which were most Graciously Accepted—they Represented the free *Indians of Guiana* & negroes *slaves of Surinam* in Different Occupations on an Island Supported by a Crystal Miror, & Ornamented with Solid Gold—I now also made a present of my true & Faithful Black boy *Qwaccoo* by *his own Consent* to the Countess of *Rosendaal,* to Which family I was under very high Obligations & who Since on Account of his Honesty & Sober Conduct not only Christned him by the name of *Stedman* at my desire but Created him to be theyr Butler, with a promise to take Care of him as Long as he Lived—& which was a Blessing I Could never have Bestow'd on him myself—

About this time I was offered by the directors of the Settlement to be Sent over a Lieutenant Governor to the Colony of *Berbice* next to Surinam. In Consequence I went to Amsterdam to wait on them & hear the proposals, by which they indeed offer'd me a higher Salary, & Greater Advantages than they had ever Offer'd to any other Gentleman in that line, but I insisting on either the Survivancy of the *Government,* or a Pension after a Certain number of Years at my Return, which being out of their Power /they Said/ to Grant me, I Relinquished the plan Altogether Preferring to Regain my health & Vigour in Europe with a Scots Company, Rather than to broil any Longer under the Torrid Zone, without a prospect once more to Settle at home both with Honour & a Competant Fortune, & indeed my fine Constitution was Such that in a few months, I Again became as Plump & Healthy as ever I had been in my Life, Which happiness not one amongst a hundred of my poor Shipmates Could boast of, it being now exactly 5 Years since I set on this Cursed Expedition—

Amongst Others poor *Fourgeoud* was one who Could not boast of *this good Fortune* for he now no sooner Came to Holland with the remaining few we left behind, than his beloved *Teasan* gave him the Slip, while himself Also gave the Slip to that Justice which was Ready to Call him to an Account—that is he was Suddenly found *dead* in his bed Attended only by a negro, & buried at the Hague without the Regret of any one that ever knew him before—

Thus ended the Life of that man who had been the death of so many—Snacht Off without having time to Say God help me, & Call'd unprepared to Appear at the Bar of Heaven Charged with a life of Complicated Misdemeanours

> And Could that mighty Warrior Fall?
> And so inglorious, after all!—
> Well, since he's gone, no matter how,
> The last loud trump must wake him now:
> And, trust me, as the noise grows stronger,
> He'd wish to sleep a little Longer
> * * * * * * *
> This world he Cumber'd long enough;
> He burnt his Candle to the Snuff;
> And that's the Reason some Folks think
> He left behind so great a S——k.
> Behold his Funeral Appears,
> Nor Widow's Sighs, nor Orphans tears
> Wont at such times each heart to pierce
> Attend the progress of his herse—
> But what of that his friends may say
> He had those Honours in his day
> True to his profit & his pride
> He made them weep before he dy'd
> * * * * * *
> Til from his ill got honors flung—
> He turn'd to dirt from whence he Sprung.
> —Swift—

As for his ill got Stores they were sent to Switzerland amongst his poor Relations—And not long after this expired in Surinam Fourgeouds mortal enemy the Governor of the Colony to evidence against him in the other World in whose place was Created as I have said before the deserving Mr. Wighers—but to proceed.

The Emperor of Germany having now retaken the barier towns from the states of Holland Gen.ˡ Stuarts Reg.ᵗ was the last that evacuated the City of *Namur* & on the same day the imperial troops march'd in to take possession, after which the Aspiring *Joseph* demolish'd all the Fortifications—

‍‍‍ Soon after this the Scots Brigade were naturaliz'd, that is form'd into 3 duch Reg.ᵗˢ on Account of the war with Britain where most of the Principal Officers refusing to serve against their King & Country left it, who were in Consequence of their Loyalty taken under his Majesty's protection—

‍‍‍ On the Eighteenth of June Eleven of them /of which number I was so happy to make one/ were introduc'd at S.ᵗ James where they had the

‍‍‍ honour to kiss the Kings hand—& in the same month the half pay was Voted for them all by the British house of Commons each individual According to his Rank Abroad*—

That the Reader may have some fent [faint] idea of what is meant by the Scots Bregade & of what they formerly Consisted I will beg leave to insert the following short Acco.ᵗ

In 1570 they were Supposed to Come over to holland as independant Companies Commanded by some of the first noblemen in Scotland—

1578 theyr Gallant Behaviour together with the English at the Battle of *Reminat* near Mechlen is mention'd particularly by *Strada*—

1579 *Menin* was surprised & the Spanish & Waloon guards taken prisoner by Col: *Balfour* with his Reg.ᵗ Alone—

1588 at the memorable blockade of *Bergen up Zoom* by the prince of *parma* the Scots under the Command of Gen.ˡ *Balfour* & Col: *Scott* made a Sortie & demolish'd the greatest part of the Spanish lines by which the enemy were forced to break up the Seige with Considerable loss of men & Ammunition—

1590 at the Siege of *Zutphen, Deventer Nimegen* & *Hulst* theyr Behaviour was Conspicuous &

1593 they shared so much of the Glory at the taking of *Geertrudenbergh* that both Gen.ˡ Balfour & his Reg.ᵗ were highly distinguished by Prince *Morice* the first he made Governor to Command the Garrison in place of his Brother *Prince Henry* & the 2.ᵈ he Appointed as the most Spirited to defend it—

1594 a Deputation from Holland having presented to King *James* two

---

• —That is According to the Rank in which he had Serv'd abroad, Since on the very day of my dismission I was amongst others Complimented with that of a Lieutenant Colonel—

I ought Still to Observe that on the Scots Officers receiving theyr Commission in the Duch Service it was Usual for them before the British ambassador to take the Oaths of *Allegiance* to his Britannic majesty & *abjuration* to the Pretender of which the Certificates were sent over to the Secretary of state & Register'd at the war office

1783—JUNE 27

Golden Cups in a box of the same mettal, & beg'd leave to Stand Godfather for the young prince who was then Born, they returned Accompanied with 1500 men & Severals of the Nobility who all enter'd into theyr Service, and on whom they put the very Greatest Value—

1599 At the taking of *Bommel* the Scotts suffered most Considerably & in *1600* two Field officers & Captains &c With Above 600 private men were left dead on the field After the famous *Battle of the Downs* near *Newport* when both they & the English behaved with the greatest gallantry & to whom Conjunctly was attributed the Success of the day—

1601 at the Siege of *Ostend* which lasted 3 Years & at which was Level'd the whole pow'r of Spain nothing Could equal the Valour & Courage both of the Scots & English the first Commanded by Gen! *Balfour*—& S! *Clair* the latter by Lords *Willoughby* & *Vere* who after killing 78,000 Spaniards including all the best officers, & putting theyr nation to the expence of an immense Sum of money still forced the haughty dons to break up the siege & Retreat with great Shame & Confusion to whence they Came from—

1609 the 12 Years time being Concluded there were for some time few Remarkable Actions, but let it Suffice that during the Reign of the 3 first princes of Orange—*William*—*Maurice* & *Frederick Henry* the Scots behaved with so much bravery, Honour, & Reputation that by the last /besides many other marks of distinction/ they were Cal'd the *Bulwarks of the Republick*—

In Short to innumerate the many Services this distinguished Corps of men has Rendered to the Provinces of Holland I Will only step over to the *last Siege of Bergen up Zoom* in 1747 by the French where while others Shamefully Ran away, a Whole Reg! of the Scots in the middle of the town Sooner Allow'd themselves to be Cut to pieces, many of Whom were Observ'd to fight even on theyr bleeding Stumps & d——ning the French after both theyr legs had been Shot away by the enemy—

Such is the History of the late Scots Bregade in the Duch Service, & such are the outlines of its General Character till the day of its desolution as I have said in 1783—

I Nevertheless Wilfully Acknowledge & from my heart my early wishes to have enter'd in the English *Army* or *navy*, but, though born a Gentleman, I wanted the Chief ingredients /Viz/ money and interest & on which Account with many Others my Ardent desire was Frustrated—

I must now draw this Narrative to a final Conclusion by *once* more mentioning the name of Poor *Joana* & by Acquainting the Reader that Alas—*Joana is no more*—

1783—AUGUST 7

From Mr *Gourlay* in August did I receive the melancholy tidings which pierc'd me to the Very Soul that on the Fatal 5 day of Last November /a day ever Remarkable for treason in the Annals of this Island/ this virtuous young Creature had died by *poison*, administred by the hand of Jealousy & Envy on Account of her prosperity & the marks of distinction, which her Superior merit so Justly Attracted from the Respectable part of Mankind—While others insisted that her death was the Consequence of a Broken heart•—

Be that as it may—she is no more—Reader the deserving Joana is no more. her adopted mother Mrs Godefrooy who bedued her Beauteous body with tears, now order'd it to be interred with every mark of Respect under a Grove of Orange Trees, on which Occasion I wrote the following lines, dictated only by Sensibility & Affection

> Approach with gentle Step with sacred awe inspir'd
> With simpathyzing heart, with gen'rous pity fier'd
> Then read, *O Christian* Read, while nobly down let flow
> One Tributary tear—let Rose & myrtle blow
> Upon this verdant tomb—An Angel not a Slave
> In prime of Beauteous youth, Alas Rests in this Grave
> Obscure but for that Gold her *mothers* Country stor'd
> Sad Sable *Africa* on her *European* Lord—
>   Strew Garlands will not blush, nor let thy pity Cease
> While dear Joana Slumbers in eternal peace
> Whose Virtuous Soul on earth so hard her due was giv'n
> Now Shines and blazes with her Sister stars in heaven
>   And thou O Fragrant Grove thy Cluster'd branches spred
> Waft thy Ambrosia insence round her pratious head.
> Twas *she her Stedman* sav'd from the pale jaws of death
> Beneath thy golden fruits now lies depriv'd of breath
>   In Gratitude now Stedman to the world doth give
> These lines to Teach mankind how by her death to live
> Then wilt thou Soar to heaven draw to thy maker nigh
> Learn first O Christian like this virtuous slave to die
> While he'll incessant strive since no more Can be done
> To make her Virtues shine immortal in her Son
> Here ends my Theme—Farewell—nor more let me Complain
> Till bounteous Heaven shall please perhaps to make us meet again

And art thou then no more, who saved my life so often—Cut off in the bloom of thy youth—so Accomplish'd—so nearly arrived at Perfection—

• —It is to be Remark'd & Lamented that her younger *brother henry* who had Also Obtain'd his manumission expired in the Same Year & in the same languishing Condition—

1783—AUGUST 7; 1784; 1787

Reader if you have a heart—but oh! I must drop the Melancholy Subject—

Now her Lovely boy was sent over the Ocean to my longing Arms with a Bill for near £200 his private Property* & whose faithful Guardians both Expired soon after the death of his well deserving Mother—

Not long had I been in this Situation, when now a young Lady whom I thought nearest Approach'd to her in every Virtue help'd to Support my Grief by becoming my Other Partner.—She was of a very Respectable Family in Holland—I Sought no other Fortune & with this Amiable new Companion & my boy, whom she tenderly Loves, I peacably Retired to the Fruitful Country of *devon in* England where with my half pay for all Allowance I make Shift to make ends meet, & thank God for all his mercies.—And where our two first English born Children a beautiful boy & Girl we in Gratitude to our Bounteous Sovereign Christne'd George William & Sophia Charlotte after theyr Majesty's the King & Queen, praying Unanimously for theyr lasting Welfare & the uninterrupted Prosperity of this happy Nation—

> This Royal Throne of Kings, this Chief of Isles;
> Where Scepter'd majesty in Grandeur smiles:
> This other Eden fam'd in peace, & War,
> This Fortress built by natures Guardian Care:
> Whose safety, while her sons unite, is sure,
> From foreign foes, & pestilence Secure.—
> This little World, whose Blessings Liberty;
> This precious stone, set in a Silver Sea;
> This House, surrounded by Great neptunes moat,
> Whose Walls are waves, & whose strong Castles Float.
> This nurse, this womb of Kings; of royal worth;
> Fear'd from their breed, & famous for their Birth.
> Rever'd for Arts & Sciences at home;—
> Renown'd for deeds as far as fame Can roam.
>   —alter'd from Shakespear

Still one Singular Anecdote let me Relate—Having innoculated most of the Family for the *Small Pox* but not the Youth born in Guiana, Who Reported to have had them in Surinam—he nevertheless would go through the whole Operation only to encourage his Brother &c the happy Consequence of which was that having only had the *Watter Pox* before, he took the infection to our Great surprise with the Rest, & by not taking the disease in the natural way escap'd possibly that fatal fate

---

* —in a *female negro Slave* & *three Score Sheep* had Consisted the Live Stock of Poor Joana—

that attended the unfortunate Prince *Lee Boo* who Came from the islands of Pelew—

Since this having made the Greatest progress in Education, he went two west india Voyages as a Sailor & is at this moment on board of the *Southampton* Frigate under Cap.t *Cates,* ready to Strike a blow at the Spaniards should they dare to Quarrel with the Kingdom of Great Britain, while my own Remaining Wish is Confin'd to that of Horace in his VI.th Ode 2.d Book

> Tibur Argeo Positum Colono
> Sit meae sedes utinam senectae;
> Sit modus lasso maris, & Viarum
>   Militiaeque.
> ———
> Quite tir'd of Foreign lands and mains,
> Of Journeys great, and dire Campaigns;
> My age at Tibur let me spend,
> At Tibur all my Labours end.

And now Farewell my Patient Friends who have been pleas'd to peruse this Narrative of my Sufferings with any Degree of Sensibility, particularly those whose Simpathetick Feelings have been Rous'd by the Distressing Scenes they may have met with in reading, & whose good nature is ready to forgive the inacuracies annext to the pen & pencil of a Soldier debar'd from his youth from a Classical Education—I say Farewell, Claiming no other merit whatever than in having spoke the simple Truth & without which may the pages annex'd die with theyr Author, but should this Gift so Rarely to be met with Chance be found in my Performance—

> Let one poor Sprig of Bays around my head
> Bloom while I Live & point me out when dead

While, long, long, may you live & be happy in this Bless'd Island, accumulating wealth with honor & Surrounded with victory, till the Lowest subject amongst you shall have Ascended to the highest pinnacle of unfading Glory—

Finis

Names of the Gentlemen Officers
Belonging to Col: Fourgeoud's Regiment of Marines

Fourgeoud	Meyer	Immink
Baron van Gersdorff	Rulagh	Van Halm
Landman	Meervus	Van Aelst
Westerlo	Noot	Streck
Becquer	Pape	DeBorde
Ruhkopff	Esselink	Morack
Desborgnes	Mc Donnald	Boom
Middelaar	Franson	DeLand
Tulling V:O:D: Barneus	Fradaricy	Small
Brandt	Neys	Van Guricke
Stedman	Luk	Hogenhuyse
Vangeuricke	Matthiew	Pineda
Van Coeverdon	Cooneu	Buno
Van Halm	Cabanes	Lang
Portugees	Gamb	Burgers
Perret Genteel	Seiborgh	Oottinger
Baron de Bush	Seiborgh	Noot
Kandwyk	Hamell	Geovanony
Du Moulin	Brugh	Stam
Heeneman	Bols	Hents
Du Perron	Orligh	De Shorsin
Stroomer	Van Dhale	Van der Salm
Van Zande	Esselink	DeStetfeldt
Campbell	Chataar View	Knollart
Geelkin	Smith	Stagger
Swildens	Gibhart	Niseus
De Haamer	Straws	Renard
Cattenburgh	Morack	Meyer
Baron van Ower	Wischer	Scheffer
Dederling		

List of Subscribers

[A]

Acland Bar{t} / Sr Thos Dyke / Hillerton
Anderson / Lady / –Yorkshire

B

Bamff. Right Hon{b} Lord 6 Dragoons
Baring Esqr / Chas / 5 Coppies
Bates Captn / Ralph / 6 Dragoons
Broadley Esqr / Isaac /
Boundler / Mrs /–Bath
Besley / Mr Willm / Tiverton
Black / Mr John / London

C

Chichister / Sr John / Bar{t}
Chichister / Mrs / Arlington
Chichister / Miss
Chichister / Miss Mary M{c}Donald
Cholwich Esqr / John B /
Cholmly Esqr / N /
Croft Esqr / J{no}

D

Duntze Bar{t} & M:P/ P{r}Jn{o} / Rocksbearhouse
Drew Esqr / Richard / Exon
Dennys Esqr / N /
Dunsford / Mr M / Tiverton

[E]

Elliott R Honble / Fred: Agustus / 6 Dragoons
Edwards / Mr / pallmall 12 Coppies

F

Fitzgerald / Miss
Follett Revd / Mr /
Ferrier, / Lieut Col: / Edinburgh
Flower / Mr / London
Flower / Mr B / Tiverton

G

Gray / Miss
Grimston Esqr / Henry

H

Hunter Esqr / M:D: York
Heathfield Esqr Nutwell
Hume / Lieut Col: London
Harding / Revd John / Barnstaple
Hilyard, Bar{t} / Sr Robt Darcy / York

I

Incledon / Robt Newton Esqr / Pilton House
Incledon Captn

[L]

Lardner Esqr / Richd
Lardner Esqr / John /

LIST OF SUBSCRIBERS

Lardner Esqr / James
Louis / Mr John / Exeter

M

McPherson Bar^t / S^r Jno / London
McAwley Esqr / Alex^r / London
McLoud, Lieu Col. London
McAwley Esqr / Angus / Bath
McQueen Esqr / Dundas / Edinburgh
Maddison Esqr / M:P: / John /
Martyn / M^r / London
Moore Esqr / Jno / Tiverton

N

Nibbs Esqr / JL / Beauchamp 2 Coppies
Neagle Esqr / Jo^s / Calverleigh
Neagle Esqr / David / Bath
Needham Esqr / Jno / of Grays Inn
Newte, Rev^d / Miss / Titcomb
Northcote, Bar^t / Sr Staff. Hen^ry / Pynes House

P

Peachey Esqr / M:P: / John
Palmer / Hon^b Thos / Barclay square
Popple, / Rev^d M^r / York
Pleydell Lieu / J M / 6 Dragoons

[R]

Ryder / M:P: Right Hon^b Dudley
Reah, Esqr / Northumberland
Ridsdale, Cornel / G W / 6 Dragoons
Rolland, Esqr / Adam / Edinburgh

S

Strickland, Bar^t / Sr Geo / Boynton House
Strickland, Lieu^t / Geo / 8th Reg^t Foot
Strickland, Esqr / Willm
Strickland. / Lady
Strickland, Miss Charlotte
Sutherland, D^r – Westminster
Stedman Esqr / M:D: / John / Edinburgh
Stuyvesant, M:D: Surinam
Suttel, Mr Geo / York
Sheldon, Miss Ann / Exeter

T

Todd, M^r / T / York

W

Worth, Mrs Mary / Tiverton
Worth, M^{rs} / Worth House Devon
White, Esqr / Counsellar / Ja^s / Exeter

Editors' Notes to Stedman's "Narrative"

8. **Admir! Anson** . . . British admiral (1697–1762), whose famous voyage round the world (1740–44) inflicted great damage on Spanish shipping; he later served as first lord of the admiralty.
8. **Alex! Selkirk** . . . Scottish sailor (1676–1721) who, after a quarrel with his captain in 1704, asked to be marooned on Más a Tierra (one of the Juan Fernández Islands), where he lived for over four years. His adventures are said to have served as model for Defoe's *Robinson Crusoe* (1719).
9. **Do. Stedman** . . . Dr. John Stedman (1710–91), author of *Laelius and Hortensia; or, Thoughts on the Nature and Objects of Taste and Genius, in a Series of Letters to Two Friends* (Edinburgh, 1782). This was the Scottish uncle with whom the young Stedman was forced to live for two relatively unhappy years (see Introduction).
9. **Miss Merians Surinam Drawings** . . . Maria Sybilla Merian (1647–1717), naturalist and painter, who lived in Suriname 1699–1701. Her famous book, *Metamorphosis Insectorum Surinamensium*, with vivid colored illustrations, was first published in 1705 at Amsterdam. Stedman followed in a long line of learned critics and defenders of Merian's drawings (see Stuldreher-Nienhuis 1944, 119).
10. **the ingenious Cowley** . . . Hannah Parkhouse Cowley (1743–1809), dramatist and poet. A native of Tiverton, where Stedman lived while writing the "Narrative," she was the author of very successful comedies, such as *The Runaway* (1776) and *The Belle's Stratagem* (1780), as well as being the leading English Della-Cruscan, writing poetry under the name of Anna Matilda. See entry for page 388 in Appendix B.
10. **the immortal Reynolds** . . . Sir Joshua Reynolds (1723–92), England's

greatest portrait painter and first president of the Royal Academy. Stedman again describes Reynolds's reactions to his paintings on page 392.

11. in the Language of Eugenious . . . Stedman is alluding to Laurence Sterne's character Eugenius in *The Life and Opinions of Tristram Shandy, Gentleman* (1760) who, upon the death of his friend Yorick, quotes Shakespeare by inscribing on his tombstone, "Alas, poor YORICK!" (bk. 1, chap. 12).

22. Snake . . . See Introduction, note 28.

24. The Chastisement . . . See Introduction, note 28.

32. negro insurrection in the Colony of *Berbice* in 1763 . . . One of the largest slave revolts in the history of the Americas. Nearly the entire slave population rebelled and took control of the sugar colony of Berbice. The rebels' plans to establish an independent kingdom failed within the year, however, as much from internecine strife as from European pressures (Blair 1984). For Stedman's account of the insurrection, see pages 76–77.

41. *Black Soldiers* . . . In 1772, the elite "Neeger Vrijcorps," or corps of Rangers, was formed, when the government purchased plantation slaves from their masters and promised them their freedom and other material benefits in return for fighting the Maroons. See Introduction, note 8.

43. but here *wousky* pursued me again . . . Wowski, a "comic" female character—black, ill-mannered, slow-witted—in *Inkle and Yarico,* a very popular opera by George Colman the Younger produced in London in 1787. See also the note to page 98.

46. in *Quirpo* to battle with the Gnats or Muskitos . . . "In cuerpo" = in undress, naked.

49. the Governor Mr *Nepveu* . . . Jan Nepveu (1719–79). Although Stedman writes that Nepveu "was said to be a man of Sense more than Learning" (p. 108), Nepveu wrote a detailed and ethnographically important monograph in the form of commentaries on Herlein's 1718 description of Suriname ("Annotatiën," Societeit van Suriname 556, and Collectie Nepveu 19, Algemeen Rijksarchief, currently being prepared for publication by Silvia W. de Groot), as well as commentaries on Hartsinck 1770 (Collectie Nepveu 18, Algemeen Rijksarchief), and Stedman may have depended on Nepveu more than he admits for the ethnographic portions of the "Narrative."

50. Sir Godfrey Kneller . . . Fashionable English portrait painter (1646–1723), born in Germany, and named principal painter of the court in 1688.

51. Doctor Bancroft . . . Edward Bancroft (1744–1821), naturalist and chemist, who visited North and South America several times. He wrote *An essay of natural history of Guiana in South-America in several letters from a gentleman in the medical faculty* (London, 1749). Stedman's latitudes and longitudes for "Guiana" are approximately correct, given the broad definition he gives the term in his map (pl. 1).

53. Mr Hartsink . . . Jan Jacob Hartsinck (1716–79), author of the most important eighteenth-century history of Suriname, *Beschrijving van Guiana of de Wilde Kust in Zuid-Amerika* (Amsterdam, 1770). Hartsinck worked exclusively in the Netherlands, using the correspondence and reports sent from Suriname by colonial officials. Stedman's sunrise and sunset figures are correct (Bruijning and Voorhoeve 1977, 344).

53. two *rainy* and two *dry* Seasons . . . Suriname's seasons are, as Stedman reports, highly variable from one year to the next. The seasons are usually reckoned as Short Rainy Season (December–January), Short Dry Season (February–April), Long Rainy Season (May–mid-August), and Long Dry Season (mid-August–November) (Bruijning and Voorhoeve 1977, 340).

53. M.͞ *Guthrie* . . . William Guthrie (1708–70), a writer on politics, history, and geography. He was author of *Geographical, historical and commercial grammar* (London, 1770), reissued as *A new system of modern geography* (Philadelphia, 1794).

53. D.͞ *Fermyn* . . . Philippe Fermin, physician from Maastricht who served as a doctor in Suriname 1754–64. Stedman apparently met him during the 1780s (see p. 114). His main works, written in French but translated into Dutch, German, and English, are Fermin 1769 and 1778.

55. The limits of Surinam . . . The modern borders of Suriname are the Corantijn on the west and the Marowijne on the east.

56. its source never being discovered by Europeans . . . The source of the Suriname River was first reached by Europeans only in 1908, in an expedition led by Saramaka Maroon guides (Eilerts de Haan 1910).

58. the *Orange Path* . . . See Introduction, note 11.

58. Admiral *Rodney* the last war . . . It is unclear whether Stedman is referring to Rodney's exploits during the Seven Years' War (1757–63) or to his final voyage, when he soundly defeated the French fleet off Dominica in 1782.

58. That part of Terra Firma which is called *Guiana* . . . In writing certain of the descriptive portions of the "Narrative" (especially on the geography of the Guianas and the historical background of the colony, and in the Amerindian descriptions), Stedman drew liberally on the works of earlier authors, in particular Hartsinck 1770, Fermin 1769 and 1778, and Bancroft 1749 (see notes to pp. 51 and 53).

58. the relation of David *piterse devries* . . . D. David Pietersz. de Vries (1593–1655), a Dutchman who attempted unsuccessfully to establish a colony in Cayenne in 1634, wrote *Korte historiael, ende journaels aenteyekeninge, van verscheyden voyagiens* (Hoorn and Alckmaer, 1655).

59. a strong Fortress . . . Fort Zeelandia has had a checkered history. During the twentieth century it has served as a prison, as the home of the Surinaams Museum, and currently as the headquarters of the military government. See Fontaine 1972.

60. Capt.͞ Abraham *Cruisen* . . . Crijnssen (or Krijnsen), lieutenant admiral of the province of Zeeland, who commanded the troops that captured Suriname from the English in 1667. Seven ships and 700 men are the figures usually cited today (Bruijning and Voorhoeve 1977, 140).

60. Surinam was never more in the possession of Great Britain . . . After

Stedman wrote the "Narrative," Suriname again came under British rule (1803–12), but this had little lasting effect on the colony.

61. *Cornelis van Aarssens Lord of Somelsdyk*... Cornelis van Aerssen, Lord Sommelsdyk (1637–88), who owned one-third share of the colony and became governor in 1683. His treaties with Indians and Maroons served as models for those of the mid-eighteenth century (R. Price 1983b). For a twentieth-century biography, see Oudschans-Dentz 1938.

64. Paramaribo which is said to be the true *Indian* Name... The etymology of Paramaribo continues to be debated. For recent references, see Bruijning and Voorhoeve 1977, 462; van Lier 1971, 454.

67. Governor Mauricious... Johan Jacob Mauricius (1692–1768), governor of Suriname 1742–53. The complex story of his attempts to make peace with the Saramaka Maroons is discussed in detail, with supporting documents, in R. Price 1983b. Stedman's confused version of these events comes largely from Hartsinck 1770, 768–814.

67. the rebels on the Island of Jamaica... In 1739, the Maroons of Jamaica signed treaties with the colonial authorities, ending temporarily seventy-five years of active guerrilla warfare.

69. By this accident the peace was immediately broke... Stedman's account of the peacebreaking, derived from Hartsinck, is false. The promised presents were never dispatched and the government "detachment" did not travel to Saramaka at the time agreed upon by the two parties. Both government and Saramaka versions of these events may be found in R. Price 1983a and 1983b.

69. run away Negroes... alongst the banks of the *Jocka* Creek... These were the Aukaner (Auca or Djuka) Maroons.

74. This same Year 1761 the peace was also a Second time concluded... Stedman, loosely following Hartsinck 1770, has conflated several discrete incidents, badly confusing his account. Musinga's difficulties with the government, and with other Saramakas, occurred in 1766, and his separate peace was not established until 1769.

74. a handsome Quantity of Arms and Ammunition from the Colony... For the full lists of these tribute goods, see R. Price 1983b.

75. Both these tribes... computed to be no less than 15 or 20000 people... Stedman's combined population figures for the Djuka and Saramaka probably exaggerate reality by a factor of approximately two.

76. the Year 1761... The Berbice insurrection in fact occurred in 1763. See note to page 32.

76. Indians, who are natural enemies to the Negroes but friends to the Europeans... The relationship between Indians and Maroons in Suriname was, in fact, much more variable than Stedman implies. During the early years of the colony, Indians and Africans toiled side by side as plantation slaves; in some cases, Indians facilitated Africans' escapes and harbored them in the forest; and settled groups of Maroons, likewise, assimilated some small groups of Indians. However, Indians were also prominent as guides on military expeditions against Maroons and were often particularly successful bounty hunters. In the neighboring Dutch colonies, during the Berbice rebellion of 1763, the frightened colonists were able to mobilize some two thousand Carib warriors to their cause.

79. a free Negro Woman call'd Eliz. *Sampson* going to be married to an European . . . This marriage, celebrated in 1767, was the first of its kind in the colony and caused considerable discussion and scandal. See van Lier 1949, chap. 3.

81. The barbarous Captain *Coolingward* . . . Clarkson's widely read *Essay* (1788, 98–99) describes this incident in detail: in September 1781, a captain (whose name is not mentioned), after suffering considerable loss of slaves from illness, threw 132 others overboard in order to cheat the vessel's underwriters. Clarkson calls this "a deed, unparalleled in the memory of man . . . and of so black and complicated a nature, that were it to be perpetuated to future generations . . . it could not possibly be believed" (ibid.).

82. who Commands them in the forest by the different Sounds of his horn . . . Both the black troops fighting for the colonists and the Maroons used signal horns in battle. For a photo of a Saramaka signal horn (*tutu*), see S. and R. Price 1980, 182.

82. a scarlet Cap . . . Because of their caps, these soldiers were commonly called *redi moesoe* (Sranan for "red caps").

84. Another Settlement of the Rebels . . . Maroon villages in this particularly inhospitable area, also known as "Devil's Marsh," date from at least the early eighteenth century and persisted for a century and a half (R. Price 1983a, 74–75).

84. Lieut. *Fredeiricy* . . . Juriaen François de Friderici (1751–1812). Later, governor of Suriname (1792–1802). See also page 86.

85. Baron . . . Recent archival research makes clear that though Baron was a military commander of some importance, he was never a real chief and that Boucou was ruled by Boni (Hoogbergen 1985, 80–85). The vivid story of Baron's mistreatment and escape from slavery, first published by Stedman, was repeated by later historians (see, for example, Wolbers 1861, 327; Debien and Felhoen Kraal 1955) but remains controversial. Oudschans-Dentz (1928/29) has cited a public announcement placed by Baron's former master, Dahlberg, in a 1775 issue of the *Wekelijksche Surinaamsche Courant* which denies that Baron ever left Suriname, was sold to a Jew, was deceived or mistreated, and so forth, and Oudschans-Dentz concludes that the story reported by Stedman is false. Other historians, however, suggest that Stedman's version has withstood the test of time (de Groot 1975, 33). The date of Baron's death, previously given as 1776 (ibid., 43), appears from recently published documents to have been instead 1774, during a battle in which his well-known comrade Joli Coeur may also have been killed (de Beet 1984, 21, 213; Hoogbergen 1984, 10; 1985, 85, 207). News of the death of these renowned Maroons was characteristically kept from the whites; in August 1775, Stedman remained unaware of their deaths (p. 400).

85. **Cutting of[f] the Ears—nose—and lips** . . . Stedman refers here to a complex 1772 incident, described in more detail in recently published contemporary documents, in which a Ranger was captured by Baron's men and, at the behest of their gods, instead of being executed was whipped, had an ear cut off and his head shaved, and was then sent back to the whites with a defiant message (de Beet 1984; 135–36). The maiming and sending back of a traitor—a slave siding with the whites against the Maroons—is an important theme in Maroon historiography (see R. Price 1983a, 153–59).

90. **the Protector of Cery with their Children** . . . *Jolycoeur* . . . That Joanna, the supremely cultivated house slave, spent her childhood under the protection of Joli Coeur, who became a well-known guerrilla warrior, should not surprise. Ties of kinship, adoption, and friendship among Suriname's slave community were extensive. (Note, for example, how often Joanna's various relatives appear in the "Narrative.") Indeed, close relatives often found themselves separated, with one a slave and one a Maroon, and this fact had important implications for the success of ongoing Maroon intelligence operations.

92. **Do. *Bancroft* in his Letters to Do. *Pitcairn*** . . . See note to page 51.

95. **a few dreadful Executions** . . . Stedman's diary specifies "3 negroes were hangd on the b! and 2 whipt below the gallows" (*9 March 1773*).

95. **prickly-heat—by the Colonists [called] rootvont** . . . The symptoms described by Stedman seem to correspond to true "prickly heat," an inflammation of the skin around the sweat ducts, more than they do to those of *roodvonk* (the Dutch term for scarlet fever or scarlatina).

95. **a Curious Paper Something Similar** . . . Stedman refers here to "Conjectures upon a Discovery," a quasi-scholarly discourse on the salutary intellectual and emotional effects of scratching the skin regularly, and a recommendation that the "body brushes" of the East Indies be adopted in England (*European Magazine,* July 1785, 30–31).

98. **the history of *Incle* and *Yarico*** . . . Stedman refers here to the version of the Inkle and Yarico story published by Addison in the *Spectator* (no. 11). There were also poems, plays, and operas (see the note to p. 43) based on this very popular Noble Savage tale, which seems to have been first published in relatively full form in Richard Ligon's *A True & Exact History of the Island of Barbadoes* (1657, 54–55). See Sypher 1942, 122–37.

98. **Lavina** . . . "The lovely young Lavinia," poor but virtuous, in *The Seasons* ("Autumn") by the very popular James Thomson (see Introduction, n. 56) has a tragic affair with her social superior Palemon, "the pride of swains . . . the generous, the rich."

99. **For every Rebel Prisoner a reward is paid** . . . By 1685, the colonial government had already established bounties for the capture of maroons. At first, it was set at five guilders; two years later it was increased to three hundred pounds of sugar if the maroon had been expressly hunted down, and one hundred pounds otherwise; in 1698, it was increased to twenty-five

to fifty guilders, depending on the specific circumstances of capture; and in 1717 bounties of fifteen hundred guilders each were earmarked for the discovery of two notorious Maroon villages, and six hundred guilders for any other village, plus a ten-guilder bonus per inhabitant (which was later expanded to the granting of freedom in addition to the usual bounty to any slave or maroon who disclosed the whereabouts of a Maroon village) (Hartsinck 1770, 2: 756–57). Stedman describes bounties during the 1770s on page 387.

107. the rebels being apprized . . . by theyr Spies . . . Maroon intelligence was well organized and efficient, consisting of slave informers, Maroons who allowed themselves to be recaptured only to escape again, and double agents (R. Price 1983a, 1983b).

111. in this hot Country where putrefaction so very soon takes place . . . In fact, modern non-Christian Maroons bury their dead only after many days, the number increasing with the dead person's social status and reaching two months or more for the tribal chief.

111. *putred-fever* . . . Stedman appears to be describing jaundice caused by yellow fever.

111. *Belly-hatty* or dry Gripes . . . Apparently caused by drinking rum that had been contaminated by lead during the manufacturing process. For details on this ailment, which was widespread in the eighteenth-century West Indies, see Handler et al. 1986.

114. *Akera* and *Gowsary* two desperados . . . Akara and Gousari, leaders of the Berbice rebellion under Coffy, surrendered after Coffy's downfall and offered their services to the Europeans. As scouts and rebel-catchers, they were credited with bringing in some six hundred rebels in Berbice and were granted a full pardon. Fourgeoud, who was sent out from the Netherlands as commander of the state troops in Berbice after the rebellion, met Akara and Gousari there and, in 1765, they were brought to the Netherlands as part of a regular regiment. Fourgeoud was responsible for bringing them to Suriname (Blair 1984, 74–75).

114. Merian, Zeba and some random Historians . . . On Merian, see note to page 9; Albertus Seba (1665–1736) was a Dutch naturalist who visited the tropics and made a collection, which was sold to Peter the Great. His major work was *Locupletissimi rerum naturalium thesauri accurata desciptio et iconibus-expressio per universam physicis historiam* (Amstedam, 1734–63). On Hartsinck, see note to page 53. John Benjamin Wesley (1703–91), Methodist leader, wrote a natural history to which Stedman occasionally refers: *A survey of the wisdom of God in the creation; or, A compendium of natural philosophy* (Bristol, 1763).

115. a *Jewes*[s] . . . Stedman's depiction of Jews as particularly cruel masters and mistresses perpetuated a longstanding Suriname stereotype. However, modern scholarship, based on archival research, suggests that there is no factual basis for such charges (Hoogbergen 1985, 37–38).

117. card Money . . . Because of a shortage of silver coin, cardboard money resembling playing cards was introduced for local use in Suriname in 1761. See, for illustrations, Schiltkamp and de Smidt 1973, pls. 10–16.

120. Gordons Geographical Gramar . . . Patrick Gordon, *Geography Anatomiz'd: Or, The Compleat Geographical Grammar. Being a Short and Exact Analysis Of the whole Body of Modern Geography, after a New and Curious Method*, 2d ed. (London, 1699). Stedman's description in fact closely followed Gordon's: "In some Rivers of *Guiana*, is a certain little Fish, about the Bigness of a Smelt, and remarkable for having Four Eyes, two on each side, one above the other; and in swimming, 'tis observ'd to keep the uppermost two above, and the other two under Water" (ibid., 359).

124. cutting of[f] the Heads of the Slain . . . Although Stedman interprets the Maroons' headcutting as trophy taking, the practice in fact involved a whole complex of ritual and belief relating both to self-protection against the avenging spirit of the deceased and to central West African-derived notions of manhood. The proper handling of a severed head was undoubtedly complex. The related hunting rites carried out by modern Maroons after killing a large animal (especially a tapir) have the same goal—to settle its spirit so it will not return to take vengeance. For further discussion, see R. Price 1983a, 145–46.

127. Doctor *Armstrongs* beautiful poem . . . John Armstrong (1709–79), poet, physician, and essayist, was author of the didactic poem *The Art of Preserving Health* (London, 1744).

131. in what manner heavy loaded Muscatoons ought always to be fired . . . Until the middle of the twentieth century, most Saramaka Maroons fired their shotguns (used for hunting) in this same "under the hand" manner, rather than from the shoulder, because of the uncertainties of the force of the homemade charge.

134. a Negro Woman and sucking Child who had formerly been Stole by the Rebels, and had now found means to make her Escape . . . It was not uncommon for slave women who were taken by Maroons on raids to attempt to return to their plantations, almost always because of conjugal or kin ties there.

134. Several Jews were Soldiers . . . The Jewish population of mid-eighteenth-century Suriname, largely descended from Portuguese Jews who had arrived as already-experienced sugar planters via Brazil, was concentrated on the Suriname River plantations, with the settlement of Jews Savannah (see pl. 70) their center. A separate Jewish militia was very active in pursuing escaped slaves during the first half of the eighteenth century, and Jewish soldiers played a special role in many of the massive anti-Maroon military operations of the middle of the century (R. Price 1983b).

136. Sharp Pins stuck in the Ground . . . The use of such devices was not limited to this village (R. Price 1979b, 6).

136. ryst, Yams and Casadas . . . Stedman sprinkles his text with information about Maroon crops and other foods. Together with the more detailed eighteenth-century missionary diaries and dictionary from Saramaka (R.

Price n.d.), his reports permit a rather full reconstruction of Maroon diet, the staples of which were (unirrigated or hillside) rice and manioc (cassava), combined with a variety of root crops, plantains, maize, peanuts, okra, capsicum, and many other cultigens. See also notes to pages 309, 536, and 563.

139. *Ah Poty backera* . . . "Ah, poor whitefolks."

140. Letters to Holland with an account of his already begun Exploits . . . Fourgeoud's correspondence is now in the Algemeen Rijksarchief (Coll. Fagel), the Hague.

148. the Negro's now cut him in Slices in order to dress him and eat part of him . . . Neither the killing nor the eating of anacondas is conceivable by twentieth-century Maroons who, like contemporary coastal Afro-Surinamers, consider them vehicles of important deities, with the power to become avenging spirits. Among Saramaka Maroons, these beliefs were clearly present during Stedman's time (R. Price n.d.). Perhaps Stedman's companions in this venture were slaves who hailed from African societies in which such snakes were not sacred. Stedman himself describes the ways boa constrictors were venerated (p. 522), as they still are today, but unlike Saramakas he does not view them and anacondas as vehicles for two closely related deities.

148. M: Parkinsons Museums . . . In 1795, Stedman presented "eighteen Surinam curiosities" to James Parkinson's Leverian Museum, which since the mid-1780s had been attracting crowds in London (1795). See also note to page 540.

153. I was now obliged to make Slaves to Soldiers . . . Stedman's fears were not idle. Throughout the early and mid-eighteenth century, it had been customary for slaves to constitute the numerical core of antimaroon military expeditions, but their role was almost always as unarmed bearers. Even so, the threat that these unarmed slaves posed keenly worried the white commanders and troops, as vividly evidenced in the documents in R. Price 1983b.

155. the Negro Slaves being interspersed between the Men to be guarded themselves . . . The fear of slaves on such military expeditions deserting to the enemy was realistic. The extensive documents in R. Price 1983b demonstrate that it was not unusual for 50 percent of the slaves on some of the larger eighteenth-century expeditions to desert, in spite of the extraordinary measures taken to surround them at night with armed guards.

163. *Ring-Worm* . . . A mycosis that particularly plagued newly arrived Europeans in Suriname. A Moravian contemporary of Stedman in Suriname wrote,

> [In 1780] I was itching all over. . . . There were little red rings, the size of sixpence coins, all over my body. . . . This itching never gave me any peace . . . and even though I tried to tie my hands together so I wouldn't scratch, I could never sleep more than a half hour at a time.

The only way I could find relief was to disrobe and throw myself into the Suriname River, but I had to keep constantly moving so I wouldn't be attacked by the piranhas. (Staehelin 1913–19, 3[2]: 226)

168. M: Clarkson's Essays . . . Thomas Clarkson (1760–1846), a leading abolitionist who, with Wilberforce, was largely responsible for getting passed the 1807 act abolishing the British slave trade. The essays to which Stedman refers were *An Essay on the Slavery and Commerce of the Human Species, particularly the African* (1786), and *An Essay on the Impolicy of the African Slave Trade* (1788).

170. These 100000 [Africans] . . . transported yearly . . . Modern estimates for the 1780s would place the annual number of Africans transported at closer to 60,000 (Curtin 1969, 266).

172. Bottany Bay . . . Botany Bay (New South Wales) was visited in 1770 by Captain Cook, who proclaimed British sovereignty over the entire east coast of Australia. In 1788, the first British settlement, a penal colony, was established.

172. 20000 *Ouca* and *Serameca* free Negroes . . . For Auka (Djuka) and Saramaka population figures, see note to page 75.

173. Abe *Renald* . . . Abbé G. T. F. Raynal, author of the *Histoire philosophique et politique des établissements et du commerce des Européens dans les deux Indes*, 8 vols. (The Hague, 1774), translated as *A Philosophical and Political History of the Settlements and Trade of the Europeans in the East and West Indies*. For British readers this was "the best known . . . anti-slavery manifesto of the French Enlightenment. . . . Between 1776 and 1806 the work appeared in no less than fifteen English editions" (Anstey 1975, 123).

174. all Captains are not *Cooling Woods* . . . See note to page 81.

175. the Negroes are composed of different Nations or Casts . . . The interpretation of such lists, produced by many colonial writers, contains multiple pitfalls. A summary of information on the African provenience of peoples referred to by Stedman's labels would include: *abo*—from what is now northwestern Cameroon; *bonia*—uncertain; *blitay*—possibly from Togo; *Coromantin*—the Dutch shipped Fantis, Ashantis, and members of other interior Gold Coast peoples through their fort at Koromantin; *Congo*—various Bantu-speaking peoples were shipped under this label from the ports at the mouth of the Congo; *gango*—Mandingo from what is now Southwestern Mali; *konare*—uncertain; *kiemba*—uncertain; *Loango*—from the great kingdom and port of that name near the mouth of the Congo, through which large numbers of slaves were shipped to Suriname; *N'Zoko*—uncertain, because both Bantu-speaking and interior Gold Coast peoples have similar names; *Nago*—the Ewe word for Nigerian Yorubas; *Papa*—from the area around Grand and Little Popo, in what is now Togo; *pombo*—a term derived from Mpumbu, the Kongo word for Malebo [Stanley] Pool on the Congo [Zaire] River, used in colonial accounts to refer to a large region in the interior of the Kongo; *wanway*—an interior Gold Coast people. (N.B. In the 1796 edition [1:207] *bonia* became *Conia* and *kiemba*,

Riemba, leaving unclear Stedman's own intentions.) For more detailed discussion of the African provenience of Suriname slaves, with references to a number of other colonial lists besides Stedman's, see R. Price 1976, 13–16. In general, Bantu-speaking slaves from Loango/Angola made up one-fourth to one-third of all imports to Suriname, with most of the remainder, during Stedman's day, coming from what is now Guinea, Sierra Leone, Liberia, Ivory Coast, and Ghana. The Slave Coast (modern Togo and Benin)—Suriname's major supplier until 1735—was providing few new slaves by the 1770s (ibid.).

176. the Estate at present belonging to only two Masters . . . By the 1770s, particularly after the Amsterdam stock market crisis of 1773, planter absenteeism reached an all-time high for Suriname, with large numbers of plantations being put into receivership.

176. two *more* Anchors of best Claret . . . An anker measured between 30 and 40 liters of wine.

176. like Doctor Slop by Obadiah . . . Stedman's allusion is to Laurence Sterne's *The Life and Opinions of Tristram Shandy, Gentleman* (1760, bk. 2, chap. 9), where the comic "man-midwife" Doctor Slop, surprised by Obadiah on his horse, "left his [own] pony to its destiny, tumbling off it diagonally . . . being left . . . with the broadest part of him sunk about twelve inches deep in the mire."

177. the Celebrated Count De Buffon . . . Georges Louis Leclerc, Comte de Buffon (1707–88). French naturalist and academician. His magnum opus was *Histoire naturelle, générale et particulière, avec la description du Cabinet du Roi,* 44 vols. (Paris, 1749–1804). Stedman seems to have used the first or second edition of Smellie's English translation, which we have been unable to examine. Instead, we have consulted the (apparently very similar) third edition—*Natural History, General and Particular,* trans. William Smellie (London, 1791)—in which the page references also correspond to Stedman's citations.

178. Cotton . . . which has only been Cultivated in Surinam since about the Year 1735 . . . Small amounts of cotton had in fact been exported since the first decade of the century (van Lier 1971, 459) but it became economically significant only in the 1760s. By the 1780s, its value was approximately 40 percent as much as the colony's sugar exports (R. Price 1976, 18).

181. hats wigs. bottles and Glasses flew out at his Window . . . John Greenwood (1727–92), an American painter who spent nearly six years in Suriname, depicted a similar scene in his "Sea Captains Carousing in Surinam" (1758), now in the St. Louis Art Museum. (For a reproduction of this painting, see R. Price n.d.)

183. from which it takes its Name . . . It was called Sporkesgift.

184. *kay Mimasera da wan See Cow* . . . "[Exclamation] Master! That's a seacow."

188. one *bony* a relentless Mullatto . . . About 1765, the thirty-five-year-old Boni, together with his senior, Aluku, became joint leaders of the largest rebel group. Born in the forest, as Stedman notes, Boni had, according to different sources, either a white or an Indian father. Stedman is incorrect in asserting that Boni was not involved with Baron at Boucou; indeed, it was Boni, not Baron, who was chief of that fortress-village. It was sometime before Fourgeoud's conquest of "Rice Country," in 1773, that Baron and some fifty others left Boni's group. (For details, see Hoogbergen 1985, 78–85).

199. like Mahomet betwixt the two Load Stones . . . After Islamist colleagues in Baltimore and elsewhere failed to elucidate this reference, we wrote a note saying that we were unable to identify its source. But while this critical edition was in production, we received a letter from Claude Lévi-Strauss, who had noticed the lacuna in our already published commentary on Stedman's "Poetical Epistle" (R. and S. Price 1985). The relevant portion (in translation) reads as follows:

> In seventeenth- and eighteenth-century Europe, a widespread legend held that Mohammed's coffin, made of iron, was under an arch of loadstones, which held it suspended in mid-air. . . . This was an ancient legend, applied only later to Mohammed. In his *Natural History* (book 34, end of chapter 14), Pliny attributed its origin to an Egyptian king. Authors from the beginning of the Christian era (Ausone, St. Augustine) also mentioned it. I believe that it was an Arabist from Oxford named Pockoke or Pokoke who, in the seventeenth century, made the connection with Mohammed's tomb. But there are a number of variations on the theme in the literature of antiquity. There is nothing surprising, then, that it was familiar to a man of the eighteenth century.

201. *feegh Shinder-kneghte* . . . This German curse permits multiple translations, from "cowardly knacker" to "rotten nigger driver."
204. Panting Corviser . . . This may be an allusion to a tale or fable concerning a shoemaker (corviser), but we have been unable to identify it.
205. *houndsfuss* . . . German, "scoundrel."
206. one of whom call'd *Pass-up* . . . See note to page 524.
208. that line with which Smollet begins his Roderic Random . . . *Roderick Random* (like *Tom Jones,* as mentioned in our Introduction) was one of Stedman's favorite books. This Horatian adage appeared on the title page of each of the two volumes of the 1748 first edition.
210. Doctor Cook . . . We have been unable to identify this authority.
211. Do. Bancroft says . . . See note to page 51.
211. vide Westlys Philosophy . . . See note to page 114.
211. In the Town of Maestricht . . . Stedman writes here from personal experience, having himself lived in Maastricht.
214. grog . . . After "Old Grog," the nickname of Admiral Edward Vernon, who habitually wore a grogram cloak in foul weather and who, in 1740, issued the order that British sailors' rum ration would henceforth be diluted

to prevent drunkenness. Grog referred to any unsweetened mixture of rum and water, but the usual mixture was a ratio of 1:2.

215. the rich Man *Dious* when he beg'd Water from Lazarus . . . Stedman alludes here to Luke 16.24, part of the parable of the rich man and Lazarus.

216. creeping on all fours like Nebuchadnezar . . . Stedman alludes here to Daniel 4.33.

216. the berbician Negro Gausarie . . . See note to page 114.

218. the bloody flux . . . Probably acute bacillary dysentery.

220. *Consaca* . . . The Sranan word for a mycosis, like athlete's foot, that is highly vulnerable to secondary bacterial infection in the tropics.

222. open Sores and ulcers . . . Possibly filariasis with secondary infections, but an alternative possibility is "bush-yaws" (leishmaniasis).

224. Harway, Needham, Bradley, . . . Sir *Joseph Banks* . . . Harway, possibly William Harvey (1578–1657), who wrote extensively on animal anatomy and behavior; John Tuberville Needham (1713–81), English physician and naturalist whose main work was *Microscopical discoveries in the natural history of animals, plants, etc.* (London, 1745); Bradley, possibly Richard Bradley (d. 1732), author of popular horticultural manuals and professor of botany at the University of Cambridge from 1712 until his removal for "unbecoming conduct"; Sir Joseph Banks (1743–1820), English naturalist who sailed with Cook around the world, was president of the Royal Society from 1778, and was honorary director of the Royal Botanical Gardens at Kew.

225. these Mountains might be made of use in finding Metals . . . In fact, the major twentieth-century wealth of Suriname is contained in its bauxite deposits.

225. *Cosivail Mondo* . . . *Cosí va il mondo.* Italian, "that's the way the world goes."

225. the Spanish Duke D'Alba . . . Being brought up in the Netherlands, Stedman would have been familiar with the strength of legends about the Spanish occupation of the sixteenth century. Often described as ruthless and fanatical, the Duke of Alba (1507–82), who was Philip II's captain- and governor-general in the Netherlands, tried to crush local attempts at religious toleration and political self-government. Leiden still actively celebrates the lifting of the famous siege of 1574.

226. the Honble Gen! *Stuart* . . . The Honorable General John Stuart, titular commander of Stedman's regiment in the Scots Brigade.

227. improved from Miss Merian . . . Stedman based his drawing (pl. 29) on Merian's plate 9 (see notes to p. 9).

229. *Bampfield-Moore-Carew* . . . Stedman's "kindred spirit," the King of the Gypsies near whom he was buried. See Introduction, note 4.

229. *Hannibal* had lost his Army at *Capua* . . . Stedman here alludes to the battle during the Second Punic War in which Capua was retaken by Rome (211 B.C.).

230. to keep from Starvation only, having been theyr Motive . . . The motives of "rebels" who turned themselves in to the whites were as difficult for the whites to judge as those of new maroons who turned up in the rebels' camps were for the rebels to judge. In the first case, given the destruction of crops and forced mobility of rebels in the Cottica area, starvation may indeed have been at play, but Maroon groups also frequently ran spies by having members of their groups "desert" back to the whites to gather intelligence and then escape again (R. Price 1983a). And slaves liberated by the Maroons sometimes chose, for family or other reasons, to escape back, on their own initiative, to slavery (see, for example, p. 134).

233. **that [house] lately built by Governor Nepvew** . . . Nepveu's house at Gravenstraat 6 was built in 1774 and named "Cura et Vigilantia." It is today owned by the government. For a description and illustrations, see Temminck Groll 1973, 125–30.

233. **the Negro-Slaves excepted, who mostly lay on the Ground** . . . Saramakas still remember having to sleep on the ground on banana leaves, instead of in hammocks, as one of the most vivid humiliations of slavery (R. Price 1983a, 77).

236. **an European Man or Maid Servant being almost never to be met with** . . . During the first decades of Suriname's colonial history, indentured Europeans labored alongside Indian and African slaves, but by the time of Stedman's visit to be white meant to be free and (aside from a scant one percent) to be black meant to be a slave.

236. **The Negro Slaves never receiving Paper Money** . . . The 1796 edition adds as prime reason that "as they cannot read they do not understand its value" (1:290).

239. *Caleebasee* **(that is a Maid)** . . . The fruit of the calabash tree (*Crescentia cujete*) plays a number of related symbolic roles regarding female sexuality and fertility in Suriname; the act of breaking or smashing a calabash may, for example, be part of rituals of divorce and childbirth.

240. **they keep singing a loud Chorus** . . . This is a rare reference for Suriname of African women singing in chorus while performing labor; Stedman also describes (but in more detail) male slaves singing while rowing: see note to page 516.

241. **Negro fisher-Men** . . . Slave fishermen enjoyed special privileges throughout the Caribbean, in part because of their access to boats with which they could, if they desired, escape (R. Price 1966). Suriname fishing slaves are also mentioned in a 1749 document (R. Price 1983b, 81).

241. **I have known Slaves, to *buy* Slaves for their own use** . . . The practice of slaves owning slaves, though not common, is mentioned several times by Stedman; at the time of her death, Joanna owned a female slave (p. 625). The practice of masters permitting their slaves to hire themselves out independently and remit a fixed sum to the master each week was common throughout the eighteenth-century Caribbean; men ranged from carpenters to blacksmiths, and women were often prostitutes (R. Price 1966).

244. **Sir Hans Sloane** . . . Sir Hans Sloane (1660–1753), British physician

whose collection of books, manuscripts, plants, animals, and ethnographica formed the basis of the British Museum. Sloane visited Jamaica, Barbados, and other West Indian islands during the 1680s.

245. Hider-Aly . . . Haider Ali (1722–82) was the brilliant military ruler of Mysore who, from the 1760s until shortly before his death, successfully expanded his kingdom, several times badly defeating British forces.

246. what *Voltaire* says in his Candide . . . For the relevant passage from *Candide,* see the opening paragraph of our Introduction.

250. Of the Deer Species there are in Guiana 2 kinds . . . In fact, there are at least three species of deer in Suriname, but Stedman's descriptions and depictions (pl. 33) omit the most common variety, the Large Red Brocket (*Mazama americana americana* [Erxleben]). See Appendix A, s.v. *Bajew; bossee cabritta.*

254. M^ch 28.73 . . . This is Stedman's shorthand reference to his own diary entry for 28 March 1773, which describes a visit to Schoonvort and other plantations.

255. Sugar Cane, which is supposed to be natural to Guiana . . . Van Lier claims that sugar—which is not in fact native to the New World—was introduced into Suriname by the French in 1640 (1971, 461). In the 1796 edition, Stedman adds that sugar was first refined in Suriname in 1659 (1796, 1:317).

259. geneva . . . Genever, Dutch gin.

259. Wooden-locks and keys . . . Wooden door locks, using mechanisms that were widespread in Africa, were reported as well by Hartsinck for eighteenth-century Suriname (1770, 17), and they continued to be manufactured by coastal Afro-Surinamers well into the twentieth century (van Panhuys 1925, 273). For examples made by Suriname Maroons, see S. and R. Price 1980, figs. 144–46.

261. Spoken . . . by George Dallas'd Esqr at Calcutta . . . George Dallas (1758–1833) quoted Addison's "Epistle" at a 1785 meeting of opponents to Pitt's East India Bill and was deputed by the local British community to present a petition against the bill to the House of Commons.

270. *Leander* had determined to visit Hero . . . Leander and Hero, lovers celebrated in Greek mythology, whose story was preserved by poets from Ovid to Marlowe. Leander died while swimming the Hellespont at night to meet Hero.

270. Flora Macdonald and Genny Cameron . . . Flora Macdonald was the Scottish Jacobite heroine who helped Bonnie Prince Charlie to escape from Scotland to France in 1746. Jenny Cameron's alleged romance with the Young Pretender captured the popular imagination at mid-century, forming the basis for a grubstreet novel and earning a brief mention in *Tom Jones* (bk. 11, chap. 2). Their relationship appears to have been a fabrication, and Jenny Cameron seems not to have participated in the prince's escape; the widely discussed story constitutes "one of the most obscure affairs connected with the insurrection" (Chambers 1869, 251).

271. "true to the Europeans" ... Precious metal ornaments engraved with similar marks of planter gratitude are reported elsewhere for eighteenth-century Suriname: in 1730, Stedman's "celebrated Graman Quacy" (engraved by Blake in pl. 76) had been given "a golden breastplate on which was inscribed 'Quassie, faithful to the whites'" (van Sijpesteijn 1858, 92).

271. *Jolly Coeur* ... **one of the fiercest Rebels in the forest** ... Joanna's uncle's account of Joli Coeur's revenge on Schültz, his former plantation manager, is complemented by that of two other eyewitnesses, one claiming that Joli Coeur killed the plantation's white overseer while Boni himself shot Schültz, the other that Joli Coeur brought Schültz to Boni who then shot him (Hoogbergen 1985, 84–85).

277. at Paramaribo an insurrection was discovered amongst the Negroes ... A half-century later, the planters were not so fortunate. In 1832, three young slaves led an insurrection and succeeded in burning down much of the capital before being captured and brutally executed.

279. sent their heads barbacued to Paramaribo ... In the 1796 edition, the barbecued heads became "right hands." The latter were, in fact, often used during the eighteenth century as tokens that a maroon had been killed, each right hand being worth a bounty (see p. 387). Stories about the taking of Chief Boni's head circulated widely in the colony over many years; modern versions and analyses may be found in de Groot 1980, Hoogbergen 1985, and Pakosie 1972.

282. ouca-Negroes, /who were our alies by treaty/ ... The Auca, more commonly called Djuka, signed a treaty with the government in 1760. Something of their complex attitudes toward the Boni during the 1770s can be gleaned from the documents in de Beet 1984 and Hoogbergen 1984, and from de Groot 1975 and Hoogbergen 1985.

283. my friend M: Heneman ... J. C. Heneman (1738–1806), military engineer and the most important cartographer of eighteenth-century Suriname. His two great maps of the colony, completed in 1784 and 1787, are at scales of 1:177,000 and 1:40,000, respectively (Bubberman et al. 1973, 65–66).

285. the late Duke of Brunswick-wolfenbuttel ... See Introduction, n. 35 (7).

289. a Medicine he cal'd *teasan* ... In French (Fourgeoud's native language), *tisane* refers to an infusion or decoction, usually of herbs.

290. but even King-*Solomon* **supports** ... "Go to the ant, thou sluggard; consider her ways, and be wise:/ Which having no guide, overseer, or ruler,/ Provideth her meat in the summer, *and* gathereth her food in the harvest" (Proverbs 6.6–8).

292. *Loango-Dancing* ... Although rapid religious syncretisms among slaves of diverse African provenience were an earmark of colonial Suriname's first one hundred years (R. Price 1976), rituals and other performances associated with Loango, Papa, Nago, and other "nations" were still an important feature of late eighteenth-century plantation life. About seventy percent of plantation slaves were still African-born, with some thirty-five percent having arrived during the previous ten years (ibid.), so the occasional assertion of African ethnicity seems hardly surprising. In contrast, by Stedman's time similarly named performances among the Saramaka Maroons (e.g., "Luángu" or "Papá" rites and dances) clearly included people and ideas of quite varied African ancestry; there were hardly any African-born Saramakas still alive, and marriage was not in any sense endogamous by place of origin. Stedman's allusions to spirit possession are not intended to be limited to "Loangos"; it was and remains a central feature of Afro-Suriname religions in general. For a discussion of Luango dancing and rites among the modern descendants of Suriname slaves in the Para region, see Wooding 1981, 166–72.

293. European dancing as the height of incipidity . . . The 1796 edition adds here a lengthy footnote describing (in the words of Emanuel Martinus) Spanish fandangos, which are so lascivious that the whole quotation—except for one word in Greek—is printed in Latin (1:365).

299. John Hunter Esq*r* F.R.S. . . . John Hunter (1728–93), a leading London anatomist and surgeon who, among his many other studies, explored natural history and comparative embryology.

302. Caribbees . . . Piannacotaws . . . Stedman's "Caribbees" are the Caribs (Kalina or Galibi), most of whose descendants today live along the lower Marowijne in coastal Suriname, though during Stedman's time the great bulk of Caribs in the Guianas lived outside Suriname's borders, to the west. His "Accawans" are the Akawaio, whose descendants live in the interior of Guyana. His "Worrows" are the Warau, whose descendants live in the delta of the Orinoco. His "arrowouks" are the Arawaks, whose descendants live in coastal Suriname. His "tawiras" might be the group sometimes called "Attoria" (Menezes 1977, 20); they might be the Taira who lived in the interior of what is now French Guiana, next to the Emerillon near the Brazilian border; but our own reading of Hartsinck (1770, 3), whence Stedman apparently got the term, suggests that Stedman might simply have misunderstood that writer, who was not naming a "tribe" but rather an Indian term allegedly meaning coastal, as opposed to inland, Indians. Finally, Stedman's "Piannacotaws" are the Pianakotos, a Carib group that lived far inland, from the upper Corantijn toward the east, along the Suriname-Brazil border (Benjamins and Snelleman 1914–17, 175).

303. the most Plausible Causes why the Americans are a Copper-Colour . . . Environmental explanations of skin color were, by the time Stedman wrote, part of received wisdom, in spite of the several contradictions they encapsulated. They were accompanied by a widespread belief, deriving from Erasmus Darwin and Lamarck, that the effects of environmental influences were, at least to some degree, inherited (Jordan 1968, 13–20, 240–52, passim; see also Todd 1946).

304. the Speech of an Indian in reply to a Sermon . . . This may be a reference to the treaty signed by William Penn, the Susquehannas, and a band of Shawnees at Conestoga Creek in 1701.

304. Moravian Preachers . . . The Moravians, who arrived in Suriname in 1735, were the first missionaries who actively proselytized among slaves, Indians, and Maroons. In 1757 they established an Indian mission on the Saramacca River; eight years later they began to work with the Saramaka Maroons; but the first slave was baptized by them in Paramaribo only in 1776, owing to widespread planter disapproval (see note to p. 341). Today the Moravian church (Evangelische Broedergemeente) is the largest Protestant denomination in Suriname.

304. All the Guiana Indians believe in God. . . . But they *Worship* the Devil whom they Call *Yawahoo* . . . Stedman's understanding of Suriname Indian religions is slight and derivative. The idea that "Yawahoo" is the Devil is copied, like a good deal of Stedman's Indian "ethnography," from Hartsinck (1770, 33), who himself never set foot in Suriname. In fact, Yawahu or Yoleka is an evil spirit of the Caribs which causes sickness and misfortune (Benjamins and Snelleman 1914–17, 110).

304. *Peii*, or *Pagayers* . . . *Pïyei* is the Carib word for shamans who, in trance, communicate directly with the spirit world (see Kloos 1971, 209–33).

306. *Camisa* . . . This word continues to be used by Indians and Afro-Surinamers today to refer to loincloths or breechcloths, not (as in Spanish or Portuguese) to shirts.

306. *Queiou* . . . Twentieth-century Indian women and Maroon teenage girls continue to wear similar aprons, called in Saramaccan *koyó*.

308. *Cotton Garters* . . . These characteristic Indian legbands were adapted and developed by Suriname Maroons, drawing also on African models, and continue to be worn today. For historical and contemporary illustrations, see S. and R. Price 1980, figs. 49, 52, 273.

308. *Caracoly* . . . Kulukuli is the Carib word for gold trinkets, and close cognates refer in Arawak to brass, and in Wayana to silver.

308. *Carbets* . . . Although the provenience of this word troubled van Lier (1971, 464), it is the standard Island Carib term for their houses. Like a good deal of Stedman's Amerindian ethnographic description (which followed Hartsinck, Fermin, and others), it ultimately comes from Labat and other travel authorities who reported on life in the insular Caribbean—where Europeans had already been living in contact with Indians for a long time—rather than from experience on the mainland. A solid, traditional overview of Suriname Indian ethnography may be found in Benjamins and Snelleman 1914–17, 101–17, 170–77.

308. *Calebasses* or *gourds* . . . Suriname Indians used both calabashes (the fruit of *Crescentia cujete*), which grow on trees, and gourds (*Lagenaria siceraria*), which grow on vines. For details, see S. Price 1982.

309. The Manner in which the Indians prepare it [manioc] . . . Stedman's description slightly simplifies the standard preparation of manioc roots for cooking. Suriname Indians generally grated the roots on a wooden board into which sharp pebbles had been fixed with gum (rather than grinding it on a stone), then squeezed it as he described in a *"matappy,"* then sifted the flour in a basketry sieve (*"manary"*), before baking it on a griddle into bread.

309. Experimental Proof taken of this Poison . . . Manioc contains hydrocyanic, or prussic, acid, in variable concentrations, which must be expelled or transformed by cooking before it can be eaten. We have been unable to examine Fermin 1769 to locate the precise reference.

310. the *Sweet or innocent* Cassava Root . . . In fact, one species (*Manihot esculenta*) includes both the "bitter" and the "sweet" manioc or cassava root.

310. all these beveridges are inebriating . . . For discussion of the uses of *kasilí* and other alcoholic drinks among modern Caribs, see Kloos 1971.

312. the *woorara* poison . . . As prepared by Suriname Indians, the main ingredient of curare (Carib *urali*) is *Strychnos guianensis,* a liana whose roots are boiled with other ingredients to make the arrow poison (Ostendorf 1962, 186–87).

313. Baskets . . . cal'd *Pagala* . . . For illustrations of modern examples, see Wilbert 1975, 70.

314. Doctor Smollets discription of a burial . . . Van Lier (1971, 465) attributes this reference to a book we have been unable to examine: Tobias George Smollet's *The Present State of All Nations, Containing a Geographical, Natural, Commercial and Political History of All the Countries in the Known World* (London, 1768–69). As mentioned in our Introduction, Stedman was a devotee of Smollet's novels, and his autobiographical sketch (*1786*) clearly alludes to events in *Roderick Random,* which he says he read; in fact, it seems likely that Smollet's *Peregrine Pickle* and *Humphry Clinker* also influenced the manner in which Stedman depicted himself in that work.

315. these kind of Slaves are only for Show and Parade . . . During the seventeenth century, significant numbers of Guiana Indian slaves worked on Suriname plantations alongside Africans. During the eighteenth century, Indian slaves were regularly sold to planters in the Lesser Antilles, who used them both in domestic roles and to hunt and fish for their tables (R. Price 1976, 7–8; 1966, 1368). A rather extensive slave trade between the Caribs and the Dutch flourished between the mid-seventeenth and early nineteenth centuries (Whitehead 1987).

315. Three famous battles . . . Stedman's dating of these Hundred Years' War battles is inexact; the English defeated the French at Crecy in 1346, at Poitiers in 1356, and at Agincourt in 1415.

315. the Honourable Daines Barrington . . . Apparently a reference to Daines Barrington (1727–1800), who was a judge, antiquarian, and naturalist. His connection to archery is not mentioned in such biographical sources as the *Dictionary of Welsh Biography.*

316. Don Antonio *Ulloa* . . . Antonio de Ulloa (1716–95), Spanish naval officer and scientist who lived for some years in Peru and published works on South America.

318. **furniture, ornaments, and Arms [of the Indians]** . . . See note to page 540.

318. **A bow tow or Indian Club** . . . In the 1796 edition, the club is called *apatou*, its Suriname Carib name. Stedman's initial use of "bow tow" (*boutou*), which is the Island Carib name for this implement, again suggests the mixed sources from which Stedman's Amerindian ethnography sprang.

320. **the Ingenious *Doctor Bancroft*** . . . Stedman appears to be publicly, if indirectly, acknowledging his scholarly debt to Bancroft—and he could have added the names of Hartsinck and Fermin—for his Amerindian ethnography, a part of his book (like the portions on general geography and historical background) that is not based on his personal experience.

322. **the Playhouse where the *Death of Caesar* and *Crispin-Doctor* were Performed** . . . The Playhouse was brand-new at the time. Stedman probably witnessed *De dood van Caesar*, a Dutch translation by Charles Sebeille of Voltaire's *La mort de Caesar*, and *Crispin Doctor*, a Dutch translation by de la Croix of Le Breton's *Crispin medecin* (van Lier 1971, 466).

323. **like Sir John Lade or Lord Molesworth** . . . We have been unable to identify this allusion.

324. **the Plantations were all Lay'd in Ashes by the Rebels in 1757** . . . Stedman refers here to the great Tempati rebellion of that year, in which hundreds of slaves on several plantations successfully rebelled, with many joining the Djuka Maroons.

324. ***Gold* and *Silver* Mines Might be met with** . . . Goldmining became an important economic activity during the late nineteenth and early twentieth centuries, until the alluvial deposits were apparently exhausted. During the 1980s, changing economic conditions reawakened interest in this activity. See also note to page 225.

329. ***Lord Munboddo*** . . . See note to page 515.

341. **he Could not yet be Christned** . . . Stedman here alludes to the fact that the major churches of the master class, the Dutch Reformed and the Lutheran, were generally opposed to the conversion of slaves. The Moravian and Roman Catholic churches, in contrast, were by Stedman's time beginning actively to seek converts among both slaves and Maroons. The large-scale conversion of Suriname slaves took place only during the second quarter of the nineteenth century (Van Lier 1949, chap. 6; Lamur 1985).

343. **f——tu B——gres** . . . "Foutu Bougres." French, roughly "damn buggers."

344. **Goldsmiths Animated Nature** . . . Oliver Goldsmith's *An history of the earth, and animated nature* (London: J. Nourse, 1774), which Jordan (1968, 254) describes as "indiscriminately eclectic."

348. **an Inverted Straight Trump or Tube** . . . Trump (obs.) meant "proboscis."

349. **M*r Allamand* in the *Count-De-Bufon*** . . . Johannes Allamand (1713–87), naturalist and professor in the Netherlands, was one of the contributors to Buffon's *Histoire Naturelle*. Stedman's citation may be found on the indi-

cated pages in the third English edition (see note to p. 177): "M. Allamand gave the first description and figure of it under the name of *grison,* in the 15th volume of the Dutch edition of my work."

352. he proposed to me to Paint his Figure at Large ... The engraving modeled on Stedman's drawing is reproduced in our Introduction, fig. 2.

356. Bankes's Sistem of Geography ... Thomas Bankes et al., *A new royal authentic and complete system of universal geography antient and modern* (London, n.d. [ca. 1787]). The indicated page quotes *in extenso* Bosman's dramatic description of the capture of a tiger on the Gold Coast.

358. M.: *Sonini De Manoncourt* in *Buffons* Natural history ... M. Sonini de Manoncour contributed the section on "the JAGUAR of Guiana," which appears in the 1791 English edition in vol. 5, pp. 194–96.

358. M.: Fermyn, While he Compares it to a *Dog* ... Stedman probably used the Dutch translation of Fermin 1769, *Nieuwe algemeene beschrijving van de colonie van Suriname* (Harlingen, 1770). We have been unable to examine this volume to locate the precise reference.

367. M.: *Smiths* tour through the United States ... M.: *Glen's* Act of Barbarity ... John Ferdinand Dalziel Smyth (1745–1814), author of *A Tour in the United States of America,* 2 vols. (London, 1784), described how while visiting Virginia he and Mr. Glen went for a swim in the river: "whilst we were there, his wife and her sister, who were both young and handsome, came down to the water-side, and in a frolic hid our cloaths." The women soon disclosed the location of the clothes, and Smyth dressed. Glen, however, pursued his wife stark naked, brought her into the room where Smyth and the sister were, locked the door, and

> threw her down on the bed, and notwithstanding her utmost endeavors to prevent him and disengage herself, committed an act that a mere savage would have been ashamed to have attempted in public.
>
> This he would afterwards boast of in all companies, in the presence of his wife and every other lady, as an excellent joke, and prodigious piece of humour. (1784, 1:133)

381. the Court of *Polity,* and *Criminal* Justice ... Van Lier (1971, 469–70) corrects some of the details of Stedman's description of the composition of the courts as well as those, on subsequent pages, of the militia and the arms of Suriname.

384. Lord North ... Isaac Hopkins ... Frederick, 8th Lord North (1732–92), was prime minister of Great Britain during the American Revolution; Esek Hopkins (1718–1802) was a successful sea captain who became a naval hero during the Revolution and commander in chief of the Continental Navy.

386. Without the Consent of Parents ... no Respectable Slaves are *individually* Sold in Surinam ... Suriname indeed differed from most Caribbean slave societies in that, from the founding of the colony, it was standard policy not to break up slave families (mothers and children, husbands and wives) through sales. In general, slaves were sold not as individuals or family units but only as a large group, when the estate itself changed hands, and even this required special approval from the governor. Following the financial crisis on the Amsterdam stock exchange in 1773, with its attendant credit problems for Suriname planters, both absentee ownership and violations of these longstanding policies became more frequent, and it is possible that "respectable" (i.e., "house") slaves remained the main beneficiaries during this period. For discussion, see R. Price 1976, 19–20.

387. **the Rangers . . . Chop off the *right* hand of Ev'ry Rebel Negroe they Kill . . .** See note to page 99.

390. **hair . . . Plaited Close to his head, by way of Distinction from the Rangers . . .** Male hairbraiding continued to be a special prerogative of Suriname Maroons, in contrast to coastal Afro-Surinamers, well into the twentieth century (see, for illustrations, S. and R. Price 1980, figs. 42, 43).

392. **Sir *John* Reynolds . . .** Stedman's amanuensis apparently meant to write Sir Joshua Reynolds. See note to page 10.

392. **Messrs. *Cossway, Rigaud, Cross, Humphreys* . . .** Richard Cosway (1740–1821), well-known miniaturist who was born in Tiverton. John Francis Rigaud (d. 1810), a historical painter and member of the Royal Academy. Ozias Humphry (1742–1810), miniaturist and Royal Academician born in Devonshire. We are unable to identify Cross.

394. ***an Essay on the Subject of Chimistry* . . .** The correct reference is "On the Analogy between Animals and Vegetables," by Dr. Richard Watson, Lord Bishop of Llandaff (extracted from an unpublished pamphlet entitled "An Essay on the Subjects of Chemistry, and their General Division"), *European Magazine,* November 1784, 354–58.

395. ***Crassy-Crassy* . . .** The Sranan word for scabies.

398. **to Carry Away the Dead Body, And Prevent it from falling in the hands of the Adversary . . .** This practice, as well as what Stedman describes as "Mangling and tearing" the bodies of their slain adversaries, relates to rituals of power and protection (see note to p. 124).

398. **Mr. Smiths tour . . . in that Passage Where Major Lewis was kill'd . . .** In his *Tour* (see note to p. 367), Smyth describes the battle between twelve hundred white men and "the Shawnese, joined by the Delawares, and some other warriors of different nations, to the number of near nine hundred" (1784, 2:163). The "Major Lewis" whose death Smyth reports (2:167) was "Major Charles Lewis, a sensible, worthy, and enterprising man, and a brave gallant officer" (2:170).

405. **Clarksons essay on the Slave trade . . .** In fact, "Andrew Sparman, M.D. Professor of Physick at Stockholm" is quoted by Clarkson as reporting that "the balls discharged by them [the Dutch colonists] will sometimes . . . go through the bodies of six, seven, or eight of the enemy [the Hottentots] at a time" (1788, 46).

405. **like *Gill Blas* when he was amongst the Robbers . . .** In Alain-René Lesage's *Histoire de Gil Blas de Santillane* (Paris, 1715–35), the protagonist is

forced by his robber-captors to participate in a gun battle during which he looks the other way while firing in order not to be held accountable, in the next world, for murder (bk. 1, chap. 9).

408. both Parties Cursing And Menacing each other at a Terrible Rate ... Pitched verbal battles, replete with insults and threats, were frequent in encounters between Maroons and black government troops, whenever they were in close proximity, especially at night. For a striking example from 1755, see R. Price 1983b, 116.

409. The Hardships suffered since by the British Troops at Gibraltar ... The Great Siege of Gibraltar by Spanish (and French) troops (1779–83) inflicted terrible suffering on the defending forces.

409. See Guthry Page 685 ... See note for page 53. We have been unable to examine this work.

413. Which the Negroes Generally Adorn by Carving ... In his description of calabashes and their decoration, Stedman draws directly on the words of Fermin (which he probably read in the 1770 Dutch translation, unavailable to us): "Il y a des Negres qui gravent sur la convexité de ce fruit, des compartiments & des grotesques à leur maniere, dont ils remplissent ensuite les hachures de craie; ce qui fait un fort joli effet" (1769, 1:194).

423. a Letter Dated March 24 ... The letter from "I. H.," entitled "A Cure for the Bite of a Viper," is indeed found in the *Grand Magazine of Universal Intelligence* 1 (1758): 192–93.

426. See Jan 6—1774 ... The reference is to page 226.

426. *Gramans Qwacy,* A Celebrated And Cunning Old Negro ... See note to page 581.

426. According to M:ʳ *Bruce* ... James Bruce (1730–94), Scottish explorer of Africa and author of *Travels to discover the sources of the Nile, 1768–73* (first published as a whole in 1790, though Stedman must have seen portions of it earlier).

428. more Frightful than that of Tom Jones ... In *Tom Jones,* Fielding himself refers to the incident in question as "A most dreadful Chapter indeed; and which few Readers ought to venture upon in an Evening, especially when alone" (bk. 7, chap. 14).

429. a Bat is Represented With only but 3 Toes ... Stedman is correct: bats have five toes on each foot and five digits on each wing, including the rather distinctive thumb (which Stedman was presumably not counting). Buffon, however, clearly knows this (see the 1791 English edition, vol. 4, p. 318), and only the illustration (ibid., facing p. 324) appears to be faulty.

429. *Linaeus, Seba,* and M:ʳ *Vosmeer* ... Carolus Linnaeus (1707–78), the great Swedish botanist and taxonomist whose *Systema Naturae* (1735) and *Species Plantarum* (1753) established the basis for the binomial system of nomenclature and the modern classification of plants and animals. For Seba, see note to page 114. Arnaut Vosmaer (1720–99) was director of the natural history and art collection of Willem V, Prince of Orange. He edited and published part of Seba's natural history corpus and, in 1767, published at

Amsterdam the book to which Stedman probably refers: *Algemene natuurkundige en historische beschrijving der zeldzame en verwonderingswaardigste schepselen die gevonden worden in de Kabinetsverzameling en dergelijke van den heere prince erfstadthouder met nauwkeurig afbeeld.*

429. See Buffon Volume 5 Page 282 . . . Stedman is actually copying here from Buffon, who writes in the 1791 English edition (vol. 5, p. 282), "Linnaeus is wrong, when he says, that all bats have four cutting teeth in each jaw."

435. See Buffons Natural History Vol: 5 Page 398 . . . Stedman is correct about the mobility of the *paca,* as R. P. can attest from numerous hunting encounters in the Suriname forest. Buffon, in the 1791 English edition (vol. 5, p. 398) had erroneously written: "This animal, notwithstanding, is gross and corpulent. His body is neither delicate, nor smooth, nor nimble, but rather heavy and lurid, having nearly the gait of a small hog. He runs seldom, and, when he does, it is always with a bad grace."

442. M:̲ *Pater* . . . A group of Mr. Pater's slaves who escaped to the forest were apparently the ancestors of the modern Pata clan of the Djuka Maroons (Köbben 1967, 13–14).

444. as no *Tommohawk* is ever to be seen in All this Country . . . In the 1796 edition, Stedman substitutes in a footnote, "as we were at peace with all the *Indians,* and scalping was never practised by the *negroes*" (2:160). Stedman's unsupported attribution of scalping to Suriname Indians may be the only such mention in the literature on the colony (Benjamins and Snelleman 1914–17, 105). For an excellent analysis of scalping (and accusations of same) among Indian and European adversaries elsewhere in the Americas, see Axtell and Sturtevant 1980.

445. Bonys House . . . Stedman later built himself a house modeled on this one and in 1776 made a detailed pen-and-ink drawing of it (see Introduction, n. 35 [5]).

445. the Private Baths . . . Where his Women wash'd Themselves Morning and Evening . . . Maroon women's ablutions still occur in the privacy of small enclosures behind their houses. These warm herbal baths, applied particularly to the genital area, are intended both to counter female pollution and to enhance sexuality. See S. Price 1984, 203.

446. *Ants Hillocks* . . . Van Lier (1971, 472) suggests that these are nests of *Atta cephalotus.*

447. the Fable of the Man the Boy And the Ass . . . One of Poggio's fables, concerning the difficulties of an old man who, with a boy, took an ass to market and, by trying to please every person he encountered along the way, ended up displeasing them all and losing his ass in the bargain.

450. a Letter from his Mistress in Europe . . . In the 1796 edition (2:170), the letter from Magy Fowler that appears above on page 286 is, instead, reproduced at this point in the text.

453. none of his People were trusted with Arms Except such as had first served him some years as Slaves . . . Though Boni's sense of discipline, and the alleged length of the period during which he kept newcomers in servile roles, was extreme among Suriname Maroons (see also pp. 482 and 493), new maroons were perceived as a serious security threat by all established groups. For discussion and examples of the realities behind these fears, see R. Price 1983a, and for comparative materials on other Afro-American Maroons, see R. Price 1979b, 16–18.

453. Yorica Signifying the Devil . . . Though the Carib word *yoloka* refers to "spirits," in both Sranan and the Maroon languages *yorka* or *yooka* refers only to "ghosts," the spirits of the dead.

456. Lord Munbodo . . . See note to page 515.

457. the Watra Mama . . . A female water spirit that plays a role in Afro-Suriname religions and who has widespread antecedents in Africa. The animal that some observers confuse with this spirit is the manatee, which Stedman describes on page 453 and depicts in plate 59. An engraved depiction of a watra mama spirit, made by a Suriname slave shortly after Stedman's time, is found on a calabash now in the Völkerkundemuseum Herrnhut (Neumann 1961).

457. Chopt off the Limb of a Mullotto Child in Revenge to its Father . . . Maroons, like Suriname slaves, were deeply ambivalent about mulattoes, who were at once innocent victims of their parents' behavior (whether a white father's rape of a slave mother, or a mother's currying favor by sexual means), visible symbols of such master-slave violence or collusion, and often-"privileged" members of the slave hierarchy. Joanna represented one common type of mulatto adjustment to the sharply divided society; Boni, who was also a mulatto, represented the other extreme, and the details of his birth are often used to explain his especially violent hatred of whites. A particularly nuanced picture of Maroon ambivalence toward mulattoes in the eighteenth century may be read in "Paanza's Story" (R. Price 1983a, 129–34).

458. Timpany Calld here the *Kook* . . . Apparently, a fermentative dyspepsia (van Lier 1971, 472).

459. the Lions in the Tower . . . Ever since Henry I had moved the royal menagerie, including "lions, leopards, lynxes, porcupines, and several other uncommon beasts," to the (now-demolished) Lions Tower of the Tower of London, it had been considered one of London's prime "curiosities" (Pennant 1813, 2:22–24).

459. at S: Jos: Bankes's in 1788 . . . It is not clear whether Stedman is referring to a personal visit to Sir Joseph Banks or to a visit to Kew Gardens, as his diaries for 1788 are apparently lost.

459. D: Bancrofts . . . See note to page 51.

463. *Fumming Watra* . . . Sranan *fon* = "to beat."

465. a Mullatto-Ball . . . In late eighteenth-century Suriname, free blacks and mulattoes composed a much smaller proportion of the nonwhite population (approximately 1 percent) than in most New World plantation societies, but their balls and dance societies were a subject of considerable interest to whites, for example, "The free Negroes and colored as well as many slaves have among themselves dance societies. . . . They call such a group a *Doe,* and thus have the 'gold *doe,*' the 'silver,' the 'amber,' the 'fashion,' and the 'love' *doe*" (F. A. Kuhn, 1824 letter, cited in R. and S. Price 1979, 134–35); see also Nassy's better-known discussion (1788, 2:38).

466. Abe Renald . . . Abbé Raynal. See note to page 173.

469. the Club Call'd Abowtow . . . See note to page 318.

469. the Chareebee Indians . . . even Devoured the Negroes whom they kill'd . . . The factual basis of Carib cannibalism remains the subject of much scholarly controversy. For two recent assessments, see Myers 1984 and Whitehead 1984.

470. Mr Roux's Cabinet of Curiosity . . . By the eighteenth century, collections of natural history specimens, assorted ethnographica, and so on—so-called cabinets of curiosity—had ceased to be the sole prerogative of European royalty. Public and private exhibitions apparently took place not only in the great European capitals (see note to p. 148) but even in colonial outposts, such as Suriname, where not only Mr. Roux but others entertained guests with their private cabinets (see, for example, *23 March 1776* and *6 August 1776*). See also note to page 540.

471. a Letter to the Editors of the new Universal Magazine for October 1787 . . . We have examined this issue of the periodical but find no relevant letter.

472. the Last was Improved from Miss Merians Collection . . . See Appendix A, s.v. *[Green] Butterfly of South America.*

474. the Following Table for 4 Successive Years . . . For a discussion of these and related figures, see R. Price 1976, 18.

478. they Can here make no Rum . . . Stedman refers here only to rum made from molasses. An inferior rum, known as "killdevil," distilled instead "from the Scum and dregs of Sugar chaldrons," was produced locally and consumed in quantity (see p. 96).

480. the first Crop was Exported to Holland in 1733 . . . Cacao is, indeed, native to Suriname, though François de Chatillon may have planted the first large groves. Cacao was already a significant export by 1706 (van Lier 1971, 473).

480. the Celebrated Free Negro Qwaci . . . See note to page 581.

482. on the Wana Path behind Paramaribo . . . The 1796 edition corrects this phrase to read "*Wanica* path" (2:211). This area, like the Devil's Marsh a few miles to the north, provided hospitable ground for small villages of maroons. The Wanica path, leading to the Saramacca River, was also a frequent escape route for slaves fleeing the city.

486. an Embassy to the *Ouca,* and Sarameca Free Negroes . . . These "embassies" are discussed in R. Price n.d. See also note to page 558.

486. he kill'd the King of Pongar . . . And Dethron'd Also the King of Salangoor . . . Stedman is referring not to the Moluccas in Eastern Indonesia but to Malacca, on the Malay Peninsula. Selangor is one of the traditional states on the west coast of the peninsula. "Pongar" is probably Pangkor, an island off the coast of the state of Perak, just north of Selangor. Hamel, by then a major, sailed out from Texel in 1783 as part of a 1544-man expedition under the command of Jacob Pieter van Braam. In the 1784 attack on Selangor, in which Hamel led a 734-man landing force, one native leader was killed and another escaped. For details, see Mollema 1941, 313–18.

490. Miss Merian says the humming bird sits on 4 Eggs . . . In fact, hummingbirds sit on only two eggs, as Stedman states (van Lier 1971, 340).

493. a Rebel . . . was Sabred to Pieces . . . The 1796 edition specifies further that this execution of a maroon was ordered by Boni himself (2:223).

494. this Plant derived its name from the Island of *Tobago* . . . Stedman here repeats a common but erroneous British folk etymology. In fact, "when Christopher Columbus stepped on American soil for the first time in Guanahaní on October 12, 1492, the Indians of the island greeted him with an offertory rite, a gift of tobacco: 'Some dried leaves, which must be a thing highly esteemed among them, for in San Salvador they made me a present of them'" (Ortiz 1970, 14). The plant, its uses, and its name were well known to Europeans long before the "discovery" of Tobago.

494. *Seven boom* Which is too Frequently Used by the Young negro Wenches to promote Abortion . . . In Suriname, as elsewhere in plantation America, slave women seem to have used abortifacients frequently. Merian provides an early description of the use of the seeds of "Flos Pavonis" (*Poinciana pulcherrima?*) for this purpose (1705, pl. 45).

496. the negroes had taught them to make Proper Traps . . . Saramaka and other Suriname Maroons still use these (and other) fishtraps regularly, calling Stedman's "Spring Hook" *seti huku* and his "Spring Basket" *bakisi* (a word already in use among Maroons in the eighteenth century). Among Saramakas, the *masua* is an entirely different fishtrap, some six to ten feet long, designed to trap whole schools of fish.

499. "many Christians are a Parcel of Damn'd Monkeys" . . . Such "Repartee," using monkeys as metaphors, continues today. For a fine exchange between an urban Afro-Surinamer and a modern Maroon, see R. Price 1983a, 12.

510. a Shameful Peace . . . The idea that the 1760 and 1762 treaties with the Djuka and Saramaka, respectively, were "shameful" was commonplace among eighteenth-century colonial whites. One planter wrote in 1778 of the whites having "submitted to conditions so humiliating for us and so glorious for them" (cited in R. Price 1983b, 38). Stedman writes below of the whites' "Shameful Capitulation" (p. 510).

510. they [the Maroons] are unfairly Dealt with . . . It seems significant that Stedman (and presumably his friend and informant on such subjects, Governor Nepveu) admitted in private that the government had reneged on its part of the treaties. During the 1770s, Saramakas consistently argued to Suriname officials that this was the case, but the officials just as consistently denied it in public.

512. **two *White Negroes*** . . . White "black" men or women—albinos—"aroused [eighteenth-century] interest which ranged all the way from scientific speculation to side-show curiosity" (Jordan 1968; 250). Jordan provides an excellent summary of the relevant mid-century scientific debates in France and England (ibid., 250–52). In Suriname, albinos continue to be relatively common and, among Maroons, are associated with water spirits (R. Price 1983b, 228).

513. **M.ʳ *Broughton* the Late Famous Boxer** . . . John Broughton (1705–89), often called the father of British pugilism, who—upon his retirement—established various boxing arenas in London.

514. **a Negress Call'd *Louisa Truxo*** . . . The *London Chronicle* for Tuesday, 3 October 1780, indeed describes the evidence, largely oral, that "demonstrates" Louisa Truxo's age to be "175 years."

514. **Names of above a Dozen Negro Tribes** . . . See page 175 and our accompanying note. For a detailed discussion of body cicatrization among Suriname slaves and Maroons, see S. and R. Price 1980, 88–92.

514. **by Linaeus the Whole human Race . . . is Classed amongst the Monkeys** . . . See page 144 and Introduction, note 3.

514. ***Accorees* or *two fingers*** . . . The "Twofingers" were a group of eight to ten tropical forest Indians with varying degree of genetic deformity, who had come to live with the Saramaka about 1760. Suriname whites were absolutely fascinated by the Twofingers, who joined the lengthy lineage that included, among other exotic creatures of the European imagination in the Guianas, the Ewaipanoma (a race of headless people) and the Amazons. Details regarding the Twofingers, including contemporary illustrations, may be found in R. Price 1983a and 1983b. Stedman's "Accorees" refers to Akurio Indians, a small group of whom were also discovered, like the Twofingers, to be living with the Saramaka in 1763, when the first white person visited them in peacetime (ibid.).

515. **Lord Munbodo's *Ancient Metaphisiks*** . . . *Antient Metaphysics; or, the Science of universals* (1779–99), by James Burnet, Lord Monboddo (1714–99). Monboddo was a pioneer anthropologist and early evolutionist and would, naturally, have been intrigued by the "Twofingers."

515. **a Few Words for that Call'd the *Coromantyn*** . . . The 1796 edition adds here that "they [Coromantyns] break off their words very short, in a kind of guttural manner, which I cannot easily describe" (2:257). For a Komanti word list from twentieth-century Maroons in Suriname, see Hurault 1983, 38–41.

515. **that [language] Spoke by the Black People in Surinam** . . . The history of Sranan, the creole language of Suriname slaves and still that country's lingua franca, is more complex than Stedman implies. For bibliographical and historical references, see Voorhoeve and Donicie 1963, R. Price 1976, and the ongoing periodical *Amsterdam Creole Studies*.

515. **a Printed Grammar** . . . Stedman is probably referring to C. L. Schu-

mann's *Neger-Englisches Wörter-Buch* of 1781 (see Voorhoeve and Donicie 1963, 23).

516. *Sweety muffo* [etc.] ... Stedman's translations from Sranan to English tend to be at once over-literal (relying too heavily on cognates) and subjectively embellished.

516. the Chorus is Renew'd a Second time & So ad perpetuum ... The 1796 edition adds here, "This kind of singing is much practiced by the barge rowers or boat negroes on the water, especially during the night in a clear moonshine; it is to them peculiarly animating, and may, together with the sound of their oars, be heard at a considerable distance" (2:258). This type of call-and-response singing is, of course, characteristic of much Afro-American, and African, music.

516. one bus adiosio ... The 1796 edition gives an interlinear translation of the song. The English reads, "One buss good-by o 'tis so good-by girl I must go I love for to fight like a man o Amimba I go to the woods o 'tis so good-by girl, I must go" (2:259).

517. *Phillis Wheatly* ... Clarkson quotes three of Phillis Wheatley's poems and discusses her brief life (ca. 1753–84), as well as that of Ignatius Sancho, as examples of "African genius" (1788, 120–22).

517. *Ignatius Sancho* ... Famous black actor who specialized in the roles of Othello and Oroonoko, friend of Hogarth and Sterne, painted by Gainesborough. Stedman may have been among the original subscribers to his book, *Letters of Ignatius Sancho, An African* (London, 1782, xlix).

517. *Tho.! Fuller* a Negro Slave ... Thomas Fuller, born in Africa ca. 1710 and the slave of Mrs. Elizabeth Cox near Alexandria, was interviewed in or about 1788 by two Pennsylvanians, who posed three questions, (1) how many seconds are there in a year and half? [47,304,000]; (2) how many seconds has a man lived who is seventy years, seventeen days, and twelve hours old? [2,210,500,800]; and (3) if a farmer has six sows, and each sow has six female pigs the first year, and they all increase in the same proportion to the end of eight years, how many sows will the farmer then have? [$7^8 \times 6 = 34,588,806$]. Fuller answered all three correctly. The most accessible source for Dr. Rush's letter is *American Museum* 5:62–63. Fuller's life and feats of mental calculation are discussed in Smith 1983, 178–80.

518. the Supplement to the town and Country Magazine for 1788 ... We have been unable to locate Benjamin Rush's letter in this periodical. The only related essay in the Supplement (p. 623) is entitled "The Slave" and concerns courage and gratitude rather than intellectual prowess. See the previous note.

520. not that if they die Abroad they will Rise in theyr Own Country ... The idea that death would bring diaspora Africans back to their "Own Country" was both widespread and sporadic. We believe that it is not a question of whether Merian, Clarkson, or Stedman was correct, but rather who the African or Afro-American informant happened to be. Many Africans in Suriname clearly did believe that, upon their death, they would fly back to the land of their birth; others believed they would, as Stedman suggests, pass into the land of the ancestors but never again cross the great ocean. The libations described by Stedman are intended as a way of sharing drink with the ancestors.

521. *Winty Play* . . . Spirit possession was (and remains) a core feature of Afro-Suriname religious behavior. Today "Winti" has become the general name for coastal Afro-Suriname religion and has been described in detail by several authors (see, for example, Wooding 1981). For vivid descriptions by missionaries of eighteenth-century spirit possession dances among Maroons, see R. Price n.d.

522. to Charm the *Ammodytes* or Papaw Serpent . . . Today, the *papa-gadu* cult remains a central part of the religion of both coastal Afro-Surinamers and Maroons. Boa constrictors, known as *papa, daguwe,* or *vodu* snakes, are the vehicles for gods; when such a snake is accidently disturbed or killed, these gods may possess humans as avenging spirits. These snakes (like anacondas, which house related spirits) are sacred and protected.

523. every Family is distinctly Prohibited, from Father to Son, to Eat . . . Among Afro-Surinamers, paternity is symbolically marked by the transmission from father to child at conception of a taboo, usually alimentary, the violation of which leads to a variety of sicknesses. In twentieth-century Suriname (M. and F. Herskovits 1936, 36–37), coastal people still call these *treef* or *trefu* (see also Stedman 1796, 2:264), deriving from the Hebrew *tereefa* (= prohibited food) of the large Suriname Jewish community, while Saramaka Maroons instead use the term *táta-tjína* ["father-taboo"], deriving from Bantu sources. In both cases, the belief seems related to prior African models such as the Ashanti *ntoro* complex (see Rattray 1923, 45–54; R. Price 1975, 52).

524. thy Canting Meravians . . . See note to page 304.

524. The Above names are Generally given to Imported Negro Slaves . . . In fact, the naming system for eighteenth-century Suriname slaves was far more multifaceted, with a host of African names—often, during the late eighteenth century, Akan day names such as those Stedman cites—appearing in colonial documents alongside "classical" names such as Nero, Neptune, and Medusa and "fanciful" names such as Chocolate, September, or Pasop (Dutch for "Watch-out!"). The name of a plantation or owner was often added as a second name in the documents, for example, Kofi Charprendre or Kwaku van [of] Sara de la Para. Whether such names were given by masters or slaves, and the differing but overlapping ways each group used them (as well as other kinds of personal names that were not recorded by whites), is a complex issue. For discussion, see R. and S. Price 1972 and R. Price 1983b.

525. Other Horrors too dreadful to Relate . . . The 1796 edition adds here, as a footnote:

> It is a well-known fact, that a negro, having been ill-treated by the family in which he lived as a servant, one day took the following

desperate revenge:—The master and mistress being from home, he, having locked all the doors, at their return presented himself with their three fine children on the platform at the top of the house. When asked why he did not give admittance, he only answered by throwing an infant baby to the ground: they threatened—he tossed down the brother: they intreated, but to no purpose, the third sharing the same fate, who all lay dead at their parents' feet—then calling out to them that he was now fully revenged, leaped down himself, and dashed out his own brains amongst the amazed spectators.—Another stabbed the inoffensive husband to be revenged on the guilty wife; declaring, that to kill herself was only temporary, but to lose all that was dear to her must be eternal bitterness, while to himself it was the sweetest satisfaction. (2:266)

525. *Wissy men* . . . Sorcerers, often accused of being poisoners as well. The term is usually considered to have derived from English "witch." Among eighteenth-century Maroons, convicted sorcerers were burned at the stake; for a contemporary illustration, see S. and R. Price 1980, 58, and for contemporary accounts, R. Price n.d.

526. *Gango* Negroes . . . Mandingos. On the realities and myths of cannibalism among Africans, see Evans-Pritchard 1965 and Arens 1979, 83–96.

526. Particularly the *Coromantyn* & these of *Nago* . . . See note to page 175.

526. I dont Remember ever . . . to have Seen one Offer a Kiss in public to a Woman . . . Stedman's observation fits with modern Maroon sensibilities on the subject. There is, however, one apparently contradictory piece of visual evidence: in Valkenburg's 1707 painting of a "play" on a Suriname River plantation, there is a couple clearly kissing in the foreground (R. Price 1983a, 109). We suspect that, in spite of the otherwise "realistic style" of this painting, the artist posed this particular couple in a conventional European posture.

526. the Case of Lesperanza . . . See page 513. The lengthy post-partum sex taboo, usually associated with prolonged breast feeding, was a significant feature of child spacing in many parts of plantation America (see Higman 1984, 353–54), and it is still practiced (in truncated form) among Suriname Maroons.

527. eating Common Earth . . . Earth eating by slaves was a common but perplexing problem for masters throughout the Caribbean. Geophagy not only had a strong cultural focus, with West African antecedents, but it was related, unbeknownst to contemporary medical science, to intestinal helminthiasis (hookworm) as well as to malnutrition (particularly, calcium and iron deficiencies). Iron masks to prevent geophagy were common sights among Caribbean slave crews, yet the practice remained widespread, particularly for children and pregnant women. An excellent recent discussion may be found in Higman 1984, 294–98.

527. Philemon & Onesima . . . St. Paul's Epistle to Philemon exhorts him to take back and forgive the runaway slave Onesimus.

528. the *Captive-Prince* . . . The number of references to captive princes and princesses in eighteenth-century writings on Suriname (and other Caribbean slave societies) attests to the importance of this literary theme. Aphra Behn's *Oroonoko* (1688), about mid-seventeenth-century Suriname, was the enormously popular prototype of the genre.

530. *Lota* . . . Probably the superficial mycosis *pityriasis versicolor* (van Lier 1971, 476).

530. *Yaws* . . . This description fits "bush-yaws," cutaneous leishmaniasis (van Lier 1971, 476).

530. to put them under a Salivation . . . The descriptive phrase for a common eighteenth-century European treatment used for various ailments (most notably syphilis), whose goal was to produce an excessive flow of saliva by the administration of mercury. If this form of yaws were treponematous, it would of course be closely related to syphilis.

530. *Clabba Yaws* or *Tubboes* . . . Probably treponematous yaws (van Lier 1971, 476).

530. the *Guinea* or Lint Worm . . . Van Lier (1971, 477) identifies this as *Filaria medinensis* or *Draculus persarum*.

531. *Basha* . . . Usually written *basia, busha,* or *bastiaan*. Black overseer or slave driver on Suriname plantations.

533. 50,000 Healthy people is Exactly Extinct one every 20 Years . . . Some of the details of Stedman's demographic model are faulty, but his general picture of the costs in human lives of the Suriname slave system—one of the most extreme cases in the Americas—is generally correct. For detailed discussion of the historical demography of Suriname as a plantation colony, see R. Price 1976, 6–16.

534. *Ramsay & Clarkson* . . . James Ramsay (1733–89), who had lived as a missionary for nineteen years in St. Kitts, became a leading abolitionist in England, viewing slavery both "as an affront to humanity and as inhibiting missionary activity" (Anstey 1975, 248). Stedman would have known two of his pamphlets, *An Essay on the Treatment and Conversion of the African Slaves in the British Sugar Colonies* (1784), and *An Enquiry into the Effects of the Abolition of the Slave Trade* (1784). For Clarkson, see note to page 168.

534. no Negroes work is more than a Healthy Exercise . . . Note that even Stedman's idealized depiction of the slaves' work day in their master's fields, which he says allows generous time *afterwards* for hunting, fishing, cultivating a garden, making crafts for sale, and so forth, does not end until sunset!

536. *Braff.* . . . *Tom-Tom.* . . . *Gangotay.* . . . &c . . . All named items on Stedman's list of recipes appear also on the more extensive lists gathered contemporaneously among Saramaka Maroons by Schumann (1778), though ingredients often vary. For discussion of eighteenth-century slave and Maroon foods, see R. Price n.d. The foods mentioned by Stedman continue to be prepared today by both coastal Afro-Surinamers and Maroons (see, for example, M. and F. Herskovits 1936, 15).

537. **the Funeral Rites are quite Ended by a Second Feast** . . . The funeral rites scenario so briefly sketched by Stedman covers the most extensive rituals practiced by Suriname slaves and Maroons, which involved—over the course of about a year—a rich cultural complex of economic exchanges, large social gatherings and feasting, complex communications with the ancestors and gods, and a tremendous variety of specialized song/drum/dance performances.

537. *Soesa* . . . An African-derived martial arts game/exercise/dance played by pairs of men and still known today, with affinities to Bahian *capoeira*.

537. *Awaree* . . . This board game of nearly worldwide distribution, brought to Suriname from Africa, is known among coastal Surinamers as "awari" and among Saramaka Maroons—who play it only at funerals—as "adjiboto." For discussion, see Herskovits 1929 and 1932.

538. Otaheytee . . . The usual eighteenth-century designation for Tahiti.

540. **Such are the *musical Instruments* of our African Brethren** . . . Several years ago, we were fortunate to discover in the Rijksmuseum voor Volkenkunde, Leiden, a manuscript list demonstrating that thirty-nine of the forty-two objects described and depicted by Stedman on pages 318 and 538–40 (and in pls. 40 and 69) had, at one time, been accessioned by the museum. We were able to locate several, including the *great Creole drum*, the *Loango too-too*, and, most important, the *Creole-bania*, which represents the oldest Afro-American banjo still in existence anywhere. (See, for photographs and discussion, R. and S. Price 1979 and S. and R. Price 1980.) The complex route by which Stedman's Suriname collection reached the Rijksmuseum voor Volkenkunde, possibly via the Leverian Museum (see note to p. 148) is discussed in R. and S. Price 1979, 140.

541. **the Negroes dance Always in Couples** . . . For a fine depiction of a Suriname plantation dance in the slave quarters, see Valkenburg's 1707 painting reproduced in R. Price 1983a, 109.

541. **Living till they die With their Parents and Nearest Relations** . . . See note to page 386.

542. **"Cursory Remarks upon the Reverend Mr Ramsays Essay . . . "** The author of this antiabolitionist pamphlet, which was published in London, was James Tobin (d. 1817).

543. **the long Projected Cordon or Path of Circumvolation** . . . See Introduction, note 11.

546. *Neptune*. . . . **Sentenced to be brook *Alive* upon the Rack** . . . Several literary specialists have suggested to us that Stedman's description of Neptune's death seems derivative from Aphra Behn's fictionalized account of the death of Oroonoko, set in Suriname a hundred years earlier:

> He [Oroonoko-Caesar] had learned to take Tobacco; and when he was assur'd he should die, he desir'd they would give him a Pipe in his Mouth, ready lighted; which they did: And the Executioner came, and first cut off his Members, and threw them into the Fire; after that,

with an ill-favour'd Knife, they cut off his Ears and his Nose, and burn'd them; he still smoak'd on, as if nothing had touch'd him; then they hack'd off one of his Arms, and still he bore up, and held his Pipe; but at the cutting off the other Arm, his Head sunk, and his Pipe dropt, and he gave up the Ghost, without a Groan, or a Reproach. . . . They cut Caesar [Oroonoko] into Quarters, and sent them to several of the chief Plantations. (Behn 1722 [1688], 199–200)

Scholars familiar with the realities of eighteenth-century Suriname, however, will realize that the event Stedman describes as an eyewitness needed no literary precursor. From other contemporary sources, we know that such theatrical public executions—and the victim's stoic or defiant reactions—were relatively frequent during this period, and we see no reason to doubt the directness or veracity of Stedman's description.

549. Which days of Martyr are Absolutely a Feast to many Planters . . . The 1796 edition here strengthens the chauvinistic tone of Stedman's following lines by substituting:

Though I never recal to my remembrance, without the most painful sensation, this horrid scene ["The Execution of Breaking on the Rack"], which must revolt the feelings of all who have one spark of humanity, I cannot forbear exhibiting to the public the dreadful spectacle in the annexed drawing. If the reader, however, should be offended with this shocking exhibition, and my dwelling so long on this unpleasant subject, let it be some relief to his reflection, to consider this punishment not inflicted as a wanton and unprovoked act of cruelty, but as the extreme severity of the Surinam laws, on a desperate wretch, suffering as an example to others for complicated crimes; while at the same time it cannot but give me, and I hope many others, some consolation to reflect that the above barbarous mode of punishment was hitherto never put in practice in the British colonies. (2:297–98)

Stedman's several-page-long description of Neptune's suffering and death was quoted in full in Andrew Knapp and William Baldwin's *The Newgate Calendar*, 5 vols. (London, 1824), where it formed the centerpiece of their discussion of torture (1:136–43). "No longer deemed compatible with freedom . . . [execution by torture] was therefore abrogated in the year 1772. Yet . . . the inhuman practice still prevails in some of the English settlements abroad" (1:136).

555. a Mrs *Van Eys* Alleging she had Affronted her Only by her Looks . . . Stedman's Suriname diary for this day explicitly attributes the punishment to Mrs. van Eys's own sexual frustrations: "Frow van Eys is in low Spirits for the absence of her d^r de g——v [apparently, her lover, the wealthy planter G. A. D. de Graav], it was that bich that gave poor brands [slave] mistres a Spance-bok [torture] at the Fort because he would not fuk herself, damn her" (*7 September 1776*).

556. The Punishment Call'd a Spanso bocco . . . Governor Nepveu's description of the *Spaanse bok* (Spanish whip) reads:

> [T]he hands are tied together, the knees drawn up between them, and a stick inserted through the opening between the knees and the hands and fixed firmly in the ground, around which they then lie like a hoop and are struck on the buttocks with a guava or Tamarind rod; one side having been struck until the skin is completely broken they are turned over to have the other side similarly injured; some use hoopsticks for this, although this is an extremely dangerous practice as it generally results in the slave's death, even though the chastisement is less than with the abovementioned rods. (Nepveu, cited in R. Price 1983b, 7–8)

Stedman's drawing of this punishment, planned as a plate, may have been omitted by the publisher as too gruesome. No known copy exists, and the plate was apparently never engraved.

557. M.r Belknaps History of New Hampshire . . . Jeremy Belknap, *The History of New Hampshire*, vol. 1 (Philadelphia, 1784).

558. a Libel against the Good Fourgeoud . . . Stedman appears to be referring to a brief report in the *Utrechtsche Courant* of 30 August 1776, in which Fourgeoud is accused of having sent the delegations to the Djuka and Saramaka Maroons "without the knowledge of the colonial government."

559. the Indians Who had Voluntarily Fought & Defeated the Enemy there . . . The Lee Shore settlements are those referred to in the note to page 84. Arawak Indians fought against such a community, alongside whites and slaves, as early as 1711 (R. Price 1983a, 75).

561. the noted Free Negro Gousary . . . See note to page 114.

563. The *Oryza* or *Rice* . . . Almost all rice grown by the Maroons was upland or dry (unirrigated) rice, grown like wheat, and it was often their staple food. For stories relating to the origins of rice among the Maroons, see R. Price 1983a, 129–34.

564. my Own Habitation . . . A sketch of this house was drawn by Stedman directly into his journal. See Introduction, note 35 (3). The unusual entrance is not visible in the sketch.

574. D.r Brooks . . . Richard Brookes discusses the "Wood-Lice of the *West-Indies*" on pages 271–72 of *The Natural History of Insects*, vol. 4 of his *A New and Accurate System of Natural History*, 6 vols. (London, 1763).

579. the End of my 7.th & Last Campeign . . . The 1796 edition adds as a coda:

> [at Paramaribo] I was most heartily welcomed by my many friends with the warmest congratulations on my still existing, after having escaped so many dangers, and been so long deprived of every comfort—torn by thorns, stung by insects—starved, tormented, emaciated, and wounded—often without clothes, health, rest, money, refreshments, medicines, or friends;—and after having lost so many of my brave companions, who lay buried in the dust.—Thus ended my seventh and *last* campaign in the forest of Guiana. (2:344)

581. the Celebrated *Graman Qwacy* . . . Other colonial sources, when combined with Stedman's descriptions, permit the following capsule biography of this extraordinary man (for bibliographic references, see R. Price 1983a, 155–57). Kwasi was born in West Africa ca. 1690 and enslaved and transported to Suriname as a child. By 1730, he had discovered the medicinal properties of the tree that Linnaeus named in his honor *Quassia amara* (called in Suriname "Quassiehout" or "Kwasi-bita"); and during the next six decades, amidst his many other activities, Kwasi served as the colony's leading *dresiman* (curer) and *lukuman* (diviner), with vast influence not only among blacks and Indians but also among European colonists. Kwasi's fame among Europeans was not, however, based solely on his medical talents; for more than forty years he was the colony's principal intermediary in dealing with maroons, serving first as a scout, then as a negotiator, and finally as spiritual and tactical adviser of the Rangers. Always the opportunist, Kwasi—who as early as 1730 had received from a member of the Council a golden breastplate on which was inscribed "Quassie, faithful to the whites"—became in 1744 the slave of Governor Mauricius. His varied antimaroon activities during the next decade won him a letter of manumission, but personal freedom did not significantly alter his customary activities: he continued to conduct expeditions against maroons and to hunt them for a bounty, and he continued his varied medical practice.

In due course, Kwasi became a planter in his own right and, in 1776, as Stedman reports, in recognition of his many services to the colony the governor sent him all the way to The Hague, to be received by Willem V, Prince of Orange, who feted him with gifts. After his triumphant return to Suriname, Kwasi remained active on behalf of the colonists into his nineties, while he lived in a fine house in Paramaribo, given him for his use free of charge by the government. And it was during those final years that he became accustomed to receiving letters from abroad addressed to "The Most Honorable and Most Learned Gentleman, Master Phillipus of Quassie, Professor of Herbology in Suriname."

But the view of Kwasi given in the documents forms only half the available picture. Saramaka Maroons today preserve rich and powerful memories of this same man (whom they call Kwasimukamba), who came to live with them as a spy in the mid-1750s, escaped back to the whites, led a giant military expedition against them and, ultimately, had his right ear cut off by the Saramaka chief (see pl. 76). For details of this story, with both documentary and oral historical evidence, see R. Price 1979a and 1983a, 153–59.

586. [coffee] Was first planted in Surinam by the Count *De Neale* . . . Van Lier states that coffee was first planted in Suriname between 1711 and 1713 and first exported in 1721 (1971, 478). In the decades following 1750, coffee outweighed sugar as the colony's most valuable export (R. Price 1976, 17).

586. Count Gentilly . . . We have been unable to identify this traveler.

590. the Bruised [coffee beans] which are Consumed in the Colony . . . This is an interesting example of a pattern that persists today throughout the Caribbean, the oldest continuously colonized region in the modern world system.

591. Benjamin Mosely, M:D . . . Benjamin Mosely (1742–1819) became surgeon-general of Jamaica in 1768. His treatise on coffee was published in 1775.

591. Dr. *Fermyn* which Gentleman is highly Correct & Preferable to All that I have read . . . Stedman's admiration for Fermin's reportage was not shared by Governor Nepveu, who described his book as "so Superficial, inaccurate, and filled with contradictions that it is not even worth looking at" ("Annotatiën," unpublished document, Sociëteit van Suriname 566, Algemeen Rijksarchief).

591. an Avarige About 75,000 negro Slaves . . . Stedman overestimates the slave population by about 50 percent and similarly exaggerates the number of plantations (van Lier 1971, 479). See also note to page 533.

594. "letters to a young planter" . . . *Letters to a Young Planter; or, observations on the management of a Sugar-Plantation,* by Gordon Turnbull (London, 1785).

596. *Monsieur Godins* well Authenticated Letter . . . "Lettre de M. Godin Des Odonais à M. de la Condamine" (20 October 1773), published under the title "Relation du naufrage de Madame Godin, sur la rivière des Amazones," in C. G. T. Garnier, *Voyages Imaginaires* (Amsterdam, 1787–89), 12:385–421. For biographical details on Jean Godin des Odonais (1717–92) and Charles-Marie de la Condamine (1701–74), see van Lier 1971, 479. As a modern authority on the Amazon has written,

> There is no more valiant a symbol of the hardship of colonial Amazonia than Madame Godin, the determined wife of a member of La Condamine's party who was compelled to leave her brother and their two children in Quito. For fifteen years the lady awaited news of a "sloop" that her husband, before continuing into Amazonia, had promised would come to fetch her. Upon hearing a report of a rescue party on the upper Marañon, she decided to try to expedite the rendezvous by setting forth across the Andes with the children, her brother, and several servants. To her dismay, she found the village for which she was headed to have been totally eradicated by smallpox. She therefore was compelled to continue down the Marañon without guides or maps or food. Next she lost her canoe in rapids, and the party continued on foot. Everybody but she died of hunger and fatigue; after nine days of struggling forward alone, she was found by Indians and taken to a mission village. Eventually, after a separation that lasted fully nineteen years, the bedraggled lady was reunited with her husband in Belém. (Stone 1985, 43)

599. *Incle & Yarico* . . . See note to page 98.

600. a Spleet new Suit of Blue . . . "Spleet" is Scottish for "split"; "spleet new" means "brand new."

600. to Appoint a day when the boy was to be Christned . . . The 1796 edition adds here as a footnote:

> I should not here omit to mention that in the colony of Surinam all emancipated slaves are under the following restrictions, *viz*.
>
> They are (if males) bound to help in defending the settlement against all home and foreign enemies.
>
> No emancipated slave, male or female, can ever go to law at all against their former master or mistress.
>
> And finally, if any emancipated slave, male or female, dies in the colony, and leaves behind any possessions whatever, in that case one quarter of the property also goes to his former owners, either male or female. (2:372-73)

604. more dejected than *Sterns Maria* . . . The narrator of Laurence Sterne's *A Sentimental Journey* (1768), who had first been told Maria's sad tale by his "friend Mr. Shandy," seeks out "that disorder'd maid . . . [that] poor luckless maiden . . . [who is] crying . . . wandering somewhere about the road . . . the tears trickl[ing] down her cheeks" (Sterne 1941, 115-19).

607. out of a number of near twelve hundred Able bodied men . . . For discussion of the contradictory figures regarding the size of Fourgeoud's troops, see Introduction, page xxvi and note 12.

612. the small island of *Urk* . . . Van Lier (1971, 480) points out that Urk is not in fact a rock.

613. *watter Manakins* . . . Van Lier (1971, 480) identifies these craft as having been owned by fishermen from Marken, who traditionally provided these towing services.

614. *Scaardam, Haarlem, & Tergow* . . . Zaandam, Haarlem, and Gouda (van Lier 1971, 480).

617. the fate of poor *Madan Blanchard* . . . Madan Blanchard, an English seaman who fell in love with Palau after a 1783 shipwreck and elected to stay there when the rest of the crew of his ship returned to England. George Keate embellished the journal of Captain Wilson, which described these incidents, to produce his own popular *An Account of the Pelew Islands* (London, 1788).

617. Admirals *Van-Tromp, Peet-Heyn, Obdam & DeRuyter* . . . *Zoutman* . . . These Dutch naval heroes include one or the other of the seventeenth-century Tromp father-son pair (Maarten and Cornelis); Piet Heijn (1588-1629), who saw considerable action off Brazil and in the Caribbean; the hero of a 1658 battle with the Swedish fleet named Obdam; Michiel A. de Ruyter (1607-76), who fought alongside both Maarten and Cornelis Tromp and succeeded Obdam in the Baltic theater; and Johan Zoutman (1724-93).

620. *Lord Cutt* . . . Lord John Cutts (1661-1707).

620. I Complimented his Serene highness With 18 Figures in Wax . . .

An extensive search in the Netherlands for this remarkable object, aided by more than a dozen Dutch scholars, uncovered no trace, and we presume it to have been destroyed, probably during the Napoleonic wars.

620. a Blessing I Could never have Bestow'd on him myself ... The 1796 edition adds here:

> Here I cannot omit an anecdote of attachment in this boy:—Having set out by myself on a short journey, I found a crown-piece more than I expected in my purse, and for which I was at a loss to account; till on my return, when I questioned Quaco, he said, "that fearing I might be short of cash, where people seemed so fond of it, he had put his five-shilling piece in my pocket."—This action was the more generous, not only in the manner it was done, but being at that time the only crown poor Quaco possessed in this world. (2:396)

621. M:r Wighers ... Upon Governor Nepveu's death in 1779, Bernard Texier (d. 1783) became governor and was in turn succeeded by Jan Wichers in 1784.

625. in a *female negro Slave* & three Score Sheep had Consisted the Live Stock of Poor Joana ... See note to page 241.

626. Prince *Lee Boo* ... A Noble Savage from Palau who was taken to England with Captain Wilson and his crew in 1784 to be "civilized," was greatly admired by the British public, but died there soon after from smallpox. His story was first popularized in George Keate's *An Account of the Pelew Islands* (London, 1788), and he became a popular figure in the literature of the age—from Coleridge's poetry to *The Interesting and Affecting History of Prince Lee Boo,* which ran through twenty editions after its publication in 1789 (Fairchild 1928, 117).

628. List of Subscribers ... The 131 subscribers who were added between the time of this compilation (February 1791) and publication in 1796 include (in order of the listing in 1796, 1:vii–xiv):

> Auckland (Lord) British Ambassador at the Hague.
> Ashmead (Wm.) Esq. London.
> Bute (Rt. Hon. Earl of).
> Bristol (Rt. Hon. Earl of).
> Barrington (Rt. Hon. Lord Viscount).
> Boydell (Rt. Hon. John) Lord Mayor of London.
> Barwell (———) Esq. London.
> Broadley (R. Carlisle) Esq. York.
> Barker (Thomas) Esq. Jamaica.
> Bain (———) Esq. M. D. Bath.
> Burk (Geo.) Esq. Waddon Court, Devon.
> Batt (J. F.) Esq. Richmond.
> Brown (E. H.) Esq. Richmond.
> Bastard (John P.) Esq. Kitley, M. P.
> Brown (Wm.) Esq. Wiveliscombe.
> Bush (Baron de) Commandant at Curacao.

EDITORS' NOTE TO PAGE 628

Bolls (And.) Esq. Capt. in the Dutch Navy.
Bloys de Treslon (Cor.) Esq. Capt. in the Dutch Navy.
Brown (——) Esq. Bristol.
Bulguin (Mr. ——) Bristol.
Blake (Mr. Wm.) London.
Canterbury (His Grace the Archbishop of)
Cambridge (R. O.) Esq. Twickenham.
Cowley (John) Esq. London.
Campbell (Rt. Hon. Ilay) Edinburgh.
Cholmondeley (G.) Esq. London.
Cooksley (J. Sparkes) Esq. Ashburton.
Dover (Rt. Hon. Lord).
Douglas (Gen. Robert) Holland.
Dowce (Francis) Esq. Richmond.
Danby (Wm.) Esq. Swinton.
Drummond (J.) Esq. M. D. Jamaica.
Ducarrell (——) Esq. Exmouth.
Delaval (E. Hussey) Esq. London.
Dickenson (Benj.) Esq. Tiverton.
De Graav (Gid. And. D.) Esq. Surinam.
Des Borgnes (Col. Briseval) Fourgeoud's Marines.
Erving (George) Esq. London.
Euler (——) Esq. for the Library of his Serene Highness the Prince of Orange.
Fitzwilliam (Right Hon. Earl)
Fredericy (——) Esq. Governor of Surinam.
Freeman (——) Esq. Chute Lodge.
Freeman (Mrs. Elizabeth).
Fattet (Mr. Barth. Francois).
Guildford (Right Hon. Earl of).
Gordon (Col. Robert) Deputy Governor at the Cape of Good Hope.
Graham (John) Esq. M. D. Jamaica.
Grinstone (Thomas) Esq. Kilnwick.
Goodwin (G. R.) Esq. Bath.
Godefrooy (Mrs. Eliz.) Surinam.
Gray (Miss Jane) Edinburgh.
Heathfield (Rt. Hon. Lord).
Harrowby (Rt. Hon. Lord) Sandon, Staffordshire.
Hamilton (Sir Alexander) Bart. Retreat.
Hastings (Warren) Esq. late Governor General of Bengal.
Hamell (Colonel) Cape of Good Hope.
Hamilton (Robert) Esq. of the Hon. East India Company's Service.
Hamilton (Major) Exon.
Hilton (William) Esq. Jamaica.—2 Copies.
Hecke (C. A.) Esq. Demerary.
Heneman (Gysbert) Esq. Hague.
Haringman (John) Esq. Admiral in the Dutch Navy.
Hogg (Jos.) Esq. Tiverton.
How (J. M.) Esq. Wiscome Park.

Hartford (Jos.) Esq. Bristol.
Hobroid (Mrs.) Richmond.
Jermain (Thomas) Esq. Bristol.
Johnson (J. R.) Esq. Jamaica.
Keates (Rev. Richard) Tiverton.
Kincaid (Patrick) Esq. Exon.
Knight (Mr. Charles) Knightsbridge.
Kennedy (H. J.) Esq. Cleves.
Knollaerdt (———) Esq. Fourgeoud's Marines.
Macallester Loup (Duncan) Esq. Hague.
Mackay (John) Esq. London.
Mackay (Hector) Esq. War Office.
Mowbray (Robert) Esq. M. D. Cockayrny.
Marshall (Mr. Robert) Tiverton.
Moens (Mr. Adrian) Rotterdam.
Medlaer (George Crawford) Esq. Fourgeoud's Marines.
Noot (Captain) Fourgeoud's Marines.
Nichols (Rev. Mr.) Richmond.
Newte (Thomas) Esq. late Captain in the Hon. East India
    Company's Service.
Newbiggen (Miss Jane) Edinburgh.
Owens (George) Esq. Tiverton.
Pepperel (Sir William) Bart. London.
Palmer (William) Esq. London.
Prince (J. D.) Esq. Holland.
Perret Gentilly (Major) Fougeoud's Marines.
Polson (Hugh) Esq. Exmouth.
Rockby (Right Hon. Lord) Horton Kent.
Ricketts (Hon. W. H.) Jamaica.
Ricketts (E. Jarvis) Esq. Jamaica.
Rosendaal (Countess de) Holland.
Rolle (John) Esq. M. P. Tidwell.
Robinson (William) Esq. Writer to the Signet, Edinburgh.
Robinson (Capt. Thomas) of the Hon. East India Company's
    Service.
Rigaud (P.) Esq. R. A.
Reynsdorph (Andrew) Esq. Surinam.
Spencer (Rt. Hon. Lord Henry).
Sykes (Sir Christopher) Bart. York.
Small (Major Charles) Isle of Man.
Small (Peter) Esq. Montreal, Canada.
Stuart (Hon. General John).
Sampson (James) Esq. late His Majesty's Consul General at
    Morocco.
Sturgeon (T. W.) Esq. Trowbridge.
Swale (———) Esq. London.
Sheriff (Mr. Robert) Leith.
Stedman (John) Esq. M. D. Edinburgh.
Stedman (Capt. Wm. George).

EDITORS' NOTE TO PAGE 628

Stedman (Miss Catherine) Edinburgh.
Sharrat (Mr. John) Walfall.
Somerville (Miss Elizabeth) Edinburgh.
Tozer (Aaron) Esq. of the Hon. East India Company's Service.
Vance Agnew (Robert) Esq. Edinburgh.
Van Coeverde (Colonel) Fourgeoud's Marines.
Willoughby de Broke (Rt. Hon. Lord).
Westerloo (General) Holland.
Wemyss (Major) 11th Regiment of Foot.
Wierts (Francis) Esq. Captain in the Dutch Navy.
Winsloe (Thomas) Esq. Collipriest.
Woolery (R. P.) Esq. Jamaica.
Williams (Jos.) Esq. Jamaica.
Wyville (Rev. Christopher) York.
Wray (G. Lewis) Esq. Spence Farm.
Wood (Bevis) Esq. Tiverton.
Wray (Mrs.) Richmond.
Watt (Mr.) London.
Wardlaw (Mrs. Susan) Edinburgh.
York (His Grace the Archbishop of).
Yorke (Hon. John).

A cursory check of lists of prominent pro- and antiabolitionists turns up few matches with Stedman's subscription list. Of the "hard-core abolitionist vote"—twenty-six committed abolitionists in 1791 (Anstey 1975, 282)—none were listed as subscribers to Stedman's work.

Appendix A: Flora and Fauna Identifications

In his original preface, Stedman—referring to his extensive natural history descriptions and depictions—offhandedly remarked that "the Linaen names may easily be added by the Connoisseurs" (p. 8). In fact, however, few aspects of the preparation of this critical edition created more headaches. Not only are certain local plant and animal families still incompletely known; correct distinctions between species often rest on an obscure bit of nonbotanical or non-zoological knowledge, for example, regarding the local perceptions or uses of a plant or animal by Maroons or Indians. We have drawn on a large number of sources, published and unpublished, as well as on our own two-decade-long acquaintance with the Suriname forest and its inhabitants (observing, hunting, fishing, cooking, eating), in compiling these lists. Undoubtedly, errors and uncertainties remain. While we must accept ultimate responsibility for these identifications in their present form, we are also pleased to acknowledge our debt to the work of other specialists.

For flora, the published sources most important for our identifications were Bruijning and Voorhoeve 1977, Hurault 1965, van Lier 1971, Ostendorf 1962, Stahel 1944, and Vink 1965. In addition, R. A. J. van Lier generously provided us with the original letters containing the identifications made for him by the botanists J. C. Lindeman and J. G. Wessels Boer, then of the Instituut voor Systematische Plantkunde, Rijksuniversiteit Utrecht, in connection with his 1971 edition of Stedman's *Narrative*.

For fauna, the most useful sources were Bruijning and Voorhoeve 1977, Dunning 1982, Haverschmidt 1968, Herklots 1961, van Lier 1971, Sanderson 1965, and Walker 1975. Once again, R. A. J. van Lier kindly provided us with the original letters containing the identifications made for him in connection

FLORA IDENTIFICATIONS

with his 1971 edition—by F. Haverschmidt for birds; by H. Nijssen, then of the Zoologisch Museum, Universiteit van Amsterdam, for fish; by P. H. van Doesburg, Jr., then of the Rijksmuseum voor Natuurlijke Historie, Leiden, for insects and reptiles; and by A. M. Husson, then of that same institution, for mammals.

For Sranan words (Sr), we have employed the standard orthography, which derives from Dutch; for example *oe* = English *u*. Carib, Arawak, Wayana, and Saramaccan words are here written with an English-based orthography, for example *y* rather than (Dutch-derived) *j*. Note that variant spellings of a particular term often appear in the text of the "Narrative."

The page numbers that follow the names of plants and animals signal the location of Stedman's primary description of each one. When Stedman gives both an Afro-American and an Amerindian term for a plant or animal, we have generally listed it under the former.

FLORA

Acajou (310, 426). The cashew and bush cashew tree, *Anacardium occidentale* and *A. giganteum* Hancock. Sr *kasjoe* and *boesi-kasjoe* ‹ Carib *akayu*.

agoma (249). *Solanum americanum* Miller. Sr *agoema*.

ambergine (249). Eggplant, *Solanum melongena*.

American Aloes Tree (502). *Aloë barbadense* Miller.

Annana (484, pl. 64). Pineapple, *Ananas comosus*.

Arnotta (305, 334–36, pl. 43). Roucou, *Bixa orellana*. Sr *koesoewe* ‹ Carib *kuswe*.

arracocerra (316). Acouchi resin, from the bast of *Protium aracouchini* March. ‹ Arawak *alakuseri* and Carib *alakseri*.

avigato-Pear (244). Avocado, *Persea americana* Miller. Sr *afkati*.

awara (44, pl. 5 [*top*]). *Astrocaryum segregatum* Drude. Sr (and Arawak and Carib) *awara*. Both Maroons and Indians use this palm fruit to make cooking oil.

baboon Knyfee (221). Probably *Scleria secans* Urb. or *Flagellum nigrorum* Berg., but other *Cyperaceae* also bear this name. Sr *baboen-nefi*.

Balsam-Capivi (316). Apparently an oleoresin from *Hymenaea courbaril* rather than from *Copaifera guianensis* Desf. (to which the name—copaiba balsam—usually refers). ‹ Arawak *kupai*.

Banana (297, pl. 38). *Musa* spp. Sr *bakba*. Includes only fruits that can be eaten raw.

Bee Bee (410). The corkwood tree, *Pterocarpus officinalis* Jacq. Sr *watra-bebe*.

Berklack (561). *Eschweilera* spp. Sr *barklaki*.

Black Cabbage Tree (446). The tatabu, *Diplotropis purpurea* (Rich.) Amsh. Sr *blaka kabisi*.

Bonjera (502). Sesame, *Sesamum indicum*. Sr *abongra*.

Bourracourra (333). Letter- or leopardwood, *Piratinera guianensis* Huber. ‹ Arawak *burukoro*. Sr *letr'oedoe*.

Brown Heart (573). *Vouacapoua americana* Aubl. Sr *broin-ati*.
bullet Tree (573). The balata or bullet-wood tree, *Manilkara bidentata* (A.DC.) Chev. Sr *bortri*.
Cacao Tree (479, pl. 63). *Theobroma cacao*. Sr *kakaw*.
Canavatepy (561). The trebol, *Platymiscium trinitatis* Benth. and *P. ulei* Harms. ‹ Arawak *kunatepi*.
Caraba (316). The crabwood tree, *Carapa procera* DC. or *Carapa guianensis* Aubl. Sr *krapa* ‹ Arawak *karaba*, Carib *karapa*.
cassava (309). *Manihot esculenta* Crantz. One species includes both "bitter" and "sweet" manioc. Sr *kasaba*.
Cassia (494). *Cassia* spp., most likely *C. spectabilis* DC., though JGS's description is inexact.
Castor or *Palma-Christi* (316). *Ricinus communis*. Sr *krapata*.
Cayenne Pepper (264). *Capsicum annuum* or *Capsicum frutescens*.
Cedar (573). The Spanish cedar, *Cedrela odorata*. Sr *sedre*.
China-Apples (245). Oranges, *Citrus sinensis*. Sr *apresina*.
Cica Pepper (377, pl. 52). A variety of *Capsicum frutescens*. Sr *sika*[chigoe]-*pepre* ‹ Wayana *šika*.
Cocareeta (201). Probably *Bactris major* Jacq.
Cocoa-Nut Tree (193, pl. 26). The coconut palm, *Cocos nucifera*.
cocoes (263). See *naapjes*.
Coffee (586, pl. 77). *Coffea arabica*.
Consaca-Weeree-Weeree (342). *Peperomia pellucida* H. B. K. Sr *konsaka-wiwiri* [athlete's foot weed].
Cotton (178, pl. 23). *Gossypium barbadense*. Sr *katoen*.
Coumoo (310). A palm, *Oenocarpus bacaba* Mart. Sr *koemboe* ‹ Carib *kumu*.
Crassy-Weeree-Weeree (342). Van Lier (1971, 467) suggests *Mucuna sloanei* Fawc. et Rendle.; other sources give *Jatropha urens*. Sr *krasi-wiwiri* [itch weed].
Crassy-Woodo (342). Unidentified.
Cupy (237). Kopie, *Goupia glabra* Aubl. Sr *kopi* ‹ Carib *kupi-i*.
Curetta or *Indian Soap* (221). *Furcraea foetida* Haw. Sr *ingi-sopo*.
Cutty Weeree-Weeree (342). Various Gramineae and Cyperaceae. Sr *koti-wiwiri*.
Dago peepee (377, pl. 52). A variety of *Capsicum frutescens*. Sr *dagoe*[dog]-*pepre*.
dates (439). The description most closely matches *Astrocaryum segregatum* Drude, already described by JGS in somewhat different terms (see *awara*).
Dea Weeree-Weeree (342). Possibly *Centropogon surinamensis* Presl. Sr *diaklaroen*.
Ducolla Bolla (573). Suriname satinwood, *Brosimum rubescens* Taub. ‹ Arawak *dukaliballi*.
Duncane (263). Dumb cane, *Dieffenbachia seguine* Schott. Sr *donke*.
Eta-Tree (310, 426). The miriti palm; see *Maureecee Tree*. Stedman's observation (426) that this tree is smaller than the miriti seems confused. ‹ Arawak *ité*.
Ginger (508). *Zingiber officinalis* Roscoe. Sr *djendja*.
Gourd or *Calebas Tree* (413). The calabash, *Crescentia cujete*. Sr *krabasi*. See note to page 308.
green-heart (310). The greenheart, *Tabebuia serratifolia* (Vahl)Nich. Sr *groen-ati*.

FLORA IDENTIFICATIONS

Guaba or *Guava-Tree* (322). *Psidium guajava*. Sr *goejaba*.

Hiarree (312). JGS means here *Lonchocarpus* spp. (‹ Arawak *hiari*), not *Helicostylis tomentosa* Machr. (also Arawak *hiari*). Not = *tingee-Woodo* (see below), another indigenous fish drug.

indigo (552, pl. 72). *Indigofera suffruticosa* Miller.

Iron-Wood Tree (333). *Swartzia prouacensis* (Aubl.) Amsh.

Jesmin (498). Jasmine, *Jasminum* spp.

Lattacaca [*Pepper*] (377, pl. 52). A variety of *Capsicum frutescens*. Sr *alatakaka*[ratshit]-*pepre*.

Lawna-Tree (306). The genipap, *Genipa americana*. See *Tapouripa*. ‹ Arawak *lana*.

Limes (377, pl. 52). *Citrus aurantifolia* Sw. Sr *lemki*.

Locust Tree (447). The courbaril, *Hymenaea courbaril*. Sr *loksi*.

Maize (263). *Zea mais*.

Mammee-Apple (379, pl. 52). The mammee, *Mammea americana*. Sr *mami*.

Mangrove (125). There are in fact three species in Suriname: *Rhizophora mangle*, which JGS discusses here, *R. harrisonii* Leechman, and *R. racemosa* G. F. W. Meyer.

Manicole or *Latanie* (191). See *Pina*.

Manioc (309). See *cassava*.

Marcusas (138). Passion fruit. Sr *markoesa*. There are several related species in Suriname. JGS here refers to *Passiflora laurifolia*.

Maripa (201). The maripa palm, *Maximiliana maripa* Drude. ‹ Carib *maripa*.

Markoory (459). Unidentified.

Marmalade Box (561). *Duroia eriopila* L. fil. Sr *marmadosoe*.

Matakee (201, 459). *Symphonia globulifera* L. fil. Sr *mataki*, Arawak and Carib *mani*.

Mawna tree (305, 316). Van Lier (1971, 465) suggests that JGS means here *mani* (see *Matakee*).

mawrisee tree (214). See *Maureecee Tree*.

Maureecee Tree (372, pl. 50). The miriti palm, *Mauritia flexuosa* L. fil. Sr *morisi*.

Medlars (449). Possibly *Mouriria* spp.

Mocco-Mocco (132). *Montrichardia arborescens* Schott. Sr *moko-moko*.

Monbiara (459). Unidentified.

Monpe (449). *Spondias mombin*. Sr and Carib *mope*.

Mountain-Cabbage-Tree (371, pl. 50). Probably the cabbage palm, *Roystonea oleracea* O. F. Cook.

Musk-Melon (484, pl. 64). *Cucumis melo*.

naapjes (263). *Dioscorea trifada*. Sr *napi*.

nebees (192). JGS uses this term quite generally for "lianas" or "vines," of which many species exist in Suriname (e.g., 214, 220), as well as for the aerial roots of *Araceae* (142).

[*Large*] *Nuts* (333). The monkeys appear to have been eating nuts from *Lecythis* spp.

FLORA IDENTIFICATIONS

ocro or *Althea* (238). Okra, *Hibiscus esculentus.* Sr *okro* ‹ any of several African languages.

Oryza (563). Rice, *Oryza sativa.*

Papau or *Papaya* (507). The papaya, *Carica papaya.* Sr *papaja.*

Physick nut Tree (494). Probably *Jatropha curcas,* though the seed has no "white skin." Sr *po-oka.*

Pigeon or *Angola Peas* (397). *Cajanus cajan* Millsp. = *C. indicus* Spreng.

Pina or *Manicole Tree* (191, pl. 26). A Palm, *Euterpe oleracea* Mart. Sr *pina, prasara.*

Pinda (379, pl. 52). The peanut or groundnut, *Arachis hypogaea.* Sr *pinda* ‹ kiKóongo *pindá.*

Pine Apple (pl. 64). See *Annana.*

Pistachio (379, pl. 52). The true pistachio (*Pistacia vera*), as depicted in pl. 52, is not otherwise reported for Suriname. See *Pinda.*

Plantains (296, pl. 38). *Musa* spp. Includes only fruits that must be cooked before eating. Sr *bana.*

Pomegranets (498, pl. 29 [flowers]). *Punica granatum.* Sr *granaki-bon.*

Pomme de Canelle (558). The sweetsop, *Annona squamosa.*

Purple-heart Tree (333). *Peltogyne pubescens* Benth. or *P. venosa* (Vahl) Benth. Sr *popo-ati.*

Qwacy Bitter (582). *Quassia amara,* named by Linnaeus in honor of "Graman Quacy." Sr *kwasi-bita.*

Sandkooker Tree (446). The sandbox tree, *Hura crepitans.* Sr *posentri.*

Sapadilla (507). The sapodilla or naseberry, *Manilkara zapota* Van Royen. Sr *sapatia.*

Sevejaars boontie (494). The civet bean, *Phaseolus lunatus.* Sr *sebijari-bonki.*

Seven boom (494). Unidentified.

Shaddock (44, pl. 5 [bottom]). The pompelmous, *Citrus grandis* Osb. Sr *poeploemoesoe.* A fruit somewhat resembling and probably ancestral to the grapefruit (*Citrus paradisi* Macf.).

Shame-Shame (498). Probably *Mimosa pudica.* Sr *sjensjen.*

Snakee Weeree Weeree (494). Button snakeroot, *Eryngium foetidum.* Sr *sneki-wiwiri.*

Soete Boonties (494). *Inga* spp. Sr *swit'bonki.*

sower-Orange (240). *Citrus aurantium.* Sr *swa'alanja.*

Sugar Cane (255, pl. 34). *Saccharum officinarum.* Sr *ken.*

Surinam Cherries (249). *Eugenia uniflora.*

Tamarind (92, pl. 9). *Tamarindus indica.* Sr *tamaren.*

Tapouripa (306). The genipap, *Genipa americana.* Sr *taproepa* ‹ Carib *tapurupo.* See *Lawna-Tree.*

tas (308). *Geonoma baculifera* Kunth. Sr *tasi.* The longest-lasting and most sought-after palm-roofing material in Suriname.

Tayars (493). Various *Araceae*: *Xanthosoma sagittifolium* Schott, *Alocasia macrorrhiza* Schott, *Colocasia esculenta* Schott. Sr *taja.*

tingee-Woodo or *konamee* (312). *Clibadium sylvestre* Baill. ‹ Carib *kunami.*

FAUNA IDENTIFICATIONS

Tobacco (494). *Nicotiana tabacum.*

Tomate (494). Tomato, *Lycopersicon esculentum* Miller.

Tonquin (601). The tonka-bean tree, *Dipteryx odorata* Willd. Sr *tonka.*

trooly (308). *Manicaria saccifera* Gaertn. Sr *troeli* ‹ Carib *turuli.*

Vanillas (502). *Vanilla* spp. Sr *baniri.*

Wana (237). The red louro, *Ocotea rubra* Mez. Sr *wana* ‹ Carib *wonu.* Still the wood most favored by Maroons and Indians for canoe making.

warimbo (221). *Ischnosiphon gracilis* Korn. Sr *warimbo.* Still the most important source of basketry fiber in Suriname.

Water-Withy (216). One of the *Dilleniaceae.*

Watter-Melon (484, pl. 64). Watermelon, *Citrullus vulgaris* Schrad. Sr *watramoen.*

Wild Cotton tree (520). The silk-cotton tree, *Ceiba pentandra.* Sr *kankantri.*

Wild Purslana (413). *Portulaca oleracea.*

woorara (312). *Strychnos guianensis* Baill. ‹Carib *urali.* See note to page 312.

Yamesy or *Yams* (263). *Dioscorea cayennensis* L.fil. or *D. alata.* Sr *jamsi* ‹ any of several West African languages.

Zurzack (507). The soursop, *Annona muricata.* Sr *soensaka.*

FAUNA

aboma (148, pl. 19). The anaconda, *Eunectes murinus.* (*Not* the boa constrictor, *pace* van Lier 1971, 458, and Bruijning and Voorhoeve 1977, 14.) Sr *aboma.*

Agama (334). Probably the Mexican chameleon, *Polychrus marmoratus.* Sr *agama,* but this term also includes other species of lizards.

Agamee or *Cani Cani* (213, pl. 27 [*top*]). The common trumpeter, *Psophia crepitans.* Sar *akamí,* Sr *kamikami.*

Agouti Pacarara (436, pl. 58 [*top*]). See *Indian Coney.*

Aligator (128). See *Kaiman.*

Amakee (579). The Bahama or white-cheeked pintail, *Anas bahamensis.* Sr *anaki.*

Amazone-Macaw (166, pl. 21 [*bottom*]). The scarlet macaw, *Ara macao.* Sr *bok rafroe.*

Ambulatory or *walking Leaf* (394). See *foeille Ambulante.*

Ammodytes or *Papaw Serpent* (522). The boa constrictor, *Constrictor constrictor.* Sr *papasneki.* See note to page 522.

Amphisboenoe (471). A limbless lizard, *Amphisbaena fuliginosa.* Sr *toe-ede-sneki* [two-headed snake].

Annamoe (344, pl. 45 [*bottom*]). The great tinamou, *Tinamus major.* Sr *mamafowroe anamoe.*

Ants (425). JGS's descriptions are inexact. His "Perfectly Black" ants are probably *Paraponera clavata,* which do not cut leaves. The two species of Suriname leaf-cutting ants are *Atta cephalotes* and *A. sexdens.* The army ants are *Eciton* spp.

Arlacacca (446). *Geoemyda punctularia.* Sr *arakaka.*

FAUNA IDENTIFICATIONS

Armadillo (pl. 24 [*bottom*]). See *Capasee*.
Bajew (250, pl. 33 [*top*]). The Guiana white-tailed deer, *Odocoileus virginianus cariacou* Boddaer. Sr *awojo-dia*.
bat (206, 428). The South American vampire bat, *Desmodus rotundus* E. Geoffroy. Typically bites humans on the big toe.
Blatta (162). See *Cockroach cald Cakrelaca*.
Blew-and-Yellow Macaw (164, pl 21 [*top*]). The blue-and-yellow macaw, *Ara ararauna*. Sr *tjamba rafroe*.
Blue Dipsas (471, pl. 62 [*bottom*]). Unidentified.
boossy-Calcoo (200). The marail guan, *Penelope marail*. Sr *marai*.
bossee cabritta (250, pl. 33 [*bottom*]). The brown or grey brocket, *Mazama gouazoubira nemorivaga* F. Cuvier. Sr *boesi-krabita*.
Bush-Rat (436). See *Wood-Rat*.
Bush-Spider (395). The South American bird spider, *Avicularia avicularia*. Sr *boes'anansi*.
Bush-Worms (460). Any of several species of grubs carried by mosquitoes, e.g., *Dermatobia hominis* Say. Sr *maskitaworon*.
[*Azure blue*] *Butterfly* (pl. 29). Merian depicts this butterfly in her pl. 9 (1705).
[*Beautiful*] *Butterfly* (336, pl. 44 [*top*]). *Ageronia* spp. Merian depicts this butterfly in her pl. 8 (1705).
[*Blue & Crimson*] *Butterfly* (pl. 44 [*top*]). See [*Beautiful*] *Butterfly*.
[*Green*] *Butterfly of South America* (472, pl. 62 [*top*]). *Urania leilus*. The same moth is depicted in Merian's pl. 29 (1705).
[*large Diurnal*] *butterflies* (227, pl. 29). *Morpho menelaus*. See [*Azure blue*] *Butterfly*.
Cabbage-Worms (338, pl. 44 [*bottom*]). Palmnut grubs, larvae of *Rhynchophorus palmarum*. Sar *sómbi*.
Cabiay (423). The capybara, *Hydrochoerus hydrochaeris*. Sr *kapoewa*.
Calapee (38). The green turtle, *Chelonia mydas*. Sr *krapé*.
Camawerry (459). The white-necked or cocoi heron, *Ardea cocoi*. Sr *koemawari*.
Capasee (185, pl. 24 [*bottom*]). There are five known species of armadillo in Suriname. "The largest," which JGS discusses, is the giant armadillo, *Priodontes giganteus* E. Geoffroy, Sr *granman-kapasi*. Pl. 24 depicts either of two similar species: the nine-banded armadillo, *Dasypus novemcinctus novemcinctus* (Sr *kapasi*), or Kappler's armadillo, *D. kappleri kappleri* (Sr *maka-kapasi*).
Carett (38). Caretta or loggerhead turtle, *Caretta caretta*. Sr *karet*.
Caribean-Wren (109). See *Gado-fowlo*.
cerfvolent (224). Lucanidae. Otherwise undocumented for Suriname.
Chigoes (136, 283). Chigoes or sand fleas, *Tunga penetrans*. Sr *sika*.
Coata Monkey (419). The spider monkey, *Ateles paniscus*. Sr *kwata*.
Coati Mondi (356, 567, pl. 74 [*top*]). The coatimundi, *Nasua nasua*. Sr *kwas'-kwasi*.
Cocatoos (316). Probably the red-fan parrot, *Deroptyus accipitrinus*. Sr *fransmadam*.
Cockroach cald Cakrelaca (162). *Periplaneta americana*. Sr *kakalaka*.

FAUNA IDENTIFICATIONS

Coemma-Coemma (203). One of the Suriname sheatfish, *Sciadeichthys emphysetus*. Sr *koemakoema*.

Common Parrot (343, pl. 45 [*top*]). The orange-winged or common Amazon parrot, *Amazona amazonica*. Sr *koele koele*.

Coot-Eye (120). The four-eyed fish, *Anableps anableps* or *A. microlepis*. Sr *koetai*.

Couguar or *Red Tiger* (359). The puma, *Puma concolor discolor* Schreber = *Felis concolor*. Sr *dia-* or *reditigri*.

Cowereekee (579). Unidentified.

Cowflie (224). *Tabanus* spp. Sr *kawfré*.

Crabbo-Dago (349). The crab-eating raccoon, *Procyon cancrivorus*. Sr *krab'dagoe*. Not = the grison, which JGS depicts (after Buffon) in pl. 46 [*bottom*].

Crane of Surinam or *Jabiru* (579, pl. 75 [*bottom*]). The American wood-ibis or wood-stork, *Mycteria americana*. Sr *nengrekopoe*.

Cras-Pinco (286). Probably the older male white-lipped peccaries (see *Pingo*).

Crested Eagle (550). The harpy eagle, *Harpia harpyja*. Sr *gonini*.

Crocodile (130). See *Kaiman*.

Crocro (459). Haverschmidt suggests the greater ani, *Crotophaga major*, (Van Lier 1971, 473) but elsewhere (1968, 154) notes the similarity of its "krokrokro" call to that of the green ibis, *Mesembrinibis cayennensis*, which is the usual referent of Sr *korokoro*.

Cromback (459). The American whimbrel, *Numenius phaeopus*. Sr *krombek*.

Curema (464). One of the Suriname mullets, *Mugil curema*. Sr *prasi*.

Curliew (578). Probably one of the Scolopacidae.

Dago-Fisee (353, pl. 47 [*top*]). *Acestrorhynchus falcatus*. Sr *dagoefisi*, which also refers to *A. microlepis*.

Devil-of-the-Woods (334). Possibly *Plica umbra* Gray. Sr *agama*.

Dolphin (31, pl. 2). The dorado, *Coryphaena hippurus*.

Dung-fish (452). Unidentified.

Falcon or *Hawk* (300). See *Surinam Falcon* or *Hawk*.

firy-Ants (393). Probably *Solenopsis geminata* F.

Flycatcher (109, pl. 12 [*bottom*]). See *Sun fowlo*.

flying fish (34, pl. 2). Possibly *Exocoetus volitans*, as JGS suggests, but there are other similar species in the mid-Atlantic.

Flying-lice (574). JGS is correct; these are the sexuales of his *Wood Lice (Isoptera)*.

foeille Ambulante (394). Probably *Pterochroza* spp., but there are several other similar walking-leaf grasshoppers in Suriname.

Four-Miller (569). The pygmy anteater, *Cyclopes didactylus didactylus*, described here by JGS following Buffon. Sr *likanoe*.

Gado-fowlo (109). The house wren, *Troglodytes aedon*. Sr *gadofowroe*.

Gelenies (500). See *Tokay*.

Grampus (608). *Grampus orca*.

Grass-Snipe (294). The common snipe, *Gallinago gallinago*.

Grass-Sparrow (490). Probably the green-rumped parakeet, *Forpus passerinus*. Sr *okro-prakiki*.

Great Ant eater (568, pl. 74 [*bottom*]). The giant anteater, *Myrmecophaga tridactyla tridactyla*. Sr *tamanwa*. Mislabeled "Tamandua" in pl. 74 [*bottom*]. See *Tamandua*.
Green Parrots (pl. 45 [*top*]). See *Common Parrot*.
Grison (350, pl. 46 [*bottom*]). The Guiana marten, *Galictis vittata vittata*. Sr *weti-aira*. Not = *Crabbo-Dago*.
groegroe (338, pl. 44). See *Cabbage-Worms*.
grow-Muneck or *gray-frier* (240). A sea bass, either *Hypoplectrus chlorurus* or *Epinephelus itajara*. Sr *granmorgoe*.
Guiana-Curlew (276, pl. 36 [*bottom*]). The scarlet ibis, *Eudocimus ruber*. Sr *kori kori* or *flamingo*.
Guiana-Porcupine (185, pl. 24 [*top*]). The South American tree porcupine, *Coendou prehensilis prehensilis*. Sr *djindja-maka*.
Haddock (506). *Cynoscion acoupa* (Lac.) Jord. Sr *koebi*.
Hedge hog (187). Unidentified.
Herring-Gulls (611). *Larus argentatus*.
Hippocampus or *Sea Horse* (607). Various species of *Hippocampinae*.
Howling Baboons (502). The red howler monkey, *Alouatta seniculus straminea* Humboldt. Sr. *baboen*.
Humming Bird (pl. 65). See *Trochilus*.
Indian Coney (436, pl. 58 [*top*]). The red-rumped agouti, *Dasyprocta leporina leporina*, also sometimes designated *D. aguti*, *D. cayana* Lacépède, and *D. aguti cayana* Lacépède. Sr *kon'koni*.
indian-Rat-Coney (436). Probably the red acouchi. See *Wood-Rat*.
Jackee (114). In fact, the larvae of a frog, identified by van Lier (1971, 456) as *Rana piscatrix*, and by Bruijning and Voorhoeve (1977, 308) as *Pseudis paradoxa*. Sr *todo-djaki*.
Jackee (203). A fish, *Rhamdia quelen*. Not = the frog mentioned on 114. Sr *djaki*.
Jaguar (358, pl. 48 [*top*]). *Panthera onca* = *Leo onca*. Sr *penitigri*.
Jaguaretta (359). The jaguarondi, *Felis yagouaroundi* = *Herpailurus y.* E. Geoffroy. Sr *boesikati*.
Kaiman (128, pl. 15 [*bottom*]). There are three species of *Alligatoridae* in Suriname. Pl. 15 depicts *Caiman crocodilus*, which JGS claims reaches 20 feet, though modern authorities claim only 8 feet. JGS's *Crocodile* description (130) is insufficiently exact to permit the choice between *Paleosuchus palpebrosus* and *P. trigonatus*. Sr *kaiman*.
Kawiry (269). Van Lier (1971, 462) suggests *Mugil brasiliensis*, Sr *kweriman*, but JGS's description does not at all match that in Bruijning and Voorhoeve 1977, 359.
keesee-keesee (142, pl. 18 [*top*]). There are eight species of monkeys in Suriname. Although JGS's reports of relevant local terminology seem confused, his descriptions and plates permit identification. JGS's *Keesee-keesee*, the two monkeys depicted in pl. 18 [*top*]), are brown capuchins, *Cebus apella apella*. Sr *keskesi*, *mekoe*, and *granmonki*. See *Monkee-Monkee*.

Kibry-fowlo (284). Unidentified.
King of the Vultures (550). The king vulture, *Sarcoramphus papa*. Sr *granmantingifowroe*.
Lamper (269). Unidentified.
Land Scorpion (560). There are many species in Suriname. Sr *kroektoetere*.
Land Turtle (445). Van Lier (1971, 472) gives *Geochelone* spp.
Leguana (130, pl. 15 [*top*]). The iguana, *Iguana iguana*. Sr *legwana*.
lipee-banaw (299). JGS describes two species: the yellow-rumped cacique, *Cacicus cela* (Sr *banabeki*), and the red-rumped cacique, *C. haemorrhous* (Sr *redi banabeki*).
Locusts (452). Probably *Schistocerca* spp.
logo-logo (299). Not an eel but a fish, *Gymnotus carapo* or *G. anguillaris*. Sr *logologo*.
Long Nosed Caviay (436). See *Indian Coney*.
Macrely-fisy (269). The tunny, *Thunnus thynnus*. Sr *makrede*.
Manatee (184, 453, pl. 59 [*bottom*]). The American manatee, sea cow, or lamentin, *Trichechus manatus manatus*. Sr *sekoe*.
Marobonso (277). A wasp, *Poliatis canadensis* or *P. infuscatus* Lep. Sr *marbonsoe*.
Matuary (299). A fish, identified by van Lier (1971, 463) as *Crenicichla saxatilis*. Sr *matoewari*.
Mawkers (46). Probably one of the larger local species of mosquitoes (see *Muskitos*), but possibly stinging flies, *Tabanidae*. Sr *makoe*.
Meecoo (142). See *Keesee-keesee*.
Monkee-Monkee (142, pl. 18 [*bottom*]). The common squirrel monkey, *Saimiri sciureus sciureus*. Sr *monkimonki*. Two are clearly depicted in pl. 18 [*bottom*], though erroneously labeled there *kishee-kishee*.
Monpeira (252). Gnats, *Ceratopogonidae*. Sr *mampira*.
Murine or *Mouse Oppossum* (429, pl. 57 [*top*]). See *Philander* or *Mexican Oppossum*.
Muskitos (46). Any of a variety of *Culicidae* found in Suriname, e.g., *Aedes* spp., *Anopheles* spp., or *Culex* spp. Sr *maskita*.
Naaynaay Fisee (452). Probably the freshwater garfish *Potamorrhaphis guianensis*. Sr *nanaifisi*.
Narval (36). The narwhal, *Monodon monoceros*.
New-mara (353, pl. 47 [*bottom*]). *Hoplius macrophthalmus*. Sr *anjoemara*.
North-Caper (608). Unidentified.
Oisters (301). In fact, mussels, *Mytilla charruana* d'Orb.
Oroccoco Snake (422). The fer-de-lance, *Bothrops atrox*. Sr *owroekoekoe-sneki*.
Ouriwifee (452). Van Lier's authority (1971, 314) suggests *Cichla ocellaris* (Sr *toekoenali*), but *Chiclosoma bimaculatum* (Sr *owroewefi*) seems more likely.
Paca (435, pl. 58 [*bottom*]). The paca, *Agouti paca*. Sr *hei* or *é*.
Pakeira (286, pl. 37 [*bottom*]). The collared peccary, *Tayassu tajacu*. Sr *pakira*.
Parrot of a Deep Slate Blue Colour (343). The dusky parrot, *Pionus fuscus*.
Passay (464). *Brachyplatystoma vaillanti*. Sr *pasisi* or *lalaw*.
Patakee (452). *Hoplias malabaricus*. Sr *pataka*.

Pattat (39). *Trombicula batatas.* Sr *patataloso.*

Peroquets (344). JGS's descriptions are inexact. "The finest" may be the seven-colored parakeet (= lilac-tailed parrotlet), *Touit batavica,* and the other the green-winged parakeet (= green-rumped parrotlet), *Forpus passerinus* (Sr *okro-prakiki*).

Pery (127). The piranha, *Serrasalmus rhombeus.* Sr *piren.* JGS's claim that this fish is "sometimes near 2 feet long," which was dismissed as false by van Lier's authority (1971, 457), is in fact correct, as we can attest from considerable first-hand experience.

Philander or *Mexican Oppossum* (567, pl. 57 [*top*]). The four-eyed opossum, *Philander opossum.* Sr *fo-ai-awari.* Although mislabeled "Murine Oppossum" there, pl. 57 [*top*] and JGS's description (429) clearly depict the four-eyed opossum.

Picui-nima (248). Probably the common ground dove, *Columbigallina passerina,* rather than *C. talpacoti,* the ruddy ground dove. Sr *stondoifi.*

Pilot Fish (609). *Naucrates ductor.*

Pingo (286, pl. 37 [*top*]). The white-lipped peccary, *Tayassu pecari.* Sr *pingo.*

Pipa (210). Van Lier (1971, 460) gives *Bufo marinus,* which fits JGS's comments on size, but the rest of the description suggests rather the Suriname water-toad, *Pipa americana* (= *Pipa pipa*). Sr *swampoetodo.*

Plover (489). Probably *Charadrius* spp.

Porcupine (pl. 24, [*top*]). See *Guiana-Porcupine.*

Porpuses (611). Porpoise, probably *Phocaena* spp.

Portuguee manowar (33). Portuguese man-of-war, *Physalia* spp.

Powesa (213, pl. 27 [*bottom*]). The black or crested curassow, *Crax alector.* Sr *powisi.*

Prare-Prare (464). *Ageneiosus brevifilis.* Sr *prarprari.*

Provost (464). Unidentified.

Quarta (328, pl. 42 [*bottom*]). The spider monkey, *Ateles paniscus.* Sr *kwata.*

Que-Quee (131). *Hoplosternum thoracatum.* Sr *kwikwi* (which also includes other species).

queese-queedee (248). The great kiskadee, *Pitangus sulphuratus.* Sr *gritjibi.*

Qwacy-Qwacy (567). See *Coati Mondi.*

Rattle Snake (470, 596, pl. 62 [*bottom*]). *Crotalus durissus.* Sr *sakasneki.*

Red-Breast (489). The red-breasted blackbird, *Leistes militaris.* Sr *rediborsoe.*

Red Curlew (pl. 36). See *Guiana-Curlew.*

Remora (609, pl. 79). Various species of Echeneididae.

Rhinocerous beetle (223). *Megasoma actaeon.* Sr *asege.*

Rock Cod (353, pl. 47 [*bottom*]). See *New-Mara.*

Sabacoo (264). Probably the little blue heron, *Florida caerulea.* Sr *sabakoe* includes several other small herons.

Saccawinkee (329, pl. 42 [*top*]). The red-handed tamarin, *Saguinus midas.* Sr *sagoewenki.*

Salamanders (334). Otherwise not reported for Suriname.

FAUNA IDENTIFICATIONS

Sapagala (250, 448). The tegu lizard, *Tupinambis negripunctatus* Spix. Sr *sapakara*.

Sara-Sara (310). A crayfish, *Macrobrachium carcinus*. Sr *sarasara*.

Saw fish (36). The sawfish, *Pristis pectinatus*.

Scaar-Sleep (347). A cicada, probably *Fidicina plebeia*. Sr *siksijoeroe*. Not = JGS's *Vieleur*.

Scolopendras or *Centipedes* (448). Chilopoda. Sr *loesoembe*.

scrapat (39). Larva of a tick, probably *Amblyomma americanum*.

Sea Snails (464). Mollusca/gastropoda.

Seereeca (310). A crab, *Callinectes bocourti* A. M. Edwards. Sr *srika*.

Separee (506). Either of two sweetwater stingrays, but probably *Potamotrygon reticulatus*. Sr *spari*.

Shoveler or *Spoon Bill* (579, pl. 75 [top]). The roseate spoonbill, *Ajaia ajaja*.

Siliba (496). Any of several Characidae. Sr *sriba*.

Sloth call'd loyaree or *Hiaey* (132, pl. 16). There are indeed two species in Suriname: the three-fingered sloth, *Bradypus tridactylus* (pl. 16 [bottom], Sr *sonloiri*), and the two-fingered sloth, *Choloepus didactylus* (pl. 16 [top], Sr *skapoeloiri*).

Snakefish (367). *Synbranchus marmoratus*. Sr *snek'fisi*.

Snipe (578). See *Grass-Snipe*.

Sokay (496). *Hoplosternum littorale*. Sr *soke-* or *hei-ede kwikwi*.

Sookooroorkee (579). The black-bellied tree-duck, *Dendrocygna autumnalis*. Sr *skroerki*.

Spaanse-Juffer (347). Although this name usually refers to the praying mantis, JGS here describes the walkingstick insect, Phasmidae.

Spotted-Cat (367). Probably *Pseudoplatystoma fasciatum*. Sr *spigrikati*.

Spur-wing'd Water-Hen (274, pl. 36 [top]). The wattled jacana, *Jacana jacana*. Sr *kempanki*.

Squirls (332). There are two species of squirrels in Suriname: the Guiana tree squirrel, *Sciurillus aestuans*, and the South American pygmy squirrel, *S. pusillus* Desmarest. Neither JGS's "white" nor his "flying" squirrel is otherwise reported for Suriname. Sr *bonboni*.

Storm Bird (30). Storm petrel, *Hydrobates pelagicus*.

Strix or *Night Owl* (504). The tropical screech-owl, *Otus choliba*. Sr *owroekoekoe*.

Sunfish (367). Probably *Pomacanthus arcuatus*. Sr *sonfisi*.

Sun fowlo (109, pl. 12 [bottom]). The sunbittern, *Eurypyga helias*. Sr *sonfowroe*.

Surinam Falcon or *Hawk* (300). There are some 43 species in Suriname, and JGS's description is insufficiently precise for identification.

Sword Fish (36). The swordfish, *Xiphias gladius*.

Tamandua (569). The lesser anteater, *Tamandua longicaudata longicaudata* Wagner. Not the animal depicted in pl. 74 [bottom], which corresponds to JGS's *Great Ant eater* or *Tamannoir*. Sr *mirafroiti*.

Tamannoir or *Antbear* (330, pl. 74 [bottom]). See *Great Ant eater*.

Tapira (454, pl. 59 [*top*]). The South American tapir, *Tapirus terrestris*. Sr *bofroe*.
Tarpoon (496). The tarpon, a saltwater fish, *Megalops atlanticus*.
Tavous (144). The smaller animal is the Guiana otter, *Lutra enudris* F. Cuvier; the larger is the giant or flat-tailed otter, *Pteronura brasiliensis brasiliensis*. Sr *watradagoe*.
Tiger-Cat (359, pl. 48 [*bottom*]). The ocelot, *Felis pardalis* = *Leopardus p. melanurus* Ball. Sr *tigrikati*.
tigri-fowlo (126). The rufescent tiger-heron, *Tigrisoma lineatum*. Sr *tigrifowroe*.
Tokay (500). The common guinea fowl, *Numida meleagris*, originally from West Africa. Sr *toke*.
Toreman (294). Van Lier's authority (1971, 463) suggests the marail guan, *Penelope marail*. Sr *marai*.
Torporific or *Electrical Eel* (114). The electric eel, *Electrophorus electricus*. Sr *prake*.
Torro-Torro (496). Van Lier's authority (1971, 474) suggests *Nebris microps*.
Towcan (109, pl. 12 [*top*]). The toco toucan, *Ramphastos toco*. Sr *koejake*.
tree-frog (187). JGS's description is too inexact to choose between *Dendrobatidae* and *Hylidae*.
Trochilus or *Humming-birds* (490, pl. 65). The tufted coquette, *Lophornis ornata*. Sr *kownoebri*.
turtles (248). Any of several local *Columbidae*.
Tuyew or *Emu* (200). Van Lier's authority (1971, 133) suggests the horned screamer, *Anhima cornuta*.
Vampier or *Spectre of Guiana* (428, pl. 57 [*bottom*]). The first part of JGS's description and pl. 57 depict the tropical American false vampire bat, *Vampyrum spectrum*, the largest New World bat. The true bloodsucking bat of Suriname, the South American vampire bat, *Desmodus rotundus* E. Geoffroy, is quite small. See *bat*.
Vieleur (347). The Suriname lanternbearer, *Fulgora laternaria*. Not = JGS's *Scaar-Sleep*.
Vultures or *Tingee-Fowlo* (550). There are four species in Suriname. JGS seems to be referring to the black vulture, *Coragyps atratus*. Sr *tingifowroe*.
Wanacoe (329). The pale-headed saki, *Pithecia pithecia*. Sr *wanakoe*.
Waracoo (597). *Schizodon fasciatus* (Sp.) Ag. Sr *warakoe*.
Warappa (203, 452). *Hoplerythrinus unitaeniatus*. Sr *warapa*.
Waree Hogs (422). See *Pingo*.
wassy-wassy (157, 502). Various wasps, members of the superfamily *Vespoidea*. Sr *waswasi*.
Weepee (597). Van Lier (1971, 479) identifies this as the stringray, *Potamotrygon reticulatus*, but this seems unlikely.
Whip Snake (423). Van Lier (1971, 294) identifies this as *Oxybelis argenteus*. Sr *wipi-sneki*.
white *Shark* (608). Unidentified.
Wirrebocerra (252, pl. 33 [*bottom*]). See *bossee cabritta*.
Wood-Cock (334). Probably the great tinamou. See *Annamoe*.

Wood-Lice (574). Termites (*Isoptera*). The massive nests on trees are built by *Nasutitermes* spp. Sr *oedoeloso*.

Woodo-Louso fowlo (500, pl. 67 [*top*]). The black-tailed trogon, *Trogon melanurus*. Sr *oedoeloso-fowroe*.

Wood Pecker (500, pl. 67 [*bottom*]). The chestnut woodpecker, *Celeus elegans*.

Wood-Rat (349, pl. 46 [*top*]). The red acouchi, *Myoprocta exilis* Wagler = *M. acouchy* Erxleben. Sr *maboela*.

Yellow Back (597). *Sciadeichtys luniscutis* C & V. Sr *jarabaka*.

Yellow Woodpecker (pl. 67). See *Wood Pecker*.

Yombo-Yombo (261). Van Lier (1971, 461) gives *Hylanubra laurenti*. Sr *djompo-djompo*.

Appendix B: Sources for Literary Citations

In writing his "Narrative," Stedman made liberal use of literary citations, about two-thirds of which were deleted in the 1796 publication. The sources of some of these were indicated in the 1790 text; for many of the Latin passages, translations were also given, either in a section at the end of the manuscript, entitled "Explination of the Latin Verses," or, occasionally, in the text itself. Stedman drew on classical works, the Bible, and the writing of Milton, Pope, Shakespeare, Swift, James Thomson, Voltaire, Phillis Wheatley, members of the Della Cruscan school, and many others, often altering the original wording for the "Narrative." In some cases, the modifications were clearly intentional; in a passage taken from the *Iliad* in which Andromache is bidding farewell to Hector, for example, he changed "he" to "I" to adapt it for a scene in which he is parting from Joanna. In other cases, the discrepancies seem to be simple mistakes in wording, spelling, or punctuation; a passage from Pope, for example, that read "Why has not man a microscopic eye? / For this plain reason, man is not a fly" was rendered as "Why has not Man a Microscopic Eye? The reasons Plain because Man's not a fly" (p. 169). And the non-English passages contain countless errors of spelling and grammar. In this edition, we have retained intact the versions that appeared in Stedman's manuscript. We offer below notes on Stedman's citations, indicating by the initials "JGS" those translations and attributions that have been taken directly from the 1790 "Explination of the Latin Verses."

There remain a substantial number of citations that we have not been able to identify. Many of these were taken from either the large body of antislavery verse or the equally voluminous output of bucolic poetry that was being produced during this period. Clearly, some of the verse was penned by Stedman himself, who was known to express himself in verse from time to time and who had several of his poems published during the 1780s and 1790s (see, for example, the printed pages from various issues of the *Weekly Entertainer* pasted into Stedman's diary between entries for 28 September 1790 and 4 February 1791, in the March 1795 entry, and facing the entry for April 1795); see also his lengthy poem about his outward voyage to Suriname (published for the first time in R. and S. Price 1985). But because Stedman was also given to quoting mediocre verse without noting its source, it has often not been possible to determine which passages are his own. We hope that readers of this book will, over the course of time, recognize some of the passages that we have not been able to identify and supply their original sources for a future edition.

3. O Quantum terra . . .
Valerius Flaccus, *Argonauticon* 1.168–73.
11. Non, qui Sidonio . . .
"The Man, who cannot with Judicious eye / Discern the Fleece, that drinks the tyrian dye, / From the pale Latian; yet shall ne'er sustain / A Loss so touching, of such Hart felt pain, / As he, who can't, with Sense of happier kind / Distinguish Truth from falshood in the Mind. / —Horace—" (JGS). *Epistle* 1.10.26–29.
27. No Art without a Genius . . .
Source not identified.
30. This day a Day . . .
Source not identified.
30. Sic transit . . .
"Thus passes the glory of the world." Thomas à Kempis, *The Imitation of Christ* 1.3.
44. Exotic of Cerean dye . . .
Anonymous, "Jamaica, a Poem in Three Parts. Written in that Island, in the Year MDCCLXXVI" (1777), I, vv. 114–17.
50. Living great . . .
Alexander Pope, "Epitaph on Sir Godfrey Kneller" (1730), vv. 7–8.
73. Then loudly . . .
Homer, *Iliad* 3.275–80, 298–301.
92. The Wanton Courser . . .
Alexander Pope, *Homer's Iliad* (1715–20), 6.652–55.
98. But lo! with graceful Motion . . .
Source not identified.
108. Vera dicuntur . . .
"True things are spoken in darkness." Source not identified.
117. Ede bibe lude . . .
"Eat, drink and be merry for after death is no more Happiness.—" (JGS). Motto of the Epicureans.
117. Cast a mournfull . . .
Alexander Pope, *Homer's Iliad* (1715–20), 6.506–9.

SOURCES FOR LITERARY CITATIONS ON PAGES 127–249

127. If you Phisitians want . . .
   Source not identified.
139. Timeo Danaeos . . .
   "I fear Greeks even when bearing gifts." Vergil, *Aeneid* 2.49.
152. You Gallant . . .
   James Thomson, *The Seasons* (1730), "Summer," vv. 1041–46.
169. Why has not . . .
   Alexander Pope, *An Essay on Man* (1733), "Epistle I," vv. 193–94.
184. Hail Holy light . . .
   Paraphrase of John Milton, *Paradise Lost* (1667), 3.1–3. John Armstrong adapted Milton's lines in the opening of his 1744 poem, "The Art of Preserving Health."
194. From yonder Monarch . . .
   Anonymous, "Jamaica" (1777), 1, vv. 102–7.
206. Behold the Castle . . .
   Source not identified.
208. Et genus et virtus . . .
   "Both rank and virtue without reality are more vile than seaweed." Horace, *Sermones* 2.58.
226. Pudet hoec oprobria . . .
   "One is ashamed to be told opprobrious Language but more so when not able to retaliate with propriety.—Terence" (JGS). Ovid, *Metamorphoses* 1.758. Note that Stedman was incorrect in attributing this passage to Terence.
226. vas grandeur . . .
   Roughly: "Your airs are mascarades, children's games, like all your enterprises. When the curtain falls, emperors and subjects are all equals and comrades." Although Stedman attributes this passage to Voltaire, we have been unable to identify it.
230. Ibit eo quo . . .
   "None will behave in Action so desparately as those that are tired of their Lives—Horace" (JGS). *Epistle* 2.2.40.
242. The Samboe dark . . .
   Anonymous, "Jamaica" (1777), 2, vv. 27–28.
244. How great thy fame . . .
   Anonymous, "Jamaica" (1777), 1, vv. 79–82.
247. experienca . . .
   "Experience teaches." Source not identified.
249. Ne sit ancillae . . .
   "Let not my Phoceus think it shame / For a fair slave to own his flame; / A slave could stern Achilles move, / Abend his haughty Soul to Love: / Ajax, invincible in Arms, / Was Captiv'd by his Captiv's Charms. / Atrides, 'midst his triumph mourn'd, / And for a ravish'd Virgin burn'd, / What Time, the fierce Barbarian Bands / Fell by Pelides' conquering Hands / And troy (her Hector swept away) / Became to Greece an easier prey. / Who

knows, when Phillis is your Bride, / To what fine folks you'll be allied? / Her Parents dear, of gentle Race, / Shalt not their Son-in-law disgrace. / She sprung from Kings, or Nothing less, / And Weeps the Family's distress— / —Horace" (JGS). *Odes* 2.4.1-16.

257. Who toil and sweat . . .

Anonymous, "Jamaica" (1777), 2, vv. 42-54.

260. Here in close . . .

John Milton, *Paradise Lost* (1667), 4.708-15.

261. Orea libertas

"Golden liberty." Source not identified.

261. O Liberty . . .

Joseph Addison, "A Letter from Italy to the Right Honorable Charles, Lord Halifax" (1701), vv. 119-26.

262. Undeck'd save . . .

John Milton, *Paradise Lost* (1667), 5.380-85.

268. Teach Britain . . .

Anonymous, "A Poetical Epistle, from the Island of Jamaica, to a Gentleman of the Middle-Temple," published with the author's "Jamaica" (1777), vv. 37-38.

272. Her heavenly . . .

John Milton, *Paradise Lost* (1667), 9.457-62.

274. Pone me pigris . . .

"Place me where never Summers breese / Unbends the glebe or warms the Trees / Where everlowring Clouds appear / And angry Jove deforms th'inclement Year / Place me beneath the burning ray / Where rolls the rappid Car of Day / Love and the Nymph shall charm my toils / The Nymph who sweetly speaks and sweetly smiles—Horace" (JGS). *Odes* 1.22.17-24. In all probability, Stedman copied both the Latin and the English translation of this passage from Fielding's *Tom Jones* (bk. 12, chap. 10).

277. While I recline . . .

Anonymous, "Jamaica" (1777), 1, vv. 83-86.

278. Say not I died . . .

Source not identified.

279. T'is folly . . .

Doctor Cotton is probably Charles Cotton (1630-87), poet and translator of Montaigne, but we have not been able to identify this passage.

282. veritas audium . . .

"Truth gives birth to hate." Terence, *Andria* 68.

293. The Cloud Capt towers . . .

William Shakespeare, *The Tempest* (1611), 4.1.152-54.

295. nemo homnibus . . .

"No one knows in every hour." Source not identified.

297. But what kind fruit . . .

Anonymous, "Jamaica" (1777), 1, vv. 140-43.

SOURCES FOR LITERARY CITATIONS ON PAGES 303-75

303. Lo the Poor . . .
Alexander Pope, *An Essay on Man* (1733), "Epistle I," vv. 99-113.
304. For modes of . . .
Alexander Pope, *An Essay on Man* (1733), "Epistle III," vv. 305-6.
316. Now with full . . .
Alexander Pope, *Homer's Iliad* (1715-20), 4.152-57.
327. Let others brave . . .
James Thomson, *The Seasons* (1730), "Autumn," vv. 1278-79, 1284-86, and 1299-1302.
334. Rocks rich in Gems . . .
James Thomson, *The Seasons* (1730), "Summer," vv. 646-50.
334. But Chiefly. . .
James Thomson, *The Seasons* (1730), "Spring," vv. 83-86.
352. Ille Flagranti . . .
"Deep horror seizes ev'ry human Breast, / Their pride is humbled, and their fear confess'd: / While he from high his rolling thunder throws, / And fires the Mountains with repeated Blows: / —Virgil" (JGS). *Georgics* 1.331. Note that only the last two lines of the English passage translate the Latin given in the text. The beginning reads: Fugere ferae, et mortalia corda / Per gentis humilis stravit pavor.
355. Si quoties peceant . . .
"If Jupiter used his thunder Bolts as often as Men deserve he soon would have none to use" (JGS). Ovid, *Tristia* 2.33-34.
357. P. M. S. Edwardi Wynter . . .
"Sacred to the divine spirit of Edward Wynter, a knight who, still in his early youth, set out from his fatherland for the East Indies, where he engaged in business and amassed a large fortune, which could have been even greater had he not scorned it, living there in splendor and with honor. After 42 years he returned to England and took as his wife Emma, the daughter of Richard Howe, Squire of Norfolk. He died on March 2, at the age of 69. A.D. 1685/6. Erected by his most sorrowful wife in honor of a husband who treated her well." (Note that "P. M. S." should have been written "D. M. S." [Dis Manibus Sacrum].)
357. Nita Peregrinatio . . .
Finita peregrinatio = "The journey is over." Source not identified.
360. Some Afric Chief . . .
Anonymous, "A Poetical Epistle, from the Island of Jamaica," (1777), vv. 77-82.
362. Curse him with . . .
Source not identified.
362. Hodie tibi . . .
"Today is yours, tomorrow mine." Source not identified.
375. Should their Sins be as Scarlet . . .
Isaiah 1.18.

SOURCES FOR LITERARY CITATIONS ON PAGES 376-432

376. Bear me, Pomona . . .
James Thomson, *The Seasons* (1730), "Summer," vv. 663–68.

376. as Cold Water . . .
Proverbs 25.25.

387. Accidit in Puncto . . .
"What is not hoped for in a year happens in a moment." Source not identified.

388. If as Philosophy . . .
Anna Matilda [Hannah Parkhouse Cowley], *The Poetry of Anna Matilda* (1788), "Stanzas to Della Crusca," vv. 73–80. The Della Cruscans were a minor school of English poets who wrote a kind of overwrought, highly affected verse during the late eighteenth century. They took their name from the Florentine academy of that name, of which their leader, Robert Merry, was a member. Merry wrote the two poems attributed to "Della Crusca" that Stedman excerpts on pages 401 and 432. The other leader of the school was Stedman's Tiverton acquaintance Hannah Parkhouse Cowley, who wrote under the name of Anna Matilda.

389. Though they Dig . . .
Amos 9.2.

397. Now Black and Deep . . .
James Thomson, *The Seasons* (1730), "Autumn," vv. 1138–43.

400. But yonder . . .
James Thomson, *The Seasons* (1730), "Summer," vv. 81–85.

401. And 'tis most True . . .
Della Crusca [Robert Merry], "To Anna Matilda," vv. 65–81, published in *The Poetry of Anna Matilda*. (See entry for page 388 in this appendix.)

409. Inventas qui Vitam . . .
Source not identified.

414. Behold how good . . .
Source not identified.

415. Hic Labor . . .
"This Laborous bount, this Battle produc'd a rest for many Days, and both sides laying by their arms were quiet—Ovid" (JGS). *Metamorphoses* 12.146–47.

423. But still more . . .
James Thomson, *The Seasons* (1730), "Summer," vv. 907–11.

428. Be thou a Spirit . . .
William Shakespeare, *Hamlet* (1602), 1.4.40–41.

432. So two Young . . .
Alexander Pope, *Homer's Iliad* (1715-20), 5.681–88.

432. But Sure 'tis . . .
Della Crusca [Robert Merry], "Elegy, written on the Plain of Fontenoy," vv. 21–24, published in *The Poetry of Anna Matilda*. (See entry for page 388 in this appendix.)

SOURCES FOR LITERARY CITATIONS ON PAGES 433—68

433. Dependants, friends...
James Thomson, *The Seasons* (1730), "Summer," vv. 1080—82.
438. Voxet Pretera...
"A voice and nothing more." Source not identified.
441. Take back the...
Alexander Pope, *Homer's Iliad* (1715—20), 4.404.
442. Forget the Dunghill...
Source not identified.
442. Prive de tout...
Roughly: "Deprived of all my possessions in a deadly climate, I adore you and lose you. Only the dagger remains for me. But oh, I am *Pater*, and have been marked for suffering. I would still be able to live, and to do more than die." Although Stedman attributes this passage to Voltaire, we have been unable to identify it.
448. Flaming Up...
James Thomson, *The Seasons* (1730), "Summer," vv. 199—200, 209—11.
448. Who far from...
James Thomson, *The Seasons* (1730), "Autumn," vv. 1236—39, 1273—77.
453. Visa fugit...
"The Nymph when seen, fled, as the frighted doe does the yellow Wolf, and the River Duck, catch at a distance from the water left by her, flies the Hawk... She flies as swift as winds that sweep thro' air / Nor stop to hear this fond recalling prayer. / Stay, Nymph I pray thee stay, I am no foe; / So Lambs from Wolves, Harts fly from Lyons so: / So from the Eagle spring the trembling Dove; / —Ovid—" (JGS). *Metamorphoses* 11.771—72 and 1.500—505.
456. Far in the Deep...
Homer, *Iliad* 18.35—38.
456. Nos Cantabimus...
"With voices alternate, the sea Potent King / And the Nereids, with Ringlets of azure, we'll sing; / Lotona's, and swift darting cynthis's praise / The gay smiling goddess &c— / Horace" (JGS). *Odes* 3.28.9—13. (Latona, the Roman equivalent of Leto, was the mother of Apollo and Diana/Artemis.)
456. Nais an ut...
"Or how the Nai's pow'rful Herbs and song / Chang'd list'ning Youths into a sealy throng, / Till in their fate she shared who did $\frac{c}{y}$ wrong;—Ovid" (JGS). *Metamorphoses* 4.49—51.
460. *Life* makes...
Edward Young, *Night Thoughts* (1742—45), "Night the Third" (1742), vv. 450—59.
466. Such as Arcadian...
Source not identified.
468. She takes the Bow...
Homer, *Iliad* 23.870—81.

693

469. Mollis illa . . .
"That soft education that we call indulgence breaks all the muscles of the mind and the body." Quintilian, *Institutionis Oratoriae*, bk. 1, chap. 2.6.
483. Then to the . . .
James Thomson, *The Seasons* (1730), "Summer," vv. 1321–24.
484. O thou fair Melon . . .
Anonymous, "Jamaica" (1777), I, vv. 87–90.
486. Lo the poor . . .
William Shakespeare, *Measure for Measure* (1604), 3.1.79–81.
486. Should fate Command . . .
James Thomson, "A Hymn on the Seasons" (1730), vv. 100–106.
492. This is the . . .
James Thomson, *The Seasons* (1730), "Summer," vv. 1257–58, 1263–66.
500. For Natures hand . . .
James Thomson, *The Seasons* (1730), "Summer," vv. 735–40.
504. Even so a . . .
James Thomson, *The Seasons* (1730), "Spring," vv. 680–84.
507. Their Joice Combin'd . . .
Anonymous, "Jamaica" (1777), I, vv. 110–11.
508. Thou Land of . . .
James Thomson, *The Seasons* (1730), "Summer," vv. 781–83.
510. To put up . . .
John Pomfret, "The Choice" (1700), vv. 148–49.
514. Alba ligustra . . .
"How much more easy was to sustain / Proud Armarillis, and her haughty reign, / The scorns of young Menaleas, once my care / Tho' he was Black, and thou art heav'nly fair—Virgil—" (JGS).
517. Now here now . . .
Phillis Wheatley, *Poems on Various Subjects* (1773), "On Imagination," vv. 9–20, 22.
518. No Sooner *Irvan* . . .
William Mavor, *Poems* (1793), Ode 22, "Carloc and Orra. In Imitation of Ossian. Supposed from the Erse," vv. 37–64. In the "Advertisement" to the volume, Mavor notes that "many of these poems have been published in various forms, and on various occasions." Undoubtedly, Stedman referred for his text to one of these earlier versions.
519. Last Morn Proud Dano . . .
Source not identified.
520. Stay till I bring . . .
Alexander Pope, *Homer's Iliad* (1715–20), 6.322–26.
520. Add hither . . .
James Thomson, *The Tragedy of Sophonisba* (1730), 5.vii.
521. Talibus affatta . . .
"This said, the servants urged the sacred rites; / While to the Temple she the Prince invites / A spacious cave within its farmost part, / Was hew'd

SOURCES FOR LITERARY CITATIONS ON PAGES 521–24

and fashion'd by Laborious Art, / Tho' the Hill's hollow sides: before the Peace / A hundred doors, a hundred entries grace: / As many Voices issue: and the sound / Of Sibyl's Word as many times rebound. / Now to the Mouth they come: aloud she cries, / This is the Time, enquire your destanies— / He comes, behold the God! thus while she said / (And shiv'ring at the sacred entry staid) / Her colour chang'd, her face was not the same / And hollow grones from her deep spirit came / Her hair stood up; convulsive rage possess'd / Her trembling, and heav'd her lab'ring Breast. / Greater than human kind she seem'd to Look / And with an accent, more than Mortal, spoke / Her staring eyes with sparkling fury roll; / When all the Gods came rushing on her soul. / Swiftly she turn'd, and foaming as she spoke / Why this delay, she cry'd; the pow'rs invoke / Thy pray'rs alone can open this abode, / Else, vain are my demands, and dumb the God / She said no more: / —Virgil" (JGS). *Aeneid* 6.40–55.

522. *Finem dedit* . . .

"Struggling in vain, impatient of her Lord, / And lab'ring underneath the pond'rous God, / The more she strov'd to shake him from her Breast, / With more and far superiour force he press'd: / Commands his entrance, and without Comtroul; / Usurps her Organs, and inspires her Soul. / Now with a furious Blast the hundred doors / Ope of themselves; a rushing whirlwind soars / With in the Cave; and Sibyl's voice restores— / Thus, from the dark recess, the Sibyl spoke / And the resisting Air, the Thunder broke; / The Cave rebbellow'd; and the Temple shook. / Th'Ambiguous God, who rul'd her labring breast / In this mysterious words his mind expresst / Some truths reveal'd, in terms involv'd the Rest / At length her fury fell; her foaming ceas'd, / And ebbing in her Soul, the God decreas'd.—Virgil" (JGS). *Aeneid* 6.76–80, 98–103.

522. *Has ubi Praeteriit* . . .

"After he had passed these, and left the Parthinopian City on the right, and on the left side the Tomb of the Trumpeters, the Son of Aeolus, and places filled with fenny Sages; he enters upon the shores of Cumae, and the Cave of the long lived Sibyl; and begs to his Father's Ghost through Averna— But she raised at last, her Countenance fixed a long Time upon the Earth; and at length being distracted with the God she received into her, she said you designed great Things, O Man remarkable for great Achievements; whose right Hand has been proved by the Sword, and your piety by fire— Yet Trojan lay aside all your fear; you shall have your request; and with me for your guide, you shall visit the Elisaen abodes, and the lowest Kingdom of the World, and the Dear Image of your Father, no Way is unpassible to Courage— / —Virgil—" (JGS). Note that Stedman's attribution of this passage to Ovid in the text of the "Narrative" is correct; the reference is *Metamorphoses* 14.101–13.

524. *What Good man* . . .

Anonymous, "Jamaica" (1777), 3, vv. 57–64.

SOURCES FOR LITERARY CITATIONS ON PAGES 525–76

525. A Generous Friendship . . .
Source not identified.
529. The naked Negro . . .
Oliver Goldsmith, "The Traveller" (1764), vv. 69–74.
529. While he delv'd . . .
Source not identified.
531. Dictio testimonii . . .
"The recitation of testimony is not as a slave for man." Source not identified.
532. From Egypt first . . .
Samuel J. Pratt, *Humanity, or the Rights of Nature, a Poem* (1788), 17.
532. Detested Hawkins arm'd . . .
Samuel J. Pratt, *Humanity, or the Rights of Nature, a Poem* (1788), 22.
532. All! All is Lost . . .
Samuel J. Pratt, *Humanity, or the Rights of Nature, a Poem* (1788), 28.
533. But Hark! the Afric' Genius . . .
Anonymous, "Jamaica" (1777), 2, vv. 76–77.
533. O Slavery! thou Fiend . . .
Source not identified.
540. Saltantes Satyros . . .
"Alphesiboeus, tripping, shall advance; / And mimic satyrs in his antic dance— / —Virgil—" (JGS). *Eclogues* 5.73.
547. Disdains / Lo! tortures . . .
Anonymous, "Jamaica" (1777), 1, vv. 186–90.
549. Why *Christians* Rag'd . . .
It is possible that the American poet David Humphreys, senior author of the satirical poem *The Anarchiad: A New England Poem* (1786–87), is the author of these lines, but we have been unable to identify them.
549. And in those times . . .
Daniel 11.14.
549. After this Shall he . . .
Daniel 11.18.
557. Hence ev'ry Harsher . . .
James Thomson, *The Seasons* (1730), "Autumn," vv. 1208–10.
561. Live Sit quod . . .
"A Burthen is lightest when it is well born—" (JGS). Ovid, *Amores* 1.2.10.
561. All Conquering . . .
James Thomson, *The Seasons* (1730), "Summer," vv. 451–57.
572. Strength is Derived . . .
Alexander Pope, *Homer's Iliad* (1715–20), 19.159–68.
575. But vain theyr . . .
James Thomson, *The Seasons* (1730), "Summer," vv. 1083–86.
576. Sad Noisome Dark . . .
Source not identified.

SOURCES FOR LITERARY CITATIONS ON PAGES 577–612

577. Ah Little think . . .
James Thomson, *The Seasons* (1730), "Winter," vv. 322–28, 346–48.

579. Acti Labores . . .
"Labors that have been performed are pleasant." Cicero, *De Finibus Bonorum et Malorum* 2.32.

584. Soli deo Gloria . . .
"Glory to God alone. The Fortuna [Roman goddess of fortune] of the Baetici [inhabitants of an area of Spain corresponding to Andalusia and part of Grenada]."

585. Finis Coronant . . .
"The end crowns the work." Source not identified.

594. No *holy Fury* . . .
James Thomson, *The Seasons* (1730), "Summer," vv. 755–61.

599. What Conscience dictates . . .
Source not identified.

602. Si possem . . .
"Smit by new Pow'rs, my Heart unwilling bleeds, / Discretion there, and here affection pleads; / —Ovid—" (JGS). *Metamorphoses* 7.18–19.

602. Zaire il est . . .
"It is too true that I am commanded by honor, / That I loved you, that I am abandoning you, / That I am renouncing you, that you desire it, / That under another law [in other circumstances], . . . Zaire, are you weeping?" Voltaire, *Zaire* (1732), vv. 1151–54.

602. Atque ope nescio . . .
"And shall I then betray my Father's throne, / To save an Idle, wand'ring Youth, unknown? / Who by my aid preserv'd, shall prove unkind, / Sail off, and his preserver leave behind, / Then with his beauties bless some happier dame, / While I am left to punishment and shame / Could he scorn me, and to another fly? / Then without Pity let the traytor dye; / —Ovid—" (JGS). *Metamorphoses* 7.39–43.

605. Ne'er did my heart . . .
Probably excerpted from one of the antislavery poems written by Captain J. Marjoribanks, a British soldier stationed in Jamaica during the 1780s. In his journal, Stedman mentions being given a copy of "Majoribanks triffles in verce" (*14 September 1784*); these may be the poems referred to in Marjoribanks (1792, 5).

605. By my Sad Follies . . .
Source not identified.

607. Of all things . . .
Source not identified.

612. Sic ubi pucsarant . . .
"Thus after the violent Waves have beat the high sides of the Ship, the fury of the tenth Wave, rising vastly above the rest, rushes on, and ceases not to attack the Sides of the wearied ship before it descends into the sides of the taken Ship— / —Ovid—" (JGS). *Metamorphoses* 11.529–34.

SOURCES FOR LITERARY CITATIONS ON PAGES 613–26

613. In vain we Strove . . .
Source not identified.

613. But where am I? . . .
Source not identified.

615. Hail Source . . .
James Thomson, *The Seasons* (1730), "Spring," vv. 556–59.

615. Vox andita . . .
"The word once given out perishes, the written letter remains." Source not identified.

618. Per Varios . . .
"An Hour will come, with Pleasure to relate / Your Sorrows passt, as Benefits of Fate— / Through various hazards, and Events we move / To Latium, and the Realms foredoom'd by Jove.— / —Virgil—" (JGS). *Aeneid* 1.204-5, 203.

620. Magna est . . .
"Truth is great and will prevail." Source not identified.

621. And Could that . . .
Jonathan Swift, "A Satirical Elegy on the Death of a Late Famous General" (1722), vv. 3–8, 13–24, 31–32.

625. This Royal Throne . . .
Paraphrase of William Shakespeare, *King Richard II* (1593–94), 2.1.40–53.

626. Tibur Argeo . . .
Horace, *Odes* 2.6.5–8.

626. Let one poor Sprig . . .
Source not identified.

REFERENCES CITED

Anonymous
1818 "William Thomson, LL.D." *Annual Biography and Obituary*, 2: 74–117.

Anstey, Roger
1975 *The Atlantic Slave Trade and British Abolition, 1760–1810*. London: Macmillan.

Arens, W.
1979 *The Man-eating Myth: Anthropology and Anthropophagy*. Oxford: Oxford University Press.

Axtell, James, and William C. Sturtevant
1980 "The Unkindest Cut, or Who Invented Scalping?" *William and Mary Quarterly* (3d ser.) 37: 451–72.

Bancroft, Edward
1749 *An Essay of Natural History of Guiana in South-America in Several Letters from a Gentleman in the Medical Faculty*. London.

Beers, Henry Augustin
1899 *A History of English Romanticism in the Eighteenth Century*. New York: Holt.

de Beet, Chris
1984 *De Eerste Boni-Oorlog, 1765–1778*. BSB 9. Utrecht: Centrum voor Caraïbische Studies, Rijksuniversiteit Utrecht.

Behn, Aphra
1722 "The History of Oroonoko; or, the Royal Slave" [1688]. In *All the*

Histories and Novels Written by the Late Ingenious Mrs. Behn, Intire in Two Volumes, 75–200. London: A. Bettesworth.

Benjamins, H. D., and Joh. F. Snelleman, eds.
1914–17 *Encyclopaedie van Nederlandsch West-Indië.* The Hague: Martinus Nijhoff.

Bentley, G. E., Jr.
1977 *Blake Books.* Oxford: Clarendon Press.
1980 "The Great Illustrated-Book Publishers of the 1790s and William Blake." *Editing Illustrated Books,* edited by William Blissett, 57–96. New York: Garland.

Blair, Barbara L.
1984 "Wolfert Simon van Hoogenheim in the Berbice Slave Revolt of 1763–1764." *Bijdragen tot de Taal-, Land- en Volkenkunde* 140: 56–76.

Blake, William
1793 *America: A Prophecy.* London.

Bogan, James
1976 "Vampire Bats and Blake's Spectre." *Blake Newsletter* 37, 10(1): 32–33.

Bruijning, C. F. A., and J. Voorhoeve, eds.
1977 *Encyclopedie van Suriname.* Amsterdam: Elsevier.

Bubberman, F. C., A. H. Loor et al., and C. Koeman, ed.
1973 *Links with the Past: The History of Cartography in Suriname, 1500–1971.* Amsterdam: Theatrum Orbis Terrarum.

Buckley, Roger Norman
1979 *Slaves in Red Coats: The British West India Regiments, 1795–1815.* New Haven: Yale University Press.

Chambers, Robert
1869 *History of the Rebellion of 1745–46.* 7th ed. Edinburgh: W. & R. Chambers.

Clarkson, Thomas
1788 *An Essay on the Slavery and Commerce of the Human Species, Particularly the African.* 2d ed. London: J. Phillipps [orig. 1786].

Corncob, Jonathan [pseud.]
1787 *Adventures of Jonathan Corncob, Loyal American Refugee.* London [1976 ed. Boston: Godine].

Counter, S. Allen, and David L. Evans
1981 *I Sought My Brother: An Afro-American Reunion.* Cambridge: MIT Press.

Craton, Michael
1975 "Jamaican Slavery." In *Race and Slavery in the Western Hemisphere: Quantitative Studies,* edited by Stanley L. Engerman and Eugene D. Genovese, 249–84. Princeton: Princeton University Press.

REFERENCES CITED

Curtin, Philip D.
1969 *The Atlantic Slave Trade: A Census.* Madison: University of Wisconsin Press.

Darnton, Robert
1984 "Working-Class Casanova." *New York Review of Books* 31(11): 32–37.

Davis, David Brion
1966 *The Problem of Slavery in Western Culture.* Ithaca: Cornell University Press.
1975 *The Problem of Slavery in the Age of Revolution, 1770–1823.* Ithaca: Cornell University Press.

Davis, Michael
1977 *William Blake: A New Kind of Man.* London: Paul Elek.

Debien, Gabriel, and Johanna Felhoen Kraal
1955 "Esclaves et plantations de Surinam vus par Malouet, 1777." *De West-Indische Gids* 36: 53–60.

Dunning, John S.
1982 *South American Land Birds: A Photographic Aid to Identification.* Newton Square, Pa.: Harrowood Books.

Edwards, Bryan
1794 *The History, Civil and Commercial, of the British Colonies in the West Indies.* 2d ed. London: J. Stockdale.

Eilerts de Haan, J. G. W. J.
1910 "Verslag van de expeditie naar de Suriname-Rivier." *Tijdschrift van het Koninklijk Nederlandsch Aardrijkskundig Genootschap* (2d ser.) 27: 403–68, 641–701.

Erdman, David
1952 "Blake's Vision of Slavery." *Journal of the Warburg and Courtauld Institutes* 15: 242–52.
1969 *Blake: Prophet against Empire.* Princeton: Princeton University Press.

Essed, Hugo A. M.
1984 *De binnenlandse oorlog in Suriname, 1613–1793.* Paramaribo: Anton de Kom Universiteit van Suriname.

Essick, Robert N.
1973 "Blake and the Traditions of Reproductive Engraving." In *The Visionary Hand: Essays for the Study of William Blake's Art and Aesthetics,* edited by Robert N. Essick, 492–525. Los Angeles: Hennessey and Ingalls.
1980 *William Blake, Printmaker.* Princeton: Princeton University Press.

Evans-Pritchard, E. E.
1965 "Zande Cannibalism." In *The Position of Women in Primitive Societies and Other Essays in Social Anthropology,* 133–64. London: Faber & Faber.

REFERENCES CITED

Fairchild, Hoxie Neale
1928   *The Noble Savage: A Study in Romantic Naturalism.* New York: Columbia University Press.

Fermin, Philippe
1769   *Description générale, historique, géographique et physique de la colonie de Surinam.* Amsterdam: E. van Harrevelt.
1778   *Tableau historique et politique de l'état ancien et actuel de la colonie de Surinam, et des causes de sa décadence.* Maestricht: J. E. Dufour & Ph. Roux.

Fielding, Henry
1742   *The History of the Adventures of Joseph Andrews.* London: A. Millar.

Fontaine, Jos
1972   *Zeelandia: de geschiedenis van een fort.* Zutphen: De Walburg Pers.

Goveia, Elsa V.
1956   *A Study on the Historiography of the British West Indies to the End of the Nineteenth Century.* Mexico: Instituto Panamericano de Geografia e Historia.

de Groot, Silvia W.
1970   "Rebellie der Zwarte Jagers: de nasleep van de Bonni-Oorlogen, 1788–1809." *De Gids* 133: 291–304.
1975   "The Boni Maroon War, 1765–1793: Suriname and French Guiana." *Boletín de Estudios Latinoamericanos y del Caribe* 18: 30–48.
1980   "Boni's dood en Boni's hoofd: een proeve van orale geschiedenis." *De Gids* 143:3–15.

Handler, Jerome S., Arthur C. Aufderheide, Robert S. Corruccini, Elizabeth M. Brandon, and Lorentz E. Wittmers, Jr.
1986   "Lead Contact and Poisoning in Barbados Slaves: Historical, Chemical, and Biological Evidence." *Social Science History* 10:399–425.

Hansard
1848   *Parliamentary Debates* (3d ser.), vol. 96. London: G. Woodfall & Son.

Hartsinck, Jan Jacob
1770   *Beschrijving van Guiana of de Wilde Kust in Zuid-Amerika.* Amsterdam: Gerrit Tielenburg.

Haverschmidt, F.
1968   *Birds of Surinam.* Edinburgh: Oliver & Boyd.

Hepburn, James
1968   *The Author's Empty Purse and the Rise of the Literary Agent.* London: Oxford University Press.

Herklots, G. A. C.
1961   *The Birds of Trinidad and Tobago.* London: Collins.

REFERENCES CITED

Herlein, J. D.
1718 *Beschryvinge van de Volk-plantinge Zuriname.* Leeuwarden: Meindert Injema.

Herskovits, Melville J.
1929 "Adjiboto, An African Game of the Bush-Negroes of Dutch Guiana." *Man* 29: 122–27.
1932 "Wari in the New World." *Journal of the Royal Anthropological Institute* 62: 23–38.

Herskovits, Melville J., and Frances S. Herskovits
1936 *Suriname Folk-lore.* New York: Columbia University Press.

Higman, B. W.
1984 *Slave Populations of the British Caribbean, 1807–1834.* Baltimore: Johns Hopkins University Press.

Hoogbergen, Wim S. M.
1984 *De Boni's in Frans-Guyana en de Tweede Boni-Oorlog, 1776–1793.* BSB 10. Utrecht: Centrum voor Caraibische Studies, Rijksuniversiteit Utrecht.
1985 *De Boni-Oorlogen, 1757–1860: marronage en guerrilla in Oost-Suriname.* BSB 11. Utrecht: Centrum voor Caraibische Studies, Rijksuniversiteit Utrecht.

Hurault, Jean
1965 *La vie matérielle des Noirs Réfugiés Boni et des Indiens Wayana du Haut-Maroni.* Paris: Office de la Recherche Scientifique et Technique Outre-Mer.
1983 "Eléments de vocabulaire de la langue Boni (Aluku Tongo)." *Amsterdam Creole Studies* 6: 1–41.

Jones, James T., John Elting, and Anthony F. Gero
1981 "Netherlands 21st Marine Regiment in Surinam (Service Uniforms), 1772–1779." Plate no. 509. *Military Uniforms in America.* Providence: Company of Military Historians.

Jordan, Winthrop D.
1968 *White over Black: American Attitudes toward the Negro, 1550–1812.* Baltimore: Penguin Books.

Keynes, Geoffrey
1921 *A Bibliography of William Blake.* New York: Grolier Club of New York.
1969 "Introduction." In Charles Ryskamp, *William Blake, Engraver: A Descriptive Catalogue of an Exhibition,* 1–18. Princeton: Princeton University Press.
1971 *Blake Studies: Essays on His Life and Works.* 2d ed. London: Oxford University Press.

Kloos, Peter
1971 *The Maroni River Caribs of Surinam.* Assen: Van Gorcum.

Köbben, A. J. F.
1967 "Unity and Disunity: Cottica Djuka Society as a Kinship System." *Bijdragen tot de Taal-, Land- en Volkenkunde* 123: 10–52.

Lamur, Humphrey E.
1985 *De kersteningen van de slaven van de Surinaamse Plantage Vossenburg, 1847–1878*. Amsterdam: Antropologisch-Sociologisch Centrum.

Lewis, Gordon K.
1983 *Main Currents in Caribbean Thought: The Historical Evolution of Caribbean Society in Its Ideological Aspects, 1492–1900*. Baltimore: Johns Hopkins University Press.

van Lier, R. A. J.
1949 *Samenleving in een grensgebied: een sociaal-historische studie van Suriname*. The Hague: Martinus Nijhoff.
1971 *Narrative of a Five Years' Expedition against the Revolted Negroes in Surinam . . . by Captain J. G. Stedman*. Edited and introduced by R. A. J. van Lier. Barre, Mass.: Imprint Society.

Long, Edward
1774 *History of Jamaica*. London.

Marjoribanks, J.
1792 *Slavery: An Essay in Verse*. Edinburgh: J. Robertson.

Menezes, Mary Noel
1977 *British Policy towards the Amerindians in British Guiana, 1803–1873*. Oxford: Oxford University Press.

Merian, Maria Sibylla
1705 *Metamorphosis Insectorum Surinamensium ofte Verandering der Surinaamsche Insecten*. Amsterdam.

Mollema, J. C.
1941 *Geschiedenis van Nederland ter Zee*, derde deel. Amsterdam: Uitgeverij Joost van den Vondel.

Myers, Robert A.
1984 "Island Carib Cannibalism." *New West Indian Guide* 58: 147–84.

Nassy, David de Ishak Cohen et al.
1788 *Essai historique sur la colonie de Surinam . . . Le tout redigé sur des pieces authentiques y jointes, & mis en ordre par les régens & représentans de ladite Nation Juive Portugaise*. Paramaribo.

Neumann, Peter
1961 "Eine verzierte kalebassenschüssel aus Suriname." *Veröffentlichungen des Städtischens Museums für Volkerkunde zu Leipzig* 11: 481–98.

Ortiz, Fernando
1970 *Cuban Counterpoint: Tobacco and Sugar*. New York: Random House (Vintage Books) [orig. 1940].

REFERENCES CITED

Ostendorf, F. W.
1962 *Nuttige planten en sierplanten in Suriname*. Landbouwproefstation in Suriname Bull. No. 79. Amsterdam: Van Leeuwen.

Oudschans-Dentz, Fred.
1928/29 "Het einde van de legende Dahlberg-Baron." *De West-Indische Gids* 10: 165–67.
1938 *Cornelis van Aerssen van Sommelsdijck*. Amsterdam: P. N. van Kampen.

Pakosie, André R. M.
1972 *De dood van Boni*. Paramaribo.

van Panhuys, L. C.
1925 "Contribution à l'étude de la distribution de la serrure à chevilles." *Journal de la Société des Américanistes* (Paris) 17: 271–74.

Paulson, Ronald
1983 *Representations of Revolution (1789–1820)*. New Haven: Yale University Press.

Pennant, Thomas
1813 *The History and Antiquities of London*. London: J. Coxhead.

Price, Richard
1966 "Caribbean Fishing and Fisherman: A Historical Sketch." *American Anthropologist* 68: 1363–83.
1975 *Saramaka Social Structure: Analysis of a Maroon Society in Surinam*. Rio Piedras: Institute of Caribbean Studies of the University of Puerto Rico.
1976 *The Guiana Maroons: A Historical and Bibliographical Introduction*. Baltimore: Johns Hopkins University Press.
1979a "Kwasímukámba's Gambit." *Bijdragen tot de Taal-, Land- en Volkenkunde* 135: 151–69.
1979b *Maroon Societies: Rebel Slave Communities in the Americas*. Edited and introduced by Richard Price. 2d ed., rev. Baltimore: Johns Hopkins University Press.
1983a *First-Time: The Historical Vision of an Afro-American People*. Baltimore: Johns Hopkins University Press.
1983b *To Slay the Hydra: Dutch Colonial Perspectives on the Saramaka Wars*. Ann Arbor: Karoma.
n.d. *Alábi's World: Conversion, Colonialism, and Resistance on an Afro-American Frontier*. Book in preparation.

Price, Richard, and Sally Price
1972 "Saramaka Onomastics: An Afro-American Naming System." *Ethnology* 11: 341–67.
1979 "John Gabriel Stedman's Collection of Eighteenth-Century Artifacts from Suriname." *Nieuwe West-Indische Gids* 53: 121–40.
1985 "John Gabriel Stedman's 'Journal of a Voyage to the West Indies in

Ye Year 1772. In a Poetical Epistle to a Friend.' " *New West Indian Guide* 59: 185–96.

Price, Sally
1982   "When Is a Calabash Not a Calabash?" *New West Indian Guide* 56: 69–82.
1984   *Co-wives and Calabashes*. Ann Arbor: University of Michigan Press.

Price, Sally, and Richard Price
1980   *Afro-American Arts of the Suriname Rain Forest*. Berkeley and Los Angeles: University of California Press.

Rattray, R. S.
1923   *Ashanti*. London: Oxford University Press.

Ray, Gordon N.
1976   *The Illustrator and the Book in England from 1790 to 1914*. New York: Pierpont Morgan Library; London: Oxford University Press.

Sanderson, Ivan T.
1965   *Caribbean Treasure*. New York: Pyramid Books.

Schiltkamp, J. A., and J. Th. de Smidt
1973   *Plakaten, ordonnantiën en andere wetten, uitgevaardigd in Suriname, 1667–1816*. Amsterdam: S. Emmering.

Schlegel, Klaus
1980   *Besselich am Mittelrhein*. Cologne: Verlag J. P. Bachem.

Schumann, C. L.
1778   "Saramaccanisch Deutsches Wörter-Buch." In *Die Sprache der Saramakkaneger in Surinam*, edited by Hugo Schuchardt, 46–116. Verhandelingen der Koninklijke Akademie van Wetenschappen te Amsterdam 14 (6), 1914. Amsterdam: Johannes Muller.

van Sijpesteijn, C. A.
1858   *Mr. Jan Jacob Mauricius, Gouverneur-Generaal van Suriname van 1742–1751*. 's Gravenhage: De Gebroeders van Cleef.

Sitwell, Sacheverell
1940   *Sacred and Profane Love*. London: Faber & Faber.

Smith, Bernard
1960   *European Vision and the South Pacific, 1768–1850: A Study in the History of Art and Ideas*. Oxford: Clarendon Press.

Smith, Steven B.
1983   *The Great Mental Calculators*. New York: Columbia University Press.

Snell, F. J.
1904   *Early Associations of Archbishop Temple: A Record of Blundell's School and Its Neighborhood*. New York: Thomas Whittaker.

Staehelin, F.
1913–19 *Die Mission der Brüdergemeine in Suriname und Berbice im achtzehnten*

Jahrhundert. Hernnhut: Vereins für Brüdergeschichte in Kommission der Unitätsbuchhandlung in Gnadau.

Stafford, Barbara Maria
1984 *Voyage into Substance: Art, Science, Nature, and the Illustrated Travel Account, 1760–1840*. Cambridge: MIT Press.

Stahel, Gerold
1944 Notes on the Arawak Indian Names of Plants in Surinam. *Journal of the New York Botanical Garden* 45: 268–79.

Stephen, Leslie, and Sidney Lee
1967–68 *The Dictionary of National Biography*. Oxford: Oxford University Press.

Sterne, Laurence
1941 *A Sentimental Journey through France and Italy*. New York: Heritage Press [orig. 1768].

Stone, Roger D.
1985 *Dreams of Amazonia*. New York: Viking Press.

Stuldreher-Nienhuis, J.
1944 *Verborgen paradijzen: het leven en de werken van Maria Sibylla Merian, 1647–1717*. Arnhem: Van Loghum Slaterus.

Sypher, Wylie
1942 *Guinea's Captive Kings: British Anti-Slavery Literature of the Eighteenth Century*. Chapel Hill: University of North Carolina Press.

Szwed, John F.
1985 Review of Richard Price, *First-Time: The Historical Vision of an Afro-American People*. *New West Indian Guide* 59: 225–28.

Temminck Groll, C. L.
1973 *De architektuur van Suriname, 1667–1930*. Zutphen: De Walburg Pers.

Thompson, Stanbury
1962 *The Journal of John Gabriel Stedman, 1744–1797*. Edited by S. Thompson. London: Mitre Press.
1966 *John Gabriel Stedman: A Study of His Life and Times*. Stapleford, Notts.: Thompson.

Todd, Ruthven
1946 *Tracks in the Snow: Studies in English Science and Art*. London: Grey Walls Press.

Tooley, R. V.
1954 *English Books with Coloured Plates, 1790 to 1860*. London: B. T. Batsford.

Tyson, Gerald P.
1979 *Joseph Johnson: A Liberal Publisher*. Iowa City: University of Iowa Press.

Vink, A. T.
1965 *Surinam Timbers.* 3d ed., rev. Paramaribo: Surinam Forest Service.

Voorhoeve, Jan, and Antoon Donicie
1963 *Bibliographie du Négro-Anglais du Surinam.* The Hague: Martinus Nijhoff.

Walker, Ernest P., ed.
1975 *Mammals of the World.* 3d ed., rev. Baltimore: Johns Hopkins University Press.

Whitehead, N. L.
1984 "Carib Cannibalism: The Historical Evidence." *Journal de la Société des Américanistes* (Paris) 70 (1): 69–88.
1986 "John Gabriel Stedman's Collection of Amerindian Artifacts." *New West Indian Guide* 60:203–8.
1987 *The Carib Conquest, 1500–1800.* Leiden: Koninklijk Instituut voor Taal-, Land- en Volkenkunde.

Wilbert, Johannes
1975 *Warao Basketry: Form and Function.* Los Angeles: UCLA Museum of Cultural History.

Wolbers, J.
1861 *Geschiedenis van Suriname.* Amsterdam: H. de Hoogh.

Wooding, Charles J.
1981 *Evolving Culture: A Cross-Cultural Study of Suriname, West Africa, and the Caribbean.* Washington, D.C.: University Press of America.

Lightning Source UK Ltd.
Milton Keynes UK
UKHW031235030220
358073UK00013B/3177